BLACK JUDAS

BLACK

William Hannibal Thomas
and *The American Negro*

JUDAS

JOHN DAVID SMITH

The University of Georgia Press

Athens and London

© 2000 by the University of Georgia Press
Athens, Georgia 30602
All rights reserved

Designed by Erin Kirk New
Set in 11.5 on 13.5 Bulmer by G & S Typesetters, Inc.
Printed and bound by Maple-Vail Book Group

The paper in this book meets the guidelines for
permanence and durability of the Committee on
Production Guidelines for Book Longevity of the
Council on Library Resources.

Printed in the United States of America
04 03 02 01 00 C 5 4 3 2 1

Library of Congress Cataloging in Publication Data
Smith, John David, 1949–
Black Judas : William Hannibal Thomas and The American Negro
/ John David Smith.
p. cm.
Includes bibliographical references (p.   ) and index.
ISBN 0-8203-2130-3 (alk. paper)
1. Thomas, William Hannibal, b. 1843.   2. Afro-Americans—
Biography.   3. Afro-American intellectuals—Biography.
4. Thomas, William Hannibal, b. 1843. American Negro.
5. Afro-Americans—Social conditions—To 1964.   6. Racism—
United States—History—20th century.   I. Title.
E185.97.T545S55   2000
305.896'073'0092—dc21
[B]   99-25538

British Library Cataloging in Publication Data available

Frontispiece: William Hannibal Thomas, ca. 1901, from an
announcement in the *Book Buyer*

Für Sylvie

Contents

Acknowledgments

AS MY FAMILY, FRIENDS, and generations of former students have reminded me at every opportunity, this book has had an unusually long life — seemingly as long as that of William Hannibal Thomas. I first encountered Thomas in the mid-1970s while researching post-Civil War racial thought. In 1984, after completing *An Old Creed for the New South: Proslavery Ideology and Historiography, 1865–1918* (1985), I began working full time on Thomas, only to encounter one methodological snag after another. Thomas purposely covered his tracks and left few records behind, so gaps remained in establishing even his basic chronology. There also were at least nineteen African Americans with the name William H. Thomas who had been confused with William Hannibal Thomas at one time or another. But most problematic of all was analyzing Thomas and *The American Negro* fairly and dispassionately — explaining why a Negro would write one of the most racist books ever published.

To some extent my work on Thomas forced me to retool. Over the last fourteen years I immersed myself in disciplines and methodologies new to me, including genealogy, military medicine, chronic pain, personality theory, and trauma recovery. I logged many research miles, from Atlanta's Fulton County Court House to Ohio's Wilberforce University, from the Wellcome Institute for the History of Medicine in London to the Arquivo Nacional da Torre do Tombo and the Arquivo Historico Ultramarino in Lisbon, Portugal. In the course of my research, I encountered many roadblocks and made some wrong turns, but researching and writing about William Hannibal Thomas has been an enriching and rewarding journey. I am delighted to acknowledge my many debts to historians, archivists, librarians, medical professionals, public officials, friends, family, and students who helped me find my way.

Over the years several institutions and organizations invited me to lecture on Thomas and provided productive opportunities to test my ideas before varied audiences. These include the University of Georgia, Athens; the University of Nottingham, England; Cambridge University, England; the University of Sydney, Australia; Otterbein College, Westerville, Ohio; Baldwin-Wallace College, Berea, Ohio; the W. E. B. Du Bois Institute, Harvard University; the John F. Kennedy Institut, Freie Universität, Berlin; the Amerika-Institut, Ludwig-Maximilians-Universität, Munich; the Historical Society of North Carolina, Chapel Hill; the North Carolina Library Association, Chapel Hill; the Kentucky Department for Libraries and Archives, Frankfort; and the Ohio Valley History Conference, Bowling Green, Kentucky. Similarly, I received valuable comments on my work on Thomas when presenting conference papers before the Society for the History of Authorship, Reading, and Publishing, Cambridge, England; the British Association for American Studies, Leeds, England; the Australia New Zealand American Studies Association, Melbourne, Australia; the Association Française d'Études Américaines, Dourdan, France; and the Organization of American Historians, Minneapolis, Minnesota.

Many friends and colleagues have gone to great lengths to assist me in writing and researching this book. Through the years Jeffrey J. Crow and William C. Harris read numerous drafts of the entire manuscript with painstaking thoroughness, care, and good cheer. I am immensely grateful to Jeff and Bill for their support and endurance. David P. Gilmartin always asked tough questions about Thomas. Though he rarely found my answers satisfactory, David boosted my spirits, especially when we discussed writing in the active voice. Will Kimler read significant portions of the manuscript and shared with me his vast knowledge of early-twentieth-century science and late-twentieth-century word processing. John C. Inscoe and Gary W. Gallagher read portions of the manuscript and provided timely research support. Robert J. T. Joy assisted my early research on military amputations and Carol Reardon kindly obtained a copy of an obscure diary for me at Carlisle Barracks, Pennsylvania. Noah A. Trudeau unselfishly shared with me his research on a writing competition that Thomas entered for Civil War amputees in 1865. Mary-Louise Mussell provided invaluable help in sorting out Thomas's Methodist affiliations and R. Bruce Mullin, blessed with the patience of Job, answered my seemingly endless questions regarding

Thomas's biblical references. While curator at the South Carolina Historical Society, David Moltke-Hansen generously provided me access to the Theodore D. Jervey Papers, the richest manuscript collection containing Thomas materials.

At the National Archives, Walter B. Hill Jr. enthusiastically provided access to record groups that filled many gaping holes in Thomas's life. Early in the project Jacqueline A. Goggin, then at the Library of Congress, generously copied for me the valuable report on Thomas's *The American Negro* from the Fifth Hampton Negro Conference deposited in the Carter G. Woodson Papers. Paul R. Begley went to great lengths on my behalf, locating documents at the South Carolina State Archives and critiquing chapter 4 of this book. Thomas H. Pope graciously shared his research materials with me on Thomas's life in Newberry, South Carolina, where Thomas tangled with one of Pope's forebears. Merton L. Dillon uncovered information for me on Thomas's early years in Michigan and Eldon W. Ward and Wendy S. Greenwood helped me reconstruct Thomas's later life in Columbus, Ohio. The late John Becker, Melinda Gilpin, Alberta E. M. Messmer, and the late Harold Hancock welcomed me twice to Otterbein College and made my visits there both profitable and memorable. I fondly recall trekking with Professor Hancock and Mrs. Messmer through the Otterbein Cemetery looking for Will Thomas's grave. After an hour on the prowl, we finally found the right grave, only to discover that factual errors regarding Thomas's life had been engraved on its stone.

Several individuals prodded me to expand my interpretive horizons, ultimately leading to my interest in the role of Thomas's emotional and physical traumas as sources of his behavior. Special thanks for encouraging me in this direction go to Clarence E. Walker, University of California, Davis; Bertram Wyatt-Brown, University of Florida; Jennifer Fleischner, State University of New York, Albany; Leslie S. Rousell and Charles Rousell, Northeast Center for Trauma Recovery, Greenwich, Connecticut; and Ken Lessler, Human Resource Consultants, Chapel Hill, North Carolina.

Raleigh is an excellent place to work on the history of the South. There I have enjoyed superb library resources, splendid colleagues, and talented research assistants. At North Carolina State University's D. H. Hill Library, librarian Cindy Levine helped me track down numerous obscure references and Baker S. Ward procured rare texts and microfilm with extraordinary precision and dispatch. Other colleagues at D. H. Hill Library, including the late Marta A. Lange, Deborah L. Marshall, Bryna R. Coonin, Mark Howell,

Bev Loseke, Maude Jones, the late Liz Carroll, Sherry Johnson, Ann Smith, Jean Porter, Sonya Dean, Margaret Hunt, Sandra Lovely, Orion Pozo, and Steven M. Backs eased my research tasks immeasurably.

North Carolina State's Department of History and the College of Humanities and Social Sciences have generously supported my years of research for this book. Colleagues John M. Riddle, Linda O. McMurry, Walter A. Jackson, Richard W. Slatta, Jim Clark, Steve Middleton, David Zonderman, Joseph P. Hobbs, Kenneth P. Vickery, Alexander J. De Grand, Nancy Mitchell, Holly Brewer, Gail W. O'Brien, Mimi Kim, Norene Miller, and Helga G. Braunbeck helped me in various ways. So too did Joe Mobley of the North Carolina Division of Archives and History.

Over the course of many years my graduate assistants at N.C. State provided extraordinary research support. Sarah Minor, Julie Doyle, Yvette M. Stillwell, and the late David Jackson, in particular, were instrumental in my decoding Thomas's often incomprehensible prose. Daniel J. Salemson, Chris Graham, Alexandra Gressitt, Lee Bumgarner, Dorothy Frye, Dennis Rush, Michelle Justice, Annette McDaniel, Jennifer L. Bryan, Troy Burton, Debra Blake, Jo Frost, Corinne Frist Glover, Ellen Turco, and Ellen Uhl assisted me as well. Bernard Taylor served as my research assistant in Boston and Felton Best performed similar work in Columbus, Ohio. I would be remiss if I failed to thank students in my graduate and undergraduate seminars at N.C. State, including Angela Brendle, Judy Sadler, Hays Poole, Harry J. Kane, Richard W. Hite, Paul Peterson, and Bethany Parrish, who supplied me with information or assisted me in some meaningful way. Over many years I have kept Richard Costello, B. D. Sossomon, Brett Larson, Anne Cecil, and Hilme Lahoud amused by my "proficiency" with computers and printers. In the last stretch, Jennifer Comeau of the University of Georgia Press, a true software wizard, came to my rescue on several occasions. Many thanks, too, to my project editor, Kristine M. Blakeslee, and Stephen Barnett, who copyedited the manuscript. Nancy Kaiser prepared the index.

As I neared the end of this book, a number of historians commented on my arguments and offered support in various ways. I owe special thanks to John B. Boles, Rice University; Fitzhugh Brundage, University of Florida; Dietmar Herz, Rheinische-Friedrich-Wilhelms-Universität, Bonn; Gert Raeithel, Ludwig-Maximilians-Universität, Munich; Henry Louis Gates, Harvard University; Willi Paul Adams, Freie Universität, Berlin; Anthony Badger, Cambridge University; Shane White, University of Sydney; Richard King, University of Nottingham; Mark A. Huddle, Bradford College; Reginald D. Hildebrand, University of North Carolina at Chapel Hill; Randall M. Miller,

St. Joseph's University; Nell Irvin Painter, Princeton University; Richard J. M. Blackett, University of Houston; and David W. Blight, Amherst College.

Over the course of many years various other scholars also replied to my queries, supplied me with information, or read early drafts of my work on Thomas. They include Thomas H. Appleton Jr. and James C. Klotter, Kentucky Historical Society; D. L. Smith and Dennis C. Dickerson, Williams College; Paul H. Bergeron, University of Tennessee; Joseph T. Glatthaar, University of Houston; Leslie S. Rowland, University of Maryland; Walter L. Williams, University of Southern California; Edwin S. Redkey, State University of New York at Purchase; Stephen W. Angell, Florida Agricultural and Mechanical University; Will Gravely, University of Denver; Willard B. Gatewood, University of Arkansas; Walter B. Edgar and the late George C. Rogers Jr., University of South Carolina; Richard B. Sherman, College of William and Mary; David W. Wills, Amherst College; John Y. Simon, Southern Illinois University; Todd L. Savitt, East Carolina University; David Levering Lewis, Rutgers University; James O. Horton, George Washington University; David M. Katzman, University of Kansas; Richard H. Abbott, Eastern Michigan University; Werner Sollors, Harvard University; Louis R. Harlan, University of Maryland; Joe M. Richardson, Florida State University; Louis Filler, Ovid, Michigan; James A. Ramage, Northern Kentucky University; James H. Madison, Indiana University; Patrick J. Kelly, Cambridge, Massachusetts; Bill Donovan, Loyola College in Maryland; John A. Hardin, Western Kentucky University; Bob Hall, Northeastern University; Charles W. Joyner, Coastal Carolina College; John H. Roper, Emory and Henry College; Gerald L. Smith, University of Kentucky; Clark G. Reynolds, University of Charleston; Glenda E. Gilmore, Yale University; Allen W. Trelease, University of North Carolina at Greensboro; William C. Hine, South Carolina State College; Edmund L. Drago, College of Charleston; August Meier, Kent State University; Paul A. Cimbala, Fordham University; Jerry Thornbery, Baltimore, Maryland; Ralph E. Luker, Antioch College; Robert Sawrey, Marshall University; and Daniel W. Stowell, Lincoln Legal Papers Project.

Many archivists, librarians, and historians also have assisted me with this book. I especially wish to thank Donald L. DeWitt, University of Oklahoma; Paul K. Baker, Fayetteville State University; James S. Rush Jr., Mary Frances Morrow, Mike Meier, Charles E. Schamel, Stuart L. Butler, William E. Lind, Rodney A. Ross, Cathy NiCastro, and Elizabeth K. Lockwood, National Archives and Records Administration; Joseph Allan Stroble, Ted Sargosa, Gregory Strong, William C. Beal, and C. Jarrett Gray Jr., Drew University

Library; Mary Ellen Scott and Andrew J. Sopko, Pittsburgh Theological Seminary Library; Linda Caskie and Beth Weinhart, Westerville, Ohio, Public Library; Ann Sizer, Church of the Master, United Methodist Church, Westerville, Ohio; Frank R. Levstik, Kentucky Department for Libraries & Archives; Roland M. Baumann, Oberlin College; Betty Dawley, Pickaway County, Ohio, Historical and Genealogical Library; George W. Bain, Sheppard Black, and Michel Perdreau, Ohio University Library; John P. Adams, Joan Williams, Susanna Austin, and Mark J. Parisi, Parlin Memorial Library, Everett, Massachusetts; James Shannon, Glenn V. Longacre, Janet A. Thompson, George Parkinson, and Gary J. Arnold, Ohio Historical Society; Paul Comstock, Delaware, Ohio; James L. Hansen, Harold L. Miller, F. Gerald Ham, and Peter N. Gottlieb, State Historical Society of Wisconsin; Charles L. Metze, II, Allen University; Allen H. Stokes Jr. and Eleanor M. Richardson, University of South Carolina Library; Linda Ziemer, Chicago Historical Society; James Bantin, University of Missouri; Denise Green and Paul Burnam, Ohio Wesleyan University; Stephen P. Pentek, New England Methodist Historical Society; Wanda L. Crenshaw and Fritz J. Malval, Hampton University Library; Laura Linard, Chicago Public Library; Edwin G. Sanford, Boston Public Library; Melinda Rhoads, Deputy Clerk, Pickaway County, Ohio; Sam Roshon, Columbus, Ohio, Metropolitan Library; Thomas Nixon, Yale University Library; the Reverend Bennie D. Warner, St. Paul United Methodist Church, Little Rock, Arkansas; Julie Orenstein, Jean K. Mulhern, and Jackie Brown, Wilberforce University Library; Susan E. Davis, Charles Kronick, John D. Stinson, Anastacio Teodoro, Genette McLaurin, and Robert C. Morris, New York Public Library; Cliff Sanderson, Duke University Library; Malik A. Azeez and Esme E. Bhan, Howard University Library; Betty Ammons, Baltimore Conference United Methodist Historical Society; Jane E. Mason, United Brethren Historical Center, Huntington College; Raymond M. Bell, Washington, Pennsylvania; Victor Lieberman, Newberry Library; Jacqueline Mazza, formerly of the Democratic Study Group, U.S. House of Representatives; Harold Lawrence, First United Methodist Church, Milledgeville, Georgia; Ruby C. Boyd, Historical Commission, Mother Bethel A.M.E. Church, Philadelphia; Gerry Reiff, Millsaps College Library; Joan L. Clark, Cleveland Public Library; Cyprian Davis, St. Meinard Archabbey, Indiana; Alexander Moore, Robert Mackintosh, and Charles H. Lesser, South Carolina Department of Archives and History; Phil Lapsansky, Library Company of Philadelphia; Lee Albright and Pam Toms, North Carolina State Library; Jacqueline D. Kinzer, Rome-Floyd County, Georgia, Library; Rene Shoemaker, University of Georgia Library; Randall K. Burkett and Richard Newman, W. E. B. Du Bois Institute, Harvard University; Pierre-Rene Noth, *Rome News-Tribune;* John Parascandola, National Institutes of Health, National Library of Medicine; Jeanne Roberts, Historical Society of Pennsylvania; Harry McKown, Nidia T. Scharlock, and Cynthia Clay Adams, University of North Carolina Library, Chapel Hill; Mary Giles, South Carolina Historical Society; Manfred F. Boemeke, Papers of Woodrow Wilson, Princeton University; Helen M. Wilson, Historical Society of Western Pennsylvania; Shannon H. Wilson and Gerald F. Roberts, Berea College Library; N. Louise Bailey, State of South Carolina State Budget and Control Board; Virginia H. Smith, Massachusetts Historical Society; Philip N. Dare, Lexington Theological Seminary Library; Robert H. Reid Jr., editor, A.M.E. *Christian Recorder;* Carson Holloway, Durham, North Carolina; Elinor S. Hearn, Archives of the Episcopal Church; Joseph C. McKinney, African Methodist Episcopal Church Financial Department; Daniel T. Williams, Tuskegee University Library; John V. Cinciarelli, Jersey City Public Library; the Reverend Bill Easley, Durham, North Carolina; John Walker and Michelle Francis, Department of History (Montreat), Presbyterian Church (USA); Anthony J. Kostreba, Charles Bean, Carl Crosby, James H. Hutson, Jeffrey M. Flannery, and Irene Schubert, Library of Congress; Nancy E. Wight and Sara Saunders, Atlanta Historical Society; Voorhees Dunn, State of New Jersey, Archives and Records Management; Joyce Ann Tracy, American Antiquarian Society; Thomas Rosenbaum and Kenneth W. Rose, Rockefeller Archive Center; Olivia J. Martin, Western Reserve Historical Society; William O. Harris, Princeton Theological Seminary Library; Jan Marshall, Lexington, Kentucky, Public Library; Frank A. Zabrosky, Archive of Industrial Society, University of Pittsburgh; Linda Anderson and James Russell Harris, Kentucky Historical Society; James J. Holmberg and Nelson A. Dawson, Filson Club, Louisville, Kentucky; Charles Lindquist, Lenawee County Historical Society, Adrian, Michigan; Jeanine K. Wing, Suzanne Wayda-Slomski, Adrian, Michigan, Public Library; Charles Niles, Boston University Library; Karl Kabelac, University of Rochester Library; Melissa Rumbarger Smith, Department of Veterans Affairs, Medical Center, Dayton, Ohio; Eugene Jones and David M. Bradley, Veterans Service Commission, Columbus, Ohio; Mary Du Mont and James W. Geary, Kent State University Library; Michael Roy, Black Periodical Literature Project, Cambridge, Massachusetts; Donald D. Dykstra, Indianapolis, Indiana; Mrs. G. Donald Riley Jr., Historical Society of Carroll County, Maryland; Kenneth J. Ross, Presbyterian Historical Society, Philadelphia; Laura H. Randall and Richard P. Heitzenrater, Perkins xvi — Acknowledgments

School of Theology, Southern Methodist University; Charles Stuart Kennedy, Foreign Affairs Oral History Program, Georgetown University; Susan Ravdin, Bowdoin College Library; Chris Jeffries, Margaret N. Burri, and Jennifer A. Bryan, Maryland Historical Society; Manuel Damazio Sousa, my driver in Lisbon, Portugal; Elaine W. Williams, Atlanta University Library; Brenda Wagner, Veterans Service Office, Circleville, Ohio; Bill Bigglestone, Tucson, Arizona; Ellick G. Stevenson, Hobbs, New Mexico; Rod Gragg, Conway, South Carolina; the Reverend Beaumont Stevenson, Oxford, England; M. Patrick Graham, Emory University Library; Clifton H. Johnson and Andrew Simons, Amistad Research Center, Tulane University; Thomas J. Culbertson, Janice L. Haas, and Leslie H. Fishel, Rutherford B. Hayes Presidential Center, Fremont, Ohio; Barry Jones, Chapel Hill, North Carolina; Steven M. Rowe, Raleigh, North Carolina; Michael R. Kornegay, formerly of Oxford University Press; Jennie Rathbun and Henri J. Bourneuf, Harvard University Library; Regina Entorf and Kathy Schulz, Wittenberg University Library; Laurann Figg, Vesterheim, Decorah, Iowa; Jane Farrell-Beck, Iowa State University; Lynn Hobbs, Barratt's Chapel & Museum, Frederica, Delaware; Ralph L. Elder, University of Texas at Austin Library; Charlotte Ames and Jay P. Dolan, University of Notre Dame; Khalil Mahmud, Lincoln University; Richard Geyer, Adrian College Library; the Reverend Donna L. Fowler-Marchant, Cary, North Carolina; Gloria Fiddler, Ohio Veterans Home, Sandusky, Ohio; Harmon Smith and Dale Couch, Georgia Department of Archives and History; Clara M. Lamers, Brooklyn Historical Society; Rachel Davies Wermann, Wellcome Institute for the History of Medicine; Don Ritchie, U.S. Senate Historical Office; Agnes Fisher and Mary Anne Thompson, Macmillan Publishing Company; Beth M. Howse, Fisk University Library; Joseph F. Spaniol Jr., Clerk of the Supreme Court of the United States; Elizabeth C. Bouvier, Supreme Judicial Court Archives, Boston, Massachusetts; Rosalie Bookston, Brookline, Massachusetts, Public Library; Nancy R. Horlacher, Dayton and Montgomery County, Ohio, Public Library; Russell Mobley, Office of Information and Image Management, Fulton County, Georgia; Richard C. Kaplan, Massachusetts Archives at Columbia Point; and Mary C. Downing, Assistant Registrar of Voters, City of Everett, Massachusetts.

Friends and family also have provided valuable help in the researching and writing of this book. My editor and friend Malcolm Call of the University of Georgia Press has waited patiently for me to finish *Black Judas*. He has believed in this project even when I wondered whether I would ever sort out the multiple William H. Thomases. I am immensely grateful to Malcolm, as well as to Karen Orchard, director of the press, for their confidence in me and their longstanding enthusiasm for the project. As always, my parents, Doris and Len Smith, have lovingly supported me during this book's long gestation period. My three stepchildren, Alex, Lisa, and Lorenz Andrusyszyn, small children when they first heard about "Black Judas" but now on the verge of adulthood, have provided me with wonderful diversions and have followed the book's progress with keen interest.

Finally, almost from our first meeting, Sylvie, who later became my wife, and I discussed what she's always referred to as "that Thomas book." Her lawyer's eye for detail, her uncommon good sense, and her unflagging support have helped me finish "that Thomas book" at long last. *Ich widme ihr dieses Buch in grenzenloser Liebe und Hochachtung.*

John David Smith
Amerika-Institut
Ludwig-Maximilians-Universität
Munich

An African American Enigma

Heretofore, enemies have been our historians, as was the fate
of Hannibal, the great Carthaginian general, whose record of
achievements was written by hostile Roman hands.
—William Hannibal Thomas, "Race Problems," August 1886

"DESPITE SUPERFICIAL AND TEMPORARY SIGNS which might lead one to
entertain a contrary opinion," Booker T. Washington wrote in 1901, "there
was never a time when I felt more hopeful for the race than I do at the
present." Ever the optimist and propagandist, Washington was "the supreme diplomat of the Negro people through a generation filled with severe
trials," in the words of Swedish sociologist Gunnar Myrdal. Yet Washington's
rhetoric belied reality. He knew full well that in 1901 white mobs were mur-
dering blacks for many alleged crimes, lynching 105 that year alone. "Violence and the fear of violence," historian Leon F. Litwack writes, "helped to
shape black lives and personalities." The turn of the century was a violent
and fearful era for blacks, the low point in the history of race relations in
America.[1]

Whereas Washington was measured and circumspect in his public statements on the contemporary "Negro problem," another African American,
the Ohio freeborn mulatto William Hannibal Thomas (1843–1935), openly
disagreed with Washington and presented a strident, unbridled, and dramatically different interpretation of black life in the age of Jim Crow. While
Washington exuded guarded optimism, Thomas erupted in overblown pessimism. As Myrdal understood, Washington and Thomas operated at markedly different levels in the black community and spoke with diametrically

opposite voices. Never close to Washington's stature or importance and lacking Washington's national following, in 1901 Thomas nevertheless catapulted from relative obscurity to the center of the nation's discourse on race by arming extreme white racists with a powerful new weapon, a book, that produced outrage among blacks. In that year the prestigious Macmillan Company published Thomas's *The American Negro: What He Was, What He Is, and What He May Become.* Blacks feared that this book would help keep them suppressed legally, socially, and economically. Indeed, with this book Thomas single-handedly stoked the fires of white racism with a force that scores of white bigots could not have hoped to achieve.[2]

In *The American Negro* Thomas denounced blacks in the harshest and crudest of terms as physiologically, intellectually, morally, and culturally inferior to whites. He identified blacks, not whites, as the cause of the contemporary "Negro problem" and differentiated between mulattoes like himself, whom he considered superior, and Negroes, whom he judged to be hopelessly depraved. Light skin alone, however, according to Thomas, did not necessarily free a person of African descent from what he considered offensive Negroid traits. Thomas insisted that character, not color or environment, held the key to what he termed "the full stature of manhood and womanhood." In order to mature as a race, he argued, blacks needed to model themselves after white and exemplary mulatto role models, men like William Hannibal Thomas.[3]

Throughout 1901 and afterward blacks were shocked that a Negro, one of their own, would defame them so egregiously. Blacks took Thomas and his book very seriously and rallied forcefully against him. Predictably, Booker T. Washington reviewed *The American Negro* anonymously in a straightforward, gentlemanly, and thoughtfully critical vein. W. E. B. Du Bois critiqued it more harshly in a signed review, interpreting Thomas as yet another victim of life under the veil of white racism. Other African Americans systematically dug up damaging information on Thomas's past and publicized it in order to embarrass and discredit him. Blacks even worked behind the scenes to convince Macmillan to withdraw *The American Negro* from the market. Thomas's many African American critics argued that his book really was his autobiography, not an analysis of their race. They underscored the details of his dishonest and corrupt life and denounced him as a rank hypocrite. He was a man of color to be sure, they said, but also a man of unquestionably bad character. Just as Thomas had severed his ties with them, so too did African Americans sever their ties with him.

Thomas's book was so explosive and received so much notoriety that it united all segments of the black community against it, including the warring Washington and Du Bois factions. Editors of African American newspapers and journals ran exposés on *The American Negro,* and black preachers delivered vitriolic sermons damning its author. Black women's clubs met to denounce Thomas and to ban his book from public libraries. In July 1901 blacks congregated in Virginia at the Fifth Hampton Negro Conference and devoted an entire session to responding to Thomas's anti-Negro allegations. Many blacks at the conference and throughout the country branded Thomas a race traitor, a good Negro gone bad.

By the time of the book's publication, however, Will Thomas no longer considered himself a Negro. Burying his Negro origins, disassociating himself from all but a small number of blacks, Will assumed a new identity as an exemplary mulatto. Egotistical and myopic, bitter and angry, Thomas believed that he had transformed himself into someone far superior intellectually, culturally, and morally than the average mixed-race hybrid. He was a self-proclaimed leader but had no one to lead. Shunned by his race after 1901 and in constant pain from a severe Civil War wound, Thomas led a lonely and peripatetic life until his death in 1935 at age ninety-two. Little studied, the details and meaning of Thomas's biography remain dimly lit. This book attempts to shed light on the shadowy life of William Hannibal Thomas and *The American Negro.*

Over the course of the twentieth century historians have mentioned William Hannibal Thomas in passing, usually dismissing him as too idiosyncratic and too insignificant to warrant careful and thorough analysis. Upon examining *The American Negro,* most have interpreted him to be an aberration, an accommodator, an appeaser, a bitter and desperate man, an eccentric, an enigma, a man mired in self-hate, or an uninformed middle-class northern critic. Thomas cared little for historians, writing in 1886 that "enemies have been our historians, as was the fate of Hannibal." Yet historians have paid relatively little attention to him.[4]

It was a pioneer black sociologist, Bertram Wilbur Doyle (1897–1980), who provided the earliest scholarly analysis of Thomas and his book. Doyle credited Thomas with being "one of the first of his race to make a study of Negro traits." A graduate student under Professor Robert E. Park at the University of Chicago in the 1920s, Doyle researched how blacks assigned racial characteristics to themselves. Whereas most blacks shied away from self-criticism, Doyle argued that in *The American Negro* Thomas made "an avowed effort to bring to light the failings, shortcomings and vices of the Negro." Doyle remarked that "the result was so perfect that the book brought forth a storm of protest from Negroes themselves." *The American Negro*, Doyle said, "showed the seamy side [of African American life] with a caustic clearness. At times [Thomas's] vindictiveness and bitterness were so evident that even we were inclined to question the scientific validity of his conclusions." Nevertheless, Doyle appreciated Thomas's book because it represented a lone critical voice in the literature about Negroes by a man of color. Doyle agreed with Thomas's observation that the Negro was incapable of self-criticism, "that he resents rebuke for obvious shortcomings, and treats all racial criticism, despite its elements of suggestive helpfulness, as the accusation of enemies." Curiously, aside from a single bibliographical citation, Doyle disregarded Thomas's book in his study of social distance between the races, *The Etiquette of Race Relations,* published in 1937.[5]

Much more surprising is the decision of August Meier, one of the most thorough, insightful, and influential historians of Jim Crow–era racial thought, to exclude Thomas from his important analyses. In 1957 Meier cited *The American Negro* in the bibliography of his Columbia University dissertation but ignored him in the text. And Meier completely omitted Thomas from his pathbreaking *Negro Thought in America, 1880–1915,* published six years later.[6]

Comments by three modern scholars—Lawrence J. Friedman, James M. McPherson, and Ralph E. Luker—generally suggest how contemporary historians have interpreted Thomas. In 1970 Friedman explained that in *The American Negro* Thomas "may have been hoping to dissociate himself from the black masses. But at the same time, he sensed his lot was inextricably tied to theirs." Writing in 1975, McPherson described *The American Negro* as "one of the most extreme racist polemics of its time." Contemporary blacks and their white allies "repudiated this product of a sick mind that sought to escape blackness by identifying with the most virulent white stereotypes of Negroes. Thomas was a living illustration of the 'tragic mulatto.'" Most recently, Luker remarked in 1991 that in the early twentieth century, "more than any other black writer, William Hannibal Thomas absorbed the anti-Negro sentiment of his age." While these historians have raised interesting questions about Thomas's motivations and significance, they have provided only the slightest clues into his identity and why he wrote *The American Negro.*[7]

Thomas is puzzling for several reasons. First, his book had questionable legitimacy. Thomas grounded his racist opinions on decades of subjective observation, not on "scientific" data or method. *The American Negro* represented no school of sociological thought, and, after the furor over its publication ceased, it generated little debate. Though many newspapers reviewed the book favorably, Thomas had no devoted following. Only white supremacists, most notably Theodore D. Jervey (1859–1947), a conservative South Carolina attorney and author, enthusiastically welcomed Thomas's book. Scholars, especially those inclined to interpret *The American Negro* as the product of a "sick mind," paid it no heed.

Second, Thomas is an extremely difficult subject for a biography. Like other nineteenth-century free blacks, few public records remain to document his life. But Thomas's case is unique to a significant degree. Throughout his long life he rarely remained in one place very long. At major turning points in his life, Thomas invariably got into trouble, sometimes serious trouble, and he often absconded to avoid sheriffs, lawyers, judges, and bail bondsmen determined to find him. To escape capture, Thomas purposely left a spotty paper trail. As if determined to cheat his biographer, Thomas kept no diary, retained no body of private papers, and recorded only a few autobiographical fragments, some of which are contradictory and confused. To complicate matters, those in search of him frequently mistook William Hannibal Thomas for other black men—as many as nineteen—named William H. Thomas (see appendix 1). Basic elements of his biography, particularly his childhood, remain unknown, and it is impossible to account for him during several years of his life. Obscure, frequently on the run, and easily mistaken for others, Thomas has resisted those who have tried to pin him down.

Third, Thomas's racist arguments and insulting language understandably have repelled researchers. No subject for a biography could be more "politically incorrect" than an embittered "black" Negrophobe who wrote when racial tensions in America were as volatile as a powder keg. Thomas is an especially unlikely candidate for an intellectual biography during the culture wars of the late twentieth century, when historians have celebrated African American heroes, not renegades, and have contributed numerous important studies that repudiated the arguments that Thomas espoused. Not surprisingly, scholars have uniformly relegated Thomas and his book to the trash heap of black historiography. Despised and virtually forgotten, Thomas has been an African American enigma, an outcast shunned by his black contemporaries and at best marginalized by scholars. Yet by allowing Thomas's foul ideas to rot, historians have missed an important opportunity to study a man who was both part of and apart from turn-of-the-century African American intellectual life.[8]

Will Thomas was neither as peripheral nor as eccentric as previous historians have assumed. After distinguished service with the U.S. Colored Troops in the Civil War, in which he lost his right arm, he labored for many years to reform his race from within, identifying clearly with and working for blacks. For three decades following the Civil War he exhibited considerable ability as a preacher, teacher, lawyer, trial justice, state legislator, and journalist in Ohio, Pennsylvania, Georgia, South Carolina, and Massachusetts. Thomas promoted racial reform that consistently challenged black leaders to serve their race in more productive ways. While often sharp in his judgments of African Americans, he clearly sided with the South's ex-slaves, believing that their lot could be improved by a combination of private and public philanthropy.

Thomas grounded his ideas on a sweeping program of moral uplift, church reform, manual training, and land distribution. He proposed the same kinds of self-help, group solidarity, and petit-bourgeois values as such mainstream black leaders as Bishop Daniel A. Payne of the African Methodist Episcopal (A.M.E.) Church, Booker T. Washington, and W. E. B. Du Bois. As a measure of his growing reputation, in 1885 Thomas participated, along with such influential black leaders as Frederick Douglass, T. Thomas Fortune, William Still, P. B. S. Pinchback, Bishop Henry McNeal Turner, and William S. Scarborough, in a national roundtable forum on "The Democratic Return to Power—Its Effect?"[9]

In many articles in religious publications, especially the A.M.E.'s *Christian Recorder* and the *A.M.E. Church Review,* and in a short book, *Land and Education* (1890), Thomas worked systematically and largely constructively to combat white racism, help redeem his race, and improve the operations of the A.M.E. Church. He consistently urged blacks to improve themselves, to reform the race from within. Because of his many publications, by the turn of the century Thomas was reasonably well known, especially among a national audience of African Methodists. Many recognized his sobriquet "Hannibal" in the *Christian Recorder* and expected sharp and spirited criticism on a broad range of secular and religious topics from his pen.

But there was another side to Will Thomas, one that undermined him throughout the post–Civil War years: his pattern of self-destructive behavior. Again and again, just when his ability, insight, intelligence, and Civil War record positioned him close to real leadership in the black community, he stumbled over an ethical or moral issue, sabotaging opportunities to use his keen mind, gift of persuasion, and grasp of the language for the betterment of his race. In Pennsylvania a divinity school expelled him for his hypocrisy. In Ohio a black university cashiered him for alleged financial irregularities. In Pennsylvania he lost a church position for alleged financial improprieties. In Georgia and South Carolina he reportedly stole money and property entrusted in his care. From 1865 to 1900, he abandoned his wife and children in Pennsylvania and, according to his later critics, lived in South Carolina and Massachusetts in sin.

Thomas reinvented himself after every brush with civil or clerical authorities. Each time he got into trouble he would deny allegations of his misdeeds and then flee, usually returning to Delaware, Ohio, to lose himself in the protection offered by this town's friendly mulatto community. Then he began anew, relocating, blending into the community, and then getting into trouble again. Thomas's attempts to secure consular appointments with the U.S. State Department in the late 1870s and early 1880s illustrate his disingenuous strain most clearly. A man blessed with obvious talent, he also possessed the uncanny knack of blending into communities, running afoul of the law, and making quick escapes. Some considered him a con artist; others judged him an artful dodger. In any case, throughout his life Thomas climbed to positions of trust and responsibility only to tumble, raising serious questions about his character and integrity.

Nonetheless, in the 1880s Thomas sustained consistent success as a journalist. In these years he traveled widely in the South, observing the freedpeople and preparing a book-length manuscript that ultimately became *The American Negro*. In 1886 Thomas edited the short-lived periodical *The Negro* and four years later published *Land and Education,* a serious and constructive attempt at racial reform that received a positive reception from contemporary critics. In this book Thomas openly sympathized with black southerners, blaming their social and economic problems on environmental factors and white racism, not inherited race traits. He optimistically advocated race pride, self-respect and, more pragmatically, land distribution and manual training, for what he still termed the "freedmen."

By the mid-1890s, however, Thomas had once again changed direction, this time falling headlong in a self-destructive spiral from which he never recovered. During this decade he cut himself off permanently from his race. Latent emotional and physical forces, present since his young adulthood but never fully manifested, exploded in a rage of racial hatred. In 1894 Thomas became utterly pessimistic, viciously intolerant, and indiscriminately critical of blacks, especially black southerners. Though always prone to reproach the race's leaders, especially black teachers and preachers, in 1894 and again in 1897 Thomas published articles that were captious, rambling bromides filled with sweeping denunciations of virtually all blacks. His reckless fulmination of African Americans seemingly knew no bounds. Hyperbolic and accusatory, Thomas's voice became shrill and his ideas extreme, even to the point of proposing "surgical castration" as a deterrent for blacks who raped white women. By the turn of the century, Thomas had concluded not only that blacks were inherently inferior to whites but that blacks, not whites, were the source of the "Negro problem." Negroes, he concluded, required a thorough and radical redemption. That was his justification for publishing *The American Negro,* a work Thomas considered a critical and practical discussion of the contemporary race problem.

In this book Thomas drew a color line between himself and others of his race, subjecting blacks to relentless attack—all in the name of racial reform. *The American Negro* overflowed with gratuitous negative racial stereotypes. Never before had a person of color so thoroughly slandered his race. "Nothing that any of the old Southern planters or their official apologists ever said about the negro slaves was half so bad as this," a London reviewer observed. Indeed, this racist and disturbing book remains one of the most offensive works ever written about African Americans by a member of any race. The brainchild of a Negro, it played right into the hands of white supremacists who cited *The American Negro* as justification for the proscription of black southerners.[10]

In 1901 a broad range of blacks, scrambling to offset the damage of Thomas's book, constructed an image of him as a conspirator, a brother who brazenly fell from grace and sold out to the enemy. African Americans feared that in the racially tense early twentieth century, his ideas would become the standard by which whites would judge blacks. Outraged by and consumed with Thomas's book, members of the race campaigned rigorously to besmirch his reputation, and Thomas quickly lost whatever credibility he had attained in the years before *The American Negro* appeared. His African American critics crucified Thomas, the man who wanted to be their savior. They called him "Black Judas" and orchestrated a campaign that transformed him into one of the most hated African Americans of all time. In 1901 Thomas's actions finally caught up with him. He had betrayed his race, a betrayal that haunted him for the more than three decades that remained in his long and tragic life.

BLACK JUDAS

CHAPTER ONE

Student, Servant, Soldier

FULLY IN KEEPING with a life shrouded in ambiguity, controversy, and secrecy, William Hannibal Thomas purposely left few records of his origins and early life. Much of the documentation that remains—mere scraps of information—is as confused and contradictory as the man himself. Two things, however, are certain. First, none of Thomas's immediate ancestors had been slaves. That distinction mattered much to him because throughout his life he distanced himself from slaves and former slaves and what he believed was their inferiority. Yet even as a free man of African descent, he inherited the social and political status that the white majority accorded slaves and former slaves. And second, Thomas identified himself as a light-skinned mulatto.

No characteristic had more influence on Thomas than the color of his skin. Just as he created a barrier between his free black origins and that of the slaves, so too did he differentiate between mulattoes and blacks. To an important extent, the lightness of his skin empowered and energized him; it set him apart from "Negroes," whom he considered intellectually, culturally, and morally subordinate. Will's skin color positioned him in a racial twilight—caught between two racial worlds. Though in his writings he classified himself with other "people of color"—part of an amorphous nonwhite racial group—by 1901 Thomas subtly but clearly drew a pejorative color line between mulattoes like himself and black Americans (whom he generally called "negroes" or "colored Americans"), especially those descended from slaves. His obsession with color and race ran through his long and painful life like a leitmotif.[1]

Will Thomas was descended from two generations of American mulattoes. Caucasian racial characteristics dominated both sides of his lineage. On several occasions whites, including the surgeon who discharged him from a Civil War military hospital, described the complexion of the five-foot-ten, dark-eyed Thomas as "yellow." His mother's family had English and German roots. Thomas's grandfather, Isaac Fisher, born about 1758 at Bedford, Pennsylvania, was descended from a white indentured female servant and a free Negro. Thomas's grandmother, born in 1770 in either Germany or a German community in the American colonies, was reared in Hagerstown, Maryland. "This branch of my ancestry," Thomas wrote in 1901, "emigrated to Ohio in 1792, and settled near the town of Marietta" in southeastern Ohio along the Ohio River opposite what was then Virginia.[2]

Will's mother, Rebecca Fisher, was born in 1812 in Marietta, Ohio. Founded in 1788 at the confluence of the Muskingum and Ohio Rivers, Marietta was the first permanent settlement in the Northwest Territory in an area settled by Germans, Scotch-Irish, and New Englanders. By 1800 Washington County and Marietta contained about five thousand settlers. From Marietta the Fishers traveled up the Muskingum River and were among the first to settle Zanesville, Ohio. In 1830 the federal census taker for Wayne Township, Muskingum County, judged Isaac Fisher to be so light-skinned that he listed him as head of a household of seven "Free White Persons." Both of Thomas's grandparents on his father's side were Virginians, also of mixed racial heritage. Though he conspicuously never mentioned his father by name, Thomas recorded that he was born in 1808 near Moorefield in Hardy County in present-day West Virginia. Thomas's father also moved westward to Ohio "before attaining his majority." He probably traveled west from Wheeling along Zane's Trace to the Scioto River and then north to Pickaway County. Like countless other free blacks and escaped slaves of the day, Thomas's parents came to Ohio to carve out a new life in the Old Northwest.[3]

"I was born on a farm, in a log cabin, on the fourth day of May 1843, in Jackson Township, Pickaway County, Ohio," Thomas wrote in 1901 in *The American Negro*. Thomas, who always boasted of having influential friends and connections, believed that he was born on the southcentral Ohio farmland owned by Mrs. Harriet L. Woodrow, stepgrandmother of President Woodrow Wilson. Despite Thomas's statement about his birthplace, no record exists of the Thomas family in the 1840, 1850, or 1860 federal manuscript census for Pickaway County. Will did appear in the 1850 and 1860 enumerations—described correctly as a mulatto—but the census taker inexplicably recorded him both times as having been born in Michigan, not Ohio. To complicate matters further, in 1850 Will, then seven years old, was listed as residing not with his parents but with the family of Henry Whiting, a black farmer. A Virginia native, Whiting lived with his wife, their three children, and an eighteen-year-old mulatto woman who, like Will, apparently was not related to the Whitings. In 1860 Will, then age seventeen, once again was listed as living with the Whitings, one of their children, and two young girls, a black and a mulatto, who again were apparently not kin to the Whitings.[4]

Though Will never mentioned living with another family, evidence suggests that he resided off and on with the Whitings, possibly as an apprentice farm hand. His parents meanwhile searched for a homestead and economic opportunity for their family. "Like Americans in general," historian Kenneth J. Winkle writes, "most Ohioans moved frequently during the nineteenth century, over long distances as part of the westward movement or in shorter moves within their own state." That movement was especially pronounced in Ohio's "canal counties" like Pickaway, which "were renowned for their restless migration." According to Winkle, such counties "gained population much faster than did" Ohio's other counties, "especially during the peak settlement years of the 1840s, and they attracted the most migrants." In 1850 Will's parents moved to Indiana (possibly without him), in an example of Winkle's "frequent, short-term migration." This frequent moving also explains the difficulty of pinpointing the Thomases in the 1840s. The identification of Michigan as Thomas's birthplace remains puzzling, all the more so because two census takers recorded the same data a decade apart. To compound the problem, Thomas and his family did reside briefly in Michigan in 1857. In the end it remains impossible to determine the exact circumstances of Thomas's childhood because the details simply are unavailable. Pickaway County did not document guardianships until 1852 and Ohio did not record births and deaths until 1867.[5]

But it is certain that Thomas spent the first six or seven years of his life, and later periods as well, in the vicinity of Circleville, the county seat and Pickaway County's marketing and commercial center. Even though Thomas left Ohio in 1865 and spent much of his adulthood away from the state, he always considered southcentral and central Ohio his home. He returned frequently to visit family and friends in Delaware and Westerville, and ultimately lived out his last years in Columbus. At critical times in his life, he ventured to Ohio to seek refuge and anonymity in mulatto and black communities in order to escape the grasp of those determined to hold him accountable for his misdeeds.

Though its population in 1840 totaled only 2,329 (including 112 blacks), Circleville nevertheless was one of Ohio's principal towns before the Civil War. Founded in 1810 on the site of a round prehistoric earthwork (by mid-century the circle had become square), Circleville and its environs were settled largely by migrants from Virginia and Pennsylvania. Located in the agriculturally rich Scioto Valley, Pickaway County attracted many settlers. By 1840 it contained 19,725 inhabitants, including 333 blacks. A decade later Jackson Township, northwest of Circleville along Darby Creek, where Thomas lived with the Whitings, contained 1,042 people, including 58 blacks. By 1860 the number of blacks in the township had increased to 115, making its black population the third largest in the county behind two of Circleville's wards. In 1860 Circleville proper contained a substantial black community of 495. In contrast, in the same year Cleveland and Columbus, cities with considerably larger white populations and of more importance to Ohio's economy, had 799 and 997 blacks, respectively. In the 1860 census, Pickaway County had a total of 936 people of African heritage, 631 blacks and 305 mulattoes.[6]

Local lore around Circleville held that Virginians settled on the west bank of the Scioto River near Jackson Township. They reportedly were wealthier, more conservative, and more homogeneous than the heterogeneous Pennsylvanians who settled on the east bank. Both Circleville and Pickaway County were envied throughout the state as agricultural marketing and production centers. The Scioto River linked Circleville to Columbus to the north and Chillicothe and the Ohio River to the south first by flatboats, after 1818 by steamboats, and, in 1831, by the Ohio and Erie Canal. A wooden aqueduct carried the canal over the Scioto River at Circleville, which benefited from its status as a canal town. The canal brought new settlers and new ideas to rural Pickaway County and, significantly, connected it commercially to the East (via the Great Lakes) and to the South (New Orleans). Circleville had a reputation as a hog- and cattle-packing center. Meat was shipped south on the canal to the Ohio River and then distributed throughout the Mississippi Valley. This agricultural trade was the lifeblood of southcentral Ohio. Containing some of Ohio's richest soils, the Scioto Valley reaped rich harvests of apples, corn, hay, and wheat. According to an early historian, "with such soil, with beautiful and clear streams, and a fine climate, the farmers of Pickaway have a 'goodly heritage.'"[7]

Living in this agriculturally abundant area, the black minority encountered little difficulty in finding employment. Pickaway's black community emerged soon after Ohio became a state in 1803. By 1820 twenty-three black families had settled there, mostly emancipated Virginia slaves who worked as farm laborers. Over the next decade Pickaway's black population doubled and thrived. In 1830 the county had twenty-five black heads of families. Jackson Township contained five. In Darbyville, Charles McFeeters, a mulatto, established his own blacksmith shop. Some blacks purchased their own farms, while most labored for others or worked in service industries. In 1860 Henry Whiting had accumulated a modest $200 in private property. This amount is significant because, according to economist Lee Soltow, in 1850 only 45 percent of male Ohioans aged twenty and older owned land, and the "probability of a free colored male's owning property was very small indeed, about one-fourth of that of all freemen." Whiting's son, Samuel Whiting, and Will Thomas were employed as farm laborers. They comprised part of a small and insular but vibrant black community in Circleville.[8]

Since 1834 Circleville had supported an active congregation of the African Methodist Episcopal (a.m.e.) Church and later, in the 1850s, an African Baptist Church. A white teacher, Miss Raymond, reported in 1840 that she had taught a five-month term in a "colored" school in Circleville. She observed that the "mental capacities" of her black pupils were "equal to the whites in similar circumstances." The black community received guarded support from some local whites, especially the editor of the moderate Whig (and later Republican) *Circleville Herald*. Writing in 1854, for example, editor Gamaliel Scott attacked the increasing power of the slave states as a threat to "Republicanism." "If," Scott asked, "the increase of slavery, and the power of slavery be sanctioned and encouraged, why not the increase of Monarchy, or any other form of Despotism?" Because since 1804 Ohio's blacks had suffered from the state's discriminatory "black laws," Pickaway's residents of African descent needed all the support they could get from whites. In addition to mandated proscription and exclusion based on race, during the 1850s reports surfaced regularly of fugitive slaves being kidnapped in the county by slave catchers and being returned to the South.[9]

Circleville reportedly constituted part of a main artery of the Underground Railroad, the informal network of hundreds of escape routes that crisscrossed Ohio and assisted runaway slaves on their journey to freedom. Ohio's location—bordering slave states on its southern and southeastern boundaries—made the state a logical haven for runaway slaves. Over time, as historian Wilbur H. Siebert has argued, the various "lines" of the Underground Railroad came together and established "a great network" in Ohio. In 1842 an anonymous writer concluded that "there exist some eighteen or nineteen thoroughly organized thoroughfares through the State of Ohio for the transportation of runaway or stolen slaves." A half-century later, Siebert raised the number of "lines" in Ohio to no fewer than twenty-two or twenty-three. They allegedly ran from the border states up to Chillicothe, then to

Circleville, and up through Columbus to the village of "Africa" (named in the mid-1840s for its antislavery sentiments) in southern Delaware County. From "Africa," the escapees were led north to Canada. Siebert identified three "operators" of the Underground Railroad in Pickaway County, including Bishop William Hanby of the Church of the United Brethren in Christ (UBC).[10]

While living in Circleville, Will Thomas and his family came under the influence of the UBC, which located its administrative offices and publishing house there before moving to Dayton. The UBC was founded in Frederick County, Maryland, by the German Reformed pastor Philip William Otterbein, the Swiss-American Mennonite evangelist Martin Boehm, and other reform evangelists who sought a renewal of faith in established frontier churches, not in the establishment of a new sect. Otterbein migrated to America from Ockersdorf, Germany, in 1752 and ministered German Reformed churches in Pennsylvania and Maryland. He espoused a merger of Calvinist and German pietism, following Methodist and Arminian patterns, and believed that faith was developed through commitment to God. Faith was achieved, he believed, not by baptism but by emphasizing the Trinity, reading the Bible, praying, singing hymns, and performing good works. He rejected the idea of strict adherence to a specific creed. The sect, identified as "German Perfectionist," differed little from Methodism except for its insistence on preaching in German. Like John Wesley, Otterbein, Boehm, and their disciples stressed an intimate, personal, experiential relationship with God.

Despite their intentions, in 1800 a new church took shape, though the UBC name was not decided upon until 1821. At first it considered itself an "unsectarian" religious movement and evolved gradually into an independent denomination. The UBC's confession of faith and book of discipline were printed in both German and English. In practice the church adapted the Methodists' quarterly, annual, and general conferences, although the ministry had only one order, the elders. In 1841 the UBC constitution prohibited membership in secret societies like the Freemasons and opposed racial slavery. Will Thomas's father, a literate mulatto, subscribed to the *Religious Telescope,* the UBC's official organ. Years later Will would publish several articles in the denomination's scholarly journal, the *United Brethren Review.* The *Religious Telescope,* Thomas explained, appealed to poor, working-class people such as his kin. Like the contributors to the newspaper, the Thomases were "fresh from plow and ax." They too lived in "rustic simplicity," were "foes to all carnality," and "stood for absolute faith in an incarnate God, a militant church, and actual devil." [11]

In 1850 Thomas's parents moved to Indiana, he recalled, "in search of material betterment." No record exists to indicate whether seven-year-old Will accompanied them, and, if not, who cared for him. Most likely he was apprenticed to Henry Whiting. Nor did Thomas ever explain where in Indiana his parents relocated or for how long. One thing, however, is certain: in 1851 Indiana legislators passed Article XIII of the new state constitution, prohibiting blacks or mulattoes from entering or settling in the state and voiding all future contracts between whites and persons of African descent. Blacks who already resided in the state were required to register with county clerks. Although historian Emma Lou Thornbrough found that this legislation "was not systematically enforced," it nonetheless signified overt "racial prejudice, and as such it probably deterred Negroes from coming into the state." Confronted by such a negative racial climate, after only a short residency in Indiana the Thomases returned to Ohio. [12]

Will and his family spent approximately the next five years in Ohio, probably in Pickaway County. Years later he wrote that in 1856, at age thirteen, he finally "saw the inside of a schoolroom," attending an eleven-week term at a rural district school. That, he said, was "the first and only colored school I ever attended." Ohio's country district schools, Thomas complained, offered at best "only the most rudimentary instruction." Luckily, he explained, years earlier his mother, Rebecca, had taught him how to read and he developed "an extraordinary fondness" for books. "Therefore, having read some books of history and travel, though I was chiefly familiar with the Bible, I found myself, when I entered my first school . . . ahead in intelligence of many who were twice my age." Another two years would pass before Thomas again entered a schoolroom. In the meantime, in 1857, his parents once more were on the move—this time accompanied by their children. They ventured "with a hope of opportunity to educate their children" to Adrian, Michigan, fifty-nine miles southwest of Detroit and just north of the Ohio border. [13]

Michigan, however, like Ohio and Indiana, was no bastion of racial liberalism. Rather, according to historian Ronald P. Formisano, it "was a caste society, by custom and by law." The state's legislature grudgingly agreed to incorporate schools for blacks only after forceful protests by blacks and the passing of an amendment segregating the races. Its black laws, Formisano explains, "discouraged both blacks and slave catchers from coming to Michigan—an early display of the co-existence of anti-black and anti-slaveholder sentiments that prevailed in the 1850s." [14]

Adrian had slightly under 3,000 white residents and only 18 blacks in 1850. The surrounding Lenawee County, however, had a black community where 92 people of African descent lived in 1850. This number increased to 243 a decade later. During the 1850s Adrian, thanks to its railroad industry, grew into Michigan's second-largest city. Foundries and ironworks of various kinds lured workers in search of jobs. In these years the city's white population doubled and, despite the racial hostility exhibited by whites elsewhere in Michigan, the number of blacks in Adrian increased almost sevenfold. Blacks migrated there because Adrian had the reputation of being Michigan's foremost antislavery enclave. After speaking in Adrian in 1853, William Lloyd Garrison remarked, "it is impossible to say anything new here on the subject of slavery, as they have had all our able lecturers in superabundance. It is almost like 'carrying coals to Newcastle.'" In 1857, when the Thomases arrived in Adrian, the escaped Kentucky slave William Wells Brown visited the town to lecture against slavery. Brown "was once a slave," wrote the editor of the *Adrian Expositor*. "He is now a man, and an intelligent one at that." [15]

Adrian offered Will Thomas one of the better school systems in Michigan. In 1849 several of the town's school districts were consolidated into the Union School, which, in the late 1850s, was augmented by the addition of four branch schools. No doubt Will attended integrated classes. In Adrian the Thomases came under the influence of the local UBC minister, a Mr. Miller, and joined his small congregation that had been established in the summer of 1856 on Maumee Street. In the winter of 1857, Will, then fourteen years old, and his brother Prescott S. Thomas, age twelve, attended revival meetings at the church and were converted to the UBC church. Thomas wrote that while both he and his brother were deeply religious, they nonetheless "were quite unlike in character and temperament." He described Prescott as being "impulsive and emotional" and one who "in our weekly church meetings spoke and prayed with great fervency, so much so that he was accredited with gifts and graces that seemed to set him apart for the ministry." Years later, possibly with Prescott in mind, Thomas castigated "negro religionists" whom he had known since his youth, blasting their hypocrisy, immorality, and insincerity. [16]

In the fall of 1857, reportedly in order to gain theological training for Prescott, who was barely a teenager, the Thomas family moved once more—this time to Westerville, Ohio, where Prescott was promised a scholarship to attend the UBC's Otterbein University by one of the school's trustees. Westerville, located twelve miles north of Columbus in Franklin County, was connected to the state capital by a four-horse omnibus that traversed a plank toll road. In 1859 Westerville passed one of Ohio's earliest local prohibition ordinances, outlawing the sale of wine, fermented cider, beer, and hard liquor. In 1909 the town became even more identified with temperance when the Anti-Saloon League located its printing plant and national headquarters there. Westerville, however, has largely been identified with Otterbein. As early as 1856 a traveler remarked as he passed through Westerville, "we visited the University around which the said village is located, for the village is nothing but an appendage to the college." [17]

Life in Westerville was difficult for the Thomases. Their previous moves had left the family of nine virtually penniless. By the time they arrived in Westerville their horses had died and they had been forced to sell their cattle and hogs in order to survive. Though a college town, most of Westerville's population supported themselves by farming. Virtually all of the male students also performed manual labor to meet their expenses. As a result, Thomas explained, "the excessive supply of crude labor reduced the compensation to a very low rate." Thomas thus competed with the white college students for winter work, sawing and splitting wood for the village families, and for farm labor during the spring, summer, and fall. Despite the economic pressures on his family, Thomas shared a bond with other working-class residents. "As comparative poverty was the common lot," he recalled, "neither ostentatious vulgarity, nor obsequious servility disturbed the community." [18]

Residents of Westerville and its environs were not only almost totally poor, they were also almost exclusively white. With the exception of only one other man, who labored for a village preacher, the Thomases were the only blacks in Blendon Township when they settled there. In 1850 the U.S. census reported none residing in Westerville or Blendon Township. A decade later it listed Westerville's and Blendon's total population as 1,747, including 12 "free colored." Harold B. Hancock, historian of both Westerville and Otterbein, has argued, "in view of the abolitionist sympathies of the faculty at the college and of many residents," Westerville's minuscule black population "is surprising." Local legend long held that Westerville in general, and the homes of Otterbein president, the Reverend Lewis Davis, and UBC bishop and *Religious Telescope* editor William Hanby in particular, were "stations" on the Underground Railroad. Escaped slaves reportedly spent the night in Westerville and then were passed on northward to "Africa." If

Westerville did indeed serve as a refuge for escaped slaves, local blacks no doubt played an essential role in succoring them and ushering them safely on their way northward to freedom. Professor Siebert identified four people of African descent among the thirty-seven "operators" he located in Franklin County. In his revisionist history of the legend of the Underground Railroad, historian Larry Gara argued that "the [mere] existence of Negro populations in northern towns and cities is often cited as evidence of an underground terminal."[19]

In one of his few autobiographical writings, Thomas remarked that his family was imbued with antislavery zeal. "I was bred in an atmosphere of aversion to human bondage," Thomas recalled. He credited his parents with instilling in him "positive convictions concerning life and liberty." Among his earliest memories were daily prayers for "'those who were in bonds.'" Thomas said that his family did more than simply pray for the South's slaves: "For, as far back as I can remember, my parents' home was the rendezvous of escaping slaves, from whose recital my childish heart drank in the miseries of human chattel. My father was an active conductor on the 'Underground Railroad,' and, besides sheltering and succoring slavery's unfortunate victims, spent many of his nights in transporting his passengers nearer to their haven of refuge." With uncharacteristic modesty, Thomas insisted that in aiding fugitive slaves traveling northward, his parents were not unusual. Many other Ohio blacks, he said, "put in jeopardy their lives and liberty, to protect and defend the fleeing subjects of an atrocious enthralment and bear them well on the way to a land of freedom."[20]

In Westerville, Will and Prescott joined the local UBC congregation and attended its Sunday school. Thomas credited Benjamin ("Ben") Russel Hanby, son of Bishop Hanby, "with rare mental and spiritual nobility." Ben, who taught in Westerville's common, or primary, schools while a student at Otterbein, also presided over Will's Sabbath school class, instructing him in theology and influencing him greatly. Thomas recalled that Westerville was a highly religious community. There were no fewer than ten resident preachers, including Lewis Davis, president of Otterbein University, as well as many university students who served as licentiate ministers. Thomas remarked that the village contained twenty-seven preachers, who offered considerable "quantity if not quality of preaching."[21]

In the winter of 1857–58, Will and Prescott attended the white district school in Blendon Township taught by a Miss Mercer. The two brothers were the first blacks to enter the school, whose term lasted twelve weeks and which included fifty pupils. Thomas recalled his instructor as "a nervous but conscientious teacher" and remembered being poorly prepared for school. Near the end of the term, for example, Miss Mercer asked him to prepare an "essay" to be read at the closing exercises. Thomas had no idea what an "essay" was until a classmate informed him that an "essay is what you write out of your head; a declamation is what you speak out of a book." Armed with this insight, Thomas wrote an essay on the hottest political issue of the late 1850s—"Kansas Affairs." He received high marks for his essay, including praise from one of the local ministers, the Reverend Mr. Van Anda.[22]

Thomas also attended school for twelve weeks in the winter of 1859 under Hezikiah Conley Pennell, an Otterbein graduate who befriended Thomas and inspired him to attend the same university. Pennell's ungraded "village school," located on West Home Street, was established in 1855 and was the first public school in the area with a large recitation room. It was, according to Thomas, "the best of its kind in the vicinity." Thomas flourished under Pennell, gaining admittance to the highest classes available. The two young men later would cut wood together in the local forests. Thomas retained "tender memories . . . of these school days, and from them I date the beginning of awakened mental faculties." These were "lightsome and joyous" moments in his life, "knowing nothing of life-cares, or sorrows." Years later he remarked that he had good relationships with his classmates in Westerville's district and village schools.[23]

But attendance at school was the exception rather than the rule during Thomas's youth. Like the vast majority of free blacks in antebellum America, the Thomases performed unskilled labor in order to survive. The Afro-American Communities Project, National Museum of American History, estimates that more than 70 percent of all free blacks before the Civil War were unskilled workers. Will spent most of his youth performing manual labor. In the spring of 1859 he was hired for five months by a small farmer on the outskirts of Westerville who paid him $11.00 per month in wages. Over the course of the next fall Thomas cut fifty cords of stove wood and split several hundred rails for one of the local ministers, a Reverend Mr. Bowman. Another resident preacher, the Reverend Jacob Zeller, next hired him to saw and split his winter wood and perform farm work. As compensation, Reverend Zeller, who also served as a language tutor at Otterbein, promised to provide Thomas with a scholarship to the university, where the tuition was $9.00 per term in 1860.[24]

Having completed only a few terms at the local district schools and being basically self-educated, Thomas nevertheless had a burning desire for formal education. He wanted to enter Otterbein University, an institution that given

Thomas's past experiences represented intellectual, cultural, and economic status and achievement. Even before moving to Westerville, Will was familiar with the university because of its sponsorship by the UBC. "My cherished ambition in early life," he wrote many years later, "was to become an alumnus of Otterbein University." Thomas recalled "the feeling of awe" that he experienced when he attended the school's 1858 commencement. The Latin oratory inspired Thomas, imbuing in him "a sense of harking back to forgotten ages." Since moving to Westerville, Thomas had come to know and respect many of the university students, especially his Sunday school teacher, Ben Hanby. Apparently the Thomases knew many Otterbein students from performing odd jobs for them and for other members of Westerville's white community. "Sometimes," Will recalled, "a number of them would unite in purchasing unusual edibles, which they brought to our house for my mother to cook for them. At such times they always insisted on sharing their meal with us." [25]

Otterbein, established in 1847, was the first educational institution opened by the UBC and the only UBC-related college in the pre–Civil War era. The school's founders sought to make Westerville and Otterbein "a nucleus of holy Christian influence"—distancing themselves from the crass materialism and distractions of nearby "urban" centers such as Columbus and insisting on strict discipline on the part of the students. Otterbein in no way resembled a university in the contemporary European sense, and it compared poorly even with Oberlin College, the institution to which Otterbein's founders insisted on comparing itself. Lacking the financial support that silk merchant Lewis Tappan provided Oberlin in its infancy, Otterbein more closely resembled dozens of impoverished, provincial, and isolated denominational colleges that emerged in the midwest and along the trans-Appalachian frontier in the mid-nineteenth century. [26]

These institutions tended to possess few and mediocre libraries, classrooms, laboratories, and students. Narrow and sectarian, they resulted from "the college movement" of their day—the merger of "denominational imperialism," "sectarian aggrandizement and aggression," and the ethos of the expanding middle class. Even the UBC, which prided itself on its populist creed and unpretentious clergy, joined the race to establish its own college and compete with other sects for students. Otterbein, like scores of other colleges, thus originated more from "denominational ambition" and the need for an educated clergy than from devotion to high scholarship. According to Frederick Rudolph, such schools were spirited by "a torrent of piety." Their faculties were little better—comprised largely of journeyman theologians and professors with limited training in the "classics." Otterbein's curriculum stressed Greek, Latin, mathematics, science, and philosophy. On the eve of the Civil War the school's campus consisted of two brick buildings and one frame building situated on nine acres of land. The library held 1,300 volumes. Attendance at daily religious services was required.[27]

Otterbein offered both academy (college preparatory) as well as college-level work, but until 1889 college preparatory students dominated its student body. Otterbein did not graduate its first class until 1857 but, significantly, that class included two women. Like Oberlin Collegiate Institute (founded in 1833 and chartered in 1834), Otterbein had been coeducational since its establishment. According to Otterbein's first historian, Professor Henry Garst, though Oberlin was the first college in America to graduate women (1841), Otterbein had the distinction of first admitting women without limitations or restrictions. In the 1859–60 academic year, Otterbein had eight professors and enrolled 267 students. The student body included 13 graduate students, 54 students enrolled in the Classical Course, 63 students enrolled in the Ladies' Course, and 137 students enrolled in the Scientific Course. In 1860, a majority (67 percent) of the student body studied in the college preparatory program.[28]

Though Otterbein was in no way a hotbed of abolitionism and interracial education like Oberlin or Lane Theological Seminary, Professor Garst nonetheless described it as "a center of anti-slavery sentiment and agitation." Such renowned abolitionists as Salmon P. Chase, Benjamin Wade, and Frederick Douglass spoke on campus. The school's principal commencement speaker in 1859 was abolitionist Congressman Joshua R. Giddings. Garst credited the school with "throwing open its doors to black and white alike" and asserted that only Oberlin preceded Otterbein in admitting blacks. Oberlin began encouraging black students to enroll in 1835, and its first black student, James Bradley, enrolled the following year amidst considerable dissent from some of the school's founders. "At the heart of the argument against black enrollment" at Oberlin, historian James O. Horton writes, "was the often unexpressed sexual fear of racial integration of a coeducational institution." Not until 1844 would the first black, George B. Vashon, graduate from Oberlin. Though no college before the Civil War matched Oberlin's record in educating people of African descent, the college's historian concluded that "less than one-twentieth of the students attending Oberlin in ante-bellum days were colored." Oberlin ultimately satisfied its warring factions by establishing the "liberal principle of equal access to education," not the "more radical notion of racial equality." By 1865 thirty-two black men and women completed their degrees at Oberlin.[29]

Otterbein's Professor Garst contrasted "the struggle" that integration caused at Oberlin with "the matter-of-course way in which it was done at Otterbein." As a church, the UBC prohibited slaveholding among its members and generally opposed slavery. Their stand on slavery was all the more significant because many of the denomination's early members resided in slave-holding Maryland and Virginia. Unlike the Methodist Episcopal Church, the smaller UBC never split over slavery. Otterbein's administration reportedly sympathized openly with blacks. According to Garst, "it was taken for granted that the institution would be open impartially to whites and blacks." And whereas some colleges feared the presence of black students, at Otterbein "there was anxiety because colored students were so slow in coming."[30]

Though in 1854 Otterbein's trustees had passed a resolution to recruit "colloured students," no blacks enrolled until Will Thomas's appearance in 1859. Early in that year a heated exchange occurred in the *Religious Telescope* over the treatment of blacks in Westerville's district school and at the university. A critic, "Younker," charged that local whites treated people of African descent as "*animals* of an inferior order" and denied them equal access to the common school. A "down-right fuss" resulted when critics insisted that "'niggers' had souls that might be saved, and minds that should be cultivated." Black children were ultimately admitted to the school. "Younker" went on to question why, given Otterbein's supposed "Republican sentiments and Christian principles," two blacks had been denied admission to the university. Was it "the doughfaceism so prevalent in the North?" he asked.[31]

In response, James Weaver, Otterbein's fiscal agent, defended Westerville's treatment of blacks and charged that the village's commitment to antislavery principles was beyond question. Blacks sat in integrated pews at the local church and at religious meetings. Weaver added that Otterbein contained no black students because none had ever formally applied. "Had colored people applied with testimonials of good moral character, and paid their bills as others do, they would doubtless have been admitted. *Character* and not *color*," he explained, "is the standard by which students are measured when they enter the college." Subsequent events, however, cast serious doubt on Weaver's (and later Garst's) interpretation of Otterbein's commitment to interracial education. Willard W. Bartlett, who interviewed Thomas in 1933 while researching his history of Otterbein, admits that the university had only been "saved from a serious controversy by the simple fact that colored students did not apply for admission." Circumstances soon changed.[32]

On November 11, 1859, the school's faculty considered the application of "Samuel Thomas (colored)," possibly one of Will's relatives. While the faculty expressed willingness to admit Samuel, it nevertheless rejected him because he was too young, "under 15 years." Soon after, Will, aged sixteen, applied for admission. Thomas's application sent shock waves through the tiny denominational school. The student body was deeply divided on the issue. While some students opposed Will's enrollment, others welcomed it. For its part, Otterbein's board of trustees was ambivalent on the question of admitting blacks. On November 14, three days after the faculty's decision to reject Samuel Thomas, the board's executive committee had a heated debate on Will's admission. It finally tabled, by a vote of four to two, a resolution "that it is inexpedient and unwise to admit students of color until the Board of Trustees representing the Conferences now cooperating in the building up of this Institution, shall have been permitted to pass upon this whole question." With no parliamentary means of blocking his admission, opponents of Thomas's admission reluctantly agreed to enroll him at Otterbein.[33]

According to Henry A. Thompson, who served as Otterbein's president from 1872 to 1886, Otterbein's administration really had no choice but to admit Will Thomas. Thompson, who remembered Will as a promising student at Otterbein, "a young man of sterling worth and upright character," recalled that in 1859, "the ever-present negro who for years has been the bone of contention, was at one time likely to make us some trouble, but the danger was passed. An Anti-slavery church, admitting no slaveholders to her communion, could not in good faith to the world and in keeping with her published creed do anything else than admit colored students to her colleges provided, they presented themselves for admittance." The opposition, Thompson explained, consisted of "some young men of finer birth and richer blood." Even after the resolution to bar black students was defeated, pressure continued to be exerted on the board to prevent integration at Otterbein. Although those who opposed interracial education at Otterbein may have lost the first battle, they ultimately won the war.[34]

Professor Robert M. Walker, then acting president and professor of Latin, enrolled Will in Otterbein's English preparatory course for the 1859–60 winter term. As the first black American to enroll at the school, Thomas felt the taunts and stares that have faced people of African descent who tested segregation throughout American history. No evidence suggests that Thomas sought to "make trouble" at Otterbein. Rather, he viewed his admittance as the most important opportunity in his life to better himself. Largely self-educated up to that point, Will believed that Otterbein would afford him systematic, disciplined Christian education with the opportunity to learn from his fellow students. He recalled that his plans to attend Otterbein were well known in Westerville and that no one in the university community had voiced objection to his presence on campus.[35]

At first Will received a cordial welcome from his fellow students. After about ten days, however, tranquillity turned to turmoil. According to Thomas, "a turbulent spirit awoke; a general uprising that swept the sober-minded off their feet took place, and never before nor since has Westerville passed through such an event as was occasioned by my presence in the college; nor did it end there." Will's enrollment at Otterbein was denounced vehemently throughout the village and on the campus. He was condemned by "inflammatory speeches" throughout the community. When verbal abuse failed to deter him, about a dozen male students ganged up on him, subjecting the sixteen-year-old to physical attacks. He recalled: "I was assaulted on the street; in the classroom the leaves of my books were torn out, and I was stuck with shawl-pins by those who sat around me; when I passed out of the building groups of waiting students pelted me with rocks hidden in wet snow-balls." The attack on Thomas reached a fever pitch at one Friday evening's rhetorical exercises held in the chapel. One of the students, a senior known for his "fervid oratory," announced that the university "had a surfeit of 'nigger'; that it was 'nigger for breakfast, nigger for dinner, and nigger for supper.'" The student body laughed, jeered at Thomas, and applauded loudly. When Professor Walker sought to disarm the situation with a humorous rebuke, he was met with "derision" by the students. Thomas recalled that Professor Serena W. Streeter, a UBC minister who taught philosophy, rhetoric, and belles lettres at Otterbein, "looked serious" throughout the entire proceeding but said nothing. Neither did the other faculty members, who sat "silent and uneasy." "Through it all," Thomas remembered bitterly, "I sat humiliated and angered."[36]

On the next day Will was summoned to the home of the Reverend William Hanby, where he was joined by two other members of the Otterbein board of trustees. They advised him to withdraw from the university because he was likely to be injured by his fellow students. They recommended that he return to the village school. "When I modestly expressed some ability for physical defense," Thomas said, "I was told that if I would leave Otterbein, I should be sent to Oberlin College, where the cost of my education would be met by them." When he rejected this offer, the trustees informed him that if he did not withdraw voluntarily, he would be expelled from Otterbein because his presence "imperiled the very existence of the school."[37]

Summarizing the administration's view of the incident, Professor Garst described it as a "little temporary flurry of opposition on the part of a few white students" followed by "a letter to the board by a prominent and liberal friend of the college, criticizing the authorities for receiving colored students." Unwilling to cave in to the trustees' pressure, Thomas "defied" their effort to expel him and "left [the meeting] in no amiable mood." Years later Will admitted that he might have been "blamed for not accepting the offer" to go to Oberlin, "but I had sound reasons for distrusting so exigent a promise, which, if made in good faith, was impossible to fulfill." He doubted whether in fact the Otterbein trustees could scrape together enough money to send him to Oberlin.[38]

But Thomas never questioned that the trustees were correct in their assessment of the seriousness of the crisis that his presence on campus precipitated. Within days of the Friday evening attack on him, several students, including some from Virginia, left Otterbein. With their departure, conditions quieted on campus and, Thomas explained, "the excitement subdued as quickly as it had arisen." He later interpreted the entire unpleasant experience as part of a conservative response to John Brown's October 1859 raid on the U.S. arsenal and armory at Harpers Ferry, Virginia.[39]

Brown's capture, conviction, and execution, Thomas wrote, "had wrought up the public mind to a tense pitch . . . and many of the students at Otterbein . . . shared the sentiments of his enemies." He considered Brown a "mistaken old man." Whether or not this analysis was accurate, the racial prejudice unleashed against Thomas soon was aimed at two of his brothers then attending the village school. When Thomas refused to join his brothers at the school, a trustee instructed Pennell to forbid their further attendance. Undaunted, Thomas's parents sent the boys to school the next day, where they were forcibly removed from the building and warned not to return. Rebecca Thomas ultimately resolved the issue by reportedly contacting Salmon P. Chase, Ohio's outspoken Republican governor. Chase, "with characteristic promptitude" immediately had the boys readmitted to their school.[40]

Fortunately for Will, after the departure of the southern students he experienced no more trouble at Otterbein and was treated, in his words, "in a manly fashion" by his classmates. He was even asked to join the university's Philomathean Hall Literary Society. Generally, however, Thomas segregated himself from the whites on campus. He resided "with his own people" and only met with whites in classes and in church. He credited his female student colleagues with successfully overcoming the racist barrage at Otterbein. They were, he said, "with rare exceptions . . . uniformly courteous in intercourse." He complimented "the outspoken words and courageous acts of several of these young ladies, especially one from West Virginia, who effectually held in check the mob spirit of the male students." At times, according to Thomas, the women surrounded him, shielding him from the verbal and physical abuse of the men.[41]

Will did not complete the 1859-60 winter term at Otterbein. Dismayed by his shoddy treatment by some of the students, trustees, and faculty, he departed Westerville early in 1860. He spent a total of only ten weeks on campus—one-half of the winter term. Given the controversial nature of his stay there, he probably would have been denied his scholarship even had he insisted on remaining enrolled at Otterbein. Thomas's brother, Prescott, was denied admittance by the faculty on January 25, 1860, "it appearing that he is not qualified to enter the classes to advantage." Prescott's "illusive dreams" of obtaining theological training at Otterbein "were never realized," Will solemnly wrote. He "died in his nineteenth year, in the Union army." Though Thomas had good reason to harbor resentment at Otterbein, he conceded that the university provided him certain benefits, including a "fair knowledge" of grammar, history, geography, and mathematics. He apparently made friends at the local UBC church because after the Civil War its minister, William Hanby, wrote glowingly of Thomas "as a gentleman, a scholar and Christian." Significantly, Bartlett writes that following Thomas's departure, no other blacks applied to Otterbein and "further controversy was avoided." Only a handful of blacks attended Otterbein in the post–Civil War years, but, according to Bartlett, those who did enroll were "received courteously and on equal terms in the class room and in the church." In fact, not until 1884 would the first black, William Henry Fouse, the son of two North Carolina slaves, graduate from Westerville's two-year high school program. Nine years later Fouse became the first person of African descent to earn a degree from Otterbein.[42]

Though Thomas never earned a college degree and his association with Otterbein was short-lived, he always valued higher education and longed for the opportunity to teach. Once, many years after he had left Ohio, Thomas, "in a reminiscent mood," sought permission from Otterbein's president to begin "non-resident study for the Ph.D. degree." Thomas's proposal, not surprisingly, "was curtly refused." His experiences with racial intolerance at

Otterbein deeply injured Thomas's feelings and made a deep impression on his racial views. Years later he described his anger during the Otterbein incident as "a sense of needless unfairness." The episodes at Otterbein served as his first recorded brush with overt racism and bigotry. In Westerville, Thomas began his tortured path toward a recognition of the problems that confronted blacks in general and mulattoes in particular. It was his identification as a Negro that had caused him such anguish in Westerville. Ultimately he would distance himself from blacks in order to find a separate place for himself and other mulattoes.[43]

Shunned from the white man's university and, implicitly, the white man's world, because of his identification with blacks, Thomas looked elsewhere — to God — for education and guidance. Though appreciative of the benefits of higher education, Thomas came to "believe that wise insight into the realities of life is, under God-fearing guidance, clearly within the reach of every one." Even the unlettered, Thomas argued, could attain "soul-development . . . in quest of the Infinite." "I know," he wrote in 1905, "that whatever equipment I possess of intelligent conviction, sane judgment, breadth of sympathy, strength of character, spiritual vision, and other qualities of intrinsic worth are derived from conscious kinship with God."[44]

But Thomas never forgot the pain he experienced as a sixteen-year-old boy heckled and harassed by his schoolmates at Otterbein. Reflecting years later on Ohio's black laws and layers of de facto segregation, he wrote that blacks were at best "nominally considered citizens"—"they shared all the obligations, and performed all the duties devolving upon citizens proper, yet were deprived of the advantages accruing from their citizenship." Yet for all his anger and disappointment, Thomas remained proud that in 1859 he had tested and broken the color line at Otterbein. On occasion he even wrote of the university as his "alma mater." Denied the opportunity to attend the school of his choice, he remarked in 1901 that he, like most blacks of his generation, was educated "in the school of adversity." "I would have bartered half of my life," Thomas explained with typical hyperbole, to have had the educational opportunities afforded early twentieth-century blacks.[45]

Will left Westerville and spent the remainder of 1860 and early 1861 in Pickaway County, first as a farm laborer and, later, as the foreman of a sawmill. The federal census taker visited the Whitings' farm on July 17, 1860, and recorded Thomas's occupation as "farm laborer." Meanwhile, early in the decade the rest of Thomas's family moved to the central Ohio town of Delaware, twenty-three miles north of Columbus. Though no record exists of his father's whereabouts, his mother, Rebecca, his sister, Hattie Thomas, and two brothers, Benjamin F. ("B. F.") Thomas and Walter S. Thomas, established themselves in Delaware for the next three decades. Both women worked locally as washerwomen. Rebecca reportedly also was a dressmaker and Hattie a hairdresser. "B. F." worked as a wheelwright in McElroy's Wagon Works and Walter labored as a photographer. With a white population of 22,049 in 1860, Delaware County contained only 128 people of African heritage, including 80 blacks and 48 mulattoes. Most had been free Negroes, not escaped slaves, when their families settled in town.[46]

Thomas, however, did not reside in Delaware with his mother and siblings. Rather, immediately after the Fort Sumter crisis he, like scores of other blacks, offered to join the U.S. Army. Because of the pervasive antagonism toward them in the North, and President Abraham Lincoln's unwillingness to alienate the loyal slave states and conservatives in the North, Ohio Governor William Dennison turned away black volunteers in droves. Like others Thomas was denied enlistment in the army. Will later recounted forcefully that he was "refused on account of my color,—one of not a few instances where color has militated against me." Yet he would ultimately gain his chance to serve in the army and have many opportunities to fight.[47]

In the summer of 1861, as white Union troops experienced defeat at the Battle of Bull Run, Thomas, with only ten weeks of studying in a preparatory department, became an educator. He served for a few months as acting principal of Union Seminary Institute, "which," he explained, "at that time was the sole academic school in America managed by negroes." Union Seminary was chartered in 1844 by the Ohio Annual Conference of the A.M.E. Church. The following year the conference purchased a 172-acre farm twelve miles west of Columbus in Franklin County as the site of its new school. The "seminary of learning" had a broad mission. It was to train everyone, from those who sought a common-school education to those preparing for careers as ministers. All students were expected to cultivate crops and perform other manual labor. Union Seminary of course did not pioneer the concept of education keyed to manual labor. New York's Oneida Academy and Ohio's Oberlin introduced the practice in 1827 and 1834, respectively.[48]

According to historian Bertram Wyatt-Brown, "the manual labor reform fad" of these years was premised "on the principle that learning to handle an axe instead of a whiskey bottle was the road to salvation and success." A.M.E. Church historian George A. Singleton credits Union Seminary with introducing the notion of black industrial education—"affording an opportunity" for students "to earn support for themselves while attending school"—long before Booker T. Washington popularized the "Tuskegee Idea." Despite its obscurity, Union Seminary represented the first step by blacks to offer higher education to people of African descent in Ohio. During its short history, the school had two distinguished principals, the Reverends John M. Brown and Edward P. Davis. Both men had attended Oberlin and earned strong credentials among Ohio abolitionists.[49]

Brown, a respected black activist and later an a.m.e. bishop, ran Union Seminary from its opening in 1847 until 1852. Because no structures were erected on the school's farm site, for six years Brown held temporary classes in the basement of Columbus's Bethel a.m.e. Church. In 1848 he wrote optimistically that Union Seminary was a "large and flourishing school of 53 scholars." Thomas came to know Brown and made a positive impression on him. Many years later the bishop recommended Thomas for public office. Davis, a Columbus minister, followed Brown as principal and returned the operations of the school to its original farm acreage in November 1853. Union Seminary had a shaky beginning because of inept organizing and severe underfunding by the conference and never established itself on a strong footing. In 1852, for example, Davis reported that he received only $85 to run the seminary for the academic year. Nevertheless, the school experienced steady growth under Davis during the 1850s. An observer recorded in 1852 that enrollment "varied each term, during the past year from 30 to 65." In 1854, however, only thirteen students matriculated and a.m.e. Bishop Daniel A. Payne complained that the seminary "was such a school as no intelligent parent would send a child from Columbus, Ohio, fourteen miles distant, to attend, because better schools, supported by state funds, were at their command." In 1858 Payne recommended that the school close.[50]

Thomas, hired as Davis's short-term replacement, became associated with Union Seminary at a time when the institution was in crisis. Once the Civil War began, its student body began to scatter. By 1863 only about twenty pupils were enrolled and the school ceased operations. Union Seminary, according to Singleton, had for years barely survived and finally succumbed to "poor management," apparently by Davis. "It lingered on in a miserable condition," Payne recalled, until March 1863, when the a.m.e. Church purchased Wilberforce University near Xenia, Ohio, from the Methodist Episcopal (m.e.) Church. The Ohio Conference then closed Union Seminary and sold its property "for the benefit of Wilberforce." Union Seminary's students and faculty merged with those of Wilberforce and Payne became the black school's first president. Thomas's tenure as an educator, then, lasted about as long as his career as a student. Ironically, years later he would renew these roles with quite similar results.[51]

Will Thomas's service in the Civil War provided new kinds of schooling—more painful encounters with racial discrimination, some triumphs, and a physical tragedy. Many years after the Civil War, he recalled, "I entered the army in August 1861, and remained in that service until July 1865, when I was discharged, minus a right arm." In point of fact, before 1863 he labored in the army as a noncombatant civilian. But his service from 1863 to 1865 in an armed African American regiment was the most influential event and the defining moment of his early adult years. Thomas blamed the war primarily on the South's "arrogance" and "aggressions," but held northern Democrats culpable for "bowing the knee to the cotton king. The imbecile Executive, Mr. [James] Buchanan," Thomas wrote in 1866, held "on to the skirts of his Southern lords, binding them with golden promises not to desert him, a mere tool in the hands of the Southern oligarchy." Not until Abraham Lincoln's election in 1860, however, did white northerners finally refuse to give way to "the grand aim of the South . . . the usurpation of power, and the extension of slave territory." "Great will be the judgment meted out to these Southern instigators of this unhallowed rebellion," Thomas intoned soon after war's end.[52]

To an important extent, Thomas's wartime experiences liberated him from the life of a farm worker in central Ohio. His first experience as a personal servant to an army officer enabled him to travel widely, meet educated white northerners, and become familiar with the rigors of military life. His later service as a combat soldier and noncommissioned officer introduced him to free blacks from throughout the North, slaves and freedpeople in the South, and white abolitionists. During the war he matured significantly and became a battle-scarred leader. Through his war experiences Thomas came to realize that no matter how limited his education, how circumscribed his experiences, he nonetheless could effect social change, and his racial ideology gradually began to take shape during the war.

His observations in the war-torn South inclined him to interpret blacks, especially slaves, as inferiors, people dependent upon the leadership of mulattoes such as himself. Nevertheless, in that formative period, and for almost four decades thereafter, Thomas worked largely for, not against, people of African descent. In the main he took constructive, positive steps to uplift others of his race. He made contributions to black American life that even his bitterest critics acknowledged. Not until 1901 would Thomas totally distance himself from blacks and thereby complete a lifelong cycle of self-destruction. But his first significant positions of growth, leadership, and responsibility began during the Civil War. Thomas's experiences in the U.S. Colored Troops (USCT) left him a changed man both figuratively and literally.

Spurned by the government in his earlier attempt to enter the army as a soldier, in September 1861, Thomas joined the 42nd Ohio Volunteer Infantry, then organizing at Camp Chase, Ohio, in what he quite typically obliquely termed "a civil capacity." In fact, Thomas was a servant for Captain William W. Olds of the 42nd. Olds first served as the 42nd's adjutant and later took command of Company A. As an infantry captain, Olds was allowed one servant by War Department regulations and was required to deduct from his pay the government's allotment for the servant. According to government regulations, Thomas was defined as a "private servant." In this capacity he was "not . . . allowed to wear the uniform of any corps of the army . . . [and was] required to carry with him a certificate from the officer who employs him." Though his duties were not specified, Thomas no doubt performed similar tasks as free blacks and fugitive slaves who labored as personal servants to Union officers or body servants to Confederate officers in the war. They generally washed, cleaned, cooked, foraged to supplement government-issue rations, cared for horses, split wood, blacked boots, brought water, and performed other odd jobs. According to historian Bell I. Wiley, "on at least one occasion Confederate domestics made prisoners of Negroes serving Yankee officers." In their youths such respected African American leaders as George L. Knox and James Milton Turner also served as servants to Union officers in the Civil War. So too did Milton M. Holland, who later won the Congressional Medal of Honor in the regiment in which Thomas later served. There was no indignity involved with performing such service.[53]

The 42nd, assigned to the Army of the Ohio, was commanded by Colonel James A. Garfield, the professor–turned–antislavery Republican politician–turned–self-taught military officer. In mid-December 1861, the 42nd began a campaign to drive Confederate forces out of eastern Kentucky's Big Sandy Valley and back into Virginia, thereby protecting the left flank of General George H. Thomas's First Division, Army of the Ohio. Garfield approached the campaign with trepidation. "The work," he wrote on December 17, "will be positively enormous, for a large share of the Kentucky forces are as yet unarmed and undisciplined. It is a horrible country, fully as rough as Western Virginia." Indeed, as soon as the 42nd steamed up the Ohio River to Catlettsburg, Kentucky, and then overland to Louisa, it traversed almost impenetrable mountain roads and marshlike countryside. The Kentucky campaign was characterized by blustering cold, heavy rains, swollen rivers, and seemingly endless mud. As a servant, Thomas had to brave the elements while hauling baggage, setting up and breaking camp, and preparing and serving meals. Despite the harsh conditions, the Union forces systematically pushed Confederate General Humphrey Marshall's small army back at Jenny's Creek on January 7, 1862, and occupied Paintsville the following day. The 42nd next engaged the Confederates in the Battle of Middle Creek on January 10, in which both sides claimed victory and withdrew from the field. The Union troops occupied Prestonsburg on January 11 and Pikeville on February 1 before finally taking possession of Pound Gap on March 16. The regiment occupied Cumberland Gap, Tennessee, from mid-June until early October when it was forced to retreat back to the Ohio River.[54]

Garfield's string of minor victories in the Big Sandy campaign and at Cumberland Gap earned him a brigadier's star and the 42nd considerable notoriety. At that early point in the war the northern press clamored for anything that even remotely smacked of victory in the field. Thomas, having served Captain Olds for more than a year, experienced the severity of combat, marched and camped in rugged eastern Kentucky and Tennessee, and gained familiarity with military life. Service with the army broadened him. He interacted with educated white officers and enlisted men from a variety of backgrounds and locales, captured Confederate soldiers, other free blacks, and slaves. According to historian Ira Berlin, "living in close quarters and sharing the rigors and camaraderie of camp life, servants often developed strong personal relationships with their employers." Thomas and Olds shared that experience and, in the opinion of Olds's father, became close. Nonetheless, Thomas left Olds's employ when the 42nd returned to Ohio in the fall of 1862. Olds was later killed in action at the Battle of Thompson's Hill, May 1, 1863, near Port Gibson, Mississippi. Although Thomas was attached to another Ohio regiment at that time, he served in the same campaign close to where Captain Olds fell.[55]

Thomas's next military assignment—again in "a civil capacity"—was with the 95th Ohio Volunteer Infantry, which he joined in November 1862. At that time the regiment was engaged in a major reorganization at Camp Chase. Originally mustered into service on August 19, the regiment was commanded by Colonel William L. McMillen and assigned to the Army of Kentucky, Department of the Ohio, under General Charles Cruft. No sooner had the regiment's recruits entered service, however, than the untrained and poorly equipped men were marched to Kentucky to ward off that state's invasion by Confederate General Edmund Kirby Smith. The inexperienced Ohioans proved no match for Smith's battle-tested veterans as the two forces collided at Richmond, Kentucky, on August 30. At first the 95th fought well, repulsing the Confederate attack on the Union left. But after several assaults the Union defenses folded and confusion reigned in the Federal ranks. In a stinging tactical defeat, the two brigades of Union troops totaling 6,500 men lost 206 killed, 844 wounded, and 4,303 missing (mostly captured). The 95th lost 24 men killed, 94 wounded, and 548 captured, 68 percent of its 975-man force. Most of the captured men were exchanged for Confederate prisoners of war on November 20. The remaining members of the decimated 95th regrouped at Camp Chase.[56]

No documentary record exists of Thomas's exact status with the reorganized 95th Ohio. Typically, he left few clues. But he no doubt labored once again as a "private servant" for one of the regiment's officers. On March 25, 1863, the reorganization of the 95th was complete and the unit steamed south down the Ohio and Mississippi rivers to Memphis, Tennessee, and then to Young's Point, Louisiana. It comprised part of General William T. Sherman's Fifteenth Army Corps, Army of the Tennessee, and participated in the second offensive against the Confederate Mississippi River stronghold at Vicksburg. General U. S. Grant, in command of the Department of the Tennessee, planned to attack Vicksburg from the south and east. On April 1 the 95th moved north to Duckport Landing, Louisiana, south of Milliken's Bend and northwest of Vicksburg.

There the regiment labored briefly in the construction of a canal to connect the Mississippi through a series of bayous that rejoined the river below Vicksburg. Grant's strategy was to bypass Vicksburg's heavy batteries and approach the city twenty miles to the south. The project, the second attempt to cut a canal, soon was abandoned. The 95th next engaged the enemy east of Vicksburg and south of the Vicksburg and Jackson Railroad—at Baldwin's Ferry and Mississippi Springs—smoothing the way for Sherman's capture of Jackson, Mississippi's capital, on May 14. Positioned on the enemy's right and behind its batteries, the 95th was the first Union regiment to enter Jackson. Five days later the 95th joined in the first of two failed assaults on Vicksburg (May 19 and 22). The regiment then took part in the six-week siege of Vicksburg. According to Ohio journalist Whitelaw Reid, the men of the 95th engaged in "digging canals, fighting on picket-lines, and living in bomb-proofs, until a few days before the capture of the city." Though a noncombatant, Thomas nevertheless was exposed to the rigors, hardships, and horrors of war. Even as a servant he made contacts that assisted him later in life. While serving with the 95th he met General Stephen A. Hurlbut, who commanded the Sixteenth Corps during the Vicksburg campaign. Hurlbut recalled that Thomas "was well spoken of by his officers." Thomas accompanied the regiment until after Vicksburg's fall on July 4. "I was at the surrender of Vicksburg," he informed General Oliver O. Howard many years later, and he remained with the 95th until July 9 when it began to lay siege of Jackson. Will then returned to his lifelong refuge, central Ohio. He soon would get his chance to return south, this time to fight against slavery and secession in Ohio's first African American regiment.[57]

On September 23, 1863, Thomas enrolled in the 127th Ohio Volunteer Infantry at Delaware, Ohio, and mustered into the regiment at Camp Delaware (located one mile south of town) on October 17. The 127th, renamed the 5th U.S. Colored Troops on November 1, became one of the most highly decorated black units in the Civil War, fighting in bloody campaigns in Virginia and North Carolina. Of the sixteen blacks awarded the Congressional Medal of Honor during the Civil War, four were men from the 5th — Sergeants Powhatan Beaty, Milton M. Holland, James H. Bronson, and Robert Pinn.[58] By war's end the regiment suffered 81 combat-related deaths, or almost 3 percent of the 2,894 men killed in combat or who died of wounds while serving in the USCT. In terms of total death statistics, Thomas's regiment ranked sixteenth among the 166 regiments of USCT.[59]

The 5th USCT, according to historians William and Aimee Lee Cheek, was composed of "painfully young black men" led by "idealistic, young white officers." Both temporarily subordinated notions of fairness, status, and equality "to ideas and emotions involving manhood and morality." Like other U.S. Colored Troops, for much of the war the men of the 5th received less pay ($10 per month, minus $3 for clothing) than white soldiers ($13 per month, plus clothing). Soon after the war Thomas insisted that during the first year of service his regiment "received no pay." In numerous other ways the colored troops' military experience was largely separate and unequal from that of whites. Nevertheless, the Cheeks insist that for the black Ohioans "the state's symbolic recognition of their status as men mattered deeply." Thomas agreed. "We laid the foundation for our future nation," he wrote, "when we entered the ranks of the Union army." In his opinion, Ohio's first black regiment contained "a latent power . . . which," when "developed, would make them the best soldiers."[60]

Immediately upon entering his training at Camp Delaware, Thomas made a positive impression on his superiors. The white regimental chaplain, James L. Patton, who in 1865 comforted Thomas when he was wounded in combat, recalled that the regiment judged him "a *soldier, competent & faithful*," and "a *man* of *intelligence & Christian character*." As a result the company officers appointed him second sergeant on October 18, the day following his arrival in camp. Even though until mid-1864 sergeants in the USCT received the same pay as privates, appointment as a noncommissioned officer nonetheless was a distinction. Whereas 6.7 percent of Ohio white recruits won promotion to sergeant, only 0.2 percent of Ohio's black recruits attained that rank. Thomas thus held a position of authority and responsibility among his friends, neighbors, and new acquaintances with whom he served. But with leadership came stresses and strains. As Ira Berlin has noted, there was a wide gap between the power and prestige of a white commissioned officer and the noncommissioned officers of African descent, far more than the distinction in white units. Moreover, the USCT sergeants walked a tightrope between their men and the white officers to whom they reported. Many years later Thomas wrote cynically that whites who officered black regiments often exploited them. Caucasians assumed those commands, he asserted, "for self aggrandizement . . . [and] personal notoriety." They were "unable to obtain commissions in their own ranks" and "were glad to be exalted over black men."[61]

But in October 1863 Will's appointment as sergeant symbolized a considerable achievement and underscored his potential as a leader. Until late in the war sergeant was the highest rank that blacks could attain in the U.S. Army. And even then, only about one hundred men of African descent ever received commissions, mostly as chaplains, surgeons, recruiters, and as officers with the Louisiana Native Guards. During his military service Will held several other regimental (as opposed to company) posts reserved for especially able and responsible soldiers, including mail agent (November 1863) and acting hospital steward (November–December 1863 and January–April 1, 1864).[62]

Within a month of the regiment's commissioning, in December 1863, the 5th tasted battle for the first time during a raid into northeastern North Carolina. Joining forces with two other black regiments under General Edward A. Wild, a fervid Massachusetts abolitionist, Thomas's regiment left camp near Norfolk, Virginia, on December 5 and entered North Carolina above South Mills. They then conducted forays toward Camden Court House and Elizabeth City, foraging liberally at the expense of local residents and liberating their slaves. Here was the moment that Will and his fellow soldiers had dreamed of—finally having the power to free their slave brethren. Will's first skirmish with the enemy proved sobering. He remembered the brief North Carolina raid as illustrating that "our soldiers evinced that determination for thoroughness, which afterwards rendered them such invincibles." For the next seven months, however, Union commanders consigned Will and his fellow "invincibles" to largely manning garrisons, guarding prisoners, and performing fatigue detail.[63]

It was not until mid-June 1864 that Thomas and the 5th, assigned to General Benjamin F. Butler's Army of the James, engaged in actual battle—the first assault on the outer defenses of Petersburg, Virginia. In this operation the black troops successfully drove the city's Confederate defenders back into their entrenchments and captured five artillery positions and six cannon. The 5th, positioned on the right of the City Point Road, assaulted the first row of Rebel rifle pits and captured two lines of enemy fortifications. In Will's opinion, the Petersburg assault represented "a proud, yet sad day for" the 5th. "Many of [our] comrades lay clasped in the cold embrace of death; yet the consciousness of being in the right, imparted a proud bearing to their manly forms." In the early months of the lengthy Petersburg campaign against General Robert E. Lee's army, Thomas's regiment served twenty-six days in the trenches, principally as reserve and support troops and digging earthworks. Almost daily, however, Thomas and his men skirmished with the Confederates. He remembered vividly "those long, dreary days and nights spent in the trenches, where their [the men of the 5th] moral power did as much toward keeping the enemy at bay, as their military prowess on the field of battle, the *tedium* being relieved by occasional brilliant displays of pyrotechnics, gotten up at their expense by the enemy, though more ornamental than useful." Though Thomas's regiment had been prepared to charge into the crater at the Petersburg mine assault of July 30, 1864, other troops received the assignment for the ill-timed and disastrous attack. Years later Thomas recalled observing the explosion of the mine and the resulting debacle at the "crater." "I was in front of Petersburg Va," he recalled, "and witnessed the explosion of that mine. . . . It was a never to be forgotten sight of death and devastation." Thomas's Company I, along with Company B from the 5th, supplied skirmishers on the extreme right of the charging Ninth Federal Army, but during the battle most of the men of the 5th were held in reserve.[64]

In late September 1864, however, the 5th figured prominently in the Union Army's two-pronged thrust at Richmond's outer defenses, including

Fort Gilmer, Fort Harrison, New Market Heights, Chaffin's Farm, and Laurel Hill. The fighting at New Market Heights tested Thomas and his fellow troops as never before. It represented, according to historian Noah Andre Trudeau, the black troops' "toughest combat of the war."[65]

The attack on New Market Heights began on September 29. The 5th, along with the 36th and 38th USCT, formed the second wave of Union attackers. Early in the morning fog General Robert E. Lee's veteran "Grenadier Guard" of Texans mowed down two regiments of unseasoned African Americans—the 4th and 6th USCT—as they vainly stormed New Market Heights. Undeterred, later in the day the 5th moved out of a ravine they occupied, crossed the open field where many of their comrades lay dead, and repelled skirmish fire from the woods. Will and the 5th next waded through swamp and stream to charge the heights, driving the enemy back, repeatedly charging the Confederate artillery works. Finally they engaged in hand-to-hand combat with Confederate gunners. Such fighting, according to Colonel Alonzo G. Draper, who commanded the Second Brigade of General Charles J. Paine's Third Division, made the USCT the equal of Europe's finest soldiers. "They have all the elan of the French soldier," Draper said, "and all the stubborn courage of the British."[66]

In its assault at New Market Heights and later fighting at Fort Gilmer, the men of the 5th suffered staggering losses. Sergeant Thomas recalled vividly the bloody campaign, "where so many . . . noble braves, my dear boys, poured out their blood in devotion to their country." He wrote with affection and nostalgia of the men who fought under him. There was, for example,

> Moss, the life of the sharp-shooters, and Tibbs, with his pleasant greeting for every one; and at that desperate assault upon Fort Gilmore, where our boys lay heaped upon each other, weltering in the terrible carnage of that day,—a tear starts as we remember the proud, manly form of Hall, with his clear, ringing voice, cheering on his men,—and Terrah, with his feminine appearance heightened by his glossy curls, yet withal, possessing a noble heart;— these have all fallen a sacrifice in behalf of their country.

Indeed, the 5th, a "battered regiment," had the second-highest number of casualties among the Union regiments that participated in this campaign. From among the 520 men who entered the engagement in the morning, 236 were killed, wounded, or missing by day's end. According to Colonel Giles W. Shurtleff, the former Oberlin divinity student who commanded the 5th, "twas a glorious day for col[ore]d troops. I never saw a regiment fight as the 5th did. . . . There is no longer any question about the fighting quality of negroes." Another white officer, Lieutenant Joseph J. Scroggs of Company H, agreed. Scroggs remarked that following the performance of the 5th at New Market Heights, "no man dare hereafter say aught in my presence against the bravery and soldierly qualities of the colored soldiers."[67]

The campaign was, according to historian Jack D. Foner, "the outstanding black engagement of the war." The battle at New Market Heights brought personal distinction to Thomas, national attention to his regiment, and respectability to the USCT in general. General Butler, citing their stellar performance at New Market Heights as evidence of the blacks' combat effectiveness, boasted that in this campaign they proved themselves the equals of white troops. "Their praises are in the mouth of every officer in this Army," he said. "Treated fairly and disciplined they have fought most heroically." A former Confederate soldier who fought in the campaign recalled that on September 29, "Richmond came nearer being captured, and that, too, by negro troops, than it ever did during the whole war," prior to the Confederate evacuation of the city in April 1865. For his part, Thomas received an important responsibility in this campaign. According to Lieutenant Ulysses L. Marvin, who served in Thomas's company, "from the 23rd of Sept. 1864 for a number of weeks, Sergeant Thomas was the ranking officer in his company & had command. In this position he succeeded to the satisfaction of his co. & his superior officers." Marvin, writing a few years later, judged Thomas's service during the entire war as exemplary, "his conduct as a man and a soldier was in the highest degree praiseworthy. His courage was often tested in trying positions and in every instance he showed himself a *soldier.*" Marvin noted "the good character of Sergeant Thomas as a faithful soldier & a worthy man." Colonel Shurtleff also praised Will's war record. "He . . . was brave and efficient in *action,*" Shurtleff remembered, "and entirely *trustworthy.*" He recommended Thomas as a possible officer for the USCT if the War Department authorized black officers. Like other noncommissioned officers, Thomas "gained in stature" thanks to his appointment as sergeant. He also gained in confidence. Will later applied the leadership and communication skills learned during the war to civilian life.[68]

To commemorate the gallant service of the most meritorious African Americans in this campaign, General Butler commissioned a special silver medal to be struck. He awarded it to almost two hundred blacks who fought at New Market Heights, including Thomas. Just as he had come to the attention of General Stephen A. Hurlbut during the Vicksburg campaign, Thomas also managed to gain Butler's recognition as well. The influential Massachusetts Republican wrote that in that campaign Sergeant Thomas fought "with great courage and distinction," adding that he "served with great credit, [was] honorably mentioned in General Orders, and received a silver medal for bravery in the field." Thomas carried the Butler Medal as a symbol of his military success and service for the rest of his life. The front side was inscribed "Distinguished for Courage, Campaign Before Richmond, 1864." On the reverse was inscribed *Ferro iis Libertas Perveniet* [liberty shall come to them by the sword].[69]

The 5th, its reputation as one of the most battle-tested units in the USCT well established, entrenched most of October 1864 at Chaffin's Bluff and then served along the lines at Fair Oaks and Darbytown Road, near Richmond. Following the war Thomas recalled a dreary reconnaissance that his regiment performed during this campaign along the Williamsburg Road: "Rain had fallen during the day and the road was flooded with water, this together with the darkness, rendered it almost impossible to get along. And, as the column wound slowly down the road, doubtless, we presented quite a forelorne appearance, as one after another, missing their footing would fall full length in the mud, and then call piteously for a comrade to lend a helping hand, but we bore it patiently." The regiment played only a marginal role and suffered few casualties in what amounted to yet another ineffectual Union move toward Richmond. Soon after, in November 1864, Thomas cast his first vote—for President Lincoln.[70]

On December 2, 1864, Will Thomas and his men marched from Varina, Virginia, to Bermuda Hundred, where the regiment boarded the ocean transport steamer *John Rice* en route south to North Carolina. The regiment spent most of the last two weeks of 1864 supplied with inadequate provisions, crowded among seasick comrades, horses, and mules, and tossed about in high winds and rough seas. The 5th was part of an ill-fated and poorly coordinated joint army-navy expedition concocted by General Butler and Admiral David D. Porter against Fort Fisher. The attack featured 6,500 infantry, including nine USCT regiments, and fifty-eight warships carrying 600 guns. Fort Fisher, positioned eighteen miles south of Wilmington on a point between the Atlantic Ocean and the Cape Fear River, protected blockade runners and guarded the dying Confederacy's last vital commercial link to the outside world. Butler's plan included detonating the "powder vessel" *Louisiana* (a 295-ton flat-bottomed boat laden with 235 tons of gunpowder) to destroy Fort Fisher's walls and then using the large navy guns to hammer the fort into submission. Once ashore the infantry would capture the fort. The attack, occurring on December 25, 1864, was terribly mismanaged by

Butler and Porter and, in the end, was totally botched. The *Louisiana* ran aground and exploded harmlessly offshore, and the Federal naval barrage of Fort Fisher proved generally ineffectual. Without naval support, the infantrymen who landed were immediately exposed to devastating enemy fire.[71]

The 5th was the only regiment of USCT among the approximately twenty-two hundred Union soldiers that landed in a heavy surf on the beach at Federal Point, north of Fort Fisher's landface, on Christmas Day. The 3:00 P.M. debarkation proved especially difficult because the soldiers had little training in boat drill. Once aboard the launch boats, the men made their way to shore. "We landed amid a shower of bullets from the enemy concealed in the bushes skirting the shore," Lieutenant Scroggs recalled, "[but once] deployed and advanced, a few well directed shots [resulted in] scattering the Johnnies like chaff." Soon, however, the regiment, ordered to conduct reconnaissance of Fort Fisher's strength, was pinned down by enemy fire, and, lacking reinforcements, played no significant part in Butler's fiasco. Convinced that the navy could not protect the men on the beach and certain that a large Confederate army was marching to relieve the fort, Butler abruptly canceled the assault and departed for Virginia. He abandoned 700 men on the beach without food or shelter for two days, vulnerable to rifle fire and possible capture. Thomas's unit remained on the sand for three hours, "reimbarked in heavy surf," and returned to Varina, Virginia, on December 31. Summarizing the 5th's role in the campaign, Colonel Shurtleff informed his wife, "we made a perfect failure, had no fighting of any consequence."[72]

After cashiering Butler, early in 1865 General U. S. Grant ordered General Alfred H. Terry and Admiral Porter to mount a second attack on Fort Fisher by assault or siege. No sooner had the 5th encamped in Virginia than it prepared to return to North Carolina. The second Fort Fisher campaign would have dramatic consequences for the Union cause and also for Will. In this assault, he received a wound that transformed his life.

Armed with an eight-thousand-man force, a flotilla of sixty-four vessels, and a smooth-working relationship with Porter, Terry arrived off Fort Fisher on January 12, 1865, after a stormy voyage from Fort Monroe, Virginia, via Beaufort, North Carolina. This trip the 5th USCT sailed on the *Champion*, which according to Lieutenant Scroggs was "a floating palace . . . capable of accommodating 1600 passengers." After an intense shelling of Fort Fisher, on January 13 Terry's entire force, including the 5th USCT, landed on the beach five miles above the fort's landface. "High surf, all got wet, but none hurt," Scroggs wrote. The men next marched to Flag Pond Battery, and then, under the cover of night, moved to protect the right flank across the swampy peninsula to the Cape Fear River. There the regiment guarded the river and constructed a line of breastworks covered with abatis above Fort Fisher across the sand hills of the upper neck of the peninsula to shield the Federal rear from attack by General Robert F. Hoke. From the moment Thomas and his men landed on the peninsula they were exposed to cold winds, chilling rains, and uncomfortable nights. Over the next two days the 5th's pickets skirmished with Hoke's division but did not participate in the assault on the fort. After fierce hand-to-hand combat, Fort Fisher fell to Union troops on January 15, leaving Wilmington vulnerable to Union attack.[73]

Following Fort Fisher's capture, Will's regiment remained in camp at Federal Point, north of the fort, constructing earthworks until February 11, when it was ordered to move northward toward the Confederate line at Sugar Loaf. According to Thomas, the operation was a move "up the Cape Fear River to destroy the intervening fortifications, and to occupy Wilmington." The men were provisioned with three days' rations and armed with sixty rounds of ammunition. Over the next several days the Union forces engaged in costly skirmishes with the enemy as it retreated slowly northward toward Wilmington. Along with white units, the black troops steadily forced the Confederates back and, because of their determined fighting, suffered the highest casualties among the Union troops in the campaign. The fighting of the black soldiers impressed the white troops, many of whom had never observed USCT regiments in combat. Captain Thomas Speed of Kentucky, for example, admitted that the African Americans performed "splendidly" in combat. No longer could white troops disparage the USCT. "I saw them tried yesterday," Speed reported home. "We have to give it up; . . . old nigger will fight." Another white observer remarked that they were "cool, accurate, and soldierly" in combat.[74]

On February 19 Will's regiment was ordered to follow the Confederates northward along the Federal Point Road, the main route to Wilmington. The 5th served as the Federal vanguard and first exchanged fire with Hoke's rearguard about eight miles from the city. The regiment dug in and waited for reinforcements to arrive. On February 20 the 5th, again leading the skirmish line, confronted Hoke's rearguard and proceeded slowly through shrubs, pond pines, and woody vine bamboo briar. About three o'clock in the afternoon the black Ohioans encountered the enemy at Forks Road, three miles south of Wilmington on Federal Point Road. They first met Confederate pickets, who retreated to entrenchments fortified with artillery. Grossly underestimating the size and strength of Hoke's force, General Terry ordered

Thomas's regiment to make a "valiant but futile" frontal assault. The 5th encountered not one rank of infantry and a few cannon, as Terry had assumed, but an entire infantry brigade and six field pieces. That force, according to historian Chris E. Fonvielle, "blasted the Federals with heavy volleys of musketry and barrages of lead and iron artillery cannister. The firing caused frightful Union casualties in a brief period." Two Federal soldiers were killed instantly and fifty-one others were wounded. Among the wounded was Will Thomas, who took a musket ball in the right arm. "Gen. Terry ordered the 5th to charge the works and we done it," Lieutenant Scroggs wrote, "but [we] were not able to take works manned by 4500 troops and mounted with six pcs. of artillery." An angry Scroggs noted: "I suppose it was fun for [General] Terry but little for us." Recalling the battle, Lieutenant Marvin praised Will's courage and wrote that he was hit "in the foment of the fight."[75]

The musket ball hit Will's right arm slightly above the elbow. Like the other men shot at Forks Road, he was treated in a regimental field hospital. Because of complications resulting from his wound, Dr. Henry C. Merryweather, a native of England, amputated the lower third of Will's right arm on February 20, 1865. Wounds to the extremities such as Will's were among the most common wounds in the Civil War, accounting for 71 percent of all injuries to Union soldiers. Large-caliber Civil War muskets and rifles fired conoidal Minié balls at a low velocity. On impact these tended to flatten, causing bones to shatter, splinter, or split. These projectiles proved very destructive, staying enlodged in the body instead of passing through it. Infection invariably set in quickly. Civil War surgeons, overworked, frequently hurried, and often performing surgery far from well-appointed hospitals, commonly resorted to amputations to check gangrene, osteomyelitis, or septicemia in lesions that resulted from the wounds. These amputations constituted about 75 percent of all operations performed during the Civil War; of the 29,980 amputations performed on Union soldiers, 21,753 men survived. This 26 percent mortality rate for Federal amputees was two percent lower than for Federal soldiers treated by what were considered more conservative treatments.[76]

Dr. Merryweather, the surgeon who amputated Thomas's arm, never received a medical degree, though he studied at London University, graduated from the College of Surgeons in 1854, and received a diploma from Terviter Medical College in 1856. In 1853 he became a Member of the Royal College of Surgeons and a year later held a License in Midwifery. Merryweather was, however, an experienced military doctor, having spent fifteen months at the

General Hospital at Scutari, Turkey, base of the British Army during the Crimean War and the hospital under the charge of Florence Nightingale. Three months before Dr. Merryweather amputated Thomas's arm, the surgeon in chief of the Third Division, Eighteenth Army Corps, praised the Englishman as "a well read and practical physician; a judicious and skillful operator; a man of good moral character and sound sense." He joined the 5th September 29, 1863, as assistant surgeon and during the war performed fourteen recorded amputations. Five of the men died of complications resulting from the surgery. After the amputation, Thomas confronted the prospect of a perilous recovery as his regiment entered Wilmington victorious on February 22, 1865.[77]

Thomas was admitted to Wilmington's U.S. Army General Hospital, one of almost a dozen hospitals that the army immediately converted from abandoned buildings there. In general the USCT received, according to historian Joseph T. Glatthaar, "woeful and discriminatory medical care," so much so that "nine times as many black troops died from disease as on the battlefield, and compared to white volunteers, two and one-half times as many black soldiers per one thousand died of disease." Captain Albert Rogall of the 27th USCT, sister regiment of the 5th and a unit composed almost entirely of Ohio African Americans, complained of "the meanness of the medical department in the army," providing "no assistance, no sympathy, no help." He characterized the military doctors as "a set of thieves and whoremasters, especially in the colored division." Though medical care tended to be better in regimental medical units, "post or general hospitals, which cared for seriously ill patients, regularly had separate and grossly unequal facilities for blacks and whites. Time after time," Glatthaar explains, "post or general hospitals for black troops were understaffed and poorly policed, and death rates were dramatically higher than in adjacent or nearby facilities for whites." Unfortunately, this was just the sort of medical facility, a hospital hastily set up in Wilmington within hours of the town's evacuation by the Confederates, where Thomas was treated. Such military hospitals were notoriously unsanitary and seedbeds for the spread of infection. Though he suffered decades of postoperative pain, Thomas was spared infection from his wound.[78]

Within days of his surgery, Will was transferred to an army hospital hurriedly established for the USCT in Wilmington, and then, on February 27, was sent north. On March 3 he was admitted to the U.S. Army General Hospital, G. H. McKim's Mansion, in Baltimore's northern suburbs. This hospital, located on Gallow's Hill on Greenmount Avenue, opened in mid-1862 and served as a hospital for the USCT. Thomas remained hospitalized there for five months until he was discharged for medical disability on July 25, 1865, upon which he received a $100 bounty. Five days following his muster out, the doctor in charge of McKim's Mansion praised his "soldierly deportment and excellent moral character." Though still recovering from his amputation, Thomas excelled as the hospital's "section master" and "performed his duty faithfully and promptly, and his whole conduct . . . [was] characterized by the strictest integrity." In August, he reunited briefly with his regiment in New Bern, North Carolina, and then left for Ohio.[79]

Despite his traumatic and debilitating wound, Thomas considered his military service a positive experience. It was the single most significant factor in his intellectual and personal development to that time. After a childhood marred by instability and uncertainty, his army experiences provided him a consistent, though hazardous, life. Joining the 5th USCT forced him to grow to manhood in a hurry. By twenty-two he had already traveled well beyond the confines of southcentral Ohio. He had participated in the liberation of the slaves and witnessed life in the South. These experiences introduced him to the culture of the slaves and the freedpeople. Though many years later he would radically turn against these blacks, during the hopeful postemancipation age he worked for their betterment. Service in the army prepared Thomas for the educational and religious work that he performed with the freedpeople.

The military also brought Thomas close to his fellow African Americans, mulattoes and blacks. He suffered along with them under enemy fire and in the trenches. Thomas shared their exposure to disease and ultimately sacrificed his right arm in combat. Like his African American brethren, he felt the sting of discriminatory treatment at the hands of the white government they served. Such adversity forged black soldiers into a common phalanx. Being bound together, Will wrote, by "the horrors of war, and with it the loss of friends" created "a bond of union [that] pervaded the entire ranks of the regiment." It was, he said, a "*fraternal* band." And military service developed in Thomas responsibility, leadership skills, and pride in his own manhood. As a soldier he gained self-confidence and self-esteem. His experiences in the war gave him a critical sense and an emerging political consciousness. "We are no longer the football for Southern autocrats," he wrote, "but we are *men*, standing upon the broad platform of Universal Freedom, and with that dignity, compatible with self-respect, demanding such recognition from all classes."[80]

Reflecting on his service with the 5th, Thomas brimmed with pride over the accomplishments of black soldiers. In 1865 he explained that "we regard them as representing the race to which we belong." He sang the praises "of the devotion and loyalty of the colored man to this country." Lasting friendships were made during the war, he concluded, and as the men broke ranks for the last time, tears streamed down their "bronzed cheeks." Because of the "brotherhood" experienced by members of the 5th, Thomas proposed forming a veterans association led by the same men—Powhatan Beaty, Milton M. Holland, and Robert Pinn—who had provided battlefield leadership.[81]

But Thomas harbored deep anger over the white majority's classification of men into subordinate groups by skin color. He recalled how, "in the dark hours of the rebellion," whites desperately called upon men of African descent to help smother the Confederacy. Yet once in the army, the government "refused to recognize them as soldiers, offering them a pittance for support from the treasures of the Common*wealth*, and by word and deed considering them only as menials, suitable for labor in the trenches." In spite of all that he gained from army life, Thomas left the service embittered by "the injustice and ingratitude of the American people" toward blacks. Thomas overcame numerous problems and circumvented many obstacles during his long and troubled life, but he never escaped the power that the white man's definition of skin color held over him. It ultimately became his own definition as well.[82]

CHAPTER TWO

Questions of Character

WILL THOMAS departed Baltimore by train on the morning of August 6, 1865, and arrived in Delaware, Ohio, the following day. "Home," he mused, "what a charm in that name." Thomas was delighted to be reunited with his family and friends in the central Ohio town. Yet his return to Delaware as an amputee left him dependent, despondent, and contemplative. Historian Joseph T. Glatthaar estimates that ten thousand African American soldiers received wounds in the war, with thousands more injured by accidents. Black veterans commonly suffered from poor physical conditions resulting from the war and "many," Glatthaar argues, "were physical wrecks." Thomas's amputation left him in excruciating physical pain. The stump where the lower third of his right arm had been severed failed to heal properly. Though he was fitted for a prosthesis in October 1865, the device led to the formation of ulcers on his stump that remained so painful that he was unable to wear it. Despite later fittings with several styles of artificial limbs, none proved acceptable, and through the years he suffered numerous medical complications resulting from the amputation. As he returned to Delaware that August, Thomas faced the very real prospect of being an invalid for the rest of his life.[1]

Thomas's amputation left the once-vigorous farm laborer and soldier virtually helpless. His first letters written with his left hand were all but illegible and, as a result, he was forced to dictate much of his correspondence. The very private and secretive man now had to rely on others. Thomas's disability quite naturally loomed large in his mind; it required him to reassess the direction he sought to follow after his discharge from the army. Cognizant that certain avenues would be closed forever to him, Thomas read voraciously. "I turned to the study of books and men," he recalled. Through determined self-instruction, he studied philosophy, history, and most significantly, theology and the law. During the postwar years Thomas would establish himself in both professions.[2]

Aside from his physical incapacity, the Civil War left Thomas emotionally scarred as well. His return to Ohio separately, before the mustering out of the rest of his regiment, distanced him from the comrades and the military world that since 1863 had come to mean so much to him. Despite the racism, and especially the unequal pay, he faced in the army, the military had afforded him the opportunity not only to succeed but to excel. As a member of the mulatto leadership class, in the army he found day-to-day soldierly responsibilities and comradeship with other African Americans, including free blacks, slaves, and freedmen and women. To an important degree, the 5th USCT became the home and security he never had with his own family or with the Whitings. As the train pulled into the station in Delaware, he faced many uncertainties and fears and received none of the flourish, the music, the "grand reception," or the lavish food that greeted other members of the 5th USCT upon their return to civilian life. As in so many other parts of his life, Thomas charted a solitary course.[3]

With remarkable resiliency, however, Thomas began to take charge of his life immediately upon his discharge from the army. On August 7, 1865, the day of his return to Delaware, he wrote to the Reverend George Whipple of the American Missionary Association inquiring into the possibility of a short-term teaching assignment among the South's freedmen and women. Though because of his amputation Thomas's handwriting is difficult to read, its clarity is nevertheless remarkable given the fact that he was forced to write with his left hand for the first time only months before.[4]

Determined to overcome his disability and move on with his life, Thomas worked laboriously to learn to write with his left hand. In September he entered a penmanship contest open only to disabled veterans who had lost their right arms in the war. Sponsored by William O. Bourne, editor of the *Soldier's Friend,* a New York monthly, the competition offered cash prizes for the best narratives of their military service. Bourne hoped to encourage amputees to master writing with their left hands so that they might launch postwar careers as clerks.[5]

Will drafted two documents, "A Reminiscence of the War" and "The Incidents of a Day's March," in Allegheny City, Pennsylvania, on September 27. On eight legal-sized sheets he explained his enlistment in the 5th

USCT, recalled the rigors of camp life and combat, listed the campaigns in which he participated, and summarized what he understood to be the war's meaning to black veterans such as himself. He referred to the Confederates as "would-be conquerors" and "a ruthless and mercenary foe" and recollected during the war yearning for "the happy days of 'yore,' when no traitor's hand had been lifted against our flag." Having "shared alike in the dangers and vicissitudes of the war," Thomas asked, "ought we not partake of all the immunities pertaining to the rights of citizens, even, as our Anglo-Saxon brothers?" "We ask," he continued, "that justice may be meted out to those living defenders of 'American Liberty.'"[6]

Glatthaar suggests that like Thomas, most black Civil War veterans experienced a smooth "psychological adaptation to" civilian life: "Despite the war's hardships and traumas, it was a very special time for blacks." On the lives of African American soldiers following the Civil War, historian Ira Berlin comments: "Military service provided a steppingstone to leadership in the black community, as it did in postwar American society generally." In some ways Thomas's life in the 1860s and 1870s followed those patterns. Though he was unsuccessful in securing a teaching post in 1865 with the American Missionary Association, Will nonetheless resolved to overcome his tragedy. He pinned up his empty sleeve and transformed it into a badge of honor, using the circumstances of the postwar years to create new opportunities for himself. And he capitalized on them. During Reconstruction Thomas assumed control of his life and achieved success as a journalist, as a leader of Delaware, Ohio's African American community, as a divinity student and clergyman, and as a politician. Those triumphs enabled him to minimize the effects of his serious injury, to redirect his anger and posttraumatic depression, and to turn desperation into achievement. The Reconstruction years were among Will Thomas's most productive and constructive.[7]

No sooner had Will returned to Delaware than he began sending correspondence—sometimes rambling, discursive letters, other times formal articles—to the *Christian Recorder*, the official weekly newspaper of the A.M.E. Church published in Philadelphia. The paper, "the oldest existing Negro periodical in America," commenced publishing in 1852 and had a large circulation among African Methodists and a long tradition of black protest. Gradually Thomas became known as an outspoken, sharp-tongued national correspondent who openly challenged the church and church people. He chose as his *nom de plume* his colorful and readily identifiable middle name, "Hannibal."

Identification with the Carthaginian general (245–183 B.C.) suited the icono-clastic, confrontational, and often belligerent tone of his articles. From 1865 to 1870, he published twenty-eight articles in the *Christian Recorder*. At one point the editor apologized in print to him over the backlog that had resulted in his articles not appearing. "Hannibal," he wrote, "we have not forgotten you, and will find a place for you." Over three decades Thomas used the pages of the *Christian Recorder* as his forum for a broad range of religious, social, and political commentary. In 1872 he moved briefly to Philadelphia to assist in editing the paper.[8]

Thomas also identified with and for many years participated actively in the African American community of Delaware, Ohio. After his family re-located there in the early 1860s, Delaware finally became "home" for the Thomases. Given their many previous moves, settling in Delaware gave the family a sense of permanence they had never known before. In 1863 Will had been mustered into the 5th USCT there and received his training on Josiah Bullen's farm at Camp Delaware. After Appomattox the town hosted the only recorded reunion of the 5th. Because of his military record, Thomas was known and respected in Delaware. That recognition gave him a sense of importance and heightened his self-esteem. The Thomases remained a fix-ture in Delaware's African American community for the next thirty years. Significantly, Delaware became not only Thomas's Ohio home but his home away from home as well. Exhibiting unusual mobility for his day, over the next three decades he logged numerous railroad miles, traveling back and forth with ease to Delaware from Pennsylvania, Georgia, South Carolina, and Massachusetts. He possessed the uncanny ability of slipping in and out of town casually, always blending into—sometimes losing himself in—the local black community. On several occasions over the course of many years the local postmaster even held Thomas's mail for him, seemingly awaiting his return. In short, his family and the town's closely knit African American community provided a secure home base for a man who rarely stayed in one place for any length of time. For him Delaware represented "a beautiful spot of shade and sunshine, around whose name are clustered many memories of the past." More to the point, Delaware offered Thomas a safe refuge at criti-cal junctures in his life when he required one.[9]

Though it greeted him without fanfare, Delaware's black community opened its arms to Will, welcoming him as a returning warrior. Despite his amputation, he experienced few of the problems white veterans faced finding educational opportunities and employment once the "initial show of affec-tion" toward veterans diminished after 1865. Often amputees "were beggars, messengers, . . . [who] peddled their own life stories." Thomas thrived, however, as an arm amputee, finding social benefits, status, respect, recognition, and job preference as a war hero. During the 1860s Delaware County's African American population had increased dramatically, from 131 in 1860 to 557 by 1870, 366 of whom resided in the city of Delaware. By 1880 the number of blacks and mulattoes in Delaware County totaled 610, with 446 in the city. The white population grew from 23,771 in 1860 to 26,770 in 1880. As a whole, in 1870 Ohio's African American population of 63,213 was composed of 71.8 percent blacks and 28.2 percent mulattoes.[10]

Though small and segregated, Delaware's African American community nonetheless grew and became cohesive, strong, and self-protective during Will's thirty-year association with the city. African American life centered around the A.M.E. Church, founded in 1853, on the corner of Washington and Railroad streets. The Reverends John M. Brown, who established Union Seminary Institute in 1845, and James A. Shorter began their distinguished careers at that church. Both later became A.M.E. bishops. The church, known locally as the "African Church," served as a magnet for local black reform, especially temperance, as well as social activities. For example, no sooner had Will returned from the army in August 1865 than he attended a picnic to benefit the church's Sabbath school. Bishop Daniel Alexander Payne, perhaps the most distinguished A.M.E. clergyman of his day and president at the time of Wilberforce University near Xenia, Ohio, attended the outing and spoke later that night at the church. Payne implored Delaware's blacks to seize upon education as a means to economic advancement. Political and social status, Payne argued, would occur only after economic progress was achieved. W. D. Harris, a missionary to the freedpeople of Norfolk, Virginia, also addressed the picnickers, informing them about the challenges and opportunities awaiting African Americans who went south. Thomas himself answered the call in 1871 when he left to run a freedmen's school in Rome, Georgia.[11]

Less than a month after Bishop Payne's visit to Delaware, Will met another influential A.M.E. leader, Bishop William Paul Quinn. A pioneer missionary and evangelist among blacks in the Old Northwest, Quinn admonished Delaware African Americans to take a higher ground in Christian graces than whites. They should set more pious examples in their homes and illustrate by their actions "the *real* differences between Christians and themselves." Just prior to moving to Pittsburgh in October 1865 to begin divinity school, Will also encountered a group of white German Methodists who met in Delaware. He interpreted the Christian fellowship between the German and Af-

rican Methodists as indicative of a hopeful future time when all could wor-
ship God without regard to color. Thomas's optimism, however, soon was
shattered when one of the whites preached on the "indomitable negro." Almost instantly the interracial harmony vanished and tension filled the air.
The blacks pulled back, Thomas wrote, because "our people were insulted."
Clearly identifying with the mass of African Americans, not just mulattoes,
Thomas launched the first of many attacks on whites. He advised white ministers not to patronize blacks. In their sermons whites need not continually
contrast the circumstances of slavery and the African Americans' "present
apparent freedom." "Our people," Thomas went on, "can decidedly understand a sermon about the Lord Jesus Christ, be it ever so replete with wisdom. . . . Leave out political matters especially. . . . Our people are sensitive
and cunning. From the class that has always oppressed us, we doubly feel
the wrong." Thomas, in other words, was unwilling to allow whites to continue to use sectionalism as a means to view blacks as a perpetual under-
class. Ironically, for the next thirty years he would employ sectionalism as a
weapon, *his* weapon, to attack white racism in the South and in the social
infrastructure of the North as well.[12]

After moving to Allegheny City, Pennsylvania, to attend divinity school,
Will returned frequently to Delaware. On one occasion he spoke to members
of the "African Church" on "vital questions" of the day at the church's "Murphy picnic" held on the campus of Delaware's Ohio Wesleyan University.
Nonalcoholic "Murphy drinks" were distributed free to all who attended.
The church specifically encouraged women in Delaware's black community
to assume an active role in the antisaloon campaign. Fraternal societies, such
as the Delaware Institute, the Odd Fellows, and the "Colored Masons," provided African American men with fellowship and a social network. Delaware
blacks of both sexes engaged actively in various emancipation-related festivi-
ties, celebrating West India emancipation, Abraham Lincoln's birthday, ratification of the Fifteenth Amendment, and the Emancipation Proclamation.
Crawford's Colored Brass Band—the pride of Delaware's African American
community—performed at those functions and others, promoting group
solidarity. In 1868 Will's brother, Benjamin Frank ("B. F.") Thomas, also a
USCT veteran and by then a local manufacturer, had been one of the founding
members of Crawford's Band and was also a leader in Delaware's White Sul-
phur Lodge No. 10 (Colored Masons). In the span of less than one year
Delaware's small black community sponsored two lectures by the leading
African American of the day, Frederick Douglass.[13]

Thomas took special note of the economic progress—in obtaining property and in bettering themselves—that blacks in Delaware had attained while he had been away in the army. During the war and after an African American middle class had emerged in Delaware—a grocer, a saddler, a plasterer, and a carpenter. Linking capitalism and politics, these successful businessmen established Delaware's Equal Rights League. As he looked around him in Delaware, Will observed black success stories—a talented artist, and two entrepreneurs whose investment reaped big profits for themselves and their astute bookkeeper. He wrote with pride of the city's quality black public school led by an Oberlin graduate and of Delaware's first-class boarding-house and restaurant that catered to blacks. Thomas praised those African Americans who "have done much to elevate the colored people of this city in the estimation of the dominant class, and acquire the respect and confidence of our Anglo Saxon friends." He added: "Colored friends, rally to the support of these gentlemen, and be proud of the honor thus conferred upon your city." [14]

The Thomases participated actively in Delaware's African American communal life. Rebecca Thomas, described by the local white press as "an aged and highly esteemed colored lady," assumed a leadership role among the women. In 1879, though sixty-seven years old, she was appointed to a committee by the Ladies' Christian Union of Delaware to raise money and clothing to support the black "Exodusters" who had fled the South and migrated to Kansas. Mrs. Thomas led the campaign and received praise for her success in aiding the Kansas refugees. Her sons, especially Walter, supported Mrs. Thomas during her old age. Though Will always maintained ambivalent feelings toward women, especially black women, he revered his mother, a mulatto. In 1890 he dedicated his first book, *Land and Education,* to her. Rebecca's life, Thomas wrote, had been lived "in behalf of freedom, and in defence of her race." She "aggressively and victoriously represented in character and conduct all that was noble, heroic and true in womanhood." In contrast to the way he later would ruthlessly castigate black women, Will praised Rebecca's "courage, fidelity and guidance" and credited her "for whatever measure of success" her children had achieved. Rebecca Thomas died in 1882.[15]

Though he never resided permanently in Delaware, Thomas nevertheless played a remarkably active role in the life of the town. In August 1866, for example, while a divinity student in Pennsylvania, he returned home to preach to the "African Church's" Sabbath school, "leading the lambs to the Saviour, and training them for future usefulness in the church." He also was among the most generous contributors to the "Dollar Money" fund collected by the Ohio Annual Conference from the local A.M.E. churches to support the church's national departments and bishops. In 1883 the "African Church" honored Thomas by selecting him as its representative to the North Ohio Annual Conference. Three years later, after he had settled in Boston, he still maintained links to Delaware's black community. In its summary of activities of Ohio's African Americans, the *Cleveland Gazette* reported that Thomas had been elected as a local delegate to a statewide convention. He and his brothers also assumed leadership roles in organizing a grassroots black Republican movement in Delaware.[16]

For all of the race's sacrifices during the war, by 1865 the status of blacks had changed remarkably little. The state's tenuous Unionist coalition, comprised of Republicans and War Democrats, understood well the racial fears held by the white majority. At every opportunity Ohio legislators sidestepped the implications of wartime emancipation. As a result, during the war racial change progressed at glacial speed. By Appomattox, Ohio's legislature had provided blacks with little of substance—at best additional and more centrally located segregated schools and access to public relief funds. "Four years of war had tempered the racism of the Midwest but had not purged it," historian V. Jacque Voegeli writes. During the war "few of the innumerable, subtle extra-legal devices which drew the color line in the Midwest were discarded . . . and the vast majority of [white] Republicans were apparently satisfied with the status quo." In general, Voegeli concludes, "Negroes remained fundamentally as before—victims of discrimination in travel and restaurants, of social ostracism, and of economic subordination." Indeed, most Ohio blacks continued to live segregated and proscribed lives.[17]

Activists, however, such as John Mercer Langston, president of the National Equal Rights League, were committed to racial uplift and were determined to effect change. Meeting in Cleveland in 1865, the league demanded "equality before American Law" for blacks, North and South. Downstate, people of African descent in Pickaway and adjacent counties petitioned Ohio's legislature for the vote. While campaigning for equal rights in October 1865, Langston reminded whites that "the colored man is not content when given simple emancipation. That certainly is his due, . . . but he demands much more . . . he demands absolute legal equality." Such appeals, and many others, led Republicans in 1867 to sponsor an amendment to delete the provision from Ohio's constitution that only "white male adults" could vote. Not until 1870, however, did African Americans at long last receive the franchise and began to sit on juries in Ohio. But it required many more years of petitioning and lobbying by Ohio's blacks to repeal all of the state's discriminatory laws. In the 1870s, for example, blacks in Circleville and elsewhere throughout Ohio demanded equal access to white high schools. Finally, in 1887, the legislature excised the separate school law and inter-marriage proscriptions from the state constitution.[18]

During Reconstruction and afterward Delaware's black community joined in the campaign to thwart Ohio's proscriptive laws. First it established a branch of the Equal Rights League and then launched an incipient Republican party organization. Though in that period Thomas resided in Allegheny City, Pennsylvania, studying theology and later working as a minister and journalist, he nonetheless fought racial discrimination and participated in Delaware's Republican political activities. As an articulate war hero, his opinions carried weight in the community.

Late in 1865, for example, he denounced former Ohio Governor David Tod for reneging on his wartime pledge to work for the enfranchisement of blacks immediately following the war. Thomas was outraged that Tod would deny the vote to Civil War veterans—the same men that he so eagerly had sent off to war as soldiers. "Then they were good enough to go in the place of white men, and thus avoid having a *draft*," Will wrote. He went on to charge that according to Tod, blacks were sufficient to die for whites but "not good enough to vote with the white man." Incensed by Tod's hypocrisy, Thomas wrote: "There is a day of retribution coming, when justice will be meted out to these demagogues and political aspirants. A Cromwell will be found who will secure eternal justice to our oppressed race." He assured whites that blacks no longer would tolerate "these acts of oppression." In April 1866 Thomas reminded readers of the *Christian Recorder* that "the Anglo-African" never shirked his responsibility in the fight to free the slaves. Rather, "in the hour of their country's danger," members of the race "staked their lives to maintain its honor and integrity, unsullied with treason's stains." In return, whites owed blacks the franchise.[19]

With the ability to express himself with such force on racial matters, not surprisingly Thomas became a favorite in Delaware's black and Republican circles. In 1867 he returned to deliver a public lecture, "The Conflict," at the "African Church." According to the local newspaper, Will not only was a war veteran but also one who had sacrificed dearly in the cause of freedom. "Mr. Thomas was a soldier in the Fifth U.S. Colored Infantry," noted the *Delaware Gazette*, "in which organization he remained until near the close of the war when he was wounded and lost his right arm." Thomas quite literally symbolized the emerging Republican imagery of the "empty sleeve" and the "bloody shirt." The editor underscored a point that Thomas himself reiterated at every opportunity: "Early in the war he [Thomas] tendered his services to his country but was rejected on account of his color."[20]

In 1870, though still a full-time resident of Allegheny City, Delaware's "Colored Citizens" elected Will to the executive committee of their Republican caucus. In that campaign, as in later ones, he capitalized on his war record and displayed leadership and oratorical skills. "B. F." Thomas, Will's brother, was elected to the group's central committee. Meeting at the "African Church," the caucus condemned the Democrats as the party of slavery and treason and then passed resolutions upholding the U.S. Constitution, especially the Fifteenth Amendment that then awaited ratification. It praised the Republican party for sponsoring the amendment and for enforcing the Fourteenth Amendment despite opposition from conservative white southerners. The blacks eulogized Lincoln as "the mainspring in the glorious machinery by which God in the last ten years has revolutionized American sentiment in reference to our race."[21]

Later in the 1870s, when Will was working to advance the Republican cause in Georgia, "B. F." and another brother, Walter S. Thomas, assumed leadership of Delaware's "Grant and Wilson Club," an association of blacks dedicated to Republican victory in the presidential election of 1872. Members attacked the Democrats for having "fattened for years upon the riveted chains, crushed hopes, and darkened future of our unresisting race." Should the Liberal Republican and Democratic nominee Horace Greeley defeat President Ulysses S. Grant, the group warned, then the freedmen and women of the South would once again be consigned to slavery.[22]

Walter used his experience as a Republican political operative on the local level as a springboard to a long career on the fringes of political power. He fought for the right of Ohio blacks to control their own school funds and encouraged them to vote Republican, "the party of progress and civil rights." For many years Walter served as clerk in the Republican-dominated Ohio State Senate and Ohio Department of State. In the 1880s he edited the short-lived *Columbus Free American,* an African American weekly newspaper that endorsed Republican candidates. In 1884 he was appointed one of eleven Ohio Commissioners for Colored Exhibits at the World's Exposition in New Orleans. Walter also served as an officer in the Ohio National Guard and special agent for the U.S. Census Bureau. For almost two decades he unsuccessfully lobbied for appointment, first as secretary to the U.S. minister to Haiti, then as U.S. commercial agent in Boma, capital of the Congo Free State (present-day Democratic Republic of the Congo). Place, not ideology, apparently motivated Walter as he shifted political allegiances from the

Republicans to the Democrats and then back again to the Republicans. For his part, years later Will Thomas also would seek a political career and a diplomatic appointment. But before charting this course, he first entered the ranks of the clergy and then returned to the field of education.[23]

Will's decision in October 1865 to attend divinity school in Allegheny City, Pennsylvania, was one of the most important phases of his postwar adjustment. Located on the hilly northern bank of the Allegheny River, Allegheny City was Pittsburgh's twin city positioned across the river from the site of the original Fort Pitt. From the 1860s to the 1880s it became fashionable for Pittsburgh's old-line founding families to settle there. Clean and well-manicured, Allegheny City reportedly contained only "a third of the smoke that beclouds, and the soot that well nigh buries you" in Pittsburgh. Just as the Civil War broadened Thomas's worldview, helped him to mature, and increased his self-confidence, so too would his years in the Pittsburgh area season him. Contrasted to the slow pace of rural Ohio, after the Civil War Pittsburgh, the "smoky city," emerged as one of America's industrial giants in the production of iron, steel, and glass. Life there was "busy." Drawn by jobs, swarms of immigrants from Ireland and Germany flocked to Pittsburgh in the postwar years. Between 1860 and 1870 the combined number of whites in Pittsburgh and Allegheny City increased a dramatic 60,004, from 76,075 to 136,079. In 1870, Pittsburgh and Allegheny City ranked, respectively, sixteenth and twenty-third among U.S. cities in aggregate population.[24]

Blacks, however, found few opportunities in post–Civil War Pittsburgh's burgeoning mills. According to historian Laurence Glasco, "blacks could not find work—except as temporary strikebreakers—in the region's mines, mills, factories, and offices." They tended to be confined to those trades—teamsters, refuse collectors, janitors, and laundresses—that whites, including immigrants, rejected. In 1870, 83 percent of Pittsburgh's African Americans and 84.4 percent of Allegheny City's African Americans held unskilled jobs. Indeed, blacks considered themselves fortunate if they found service jobs as waiters, barbers, porters, butlers, maids, and gardeners. Pittsburgh's long-held patterns of racial segregation in schools, local politics, and accommodations worsened such dismal prospects. These traditions did not begin to cease until the early 1870s. "Unable to guarantee their children jobs or stable homes," historian Francis G. Couvares writes, Pittsburgh's "black parents socialized them for individual survival in the industrial city." Though confronted by such bleak prospects, between 1860 and 1870 the combined African American population of Allegheny City and Pittsburgh increased by 1,333, from 1,844 to 3,177.[25]

Those blacks who migrated to the Pittsburgh area after the war came largely from Virginia and Maryland with hopes of working in the region's iron and steel mills or laboring in service jobs. On paper at least, Allegheny City and Pittsburgh appeared to be attractive havens to people of African descent. In 1860 the cities polled more votes for Abraham Lincoln and the Republicans than any other major city. "Our noble people flourish in this 'black city,' this Birmingham of America," reported the influential clergyman and abolitionist Henry Highland Garnet in September 1865. "Going into the workshops and founderies, you will see all Pittsburghers of about the same color." Five years later, a contributor to the *Christian Recorder* described Pittsburgh's blacks as frugal, hard working, and determined to succeed. "Many of them are from the South; and they show their appreciation of liberty, by *willingly* following the pursuits—many of them mechanical—which slavery made *obligatory*. Colored shoemakers and blacksmiths are now common; while almost a fourth of the wagons you meet, are driven by these sturdy sons of the South." In 1870 three wards in Allegheny City contained 933 African Americans—29.4 percent of the two cities' total population of African descent. While attending theological school, Thomas lived amid one of the heaviest concentrations of blacks in the Allegheny City–Pittsburgh metropolitan area.[26]

Black communities in postwar Pittsburgh and Allegheny City were small, geographically fragmented, and slow to become "neighborhoods." Nevertheless they progressed because of a commitment to racial uplift through education, the acquisition of land, and political activism. Religion played an especially important role in the lives of the people. Wylie Street A.M.E. Church and Allen's Chapel in Pittsburgh, for example, were well established by the time Thomas moved to Pennsylvania. Newer congregations like Brown's A.M.E. Chapel and the A.M.E. Zion Church—both in Allegheny City—served as centers for people of African descent in Pittsburgh's northern suburb. On both sides of the Allegheny River, benevolent, mutual relief, and fraternal societies bound African Americans together. Significantly, in 1849 the Reverend Charles Avery, an affluent Pittsburgh cotton merchant, endowed Allegheny Institute and Mission Church, renamed Avery College in 1858. Located in Allegheny City, Avery College was the first institution of higher education for blacks in the United States.[27]

At Allegheny City Will Thomas entered Western Theological Seminary

(WTS), affiliated with the Presbyterian Church and one of the leading divinity schools in the West. It was established in 1825 by the Presbyterian Synod of Pittsburgh to train ministers for churches in the upper Ohio Valley. The seminary's curriculum and philosophy closely paralleled those of Princeton Theological Seminary, established by Presbyterians thirteen years earlier. Described by a contemporary as "the preacher factory" on the hill—WTS held a commanding position overlooking the confluence of the Monongahela and Allegheny Rivers and the Ohio River—"The Mount of Sacred Science," as one author described it, contained a strong theological library and attracted students with training in Latin, Greek, and the classics. They came from morally strict, "pious" homes. Though the large majority of its students were white and elite, WTS had a strong commitment to foreign missions and was among just a handful of institutions in America that offered collegiate and professional instruction to blacks. As early as the 1840s William E. Walker, a leading black abolitionist and Baptist clergyman from Trenton, New Jersey, received training there. WTS acquired such a positive reputation among African Methodists that one complained to the *Christian Recorder* that "the Presbyterians are educating scores of colored ministers," and warned that the A.M.E. might lose control over the training of its ministers. The Reverend Dudley E. Asbury, himself a student at WTS and pastor of Brown's Chapel, the A.M.E. congregation in Allegheny City, agreed. Asbury explained that WTS "stands with its doors wide open for the reception of any scholars, white or colored, upon terms of perfect equality; *and it has been so for years.*" He then asked: "How soon will the Methodist colleges . . . come up to the Presbyterians in liberality?" Bishop Payne praised the young blacks enrolled at WTS. He found them "active and progressive." In 1888 Payne recalled that "it was not as common then as now for our Conferences to contain many men . . . who were pursuing a regular course of study, which . . . made it all the more an encouraging sign—a promise for the future ministry." [28]

No record exists of how Will Thomas was "induced to enter" the Presbyterian seminary, especially since he neither had completed a regular course of academic study nor was a member of a Presbytery. He most likely took a special examination to enter. Thomas and only two other members of his twenty-six-member entering class lacked college degrees. The junior class, as first-year students were called, consisted of thirteen students from Ohio, twelve from Pennsylvania, and one from Indiana. Given his limited formal education, Thomas was indeed fortunate to gain entrance into the seminary, because WTS had a rigorous three-year curriculum and a distinguished faculty. The three years of training at WTS were divided roughly into three equal parts: biblical, theological, and ecclesiastical. The curriculum emphasized Hebrew and Greek languages and scriptures and didactic theology. According to the seminary's catalog, "Original Essays, . . . weekly exercises in Debating, and in Preaching without Notes, are required throughout the whole course." [29]

The seminary's professors included such noted theologians as Dr. Archibald A. Hodge and Dr. William M. Paxton, graduates of Princeton Theological Seminary who returned to their alma mater after teaching at WTS. Hodge was renowned for his writings in didactic theology while Paxton's specialty was preaching. Thomas took classes from both men, he informed president-elect Woodrow Wilson many years later. In his opening address to the students enrolled in the fall 1865 term, Professor Hodge reminded them of their mission to the church and to their future ministry. "Mental cultivation, the acquisition of knowledge, and the formation of habits of devotion were recommended with earnestness and force." As soon as he arrived on campus, Thomas quickly befriended Jeremiah H. Turpin, a second-year (middle class) student from Philadelphia who had attended Avery College and was the only other black among the approximately 195 students enrolled at WTS. [30]

While attending seminary Thomas lived rent-free in the modern Beatty Hall in accommodations that were ideal for study. He had a single room with an individual stove and plenty of ventilation. He immersed himself right away in a demanding curriculum, studying Greek and Hebrew and preparing for the annual examinations held before the school's five professors and the board of trustees. Western Theological Seminary opened new vistas for Will. He was deeply impressed with the school's egalitarianism as well as its intellectual and Christian environment. It was a setting, he wrote, that put into practice the motto "that all men are born free and equal," and where "Christian feeling and sympathy seem to pervade the minds of all." From the very start of their theological training, Thomas and the other student ministers had opportunities to preach. He also regularly attended services at Pittsburgh's black churches, thereby coming into contact with veteran A.M.E. clergymen who became role models for him. Once, by special invitation, he was invited to a Monday evening "love-feast," and although he claimed to have witnessed many such rituals before, he considered it the biggest outpouring of the Holy Spirit he ever had witnessed. Another time Thomas attended the ritual of the "Heroines of Jericho, of Naomi Court," the female social order that performed good works for Pittsburgh-area African Americans.

Awed by these and other new religious and social experiences, the first-year divinity student wondered why people permitted Satan to come among them when God showered blessings upon them. "We have been in the bondage of sin long enough," he wrote. "Let us begin anew to work for the advancement of our Father's kingdom." [31]

Thomas found Pittsburgh's urban population driven not only by sin but also by the determination to acquire wealth. Fortunately, he said, Allegheny City and Pittsburgh's black communities were progressing steadily, thanks largely to their several churches, chapels, and schools. He wrote confidently "that a Sabbath-observing community do not retrograde, either in morals or wealth." In one instance the naive divinity student seemed shocked that partisanship within the church had led a particular minister to be assigned to an isolated chapel that, in Thomas's opinion, was well below the quality of the pastor. Sensing some intrigue, Thomas advised African Methodists: "We can never succeed as a people and organization, until we lay aside petty jealousies, and judge of men's abilities by their worth." Among his many new contacts was George B. Vashon, Oberlin College's first black graduate, a leading lawyer, abolitionist, and intellectual, and, by the time Will arrived in Allegheny City, principal of Avery College. He described Vashon as "a thorough scholar and gentleman" and praised Avery's well-appointed classrooms and laboratories. Thomas advised blacks that the best investment in the future of their race lay in the education of their children. [32]

As he settled into student life in the "smoky city," Thomas continued writing articles for the *Christian Recorder.* Although the legibility of his penmanship with his left hand improved dramatically, he joked about the problems editor Elisha Weaver must have had "deciphering" his "chirography." He also began peppering his articles with Latin phrases—showing off his newfound "classical" training. On a more serious note, in October 1865 Thomas expressed his outrage with President Andrew Johnson's condescending treatment of African Americans. Thomas viewed Johnson's behavior as part of the white backlash against emancipation that surfaced quickly after Appomattox during Reconstruction. No sooner had the war ended on the battlefield, Thomas wrote, than a new conflict emerged—"a *moral war*" waged by white southerners. It was "the jealousy of the domineering class" in the South, he explained, that led to the oppression of the freedpeople once the USCT left the region. The old slaveholding class, according to Thomas, insisted upon reasserting its "old relations with their *peculiar institutions.*" Will singled out President Johnson's attitude toward blacks as symptomatic of the problem. [33]

In an October 1865 speech to the 1st USCT before its mustering out, Johnson repeatedly questioned whether the men understood the rights and responsibilities of freedom and citizenship. On the one hand, Johnson informed the soldiers that "this is your country as well as anybody else's country." But on the other hand, the president asked: "Will you give evidence to the world that you are capable and competent to govern yourselves?" In a patronizing tone, Johnson cautioned the blacks to avoid idleness and licentiousness and to steer clear of saloons. He reminded them of "the importance of controlling your passions, developing your intellect, and of applying your physical powers to the industrial interests of the country." Johnson obliquely mentioned colonization as a solution to the race question if the blacks failed to match up to his standards. "Oh, what philanthropy on the part of the government, and our worthy Executive!" Thomas complained. "Give us our rights of citizenship, Mr. President, and we will take care of ourselves in our own country—the United States." African Americans, Thomas continued, did not need to be told to behave themselves. Though he credited Johnson with good intentions, Thomas nevertheless cringed at the president's paternalism. Blacks, he said, had proven themselves in war and expected to be treated like citizens. The twenty-two-year-old divinity student was annoyed that whites in general, and the former Democrat from Tennessee in particular, felt compelled to lecture to members of his race. He concluded that the president "partakes too much of that old party spirit which looks upon our inferiority as essential to the well-being of a community." It was, he explained in a later article, "the Jacksonian *modus operandi* re-enacted, only on a larger scale."[34]

While a theological student Will not only challenged the Democrats' conservative policies toward his race but also began to espouse several arguments that eventually dominated his thinking for the next thirty-five years. Like many other Republicans of his day, Thomas hammered away at the evils of slavery and expressed jubilation at its demise. Finally, he wrote, blacks were free from "bondage—from misery, crime, debauchery and death! No more whipping-posts, no more bloody stripes, no more parting of friends and kindred; . . . the pitiful groans of the mangled and dusky sufferer in the old out-house have been hushed to rest." But with emancipation came responsibility, he said. Blacks could not become complacent, must not fail to take an active interest in elevating their race through aggressively demanding schools and the ballot. Education and civil and political rights, Thomas argued, held the key for the success of blacks and would thwart the ever-threatening forces of neoslavery. "If we do not take heed . . . surely God will not always remain silent; but will, with terrible vengeance, smite the oppressor to the ground."[35]

Significantly, in his early articles Will openly challenged white racism and drew no color barrier between blacks and mulattoes. He pointed, for example, to the successes of Pittsburgh's black teachers as adding "another link to the largely accumulating mass of evidence, which proves that *color* is not the hinderance to a man's intellectual power." Children of both races had equal native intelligence. Thomas praised the teachers and implored them to "continue these intellectual conquests, until every vestige of caste has been forever removed, and we are permitted to stand forth in the broad sunlight of universal freedom, recognized and respected by all men." In one article Will challenged all prejudices based on race. Distinctions based on "caste," he said, "are incongruous elements that make war continually upon . . . manhood's nobler and spiritual self." "The unity and brotherhood of man is no longer a question of controversy," he added, "but a recognized fact."[36]

In 1867 Thomas was outraged, for instance, when the application of George B. Vashon was rejected by the Allegheny County bar. Though he had passed the New York State bar (Vashon was the first black lawyer to be licensed in New York) and had taught college in Haiti, according to Thomas, Vashon's "olive colored complexion, and slightly curled hair"—not his qualifications—blocked his admission to the Pennsylvania bar. "Notwithstanding the very lucid and palpable fact," Thomas argued, "that God made of one blood all the nations of the earth," whites continued to classify men by the shade of their skin. Paraphrasing Chief Justice Roger B. Taney's famous passage from the *Dred Scott v Sandford* (1857) decision, Thomas remarked that apparently "*Negroes* have no rights which *white* men are bound to respect."[37]

Though his early writings generally were optimistic, favoring self-help, self-improvement, group solidarity, and the extension of rights to blacks, Thomas nonetheless expressed a certain skepticism toward mankind of all races. He found most men capricious by nature—driven, he said, by a "chaotic mass of incongruous elements." They were selfish hypocrites, fully capable of exhibiting "polite" behavior one minute and "malicious hatred" the next. Sin enveloped the human heart, he complained, a condition that was exacerbated by the superficial demands of society. Persons erred, he wrote, in meeting the "external" demands of "polite" society and ignoring the "golden rule" in their private lives. Domestic life, Will explained, was weakened by the failure to treat family members gently, fairly, and lovingly. "If there are no outbursts of passion," he added, "there are likewise no exhibitions of tenderness and affection. . . . How far different would be the results, if every member of the household had a proper conception of his or her duty to every other member and to society." All would be improved, he wrote, if men dedicated themselves to higher moral and intellectual standards. Schools and churches should lead the way. Indeed, reforming and criticizing others would become one of Thomas's preoccupations. His comments, commonly sharp-edged, were generally captious.[38]

In 1867, for example, he attacked the Reverend Benjamin Tucker Tanner's widely acclaimed *An Apology for African Methodism* (1867). Without mentioning anything specific, Thomas faulted "the depth of [the book's] Scholastic thought" and alluded to its "many *errors*, — even *blunders*." The most substantive criticism Thomas raised concerned the poor quality of the book's binding. He also launched a gratuitous attack on one of the book's well-known contributors, the doctor, author, and abolitionist Martin R. Delany. According to Thomas, in his brief article on the relation of the African American to God, Delany went "off on a wild airy theological flight, upon a subject both absurd and untenable." He found Delany's argument "perfectly inconsistent with reason, and if followed up logically, will refute itself." Brash and impudent, Thomas proved unrelenting in his attack. Ironically, years later, after relocating in South Carolina, Thomas came to ally politically with Delany.[39]

But as a young divinity student Will took on the "establishment." He found the A.M.E. clergy—the very religious circle that he was preparing to join—most in need of cleansing from within. Writing in the *Christian Recorder* in July 1866, he declared boldly that "if every minister would look more to the improvement of his people, their religious and intellectual culture, and not seek to know how they may expect their own aggrandizement, they would not suffer for the want of sympathy and means." Too often, he continued, black ministers were "illiterate men, whose minds can grasp nothing but a mass of rude, incoherent, uncommunicating thoughts." Their sermons were "a compilation of the most incongruous matters" designed only to enhance their own prestige. According to Thomas, such clergymen engaged in petty competition amongst themselves and, in the process, held back the race. "Brethren," he admonished them, "let us lay aside this spirit of jealous simulations; consider, if we are ambassadors for Christ, we are all laboring for *one* common end, the salvation of the world."[40]

Thomas maintained constant pressure on the A.M.E. clergy to reform itself. He blamed the ministers, not the laity, for failing to support both the A.M.E. Book Concern (the church's publishing arm) and Wilberforce University. He charged many ministers with a "false, shallow philanthropy." Though he stopped short of accusing A.M.E. ministers of fraudulently withholding funds collected for the Book Concern, he referred to the "indolent, drowsy manner" in which they raised the money. As a solution to the problem he urged pastors to assess a set amount per member of their congregations. For years Thomas faulted the management of the church's finances.[41]

He also admonished A.M.E. ministers to change their pastoral and personal styles. The future success of the church and "the colored American people," Thomas wrote in 1868, depended on sweeping reforms on the part of individual clergymen. Ministers spoke too much—indulging in "spiritual dyspepsia" and "vociferous assertions"—and said and accomplished too little. He blamed them for lacking high enough intellectual standards and implored them to excise "mystical delineations" and "sensuous fancy" from their sermons. Will also faulted African Methodist clergy for shirking the day-to-day practical needs of their congregations. In his opinion the church desperately required "radical change"—higher intellectual standards for pastors, more rigorous schooling in the gospel ministry, and new and more effective leadership. Church posts, he said, should be based on ability and merit, not connections and favoritism.[42]

While Thomas advocated clerical reform, racial progress, and moral uplift in the pages of the *Christian Recorder,* he ostensibly practiced what he preached. On May 12, 1867, while in the middle class at WTS, he married Martha, a native Pennsylvanian and a widow "of his own color." She already had two young children, Charles (age seven) and George (age two). In addition to these two stepchildren, seven months later, in early December 1867, Martha gave birth to Will's son, Frank. He was born prematurely, Will explained, "in consequence of a fright." Three years later the federal census taker listed all five of the Thomases as "white," although they resided in Allegheny City's heaviest concentration of blacks. In seven city directory listings in Allegheny City (1869–80), Will was identified as "colored" only twice. Though he commonly, often proudly, wrote of himself as a person of African descent and spoke repeatedly of race "pride," at critical times in his life he may have used his light skin to "pass" as white. There is no evidence, however, to support the assertion that "Thomas usually passed as a white man." In 1868, with the new responsibilities of a family and only modest resources (in 1870 his personal estate was valued at $300) available to him, Thomas no doubt looked forward to completing his theological training and to entering the clergy. His life and career appeared to be on track.[43]

While attending WTS Will also was employed by Ohio's Wilberforce University. Though Thomas's formal association with Wilberforce began in 1868, seven years earlier he briefly had led Union Seminary, prior to that institution's merger with Wilberforce in 1863. These years were Wilberforce's most difficult, as the school struggled during its transition from control by the white M.E. to the A.M.E. Church. In 1863 the student body had dwindled to only six students and one faculty member. Will, however, watched the fledgling school's progress and kept a keen interest in it from afar. During his convalescence in Baltimore in 1865 he pledged $10.00—what for him then was a considerable sum—to the school.[44]

Wilberforce, named for English abolitionist William Wilberforce, was located three miles from the town of Xenia, in Greene County, Ohio. It was chartered in 1856 by the Cincinnati Conference of the M.E. Church, and by 1860 the school had over 200 students. Many of the first students had been freed by their masters and were sent northward for education. According to A.M.E. Bishop Daniel Alexander Payne, who arranged for the purchase of Wilberforce in 1863 by his church, the first students brought with them "nothing mentally but the ignorance, superstition, and vices which slavery engenders; but departed with so much intellectual and moral culture as to be qualified to be teachers in several of the Western States, and, . . . after the over-throw of slavery, entered their native regions as teachers of the freedmen." Under Payne's presidency (1863–76) Wilberforce emerged as America's first predominantly black university and one of the race's earliest intellectual centers. The school's mission, Payne wrote, was "to aid in giving a superior education to the youth of both sexes—to the teachers—to the educators—to the ministry of the Freedmen."[45]

Just after the school had begun to make progress in establishing itself, Wilberforce suffered a terrible setback. On April 14, 1865—the evening of Abraham Lincoln's assassination—a fire destroyed its main building, Shorter Hall. Over the next decade Wilberforce launched a major campaign to raise money to rebuild the structure. The Ohio Annual Conference of the A.M.E. considered rebuilding Shorter Hall "a necessity to our connection and our race, and in view of the mighty changes in our condition, which God is bringing about at this time, more so now than ever before." By 1869 Wilberforce had incurred a $5,500 debt in addition to its building program. Within a year Bishop Payne judged the school's financial needs so serious that he threatened to resign if funds were not acquired to hire additional faculty.[46]

Wilberforce, like many denominational schools, employed a "financial traveling agent" whose primary responsibility was to solicit donations and, secondarily, to serve as a field representative to recruit students. Such agents received a percentage of the funds they raised. The position of agent was one that required fund-raising and public relations skills, and, above all, ethics. Bishop James A. Shorter and the Reverend Thomas H. Jackson were among distinguished A.M.E. clergymen who at different times in their careers served as agents for Wilberforce. Shorter raised about three thousand dollars for the school in 1866. The position of financial agent was no doubt an attractive assignment, one that broadened a clergyman's connections and influence within the church. Success at the post certainly would serve as a steppingstone to even better assignments, more power, and more prestige.[47]

Will, though only twenty-four years old and a third-year divinity student, obtained the appointment as Wilberforce's financial agent in January 1868. Though the details of his selection are unknown, he most certainly coveted the position. While studying in Pittsburgh he had broadened his circle of professional and personal contacts, participating actively in the A.M.E. community, including Brown's Chapel in Allegheny City and the Wylie Street Church and Allen's Chapel in Pittsburgh. His articles in the *Christian Recorder* already had begun to give him some national exposure. And throughout his years in Allegheny City, Will maintained close ties to Ohio's black community. Using Pittsburgh as his base and drawing upon his growing network of contacts within the church, he no doubt anticipated being in a strong position to make connections and raise much-needed money for Wilberforce. His work for the school would enable him not only to serve the church but also to engage in what had become a particular interest—the education of the South's freedmen. In addition, Thomas would receive a commission for the funds he raised. In his agreement with the Wilberforce board of trustees, he was guaranteed 30 percent of the amount he raised as compensation. In return he was required to defray his own expenses. Indicative of his future relations with the board, in June 1868, Thomas, citing "private business which demands his immediate attention," failed to attend its meeting to report on his work. A month later the *Christian Recorder* announced that the "Rev. Wm. H. Thomas is acting as Agent for Wilberforce."[48]

Will's "private business" concerned the aftermath of serious personal problems he was experiencing at WTS. In April 1868, just days before completing his senior class examinations, allegations came before the school's faculty that questioned Thomas's "christian character." Summoned to a meeting of the professors, the faculty interrogated him about the circumstances of his wife's premature baby. Charges, they explained, had been leveled that Thomas and his wife had sexual relations before their marriage that resulted in the birth of the child. According to WTS's faculty minutes, at first Will denied having "any illicit intercourse with" his wife "previous to their marriage." But "upon further conference, he fully and explicitly confessed that such criminal intercourse had taken place between them several times within the two months immediately preceding their marriage and after they had engaged to each other to become husband and wife." [49]

No doubt shocked by Thomas's forced admission of "guilt," the faculty voted to expel him. This decision was reached "in view of the additional fact admitted by himself that this course of criminal conduct was commenced at or near the time when another colored student was expelled from the Seminary for a similar crime, which was brought to the notice of the Faculty by . . . Thomas and on whose information that student was led to confess his guilt, and thus a foundation was laid for his [Thomas's] expulsion." Because of Will's behavior in the instance of the other black student, the professors judged his "case as one of an aggravated character" and ordered "his immediate separation from the Seminary." Such hypocrisy could not be tolerated, they reasoned. The faculty, however, considered "it best for the honor of religion and the best interests of the Seminary to make no public announcement" of Thomas's dismissal. His entry in wts's matriculation records stated in small letters that he was "dismised Ap. [17]/68." Thomas, not surprisingly, never mentioned his expulsion, commenting only that "though seriously handicapped by a lack of preparatory training," he "studied theology with fair acquittance, from 1865 to 1868." A year following his departure from the seminary, the Reverend S. J. Wilson, one of his former professors there, recommended Thomas for a federal appointment. "He is quite a good scholar, has an active mind, is intelligent, and has good business qualifications." Not until more than three decades later would Thomas's severest critic, the mulatto lawyer and author Charles W. Chesnutt, first uncover this incident and use it to smear Thomas's character in the aftermath of the publication of *The American Negro* in 1901. Expelled from seminary just prior to his graduation and ordination, Thomas was defrocked before he had even been frocked. Along with his amputation, his expulsion from seminary was a major crisis in his life. But unlike his wound in battle, this incident—like others yet to come—was of his own making. [50]

Although ousted from wts by the faculty, Will nonetheless listed himself in Allegheny City's directories as "Reverend" and joined the staff of a weekly religious newspaper, the *Christian Radical.* The obscure, short-lived paper (1868–71) was edited first in Denver, Colorado, then successively in Lancaster, Pennsylvania, Springfield, Ohio, and, finally, in Pittsburgh by the Reverend Daniel Schindler (1829–93). A Maryland native, Schindler earned his undergraduate and theological degrees at Ohio's Wittenberg College in 1853 and 1854, respectively, and embarked on a long career as a Lutheran pastor in Ohio, Indiana, Illinois, Colorado, and Pennsylvania. Before establishing the *Christian Radical,* Schindler served as president of Mendota, Illinois, Female College. Through his many years of preaching and teaching, Schindler boldly proclaimed the connections between religion, science, politics, philosophy, and ethics. He favored an "elastic" church, one that related religion to everyday issues and encouraged differing opinions. Schindler denounced those who worshipped uncritically. Within the pages of the *Christian Radical,* he said, "conservatism . . . is a crime. At every moral and social evil let the Radical strike deep. Let us spare nothing which must be up rooted before the earth can bloom in the beauty of truth and bear fruit in the righteousness of Christ." Wittenberg's alumni magazine described Schindler "as an advanced thinker and radical."[51]

Thomas praised Schindler as "a man of scholarship and of great moral worth," crediting him with "the awakening of my best impulses and highest aspirations." Thomas absorbed much from the Lutheran clergyman, especially his sense of a "church" that transcended sectarian boundaries and his urgency in reforming the clergy. Schindler abhorred sectarianism. Describing the *Christian Radical*'s point of view, he explained that "it stands away from all sect-colorings, and is sublimely free from all servile ecclesiastical machinery and ritual encumbrance." In his many writings Thomas also distanced himself from rigid sectarianism (later in life he abandoned one church only to rejoin it) and favored a union of Christians. On social and racial matters, Schindler sympathized openly with the oppressed, especially blacks, and held nothing but scorn for what in 1877 he still referred to as the "slave-power." He attacked the South's unwillingness to treat the freedmen fairly and denounced leaders, especially President U. S. Grant, for their lethargy in enfranchising people of color. Schindler believed that whites never would be totally free "until the negro shall have a passage to the ballot-box as open and clear as the white man." Thomas agreed. The two men also shared the belief that racism—the "bad spirit of caste"—remained very much alive, North and South. According to the editor, "the old poison [of slavery] still lurks in the blood of many." He devoted considerable space in the *Christian Radical* to exposing the racial violence of the Ku Klux Klan.[52]

While Schindler no doubt influenced Thomas's evolving theological, social, and racial thought, the extent of Thomas's contribution to the *Christian Radical* remains far less clear. Typical of the man, Thomas exaggerated his importance, crediting himself with a much more influential role in the newspaper's production than he actually possessed. Thomas neither appeared on its masthead nor was listed as a member of the paper's staff. In fact, during the *Christian Radical*'s three-year history Thomas contributed only three articles to the newspaper. Two of these echoed Schindler's fears that American religion was being prostituted by "sectarian caste" and "denominational asperities." Thomas implored his readers to look to the Bible ("the exalted teaching of the Divine Nazarene") and away from "the credulity and prejudice of creeds." He worried that the spirit of the Reformation had been extinguished by "ecclesiastical tyranny and usurpation," especially by "Catholic Bigotry" and "Americanized German Rationalism." Thomas's work on the *Christian Radical,* no matter how marginal, along with his articles in the *Christian Recorder,* sharpened his writing skills. These experiences prepared him for the time years later when he would edit his own magazine.[53]

In addition to, and as an extension of, his journalistic work, in 1868–69 Will labored as Wilberforce's agent, drawing upon his connections in the Pittsburgh area and in central Ohio to raise funds for the school. In sharp contrast to his earlier articles, late in 1868 he published two highly complimentary articles on the A.M.E. Church, taking special pains to highlight Wilberforce's mission to the freedmen and the school's need for financial support. For a while at least Will seemed committed to his new responsibilities.[54]

In April 1869, Thomas drafted a memorial to the U.S. Congress requesting an endowment of one hundred thousand acres of public land for Wilberforce. He read the memorial before the recently established Pittsburgh Annual Conference of the A.M.E. Church that assembled at the Wylie Street A.M.E. Church (Pittsburgh-area A.M.E. churches belonged to the Ohio Annual Conference until the Pittsburgh Annual Conference was established in 1869). The first meeting of the conference, presided over by Bishop Payne, who also served as Wilberforce's president, passed a motion to provide Thomas with a list of names of its members in order to place them on the list of petitioners to support his memorial. Though two months later the university's board tabled Thomas's proposal, within a year Wilberforce began a major campaign drive that lasted until March 1870, requesting a federal appropriation of fifty thousand dollars for the education of the freedpeople of the South. In its numerous petitions to Congress, Wilberforce emphasized the school's status as the "the only Collegiate Institution in the United States *founded, owned, and controlled by colored men,* and successfully engaged in the education of the colored race." Hundreds of blacks from Ohio, Kentucky, Virginia, Tennessee, and South Carolina signed the petitions. In fact, during the period of Thomas's association with the school, Wilberforce received two major federal appropriations for capital expenditures: $3,000 from the Freedmen's Bureau in 1869 and $25,000 from the same agency (by an act of Congress) the following year. According to the Reverend David Smith, a sizable sum—over $3,000—of the money "was paid to the agent as per centage." Thomas's role, if any, in the procurement of those funds remains unclear.[55]

Without question, however, by June 1869 Will's relations with the Wilberforce Board of Trustees had soured. At its June 29 meeting he charged that the board owed him money "for expenses attending his agency," a claim that the board deemed inadmissible. When he continued to challenge the terms of his agreement, the trustees resolved that he should immediately surrender his books and records to President Payne and "be relieved from his position as agent." When the board reconvened, Thomas dropped the question of his expenses entirely and, inexplicably, presented the board with $100. The next day, June 30, the board questioned Thomas's bookkeeping. Specifically, it asked whether he had donated or loaned $1,000 to Wilberforce and questioned under what conditions the money had been acquired. The trustees appointed a committee to find out. At that point the board requested that Will's "Subscription Book and credentials" be examined by a special committee appointed by the Executive Board. It then accepted an amendment not to give him "a note for the $505. received by them until the book and credentials are delivered." Thomas's association with Wilberforce ended on a decidedly murky note. The board obviously grew suspicious of irregularities on his part concerning the money he raised on their account. Whether the suspicions stemmed from unclear instructions from the board or from sloppiness or improprieties on Thomas's part remains unclear. Years later Wilberforce President J. H. Jones informed Chesnutt that when Thomas had been "connected with Wilberforce University in a financial capacity . . . some actions on his part in relation to the institution [occurred] that were very questionable, much of which was not recorded." Following Thomas's discharge as its financial agent, Wilberforce revised its regulations and reformed its administration of fund raising.[56]

Given Wilberforce University's importance to the A.M.E. Church and the close connection between its Ohio and Pittsburgh Annual Conferences, Thomas's chances of remaining active in the church in 1869 appeared doubtful. The position of financial agent for Wilberforce was highly regarded and visible within the A.M.E., and certainly his dismissal was noted within church circles. But with Will's usual ability to bounce back from trouble, in 1870 he was admitted on probation as a minister of the Pittsburgh Annual Conference. Apparently the financial irregularities that marred his tenure with Wilberforce and his abrupt withdrawal from WTS a year earlier never surfaced. Unquestionably black clergy in the Pittsburgh area must have wondered why one of their own had so abruptly become unaffiliated with both their denomination's university and the prestigious local white divinity school. It seems unlikely that Thomas, even with his considerable skills in navigating shoals, could have failed to run aground. But he somehow remained on course, remarkably untainted by these scandals, suggesting his personal popularity and prestige. Clearly, Thomas's contemporaries considered him a man of ability, and if anyone raised questions about his professional or personal affairs, they never recorded their concerns. Typically, Will covered up his past by engaging fully in the present.

Thomas in fact had a conspicuously high profile at the Pittsburgh Annual Conference that convened in April 1870. He played a significant role at the meeting, even being appointed "special reporter for the Conference" to the *Christian Recorder* and a black newspaper from South Carolina, the *Charleston Missionary Record*. Thomas conducted the religious exercises to open one of the sessions and sat on three committees, contributing a report on the training of third- and fourth-year divinity students. After the conference approved Thomas for its "traveling connexion," recommending him for its "itinerant work," Bishop John M. Brown, who years before had established Union Seminary, assigned him to the pastorate of the Monongahela Circuit in the vicinity of Monongahela City, Pennsylvania, seventeen miles south of Pittsburgh. In 1870 that circuit, part of the Pittsburgh District, comprised several small congregations that later became the Bethel A.M.E. Church. It had 158 members. The circuit thus was an appointment of some consequence. At Monongahela, Thomas replaced the embattled Reverend W. C. West, whose "character" was scrutinized at the 1870 conference. Several complaints were raised against West: that he had improperly conducted the election of church trustees, that without authorization he had agreed to the sale of building materials for constructing a church, and that he had failed to pay his debts. Given Thomas's record at Wilberforce, he was a most unlikely candidate to restore fiscal responsibility at Monongahela City.[57]

At first Thomas prospered in his new post. He labored hard to climb the A.M.E.'s hierarchical ladder, serving "on trial" and determined to gain admittance "into full connexion." During his one year on the job, membership in the Monongahela Circuit climbed from 158 to 192, making his church the third largest among the Pittsburgh District's fifteen congregations. Under Thomas's spiritual leadership the value of its church property also increased by over $2,500. As part of his conference duties, he chaired the Committee on Education. That committee underscored the importance of compulsory public schools for all children irrespective of race. In its April 1871 report, the committee concluded that "colored Americans are moving slowly, but surely, into position and self-reliance. Education is the recognized necessity." Will's committee also urged African Methodists to examine candidates for the ministry more thoroughly, with written tests. Though Thomas had been expelled from divinity school, for many years he criticized the training of African American clergy and urged the church to reform from within. In addition, in its report Thomas's committee also urged African Methodists to support Wilberforce, which it described as "our University." In keeping with the spirit of the report (and possibly to atone for his previous fiscal transgressions with the school), Thomas spoke on behalf of Wilberforce and pledged to send it $25.00 in quarterly installments.[58]

In 1870–71 Will also served on the Pittsburgh Conference's "Committee of the State of the Country," coauthoring a report that criticized the neoslavery the South's freedmen experienced. "In too many localities," the report charged, "the Demon of Slavery still lurks, ever ready to break out in acts of violence; shorn of its old power, it retains the same spirit—substituting the weapon of the assassin for the rule of the oppressor." The committee assigned some of the blame, however, to African Americans themselves. Much like President Andrew Johnson's speech before the 1st USCT that Will had attacked, the committee advised the freedmen in a moralistic tone. Many blacks remained ignorant, it explained, "comparatively uninformed—their ideas of freedom are vague and crude. It is the especial duty of our church to instruct the ignorant, to mould the unformed character, to inculcate habits of industry and self-reliance—teaching them that freedom is not indolence—not license to follow their own devices, but a high and holy estate, to be used in fitting them for discharging their duty to God, to their country, and to the world."[59]

Yet for all his success at Monongahela, in 1871 Will again stumbled while running in full stride. Once more money served as the source of his spill. In 1870–71 Thomas collected only $281.40 to support a broad range of church responsibilities—from missions and the A.M.E. Book Concern to widows and orphans and the bishop's salary. Under Thomas's leadership the Monongahela Circuit ranked eleventh (out of fifteen churches) in monies collected in the circuit. Despite his poor performance in raising church funds, Thomas received no official criticism from the Pittsburgh Annual Conference when it met in Brownsville, Pennsylvania, in April 1871. He did, however, incur its wrath for failing to meet his obligation to bring forward his congregation's "full assessment" of bishop's salary. Other pastors, too, were slow to pay. "Considerable time," wrote the secretary, "was . . . spent settling with the pastors." After a one-half hour delay, all of the clergymen had come forward with the payment but one—"Brother W. H. Thomas." [60]

With Bishop Payne presiding, on April 18 the conference discussed Will's case. According to the conference minutes, "it was shown by his Presiding Elder that the full amount [of bishop's salary] had been placed in his (Thomas') hands; and, upon his failure to pay it over, he was, by motion of Rev. W. H. Hunter, seconded by Rev. S. T. Jones, discontinued from the Itinerant work." Hunter served as Presiding Elder of the Pittsburgh District. Just two years earlier Thomas had praised Hunter's record as a military chaplain during the Civil War. In the *Christian Recorder* he noted the pastor's moral toughness and combativeness in theological warfare, describing him as "Captain Perseverance." In the 1871 Brownsville campaign even the battle-tested "Hannibal" proved no match for the Presiding Elder: Hunter completely outflanked Thomas and forced him to surrender without a fight. As a result of his discontinuance, Thomas could receive no future clerical assignments and, to all intents and purposes, was banished from the church. Immediately the conference replaced him on the Monongahela Circuit with the Reverend J. W. Morris. [61]

So ended Thomas's affiliation with the conference and, temporarily, his career as a theologian. To be sure, his failure to deliver the bishop's salary was a dereliction of duty. But Thomas's "sins" must have been more serious, more complicated for the conference to censure him so quickly and so completely. As with the other major setbacks in his life, he never commented on the issue of the bishop's salary. Did he pocket the money? Did he oppose supporting Bishop Payne for some personal, ideological, or theological principle? Did Payne harbor resentment against Thomas as a result of his 1869 disagreement with Wilberforce?

As usual, Thomas left no record of his side of the story. Like the incidents at wts and at Wilberforce, Thomas's silence again served to confirm his "guilt," at least according to his accusers. At the very least, he proved untrustworthy with money held in his care, demonstrating again his uncanny ability to quickly raise questions in the minds of others about his honesty. Equally important, however, in explaining his problems with the Pittsburgh Annual Conference must have been Thomas's crusade to reform the A.M.E. Church. Established clergy in the Pittsburgh area no doubt took umbrage at his pointed and persistent attacks on them and everything they represented.

As early as February 1868, Thomas had anticipated a counterattack from those he criticized. "True reformers always meet with opposition," he said. "Should we," Thomas asked, "succumb to certain antagonistic forces because we happen to be in the minority? Christian zeal, intensified with pure motives . . . never suffers abatement from opposing factions, on the contrary, it will be the impetus to exciting greater action." Though unwilling to halt his barrage against the church, Thomas concluded that opportunity lay elsewhere. In 1871 he left his young family in Allegheny City (he continued to retain a residency there and be listed as a "Reverend" in its city directories until 1880), changed religious affiliation, and moved to Georgia to begin a new life. Though his surroundings changed dramatically, Thomas's character remained true to form. He packed up his old habits and took them with him to the South.[62]

CHAPTER THREE

Missed Opportunities and Unresolved Allegations

I N 1871," Will Thomas explained thirty years later in *The American Negro*, "I went South to organize schools and teach the freedmen." Though his attempt in 1865 to secure a teaching job with the American Missionary Association had failed, his problems in Pittsburgh in 1871 added a new sense of immediacy to his determination to move on. After reporting on a conference of Presbyterians in Chicago for the *Christian Radical* in June of that year, Will concluded to go south. "I want to spend the winter in the *South*," he explained to General Oliver O. Howard, commissioner of the Bureau of Refugees, Freedmen, and Abandoned Lands (the Freedmen's Bureau), "say, in Florida or Texas, or one of the other Gulf States." Thomas sought employment either with Howard's agency, which had virtually abandoned its educational work a year earlier when the U.S. Congress halted appropriations for educational purposes, or with one of the various church societies engaged during Reconstruction in educational and humanitarian work among the former slaves.[1]

Writing to the Reverend Erastus Milo Cravath, field secretary of the American Missionary Association, Thomas mentioned neither the details of his recent church work with African Methodists in Pennsylvania nor the scandals that hovered over him. Instead he listed his credentials for an appointment in the association's southern mission: "Have been preaching about five years. Am twenty-eight years of age. Have been connected with . . . the [*Christian*] *Radical* about fifteen months. Understand how to teach. Could go under my own organization, the [African] Methodist, but decline. *Compensation* not so much an object as securing a working location." Again, Thomas preferred an assignment in either Florida or Texas. He told Cravath that the American Missionary Association, not yet affiliated with the Congregational Church, appealed to him "because of its non-sectarian character and the purity of its purposes." Thomas also informed Cravath that he had applied for the post of United States minister resident to the Republic of Liberia. This would be just the first of several diplomatic appointments that he would seek.[2]

After none of his applications resulted in a job offer, Thomas moved to Washington, D.C., in November 1871, probably in search of a political appointment. Within the month, however, he relocated to Rome, Georgia, the first of two times in his life that he resided there. This was Thomas's first return to the South since his Civil War service in North Carolina. He moved to Georgia, he said, to restore his health, to gain "knowledge of southern habits and manners," and to begin a religious newspaper. He considered journalism "one of the best means for securing" the ex-slaves' "education and consequent elevation." For the next three decades Thomas became obsessed with studying the freedpeople in their native habitat. It was in Rome, Georgia, for example, that he met Albert Berrien, the son and former slave of influential U.S. Senator John MacPherson Berrien (1781–1856). Years later Will cited Albert as the ideal representative of his race, "the most intelligent and self-poised negro we have ever met . . . though he could neither read nor write, yet for sound judgment, accurate understanding, intelligent knowledge, and wise discrimination of men and things, was surpassed by but few well-informed persons of any race."[3]

As circumstances developed, however, Thomas abandoned the idea of establishing a religious newspaper in Georgia. In Rome he changed affiliation within the ranks of the Methodists, reentered the field of education, and became active in local Republican party circles. But Thomas never intended to make a home in Reconstruction-era Georgia. Amazingly, during his two years there, first in Rome and later in Atlanta, he held full-time teaching positions while somehow managing to travel extensively, frequently recording his impressions of men and measures in the *Christian Recorder*, gaining firsthand knowledge of African American life in the postwar South, and broadening his contacts and exposure nationwide. Thomas apparently had no family life, never mentioning in his correspondence or newspaper articles his wife Martha and referring only once to his young son Frank, who resided in Pennsylvania. As always, Will kept his options open and his carpetbags packed.[4]

Rome, located in Georgia's upper Piedmont region seventy miles northwest of Atlanta and fifteen miles east of the Alabama line, occupies one of Georgia's most picturesque areas. A contemporary described the area as "romantically beautiful," with "valleys, mountains, farms, and fields that rival Switzerland itself." Rome sits at the head of the Coosa River on the peninsula formed by the confluence of the Oostanaula and Etowah Rivers. Though inhabited largely by white, middle-class small farmers, not planters, in the 1850s Rome and Floyd County shared in the South's "cotton boom." This newfound prosperity resulted largely from the Rome Railroad's eastern connection to the Western and Atlantic Railroad at Kingston, Georgia, and the shipping of cotton bales down the Coosa River to Gadsden, Alabama. By 1860 Rome was a bustling railroad and river town serviced by four steamboats, a marketing center for the cotton, corn, and other crops grown in its fertile surrounding valleys and for the industrial products manufactured in its factories and iron foundries. The hills around Rome contained deposits of iron ore, bituminous coal, slate, sandstone, and limestone. In 1861 between 51 and 60 percent of the county's voters favored secession.[5]

During the Civil War Rome served as an important hospital headquarters and manufacturing and supply depot for the Confederacy. As early as 1862 the Confederate government began to extend the Blue Mountain and Selma Railroad in Alabama to Rome, but the project remained unfinished at war's end. Because of its remote location, Union troops did not occupy Rome until May 19, 1864, when a division under General Jefferson C. Davis captured it as part of General William T. Sherman's Atlanta campaign. The Union troops looted and ransacked Rome and, most important, captured virtually intact one of the Confederacy's major manufacturers of military equipment—James Noble's Ironworks and Machine Shop. According to Sherman, Rome provided "a good deal of provisions and plunder, fine iron-works and machinery." The war effectively shattered Rome's prosperity. After federal occupation the town served as a U.S. Army hospital center and, briefly before his march to the sea, as Sherman's headquarters. Prior to the start of this campaign—on November 10, 1864—Federal troops burned much of Rome's business district, including fortifications, warehouses, and industrial facilities. Disorder and confusion reigned in the town during the spring 1865 planting and lasted until the summer, when the "hill city" began to regroup. It took more than a year, however, for north Georgians to rebound from the inadequate harvests of 1865. In the countryside the freedpeople worked on shares or rented land.[6]

During Reconstruction, whites in Rome, as throughout Georgia and the South, adjusted slowly and painfully to the new order of things resulting from emancipation. Before the war, a resident explained, "slaves were part of the life pattern in a man-hungry, hard-working life, they were considered valuable property and treated accordingly, and no one had much time to discuss other fine points of ethics." Whites, according to a local historian, "remained sullen and resentful" over their defeat and occupation. This attitude took many forms, including exclusion, social ostracism, economic discrimination, verbal abuse, and violent acts—even murder. At every turn blacks faced whites who were convinced that defeat in war and emancipation had dire consequences for their race, their region, their civilization.[7]

"Our . . . merchants are exhausted of all ready means upon which to do business," Dr. Robert Battey, a prominent Rome native, remarked. He also complained of the presence of "idle negroes . . . lounging in town . . . in the prime of their manhood." They also reportedly pilfered from his garden and orchard. Cotton merchant Reuben S. Norton recorded disapprovingly that since the war had ended, the freedpeople had become "verry troublesome. . . . Negroes are moving into Town by Families, proving quite a nuisance, loitering about and having but little inclination to work; many depredations are committed night[ly], supposed[ly] by them." Martha Battey of Rome also expressed her alarm at living amidst free blacks. "I fear to hope sometimes," she wrote in June 1867, "when I look around and see the hundreds of lazy negroes that the Government is feeding." She worried that "they will not work as long as that is the case." Writing in December 1871, soon after Will Thomas arrived in Rome, white farmer John Horry Dent complained that "the negroes are ignorant, short sighted and improvident—hence they cannot be made to work for their own . . . or to the advantage of their employers." Five weeks later Dent groused that "one great error is endeavoring to enlighten the negro, for in so doing, you merely arouse his suspicions, confuse his ideas, and result in making him more persistent in believing in and doing what you have tried to make him not believe or do." Such was the mentality of the whites whom Thomas encountered as he ventured south to northwest Georgia.[8]

In 1870 Rome's population stood at 2,748, including 1,005 people of African descent. Another 1,272 blacks lived in the town's outlying areas. Throughout Reconstruction black Georgians had demanded economic and political rights and expected support, including land and education, from the government. Their assertiveness led to all manner of violent responses from whites. Though the Ku Klux Klan would not enter Georgia until 1868, as early as 1866 white Georgians began a pattern of racial violence directed at the freedmen and women. At first they intimidated blacks verbally. When that tactic failed to subdue them, whites resorted to physical abuse and murder. According to one estimate, whites murdered between 1,500 and 1,600 black Georgians from 1867 to 1871. Back in Pittsburgh, at the editorial office of the *Christian Radical,* editor Daniel Schindler and Will Thomas followed news reports of racial violence in Georgia. "The fierce spirit of Ku Kluxism is loose and busy in its work of discord and ruin," the paper charged.[9]

Not until he arrived in Georgia, however, would Will grasp the depths of abuse and degradation the blacks experienced. Meeting in Augusta early in 1866, a convention of freedmen declared "that our people are daily subjected to the most cruel abuses by men who, in defiance of law and authority, violate and outrage the simplest form of moral justice." They implored "the Government to . . . bring to speedy justice all such criminals and thus not only vindicate our cause, but the principles of liberty and right." As a result of this convention, a handful of whites joined the freedmen to create the Georgia Equal Rights Association. By early 1866 African Americans and Republican-oriented whites had established a Union League council in Rome and in other Georgia towns. From Georgia's crucible of Reconstruction emerged a contentious, unwieldy Republican party organization composed of radical and moderate scalawags, native blacks, and carpetbaggers, whites as well as those of African heritage like Thomas. According to historian Numan V. Bartley, despite its tenuous grip, in the late 1860s this coalition controlled state politics and introduced reforms. Republicans under Governor Rufus B. Bullock fought for equal access to the courts, land distribution, suffrage, and education for the freedpeople. This agenda, Bartley concludes, was "so wide-ranging that it threatened the state's tottering social and political foundations."[10]

In response, between 1868 and 1871 Democrats unleashed waves of racial violence in rural areas like Rome to undermine Republicans. In September 1868, for example, in order to disperse a Republican rally, whites opened fire on blacks in Camilla, a small town in Mitchell County in far south Georgia. Nine African Americans died and two dozen were wounded. Meanwhile, before, during, and after the presidential election of 1868, the Ku Klux Klan, the terrorist arm of Georgia's Democratic party, continued outrages against the freedpeople. In the first ten and a half months of 1868, there were 336 murders of and assaults with intent to kill Georgia blacks. Twenty-one of these occurred in Rome. According to Bartley, "the Democrats approached politics as a form of guerilla warfare." At the party's November 1869 meeting, Georgia's Republicans judged their state "as completely under the control of those who spurn the Government of the United States . . . as it was during the rebellion or during the years 1865 and 1866; and the State cannot, therefore, be recognized as either *legally* or *actually* reconstructed."[11]

Though military intervention in late 1869 enabled Bullock and the Republicans to remain in power, Democrats captured control of the Georgia legislature in December 1870 in a campaign marred by Klan violence, intimidation, and voter fraud. Fearful of impeachment, the governor resigned in October 1871. No sooner than Thomas arrived in Rome in November 1871, Benjamin F. Conley, president of the senate and Bullock's hand-picked successor, was summarily replaced in a special election by Democrat James M. Smith. The state's Republican party was in shambles. Thomas entered the state as Reconstruction in Georgia drew to a close, when Georgia's Klan violence was at its height and the federal and state governments afforded little protection for scalawags or carpetbaggers of either race. It was an inopportune time at best for a Republican, especially a sharp-tongued, one-armed black Civil War veteran and carpetbagger, to settle in northwest Georgia. Naive, or perhaps undaunted by the power of white southerners, Will Thomas made Rome his new home.[12]

Once established in Rome, Will did not engage in newspaper work as he had planned, but instead immediately secured an administrative and teaching position for the fall term (begun in October 1871) at the Rome Normal School—an institution administered by the Freedmen's Aid Society of the predominantly white Methodist Episcopal Church. In 1844 the Methodist church had split into northern (M.E. Church) and southern (M.E. Church, South) wings over disputes concerning slavery and the power of its bishops. During Reconstruction the M.E. Church made a concerted effort to enter the South and reestablish itself as the national Methodist church at the expense of the demoralized M.E. Church, South. In order to accomplish this, northern Methodists sent missionaries and teachers among both races in the South, committing, according to one historian, "ecclesiastical imperialism."[13]

The M.E. Church openly clashed not only with the southern Methodists and their 1870 creation, the Colored Methodist Episcopal Church, but with the A.M.E. Church and its rival, the African Methodist Episcopal Zion Church, as well. Once the war was over the latter two sects also fought for the souls of black southerners. According to historian Reginald F. Hildebrand, the various Methodist missionaries offered the freedpeople three alternative meanings of freedom. Whereas the Southern and Colored Methodists advanced "a new paternalism," the African Methodist denominations espoused a "Gospel of Freedom"—"a release . . . from all of the limiting aspects of the legacy of slavery." Thomas's new affiliation, the M.E. Church, promised "a radical new model of race relations"— one promulgated on an abhorrence of "caste" and a determination to integrate blacks "into the powers and privileges of the denomination." [14]

Following the Civil War these Methodists engaged in an internecine conflict of their own to win converts among the freedpeople. According to historian Ralph E. Morrow, "the interMethodist competition for African proselytes" led quickly to a "cutthroat bidding for Negro recruits." Northern Methodists, according to their southern organ, the *Atlanta Methodist Advocate,* had "the advantage of neither a sectional nor class name, . . . vast numbers, . . . wealth and influence, and the great advantage of a constant, consistent and outspoken opposition to slavery." But because of their identification with emancipation, northern clergymen like Thomas faced an uphill and often fierce battle in the former Confederacy. "The M.E., South," one minister from the North complained, "is as bitter against us as any other crowd. All make common cause against us. Our Church is titled the Northern, the Radical, the negro Church." Throughout Reconstruction southern Methodists attacked northern Methodists for "keeping up a warfare with a sister church" and for "wheedling" members away from their congregations. Northern Methodist clergy were denounced "as a set of politico-ecclesiastical propagandists; as malignants, bent on mischief; provoking the ex-slaves to hate, and take revenge on, their former masters; as disturbers of the peace and harmony of the churches." Despite such opposition, in October 1867, the northern church established its biracial Georgia Mission Conference. [15]

Though Will already had sided with editor Daniel Schindler in opposing narrow sectarianism, his 1871 shift from the A.M.E. to the M.E. Church was motivated by need. He desperately sought employment and a new field in which to operate, not a new denominational creed to follow. Church records document that he was slow to sever his ties with the A.M.E. Church: he published nineteen articles in the *Christian Recorder* in 1872–73 alone. In fact Thomas was not "admitted on trial" into the Central Ohio Conference of the M.E. Church until September 1872 and did not transfer his membership to the Georgia Conference until October 1872, eleven months after his move to Rome. Thomas's case challenges historian Jacqueline Jones's argument that the Freedmen's Aid Society, like the American Baptist Home Missionary Society, "selected teachers only from members of their respective churches. This requirement meant that successful applicants had undergone a personal religious conversion experience as evidenced by church membership." Affiliation with the northern Methodists was not a requirement for service in the Freedmen's Aid Society. [16]

Upon settling in Rome, Thomas advocated the "Christian Union" of black Methodists, worried that they already were "enfeebled and paralyzed by the circumscription of caste dogmas." In early 1872 he admonished the various sects to stop feuding over trivial issues and jealousies and to find strength in unification. Nonetheless, Thomas broke from the A.M.E. and joined the M.E. Church. His transfer to the northern branch of Methodism and moving to the South was a smart move, given that his experiences with the A.M.E.'s Pittsburgh Annual Conference made it doubtful that this church would have provided him employment. Northern Methodism, however, afforded Will a fresh start and many new opportunities. Ministers in that wing of Methodism were unaware of his past transgressions, and he could tend to the educational and spiritual needs of the ex-slaves his way, without the close supervision of the religious hierarchy. Thomas's assignment in isolated Rome would also allow him to put into practice his idealistic theories about church reform. According to Hildebrand,

> Black preachers were key figures in the success of the [northern Methodists'] mission. They interpreted the message of the denomination and conveyed it in a manner that resonated with the freedpeople's values, aspirations and modes of expression. It was the mediation of black preachers that made it possible for many black southerners to take possession of the Northern Methodist vision of the future. In a more immediate way than their white colleagues, black ministers became the embodiment of the Methodist Episcopal Church for the freedpeople, and from the very start the denomination recognized the need for cultivating a cadre of effective black emissaries.

Will realized that as a black in the largely white M.E. Church, he would be a minority, but, if successful in his work, he might advance quickly. He did so within the Freedmen's Aid Society. Thomas was one of only thirty-one teachers the agency sponsored in Georgia in the period 1865 to 1873.[17]

The Freedmen's Aid Society made a special effort to recruit teachers and missionaries like Thomas, "men of African descent, with education, who may . . . be introduced into the extreme Southern field." The Reverend Richard S. Rust, president of Wilberforce University prior to its sale to the A.M.E. Church in 1863 and first general field agent of the Freedmen's Aid Society, credited the society's missionaries with "quietly laying deep and broad foundations for the future. Intelligence and piety," he added, "are the only enduring foundations upon which the church and nation can build. Nothing else will fit the emancipated race for the appropriate discharge of the duties that await them." In contrast, the A.M.E. Church had fewer resources to devote to its attempt to win converts from among the South's ex-slaves.[18]

In Georgia the Freedmen's Aid Society collaborated with the ex-slaves and the Freedmen's Bureau to establish a system of schools and chapels. The Bureau coordinated the educational activities, commonly procuring buildings, refurbishing them, and surrendering their titles to the freedpeople, who supplied what funds they could muster. The Freedmen's Aid Society provided the teachers. The Bureau frequently offered teacher-ministers like Will with transportation to their posts and room and board. But their salaries depended upon local collections. Compensation for Methodist educators and evangelists was notoriously irregular and sparse. Tuition at Freedmen's Aid Society schools varied depending on the ability of the students' parents to pay, a consideration that invariably kept the teachers' remuneration low. Thomas obviously had not moved to Georgia for financial gain. One of his coworkers in Georgia complained in 1870 that "if I don't get help soon I shall consider that I am in the employ of nobody as nobody pays me anything."[19]

As early as October 1865, the Freedmen's Bureau organized a freedmen's school in Rome, Georgia, under a white instructor, Jonathan Holbrook. The broad range of ages of Holbrook's students suggests that he probably did well just to teach the basics—reading and writing. Among his twenty students, six were between ages five and ten, eleven were between ages ten and fifteen, one was between ages fifteen and twenty, and two were over the age of twenty. The students paid Holbrook $2 per month and attended classes in his home. In early 1868 Holbrook's school expanded beyond the confines of his house. The Bureau constructed a schoolhouse in Rome for the students and deeded the property to the M.E. Church. The Freedmen's Aid Society, though slow to respond, eventually assigned teachers to the institution, the Sibley School, named for Colonel Caleb C. Sibley, third assistant commissioner of the Freedmen's Bureau for Georgia. Sibley School was one of eleven common, or primary, schools that the Freedmen's Aid Society then maintained in Georgia. The Reverends E. Miner and Andrew W. Caldwell, assisted by Miss E. J. Girard and William B. Thompson, an African American, operated both Sibley School and Rome's M.E. chapel. As historian Ronald E. Butchart notes, northern Methodists commonly utilized churches as schoolhouses in an effort to both proselytize and educate the freedpeople. In May 1870, the Sibley School enrolled eighty students—all blacks—who attended classes for six hours per day. Of Sibley's students, only six had been free before the war and twenty-eight were over sixteen years old. The Freedmen's Bureau described Sibley as a "Day School" offering "Primary and Normal" curricula, though more than one-half of the students (forty-five) were engaged in learning to spell and read "easy lessons." In conjunction with the school, the Freedmen's Aid Society ran a Sabbath school with twenty teachers and 250 pupils.[20]

By the time Thomas left Pennsylvania, the Rome Normal School was one of eleven schools in Georgia and thirty-five in the South that northern Methodists continued to support. No record exists of its relation to the Sibley School, but as late as December 1870, the Freedmen's Aid Society reported that it maintained a preparatory school in Rome, most certainly Sibley. Rome Normal School, established sometime in 1871, no doubt replaced Sibley and occupied its building shortly before Will's appointment as principal in November. One account listed him as the school's "president" and reported the value of its property at three thousand dollars. Though the M.E. Church created Rome Normal School ostensibly to train teachers, as Morrow correctly observes, "the label of a school bore no correspondence to the caliber of its academic offerings. The Methodists had the mischievous habit of magnifying the character of institutions by the magnificence of their titles." Quite commonly students at markedly different levels of training learned under the same roof. Colleges established for the freedmen commonly had a majority of their students enrolled in elementary or preparatory departments. "Many," historian John A. Carpenter suggests, "were in . . . the normal department in which students, who had received a rudimentary training in reading and writing, learned to become teachers of these subjects." In theory at least, Thomas's school had the responsibility of educating teachers and preachers. The *Atlanta Methodist Advocate* described it as the "Normal and Biblical School at Rome, Ga."[21]

Thomas was welcomed to Georgia by Erasmus Q. Fuller, editor of the *Methodist Advocate,* a white New York minister who had served the M.E. Church in the Old Northwest. He described Thomas as "a fine scholar," one who "enters upon the work of building up this Institution with great zeal." Fuller judged that Thomas had "few superiors among his people, and we commend this enterprise most earnestly to the colored students of that whole region, and to all interested in the elevation and thorough training of the rising generation." As Fuller certainly recognized, Thomas's appointment in Rome placed him in a precarious position. Even during the period of their greatest successes, 1866–70, Freedmen's Aid Society missionaries and teachers were "assailed, stigmatized, despised" by local white churchmen. According to the Reverend John H. Caldwell, a leading M.E. preacher and organizer, they were perceived as propagandists and disturbers of the peace. By 1871 religious scalawags and carpetbaggers were, according to one of their number, "left to the mercy of the unreconstructed." A few years later an M.E. teacher predicted another civil war and feared that northern educators would be "fleeing from Georgia for our lives." Given the tense racial climate in northwest Georgia in the early 1870s—and Will's status as a black carpetbagger and religious interloper—he met with surprising success.[22]

In January 1872 Thomas hosted a "Theological Institute" on the subject of religious education at Rome's M.E. Church. The Rome conference served as his introduction to Georgia's M.E. clergy. It provided a forum to exhibit Thomas's leadership skills and to display his abilities as a preacher and teacher. The meetings featured two influential white M.E. ministers, the Reverend Lorenzo Dow Barrows (1817–78) of Boston and the Reverend James W. Lee of Atlanta's Loyd Street M.E. Church, as well as a diverse group of ministers, itinerants, and Sunday school teachers. Barrows, a distinguished religious educator, was a Vermont native who participated actively in both the abolitionist and antisaloon campaigns. He served in Methodist churches throughout New England and as president of three colleges. Barrows published *Scripture Readings for Devotion and Study in Seminaries, Sabbath Schools, and Families* (1865) and edited *The National Temperance Advocate*. Will described him as "a Christian scholar of fine culture"—"preeminently a self-made man, of a keen, clear-sighted, practical cast, with mental powers . . . rarely excelled." The Freedmen's Aid Society sent Barrows to Georgia to supervise teacher training and to establish Clark Theological Seminary in Atlanta. Will agreed with Barrows that the South offered a virgin field for northern Methodism. "The dormant energies of the multitude must be aroused, the majorities must be educated, the people should be lifted into a purer atmosphere of thought, into a new life."[23]

According to Will's account of the Rome conference, he played a role in the meetings second only in importance to the celebrated northern theologian. The twenty-nine-year-old minister joined the veteran clergyman in addressing several of the sessions and directed an afternoon program by himself. In this session Thomas delivered a sermon, conducted Bible readings and analyses, and led the conference participants in hymns. One evening Barrows, Lee, and Thomas ran a public temperance meeting, netting almost fifty signatures on an antisaloon pledge. At another session Barrows lectured the participants in "sermon-making." The clergy who attended, Will said, "are beginning to be more thoughtful, growing studious, and showing greater care in pulpit preparations, using choicer language with an observable discrimination in the selection of technical terms." Exhibiting his customary lack of modesty, Thomas concluded that his "Theological Institute" was an unqualified success. The clergymen dedicated themselves to training "a strong, active, well developed body of spiritual and intellectual preachers of the Gospel."[24]

In Rome, Will sought to ingratiate himself not only with the community of Georgia's M.E. preachers but with the ranks of the state's Republicans as well. Though by 1872 Georgia's Republican party lay in disarray, it still held pockets of strength, and Thomas naively supposed that he could succeed where others, both whites and blacks, had failed. In May 1872, for example, he informed Ohio Congressman James A. Garfield, his former commander in the 42nd Ohio Volunteer Infantry, that local Democrats had manufactured charges in order to cashier Rome's postmaster, P. M. Sheibley. Thomas considered Sheibley "a worthy, efficient Republican" and complained that "bitter rebels" and other conservatives had forged his and other names to discredit the postmaster. "I have been working for the success of the Republican Party," Thomas told Garfield. Will feared that Sheibley's removal "would cause us to suffer defeat in this part of the state." Thomas also wrote Garfield confidently that he would serve as a delegate to the Republican National Convention in Philadelphia in June 1872. Given the fact that he was a newcomer to the state, having resided in Georgia for only eight months and possessing no political base, this was an exceptionally empty boast at best. Ironically, Sheibley—not Thomas—served as an "at large" delegate from Georgia to the convention. Undaunted, Thomas nonetheless went to work to establish himself as a leader among Georgia's black Republicans.[25]

On May 30 he served as "Orator of the Day" at the "Decoration Day" ceremonies to honor the Union troops buried at the National Cemetery in Marietta, Georgia. The program was to include fellow Ohioan John Mercer Langston, who had been the primary force in recruiting the 5th USCT years earlier and was then dean of Howard University's law department. The Reverend James W. Lee of Atlanta, who had attended Thomas's "Theological Institute," and the Reverend R. Anderson, pastor of Marietta's A.M.E. Church, were the other speakers. Thomas apparently substituted for Langston as the keynote speaker at the last minute when Langston failed to appear. Thomas was introduced to the audience as the "Rev. W. H. Thomas, of Rome, Ga." A decorated USCT veteran, a minister and teacher, and an African American carpetbagger, Thomas provided an ideal speaker for the occasion at hand.[26]

Will's address, "The Heroism, Patriotism and Saviorism of the Soldiers in Blue," evoked images of the "Bloody Shirt" then popularized by Republican politicians nationwide. While Thomas acknowledged gratuitously the *"heroism"* of the former Confederate soldiers, he quickly reminded the partisan audience that "these heroes . . . *were not patriots."* White southerners, he said, fought "against their own Government, their own country, and the best interests of humanity—blindly and ignorantly, yet many of them honestly . . . to found a *Confederacy,* to satisfy the grasp for power of a few wickedly ambitious men." He urged the audience not to forget the sacrifices that Union troops had made to free the South's slaves and praised the freedpeople for the progress they had accomplished since emancipation. There was still room for improvement, though, according to Thomas. This would become the dominant theme of many of his future writings. The ex-slaves had "to improve upon the opportunities . . . offered them, and in every way prove themselves *men."* He closed his address by quoting the Apostle Paul (Philippians 2:3): "Let nothing be done through strife or vain glory. Be kindly affectioned one to another, forgiving one another, in as much as ye know that God for Christ's sake hath forgiven you." [27]

While in Rome, Thomas combined education, religion, race, and politics, hopeful to promote himself as a Republican spokesman on the national level. In the summer and early fall 1872, when the Rome Normal School was on summer recess, he ventured to Philadelphia, Pittsburgh, and New York City to assist in editing the *Christian Recorder* and to campaign among blacks for President Ulysses S. Grant, Henry Wilson, Republican candidate for vice-president, and John F. Hartranft, Pennsylvania's Republican gubernatorial candidate. Georgia Republican Amos T. Akerman, Grant's former attorney general and a champion of racial justice, informed Wilson that Thomas was "a colored man of good education and acquaintan[ce]s, and of fine character. He is a warm Republican, and having a good faculty for public speaking, is very servicable before the public." Thomas considered it essential for the good of the freedpeople that the Republicans remain in office. The Democrats, he argued in standard party rhetoric, stood for "the fossilized institution of the past, the party of oppression and enslavement; the party of northern aristocracy and Southern ologarchy; the foe of freemen and free labor; free instruction and free emigration." In contrast, Thomas asserted, the Republicans were "the party of progress, of internal improvement, of equality, of human right and universal liberty, of equal representation and recognition." In the heat of the 1872 presidential campaign, he reminded black voters that John Brown—like the Republican candidates of 1872—had exhibited "superhuman sympathy for the 'despised and enslaved race' in this country." After Grant, Wilson, and Hartranft triumphed, Thomas again assailed slavery as "an institution that in its mildest forms, left its impress upon the soul, as well as the body of its victims, the carnival of a monster in the light of American Republicanism."[28]

While in the North, Thomas met with a number of his former army friends, reportedly even General Philip M. Sheridan. Because he had no apparent previous connection to Sheridan, and because Thomas always claimed to have important friends in high places, his account of meeting Sheridan is suspect. In any case, on this trip to the North he also served as guest preacher at several black churches, including Henry Highland Garnet's Shiloh Presbyterian Church in New York City. After attending a meeting of New York's African American clergymen, Thomas blasted the poor quality of their preaching—just as he had done in Allegheny City. In his opinion, the ministers made "distorted speculations . . . from unreasonable data." The clergy's "scientific statements . . . under their plastic manipulation become unscientific jargon."[29]

In New York Thomas attended a lecture by the temperance orator John B. Gough, whose remarks on race angered him. In one of his earliest published statements on race, Thomas remarked: "It may be sensitiveness, love of race, and a regard for race dignity, but be it what it may, every man feels like promoting his ancestral honor." Whereas Gough, like the Pan-Africanist Edward Wilmot Blyden, objected to the use of the term "colored," favoring "Negro," Thomas, a mulatto, insisted that "colored is indigenous to this country, and fitly describes the class it represents." "The word *negro*," he explained, "is not generic, is not organic, is not descriptive, and is not therefore applicable to this class of American people." In the best of all worlds, he said, classifications based on racial distinctions would be unnecessary. After all, people of African descent had been Americans for two centuries and therefore constituted part of "the American race." But, he argued, because whites had dictated the term "colored," African Americans of all shades of skin color should accept it proudly. What really mattered, Thomas emphasized, was "the absolute, essential recognition of the parity of individual right, and individual citizenship." Christ's word, he believed, had the power to overturn "*caste ridden humanity*" and celebrate the "deep undercurrent of common feeling and sympathy in the hearts of all men." Ironically, thirty years later Thomas incurred the wrath of virtually all African Americans by drawing an invidious color line between Negroes and mulattoes. In 1872, however, his views on race were more mainstream than inflammatory.[30]

While en route by train back to Georgia, Will stopped in Baltimore and

Washington, D.C., and was invited to attend services at Baltimore's Mt. Vernon Place Church, an affluent white Methodist congregation constructed in 1870. Struck by the "exceedingly bad taste" of the church's "palatial edifice," Thomas again attacked the hypocrisy of white ministers in general, and those in Baltimore in particular, for excluding blacks from communion and church fellowship. This was his first attack on segregation within the church. "Yes see," Will exclaimed, "I have no feeling of tolerance for a sham Christianity," that relegated persons of color to "obscure corners in churches, . . . unclean car[s] on the railroads," and rendered them "subjects of dishonor and derision in public places." "I have grown weary of such *heartless, shameless pretensions* to piety no matter where practiced," Thomas said. Unwilling to absolve African American clergy from similar charges, he added: "Our own people are not altogether free from it" either. For years he would criticize black ministers for practicing far less than they preached.[31]

Thomas's "Saunterings," as he titled the series of twelve travel accounts published in the *Christian Recorder* in 1872 and 1873, provide among the most salient insights into his emerging worldview and complex personality. In Washington, D.C., for example, he complained that amidst all its riches, the Smithsonian Institution failed to display African artifacts. Writing from York, Pennsylvania, he described himself as "a person who has no small a share of the migratory in his nature," one "whose soul revels in the musical cadences of . . . the '*march*.'" For Thomas, "separation and isolation" served to "*awe* and *hush* the soul, into the stillness of the midnight hour." Such solitude and loneliness enabled him to reflect on a "past, full of regretfulness," and anticipate a "future, dark, foreboding and cheerless." Morose and introspective, he admitted that a life such as his required "moral heroism . . . [and] more absolute poise of soul than . . . the sensuous bravado of physical conflict." Observing the neatly trimmed cottages along the route southward, Thomas supposed that they were inhabited by young married couples. "How sad to think," he wrote, "that at sometime the *shade* will come creeping over the brightest sunshine; that sorrow's gaunt form treads close upon the footsteps of pleasure." He certainly could not have written this passage without reflecting on his self-imposed absence from his young family in Pennsylvania. Direful and downhearted, Will nevertheless went on to complain that people generally were unwilling to endure hardship in order to meet their goals. "Doubtless the hardest lesson of life," he said, "is to steadfastly, unflinchingly, heroically '*labor and wait*' to realize the full fruition of expectation." Regrettably Thomas never articulated what he considered the "fruition" of his "expectation."[32]

Despite such pessimism, upon returning to Georgia Thomas provided effective leadership at the Rome Normal School, enrolling during his brief tenure twenty-six students in the school's normal department. All of these students had either taught school or were preparing to become teachers. According to historian James D. Anderson, normal school students generally took the standard elementary school curriculum ("reading, spelling, writing, grammar, diction, history, geography, arithmetic, and music") and courses in "orthography, map drawing, physiology, algebra, and geometry, as well as the theory and practice of teaching." Seven others in Thomas's school studied theology. Freedmen's Aid Society officials complimented his "judicious management" of the institution and declared that under his leadership it had risen to "a standard of real merit." Though like Methodist educators throughout the South, Thomas labored under "poor school accommodations," especially "the absence of those essential requisites which go to make up the furniture of the school-room," his normal school nevertheless prospered. According to the Freedmen's Aid Society, under Thomas's leadership faculty and students alike "have shown courage and perseverance, and are entitled to great credit in placing their school among the best of this grade in the State." [33]

Because of this success, in 1872 the Freedmen's Aid Society promoted Thomas within its educational ranks and reassigned him to Atlanta. The Reverend T. B. Gurney, pastor of Rome's M.E. Church, and Miss M. M. Harrington, "a thoroughly educated and experienced teacher," assumed teaching duties at the Rome Normal School after Thomas's departure. It continued to suffer from the "want of suitable accommodations," however, and by 1875 the school lost Freedmen's Aid Society support and was abandoned, one of fourteen unchartered schools established by the M.E. Church. According to historian Henry Morrison Johnson, the Freedmen's Aid Society closed the Rome Normal School as part of its efforts to concentrate "its resources in the development of Clark University in Atlanta." As a result, blacks in Rome lacked educational opportunities until years later when the Rome Seminary and Rome High and Industrial School were established. Thomas meanwhile moved southward to Atlanta to join the faculty of Clark Theological Seminary. [34]

Although Atlanta lay in ruins after the Civil War, it rebuilt quickly, rapidly becoming the New South's major railroad terminus and commercial center. At war's end refugees of both races flocked to the city for food and shelter. Writing late in 1865, northern journalist John Tyler Dennett described the verve and energy of Atlanta as it rose from the ashes of defeat. "Unfinished houses," he wrote, "are to be seen on every hand; scaffolding, mortar-beds, and lime-barrels, piles of lumber and bricks and mounds of sand, choke every street, and the whole place on working days resounds with the noise of carpenters and masons. . . . Negroes of all colors abound." In fact, during and after the war, Atlanta's black population increased more than eightfold, from 1,939 in 1860 to 9,929 in 1870 and to 16,330 in 1880. African Americans represented 46 percent of Atlanta's population in 1870 and 44 percent a decade later. Indeed, over the last three decades of the nineteenth century the Gate City served as a magnet for thousands of people of color from throughout the state. This influx of migrants, however, contributed to serious social problems for the freedpeople, especially a severe housing shortage. Believing that the ex-slaves required discipline, not handouts, the U.S. Army, the Freedmen's Bureau, and northerners in general provided them only limited aid, protection, and intervention. White Atlantans generally greeted the black refugees coolly and stood determined to retain control over them.[35]

Throughout their postbellum history, black Atlantans encountered proscription and all manner of racial injustice. By 1873, for example, Atlanta provided people of African descent with only three grammar schools, two of which were supplied without rent by the American Missionary Association and the third by the Freedmen's Aid Society. The city offered blacks no secondary school facilities. Though they held voting strength in several of Atlanta's wards, the restoration of citywide elections after 1871 kept the city's freed population underrepresented and, accordingly, the African American community received few municipal improvements. Largely uneducated and forced to compete with working-class whites for jobs, most of the former slaves and free people of color in Atlanta remained unskilled and labored at manual trades.[36]

Atlanta's burgeoning African American population captured the attention of the M.E. Church as potentially fertile ground for the expansion of its southern mission. Whereas American Missionary Association missionaries worked mainly to educate Atlanta's freedpeople, the M.E. Church focused its attention on establishing churches. Because of poor white leadership and stiff competition from the A.M.E. Church, however, by 1867 the Freedmen's Aid Society decided to establish schools as a means of attracting African American converts. The agency opened its first grammar school on Atlanta's south side in 1868 — at Clark Chapel, a black church located on the corner of Jones and Fraser streets. It also established Clark University, both named for M.E. Bishop Davis W. Clark, the following year. Clark, first president of the Freedmen's Aid Society, was elected bishop in 1864 and soon after assumed responsibility for organizing the M.E. Church's southern conferences. Because the Freedmen's Bureau elected to support Atlanta University (chartered by the American Missionary Association in 1867), Clark University began modestly, initially offering only primary and preparatory training, first in Clark Chapel's basement and, in 1869, at Ayer School, a facility purchased from the American Missionary Association and renamed Summer Hill School. This large two-story brick building, also located on Atlanta's south side, accommodated 200 students. In 1870 Clark University relocated again, this time to a brick structure on Whitehall Street.[37]

Gradually Clark University's curriculum expanded to include normal and biblical departments. The Freedmen's Aid Society recognized the importance of locating a university in Atlanta, one that "might give tone and influence to . . . [its] movements all over the State." The Reverend Richard S. Rust wrote that "whoever educates this people saves them; and an institution in Atlanta, to train preachers and teachers, will exert a controlling influence in every town in the State." Administrators predicted that Atlanta would become "the gateway to the South" and were determined to erect a "normal school and theological class" that later would become "a full-orbed University" for blacks. By 1871 Clark University enrolled 130 pupils. Its enrollment swelled to 275 the following year.[38]

Clark University, like all of the Freedmen's Aid Society institutions, housed a broad range of students and curricula under the same roof—pupils ranged in age from four to sixty—including "lower English branches," college preparatory, teacher training, and a four-year liberal arts course of study. Much of the teaching, however, was at the primary level. According to an observer, Clark University teachers had to begin with such basics as instructing their pupils to pronounce English properly—overcoming "Africanisms and butcheries of the 'King's English.'" The Reverend James W. Lee, an M.E. missionary who established the first primary classes at Clark Chapel and later worked with Thomas both in Rome and in Atlanta, rejoiced that "the old 'lingo' of slavery and of the field is rapidly disappearing." Students who entered the school subscribed to strict moral standards, committing themselves "against intemperance, lewdness, idleness, and all kinds of vice." Its goals were to evangelize the freedpeople, to provide them moral uplift and to teach citizenship, to instill in them self-appreciation, and to rehabilitate the black family from the curse of slavery. Despite such good intentions, during its infancy Clark University suffered from "the lack of permanency of a chief administrator, frequent changes in site, and inadequate physical facilities." As late as 1875 it occupied one building, with "no plaster, paper, nor ceiling." Breaks in the walls allowed light and ventilation in the summer, but the school president, the Reverend Isaac J. Lansing, complained that he "could not keep it comfortably warm during the coldest weather." Three years later the Freedmen's Aid Society reported that its poor facilities and shaky financial base discouraged students from attending Clark University. "In short, the University is about equal to a New England seminary of ordinary grade. If ever a school was needy this one is." Such "universities," according to historian Robert C. Morris, went little "beyond the high school stage in the Reconstruction era."[39]

Early in 1872 the Freedmen's Aid Society used the funds that it saved from faculty expenses subsidized by the city, along with Bishop Clark's bequest, to endow a school for African American Methodist ministers. Its Cincinnati-based leadership considered it essential to prepare clergy among the freedpeople with the necessary "spiritual weapons" to fight sin and the legacy of slavery. Under the temporary direction of the Reverend Barrows and assisted by other white clergy—the Reverends Fuller, Lee, and J. H. Knowles—Clark Theological Seminary began in Atlanta's white Loyd Street M.E. Church (later located on Central Avenue) with thirty black student ministers. The theological seminary relocated to a site on the corner of Whitehall and McDaniel Streets, along Atlanta's streetcar line, and officially opened on February 20, 1872, with nineteen students. According to the Freedmen's Aid Society, "never was there a greater need, never a louder call from God, never such a golden opportunity to consecrate wealth to the high purpose of saving the redeemed millions of the South." A black woman recalled that the "Reverend Barrows was a good preacher and a good teacher, . . . Some of the most outstanding preachers of our race and of all denominations went to him by night in order to learn how to preach."[40]

While Clark Theological Seminary also enrolled students in an "academic" course, the Freedmen's Aid Society chartered it to prepare preachers and teachers for the M.E. Church's southern mission. "Its doors are open to all, irrespective of race or color," an advertisement proclaimed, but the preparation of black Methodist ministers was central to the school's purpose. Its modest campus consisted of one brick building with twelve rooms, valued at nine thousand dollars, where some students boarded and all attended classes. Those who boarded paid ten dollars per month and provided two hours of manual labor per day. Students enrolled in the preparatory and normal departments paid tuition of one dollar per month. Divinity students attended free of charge. The students came largely from Georgia but from Alabama and Florida as well.[41]

Though on paper Will continued to direct the Rome Normal School until the end of the 1871–72 academic year, he left before the academic year ended. His success in north Georgia, and no doubt his training at Western Theological Seminary and experience as a minister in Pennsylvania, earned him a call to Atlanta in early 1872. He became one of the first permanent faculty members at Clark Theological Seminary and pastor of the city's Clark Street M.E. Church—a substantial black congregation of 485 "full members," fifty-five "probationers," and three local preachers. Already known in M.E. Church circles as a powerful orator, Thomas served as one of the featured speakers at the new seminary's morning and afternoon opening day exercises. During summer 1872, the Reverend Lee replaced Barrows as the school's president. The entire Clark Theological Seminary faculty consisted of three persons: the Reverend Lee; his wife, Mrs. Lida E. Lee; and Will. A Maryland native and relative of the Lees of Virginia, Lee moved to Chicago before the Civil War and served as a U.S. Army chaplain during the conflict. Upon graduating from Garrett Biblical Institute in Evanston, Illinois, he accompanied Fuller to Atlanta and was assigned to the Loyd Street Church, supervising primary school work at Clark Chapel. Mrs. Lee graduated from Illinois Female College and supervised Clark Theological Seminary's preparatory department and served as the school's matron. She reportedly trained the first group of "jubilee singers" who toured the North to raise funds for Clark University.[42]

For his part, Thomas rose quickly within the ranks of the M.E. Church, thereby solidifying his importance as a local teacher, preacher, and race leader. But once in Atlanta, he distanced himself from politics. Late in 1872 Will was elected to deacon's orders in the Georgia Conference and was ordained by the controversial and influential M.E. Bishop Gilbert Haven. This represented the first leg in the two-step ordination process. In May 1872, Thomas published an article on the meaning of Christianity in the *Atlanta Methodist Advocate*. In his customary longwinded style, he argued that Christ stood above all other philosophers, and that his teachings transcended law and addressed man's absolute duties and obligations. Thomas differentiated between the legal prohibition against thievery and Christ's "principle . . . that all overreaching, fraudulent representations" were "theft of far greater magnitude than the burglarious midnight prowler, more to be condemned . . . because committed under pretext of apparently fair and honest motives."

"Broad, out-reaching in its beneficence to all men," he added, Christianity elevated mankind "into a purer and better atmosphere, a new life by the doctrine of eternal existence."[43]

The *Christian Recorder*—two issues of which Thomas saw through press in the summer of 1872—reprinted this article verbatim. In December 1872, however, the A.M.E. newspaper criticized him for arguing that the church was too conservative and should have acquired Howard University in Washington, D.C. According to editor Benjamin Tucker Tanner, who studied at Western Theological Seminary and whose writings Will had denounced in 1867: "We are surprised that a soldier—for Bro. Thomas went through the war, and left a right arm at Wilmington, should advise a Militant Church to dispense with its sinews of war. Our sinews are well trained METHODIST preachers; and these can no more be made at Howard, than can a Dahlgren be made at Springfield." Nevertheless, after taking note of Thomas's shift to a rival denomination, the editor of the *Christian Recorder* wished him well in his new post. Tanner described Will as "a man of genius and ready wit."[44]

Thomas served on the Clark Theological Seminary faculty during the seminary's first full term, which ended in June 1873. As with other colleges and universities established for the freedmen, Clark Theological Seminary included students at several levels. During the school's first year of operation, for example, twenty-three of its seventy-eight students were enrolled in the theological department. Seven of the student ministers served Methodist congregations as circuit preachers. The faculty examined the seminary students in Amos Binney's *The Theological Compend* (1840) and H. Crosby's *Bible Manual* (1869). The remainder of the students enrolled in the preparatory and normal departments. About a dozen of these students held appointments as teachers at Clark University's building at Summer Hill as part of Atlanta's "free school" program. M.E. Church officials encouraged "the most promising students" to enter Clark Theological Seminary, "thus making the primary-school a feeder to the higher, and thus giving to our Church a controlling influence in the training of the children." After its first year of operation the Freedmen's Aid Society declared that the Clark Theological Seminary had accomplished much despite its small faculty and limited facilities. Still, the school drastically required classrooms, a chapel, dormitories, a library, and more professors. Nevertheless, Freedmen's Aid Society administrators in Cincinnati remarked that Clark Theological Seminary "teachers have been unwearied in their efforts to promote the welfare of the institution, and these efforts have been crowned with great success."[45]

Will, apparently idealistic and committed to training African American preachers, engaged actively and fully in teaching at Clark Theological Seminary. As before, and throughout his life, he remained critical of other clergymen. In February 1873, he condemned Georgia's white ministers as hypocrites—men who preached racial tolerance but who condoned racial violence. Fearful of losing their congregations and thus their livelihoods, whites practiced a "materialistic Theism." "How," Will asked, "can one who is impure, exhort to purity; how dare the unchaste assume to exemplify chastity?" In years to come Thomas's many critics would raise similar questions about him.[46]

But Thomas also took black preachers to task, especially for what he considered to be their "flippancy, not to say rudeness, in pulpit preparation." Aware of Georgia's conservative political climate and the limited avenues of advancement for people of color, he espoused a conservative philosophy of education that stressed discipline, order, permanence, respectability, system, and wisdom. Thomas championed Clark Theological Seminary, naively envisioning the school as central to "educational reform" for the mass of ex-slaves as well as for those who sought to preach. The seminary, he explained in an April 1873 article in the *Atlanta Methodist Advocate,* was intended to be a *"school of the prophets"*—principally to educate Methodist Episcopal ministers—but also open free of charge to others irrespective of denomination. Indeed, Baptist, A.M.E., and M.E. licentiates attended classes during the school's first year.[47]

Will echoed the concerns of white Freedmen's Aid Society officials that the freedmen and women desperately required spiritual and educational leadership. They were, he wrote in language similar to that employed almost three decades later in *The American Negro,* "a degraded Humanity"—a people in need of "a conscientious, active class of educated Christian ministers." His experiences in Rome had convinced him that "no true friend of the South can look on its untutored ministry without instinctively feeling a compassionate impulse to ameliorate their condition." The freedpeople, Will argued, required "rudimentary" and continuous theological training, "an inflexible and persistent adherence to the distinctive peculiarities of organization." Educated members of the race like himself confronted "grave responsibilities," he said, including "the bigotries of ignorance, superstition, and polemical controversy."[48]

In Atlanta, Thomas finally seemed to have found his niche. As a professor of theology he pledged to challenge "the denominational barbarisms which prevail in this country and permeate society." He stood committed to reforming and uplifting his race. Writing in October 1873, Will explained that "what the colored people need in this country is unity of purpose and unity of action. Better than all the Civil Rights Bills ever enacted by Legislative assemblies, is the disposition to act in concert. Well arranged plans, with inflexibility of purpose will always insure victory. Race recognition, and not individual preferment should be the controlling desire. Capacity and availability are the important considerations that determine the issue of all crises." Unity was especially important because in the fall of that year the economic hardships of the Panic of 1873 began to unfold for African Americans in Atlanta and nationwide. The nation's financial distress forced branch after branch of the Freedman's Savings Bank to pay nervous depositors. Within a year the bank failed. According to the Freedmen's Aid Society "deep poverty and distress" ran rampant "among the colored people." And of special significance to Thomas and other M.E. clergy was the fact that by 1873 the Georgia Conference was losing converts of both races to the rival Methodist sects.[49]

In Georgia, as in Pennsylvania, Thomas's successes turned quickly to failures. As early as August 1872, apparently losing interest in the Freedmen's Aid Society, Clark Theological Seminary, and Clark Street Church, he started casting about for new opportunities. He approached Atlanta University—an American Missionary Association school and Clark University's cross-town rival—expressing his willingness to help the fledgling school obtain an endowment from the estate of the late Pittsburgh philanthropist Charles Avery. "Do you know Thomas, a colored man, who has been at Rome?" Atlanta University President Edmund A. Ware queried the Reverend Erastus M. Cravath of the American Missionary Association. Ware added: "& will he do to trust?" Ware suspected that Thomas sought a professorship at his school as compensation if he succeeded in luring Avery funds to Atlanta. During a trip to Pittsburgh Thomas lobbied on behalf of the American Missionary Association with representatives of the Avery estate and later worked to identify a teacher for the American Missionary Association's school in Savannah.[50]

Whether or not because of "the migratory in his nature," after only a brief tenure in Atlanta, Thomas determined that it was time to move on. He never explained why. Beginning in July 1873, he traveled extensively—first to visit friends in Ohio (Cincinnati and Delaware) and then to Pennsylvania (Philadelphia and Allegheny City). Will next moved east and later indulged in his characteristic name-dropping. In Ocean Grove, New Jersey, he claimed to have met with President Grant. In Boston he allegedly visited Congressman Benjamin F. Butler. And in Washington, D.C., he purportedly visited John

Mercer Langston. At every stop Thomas did work to reestablish his ties with the A.M.E. Church, condemning vice, urging piety, promoting reform of church polity, and advocating religious freedom. At one point he pointedly distanced himself from his new denomination, the M.E. Church, declaring that "*African* Methodism has a mission before it, and *African* Methodists should not be slow to realize this fact." Given Thomas's chameleonlike qualities, it is uncertain whether such a black nationalistic assertion was feigned or real. But one thing is clear: by September 1873 Will was ready to relocate from Georgia, informing the Reverend Cravath that "it is almost certain that I shall go to *South Carolina,*" where he hoped to receive a church post. Obviously Thomas knew that before long he would need to leave Atlanta. In October 1873, two weeks after the start of the fall term, his promising career at Clark Theological Seminary and in the M.E. Church ground abruptly to a halt. Soon Thomas was mired in another scandal.[51]

While the details of the case remain extremely sketchy, in the end he was expelled from the M.E. Church and charged with criminal misconduct. At its October 15, 1873, meeting, the Georgia Conference suddenly "discontinued" Thomas and referred his case to the Presiding Elder, the Reverend Fuller, "for trial." M.E. Church records remain conspicuously silent on the details and outcome of Thomas's case—underscoring just how serious and embarrassing the allegations against him were. Thomas was neither assigned a post in 1873 nor listed as having withdrawn, transferred, or having been expelled. He simply was not mentioned at all. Eleven days later, however, the *Atlanta Constitution* offered clues concerning his fall from grace. The paper's story explained that on October 24,

> Will. H. Thomas, colored, a Methodist preacher, and connected with the negro Methodist College in this city, was arrested on two warrants from Justice Hammond's Court.
>
> One charged him with cheating and swindling, and the other charged him with a larceny after a trust. These warrants were sued out by the authorities of the College. From what we are able to learn, it seems that the defendant got into his possession some $1500 of the College funds, which he is charged with having pocketed. Anyhow so far there has been no satisfactory explanation given.

On the twenty-fourth the Fulton County prosecutor brought Will before the grand jury and returned a true bill against him for "larceny after trust." He was allowed to give bond for his appearance. The court reporter concluded his story predicting that "rich developments may be expected."[52]

As with the charges raised against him by Wilberforce University's board, the A.M.E.'s Pittsburgh Annual Conference, and the M.E. Church's Georgia Conference, Thomas never responded to the allegations of the Fulton County Court. Instead he made a hasty departure, his modus operandi when faced with criminal charges. Aware that "rich developments" would only add to his problems and possibly convict him of criminal acts, Thomas was unwilling to stand trial. He made plans to surreptitiously skip bail and flee Atlanta. On October 29 Will informed the Reverend Cravath that he would "remain for a few weeks then go to Columbia," South Carolina. "I shall be happy to begin the organization of a new church," he said, "such a movement will prove a decided success, I am sure. At least," Thomas added, "I am willing to undertake it sanguine of the best results."[53]

Within four days, however, mindful of the serious legal problems that lay ahead, Will made a quick exit to Columbia—reasonably safe from the jurisdiction of Georgia law. On November 17, Fulton County's grand jury returned another true bill against him, this time indicting Thomas for forgery. But he had already slipped town, making his way across the border eastward to establish yet another fresh start. Will was never prosecuted for his alleged crimes in Atlanta, and no record exists of the monies he reportedly stole. In 1901, after Thomas published *The American Negro,* the mulatto lawyer and writer Charles W. Chesnutt contacted persons reportedly knowledgeable of the case. Chesnutt learned that in 1873, Thomas "had misappropriated funds that came into his hands as an officer of said school; that he had been indicted in the Courts of Fulton County, . . . and that the case had been settled or disposed of without trial." Bishop Haven, who had authority over Clark Theological Seminary, ultimately intervened and instructed the theological seminary to dismiss the charges. Haven did so in order "to avoid scandal" that would blemish the church.[54]

Though Thomas escaped legal prosecution, his actions in Atlanta irreparably damaged his reputation among white Protestants. Writing a few weeks after Will's departure to Columbia, President Ware of Atlanta University and the Reverend Rust of the Freedmen's Aid Society informed the Reverend Cravath of Thomas's recent brush with the law. Ware charged that Thomas had appropriated money from his church for "his own uses, was imprisoned in Penn[sylvania] for it, was arrested here [in Atlanta and], was turned out of Conference." Presbyterian clergy in Pittsburgh had informed Ware that Thomas's "name was bad with them, not in money matters, but . . . [for reasons] worse than that." The ministers no doubt alluded to his expulsion from divinity school in 1868. Ware warned Cravath about Thomas: "I judge the less you have to do with him the better."[55]

Rust informed Cravath that Thomas had "involved us in pecuniary difficulty in Atlanta, and the brethren there say all manner of evil against him." According to Rust, no matter which denomination Thomas had served, he had left "a bad record behind." Rust cautioned Cravath that Thomas "will not do you any good." The M.E. official regretted writing this, however, because even after Thomas's debacle in Atlanta, Rust still believed that he possessed "fine abilities." Rust warned Cravath, however, that Thomas would do the American Missionary Association "much harm," adding "you may save him, but he must be guarded carefully. The experiment is a little dangerous."[56]

True to form, then, during his long and controversial life, Thomas tripped in full stride. Having impressed his superiors in Rome and Atlanta with his obvious abilities, he undercut himself by the appearance—and likelihood— of wrongdoing. As in Pennsylvania, Will absconded from Georgia with a cloudy record of missed opportunities, unresolved allegations, and serious questions regarding his honesty, trustworthiness, and good judgment. Did he use the misappropriated funds to finance his "sauntering"? As before, there is no evidence to convict or absolve him from the allegations.

Following Thomas's flight from Atlanta, an M.E. minister, the Reverend George Lansing Taylor, attacked carpetbaggers who came south and disgraced the church. "No army can afford to send out its invalids to do picket duty," he wrote. According to Taylor, "we have made some bad blunders in manning our Southern work." The clergyman most certainly had Thomas in mind. If indeed Will stole Clark Theological Seminary funds entrusted to him, he committed what he had described as "theft of far greater magnitude than the burglarious midnight prowler, more to be condemned . . . because committed under pretext of apparently fair and honest motives." Thus as he left Atlanta, Thomas left a legacy of unanswered questions concerning his contributions, conduct, and character.[57]

CHAPTER FOUR

Lawyer and Legislator in South Carolina

B Y NOVEMBER 2, 1873, Will Thomas had slipped quietly away from Georgia authorities into the complex and turbulent world of Reconstruction South Carolina. He chose to move to Columbia, not Charleston, because of the capital city's healthier climate. Upon arriving in Columbia, Thomas explained disingenuously that he had been hard to reach, having been "continually on the move." He hoped to make South Carolina, a state where blacks made up roughly 60 percent of the population, his permanent home. Four years later Will would flee the Palmetto State in the midst of a major political crisis brought about, according to fellow black lawyer and politician Daniel Augustus Straker, "by blood and murder, such as had not stained the annals of history since the Inquisition."[1]

Columbia's black community, according to Thomas, welcomed him with open arms, inviting him almost immediately to preach before the city's largest black congregation. Leading members of South Carolina's black legislative delegation attended the service. Somehow procuring letterhead stationery from South Carolina's Supreme Court, Thomas wrote the Reverend Erastus Milo Cravath of the American Missionary Association to report his instant success and to make a proposition. Because Columbia's blacks greeted him so enthusiastically, Thomas believed that he could easily organize them into a Congregational church. He asked the American Missionary Association to supply him with $800 to begin the work. If the association sent him the funds, Will promised to establish a congregation with over seven thousand parishioners within just one month. An African American, he assured Cravath, would "succeed better than a white man owing to the ascendancy of the other churches" in Columbia, "and the prejudice against the mixture of races." Though Thomas professed to have several employment opportunities, including a professorship at the state university, he preferred to preach. A religious post, he said, would gratify his "life long desire . . . of being a church pastor." When the American Missionary Association failed to respond to his fanciful and unrealistic proposal, the peripatetic Thomas quickly abandoned both Columbia and the prospect of establishing a church. He moved instead to Newberry, thirty-six miles to the northwest in the state's lower Piedmont between the sandhills and the Blue Ridge.[2]

Newberry District emerged in the eighteenth century as a rich, diversified upcountry agricultural community. After the turn of the century, however, farmers experimented successfully with green-seed, short staple cotton that, thanks to the cotton gin, quickly supplanted all other crops in importance and became the county's "new panacea." By 1810, as cotton expanded in the district, white emigration began to slow. Soon the village of Newberry Courthouse (incorporated in 1832 as Newberry) became the eastern terminus of two railroads, the Greenville & Columbia and the Laurens, and the town emerged as a junction for planters to market their lucrative cash crop eastward to Columbia. By 1840 Newberry, along with neighboring Edgefield, Abbeville, and Fairfield Counties, had black majorities and plantation economies similar to cotton districts situated below the fall line. As "the leading inland cotton market of South Carolina," Newberry thrived with the approach of the Civil War. It housed the county courthouse, mercantile establishments, machine shops for both railroads, a post office, and a college. Two newspapers were published there.[3]

In 1860, Newberry was one of South Carolina's most prosperous cotton-growing districts, producing a bumper crop of 17,476 bales. Twenty-three of its 841 agricultural units contained between 500 and 1,000 acres, and eleven more covered over 1,000 acres. The district's 13,695 slaves, who represented a majority of the population, performed most of the labor. They belonged to the 937 slaveholders among Newberry's 7,000 white residents. Eleven planters held more than one hundred slaves. Among South Carolina's thirty districts, Newberry ranked ninth in the valuation of its property.[4]

Though Newberry experienced no Civil War military operations, it suffered terribly from Confederate defeat. Over one third of Newberry's 1,500 whites who fought for the Confederacy died. The war also decimated the county's agriculture, real estate, and property values. Newberry, for example, produced one-half fewer bales of cotton in 1868 than in 1860. From 1860 to 1870, Newberry's real estate values fell by forty-six percent (from $4,766,300 to $2,575,621) and the value of its personal property, consisting mostly of slaves, declined by eighty-eight percent (from $14,000,000 to $1,727,958). In an attempt to make them less dependent on African American laborers, during Reconstruction Newberry whites founded an Immigration Society. Their hopes of enticing large numbers of white Europeans to Newberry, however, ultimately failed. The county's first postwar voter registration, compiled in 1867, listed 2,251 black males and 1,131 white males. Three years later blacks outnumbered whites 13,318 to 7,457. Blacks held majorities in all but two of Newberry's twelve townships. In 1875 the district had 1,725 white as compared to 3,254 black males of voting age. According to local historian Thomas H. Pope, in the early 1870s, Newberry County was still reeling from the war's aftereffects. "The barren farm conditions were all too evident in the decaying plantations, overgrown fields, sagging buildings, rotting fences, and scrawny livestock. Swarms of freedmen were in motion; the entire labor system was in a chaotic condition." Some Newberry freedpeople, denied "forty acres and a mule" upon emancipation, migrated to Florida, Liberia, and the American West. Most, however, remained in Newberry determined to carve out new lives for themselves.[5]

Newberry's white minority, humiliated by defeat and impoverished by the war and postwar crop failures, viewed the district's increasingly assertive and mobile black majority with suspicion. Whether whites liked it or not, Newberry had a vibrant postwar black community, organized socially and politically. Freedmen's social associations included the Kindly Union Society, the Fellowship Association, and the Newberry Temperance Society. Thanks to the Fourteenth and Fifteenth Amendments, by the time Will came to Newberry he and his black neighbors enjoyed newfound civil and political rights. They savored both. After 1867 the county had an active Union League that, according to Pope, "was an important factor in preventing the white leaders of the district from securing black cooperation." In April 1868, Newberry's black majority elected its first legislative delegation: the "scalawag" Charles W. Montgomery as senator and three blacks, Joseph D. Boston, James P. Hutson, and James A. Henderson, as representatives. Boston was one of only two black politicians, the other being William M. Thomas of Colleton, a man often confused with William Hannibal Thomas (see appendix 1) to serve the entire four legislative terms of the Reconstruction period. In the gubernatorial elections of 1870, 1872, and 1874, Newberry's blacks voted overwhelmingly for Republicans and participated actively in local politics. Christian H. Suber, a white Newberry Democrat, described disparagingly how in 1870 black Republicans in Newberry "came from the remotest parts of the county to vote. . . . They congregated around the boxes at

4 o'clock in the morning, before they were opened, and monopolized all the precincts until about 10 or 11 o'clock in the day." Only in Newberry town elections—where whites had a majority—did Conservatives consistently triumph during the era of Republican control of the county.[6]

During Reconstruction Newberry's freedpeople also organized three churches that became important centers of black social and political life. The African Methodist Episcopal (A.M.E.) Church's South Carolina Conference, established by Bishop Daniel A. Payne in 1865, became the keystone of the church's southern expansion. Between 1865 and 1893 the South Carolina Conference expanded dramatically, from fifty-nine to thirty thousand members. Among them were the state's most influential black preacher-politicians, including the Reverends Richard H. ("Daddy") Cain and William M. Thomas. Cain, who tried unsuccessfully to win his party's bid for lieutenant governor in 1872, objected to Republican carpetbaggers like Thomas and advocated political reform. According to historian Julie Saville, "in South Carolina, no denomination surpassed the African Methodist Episcopal church in mobilizing voters for the Republican cause."[7]

The Reverend Simon Miller of Columbia introduced African Methodism to Newberry in 1866, and his disciples quickly disseminated the faith throughout the upcountry. In 1869 five blacks established an African Methodist Episcopal congregation on Caldwell Street in Newberry, which, by 1874, had emerged as the largest unit in the A.M.E.'s Columbia District. The Reverend Felix Torrence presided over nearly one thousand members and probationers and employed four local preachers and eleven teachers for his three Sabbath Schools. Newberry African Methodists noted with pride that Henry McNeal Turner, one of the country's leading A.M.E. ministers and prominent black politicians, was born in their village. In 1873 the Colored Bethlehem Baptist Church opened its doors on College Street. Several years later another black church, Calvary Presbyterian, was organized on a lot on Caldwell Street.[8]

Assertiveness on the part of Newberry's freedpeople contributed to racial friction, intimidation, and violence throughout Reconstruction. "After the war," ex-slave Frances Andrews recalled, "the 'bush-whackers,' called Ku Klux, rode" in Newberry. "They went to negro houses and killed the people. They wore caps over the head and eyes, but no long white gowns." White natives had a different perspective. Rumors spread widely, for example, in September 1865, that U.S. Colored Troops stationed in the district executed a white man who reportedly had savagely beaten one of the soldiers. Despite newspaper accounts that corrected misstatements (the white man acted in self-defense and the black soldier was not as seriously hurt as previously reported) whites in neighboring Fairfield County organized a militia to avenge the white man's death. In their paranoid state, whites imagined that the black troops were bent on instigating a plot to incite Newberry blacks to rebellion. Evidence of such an insurrection proved spurious.[9]

Instances of racial terrorism and violence escalated during Congressional Reconstruction as Newberry's blacks organized politically for the first time. As the November 1868 presidential election approached, two area blacks— Johnson Stuart and Lee A. Nance—were murdered by whites. Stuart was gunned down after attending a Republican gathering. Nance, a delegate to South Carolina's 1868 constitutional convention and president of Newberry's Union League Club, was murdered in his store in retaliation for an earlier assassination attempt by a group of blacks against a white. Following the murders of Nance and other up-country Republicans, a legislative investigation reported "that it was the intention of many of the leading Democrats in Newberry County to dispense with leading Republicans at all hazards." In April 1870, John T. Henderson, a black magistrate in Newberry's Maybinton Township, informed South Carolina's governor that "the colored men are much trample and intruded upon, . . . I . . . have been abused from the beginning of my commission. . . . Persons stiling themselves Democrats . . . fired into [my house] last night at the late hour of twelve." Henderson feared that the owner of the house he rented "would set fire to the house . . . rather than suffer a Radical magistrate to dwell therein." Later that year evictions of black plantation workers by white landlords in Newberry County led to what journalists described as almost a "war" between armed blacks and whites. In October 1871 President Ulysses S. Grant, as authorized by the Ku Klux Klan Act earlier in the year, suspended the writ of habeas corpus in Newberry and eight other up-country counties where "a condition of lawlessness and terror existed." Federal troops were regularly detailed to the county to maintain order. In many ways, then, in the 1870s Newberry County, with a black majority of 69 percent, was a powder magazine. Will Thomas always seemed prone to spark trouble.[10]

Upon arriving in Newberry late in 1873, Thomas steered clear, at least temporarily, of both politics and religion. Instead he accepted a post as principal of Hoge Institute, succeeding the school's first head, H. R. Morrill. A freedmen's school, Hoge Institute was established in 1867 to educate black children of both sexes. In 1869 the institution acquired a permanent home on three-quarters of an acre on Caldwell Street in the village of Newberry. An elected board of trustees held the property "in trust for the colored citizens." Soon after its establishment, Hoge Institute enrolled roughly 300 students. The school was named for Republican Solomon L. Hoge (1836–1909), an Ohio Civil War veteran who moved to Columbia, South Carolina, following the war and served on the state supreme court (1868–70), in the U.S. Congress (1869–71, 1875–77), and as comptroller general of South Carolina (1874–75). Throughout his career he maintained a keen interest in advancing educational opportunities and humanitarian care for the freedpeople. According to Pope, Hoge Institute "thrived during the entire post-war period" and served as an educational and social center for Newberry's black community until the 1890s.[11]

Though no record exists of Will's exact tenure at Hoge Institute, during Thomas's three and one-half years in the state he frequently was referred to in newspaper accounts as "Professor." In June 1875, he and State Superintendent of Education J. K. Jillson delivered the commencement addresses at what was then referred to as Hoge School. Apparently, though, Will served as principal for only a few months in early 1874. His career as an educator in Newberry, just as in Rome and Atlanta, was short-lived. That is not to say, however, that he planned to leave South Carolina. In August 1874, Thomas paid David Henry Wheeler $500 for forty-one acres of land in Helena, just west of Newberry. This was as much of a commitment as Thomas had ever made to reside permanently anywhere. Typical of the man, the details of his private life in South Carolina remain murky. Many years after he left Newberry, his enemies charged that while in South Carolina Will skipped town without paying his bills and had cohabited with two women, though no record exists of his being married. A private investigator described him as having a reputation in Newberry as "a lecherous character."[12]

No matter his domestic status, Will participated actively in Newberry's A.M.E. religious community. In June 1875, for example, "Professor W. H. Thomas" spoke before the South Carolina Annual Conference at Bethel A.M.E. Church in Columbia "concerning African Methodism." The Electoral College of the Annual Conference then selected him as a lay delegate to the church's General Conference to be held in Atlanta in May 1876. This was an important meeting because it was the first time that the General Conference assembled in the Deep South. The church still was relatively new in the region and quickly gained seven times as many southern converts as northern ones. The *Christian Recorder* reported that "Professor W. H. Thomas . . . received a majority of the votes cast, was declared the first delegate elected to the General Conference." The paper explained that

Thomas arranged to have the Greenville & Columbia Railroad provide free transportation for delegates between Columbia and Atlanta. Unfortunately, however, because he had "not been a member of the A.M.E. Church for two consecutive years," the conference ultimately decided to drop "Brother Thomas" from the list of delegates. Page Ellington went in his place. Thomas's decision to establish permanent residency and to participate in the church clearly indicated his determination to put down roots in Newberry. It no doubt, however, stemmed from his political aspirations.[13]

Eager to enter politics and to capitalize on the opportunities available for blacks in Newberry and in Republican-controlled South Carolina, in January 1874 Thomas applied for admission to the Newberry bar, the first step to enter the local political fraternity. He did so at a time, according to historian J. R. Oldfield, when most of the state's black lawyers were native-born. Like any other applicant, he stood for an examination and passed, according to a newspaper account, "in the usual manner." His examining committee consisted of white lawyers Young John Pope, B. M. Jones, and J. F. J. Caldwell. Without any legal training, and having resided in Newberry for only a few weeks, on January 30, 1874, Thomas was admitted to the Newberry bar by Seventh Circuit Judge Montgomery Moses, uncle of South Carolina Governor Franklin J. Moses Jr. Will was the first African American to be admitted to practice law in the county. Years later Thomas recalled both proudly and bitterly that he passed the bar only "after a rigid examination, and in the face of strong opposition from the Southern white lawyers." He added that his "knowledge of jurisprudence was acquired entirely from self-teaching. I had neither attended a law school nor received private instruction." Ohio Republican Governor Rutherford B. Hayes provided him with a "certificate of character." Thomas remained on South Carolina's roll of attorneys through December 1876, when he was admitted to plead cases before the supreme court of South Carolina.[14]

Empowered to practice law, Thomas next obtained a series of political appointments that broadened his influence among Newberry blacks and set him on a course for statewide recognition. In February 1874, Governor Moses appointed him captain and ordnance officer in the Second Division of South Carolina's National Guard. Seven months later he was promoted to lieutenant colonel on the staff of General P. R. Rivers. Late in 1876, no doubt as a reward for his political support, Republican Governor Daniel H. Chamberlain commissioned Will a colonel to an unassigned unit. Organized in 1869 as a deterrent to vigilantism and violence, as well as a potential source of patronage, during Governor Scott's administration the National Guard

Service of South Carolina (commonly referred to as the state's Negro militia) became "a giant political machine for use in combatting his enemies within and outside of the Republican party." The most influential leaders were company captains, according to historian Joel Williamson, "invariably . . . strong characters in the Negro community, sometimes noted for their prudence, often for their bellicosity." In Newberry's case, Representatives Boston, Hutson, and Henderson commanded National Guard companies. South Carolina counties like Newberry, where Negro militia companies were heavily armed and equipped, experienced the highest degree of racial violence. No evidence suggests that Thomas ever drilled or performed other military functions, but his militia appointments no doubt signified his emerging presence as a leader among Newberry blacks. Though his colonelcy was largely honorary, well into the next century Thomas identified himself as "Colonel William Hannibal Thomas" at every opportunity.[15]

Thomas's service in South Carolina's national guard and membership in Newberry's bar were important stepping stones for what he hoped would be his eventual entry into national Republican politics. Throughout the post–Civil War years he corresponded with influential Republican leaders, hopeful of establishing ties that would result in political patronage. In March 1874, for example, Will wrote General Oliver O. Howard, a fellow battlefield amputee and commissioner of the then defunct Freedmen's Bureau, expressing outrage against those who pilloried the agency into extinction and who sought to discredit Howard for his alleged irregular disbursement of funds. Thomas assured Howard that despite the abuse heaped upon the bureau by his critics, "four million hearts have been made glad by your untiring efforts." He praised the bureau, the government, and "the great National Republican party" for advancing "the most progressive principles in regard to the elevation, of the late enslaved Race." Thomas remained confident that Howard would be exonerated of any wrongdoing and be vindicated. While probably sincere in these statements, during his residence in the Palmetto State Thomas maintained contact with leading Republicans, determined to keep his political contacts alive and his options open. Aggressive, politically savvy, and trading on an empty sleeve, Thomas's efforts quickly bore fruit in a county with a sympathetic black majority and a state under Republican control.[16]

In May 1874, Governor Moses appointed Thomas to two posts: as a notary public and as one of Newberry County's seven trial justices. South Carolina's trial justices performed minor judicial functions similar to justices of the peace or magistrates in other states. Theoretically selected for two-year terms, in practice they were appointed by the governor and served at his pleasure. Trial justices held jurisdiction "in all matters of contract, . . . where the amount claimed does not exceed one hundred dollars, and . . . for assault and battery, and other penal offenses less than felony, punishable by fines only." They also were empowered "to bind over to keep the peace, or for good behavior." Though in terms of power and prestige trial justices stood near the bottom of state bureaucrats, historian Thomas Holt's sampling suggests that blacks held only about one in every five trial justices. Therefore, Thomas's appointment was no mean achievement.[17]

It was while serving as trial justice that Thomas first entered the internecine world of South Carolina Republican party politics. On September 25, 1874, in his first public address in Newberry, Thomas urged Republicans to join the "reform side"—the Independent Republican faction that was mobilizing to challenge the "Regular" or Union Republicans for control of the party. In the 1872 gubernatorial campaign, "Reform" Republicans had bolted against Moses, charging him with corruption. Unwilling to ally with "Conservatives" (Democrats) to defeat Moses, reform gubernatorial candidate Reuben Tomlinson lost by more than 33,000 votes. By 1874 most South Carolina Republicans agreed that years of corruption during the administrations of Governors Robert A. Scott (1868–72) and Moses (1872–74) must end. Politicians of both races had lined their pockets in railroad deals, printing scandals, fraudulent bond sales, and bribes. Scott, for example, was part of a "ring" that acquired railroad stock in the Greenville & Columbia Railroad through fraudulent means. He also speculated in South Carolina bonds and profited from corruption in the state's Land Commission, which had been created by the new political order to assist poor freedmen and whites in securing land.[18]

The Scott and Moses administrations proved so ineffective in protecting the freedpeople against South Carolina's Ku Klux Klan that President Grant was forced to suspend the writ of habeas corpus in nine counties and dispatch federal troops to the state. Tensions, however, within Republican ranks—between carpetbaggers and scalawags, blacks and mulattoes, former free blacks and former slaves—kept the party divided over most questions, including reform. Among black leaders, Holt argues, "there were subtle but distinct differences in emphasis and outlook between the largely mulatto bourgeoisie and the black peasantry, with the urban-based [former] slaves and ex-slave domestics constituting something of a swing group." Significantly, he found that from 1868 to 1876, mulattoes held considerably more political influence in South Carolina than their proportion of the black population warranted. Of the 255 blacks Holt has documented who were elected to state and federal offices, at least 78, or 43 percent of those officials whose skin color is recorded, were mulattoes. In contrast, only 7 percent of the total population was mulatto.[19]

Thomas, a mulatto, no doubt saw opportunities aplenty in Newberry and was determined to establish himself quickly in South Carolina politics. He immediately joined the bolters of 1874 to promote John T. Green's Independent Republican candidacy over Union Republican Daniel H. Chamberlain in that year's gubernatorial election. Green, a native of Sumter, was a former circuit court judge and an unsuccessful candidate for attorney general on the bolters' ticket in 1872. He lost the 1874 Regular Republican nomination for governor to Chamberlain. A Massachusetts native and Harvard and Yale graduate, Chamberlain came to South Carolina after serving briefly as an officer in the 5th Massachusetts Volunteer Cavalry (Colored). Upon failing as a cotton planter on abandoned Sea Island property, Chamberlain entered Republican politics, vacillated between the reform and regular wings of the party, and eventually joined Scott's administration as attorney general, serving from 1868 to 1872. In this capacity Chamberlain was identified with the Land Commission frauds. He practiced law during the corrupt Moses administration, and though untarnished by its scandals, the Conservative *Charleston News and Courier* considered Chamberlain "as deep in the mud as Moses is in the mire."[20]

Late in September 1874, bolters from Newberry met in Thomas's law office to select delegates to the Independent Republican convention in Charleston scheduled for October 2 and 3. According to Chamberlain's organ, Columbia's *Daily Union-Herald,* none of Newberry's bolters "had any influence in the community." It charged state Senator T. C. Dunn with involvement with the "bond ring," accused another of being an ex-convict, and identified one other as a well-known collaborator with the Conservatives. As for Thomas, the *Union-Herald* described him as a "a recent importation, whose history, as far as known, is of the most objectionable character: preacher, lawyer, trial justice, school-teacher and carpetbagger—in short, an adventurer." The caucus selected Thomas, along with Wade H. Coleman and Edward Young, as Newberry's delegates to attend the Independent Republican state convention at Charleston's Hibernian Hall.[21]

There Thomas, a political newcomer, played a prominent role in the Independent Republicans' war against "rings in high places." Elected to the committee on credentials, the platform committee, and the executive committee, he also was elected second vice president of the new organization. In

Charleston, Thomas met such well-known South Carolina reform Republicans as Major Martin R. Delany, the first black soldier to receive a field grade commission in the Federal army and a former Freedmen's Bureau agent, the Reverend Richard H. Cain, elected to the U.S. Congress in 1872, and Edwin W. M. Mackey, a scalawag from Charleston who headed that city's delegation. In addition to nominating Green for governor and Delany for lieutenant governor and adopting a nearly identical platform as the Regular Republicans, the Independent Republicans launched a broadside attack on what they considered six years of misrule by Scott, Moses, and their fellow officeholders.

They charged, for example, that during Moses's administration corruption enveloped South Carolina's state government. Delany admitted that following emancipation South Carolina's freedmen blindly accepted the political leadership of northern politicians. In the first throes of freedom they considered any tactic—including fraudulent voting—acceptable in order to gain political control of the state from Conservatives. But, Congressman Cain explained, times had changed. Over almost a decade of freedom blacks had proven themselves skilled politicians and were ready to seek political union with honest whites. Under Moses, the reformers argued, high taxes, excessive spending, corruption, graft, and bribery blanketed the government. They cited as their most poignant example South Carolina's Land Commission, an agency created with noble objectives but one that instead enabled corrupt white Republicans to get rich. Delany urged his party to lead a "departure from the old double-dyed corrupt wing of the Republican party." Though careful to assure whites that he did not favor "social equality," Delany implored Conservatives to join black and white Independent Republicans in a coalition to unseat the Union Republicans. In this election, unlike that of 1872, reform Republicans welcomed the support of dissident Democrats—"Conservatives that have persistently declared that their desire was only for good government without regard to partisan politics." Independent Republican leaders declared that they were "not hostile to the domination of the Republican party in South Carolina" but were determined "to maintain its integrity against the corrupt 'rings' which control it and at the same time protect the common interests of the white people." In response, Chamberlain supporters dubbed the Independent Republicans a "mongrel, black-and-tan party," a group of "wretched renegades who have deserted it into the sea of oblivion." [22]

Thomas, selected by his colleagues from Newberry as their county's Independent Republican Party chairman, joined Delany and Cain in addressing the convention on its opening day. This was a rather notable achievement given that Thomas was both virtually unknown in South Carolina and a political neophyte. "He made a stirring speech," according to the pro-Democratic *Charleston News and Courier,* "in which the Bond Ring were effectually shown up. It was time," Thomas exclaimed, "that a stop should be put to crime and fraud in the State." He went on to say that South Carolinians of both races demanded peace, good government, and freedom from political manipulation. According to the journalist covering the meeting, Thomas interpreted the Independent Republican movement as a move to "shake off the shackles of slavery and political bondage." He identified a parallel between conditions in South Carolina and in the American colonies before the Revolution. In both instances the masses were taxed but remained underrepresented. To implement reforms, Thomas envisioned a new biracial government led equally by intelligent and respectable men. This, he explained, would guarantee "a fair representation in the government." Joint participation in the government was essential, Thomas warned black delegates to the conference, because within four to six years whites eventually would regain an electoral majority in the state. Blacks, then, must use "common sense" and share management of the government with whites to guarantee equity in the future. "How," Thomas asked, "can we expect the Democrats to give us a share in the government, when they obtain possession of it, if we don't divide with them now?" Summarizing his speech, the reporter said that though Thomas spoke of his military service against the Confederates, he nonetheless "was willing to shake hands across the bloody chasm and forget the past, and unite with the Conservatives in securing wealth and prosperity to the State." [23]

Thomas also chaired the Independent Republicans' platform committee. On October 3 he presented its eleven planks to the convention. These included pledging allegiance to the national Republican party, introducing new tax laws to help agriculture, providing inducements to industry, and attracting more railroads to South Carolina. The Reformers also vowed to implement fair and equitable freight rates, to retire the public debt, to decrease public expenditures, and to enact sweeping financial reforms in state government. They endorsed another civil rights act and promised to protect all races and classes equally before the law. The Conservative *Charleston News and Courier* believed that the Independent Republican movement demonstrated that "when the carpet-bag corruptionists and their agents [were] excluded, colored Representatives [could] meet and transact their business in a manner satisfactory to themselves and gratifying to every true friend of the colored people." The editor urged whites and blacks to elect Green and Delany "for the redemption of the State."[24]

Though his support of the Independent Republicans won Thomas new friends in Charleston and throughout South Carolina, not surprisingly it angered Governor Moses and many Regular Republicans. Upon returning from the Charleston convention, Thomas learned that in retaliation for his breaking ranks with the party, Moses had revoked his appointment as trial justice. According to the *Newberry Herald,* Thomas "had become too 'Independent'" for Moses "and hence, the cry, 'off with his head.'" The governor was determined to utilize the powers of removing and appointing trial justices "to hold any dissidents in line." The editor of the *News and Courier,* delighted over the fissures within Republican ranks, noted that Moses had cashiered him "because Thomas supports the honest Republican State ticket." Ironically the Democratic paper, heretofore unfriendly toward black carpetbaggers, employed one of Thomas's favorite rhetorical devices to "wave the bloody shirt." "Thomas," the paper explained, "is an ex-Union soldier, and lost one arm for the freedom of his race."[25]

Undeterred by Moses's action, on October 7, 1874, Will published a typically longwinded letter in the *Newberry Herald* setting forth his political views. No doubt heady after his successful initial political foray in Charleston, he offered his services to county Republicans. Though he alleged that supporters repeatedly had urged him to run for a seat in the legislature or for probate judge, Thomas maintained that he sought no office. As the Newberry County Republican convention approached, however, he was willing to change his mind, but only as the "PEOPLE'S CANDIDATE."[26]

In a rambling, self-serving, and pompous statement in which he said he could "forecaste the future," Thomas proclaimed himself a reformer who understood Republican party goals better than any of his rivals. The freedpeople, he said, were in the midst of "a trying ordeal," experiencing "the severest tests of capacity for self-government." While blacks were responsible for improving their education and character, Thomas believed that their elected officials had to shield them from "political vandalism" that transformed the former chattel slaves into "political slaves, the subject of bargain and sale in the hands of political demagogues." Thomas promised "to emancipate the people from political servitude by the teachings of virtue and intelligence." He would lead the people "out of the chaos of political corruption and rottenness."[27]

Dedicated to equal rights and fairness, Thomas promised all things to all men—to support education, encourage economic development, improve roads, manage government more efficiently, and lower taxes. Like other Republican politicians of his day, he too waved "the bloody shirt," pointing to his "four years . . . spent in a war of internecine strife, in which I performed no humble part in the liberation of my people." Without providing details, Thomas referred to his postwar years in the South "as assiduously spent in the elevation of that race" as well. Looking back over his life, the thirty-one-year-old Thomas credited himself with having always been devoted to his race. He described himself "from birth," as "the most consistent friend of the race, my life consecrated to their social and political elevation, my influence always exercised for their best good; my services in every sense at their command; with an inflexible devotion to convictions of duty founded upon principles of universal liberty and education, the elements underlying the moral and social elevation of my race." If elected to office, Thomas promised to serve "as the friend of my people, a resident of the South, [and] a citizen of the State of my choice, South Carolina." [28]

Having announced his willingness to run for office, Thomas devoted his energies to the cause of the Independent Republicans. In mid-October Newberry hosted a statewide meeting of the party that, according to the *Charleston News and Courier,* was "probably the most orderly and attentive political meeting ever held in that section." Speakers included Senator T. C. Dunn of Horry County, Congressman Cain, and "Prof." Thomas. They attacked the corruption in Moses's administration, according to the journalist—"the present bastard government of South Carolina." In response, Chamberlain supporters held two rallies in Newberry, attacking Green, Delany, and, as a reporter described, their "local harpy, Thomas." Regular Republicans included Thomas among those they besmirched as "the scabby fellows who are parading the country in the pay of the democracy while calling themselves republicans." For the remainder of the 1874 campaign Thomas accompanied prominent Independent Republicans throughout the state promoting Green's candidacy. On October 22, for example, Thomas and the Reverend Cain addressed Independent Republicans at Laurens Court House. The following day Cain and Thomas spoke to another rally of Independent Republicans at Greenwood, South Carolina. The black spokesmen reportedly received an "enthusiastic" response from whites in the audience who endorsed the fusion of Reform Republicans and Democrats. [29]

As the November 3 election approached, Thomas's efforts at political self-promotion bore fruit. Indicative of his growing local influence, on October 21 he joined a number of officials in speaking at a Newberry town meeting following a scuffle between three whites from Edgefield County and Henry Bluford, Newberry's black town marshal. In the fracas Bluford was killed. As local blacks massed to take the law in their own hands, Thomas called for calm and the orderly apprehension of Bluford's slayers. Three days later, Governor Moses, who only recently had removed him from office, appointed Thomas to Newberry's board of commissioners to oversee the counting of ballots in the upcoming campaign. The *Newberry Herald* interpreted this appointment as a positive sign that the governor sought a fair and clean election. Obviously trying to curry Thomas's favor, shortly before the election Moses also reappointed Thomas trial justice.[30]

Despite Thomas's efforts in the November campaign, Chamberlain defeated Green in Newberry County by 1,705 votes (3,181 to 1,476) and statewide by 11,585 votes (80,403 to 68,818). Though they lost, in 1874 Green's Independent Republicans polled almost twice as many votes against the Regular Republicans' powerful machine than Tomlinson had in 1872. With substantial Conservative support, the Independent Republicans carried twelve counties. In Newberry, Democrats accused Chamberlain supporters of lining up illegal voters to pad their electoral margin. The election underscored serious rifts within Republican ranks and the potential power of Conservatives to defeat Republicans. In the 1874 election the Independent Republican–Conservative coalition garnered fifty-four seats in the state House of Representatives and fifteen in the state Senate. As historian Thomas Holt's data suggests, the election represented a turning point in the state's Reconstruction-era state politics. In 1874 white Democrats gained thirteen seats in the House while white Republicans and black Republicans lost five and ten seats, respectively, in that body. Although Democratic success in South Carolina mirrored the party's dramatic electoral victories nationwide, these successes, as Holt maintains, resulted largely from fusion and deep fissures within the state's Republicans. The party in fact went into a tailspin after 1874. Though Thomas was not a candidate for election, his name nonetheless appeared in the official returns in the race for a seat representing the Third Congressional District in the House of Representatives. The winner, Lewis Cass Carpenter, polled 3,184 votes, William H. Trescott received fifty-nine votes, and Thomas garnered six ballots, all from one Newberry precinct.[31]

Once in office Chamberlain initiated sweeping reforms designed to woo Democratic supporters. He struck an alliance, for example, with Francis W. Dawson, editor of Charleston's *News and Courier,* and worked to increase white control of his own party. The governor's attempt at fusion politics, however, deepened fissures within South Carolina's Republican factions, especially between blacks and whites, blacks and mulattoes, and natives and carpetbaggers. Chamberlain incurred the wrath of many Republicans by rejecting the legislature's nomination of W. J. Whipper and Franklin J. Moses Jr. for judgeships and by courting Conservative support. Determined to reduce the influence of blacks in his party and mindful of his comfortable but not overwhelming 8 percent electoral victory, Chamberlain replaced many black local officials, including trial justices, with white Democrats. He couched this as part of his new "reform" administration. One of Chamberlain's first acts in fact was to revoke Thomas's latest appointment as trial justice for Newberry County.[32]

A week later Will petitioned Chamberlain to reinstate him, not "for my personal enrichment but for the better protection and general good of my people." He approached the new governor in such a straightforward manner, he said, "because I always deal direct with the 'powers that be.'" To support his appeal, Thomas included a petition signed by fifteen prominent Newberry Democrats and Republicans, including the school and county commissioners, the coroner, the sheriff, two trial justices, and five members of the Newberry County Bar. They urged Chamberlain to reconsider his action because "the first requisite in the era of reform is an impartial judiciary," and the petitioners considered Thomas fully committed to protecting their personal liberties and property. Thomas's letter and the petition did the trick: early in 1875 he regained his appointment. The newly elected governor probably concluded that even though Thomas had forcefully opposed his candidacy, given his support in Newberry and new connections within Republican ranks in South Carolina, Thomas was more preferable as an ally than as an opponent. Early in 1876, for example, when lobbying for the appointment of a second black trial justice for Newberry, Thomas reminded Chamberlain that "something is *due* . . . the large colored Republican majority which this county invariably gives."[33]

Years after he departed South Carolina, Thomas asserted with typical hyperbole that he knew "Daniel H. Chamberlain better than most people." He described Chamberlain as "brilliant but erratic and . . . altogether lacking in the qualities that make sound philosophers or sagacious leaders." Chamberlain, writing in 1877—in the immediate aftermath of his most severe political defeat—described Thomas more clearly and charitably, but no less accurately, as "a lawyer of excellent standing and ability, a devoted Republican, and an able and faithful representative of the rights, wants and needs of the colored race in this state." Ironically, circumstances in 1875 would draw the two carpetbaggers close and in subsequent years ultimately drive them both from the Palmetto State.[34]

As the new year unfolded, Thomas carved out a niche for himself in Newberry's black community as a reform politician and as one of the town's twenty-one attorneys. Throughout his long life Thomas was drawn to reform schemes. Deeply interested in land redistribution, he believed that the freedpeople could not begin to improve their economic and social status until they acquired rural homesteads. Though in the 1890s Thomas would unsuccessfully propose detailed plans for land reform on the national level, early in 1875 he promoted a program in the *Newberry Herald* first outlined by Delany, the defeated Independent Republican candidate for lieutenant governor. According to Delany, "what the freedman wants is land of his own with reasonable time to pay for it."[35]

Unlike Thomas's later more complex proposals, Delany, who had opened a land and brokerage business in 1871, proposed a simple plan whereby impoverished whites would sell forty-acre tracts of land to the freedpeople at an average cost of three dollars per acre payable in five equal annual installments. Such a plan, Delany reasoned, would benefit all segments of society and provide the South's black peasants "fixed and established interests in the soil and State." Once they owned homesteads, blacks would flourish — establishing schools and churches, paying taxes, and demanding good government. He predicted that this would promote racial harmony. In addition, as soon as economic conditions in South Carolina stabilized, Delany said, northern capitalists would invest in the state. Thomas applauded Delany's plan as "the only policy that is likely to restore harmony and prosperity to the incongruous elements of the South."[36]

As a trial justice and attorney from 1874 to 1876, Thomas encountered many of South Carolina's "incongruous elements." Commenting on Thomas, who returned to Delaware, Ohio, for a visit to family in September 1875, the *Delaware Gazette* described him as "an educated and talented colored man" who, "well qualified by extensive travel through that region and careful observation," would deliver a lecture on politics and conditions in the South. The article noted that Thomas was "successfully engaged in the practice of law" in Newberry. Reflecting years later on his brief legal career, Thomas recalled "that my knowledge of jurisprudence was acquired entirely from self-teaching. I had neither attended a law school nor received private instruction; yet I am led to believe that my success at the bar was not altogether discreditable." For once Thomas's self-assessment was on target.[37]

From all reports, in 1874-75 Will apparently attended to his routine responsibilities as notary public and trial justice satisfactorily. He attested to court documents and adjudicated minor cases. In January 1876, however, the grand jury reported to Judge Montgomery Moses that Thomas, unlike Newberry's other trial justices, refused to turn over his official papers and ledger for review and audit. "We called on Trial Justice Thomas for an exhibit of his Books & papers," the clerk noted, but he failed to comply, "stating that he had no regular office, and that his books and papers were so scattered that he could not furnish them." After the grand jury recommended that "the Court take such action in this case as in its judgement may think best," Thomas smoothed matters over and thereafter maintained good relations with Governor Chamberlain's office. In May 1876, Thomas accounted successfully for the monies he had collected.[38]

Two months later, however, James N. Lipscomb, a Democrat who sought to embarrass Chamberlain, accused Thomas and fellow Newberry trial justice T. P. Slider of malfeasance in office, specifically charging that they required payment of fees before taking affidavits and issuing warrants in criminal cases. Though both Thomas and Slider denied the charges, Slider resigned. Thomas, refusing to surrender his post, argued that the charges against him were "so utterly absurd as to scarcely merit refutation." He assured Governor Chamberlain that "I do not manage my business in that way, which is apparent when I tell you that for professional services the people of this county are indebted to me [for] one thousand dollars. The office of trial justice to me, is no sinecure. I only consent to retain it on account of the protection such position gives to the poorer people of this county." After brushing aside the allegation of his official misconduct, Thomas urged Chamberlain to attend a Republican rally in Newberry on August 18. "We need your presence," he informed the governor, "though I am glad to add, that the outlook is most hopeful."[39]

Unlike his tenure as notary public and trial justice, Thomas's short career as a South Carolina lawyer attracted no controversy. His legal practice was varied but unexceptional. According to the scant records of the Court of General Sessions, on two occasions the state of South Carolina retained him as a prosecutor. In one instance, in January 1875, he appeared before the grand jury as "associate Counsel for the State" in *The State v Pink Hardy*, an indictment for murder. The case was not prosecuted and was entered in the record as nolle prosequi. In most of his court appearances, however, Thomas served clients as defense counsel. He represented them against such varied allegations as accessory before the fact of murder, grand larceny, assault and battery, assault with a deadly weapon, theft, burglary, perjury, and riot. Though court clerks failed to record verdicts in all of his cases, Thomas's clients either were acquitted or exonerated in nine of the ten cases where decisions were noted.[40]

By mid-1876 Thomas redirected his attention from law to politics. After five years of relative calm in the Palmetto State, during Chamberlain's administration economic, racial, and political relationships unraveled. Historian Richard Zuczek argues that despite outward appearances, for years white South Carolinians worked methodically to overthrow the Republicans and assert control by native Conservatives. From the inception of Republican rule in 1867, the old citizens viewed it as alien and destructive of white supremacy. Democrats battled Republicans with fraud, extortion, and intimidation perpetrated by paramilitary bands dubbed "rifle clubs." Newberry County alone had twenty-one Democratic clubs, often armed and clad in red shirts, that registered Democrats and attended Republican meetings en masse. During the 1876 gubernatorial campaign Newberry merchants refused to supply credit for purchases to Republicans. Statewide, whites openly organized and mobilized to reassert white control and to rid South Carolina of so-called carpetbag rule. In that year, Zuczek explains, "the various elements in this conflict had merged into a unified, coherent thrust against the Republican government." He considers this a counterrevolution "begun as a disjointed and disorganized effort to hamper Reconstruction programs and evolving into a deliberate, coherent drive that succeeded in removing a government." With remarkable prescience, in April 1876, Congressman Cain noted a rise in anti-black sentiment and predicted that in the course of the November gubernatorial election "a mighty revolution will take place."[41]

Open conflict erupted in May when black rice workers on Combahee and Ashepoo River plantations and in Beaufort County, hurt by depressed economic conditions, struck for higher wages and payment in cash, not promissory notes. Workers marched through the rice fields and coerced nonstrikers to lay down their hoes. When Chamberlain refused to send troops to restore order, the planters acquiesced—temporarily—to the blacks' demands. Three months later, in August, a second wave of strikes began. This time members of a Democratic rifle club confronted the armed strikers. Only the presence of two black elected officials, Congressman Robert Smalls and

Lieutenant Governor Robert Gleaves, prevented violence, and once again the planters met the workers' demands. Threats of labor unrest and racial violence hovered over the rice districts like an ominous cloud. Whites reactivated or formed new rifle clubs to counter the perceived power of Negro militia companies.[42]

Meanwhile, on July 20–21, Thomas had joined the state's leading black politicians at a Conference of Colored Citizens in Columbia to protest a more serious and bloody racial disturbance in Hamburg, an almost abandoned village in Aiken County located across the Savannah River from Augusta, Georgia. Though formerly a thriving cotton marketing and slave trading center, Hamburg suffered serious economic decline during the 1850s and emerged in the postwar years as largely an enclave of blacks. Its well-equipped eighty-man Negro militia company drilled frequently on Hamburg's streets and was a festering sore to members of nearby Edgefield County's white rifle clubs. The combination of armed former Confederate soldiers in Edgefield and armed black militiamen turned Hamburg into a tinder box.[43]

A confrontation occurred on July 4, 1876, when two whites demanded the right of way during the blacks' centennial militia drill. After a heated verbal exchange, the whites were allowed to pass. Four days later Matthew C. Butler, a former Confederate general and prominent Democrat, demanded that the blacks both apologize for blocking the path of the whites and disarm. Refusing to comply with Butler's orders, approximately forty black militiamen sequestered themselves in a brick armory. Hundreds of armed whites, equipped with a cannon imported from Augusta, surrounded the building. According to historian Joel Williamson, the "Redeemers were set to provide the Negro voter with a horrible example of the awful force which lay behind the white man's threats." Over the course of the evening of July 8–9, the white mob mortally wounded Hamburg's black marshal, captured twenty-five militiamen, murdered six blacks in cold blood, and sacked the town. One white was killed.[44]

Eleven days later Thomas met with almost sixty black leaders, including Robert Brown Elliott, speaker of the state House of Representatives, Congressman Cain, State Treasurer Francis L. Cardozo, State Representative William M. Thomas, and U.S. customs inspector D. Augustus Straker, to issue a formal protest against the Hamburg massacre. Because no whites were allowed to attend the convention, blacks apparently had lost confidence in white Republicans. In their formal response to the Hamburg slayings, "An Address to the Colored People of the United States," the signatories reviewed the facts of the bloodbath and drew the "irresistible conclusion" that the massacre resulted from a "settled and well defined purpose to influence and control" the November election. They recognized that the riot not only signaled a new phase of the Democrats' white supremacy campaign but also seriously tested the ability of Chamberlain's conservative coalition to protect black citizens. They implored the governor to request President Grant to send federal troops to the state and called upon South Carolinians to "utter the voice of the nation's condemnation of . . . the assassination of inoffensive and unoffending citizens of Hamburg." The black leaders admonished their fellow citizens "to place upon this wanton and inhuman butchery the indelible stigma of the public abhorrence."[45]

Thomas left the convention determined to support Chamberlain in the upcoming election and invited him to come to Newberry to launch his fall campaign. Despite the governor's alienation of black Republicans, and especially his inability to protect Hamburg's militiamen, Thomas remained optimistic about the Republicans' political outlook. Conservatives interpreted Chamberlain's condemnation of the Hamburg murders and his request for federal troops as a return to "bayonet rule" and began a relentless campaign to unseat him. Nine days following Thomas's invitation, Chamberlain came to Newberry by train to speak on August 17, 1876. As the governor, accompanied by Congressman Hoge and Superintendent of Education J. K. Jillson, made his way to a grove on the outskirts of town, he was accompanied by several hundred Democrats, mounted and armed, who demanded and received equal time to express their views. The governor recalled that "as I left the stand . . . I met a cordon of mounted white men, so closely 'dressed,' in military phrase, in ranks of two or three deep, that I was forced to request to be allowed to pass through, and to wait until the ranks could be broken for my exit. Every mounted white man whom I observed was armed with one or two pistols." Democrats dogged Chamberlain and Republican speakers in a similar fashion everywhere they tried to speak during the 1876 campaign.[46]

Whereas Chamberlain came to Newberry to defend his administration and solidify his party's crumbling alliance of native, carpetbag, black, white, and mulatto factions, local Democrats were committed to unseat him at any price. In July 1876, Newberry Conservatives were the first in the state to break with the fusionists and adopt a "straightout" white Democratic program. Their gubernatorial candidate was planter and former Confederate General Wade Hampton, the genteel and moderate paternalist whose Democratic followers were responsible for the Hamburg riot and other acts of racial terrorism. Hampton, who received the statewide Democratic nomination on August 17, came to Newberry on September 13 and announced a platform based on reform, meaning an end of Republican rule in South Carolina. By 1876, according to Williamson, Democrats felt burdened by taxes, declining cotton prices, scarce credit, and the specter of the state's black political majority. Though Hampton promised to enforce the Reconstruction Amendments, he appealed to white voters to curb the excesses of "Negro rule" and, not surprisingly, received a much more cordial reception from Newberrians than they gave Chamberlain. An estimated five to six thousand supporters greeted Hampton with a torchlight procession. Though Democrats promised shows of "force without violence," two days later red-shirted white terrorists began massacring blacks in Ellenton, twenty miles from Hamburg. In October another riot broke out in Cainhoy, a small village near Charleston, where five whites were killed and many were wounded. The Red Shirt campaign of political control by murder, intimidation, and fraud had begun.[47]

Committed to Chamberlain, in October Newberry Republicans nominated Thomas and two other blacks, ex-slaves Thomas Keitt and Sampson S. Bridges, for the state House of Representatives. Covering the convention, a Democratic reporter offered the first of many unflattering descriptions that plagued Thomas throughout the campaign and afterward as well. He categorized Thomas as

> a negro carpet-bagger, who has been living here for a number of years, has been very unpopular among his own people, but he has been successful at last by allying himself with the dominant faction of the convention. Thomas claims to be a personal friend of Chamberlain's and that he fought by his side during the late war. He was foremost, however, in the last gubernatorial canvass in his opposition to Chamberlain and made stump speeches for Green. He is the only one [of the Republican candidates] they have nominated who has any brains, but his moral defects are so glaring that his talents are obscured.

The pro-Hampton reporter, invoking common white racist stereotypes of his day, then commented on Newberry's black Republicans. "So great is the poverty among the blacks," he observed, "a great number of the members were in rags and tags. Half were under the influence of liquor; the other half were crazed with frenzy."[48]

It was these folk whom Thomas sought to represent in South Carolina's House of Representatives. As the November 7 election neared, Thomas further stirred white anger by campaigning for Republican candidates. At a rally in Laurens, he recalled years later, "I was met with jeers and curses; then as I proceeded, revolvers were flourished, rifles discharged, and missles thrown, both to intimidate me, and to awe the negro voters present." When speaking in Newberry's Moon Township, he branded "the Democratic Party . . . a devilish, infernal mob," one determined "to crush out rights and liberties." Reacting negatively to Thomas's strong language, a Democratic editor remarked: "We do not state this as a charge against the Republican party of the county, for many members of that party condemn it as heartily as we do; his [Thomas's] language met with no sympathy in the minds of his Republican hearers. But we desire to show the good people of Newberry what sort of a man he is—a nice character for a legislator, truly." The editorial went on to say that the "ex-reverend and present Trial Justice" Thomas informed black Republicans that "the worst Republican was better than the best Democrat."[49] His constituents soon would see for themselves.

South Carolina's controversial 1876 gubernatorial election was marred by rampant fraud, bribery, economic coercion, threats of bodily harm, and intimidation, largely by Democrats. According to an observer, the election "was one of the grandest farces ever seen." Peter L. Spearman, manager of elections in Newberry County, charged that during the November election Democrats "caused serious disturbance by challenging every vote, even those of long[time] residents, for the express purpose . . . of delaying the voting." As a result, many blacks had to walk sixteen miles to the Newberry courthouse to vote. Throughout the county whites appeared in every polling precinct armed with shotguns. A total of only sixteen U.S. troops were stationed in the county—in the villages of Prosperity, Longshore's, and Pomaria—in a futile effort to protect the freedmen.[50]

Democrats, however, also complained of voting irregularities. Commenting on the election, the *Newberry Herald* reported numerous cases of illegal voting. The paper charged that blacks from neighboring Laurens County entered the county and voted at the Jalapa precinct. "No doubt there were many fraudulent votes polled," the editor complained. Such corrupt practices and others—including threats of physical violence and economic retribution—occurred throughout the state but were especially egregious in Edgefield and Laurens Counties. As historian Thomas Holt explains, in Edgefield, the reported "Democratic majority exceeded the total white voting population by more than 2,000." According to the most careful students of the 1876 campaign, "no one knows how many ballots were stuffed, how many illegal voters cast ballots, or how many young white men of North Carolina and Georgia crossed into neighboring counties to aid the South Carolina Democrats." Historian Keith Ian Polakoff observed that "more votes appear to have been cast" in South Carolina's 1876 election "than there were eligible voters." In any case, in spite of serious rifts within the Republican camp, Eric Foner explains, "Chamberlain polled the largest Republican vote in the state's history." Apparently most black and white Republican voters were not intimidated to the extent that they stayed home.[51]

Under these circumstances, not surprisingly, both parties claimed victory and charged their opponents with voter fraud. Chamberlain and Hampton declared themselves victorious as did rival Republican and Democratic candidates for the state legislature in Edgefield, Laurens, Barnwell, and other counties. The Republican state board of canvassers was charged with the unenviable task of sorting out the election returns. Democrats, fearful that their opponents would dominate the board, appealed to the Republican-elected state supreme court to limit the power of the canvassers, whose authority was upheld by the U.S. Circuit Court. When Newberry County's votes were tallied, Chamberlain triumphed over Hampton by 565 votes for governor (2,761 to 2,196), the white Republican Henry C. Corwin was re-elected to the state Senate, and Keitt, Bridges, and Thomas were elected to the House. Will's election was a surprising triumph, all the more so because as a controversial carpetbag trial justice and relatively inexperienced politician, he defeated by 598 votes the influential Newberry attorney Young John Pope. In 1874 Pope had examined him for the Newberry bar and supported his appointment as trial justice. Unable to prevent Newberry's black majority from electing Republicans, local Democrats blasted Keitt and Thomas and contested the election. According to the Conservative *Newberry Herald,* Keitt's chief characteristic was "'gas'; he has a great deal more brass than brains." As for Thomas, the editor lambasted him as

> the worse character of the whole lot; he is a bad man, has some intelligence and education, but no principle. He distinguished himself during the last campaign as the apostle of hate, appealing to the basest passions of his race, to stir up bad blood toward the whites. The Democrats are not likely to forget him soon for calling them "a devilish, infamous mob." He has been for some time Trial Justice in town. It is bad enough when such men administer the laws, but worse still when they make them. . . . No more incompetent set of officers has ever disgraced the county.

Having garnered the wrath of local Democrats and uncertain of Chamberlain's status, Thomas went to Columbia to take his seat in the state House of Representatives on November 28, 1876.[52]

Upon arriving in Columbia, Thomas discovered that U.S. troops guarded the statehouse, that the state board of canvassers had excluded the disputed election returns from Edgefield and Laurens Counties, and, as a result, that Republicans controlled both the house and senate. While Republicans in the House of Representatives organized and elected Edwin W. M. Mackey as speaker, Democrats, unable to seat their Edgefield and Laurens delegations, bolted to nearby Carolina Hall, organizing under Speaker William H. Wallace. On November 30 the Democrats reentered the House while the Republicans were at recess, occupied the House chamber, and refused to leave. "Then began," Thomas recalled, "a political duel, the likes of which has rarely been witnessed."[53]

During the ensuing ruckus Thomas gave a speech defending Chamberlain but was interrupted by angry Democrats. According to a writer sympathetic to Hampton, "Thomas, who was full of venom as a rattlesnake in August, raised the point of order that a person not a member of the House was disturbing the proceedings." Amidst such chaos, both Wallace and Mackey declared that they were the lawful speakers and for the next four days and nights the rival houses met and tried to conduct business in the same hall. Just as neither Chamberlain nor Hampton would surrender their claims to the Governor's Office, none of the legislators dared to leave the statehouse fearful that they would not be allowed to reenter. In the sixth day of joint occupation of the House chambers, the Democrats retreated to Carolina Hall, charging Chamberlain with hiring a band of black thugs from Charleston, the Hunkidoris, to infiltrate the chamber and oust the Democrats.[54]

Years later Thomas described the "embrolia" in the statehouse, positioning himself at the center of the action: "During the whole of this period, only once was I outside the building. Much of the time I was in the speaker's chair, especially at night, and I recall with pleasure the agreeable hours I spent in the company of General Wallace. He sat beside me, and often late in the evening, during a lull in the partisan strife, he would send out for a wholesome luncheon, that was always shared with me." With his usual pomposity, Thomas claimed that during the legislative crisis, "I was much sought after . . . and had ample opportunity to study the character of the various representatives, legal and political . . . and I confess to a sense of sore disappointment at their lack of ability to deal with problems requiring immediate action."

Thomas chided Democrats for bribing Republicans, including "two negroes . . . both of whom had been educated at the expense of northern philanthropy." After taking "matters into my own hands," he explained, he put an end to further defections by examining election returns and advising the House to remove several Democratic members. "This," Thomas added with characteristic bravado, "was really a courageous thing to do in the presence of a hostile white party sitting in the same chamber." He went so far as to assert that Democrats informed him in advance of a "plan" to swap Democratic control of the state and the removal of federal troops from South Carolina in exchange for the state's disputed electoral votes for Republican presidential candidate Rutherford B. Hayes.[55]

While no documentation supports Thomas's claims, the record shows that after both the Wallace and Mackey Houses juggled the credentials of their delegates to attain quorums, the dual assemblies declared themselves the legitimate representatives of the people and inaugurated their respective governors, Chamberlain on December 7 and Hampton on December 14. "It was a unique sight," Henry T. Thompson wrote, "two bodies performing in the same hall, and at the same time, the duties, or pretended duties, of the House of Representatives without recognition from either side of the presence of the other." Commenting on the unprecedented drama and confusion unfolding around him, clerk Josephus Woodruff of the South Carolina Senate feared that the Mackey and Wallace forces would come to blows, adding that "the organization of the House and the barricade of the State House looks like revolution." In his opinion the "Republicans would stand not the shadow of a chance were it not for the U.S. troops." Reflecting on the solidarity of the black legislators, Woodruff remarked, "The colored men stick to their Republican following."[56]

Though there were in fact some defections by black representatives, including Bridges from Newberry, to the Wallace House, Thomas not only stayed loyal to the Republicans but assumed a leadership role in the Mackey House. One of the most visible and outspoken Republicans, he opened sessions with a prayer and at one point filled in for Mackey as acting speaker. During the first session of the legislature (November 28–December 22, 1876), Thomas served on several committees, including Ways and Means, Privileges and Elections, Federal Relations, and Judiciary. While Chamberlain and Hampton engaged in legal maneuvers to establish their right to the governorship, Thomas forcefully argued that Chamberlain was the legally elected governor and that those who refused to recognize the validity of his election should be cashiered.

Serving on the Privileges and Elections Committee, Thomas reviewed the credentials of those seeking entry to the legislature. In the case of Edgefield County, for example, he considered the violence "so great, and the disproportion between the voting population of said County and the vote reported by the returns to be cast at said election . . . so great as to leave no doubt in the minds of your committee that no valid election has taken place." In another instance Thomas presented a resolution requesting the governor to take steps to protect the House of Representatives against "the unlawful intrusion, interruption, and violence" caused by the Wallace House. He also took responsibility for communicating with Chamberlain, introduced a resolution to inquire into possible grounds for impeaching Chief Justice Franklin J. Moses Sr. of the South Carolina Supreme Court, and fought to get past-due school claims in Newberry County registered and engrossed to ascertain Newberry County's indebtedness.[57]

From the very beginning the Democratic press identified Thomas with the Mackey House, what it called South Carolina's "rump" or "bogus" House of Representatives. On December 8, the *Columbia Register* blasted Mackey as the leader of "ignorant fanatical men," including "Thomas, the long-winded mulatto from Newberry." The editor, who later described Thomas as the "colored carpet-bagger" who "rules the House with a rod of iron," noted that Thomas had received visiting congressmen from Washington and also favored a resolution appointing a special committee to inquire whether Chief Justice Moses had been guilty of any impeachable acts.[58]

Unimpressed by Thomas's efforts, "C.," an anonymous author, wrote the *Register* identifying Thomas as "the same shining light in the House of mis-representatives who has defrauded nearly every merchant of Newberry for large sums." "C." went on to charge Thomas with swindling the Newberry National Bank by forging checks, denying an elderly freedwoman compensation for feeding him, and refusing to turn over a financial award to a black client. "He is the same fellow," the correspondent remarked, "who opens the proceedings of his rump House with prayer, who now has two mistresses in Newberry and one wife in Pittsburg." Summing up his diatribe against Thomas, "C." considered his "rascalities . . . numerous and enormous." "Ignored by the blacks and despised by the whites in Newberry," Thomas, the writer alleged, "is just the man for the rump House." The following day the *Newberry Herald* concurred with this assessment, noting that in his letter "C." "shows up W. H. Thomas in his true colors." In an editorial the Democratic newspaper damned Thomas, charging that he "has done most of the praying for the House and much of the speaking, [and] is known by the people of Newberry to be a debased profligate and debauchee." Late in 1876, apparently convinced that smearing Thomas's reputation was proving ineffective, Young John Pope, then chair of Newberry's Democratic Party, described Thomas as "a very dishonest man." He informed Hampton, "I would suggest no delay in his decapitation."[59]

Though the stalemate between Chamberlain and Hampton and the Mackey and Wallace Houses continued well into 1877, over the course of four months Hampton gradually wrested control away from Chamberlain, whose fragile source of power was the presence of federal troops in Columbia. Soon after the election even many Republicans conceded that Hampton had received a majority of the votes for governor, but the outcome of the state's presidential electors remained in doubt. Methodically Hampton's men orchestrated their coup d'état, waiting patiently for the general population to sanction Chamberlain's ouster. Thousands of red-shirted gunmen were close by if needed to punctuate Hampton's popular support.

The show of force was unnecessary, however, because Hampton's rifle clubs already had established control over black and white Republicans in the rural areas and successfully worked to destroy Chamberlain's ability to administer the government. With the exception of the state House of Representatives, Hampton's machine was already in effect running South Carolina. In two instances judicial decisions challenged Chamberlain's authority to parole prisoners and indirectly recognized Hampton as de facto governor. When both the Mackey and Wallace Houses passed tax referendums, South Carolinians overwhelmingly paid Hampton's tax collectors, not Chamberlain's. Finally, on March 7, Associate Justice A. J. Willard of the South Carolina Supreme Court, a Republican, decided that Chamberlain was "not entitled to be recognized as Governor holding over nor as Governor de facto against the person who received the highest number of votes" and who successfully "entered upon the discharge of the duties of the office." Hampton, the judge wrote, was "at least" de facto governor. Five days earlier, on March 2, the Electoral Commission created by Congress to determine the outcome of the 1876 presidential election finally awarded the disputed electoral votes to Hayes, who was inaugurated two days later.[60]

A few weeks later President Hayes invited both Chamberlain and Hampton to Washington to make their respective cases. Hayes's support of Chamberlain, symbolized by the continued presence of federal troops in Columbia, would signal a commitment not only to the state's Republicans but to its black population as well. Removal of the troops, Chamberlain explained, would "permit Hampton to reap the fruits of a campaign of murder and fraud." On March 26, Thomas warned Chamberlain not to leave the state, fearful that the Democrats would overtake the executive branch. It was preferable, Thomas said, for Chamberlain to prepare "a paper covering the main points in our case, and submit it to the President." Thomas also informed Chamberlain that he had sent long letters to Senator John Sherman, Judge William B. Lawrence, Senator James G. Blaine, "and other friends of mine in Washington as well as the President in support of our claims." Chamberlain met with the president on March 28 and remained in Washington to await Hayes's decision after his interview with Hampton.[61]

Seriously alarmed at the prospect of the Democrats' capturing control of South Carolina, on April 2 Thomas wrote President Hayes imploring him to intervene. He warned the president that any compromise that failed "absolutely and unequivocally" to recognize South Carolina's Republican administration would doom the party's chance not only in that state but nationally as well. "Wipe out Republican Governments in South Carolina and Louisiana," Thomas cautioned the president, "and you have a solid Democratic South from Delaware to Texas for the next quarter of a century." He warned that South Carolina's Democrats were "jubilant at the prospect and can scarcely await the result."[62]

Thomas went so far as to predict that the recognition of Hampton's government would lead to "the inevitable consignment of the colored people to practical slavery." Already, Thomas explained:

> Millions of American citizens are slaves in this Republic for no crime save their ignorance and black skins. Under the old regime masters took care of their servants as a matter of pride and profit. Every slave represented a monetary investment. But since the war a colored man is simply valued at the price of a day's labor. If he sickens or dies the nominal master loses nothing [for] fifty cents will supply the place of another. From every stand point therefore absolute slavery is infinitely preferable to that which will speedily ensue if Wade Hampton is recognized as Governor of South Carolina.

Thomas predicted that despite his "fine talk and specious promises," should Hampton's administration be recognized by the president, African Americans in the state would lose their rights "either of life or property." As things then stood, Thomas said, whites routinely escaped punishment for crimes committed against the freedpeople.[63]

Thomas admonished Hayes to use the power of the government to support Republican governments in South Carolina and Louisiana. Otherwise he feared that "war or bloodshed" would ensue. In South Carolina Thomas was confident that the Democrats, "with all their bluster," would "gracefully submit to the authority of Chamberlain" if they understood that the federal government would recognize his election and support his administration. He went so far as to assert that "many" South Carolina conservatives regretted that they had supported Hampton over Chamberlain. Whites, however, had far less to fear from Hampton, a former slaveholder, than blacks.[64]

Should Hayes recognize Hampton as governor, Thomas lectured the president, "the colored people will be the greatest sufferers." The Democrats would close their schools and force white teachers, "an ignorant, vicious, and debased class," upon the ex-slaves. He also predicted that the Democrats would deny them their property, in short, shutting down "all avenues for race development into a higher manhood or purer womanhood." In terms strikingly similar to those that he employed two and one-half decades later in *The American Negro,* Thomas noted with alarm that since emancipation the freedpeople already had "sunk into a barbarism, the grossness of which is appalling." The Republicans, he said, provided the only means systematically to uplift the race. "Take away this last hope of political and social *regeneration,*" Thomas warned, "and the race relapses into abnormal debasement and ruin."[65]

Finally, Thomas reminded Hayes of the debt that both the president and his party owed African Americans. "The colored people saved the Republican party in Ohio," he wrote, referring to the state's 1875 gubernatorial campaign. In the disputed presidential election of the following year they once more rallied around the Republican banner. With characteristic immodesty, Thomas added, "I took no inconsiderable part [in these elections] without fee or reward." He considered it essential, then, that Hayes protect the fruits of Union victory in the Civil War. In Thomas's opinion, Hampton's ascendancy would represent a "cowardly" surrender to "the same men actuated by the same motives" who fought to preserve slavery. Almost literally waving the "bloody shirt," he added, "I lost my right arm on the field of battle and I justly have the right to combat any influence when it seeks to impair or deprive us of our rights of well earned citizenship."[66]

Even if his letter of April 2 would have had any effect on President Hayes, and that is highly unlikely given the political pressures on him, the president had already decided to remove federal troops from Columbia by the time Thomas's correspondence reached Washington. On April 3 Hayes and his cabinet decided to withdraw the troops on April 10. The day before, Charles J. Babbitt, Chamberlain's private secretary, informed Thomas: "You are now aware of what occurred at Washington and what the future will be the Governor cannot say. He will do what he can to maintain his rights." On April 11

Chamberlain turned over his office to Hampton and prepared to leave the state. The forces of reaction had triumphed.[67]

Thomas, however, was determined to keep his seat in the legislature, a special session of which Governor Hampton convened soon after he assumed control of South Carolina's "redeemed" state government. The Democrats demanded that members of the former Mackey House pledge an oath "purging themselves of contempt before being seated." Thomas, unwilling to "submit to such degradation," refused to take the pledge and, along with Daniel Augustus Straker, who served as a representative from Orangeburg, was charged by the new legislature's Joint Committee on Privileges and Elections with "impardonable treason." While this action failed by a vote of 48 to 28, a minority report to seat Thomas and Straker also failed. According to the *Charleston News and Courier*, "the Republicans advanced no reasons why those arch conspirators should be admitted" except that the Democrats had promised equal rights to all. The Democrats charged that Thomas and Straker were "the prime movers in the rebellion, and having much more intelligence than the common herd, should be held to stricter account." One Democratic member of the House read "the infamous resolution offered by Thomas during the deadlock last winter, declaring the legal members to be intruders, interlopers, insurrectionists . . . and calling upon the so-called Governor to use force to eject them." Others also charged Thomas with conspiring to hire the Hunkidoris ("composed of the [black] roughs of Charleston and Columbia") to provoke a violent collision with members of the former Wallace House. The Democrats concluded that Thomas and Straker had rebelled against the state of South Carolina and, like former Confederate officials, should share their fate: disqualification from office and loss of voting rights. On May 1 the majority vote passed 61 to 31 and Thomas and Straker were denied their seats. To rub insult into injury, Thomas was replaced by his old nemesis, Young John Pope. In 1906 Thomas reported that upon being expelled from the South Carolina House, he conferred with President Hayes, advising him on southern patronage, and later criticized the president for his abandonment of the freedpeople.[68]

Thomas's political enemies rejoiced at his ouster and turned his expulsion into political capital. The *Columbia Register* described him inaccurately as a "turbulent Massachusetts carpet-bag mulatto, who boasts that he was a pupil of Charles Sumner." The editor was more on the mark when he dubbed Will "one of the leading insurgent spirits in the villainous Mackey House last winter." Looking for a scapegoat, the paper blamed Thomas for "leading many better (even if they were more ignorant) men astray" through his "insolence and his knavery." Following his removal, the *Charleston News and Courier*, which supported him during the 1874 campaign, denounced Thomas as "a very obnoxious carpet-bag negro . . . as much disliked by the colored people of Newberry as by the whites."[69]

Within a week Thomas's enemies among both races settled their scores with him. On May 9, he was indicted, arrested, and bound over to the Court of General Sessions for allegedly seizing and selling private property unlawfully in his official capacity as trial justice. The indictment charged that in the fall of 1876, Thomas had illegally confiscated and later sold a bale of cotton valued at $42 belonging to J. H. Blease, an African American. The court released Will on $500 bond after four Newberry blacks—Elijah H. Phillips, a blacksmith, Burrell M. Raines, a prominent landholder and recent émigré from Liberia, Henry Kennedy, a Republican county commissioner who supported Hampton, and William H. Snead—put up bail. The *Newberry Herald* reported that Thomas fled town immediately upon his release and, the editor remarked, "it is not thought he will return." The editor hoped that "if the bond be forfeited it will be pushed to the very last dollar." Later that month Thomas's private property was confiscated by a constable and sold to satisfy his debts. "Who wants a Statesman's outfit?" the editor sarcastically inquired.[70]

While law enforcement officials no doubt searched for Thomas, in September 1877, the state of South Carolina brought charges of "official misconduct" against him and finally tried him in absentia by a jury on February 5, 1878. The court appointed Francis W. Fant as his counsel, and the state called Blease, Trial Justice James C. Packer, and A. J. Kilgore as witnesses against him. The jury returned a guilty verdict and Thomas was convicted by the Court of General Sessions. Because he failed to appear to receive his sentence, a sealed sentence was left with the clerk and a rule was ordered against his bondsmen to compromise their bond by paying $25 each. *The State v Will H. Thomas* remained on the court's docket until February 1881.[71]

Following their final victory in 1877, South Carolina's Redeemers relished in exposing the alleged corruption of former Republican leaders and issuing indictments for those who had fled the state. According to Hampton's Attorney General James Conner, "the press would revel in it & we would politically guillotine every man of them." Without question Thomas's radical oratory infuriated white Conservatives and his reputed personal behavior made him an easy target for their condemnation. Though his alleged crimes no doubt were too insignificant to warrant his extradition, as in Wilberforce, Allegheny City, and Atlanta, in Columbia and Newberry he never responded to the political or criminal charges leveled against him. His history of dishonest and unethical personal and professional practices, underscored by his repeated unwillingness to defend himself, suggests the strong possibility that he was guilty of most of the allegations against him. The sparse documentary record of Will's tenure as trial justice and state representative, however, leaves many questions about his shadowy career in South Carolina unanswerable.

Where does Thomas fit into historian Thomas Holt's continuum of "conservative" upper-status mulattoes of free origins versus "radical" blacks of free or slave origins? And if Holt is correct in emphasizing the importance of skin color differentiations and class in influencing South Carolina's political factions, why then did neither Thomas nor his black contemporaries ever mention his mulatto status? While most certainly a mulatto, Thomas was neither "conservative" nor a member of South Carolina's brown bourgeoisie. Thomas's record in fact squares best with Holt's remark that "northern free blacks [among South Carolina's legislators] were consistently among the most radical coalitions." Did Chamberlain, who after 1874 moved consistently away from radicalism and cooperated with Conservatives, "use" Thomas as his tool in 1876–77? Thomas, opportunistic and eager to gain place and position, more likely latched on to Chamberlain, not vice versa. Evidence supports no genuine ideological or personal connection between the two men. Nor can Thomas's twentieth-century reminiscences regarding his influence on Chamberlain or Hayes be given much credence.[72]

Did Thomas have any influence among blacks in the state? While he did participate in local communal and political activities in Newberry, there is very little record of how blacks judged Thomas except for the fact that they voted for him in that county. Representative Thomas E. Miller, a freeborn mulatto from Beaufort, the only colleague to comment on him, remarked in 1901 that Thomas "reeks in filth . . . has destroyed helpless innocent virtue whenever it has been entrusted to his care . . . [and] has been guilty of nearly every crime in the decalogue." Significantly, Miller made this statement in the highly charged aftermath of the publication of *The American Negro*, not within the context of Reconstruction. In 1906 Thomas wrote bitterly that the resolution to expel him from the state House "was seconded by a negro Republican, who five minutes previous had stood before the speaker's desk expressing contrition for his previous partisan acts." More telling though is the fact that four Newberry blacks willingly posted his bond after he was arrested in May and that they suffered financially when he skipped town.[73]

A likely interpretation of Thomas's years in South Carolina is that because he fought for black rights so forcefully, he was victimized by Democrats and, as a vocal carpetbagger with little property or influence, he was easily cut adrift by Republicans on a sinking ship. Writing in 1925, the conservative Charleston lawyer Theodore D. Jervey, Thomas's biggest champion, credited Will with being "in charge of the rear guard when the Negro government fell in South Carolina." The likelihood of his professional misconduct made Thomas an easy sacrificial lamb for Republicans and perfect target for the Democrats.[74]

In 1877, Will Thomas exited South Carolina in a cloud, much as he had entered the state in 1873. Though not "decapitated," he drifted silently away from South Carolina with a price on his head and ready to cash in on his empty sleeve.

CHAPTER FIVE

U.S. Consul and Racial Reformer

O N MARCH 29, 1877, less than two weeks before Governor Daniel
H. Chamberlain surrendered South Carolina's governorship to
Wade Hampton, the *Columbia Register* published a parody about
an anonymous black state official. The African American reportedly was combing the halls of federal offices in Washington lobbying for the
position of U.S. minister to Haiti, a post reserved for the most prominent
black federal appointees. According to the paper, the office seeker interviewed with William M. Evarts, chief counsel for the Republicans in the
Hayes-Tilden electoral dispute and President Hayes's new secretary of state.
Will Thomas no doubt was the subject of this political satire. The humorist
understood Thomas well. Though he would not be expelled from South
Carolina's House of Representatives until May 1, Thomas was hard at work
trying to win a diplomatic appointment from his Republican "friends" in
Washington.[1]

Thomas long had set his sights on a federal appointment, convinced that
his Civil War military record, and later his service to the Republican party,
had earned him political patronage. In the postwar years such leading African Americans as Frederick Douglass, John Mercer Langston, Richard T.
Greener, John S. Durham, and Archibald H. Grimké were rewarded for
party loyalty with diplomatic appointments. Douglass, for example, served
as minister resident and consul general to Haiti and chargé d'affaires to the
Dominican Republic (1889–91), and Grimké served as consul to Santo Domingo (1894–98). Historian Allison Blakely has identified approximately
fifty African Americans who served as diplomats and consuls from 1880 to
1920. Most, he argues, were members of the light-complexioned, upwardly

mobile African American elite and had sought political opportunities available only through patronage. Thomas viewed a diplomatic appointment as a mark of privilege and as a possible stepping stone to a higher federal appointment.[2]

Whereas the Department of State sent a limited number of diplomats to the courts of major monarchies, sovereign rulers, and capitals, it appointed hundreds of consuls to ports and cities worldwide. Most African American appointees served as consuls. They promoted American commerce, aided shippers, protected and disciplined seamen, and helped American citizens in trouble abroad. Consuls also authenticated foreign documents, certified shipping certificates, and provided commercial digests to American exporters. In contrast to the more elite diplomats, members of the U.S. consular service came largely from modest origins, held less influence and prestige, received little compensation, and generally were ignored by the State Department. According to Charles Stuart Kennedy, the history of the consular service was at best chaotic. The isolated, diverse posts were staffed mostly by temporary amateurs "acting on their own with minimal guidance, responding to local events, each according to common sense and instinct." Because of the spoils system they generally served one short term before being recalled and replaced by another political appointee.[3]

In the decades after the Civil War, the number of U.S. consular posts and agencies swelled to 644, but, according to Kennedy, the quality of men who received such appointments deteriorated. "The great adventure of the war had fostered wanderlust. For many young men consular appointments were ideal ways to escape life at home." Some "were plain adventurers, even rogues," encouraged to seek a diplomatic appointment by the political patronage system and the method of compensating consular officers by fees collected at their posts. "In fact," Kennedy explains, "a man with a commercial interest in using the consulate for personal advantage in land deals or trading was more likely to be appointed than one indifferent to commerce, as the former was more likely to lobby for the post." In sum, the consular system "attracted adventure-seeking but ill-qualified men impressed by the prestige of foreign appointments." That description fit William Hannibal Thomas to a tee.[4]

In order to win a diplomatic post, Thomas called upon an amazing number of "friends" to support his case. Though prone to hyperbole regarding his professional contacts, somehow he was able to marshal an impressive cadre of supporters who surely must have been unaware of his serious personal and professional indiscretions. Remarkably, over several years Will amassed testimonials from more than one hundred Congressmen and twenty-five U.S. senators, as well as from prominent Republican clergymen, lawyers, and businessmen. In their letters on his behalf, Thomas's many boosters uniformly praised him as an exemplary African American role model engaged in important work to uplift his race. They noted his distinguished Civil War service and praised his devotion to Christianity, his integrity, and his intelligence. He also was an unflagging Republican. In most cases those writing recommendations for Thomas commented on his battlefield amputation.[5]

As early as 1867, Congressman John Beatty of Ohio recommended Thomas for the Liberia post, describing him as "an educated gentleman" who "would serve his country abroad most faithfully and efficiently." Abolitionist James Redpath, who vigorously promoted emigration of the freedpeople to Haiti, claimed to have known Thomas since 1859. "He has a stainless record both as a soldier & citizen," Redpath said. "No colored man in Boston stands better with his people & the whites also. Every one respects him." Ohio governor Rutherford B. Hayes similarly lauded him as "a man of integrity and high character generally," and "a man worthy of entire confidence." Benjamin F. Butler, who awarded Thomas his silver medal for bravery in 1864, commended him for diplomatic service, recalling his wartime gallantry, "the evidence of which he carries in the shape of a lost arm."[6]

President Ulysses S. Grant bore the brunt of most of Thomas's requests for a diplomatic job. Thomas repeatedly asked Grant to assign him either as Minister Resident to Liberia or as U.S. Consul at Santo Domingo. Given his relative obscurity and the competition of the likes of Frederick Douglass, both posts were obviously far beyond his grasp. Nevertheless he bombarded Grant with requests.

In one letter Thomas informed Grant that he sought a place "where *strict* integrity of purpose and action on the part of the office holder, might exert, incidentally, a salutary influence upon the future condition of the colored Americans." In another he explained that he sought a diplomatic post where he could increase American foreign trade and also work to ameliorate the "spirit of caste." Expressing his desire to serve as U.S. minister to Liberia, Will added that "my aim will also be to secure to [a] higher grade of civilization than is at present enjoyed in that country, and to do this by the infusion of a spirit of emigration among colored Americans. Such a disposition will naturally ensure, when Africa's true condition shall be properly set forth." Thomas assured Grant that "I am not an office-seeker in the popular sense, else I would have entered the '*arena*' earlier, but I have the interests of my people and Government at heart."[7]

By March 1877, as Thomas's political career in South Carolina seemed on a downward course, he stepped up his lobbying campaign. Daniel Schindler, who had hired him as a journalist in Pennsylvania after the war, sang Thomas's praises and told President Grant that "besides, in our great struggle with the slave-power . . . he did his country a patriotic service." William Lawrence, one of the nation's leading international lawyers, recommended him to Grant as "my esteemed friend" who "has done much for the colored people of South Carolina." Lawrence hoped that Thomas could fill the post of minister either to Haiti or Liberia. In mid-April, Thomas informed Hayes that he would welcome either post, but would prefer the appointment to Haiti. He assured Hayes that he sought neither assignment for "honor or emoluments, but from race and humanity considerations." Still hopeful that he had a political future in South Carolina, Will informed Hayes that he could not accept a job with the State Department "until our state affairs have been satisfactorily adjusted for I have much yet to do here." Several weeks later, following Thomas's expulsion from South Carolina's legislature, former Governor Chamberlain lauded him as "a lawyer of excellent standing and ability, a devoted Republican, and an able and faithful representative of the rights, wants and needs of the colored race in this state." Chamberlain added, "his recent course here endeared him especially to all good Republicans."[8]

While these dignitaries and others were writing letters on his behalf, Thomas meanwhile was a fugitive from South Carolina justice. Determined to get out of harm's way, as before, he beat a path northward to his safe refuge: Delaware, Ohio. On August 23, 1877, the *Delaware Gazette* reported that Thomas would attend the local African Methodist Episcopal Sabbath School's nonalcoholic "Murphy picnic," where he would "address the public on vital questions." Soon after, Will wrote General Oliver O. Howard, updating him on his "fight in South Carolina for political liberty" and asking for Howard's help in securing the minister's position in Liberia. "I want to go to Liberia for many reasons," he wrote. Thomas predicted a bright future for Africa in general but especially so for Liberia. He sought to go there most importantly "for the sake of my Race and that future." In his testimonial for Thomas, Howard, himself an amputee, mentioned Will's disability and added, "I think he has a *true* character." Congressman James A. Garfield, who commanded the 42nd Ohio, Thomas's first Civil War regiment, agreed.

The future president remarked that Thomas "is highly recommended by those who knew him in Ohio & in South Carolina. I think his appointment would be a good one."[9]

Unemployed and convinced that he had sacrificed much for their lost cause in South Carolina, Thomas implored Republicans in the state to write encomiums on his behalf. Edwin W. M. Mackey, former Speaker of the state House, remarked, "if the appointment is to be given as a reward for political services, Mr. Thomas's claims are entitled to recognition. . . . If capability and competency are to decide the question . . . the government need not hesitate to appoint Mr. Thomas since he is thoroughly capable and competent." Lawyer A. Blythe, who worked with Thomas on South Carolina's eighth judicial circuit, shared this opinion, extolling Will's record "as a lawyer and as a man. His course in the Legislature of South Carolina during the stormy peril immediately succeeding the last general election," Blythe added, "won for him the position of leader in that body and stamped him as a man of high courage and ability, and [one] unswervingly devoted to the interests of the Republican party." J. K. Jillson, former South Carolina state superintendent of education, similarly praised Will's record in his state, describing him as "a gentleman of ability and culture." Most important, though, Jillson added, Thomas "is a staunch Republican."[10]

By October 1877, when his campaign for a diplomatic post still had not borne fruit, Thomas intensified his appeals for the Liberia post. Writing from the offices of the Ohio Republican Committee in Columbus, he informed President Hayes that given "all that I have endured for my adherence to the Republican party, I feel that my claim [for the position of minister resident in Liberia] should not be ignored." A month later Thomas traveled to Washington to plead his case before the president in person. Summarizing his arguments, he explained that first and foremost he deserved a diplomatic assignment because of his devoted military service. He entered the army in 1861, Thomas lectured Hayes, "when colored men were refused admission to the ranks," and remained until he suffered his amputation in 1865. Because of his skin color, Will complained, he served "without promotion or reward . . . a *commission* was denied me as well as thousands of other brave and patriotic soldiers."[11]

Thomas next argued that he deserved the position in Liberia because of his loyalty to Hayes's party and his many sacrifices on its behalf while in South Carolina. "I have always been a faithful and consistent Republican," he said, and "under the most adverse circumstances." Reminding the president of his contributions in the South Carolina House of Representatives a year earlier, Will emphasized, "and as you *are aware,* I did more than many others to secure the Electoral vote of that state for the Republicans." He credited himself, for example, for the fact that the Republicans carried New-berry County without dispute and added: "When the Legislature met, I was of no little service in securing the cohesion of the Legislature and facilitating the final action of the Republican election. I was *expelled* from the Hampton Legislature in May 1877 for my adherence to the Republican party."[12]

Finally, Thomas explained to Hayes that he could provide special leader-ship in Monrovia and improve "the future civilization of Africa." He faulted the United States for failing to establish a strong diplomatic, commercial, and humanitarian presence in Liberia, a nation that Americans had created for freed blacks. England, France, and Germany, Thomas complained, had more influence there. As America's representative in Liberia, he promised to provide the Liberians "moral and positive support" that would in turn lead to the "restoration of African civilization."[13]

After years of lobbying and cajoling, on June 26, 1878, Thomas's Repub-lican "friends" in Washington finally rewarded him with a diplomatic post—one that Will, even in his wildest fantasies, could never have anticipated. He was appointed U.S. consul at São Paulo de Luanda, Portuguese West Africa. This post was located in southwest Africa, eight and one-half degrees south of the equator. Thomas was lucky to receive even this remote tropical assign-ment—in 1880 only four African Americans held consular posts anywhere in the world. Like virtually all Americans, however, Thomas no doubt had never heard of the place.[14]

The Portuguese established the colony of São Paulo de Luanda in 1483 and its central city and major slave trading port, Luanda, in 1576. Luanda became the administrative center of Angola in 1627. Trade, largely in slaves transported to Brazil, was Portugal's primary economic activity there, and after Brazil's independence in 1822, it became Portugal's foremost colony and the city south of the Sahara with the highest population of whites. Though coffee and sugar plantations began in the 1830s, the closing of the Portuguese slave trade in July 1842 dealt the colony a deadly blow and it declined rapidly. With slaves no longer available for trade and little else to exchange, with the exception of small quantities of wax and ivory, São Paulo de Luanda became a dumping ground for Portugal's *degredados*—murderers, rapists, arsonists, and thieves. In 1875 an observer described them as "the choicest specimens of ruffians and wholesale assassins." They dominated the colony's white population and played a large part in establishing São Paulo de Luanda's negative image as a white man's grave. British diplomats jokingly defined a consulate on the southwest coast of Africa as "a corrugated iron case with a dead consul inside." [15]

Most whites lived in or near coastal settlements. By mid-nineteenth century São Paulo de Luanda was the second-largest European colony in Africa, though it contained fewer than two thousand whites, mostly soldiers, traders, colonial administrators, and *degredados*. Conditions of life were so rough there—dangerous mosquitoes, infectious diseases, and debilitating humidity—that until the middle of the nineteenth century Angola "was considered almost fatal for white women." Thomas's predecessor as consul, Joseph E. Jackson of Detroit, Michigan, took four months to reach São Paulo de Luanda and then resigned two months later. "Since my arrival here," Jackson informed the State Department, "I have suffered attack after attack of African fever until I am now very low and my staying here longer can have but one result." Several months later, in November 1878, at the start of the rainy season, the port was quarantined because of a yellow fever epidemic. [16]

Portuguese and other foreign travelers took pains to document what they deemed the low level of civilization in the port city of Luanda. Yet they praised the high standard of morality among the Africans. It was the white Europeans, they insisted, who contributed to the city's "scandalous" reputation. According to historian Gerald J. Bender, "gambling, drinking, and debauchery were the Europeans' major preoccupations and many fortunes, wives, and lives were won and lost" there. "Most visitors to Luanda were happy to leave the colony alive and few expressed a desire to return." In 1862 an anonymous Portuguese traveler summarized his sentiments upon departing. "We say goodbye, and goodbye forever, to that burning furnace called Luanda and to its cohort of mosquitoes, spiders, lizards and cockroaches." [17]

The Department of State classified São Paulo de Luanda a "Schedule C Commercial Agency," allowing the consul and vice-consul to transact their own commercial affairs while collecting fees for performing their consular duties. Occasionally American whalers would put in for fresh food and water and for medical care for sick seamen. Though the U.S. government compensated consuls for these costs, Thomas's diplomatic assignment would be far from lucrative. The Civil War severely interrupted America's once-extensive trade with Portuguese Africa, and in the years following the war this commerce declined almost to the vanishing point. The war diverted American commerce away from Africa, and Americans, who relied upon sailing vessels, found themselves unable to compete in the African market against European shippers with steamships. American merchants also encountered discriminatory ad valorem tariffs from European trade rivals. In 1867 Brazilian native Augustus Archer da Silva, a naturalized American citizen, entered the Luanda market as U.S. commercial agent. Financed by British capital, he began trading operations in palm oil, kernels, coffee, and groundnuts two hundred miles up the Cuanza River. This trade, however, amounted to only 9,000 tons in 1873. Five years later, when Thomas received his consular appointment, trade with São Paulo de Luanda was negligible. Only eight times from 1869 to 1881 did the post's consuls and commercial agents send statements of fees collected to Washington. The reports averaged a mere $32.94 per statement.[18]

Despite the post's bleak prospects both in terms of his health and potential income, Thomas accepted his appointment, which carried a $1,000 annual salary and commercial fees. News of his appointment traveled fast. On July 3 the *Newberry Herald* reported that "W. H. Thomas, well known in these parts," had been appointed consul at "a decayed settlement on the west coast of Africa." Under the terms of his appointment, Thomas was required to pay his own travel expenses to the post. On July 5, 1878, he forwarded Assistant Secretary of State F. W. Seward his oath of office and bond with sureties. These were required as guarantees of faithful execution of consular duties. After receiving his official instructions and passport, Thomas went to Boston to book his passage to Africa. He never shipped out. Because fares in August ran from $200 to $300, he sought permission from the State Department to delay his voyage until September, when the passage would cost $150. He then remained in Boston until October to visit the Reverend Edward E. Hale, the son of Boston journalist Nathan Hale and a Unitarian clergyman and author. Thomas sought a letter of introduction regarding a summer institute that he wished to attend.[19]

In early November 1878, Thomas's past finally caught up with him. Robert D. McConnicle, clerk of the Board of Directors of the Poor of Allegheny City, Pennsylvania, informed President Hayes that Will's wife, Martha J. Thomas, and their four children were on the city's relief rolls. Thomas, allegedly having provided his family no support for eighteen months, had deserted them, leaving Martha destitute and forcing her to support herself and her family by taking in wash. McConnicle, aware that Will had received "an appointment of some character to Africa," urged Hayes "to remedy the wrong that has been perpetrated by the man upon his wife and family." Hayes forwarded McConnicle's letter to the State Department, which, under the assumption that Will had sailed for his post on August 20, began an investigation. An official remarked that this was the first complaint raised against Thomas on any grounds. Will, in any case, was nowhere to be found, and the State Department never pressed him on the abandonment charge. The government simply wanted to know where he was and when he would reach his post.[20]

Writing in February 1879 from the U.S. Consulate in São Paulo de Luanda, Vice Consul Robert Scott Newton informed the State Department that Thomas still had not yet arrived. He reportedly was carrying new official consular seals and a press. Scott, who served as vice-commercial agent at the post as early as 1869 and became vice consul in 1877, worried that Thomas was aboard the mail steamer *La Plata*, due from Lisbon to São Paulo de Luanda in early January but lost at sea.[21]

On March 21, 1879, Thomas finally surfaced, not from the Atlantic Ocean, but in Philadelphia. He explained to Assistant Secretary of State Seward that he was scheduled to leave for Liverpool, England, the following day and planned to remain in England for a week. Though Thomas complained that "the passage money alone will exceed one fourth of the consular salary for the current year," he said that he was still determined to catch a steamer to São Paulo de Luanda. "My next letter to you," Thomas promised, "will be dated from that Port." He explained that he waited to sail because of "an illness of some duration" and because he wanted to wait for his confirmation by the U.S. Senate. On February 4 President Hayes had formally nominated him for the consular post. The Senate's Committee on Commerce reported favorably on it on March 3.[22]

Thomas insisted that though he had not yet gone to Africa as promised, since the date of his appointment he had "not been idle." He explained:

I have secured the cooperation of a number of merchants in Boston and New York in the African trade, and as a direct result three vessels with full cargoes have been sent to St. Paul de Loanda with orders to bring back African goods from that Port. More vessels will follow, and the indications are, that a number of vessels, heretofore engaged in the Cape and South East African trade, will find their way up the West Coast, and that St. Paul de Loanda will be the leading Port of trade with the United States on the south west coast, over one hundred thousand dollars have been secured for commercial purposes at and around this Port.

Promising to write again upon his arrival in Africa, Thomas hoped that his work over the previous several months proved "that my presence in this country has not been unproductive of good to both countries."[23]

For all his apologies, excuses, and promises, Thomas never left the United

States. In early May 1879, he was back in Delaware, Ohio, the local newspaper explained, "for a few days, previous to his departure for St. Paul de Loander, Africa, as U.S. Consul." Four months later, however, he was still there. Later in May a collection attorney in Columbus, Ohio, wrote the State Department that in April, Thomas had embezzled a railroad ticket worth $11.25 purchased for a woman friend, Miss Mamie Moore, from Ward Brothers, a Columbus ticket broker. He reportedly had purchased the ticket for Miss Moore's travel from Columbus to Bellaire, Ohio, agreeing to surrender the unused part from Bellaire to New York or its equivalent in money. Ward Brothers charged, however, that Thomas or Miss Moore "sold the ticket & pocketed the money." Miss Moore accused Thomas of retaining the ticket and Ward Brothers agreed. Their attorney, unable to track Thomas down in central Ohio, described him as "a worthless shiftless fellow." The lawyer advised his clients that probably the only way that they could obtain the ticket was to grab Thomas and "whip it out of him." Throughout the summer of 1879 Ward Brothers, convinced that Thomas had "skipped to Africa," pressed the State Department for assistance in finding him and settling their claim against him. Finally, in October, Secretary Seward informed Ward Brothers that the State Department believed that Thomas had left the country in July "and has not been heard from since." Seward assured Ward Brothers that the government would ask Thomas to respond to the charges of embezzlement.[24]

But just as the State Department never forced Thomas to answer the allegation of abandonment of Martha and his children in Pennsylvania, it never confronted him with the financial irregularities surrounding his purchase of the railroad ticket. Both cases occurred while he held a federal appointment. In fact, the State Department never pursued him and seemed unconcerned by his actions, even his failure to report to his post. Though Thomas's whereabouts in late 1879 remain uncertain, it is certain that he never set foot on Portuguese African soil. From January to August 1880, Vice Consul Newton waited in vain for his arrival and assumed charge of the consulate. Thomas resurfaced in Roxbury, Massachusetts, in March 1880, appealing to the Reverend Hale for assistance. Thomas, Hale informed the State Department, sought to establish a newspaper, *The Radical*, in Columbia, South Carolina. Perplexed, understandably, how this "colored man with one arm" could be the same individual who was supposed to be posted at São Paulo de Luanda, Hale asked the State Department to verify Thomas's handwriting. He added: "If he has lived in Loando two years it is longer than any one else has lived there. The consuls generally die in 4 months!"[25]

Not only was Thomas not deceased, but he was characteristically on the move, soon heading back to Pennsylvania. The 1880–81 Allegheny City directory listed him as residing there and, in a remarkable overstatement, credited him with serving as "consul to Africa." Convinced that he could yet again lose himself and abdicate his personal and professional responsibilities, Will never contacted the State Department or ever officially resigned his appointment. In his dealings with the government, however, Thomas was not a rarity. According to the historian Charles Stuart Kennedy, appointees commonly rejected their posts after weighing the assignments' advantages and disadvantages. São Paulo de Luanda mattered so little to the State Department, however, that it failed to appoint Thomas's successor, L. de R. du Verge, a native of Mauritius and a Maryland resident, until March 7, 1882.[26]

After more than a decade lobbying for a diplomatic job, Thomas had received one of the least desirable foreign posts available. Whereas in South Carolina political patronage had worked to his advantage, his ill-fated consular appointment was a severe blow. The history of this appointment suggests just how little influence Thomas had within Republican party circles, how minimally his alleged "friends" valued his labors on their behalf, and how unrealistic his expectations were. In any case, given the serious medical problems that resulted from Will's amputation, venturing to Portuguese Africa would have amounted to little more than a death sentence. During the period of his appointment, São Paulo de Luanda first was quarantined for yellow fever and later ravaged by a smallpox epidemic. His Republican "friends" had rewarded Thomas by exiling him to an isolated, disease-infested tropical port where he had few prospects of earning a living. Despite his statements to the contrary, Thomas was never serious about going to São Paulo de Luanda and had little interest either in encouraging American commerce or uplifting Africans.[27]

At best, Thomas's brief career with the consular service may have exhibited his wanderlust, his determination to improve himself, and, possibly, his ambivalence about uplifting African Americans in Haiti or Santo Domingo or Africans in Liberia. Yet years later—in 1889 and again in 1891—Thomas wrote General Oliver O. Howard expressing interest once more in the post of consul to Santo Domingo. Not surprisingly, Howard informed him that he could not support this request. As late as February 1897, Thomas inquired once more about a diplomatic appointment. His query fell on deaf ears.[28]

Thomas's dealings with the State Department underscored his rank opportunism, his craving for recognition, and his propensity for dishonest and unethical, if not illegal, behavior in every avenue of his life. Unquestionably, the episode exposed his abandonment of his wife and children and adds credibility to charges of sexual improprieties in South Carolina. By 1877 Thomas had exhibited clear patterns of aberrant behavior. He was corrupt, erratic, secretive, and manipulative. Not surprisingly, with the exception of the compiler of the *Directory of Pittsburgh and Allegheny Cities,* Thomas apparently never mentioned his short-lived appointment with the U.S. consular service to anyone. It was a personal disgrace, certainly nothing to brag about.

Even before leaving South Carolina in 1877, first for Ohio and then for Pennsylvania, Thomas began drifting again. He possessed extraordinary resilience. Abandoning his search for political preferment, Will soon became a nomad with ties neither to place nor to person, a rootless man driven now by one apparent obsession: observing and commenting upon the condition of black Americans. Despite an outstanding warrant for his arrest in South Carolina, Thomas returned to the South. With a mobility that was remarkable for late-nineteenth-century America, Thomas made, in 1877 and 1878, quick forays into Georgia to record with considerable detail conditions among the state's African Americans. The A.M.E.'s national publications — the *Christian Recorder* and its *Church Review* — soon provided Thomas, who revived his former nom de plume, "Hannibal," a forum for his observations on African American life. His verbose articles were long on description, short on analysis, and thin in substance. They mirrored his often conflicted and illusive mental state and underscored the disparity between his rhetoric and his conduct. But Thomas remained consistent on several points. He still was a Republican, an outspoken defender of his race, a devotee of the A.M.E. Church, an opinionated social critic, and a wanderer.

Despite his frustrations with the party after the South's "redemption" in 1877, Will nonetheless cheered isolated successes for Republicans and blacks. In April 1877, he reported the euphoria of blacks in Athens, Georgia, in the aftermath of Hayes's electoral victory. "The procession started about six hundred strong," he informed readers of the *Christian Recorder,* "and it would have made your very soul rejoice . . . to have heard their jubilant songs and proud hurrahs." To be sure, black southerners had not abandoned the Republican party. "Oh how I wish," Thomas exclaimed, "some of our [northern] friends had been here to have witnessed our procession." In later articles Will recorded with similar race pride the progress of African American teachers and their students at Atlanta University. Despite naysayers who accused the school's faculty of sectarianism and paternalism, Thomas concluded that Atlanta University "has done and is doing a noble, gigantic work for the colored people of the South." He also opposed "a few malcontents" who sought to secede from the A.M.E. Church. The church was flourishing, Thomas wrote, but required a more educated leadership so that racial progress could continue. "The times call for an educated ministry," he wrote. "Our children call for an educated ministry; the ignorance of our people calls for an educated ministry, and God calls for, and demands an educated ministry." [29]

Immediately after publishing these articles, Thomas went into seclusion. During the late 1870s and early 1880s Will left virtually no trace of his where-abouts. He most likely used Allegheny City, Pennsylvania, as his base of operations. Years later Thomas wrote in the vaguest of terms that following his tenure in South Carolina, his "chief attention" was "the educational and social advancement of the freedmen." He explained that

> in pursuance of that purpose I built churches, established school-houses, and created facilities for primary instruction in localities where such were before unknown. Nor did I cease endeavors better to observe and study the negro in every phase of his existence until I had visited every Southern state and com-munity. In my varied experience in the South I have slept in bare cabins, sat on earthen floors, and eaten corn pone, and witnessed as much genuine self-respect in log huts as I have ever beheld in the most pretentious negro homes. I have kept step with the illiterate freedman as he pursued his daily round of toil in the field or forest, and sat in rapt attention at his hearth-stone at night while he recounted his own privations or drew vivid pictures of what he dreamed, but dared not hope, his children might become.

Thomas's description, typically self-serving and lacking specifics, prefaced his 1901 attack against his race. While he may in fact have done what he claimed in the 1870s and 1880s, Will most likely exaggerated the degree of his engagement with poor southern blacks. [30]

In any case, in 1883 Thomas surfaced briefly in Washington, D.C., to ap-peal for an increase of his invalid pension, and soon after the 1884 presiden-tial election he appeared in Philadelphia at the office of the *Christian Re-corder.* He had been invited to contribute to a roundtable forum on "The Democratic Return to Power—Its Effect?" to be published in the first vol-ume of the *A.M.E. Church Review,* the denomination's new scholarly journal. This was a major opportunity for him. Contributors to the symposium in-cluded some of America's foremost black leaders and intellectuals of the 1880s. Among the notables were Frederick Douglass, classics scholar Wil-liam S. Scarborough of Wilberforce, editor T. Thomas Fortune of the *New*

York Freeman, abolitionist William Still, former acting governor P. B. S. Pinchback of Louisiana, and Bishop Henry McNeal Turner of the A.M.E. Church. This was stellar company indeed for a man who allegedly had been sitting on earthen floors, eating corn pone with the black proletariat. Though still a fugitive from South Carolina justice, in his contribution to the journal Will identified himself as resident of the state.[31]

In his article, Thomas declared New York Governor Grover Cleveland's 1884 "barren victory" a "fraud." While he predicted economic hard times as the result of Democratic economic policies, his greatest concern was the Democratic party's treatment of black southerners. Already they had been disfranchised. Whites controlled them almost as thoroughly as when they were slaves. "In his present condition," Thomas explained, "the negro is the buffet of misfortune, and the football of caprice." Distancing himself from "the colored race, credulous as they are," he urged blacks to be wary of Democrats bearing political gifts. "The Republican party has not always been just to the negro," Will admitted, "but [the] Democracy has ever been his malignant enemy." In related articles he reminded blacks that Republicans, especially President Ulysses S. Grant, had been their true friends. African Americans, he insisted, must resist overtures by Democrats to become "independent." They should marshal "cohesive race affinity—a Spartan devotion to race interests and its institutions," and, of course, support Republican candidates.[32]

But, Thomas insisted, blacks had to look to themselves for leadership and to improve as a race. "We are servile to color," he wrote in January 1885, "and deferential to caste, in the church, society and public life." As during the late 1860s, in the 1880s Will admonished blacks to embrace reform. In several articles, for example, he assailed the A.M.E. Church, criticizing its fiscal operations and, especially, its clergy. He objected to preachers entering politics and gratuitously attacked their lack of morality and their overt emotionalism. Too often, Thomas complained, African Methodists encouraged "competitive antagonism," not "concerted co-operation." He urged black ministers to teach practical lessons—"what to sow and how to reap"—and to take practical stands against the enemies of their race. Clergymen must not be surprised when their parishioners complained of receiving "husks instead of bread." Preachers, according to Thomas, also needed to elevate the race to a higher moral plane. Though he acknowledged that most blacks led Christian lives, he nonetheless condemned widespread immorality among blacks, including superstitious rituals, gambling, and drinking. Black women, whom Thomas charged with routinely engaging in illicit sex with white men and aborting babies, received special censure. "I know mothers," he said, "who affirm it to be more honorable for their daughters to fill the questionable position of mistress to a white man than to be the honest wife of a working man of color. This evil is regnant in every community." Thomas admitted, however, that many of the race's problems resulted from what he dubbed "Saxon crime during the slave period" and its legacy, white racism. He reminded readers of the *Christian Recorder* that black southerners still were subjected to a judicial system "gross, sensuous, unreasonable and vindictive in judgment, and mercilessly cruel in sentence."[33]

But blacks had to bear responsibility for much of their low status, Thomas charged. A.M.E. educators competed unwisely, and unsuccessfully, among themselves for northern philanthropy. They generally established "nondescript institutions" far inferior in quality and in endowments compared to Hampton or Tuskegee Institutes. Too often, Thomas said, blacks "put culture in the place of principle and refinement in the place of truth." Reversing his earlier endorsement of black colleges, notably Atlanta University, and blasting the white administration of the John F. Slater Fund, Will advocated a more populist, economical, practical education for blacks, one modeled on English graded schools. He lambasted the black college as "a fetich" whose "inmates are aristocrats, yet of those who enter not five per cent graduate." Thomas argued that blacks desperately required schools that imparted basic skills, "general elementary instruction." Though he was unclear whether he proposed manual training for the black masses, Thomas said explicitly that exceptional blacks should be sent north for college. To fund his proposed schools, he advanced an intricate plan whereby the principal of the Slater endowment would be invested in land, which in turn would be rented to blacks. The revenue earned from these rents would be invested in community schools. Gradually the land would be sold to upstanding black farmers. As Will would explain in this and other more detailed cooperative and federally supported land proposals, he considered "land and education" to be "the real solvents of the race problem." To his mind, providing land for blacks was an even more important goal than "literary training."[34]

In order to provide a forum for critical discussion of these and other "race problems," in 1886 Thomas began a monthly journal, *The Negro.* He did so after moving to Massachusetts—first to Somerville, then to Greenwood, and finally to Boston, where he opened his editorial office. Having spent nearly half of his life studying the freedpeople, Thomas announced that the new periodical would "present, in an unequivocal form, the actual condition of the negro race in this country," allowing the blacks to speak for themselves.

Its special focus, he explained, would be black education in the South. Though later in life he would repudiate "Negroes," in 1886 Thomas noted the importance of titling his magazine *The Negro*. He preferred the term "colored American" because it encompassed the various African American racial and cultural backgrounds, but he chose "Negro" because it represented "the most comprehensive equivalent for an otherwise inexplicable phenomenon." "The term 'negro,'" Thomas explained, "has been synonymous of obloquy and servile degradation." His hope was that the term would "become the insignia of regenerated manhood, and strong, true womanhood."[35]

Unfortunately Thomas left no record of who financed *The Negro* and provided no information concerning its editorial staff, its circulation, or why the journal ceased publication after two issues. Black journalist "Bruce Grit" (John Edward Bruce) assisted Thomas briefly ("for about three weeks") and fifteen years later became one of his severest critics. In its short publishing history, *The Negro* contained only twelve pieces, including three articles by Thomas. Curiously, the new journal also included a private letter, not intended for publication, from Frederick Douglass, in which Douglass declined Thomas's request to submit an article for publication in *The Negro*. Incredibly, Thomas edited it heavily and palmed it off as a contributed "article." Douglass wrote that "the Negro problem is a misnomer." In his opinion, it was more accurately "a white man's problem." As such it could never be solved until whites overcame their prejudices. Because of the prestige associated with Douglass's name, Thomas transformed Douglass's mundane letter into an "article" for *The Negro*. But Douglass's point also mirrored Thomas's belief—which ran through the issues of *The Negro*—that whites were responsible for the hardships of blacks. Thomas nevertheless remained convinced that blacks shared responsibility for their circumstances.[36]

Despite its modest proportions and limited content, contemporaries welcomed Thomas's addition to the small list of extant African American–run journals. Douglass remarked that compared to its rivals, *The Negro* "promises to be among the more able and useful." "It is replete with facts and fancies pretaining to the colored race," explained the *Indianapolis World*, "and judging from its contents, it has many days to accumulate negro lore and literature." The *Christian Recorder* described *The Negro* with considerable exaggeration as "brilliant and lively."[37]

The articles in Thomas's new journal today seem drab and pedestrian, but the new publication did offer positive messages about blacks in the 1880s—a decade when journals edited by whites increasingly marginalized blacks, describing them as legal pariahs, biological outcasts, and social misfits. Generally the articles in *The Negro* characterized African Americans, especially black women, in more positive terms than Thomas had employed in his own writings. Mrs. M. E. Lee's poem, for example, entitled "Afmerica," celebrated the virtues and valiant struggles of African American women. "Truth Versus Hypocrisy," a short story by B. E. Pope, another black woman, showed the condescension and hypocrisy of white northerners who funded education for black southerners on the one hand but practiced racial discrimination on the other. Pearl L. Ward told the Negro dialect story of "Aunt Harriet," a hard-working elderly ex-slave who, as a freedwoman, was victimized by prejudice and injustice in the postemancipation world. Whereas Thomas generally had emphasized the immorality of black women, contributors to his journal stressed their agency, contributions, accomplishments, and determination.[38]

Other articles published in *The Negro* highlighted the efforts of blacks to overcome slavery and postemancipation neoslavery, placing the burden of America's "race problem" squarely on the shoulders of whites, not blacks. In his exposé of "The Poor Whites of the South," "W. L. M." categorized mountain whites as dishonest, lazy, suspicious, and ignorant with no rightful claim to superiority over blacks. In articles Will's brothers—Benjamin Frank ("B. F.") Thomas and Walter S. Thomas—took whites to task as well. B. F. argued that while white industrial workers had the right to strike in order to gain better wages or self-government, they erred when they prevented others from working or destroyed property. He noted that blacks generally had steered clear of violent labor demonstrations and warned African American workers to guard their newfound labor opportunities by working within, not against, American capitalism. Labor radicalism, B. F. maintained, might compromise all that they had worked for. Walter criticized discriminatory black laws—barring mixed marriages and integrated schools—that remained on the books in Ohio, Indiana, Wisconsin, and other midwestern states. He interpreted these laws as evidence that the "blighting, withering curse of American slavery still clings, in a measure, to the negro, and cannot be lifted from him until the last vestige of obnoxious class legislation has been repealed."[39]

The Negro clearly bore Thomas's ideological and rhetorical imprint. His long, undisciplined articles restated his dog-eared arguments on the virtues for blacks of small farms, the benefits of industrial education, and the evils of sectarianism. But, significantly, in *The Negro* Thomas went beyond his usual catalog of black religious, educational, and social misdeeds and confronted contemporary white racism head on. Unlike his earlier writings, the articles in *The Negro* collectively assumed an advocacy role for blacks, interpreting them as victims whose plight had less to do with their own inferiority than with white racism.

For example, in his editorial "Notes" Will described the black man as "a patient, law-abiding citizen, eager to concede, willing to submit." In his articles he denounced Jim Crow segregation, proscription, lynching, the chain gang, and other forms of extralegal violence as "reprehensible crimes, to be condemned by all honest men, and suppressed by the government." In one piece he blasted Atticus G. Haygood's *Our Brother in Black: His Freedom and His Future* (1881) "as a truculent and vicious apology for race proscription and Southern domination." Blacks, Thomas insisted, did not favor separate churches because, as Haygood maintained, of their deficient morality, "but because caste shuts the door in the face of Christian fraternity." While Thomas identified certain race traits that set blacks apart from whites, he rejected theories that placed a ceiling on black advancement. It was proscription, Thomas said, not hereditary laws, that blocked black progress. Armed with "a practical English education," "thorough industrial training in honest work," and the ballot, blacks could compete with any race. Their future was bright, he insisted. The prospects for his journal, however, were not. *The Negro* ceased publication in December 1886, according to the *New York Freeman*, "for want of means to carry on the work." [40]

Despite *The Negro*'s demise, Thomas's publications in the late 1880s and early 1890s, including his articles in this journal, signaled a significant shift in both his racial ideology and his approach to social reform. Whereas Thomas's statements as recently as 1885 had implied that blacks were inherently inferior to whites, he increasingly came to consider blacks neither innately vicious nor depraved. Rather, their behavior resulted from a social and economic heritage grounded in slavery and perpetuated by neoslavery. The federal government, he argued, by virtue of the Negro's role in emancipation and Reconstruction, had the responsibility of righting history's wrongs. It should assist blacks in gaining access to the factors of production, supervise elections in the South, and limit congressional representation of states that trampled upon black civil and political rights. By the late 1880s, the tone of Will's writings also became less arrogant, smug, and intolerant of blacks than heretofore. Bit by bit his articles radiated optimism for the future of the race and cried out for black assertiveness. As Thomas's criticisms of the race became more nuanced, his arguments assumed a more constructive and hopeful tone. He increasingly accentuated positive qualities in blacks, defended African Americans from unfair attacks, held whites responsible for wanton discrimination and proscription, and assumed that blacks would blend into the warp and woof of American life. Education and economic success, he reasoned, ultimately held the key to racial harmony.[41]

Writing in 1888 in the A.M.E. *Church Review,* for example, Thomas implored the federal government not only to provide "seed" money and land for the landless but to offer economic stimulation and incentives for blacks engaged in southern agriculture as well. Thomas hoped that in the long run, black labor would gain "a partial ownership in production, thus joining capital and labor in confidential bonds of harmony." Once this was established, he said, "every grade of labor will fraternize with any race or creed." A year later Thomas responded boldly to charges that black men were rapists. Such accusations, he insisted, largely were fabrications by white southern women who willingly had been involved in sexual relationships with black men. The black man, he insisted, "is not a criminal reprobate bent on corrupting virtuous womanhood, but rather a long-suffering victim of caste greed and white domination, and, though perfect in neither manner nor morals, he is at worst only the product of his environment and the representative of his surroundings."[42]

In 1889 Thomas urged black men at long last to assert themselves, to use "brute force" if necessary, to protect themselves and their families from white abuse. In a remarkable passage, especially given Will's later writings and his reputation as the most heinous of "black" Negrophobes, he insisted that

> in the present state of Southern disorder and lawlessness, the shot-gun, in the hands of a fearless Negro, has no superior as a weapon of defense or as a powerful persuader to right-doing; and . . . every white contaminator of moral rectitude and lawless iniquity, remorselessly shot down at the feet of his Negro victim, is a praiseworthy and righteous vindication of Negro manhood. If there shall ever come to the race an intelligent and honorable career, it will be the product of brave, manly, wise action . . . and the time has come . . . [for] forcible and effectual resistance to these wrongs.

Thomas urged blacks to take whatever steps necessary to forge "a conscious Negro manhood" and "a considerate and decent respect for Negro womanhood." Despite all the contemporary discourse over race, he concluded that "qualities of character, and not color and features, are the determinate traits of superior and inferior characteristic distinction."[43]

According to historian David Wood Wills, Thomas's articles in the A.M.E. *Church Review* "represented the most thorough and sophisticated analysis of the economic situation of black America carried by the *Review* during this entire period." Thomas's analyses, Wills argues, "moved well beyond exhortations to individual diligence and showed a serious interest in fundamental economic reform." Historians, however, have ignored Thomas's early writings, identifying him only with the Negrophobic *The American Negro* because they simply are unfamiliar with the breadth and depth of his early publications. In many references to his work, Thomas's contemporaries ranked him among the more critical, insightful African American commentators on the "Negro problem."[44]

Thomas's first book, *Land and Education: A Critical and Practical Discussion of the Mental and Physical Needs of the Freedmen* (1890), built upon his early writing and remains his most constructive, important work on the late-nineteenth-century race problem. Like his many obscure articles, this seventy-one-page book, published in Boston, was generally ignored by his contemporaries and by later scholars who have gauged Thomas's racial thought exclusively on *The American Negro*. In contrast to that book, in *Land and Education* Thomas wrote sympathetically about the "freedmen" (a term he insisted on using three decades following Appomattox) and proffered solutions to their problems based allegedly on his years of life and labor among them. Upon its publication, Will sent a copy of *Land and Education* to ex-President Rutherford B. Hayes, the first president of the Board of Trustees of the John F. Slater Fund, hopeful that Hayes might put some of his ideas into practice. Thomas also sought Hayes's assistance in securing an invitation to speak on the race problem at a future Mohonk Conference on the Negro Question, which had omitted African American participants at its meetings in 1890 and 1891.[45]

In *Land and Education* Thomas presented the most lucid, coherent, positive, and forward-looking arguments of his entire career as a student of the "Negro problem." Though he noted negative qualities in black southerners, describing them, for example, as "a race of overgrown untutored children, rash, impetuous, wanting in self-control," Thomas suggested that these were temporary characteristics, correctable under "wholesome restraints." He concluded that what whites defined as negative racial traits or differences were based principally upon environmental factors, not forces of heredity. "It is obviously true," he declared, "that neither color or race creates distinctions in mental capacity." This is a remarkable statement given the abundance of contemporary heredity theory and the arguments of Thomas's later book. "Neither," he added, cognizant of his own light skin, "should it be said that shades of color in the same race impose any hindrance or create exceptional aptitude in mental acquirement."[46]

Focusing fully and clearly for the first time in print on the meaning of "race," Thomas said "the tints of variegation make not the slightest difference in a common humanity, that neither color, hair, form nor features among Negroes nor any other people creates exceptional advantages nor impose irrevocable drawbacks to personal achievements." "The standards of civilization," he added, "are never absolute but relative measurements." Since emancipation, he remarked, black southerners were "cruelly beset with hampering obstructions . . . increased by the augmented enforcement of caste and a deliberate and masterful political domination." Challenging glib assertions of black inferiority, Thomas observed in blacks "as much of the sacredness of living, as scrupulous regard for truth and virginal honor, as keen an appreciation . . . of the practice of Christian integrity . . . as characterizes the more pretentious white race." "The Negro," Will explained, "speaks for himself, not in the disingenuous pleading of a domestic mendicant or alien protege, but as a man fully conscious of his fellowship of aims and interests in the body politic in common with all other right-minded citizens." Significantly, in *Land and Education* Thomas urged blacks to cultivate "race pride"—"self-respect, a sense of personal dignity, a consciousness that no inherent ineradicable disability is imposed by the accident of birth and color."[47]

In his first book Thomas expanded upon his earlier articles and provided a lengthy analysis of "race" and labor relations in the South at the fin de siècle. In his view, previous attempts by whites to assist the freedpeople came up short. He believed that most whites failed to grasp the freedpeople's own efforts to overcome the harmful effects of racism. "In the natural struggle for industrial supremacy silently going on," he wrote,

the Negro is pushing to the front with a steadiness and insistence, inconceivable to those who only know him as an illiterate, menial and penniless serf, which is all the more remarkable, considering his almost insuperable obstacles and barren resources. It is my deliberate judgment that the strife for possession and permanent occupation of the south, in the future, will more and more rest with northern white emigrants and southern negroes, with the odds at its final adjustment largely in favor of the latter people, though the southern land problem may precipitate a crisis of transcendent gravity. An agrarian revolution is not improbable. It is inevitable that a change of one kind or another must come, in a system of land ownership which neither by lease or sale permits occupation, and viciously withholds from tillage the larger area of the soil.

Clearly sympathetic to black laborers at a time of rising agrarian dissatisfaction and business consolidation, Thomas argued that before blacks could lift themselves up to respectability, they desperately required an economic boost.[48]

In *Land and Education* Thomas reiterated his familiar, and all too simplistic, argument that farms and industrial schools would solve the multilayered economic and social problems that confronted late-nineteenth-century black southerners. As before, he provided detailed procedures for leasing then selling land to blacks and underscored the importance of establishing nonsectarian schools to provide manual training. Deeply concerned over the "industrial bondage" experienced by the freedmen, Thomas sought practical solutions to circumstances that kept millions impoverished, in "daily bondage" to white capitalists. In his opinion, the intervention of the federal government, along with aid from northern philanthropists and industrialists, could resolve the blacks' complex social and economic plight.[49]

Interpreting the post–Civil War years as a period of adjustment for the ex-slaves, Thomas strongly defended blacks from white critics and sharply denounced whites, especially the planters, for their treatment of the freedpeople. In a statement diametrically opposite to what he would later write in *The American Negro,* he declared that "human nature is essentially the same in all races; that what is predictable in one people may be affirmed of all when exposed to the same conditions of life." Thomas went on to emphasize "that characteristic modifications are liable to occur in the same race under different influences and epochs." Beyond that, he added that the Negro "has no greater virtues nor grosser vices than are common to other races of mankind, and like them in manhood, true and good, intelligent and upright and contributing in proportion to means and opportunity his full share of genius and thrift to national progress." He argued that just as nations progressed and retrogressed over time, so too did races. White southerners, however, had refused to accept black people's gradual evolution. This, Thomas regretted, was the source of the contemporary "Negro problem."[50]

On the day-to-day level, Thomas charged, white planters were "guilty of gross injustice in dealing with free labor." They regularly cheated blacks out of their wages, discharged them at will, and balanced accounts fraudulently in order to keep their laborers in a state of constant debt. Labor relations in the South, according to Thomas, included "nearly all the hard conditions of slavery with none of its protection and providence. All over the south the ambition and purpose to dominate the Negroes by personal control, is paramount and universal, and who are bound to a state of industrial servitude from which there is apparently no escape." Kept ignorant and helpless, the South's blacks were "fleeced on all sides, while enormous profits are made by the merchants and planters who are in collusion to keep the Negroes underneath." Thomas in fact considered the New South's sharecropping and farm tenantry systems more profitable to whites and more harmful to blacks than the old system of slavery. Like the slaveholders, New South planters retained "as absolute command of the person and movements of the freed people as before their emancipation." But under the new system of labor exploitation whites were "relieved of the expense of original purchase and that subsequent maintenance of Negro labor which the slave period imposed."[51]

Throughout *Land and Education* Thomas emphasized the economic dependence and concomitant backwardness of black southerners. Under the control of a white planter, he wrote, the African American laborer was perpetually "a pitiable and helpless victim of circumstances." As a result of this helplessness, southern blacks were incapable of self-motivation, thriftiness, or applied discipline. Landless and uneducated, they were, Thomas thought, neither shrewd nor practical. He singled out what he judged to be the egregiously lax work ethic of black females, stating that "disciplinary education" would be especially effective in making them appreciate the "nobility of labor" and would "forever eliminate that sensuous bondage which so largely dominates the entire race." After years of studying the freedpeople, Thomas believed that economic and social servility had stunted their intellectual and moral development. At the same time, he categorized the freedmen as culturally inferior to northern blacks, especially to mulattoes like himself, because of their limited exposure to the "invigorating" influences of white society. For Thomas, the ex-slaves represented "an undeveloped primitive race variety of virile stock" which, though backward, brimmed with considerable potential for advancement.[52]

Though in 1901 W. E. B. Du Bois remarked that upon publication, *Land and Education* appeared "unnoticed from the press," a section of the book in fact was reprinted in the A.M.E. *Church Review* and it received at least two positive notices. A reviewer in *Our Day*, a reform journal, contrasted Thomas's book favorably with Philip Alexander Bruce's pessimistic and racist *The Plantation Negro as a Freeman* (1889). Bruce, the reviewer complained, emphasized the black race's faults, ignored its merits, promoted racial prejudice, and excused the denial of African American civil and political rights by whites. Thomas, in contrast, espoused "the case of his race at its best." The critic judged Thomas as "thoughtful and shrewd" as Bruce and considered Thomas's intellect "quite equal to that of the white" author. He complimented Thomas's chief recommendations and acknowledged that

Thomas was realistic enough to recognize the difficulties of integrating federal aid, northern philanthropy, and self-help in order to provide land and education for the freedpeople. Writing in T. Thomas Fortune's *New York Age,* columnist W. H. A. Moore remarked that "aside from a certain ponderousness of style," Thomas's *Land and Education* was "a thoughtful and worthy contribution to the race literature of the day." It was, Moore added, "in fact one of the few by men of the race worth a second perusal."[53]

Following publication of *Land and Education,* Thomas took steps to give Americans "a second perusal" of his land reform program. For years he had considered land reform a panacea, positioning it at the center of his many proposed solutions for the race problem. Once black southerners controlled land, he reasoned, they could rid themselves of slavery's legacy and engage with their former masters from a position of strength. Though he had already published several land reform schemes, in 1890 Thomas took another tack—drafting "A Bill to establish industrial training schools and to provide land for Negroes to be held under lease with privilege of subsequent purchase" for the U.S. Congress. Before its submission to the House of Representatives, the *Christian Recorder* summarized his plan and declared that "there are many good points to the bill." On July 7, 1890, Representative William Cogswell (1838–95), a Republican from Salem, Massachusetts, formally introduced it on Thomas's behalf before the first session of the 51st Congress. In Thomas's opinion, the bill represented "the most sensible and practical measure of relief for the Freedmen and the adjustment of race problems which has been heretofore suggested." He solicited votes from congressmen, reminding them that "the Negroes of the South will be grateful for" their support. There was "no more efficient method for the uplifting of the southern freedmen," Will informed former President Hayes.[54]

Thomas's bill called for the establishment of a special commission, the Freedmen's Board of Industrial Training, to be under the overall control of the Interior Department and under the immediate oversight of the National Bureau of Education. Funded by a federal appropriation of $1 million, this commission was to purchase 6,400 acres of arable land in each of the former Confederate states with the exception of Florida. This property was to be subdivided into one hundred sixty-acre lots, then leased to one hundred "selected and approved" African American families. Though Thomas failed to mention how the families would be chosen, he specified that they would pay an annual rent of five bales of cotton. In order to "test the capacity and integrity of such tenants," they also would be subject to a two-year probationary period.[55]

The tenants, essentially segregated from whites, would farm the land using implements and livestock from surplus government stock. Thomas assumed that isolating a small number of African American families on farms would transform them into responsible, law-abiding citizens. He believed that a highly structured, supervised environment best suited the freedpeople and that such an arrangement would reduce racial tensions by keeping these families under tight control. He planned that all expenses—including the cost of housing—were to be recouped by the sale of the crops produced by the tenants. He even specified the type and amount of crops to be planted: "at least fifteen acres each in corn and cotton, ten acres in peas, potatoes and other edibles." If the tenants met all conditions during the probationary period, Thomas said, they would be granted a leasehold for a three-year term. After this period they could purchase the land from the government for an annual payment of five bales of cotton. The Board of Commissioners, however, would retain strict control over the land and its tenants until they had met all financial obligations.[56]

Under Thomas's bill the remaining four hundred acres of land would be used for educational facilities for children between the ages of six and sixteen. They would be required to attend classes for eight months of the year. In addition to reading, writing, arithmetic, and history, their studies would include industrial training for both sexes. This, according to Thomas, guaranteed "a practical knowledge of local agriculture," instruction in the use of tools for males and training in domestic service for females. Again, Thomas would empower the federal government with oversight, stipulating that special agents of the Treasury Department should conduct semiannual inspections to report on the "management and usefulness of schools, condition and fidelity of tenants, and all local agents of the Government created by this Act." Government supervision lay at the core of his plan. It basically required the tenants to be dependent on the government for at least ten years before actually owning any land. Cogswell read the bill, H.R. 11271, twice on the floor of Congress, and it then was referred to the House of Representative's Committee on Education. The bill eventually died.[57]

Undeterred, Thomas proposed another plan, one that he had shared with former President Hayes as early as June 1890. According to Thomas, the proposal outlined "the needs and wants of the colored race in a manner not heretofore emphasized." By April 1891, he had redrafted the plan, including endorsements from Hayes, former General Edward W. Hinks (under whom Thomas had served in Virginia in 1864), Edward Atkinson (Massachusetts textile manufacturer, economist, and reformer), and S. E. Peabody (president of Boston's American Loan and Trust Company). Thomas organized this land reform program under what he termed the Fountain Land and Education Fund (FLEF). In his request for a loan of one thousand dollars from the Slater Fund, Thomas assured Hayes that the plan represented "the most important step in negro education" yet attempted.[58]

This plan essentially was a privately financed and supervised version of the congressional bill Thomas had drafted a year earlier. He proposed that the FLEF should secure 12,000 acres of land for $23,000 in Camden County, North Carolina (across Albemarle Sound from Elizabeth City), divide the land into 300 farms, and lease it to 300 tenants selected from "trustworthy industrious negro families." They would raise crops for their subsistence and pay rent to the trustees. Thomas specified that the tenants were to build their own cabins from timber on the land and supply themselves with mules and implements. Because he believed that Camden County possessed ideal farming conditions, Will wrote confidently that the tenants would be able to recoup the original cost of the enterprise within three years. He no doubt recalled marching through this largely isolated, black-populated section of North Carolina with the 5th USCT during General Edward A. Wild's December 1863 raid.[59]

Thomas stated that the purpose of this plan was to provide the freedmen with the opportunity to purchase property. "The ownership of land," he explained, "lies at the root of any movement for the successful uplifting of the freedmen, and is the desire and aim of every thrifty negro." When the tenants had "proven their integrity and fitness to become landowners," the FLEF would sell each family a forty-acre homestead. In addition, Thomas specified that several hundred acres of the land would be set aside for a school, identical in function and purpose to the school he had proposed in H.R. 11271. In his FLEF plan, however, Will suggested that the school be self-supporting, financed by tuition charges and by products made by the students. The object of this plan, he wrote, would be "to introduce the most rational methods of negro culture, and practically demonstrate the feasibility of making self-supporting the existing negro institutions of the South." Though Thomas never addressed how his proposal would secure equal rights for blacks, he nonetheless concluded that his land and education scheme held the key to unlocking the South's race problem. Most important, he believed that the plan was based upon the principle of "self-help." It would encourage "habits of industry, forethought, and prudence," while contributing neither to "loss of self-respect" nor "beneficent pauperism" among the freedmen.[60]

By emphasizing self-help, Thomas's FLEF proposal broke with the paternalistic supervision of the freedpeople that he earlier had promoted in H.R. 11271. Most likely he tailored his proposals to meet the expectations of the different audiences that he addressed. In any case, both plans emphasized the need to change the behavior of the freedmen and women, not the racism of white southerners. Thomas's 1891 proposal suggested that the race problem could be solved by encouraging African Americans to become self-supporting landowners, that they could be "trained in unity of purpose" to become "contented colored producers" and, in his words, "worthy American citizens." In his view, the moral character of the freedpeople was linked directly to their economic position. His land and education reform plans reflected Thomas's belief that land ownership, combined with educational opportunity, would transform the ex-slaves from what he considered to be their degraded moral and social status into model citizens. They also suggest his vision and initiative in giving the freedmen and women an economic foothold to escape debt peonage.[61]

Despite his attempts to influence Hayes and the board of the Slater Fund, Thomas's 1891 land reform program, like his proposed congressional bill, fell on deaf ears. No record exists of the Slater Fund's loaning money to the FLEF. In fact, by September of that year Thomas had abandoned the project and, convinced that he had escaped the São Paulo de Luanda episode with his reputation unscathed, renewed his attempt to secure a diplomatic appointment—this time as consul to Santo Domingo. Much as before, he waved the "bloody shirt," underscoring his sacrifices for the Union and Hayes's party, reminding the former president that "I lost my right arm during the war and that I have served my race and the Republican party faithfully since, especially so in South Carolina in 1876." Hayes ignored Thomas's request.[62]

Much like the Civil War years, the 1890s served as a crucial defining moment for Will Thomas. After failing to fund his land reform plans he returned to the South, settling in 1890 in South Carolina as financial agent for Lincoln Institute, an A.M.E. school in Lincolnville, a railroad crossing about two miles from Summerville, twenty-two miles northwest of Charleston. Authorities in Newberry either never learned of Thomas's presence in the state or simply decided to ignore him. In any case, his tenure in Lincolnville was uneventful. The minister, editor, and later U.S. Congressman and A.M.E. Bishop Richard H. Cain established Lincolnville in 1871, purchasing plots of land and selling them as homesteads to blacks. Though Cain's settlement was mired in controversy (he allegedly sold the lots "before the previous owners foreclosed because he had failed to make the promised payments"), Lincolnville and Lincoln Institute nonetheless flourished in the early 1890s. While in South Carolina, Thomas raised money for Lincoln Institute and continued work on the "prolonged study of the race problems of the Southern States" that ultimately resulted in *The American Negro.* Meanwhile he also preached regularly to A.M.E. congregations in Charleston, where he reportedly was "greeted with packed houses of interested listeners."[63]

Typically, Will moved on, this time, however, with a new wife—Zenette, an African American woman from Ohio, twenty-six years his junior. No record exists whether Thomas and Martha ever divorced or what happened to their children in Pennsylvania. Similarly, little is known of Zenette's background. She apparently lived in Malden, Massachusetts, and met Will through activities of the A.M.E. Church in Chelsea, Massachusetts. Zenette was active in that congregation. Soon the two began traveling together. In August 1890, they were in Delaware, Ohio. Then Will and Zenette went to Charleston, South Carolina, where they stayed at the home of the city's leading A.M.E. clergyman, the Reverend L. R. Nichols of Emanuel A.M.E. Church. For approximately the next seven years the Thomases divided their time between Massachusetts and South Carolina. In an article published in the *Christian Recorder,* Zenette criticized Charleston's large African American population for its lack of ambition and its "willingness to remain in menial positions." The market existed, she said, for more black shopkeepers, and Zenette supposed that it was a lack of practical business experience that kept members of the race from establishing small businesses. She informed readers of the *Christian Recorder* that the South's race problem would be solved slowly but methodically by its African American clergymen. "I know that He whose word has gone forth, changed not; but," she asked, "couldn't we just kind of hurry matters up a little?" In 1893 the A.M.E. Tract and Bible Society published Zenette's advice on maintaining a Christian home. "Home life should be clean, healthful and sacred," she said. The undisputed head of the household, in her opinion, was the husband and father. He was to serve as "protector, friend and faithful teacher," an "example of manhood, truth, honor, integrity, industry and Christian virtue."[64]

Anyone familiar with Thomas's checkered past knew that he was the antithesis of Zenette's description of her ideal man. Nevertheless, in the early 1890s, he seemed on course to become one of the leading black experts on the "Negro problem," putting into practice the constructive spirit of *Land and Education.* In addition to traveling extensively throughout the South (venturing as far as Tyler, Texas), Thomas reestablished ties with the A.M.E. Church and befriended leading African Methodists. In 1891 he served as a lay delegate to the New England Conference of the A.M.E. Church and two years later wrote optimistically that in the future, the Negro could "stand as the best expression of Christianity and the truest embodiment of ethical perfection on the western hemisphere." In 1894 and 1896 he was selected a lay delegate to the denomination's General Conference. In the latter year Will and the Reverend William H. Thomas of Newport, Rhode Island (the two men frequently were confused in the black press—see appendix 1), representing the New England Conference, delivered papers at the A.M.E.'s Historic and Literary Congress of the First Episcopal District at Asbury Park, New Jersey. Thomas, listed on the program as the "Rev. Wm. Hannibal Thomas," read a paper entitled "Systematic Methods in Administrations and Finance." The other Thomas, "Rev. W. H. Thomas, D.D.," spoke on "Is the New Birth the Direct and Entirely the Work of the Holy Spirit, or May It Be the Result of Christian Education?" As the end of the century neared, Will contributed articles to the *Christian Recorder* in which he advocated centralization of A.M.E. Church offices, reform of its finances, and the importance of identifying new denominational leaders. Without mentioning Thomas by name, the editor chided him for "substituting theory for fact and misapplying zeal for knowledge in this and in other connections."[65]

At this time, in secular matters, Thomas communicated with Presidents Benjamin Harrison and William McKinley regarding patronage and with Booker T. Washington on matters pertaining to the race. In 1897 Thomas urged Washington to establish "a department of Domestic Industry" at Tuskegee to train young African American women to work as domestic servants for northern whites. "The servant girl question," Thomas informed Washington, "is the problem of the North; at present, our families depend on foreign help, which is more or less incompetent and unreliable." He sought to replace immigrant laborers with "trained and honest colored girls." This proposal, Thomas explained, not only would equip black females for careers but also would generate additional income for Tuskegee.[66]

In the summer of 1897 Will and Zenette finally settled down, moving permanently from Bennington Street in Boston (where the city directory noted erroneously that he worked as a "foreman") to Everett, a working-class industrial town three miles north of Boston. Everett was known for producing iron goods, paints, chemicals, and shoes. The town contained 11,068 people in 1890, including seventy-two of African descent. Everett's small African American community supported the Zion Baptist Church and a Frederick

Douglass Club. In Everett the Thomases rented a house on Tileston Street, in the southwestern part of the town near the meandering tracks of the Penn Central Railroad. Blacks occupied most of this section of Everett, though Thomas's neighborhood was interspersed with pockets of Irish Catholic and eastern European Jewish immigrants. The 1900 federal census listed Thomas as a "magazine writer" and described both Will and Zenette as "black." [67]

Thomas experienced a dramatic metamorphosis during the 1890s. By the time he and Zenette established themselves in Everett, he already had made his final and most dramatic ideological shift as an interpreter of the "Negro problem." From the mid-1880s to the early 1890s, Thomas had evolved from a sharp-edged, generally intolerant critic of African Americans to a patient, constructive supporter of the race. In these years his commentary and land distribution schemes were largely mainstream and decidedly positive and upbeat. In the mid-1890s, however, he radically reversed himself. At once his tone became singular and intensely negative and morose.

In "Southern Barbarisms, White and Black," published in the *Quarterly Review of the United Brethren in Christ* in 1894, Thomas declared that "the degradation of Southern negro men and women has scarcely a parallel in modern civilization." The debasement of Negroes, he wrote, "is largely due to physical inheritance, a growing aversion to honest toil, the poverty of the wage-earners, a love of dress, a feverish craving for ostentatious display, in-bred social distinctions, a consciousness of white superiority and negro inferiority, local environment, and the domination of the white class." While he held whites largely responsible for what he considered the Negroes' "brutality or bestiality," Will blurred the lines between the environment of slavery and the Negroes' "hereditary debasement." "Rape and murder are the two crimes for which the negro has evinced a strong preference," Thomas charged. He categorically described all Negroes as immoral, their preachers as "incompetent," and their teachers as unfit to teach. He concluded that "the negro needs moral and manly training more than a knowledge of books. The penitentiaries are crowded with freedmen," he quipped, "who can read and write." [68]

In another article, a merciless condemnation of Negro Christianity, Thomas blamed the Negro church for instilling discipline "in neither the homes nor the churches of the race." Lacking spiritual guidance, he said, Negroes "never originated a feasible movement for promoting the welfare of humanity, nor made an important or valuable contribution to American life or morals." Thomas asserted that Negroes lacked "substantial virtues" and suffered from "characteristic defects, especially those appalling hereditary weaknesses . . . inherited ignorance, inherited laziness, inherited unbridled desire, inherited apathy and cowardice." He condemned Negro churches as "debauching rendezvous" and their prayer rooms as "seances of sensuous contortions and physical frenzies." Will called Negro preachers "shameless plagiarists and reckless mutilators." Utterly pessimistic and offering no evidence to support his allegations, he predicted that "with an execrable home-life . . . and the fact that no sub-consciousness of a higher life and nobler actions exists, the plight of the race is really pitiable." Negroes would continue to languish, he concluded, until "thoroughly disciplined under competent white supervision."[69]

Convinced that Negro men required special discipline and determined to halt lynchings in the South, in 1895 Thomas drafted another congressional bill—"An Act to prevent and punish Criminal Assaults on Female Chastity, and other Felonious Acts." The draft, he informed Albion W. Tourgée, a white carpetbagger who served as a judge in North Carolina during Reconstruction, was his "contribution toward a solution of our sectional disorders." The following year Tourgée unsuccessfully represented the plaintiffs in the landmark *Plessy v Ferguson* (1896) case before the U.S. Supreme Court, in which the Court approved the "separate but equal" concept, legitimizing de jure and de facto segregation of the races in the South.[70]

Thomas's bill proposed that men (presumably blacks) convicted of rape or attempted rape (presumably against whites) should be castrated. He reasoned that the crimes committed by the freedmen against white women ultimately undermined "the character of our civilization . . . and the stability of our institutions" because they led to acts of lawless violence by the white majority. Thomas believed that only a draconian penalty like castration would serve "to punish this class of criminals, to deter others from committing like crimes, and to remove all incitement to lawlessness consequent thereon." As with his other proposals, he provided elaborate details for the implementation of this bill. "Executive Surgical Bailiffs" in each judicial district, he explained, would perform the castrations.[71]

In addition to the punishments meted out to those convicted of "criminal assaults on female chastity," Thomas's plan also provided that strict legal action be imposed against those citizens (presumably whites) who took the law into their own hands to punish blacks charged, convicted, or acquitted of rape. The penalty for such an action would be imprisonment at hard labor for no less than five and no more than ten years, as well as deprivation of all citizenship rights. He added, however, that this penalty did not prohibit "any Father, Husband, Son or Brother" from using force to avert a rape or to arrest an individual accused of that crime.[72]

Thomas explained his motives for drafting the castration bill in a printed cover letter that he sent to Tourgée. One of the primary functions of the state, he argued, was "to mould public sentiment in favor of social order and legalized authority through enforcement of its formulated laws." The raping of white women and the lynching of black men had reached crisis proportions, he said. "The time has come for American patriotism to assert itself. Let us strip these issues of every element of sectional bias, partisan strife, or race prejudice, and unite in one supreme effort for the suppression and extermination of these great wrongs." He also implored federal and state governments to protect "personal chastity, and the promotion of community morality" on the one hand and to guard against "indiscriminate retaliation" on the other. The state was obliged to protect the rights of all citizens — even those accused of rape.[73]

For all its legalistic detail, Thomas's castration plan grossly indicted the mass of black men in the South as a "criminal," "vicious class." Accepting the rhetoric of white supremacists that gratuitously defined black men as rapists, he cited no statistics of alleged rapes and provided no rationale to justify such an extreme punishment as castration. To his mind the mass of freedmen simply were moral degenerates prone to acts of violent crime. Thomas justified castration of rapists based on what he considered to be the low moral character of the ex-slaves and their descendants. Much as he would describe their racial characteristics in *The American Negro,* he referred to the freedpeople's "lack of discipline of their moral faculties and physical passions," asserting that "all classes of them, are wanting in robust integrity and moral sobriety." He purported to have observed "the social characteristics of" the freedpeople closely for a quarter of a century.[74]

By 1895 Thomas already had distanced himself from "Negroes." Though he described himself as a person of color, he insisted

> I have not the least disposition to condone or extenuate their faults and follies; I am painfully aware . . . that they set no value on chastity, and are controlled wholly by impulsive desire. I know they have but slight knowledge of moral rectitude, and we all must deplore the fact, that during these years of freedom, no instituted agency has efficiently trained them either by precept or example, in the ethics of true morality, and . . . in the face of such conditions . . . some Negroes do so far abandon themselves to unbridled sexual laxity as to commit criminal assaults on the chastity of women.

While not excusing these alleged faults, Thomas nevertheless held the nation at large partly to blame for failing to provide the freedmen with proper moral guidance. Upon emancipation, he wrote, "we gave them physical freedom and mental follies, but scorned to teach them civil duties, or train them in social obligations." Though he presumed that castration would provide a sufficient deterrent to rape, Thomas never explained specifically how this penalty would bring about the "moral redemption" of the freedmen.[75]

Thomas's proposal to punish both rapists and lynch mobs was one of the most unusual approaches of his day for solving the South's race problem. It underscored his belief that Negroes were prone to acts of violence because of their stunted moral character, essentially accepting the racist assumptions of white lynch mobs. In promoting castration as an effective punishment, he hoped to dampen the rage of whites and to mute the possibility of lawless behavior on their part. Although his cover letter to Tourgée denounced the "class discrimination" associated with lynching, Thomas failed to address the sources of white racism that motivated mob group behavior. While he proposed relatively harsh penalties for whites convicted of lynching, Thomas was obviously more concerned with preserving law and order than with protecting the lives of the freedmen. Above all, he offered no explanation for how his castration proposal, or for that matter his earlier land reform plans, would resolve the serious social and economic problems that simmered beneath the surface of racial conflict in late-nineteenth-century America.

Though according to historian Leon F. Litwack, unusual "sadism and exhibitionism" characterized late-nineteenth-century racial violence, no one stepped forward to sponsor Thomas's castration bill in Congress, probably because it was too extreme for genteel racists. Early in the new century, however, editor John Temple Graves of the *Atlanta Constitution* proposed that castrating and branding an "R" on the cheeks of black rapists would prove a more effective deterrent than lynching. Given the brutalities meted out to blacks in these years, "surgical castration" certainly was not too radical for the likes of white supremacists who mobbed, lynched, and then mutilated blacks in rituals of hate. In 1901 Thomas asserted that his castration proposal had "received the approval of many of the leading publicists of the country."[76]

To be sure, the nineties were years of volatile economic and social change. The decade's many crises—the Panic of 1893, vitriolic national debates on the money question, protective tariffs, labor and agrarian discontent, urbanization, imperialism, social reform, immigration, nativism, disfranchisement, lynching, segregation—left many Americans searching for meaning in an increasingly complex and insecure world. Though Thomas never commented on the forces that led him to become mercilessly critical of his race, his language in the 1890s suggested that he no longer considered himself a Negro. His chorus of anti-Negro rhetoric became increasingly shrill, reaching a crescendo in 1901 when he published *The American Negro.* By then Thomas blamed Negroes for contemporary racial tensions and identified not with Negroes but instead with what he considered the separate and superior mulatto racial classification. Thomas, like Georgia politician Tom Watson, would be accused of hypocrisy for his radical racial about-face and can accurately be described as a "reformer-gone-bad."[77]

A contributing factor in Thomas's reversal was the excruciating physical pain that he experienced in these years resulting from his Civil War amputation. Throughout his long life Will often complained of extreme pain and other problems with his stump that, he asserted, made him unable to wear a prosthesis. In 1887, for example, he submitted a claim for an increase in his pension based on the argument that his "stump is too short to wear an artificial arm." A board of three doctors in Boston observed that the sinew on his right arm had adhered to the bone and the muscles of the stump had atrophied. They maintained, however, that he could utilize a prosthesis just "as much as anyone when the amputation is above the elbow joint." Similar appeals by Thomas, in which he claimed "habitual soreness," a rash from use of a prosthesis, an inability to lie on his right side and to perform manual labor, similarly were rejected in 1904 and in 1909. Thomas suffered not only persistent soreness but also paralysis of his left hand and wrist and other ailments, possibly from various neurological syndromes such as neuralgia, chorea, neuritis, and sclerosis that affect stumps following amputation. Thomas's amputation was a severe adult physical trauma that likely reawakened earlier childhood psychical traumas and certainly worked in tandem with traumas associated with personal setbacks that he associated with white racism such as the 1859 incident at Otterbein University and his rejection by the U.S. Army in 1861. This combination of physical and psychical traumas fostered Thomas's pessimism and the venomous anti-Negro racial ideology he espoused in the late 1890s.[78]

Ironically, in these years both Thomas's professional and domestic life seemed decidedly on track. Despite his many past indiscretions and much self-destructive behavior, Will had emerged as a recognized, albeit minor, figure among African Methodists. He published regularly in religious journals, newspapers, and magazines and established himself as a man with a serious mind. At long last he sustained a degree of professional success without sabotaging himself. He had also found a supportive and intellectually compatible partner. Yet as the sun set on the nineteenth century, the cloud of negativism hanging over Thomas's world darkened.

As the new century dawned, Thomas's attitudes toward Negroes had hardened. Pessimistic, direful, and insular, he became obsessed with criticizing them. He did so relentlessly and in the harshest of terms. Whatever the cause of his newfound pessimism, on the eve of publishing *The American Negro,* Thomas already had described the symptoms of the "Negro problem," diagnosed its cause, and prescribed its solution. By 1900 he was less willing than before to hold slavery and environmental factors accountable for the conditions of black life. Thomas, like white Negrophobes in the age of Jim Crow, concluded that the Negro *was* the problem after all. At midlife, after five decades of being identified with Negroes, Thomas broke with the race, convinced that the only solution to the "Negro problem" was the wholesale transformation of blacks. In 1901, in *The American Negro,* he drove home this argument with relentless hyperbole. This book, his magnum opus, made him infamous.

CHAPTER SIX

Author of *The American Negro*

URING THE TUMULTUOUS 1890S, Will Thomas's racial views became severe and bitter, approaching those of the most rancorous white Negrophobes. The period was the "nadir" of race relations in American history. "Between 1890 and 1917," historian Leon F. Litwack writes, "to enforce deference and submission to whites, some two to three black Southerners were hanged, burned at the stake, or quietly murdered every week. That estimate," Litwack adds, "is conservative." Since Reconstruction, white southerners had struggled with reestablishing and then maintaining racial control over blacks. By the 1890s, even though gratuitous, random acts of violence kept black southerners in check, white legislators in every southern state nevertheless felt compelled to transform de facto segregationist practices into rigid de jure segregationist laws. Separate and unequal—backed by the constant threat of racial violence—character-ized the Jim Crow South and set a discordant tone for race relations through-out the United States. North and South, the nation was obsessed with race and racial distinctions. Rigid divisions between whites and blacks left little social space for mulattoes—men and women caught between racial worlds.[1]

Though ensconced hundreds of miles away in Everett, Massachusetts, Thomas followed conditions in the South closely. For years he had envi-sioned himself as a reformer, an uplifter, but few had paid attention to his grandiose schemes, whether to improve the A.M.E. Church and black schools, to restructure southern agricultural society, or to prevent lynchings. His most extreme views appeared in the *Quarterly Review of the United Brethren in Christ,* an obscure church publication with a limited readership. The hell-ish racial discord of the 1890s exacerbated Will's frustrations, empowering him to launch his strongest, most determined reform campaign through the pages of *The American Negro*. In this book Thomas wanted to do two things.

First, he was determined to prove, before a national audience, that Negroes were biologically and culturally inferior to whites. Assuming the role of expert advisor, he would argue that without immediate action, blacks either would be exterminated by whites or would destroy themselves. After establishing that Negroes were the source of the "Negro problem," he then would propose his own solutions for the salvation of the Negro, the South, and the nation. In his mind, he assumed the role of Joshua, leading the race across the metaphorical River Jordan and out of "industrial servitude."[2]

Second, Thomas had a personal score to settle with Negroes. Through the years he had distanced himself from the race, yet by law, custom, and contemporary ethnology the light-skinned Thomas was still considered a Negro. Frustrated and angry, he might conceivably have asked: "Can the Ethiopian change his skin, or the leopard his spots? then may ye also do good, that are accustomed to do evil" (Jeremiah 13:23). The racial milieu of the day led Thomas to respond negatively. By 1900 "people biologically black in any degree," historian Joel Williamson has explained, "could not openly aspire to whiteness," though whites "could easily descend into blackness" because of their behavior. Despite his efforts, Jim Crow America would not allow Thomas to become "behaviorally white." This was the essence of his inner turmoil.[3]

In his heart and mind Will felt that he was nothing like the blacks he had studied so minutely and had come to disdain. Not surprisingly, then, when writing about Negroes after the mid-1890s, Thomas's language became blunt, numb, and unfeeling. The hopeless tone of his 1894 "Southern Barbarisms, White and Black" and his 1897 "Characteristics of Negro Christianity" signified the sad bitterness of his recognition that he no longer considered himself a Negro and was trying to sever his ties with the race. In *The American Negro*, published in 1901, Thomas described the Negro not as a person, but rather as an anthropological "type of humanity." Wallowing in self-pity, he blamed blacks for his identification as a Negro and for what he considered his life of missed opportunities and marginalization. His pent-up anger over his racial identity erupted in *The American Negro*.[4]

In these years Thomas joined the ranks of what Williamson has termed the racial "Radicals," a small but powerful and vocal extremist wing of whites who raised the frightening specter of savage blacks unrestrained by the discipline of slavery. Radicals pointed to what they perceived as the retrogression of the freedmen toward savagery and bestiality. They predicted ultimate racial extinction, perhaps a race war. In order to prevent racial contamination and social chaos, such Radicals as politicians Benjamin R. Tillman and James K. Vardaman, and the novelist Thomas Dixon Jr. proposed to control, contain, and quarantine the black population. Theirs was a rage for order. In 1901 Thomas shared their fury, manned their lines, and all but carried their colors.[5]

But whereas Tillman, Vardaman, Dixon, and other Radicals feared African Americans, Thomas's case was different. By 1901, after years of identifying with Negroes, he concluded that the race was hopelessly inferior and divorced himself from it. In *The American Negro,* written in the guise of a self-help manual for the group he came to despise, Thomas not only cried out for personal recognition but, more important, sought a means to inform whites that not all persons of African descent, most notably William Hannibal Thomas, were Negroes.

Though in *The American Negro* Thomas almost never mentioned mulattoes per se, they nonetheless haunt every line and occupy every page. After 1900 white Americans increasingly perceived black Americans as "an undifferentiated mass of inferior beings," but in *The American Negro* Thomas identified behaviorally and culturally, though not economically or socially, with what historian Willard B. Gatewood has described as America's mulatto "aristocrats of color." Like members of the light-skinned elite, Thomas assumed a leadership role, determined to teach the black masses to behave more like the "best people" of their race. He did so, however, at a time when the status and identity of mulattoes were in serious flux. After the 1920 census the U.S. government no longer distinguished between Negroes and mulattoes. As Williamson suggests, "insofar as the Bureau of the Census was concerned," thereafter "all Negroes did look alike." Threatened by the specter of racial mixing and its implications for racial purity, white Americans, especially white southerners, denied the "mulatto" nature of American culture. This was the tide that Thomas resisted. *The American Negro* signaled his clarion call for the recognition of a respectable racial category positioned in that contested terrain, the tan world between white and black. In the process, he contributed to the growing racial prejudice in America and the relegation of blacks to an inferior status.[6]

Though Thomas insisted that he had completed *The American Negro* years before 1901, as early as 1884, this claim is hard to reconcile given his more balanced, optimistic, and judicious earlier publications, most notably *Land and Education,* published in 1890. In any case, Thomas explained that because he was unable to secure a publisher in the 1880s, he continued to observe, ruminate, research, and write about the condition of the "freed-men," a term he employed interchangeably with "negroes." In *The American Negro* Will commented on his decision not to document his sources. "It was not deemed necessary," he said, "to the verification of our statements . . . either as to person or act. Such disclosures could serve no useful end; be-sides, the characteristic data of which we have made use is everywhere pres-ent in the negro people, and readily accessible to the observant public." Some years later Thomas explained to Theodore D. Jervey, a conservative Charleston attorney and author, his method of writing: "I write mainly from memory, and as I concern myself only with significant facts, once I establish their validity, I frequently lose trace of their source." After his book's release in January 1901, scores of angry readers, black and white, challenged the "validity" of his "facts" and questioned his sweeping denunciation of Ne-groes. The publishing history of *The American Negro* sheds light on how the controversial book came into being.[7]

No documentary record exists of Will's attempting to publish *The Ameri-can Negro* until 1899, when he and Zenette were living on Tileston Street in Everett. Thomas first approached the Macmillan Company on Septem-ber 22, asking if the press, one of the most distinguished publishers on either side of the Atlantic, might consider his book manuscript, "The American Negro: What he is, What he was, and What he may become." This title was conspicuously similar to *The Negro: As He Was; As He Is; As He Will Be,* an obscure racist tract published by Mississippian Horace Smith Fulkerson in 1887. In any case, Thomas's massive manuscript contained twenty chapters and consisted of more than seven hundred typescript pages. He informed Macmillan that his particular interest was in the "several racial phases" that Negroes had experienced. Will claimed that the manuscript was written from "an original stand-point, in a vigorous spirit, but in a tone that is practical and helpful to all concerned." He considered chapters on "the Negro's char-acteristic traits, ethnic beliefs, social lapses," and "crimes and criminals" to be among the work's special strengths. The following day Macmillan asked Thomas to submit the manuscript, and he did so on September 25.[8]

Macmillan solicited referees for Thomas's manuscript quickly, first ap-proaching Columbia University's renowned sociologist, Professor Franklin H. Giddings (1855–1931). Giddings, a Connecticut native, was influenced strongly by Herbert Spencer's writings on social evolutionary development. Giddings established categories within which to analyze society, statistically and inductively, at one point proposing a systematization of the term "race."

He identified a psychological sense of group solidarity or kinship—"the consciousness of kind"—at the core of social relations. According to Giddings, this explained the racial struggle for existence.[9]

Though Giddings believed that American society was evolving in the direction of racial assimilation, he never addressed its implications, specifically how full social and political equality would be achieved. In 1896, in *The Principles of Sociology* (published by Macmillan), he declared that "mixed races, after natural selection has eliminated their weaklings, are taller, stronger, more prolific, and more adaptable than pure races." The Negro, however, when denied "the support of stronger races . . . relapses into savagery." A decade later Giddings remarked that "natural selection is as inevitable as birth and death. The unfit, the physiologically non-resistant, must perish, and doubtless Nietzsche is right in saying that it is true mercy to hasten their end." In short, like other white racist intellectuals at the turn of the century, Giddings believed in a racial hierarchy where the various races possessed different inherent abilities. As late as 1912, he judged the Fifteenth Amendment a mistake because it closed the door to gradual social change and left the South rife for race war. "It is possible to revolutionize institutions," Giddings wrote, "but it is hard to revolutionize habit."[10]

Though he reviewed manuscripts hurriedly, Giddings was far from an uncritical and unknowledgeable reader. For example, two weeks before Thomas submitted "The American Negro" to Macmillan, Giddings harshly evaluated South Carolinian William P. Calhoun's manuscript, "The Caucasian and the Negro," strongly urging Macmillan to reject the work. Giddings considered Calhoun's manuscript "rubbish of the worst description." He blasted the author for possessing "neither the knowledge nor the balance of mind, neither the sense of proportion nor the ability to write English necessary for the production of a book on this subject." Specifically, he judged Calhoun's chapter on the Negro's African background as exhibiting "an almost ludicrous ignorance of the elementary facts of ethnology. His account of efforts to educate the negro is not discussion but abuse and misinformation. His chapter on lynching is mainly a collection of southern yellow journal descriptions. . . . The book would have a real value . . . as a revelation of what is probably a common type of mind in the south, but it could not be published by a respectable house without explanations and apologies." Having only recently evaluated Calhoun's manuscript, Giddings promised to report on Thomas's manuscript within a week.[11]

Eight days later Giddings wrote a glowing reader's report on "The American Negro," enthusiastically recommending that Macmillan publish it. Giddings judged the manuscript "altogether one of the most extraordinary productions that I have ever examined," written by "a man whose own history is extraordinary." He described Thomas as a man of "narrow" education, but one who nonetheless was schooled thoroughly "in reality." Giddings continued:

> Written in the most admirable English, clearly and logically arranged, it is a record of thorough investigation and exhaustive knowledge of the subject. No such complete detailed information about the American Negro . . . has ever been given to the public from any source. As a sociological study it is one of the most valuable things to put in the hands of genuine students of american conditions that I know of. And as a book of interest to the general reader, it has qualities that will attract attention.

Giddings went so far as to praise Will as "unmistakably a scholar; and his book is a scholarly production." With extraordinary enthusiasm, Giddings remarked that "I know of nothing which . . . could do so much as to set the American people right as to the exact status of the Negro Problem in the South as the publication of this work." This was extraordinary praise, especially coming from one of America's foremost social scientists.[12]

On the same day Macmillan received Giddings's endorsement, George B. Brett (1858–1936), president of the company, offered Thomas a contract, requesting that the first two chapters—dealing with "the negro's ethnological and biological history"—be appraised by an expert, Professor William Z. Ripley (1867–1941) of the Massachusetts Institute of Technology. Brett, who in the 1890s transformed Macmillan into America's largest publisher, signed roughly six hundred new titles each year. Though generally prone to make hurried editorial decisions, in the case of Thomas's manuscript Brett wanted to be sure that these chapters were in line with "the latest scientific point of view." In addition, Brett informed Thomas, Macmillan hoped to contract with "some well known Englishman, such as perhaps Professor James Bryce, who has . . . an intimate knowledge of the negro question," to write an introduction that would boost sales of the book in Great Britain. Overjoyed, Thomas agreed to Brett's proposal and, two days later, signed a contract guaranteeing him a ten percent royalty on the retail price of each book sold. Brett meanwhile sent the chapters to Ripley, asking him to "tell us if there is anything in them which is questionable from the standpoint of the latest knowledge in ethnology and biology." Brett emphasized to Ripley that "we should not want to publish the book unless it is scientifically accurate in every respect."[13]

Ripley, born in Massachusetts, was a political economist by training but taught and wrote widely in economics, ethnology, and sociology. In 1899 he published *The Races of Europe: A Sociological Study,* an eclectic work that acknowledged some environmental influences on human physiology, but generally accepted European polygenist theories that races originated and evolved separately over time. According to George W. Stocking Jr., Ripley espoused a "professedly evolutionary, but in many respects rigidly typological approach to race." Racists and nativists welcomed Ripley's notion of static racial development and his dim view of racial mixing. For example, in *The Races of Europe* Ripley supported the argument that mulattoes were a weak hybrid, "sharing pathological predispositions of each of its parent stocks, while enjoying but imperfectly their several immunities." After the turn of the century he wrote that racial intermixture might possibly lead to a reversion to primitive types by blacks. The best hope for solving the "Negro problem," Ripley informed W. E. B. Du Bois, was in "industrial training" for the mass of black southerners.[14]

Ripley read Thomas's chapters within a week and, in stark contrast to Giddings, sent Brett a negative evaluation. Ripley said that even after he searched below Thomas's "stilted style and sometimes absurd phraseology," he found little of value in the manuscript. The chapters Ripley read had "no scientific value at all. . . . It is not only entirely irrelevant to the main subject matter, but also fantastically metaphysical." Ripley hoped that later chapters, if they contained "*concrete material*—not metaphysical padding," would be more valuable. Ripley conceded that Thomas's manuscript had the advantage that "the author is a *negro* writing about negroes." He admitted that Thomas "betrays in spots a peculiarly liberal mind toward his race problems (even acquiescing in the harmfulness of granting the suffrage after the war)." And Ripley predicted that if Thomas "ever gets down to the *plain facts* concerning the *negro* as he is, dropping matters of original creation and cosmic origins, you may discover material which would justify publication." Ripley was confident "that a future is open to a scientific book on this topic, written in freedom from social, religious and political bias." But he was quick to add that "This man [Thomas] of course cannot offer it."[15]

Late in 1899 Brett must have begun to realize that he possibly had acted too hastily in issuing Thomas a contract for "The American Negro." Macmillan Company's archives include, in addition to Giddings's and Ripley's readers' reports, a third evaluation of Thomas's manuscript. This unsigned report, probably written by one of the company's in-house editors, summarized the manuscript in one word: "worthless." The reader explained: "In the first place, it is one mass of verbiage, containing no statistics, no scientific grouping of facts. In the second place, it is simply one long abuse of the negroes, their lewdness, their ignorance, their brutishness. I do not see how it could be rewritten. It is simply rant, and rant that dwells preferably on indecency. It does not seem to me that you could publish it." Similarly, an undated in-house memorandum concerning "The American Negro" referred to Thomas's "brag and grandiose language," at one point commenting that his writing was in "bad taste." This critic described one chapter as "a worthless production" that "positively must be cut out." He appraised another chapter as neither original nor unusual in any way. The Macmillan Company thus had ample warning of the kinds of criticisms that awaited Thomas's published manuscript.[16]

Thomas, of course, knew nothing of these reports and, with a signed contract in hand, eagerly looked forward to the publication of his book as the new century began. Writing to Brett in January 1900, Thomas wanted to know the projected publication date and whether or not he could add notes to several chapters. He was surprised, however, when Brett informed him that publication would be delayed: the press still was waiting for an evaluation of the manuscript (which was *not* the case), and would require significant changes in the early chapters (which was accurate). Thomas was so impatient with the editorial process that without even being asked, he volunteered to drop the first two chapters, "Universal Biology" and "Physical Variation." Thomas admitted "the strength of this work lies in its practical treatment of complex subjects, and not in theoretical speculations." Unbeknown to him, however, Macmillan was beginning to have second thoughts about publishing his book at all.[17]

Late in January 1900, Brett informed Thomas that he was concerned with more than his opening chapters. Macmillan feared that his book might be considered "scandalous" and "libelous" and was uncertain how to proceed. Outraged, Thomas wrote Brett a blistering letter, arguing that the press had been less than candid and honest with him and apparently was reneging on its contract. On the issue of the book's possible "scandalous and libelous" character, Thomas, who had last practiced law in Reconstruction-era New-berry, South Carolina, informed Brett that legally "scandals and libels" involved individuals. He asked Brett if he realized "that impersonal statements and impersonal litigants have no legal status in our judiciaries?" Furthermore, he explained: "My manuscript discusses the characteristics of a race; in no instance are individuals the subject of comment; hence I am led to look upon its assumed scandalous and libelous character as a specious subterfuge, in fact, that is the only ground to take. Moreover, so thoroughly am I per-suaded of the soundness of this position, that I am perfectly willing to submit this question to the judgement of such jurists as Richard Olney, Moorfield Storey, and Winslow Warren." Having written this, Thomas immediately reversed himself and admitted that his chapter on "Social Lapses" might indeed fall into the category of "scandalous and libelous." In order to deter-mine its suitability, he urged Brett to consult with such respected contem-porary authorities on the "Negro problem" as Thomas Nelson Page, Philip Alexander Bruce, and John Temple Graves. "These reputable gentlemen," Thomas explained, "know the Negro as well as it is possible for white men to know him." If necessary to get the book into print, however, he volun-teered to drop the "Social Lapses" chapter.[18]

Annoyed by the confrontational and defensive tone of Thomas's response, Brett threatened not to publish the manuscript unless he accepted Macmil-lan's questions in the "spirit" in which they were sent. "There is no doubt in my mind," Brett said, "as to the value of the manuscript nor as to the correctness of our first reader's report." The publisher believed that the proj-ect "contains much valuable and interesting material that would be likely to interest a considerable public." But he remained uncertain whether the manuscript might be "scandalous and libelous," and asked Thomas to make numerous revisions. In addition to eliminating the second chapter, Brett urged him to delete the irrelevant "philosophical speculation" that marred the manuscript and to clarify his exposition throughout, substituting "for such words as 'cohabit' or 'copulate' the more generally understood terms of 'union' or 'marriage.'" Brett especially wanted Thomas to rid his manuscript of "fine writing"—the use of "difficult and complicated words, sometimes of doubtful meaning." The manuscript also suffered from needless repetition, Brett noted, urging Thomas to cut its length by one-half.[19]

Thomas spent the next five months (February to June 1900) revising "The American Negro." After Brett's frank response to his letter regarding the manuscript's possible "scandalous and libelous" material, Thomas proved completely agreeable and eager to work with Macmillan's editors. "I fear you greatly misapprehend me," Thomas informed Brett, probably fearful that the press would not publish his manuscript.

No person can be more grateful for friendly advice, or more heartily apprecia-tive of helpful suggestion than I. What I sought, was an explicit statement regarding the changes desired in my book, and now that I have it, rest assured, that I will revise this work to the best of my ability. My great regret, however, is that I did not have the benefit of these suggestions earlier. I make no attempt at "fine writing"; my physical condition renders writing of any kind difficult and painful, moreover this manuscript was prepared under conditions that few persons would care to undergo.

Upon finishing his revisions, Thomas asked Brett whether or not Bryce would contribute an introduction to his book. Thomas hinted that if Bryce elected not to do so, then Macmillan might ask either Nathaniel S. Shaler, dean of Harvard's Lawrence Scientific School, or the editor/essayist Charles Dudley Warner to write a foreword.[20]

Despite Thomas's revisions, in August 1900, Macmillan still considered "The American Negro" unprepared to go to press. Assuring Thomas that he was "more than ever convinced of the value of the manuscript," Brett asked his permission to hire an editor to prepare it for publication. Disappointed with yet another delay, Thomas agreed with Macmillan's proposal but warned Brett that "if your proposed revision contemplates the publication of a colorless namby pamby affair, it had better not be undertaken. For in that event, you will simply waste time and money in preparing something that the public do not want and will not have." Convinced that Macmillan was moving too slowly with his book, Thomas reluctantly permitted the new revisions, stipulating, however, "that no essential fact, statement, suggestion, or conclusion of mine, be omitted from the text." Brett assured him that with the exception of deleting his first three chapters, this round of emendations would be almost totally a "verbal revision."[21]

As the final editing process began, Thomas welcomed its "scholarly revision" and proposed deleting four of the original chapters: "Primitive Biology," "Racial Variation," "Chimerical Evangelasation," and "A Candid Summary." He insisted that the work should begin with "Alien Chattelism," which heretofore had served as chapter five. "The wool and web of my argument," he told Brett, "rests on what has been outlined in the chapters on Ancestral environment, Alien chattelism, and Decretal freedom. To leave these out and make Industrial bondage the opening chapter is wholly at variance with the title of the work." Thomas reminded Brett that "The American Negro" had "a deep and abiding purpose"—as "the forerunner of a movement that aims at the complete readjustment of the negro question." Brett complied with Will's request and "Alien Chattelism" appeared as chapter one. Macmillan's editing boiled the massive original manuscript down from twenty to fourteen chapters.[22]

During October and November 1900, Thomas read proof and, as his manuscript went to press, he made a positive impression on Macmillan's editors. One of them, for example, scribbled on a letter, "this shows the spirit with which Col. Thomas has worked." As he waited for the January 1901 publication of *The American Negro*, Thomas asked Brett for an advance of one hundred dollars on royalties to defray "obligations for typewriting and supplies." Brett refused, however, informing him that he could receive an advance only after the book was published. Somewhat embarrassed by his financial need and Brett's response, Thomas assured Brett that he had received money from another source and had met his outstanding debts. Whereas later critics would accuse Thomas of writing *The American Negro* in order to make money, he informed Brett "I have no idea that I shall realize any unusual sum out of this book. In fact it was not written with any expectation of profit. I believe however that you will be fully reimbursed for all outlays and that you will not regret its publication." Thomas even arranged to procure discounted copies of the book "at the best trade price" and later worked aggressively to sell them.[23]

Soon afterward, however, Thomas once again wrote Brett, requesting another advance of one hundred dollars. He informed Brett that though he had "an assured income," his military pension, he had incurred extra expenses and needed money immediately. So serious was the situation, he admitted, that he would send Brett his federal pension certificate "as additional security." Uncomfortable with Will's appeal for money, Brett again turned him down. The publisher wrote that because of "the hasty report of one of our readers we accepted . . . your work . . . before it was really ready to be sent to press. Luckily . . . we discovered the matters which have since been remedied, but the cost to us of doing [this] has been considerable." As a result of Giddings's quick reading of Thomas's manuscript, Macmillan had incurred between $300 and $400 in unanticipated editorial costs. Additionally, Brett feared that *The American Negro* would have limited sale. Serious books, he told Thomas, rarely sold many copies and, he added, "the better the books are, the smaller the sale usually."[24]

To promote *The American Negro*, Macmillan launched a national sales campaign. Prior to the book's publication, the *New York Daily Tribune*, quoting Macmillan's publicists, predicted that Thomas's work would become the "authoritative book on the American negro," and that it was only fitting that the author was a Negro. Summarizing the forthcoming book, the newspaper, which had once promoted the cause of black freedom and equality, explained that "Mr. Thomas frankly concedes the negro's inferiority and convincingly controverts the adequacy of the reformatory agencies already instituted" to elevate the race. Not only a critic of past policy, however, Thomas reportedly outlined his own steps for the Negro's elevation. The *Tribune* welcomed the appearance of *The American Negro,* especially at a time, it said, "when the vehemence of passion is being relaxed on both sides."[25]

Once the book appeared, Macmillan distributed fliers widely and ran display advertisements in New York and Boston newspapers. One circular contained Will's photograph, portraying a light-skinned, nearly bald man with bushy white hair above his ears and a full white mustache. His eyes, sunk deeply in dark sockets, were the most dominant feature. The promotional pieces included favorable blurbs drawn from advance newspaper reviews. To assist in selling his book, Will conducted what he called "a systematic canvas of the country," mailing out five hundred fliers. He also printed up business cards introducing himself as "Col. Wm. Hannibal Thomas, Author of *The American Negro.* The Macmillan Company, Publishers." After months of negotiating and revising, Will, like any author, proudly and eagerly awaited the arrival of his book.[26]

Thomas must have been pleased when he unpacked the box containing his advance author's copies of *The American Negro* in January 1901. Macmillan produced the 440-page book handsomely, binding it in attractive brown cloth, stamping the spine with gold letters, and adding top edge gilt. The book, which sold for two dollars, was on the same winter 1901 list as two distinguished Macmillan titles—the abridged edition of James Bryce's *The American Commonwealth* and Goldwin Smith's *The United States, An Outline of Political History, 1492–1871.* In terms of front matter, *The American Negro* contained no introduction, only a foreword by Thomas that included an incomplete and pompous autobiographical sketch and a rambling, prolix statement of purpose. Macmillan's editors obviously failed in significantly excising Will's book of what Professor Ripley had correctly termed his "stilted style and sometimes absurd phraseology." The narrative of the first fifty-eight years of Thomas's life conveniently left gaping holes in his biography, omitting, not surprisingly, details of his abrupt departure from Western Theological Seminary, his parting of the ways with Wilberforce and the Monongahela Circuit A.M.E. Church, and his criminal warrants in Atlanta and Newberry. Thomas purposely provided few details to chronicle his past.

But it was that history, decades of studying black southerners, Thomas said, that spirited him to write *The American Negro.* He believed that he was uniquely prepared to analyze the characteristics of the freedpeople and to lead racial reform, what he vaguely termed its "race awakening." Thomas in fact intended *The American Negro* as a primer for "race redemption." He hoped that his book would teach and inspire "all members of the race still fettered by ignorance or spiritual blindness" and empower them "to noble thoughts and deeds." Thomas dedicated it "to all American men and women of Negroid ancestry who have grown to the full stature of manhood and womanhood." This murky passage typified the ambiguous rhetoric that clouds *The American Negro*. Was the focus of his book "all" African Americans? Did Thomas employ the terms "manhood and womanhood" literally or metaphorically? From beginning to end, his stilted and cryptic language (Thomas wrote consistently in the first person plural) blurred his meaning, suggesting that he was either unclear or ambivalent or both about what he was trying to say. Incredibly, Professor John R. Commons, one of the Progressive era's leading reform economists, complimented *The American Negro*'s "entertaining literary style." [27]

Though he referred to "all" American Negroes in his dedication, Thomas generally excluded northern blacks from consideration in *The American Negro*. But when he mentioned black northerners, he tended to portray them in a more positive light than black former slaves. An Ohioan of free origins, he believed that many blacks north of the Mason-Dixon line possessed the self-motivation and desire for assimilation into white American culture that he had and desired all Negroes to have. "A mighty transformation might be wrought in the freed people," Thomas wrote, "if the professionally trained but poverty-stricken negroes struggling in Northern cities, endowed with courage and desire for serving their race, were to go South" to wage war "against the criminal ignorance and social depravity of the freedman" (384, 385). But for all their "steady patience, intelligent forethought, and strenuous purpose," northern blacks also fell short of meeting his high standards (415). After putting them on a tier above the ex-slaves and their descendants, Thomas ultimately dubbed black northerners "some of the most ignorant and degraded" of black Americans (363). In *The American Negro* he gave little credence to environment as a force capable of ameliorating what he described as engrained racial characteristics. His indiscriminate, gratuitous condemnation of American Negroes knew no regional bounds.

Who, then, among members of the race passed Thomas's muster? He explained that only persons of African descent who successfully had shed their "negro idiosyncrasies" and achieved "manhood and womanhood" were to be commended (x). In contrast, he viewed those who retained Negro "racial traits"—he also termed them "race disabilities"—as perpetual children, the scourge of the race (x, xix). Thomas believed that "environment" had "accentuated" negative racial qualities in blacks and that "an environing heredity" was "the bar sinister of negrology" (xx, xxii). The alleged pejorative Negro traits, he insisted, were not defined simply by skin color gradations but rather by "a pronounced set of characteristics, specifically exemplified in the physical, mental, and moral qualities of a type of humanity" (x). Though convinced that "negroism . . . is an attitude of mental density, a kind of spiritual sensuousness," Will admitted that the blacks' depravity and ignorance could be improved, but only by what he obliquely termed "radical treatment" (xxii).

By 1900, as Williamson maintains, the term "Negro" became an idea. Obsessed by this notion, the focus of Thomas's book was to ascertain how "negroism" came into being and "to build a feasible structure over the chasm which divides the negro as he is from that which he may become" (xxii, xxiii). "I have . . . personal knowledge," Thomas explained, "of many individuals, representing all shades of color, who are manfully engaged in a struggle to free themselves from all visible traces of racial traits" (x). This most certainly was Thomas's most accurate and revealing autobiographical statement. In fact, throughout his book he identified openly with whites, the oppressors, rather than with blacks, the oppressed. At one point in *The American Negro*, totally distancing himself from blacks, Will wrote bluntly that "negro nature requires the employment of compulsory force to induce its conformity to *our* standards of living" (392, emphasis added). The book, then, was Thomas's call to arms for "the utter extermination, root and branch, of all negroid beliefs and practices" (373). His major concern was "transforming the freedman and making a new creature of him" (417).[28]

Race obviously lay at the core of *The American Negro*, and on no topic was Thomas's language more confused, his meaning more obscure, or his message more contradictory. In striking contrast to *Land and Education* (1890), in which he took a forthright stand against biological determinist views, *The American Negro* reads at times like a poorly digested and edited social Darwinist tract. "Life," he explained, "is a ceaseless struggle for existence, and survival of species is proof of adaption to environment" (402). Thomas wrote repeatedly that Negroes stood on the lowest rung of human development. They were a people, he said, "whose history . . . is a record of lawless existence, led by every impulse and every passion" (129). He considered "the negro . . . an intrinsically inferior type of humanity . . . one whose predominant characteristics evince an aptitude for a low order of living" (139). Negroes were an alien race "whose instincts are incompatible with, and whose acts are opposed to, American-Anglo-Saxon civilization" (400). Will described "the sum total of negro contributions to the common treasury of American development" as "a pretentious imitation of civilization, a veneering over barbarous instincts" (404). "The negro is the waste product of American civilization," he declared (371). These statements and numerous others suggest that what Thomas considered to be the Negro's negative "racial traits" were inherited, having evolved over centuries from people of African heritage. While he recognized that environmental forces such as slavery and its aftermath (he termed the South's postwar labor system "industrial bondage") contributed to racial characteristics, they figured far less importantly in *The American Negro* than in his earlier writings. Despite occasional references to the impact of environment on "social development," Thomas argued that race traits were largely inherited, not acquired (420).

Though arguing that racial characteristics were immutable, Thomas paradoxically wrote that Negro qualities could indeed be diluted and, as a result, syncretic racial types had evolved over time. As early as 1894, he had predicted that "racial amalgamation," like other "evolutionary processes" in industrial America, would replace "existing racial distinctions." Mulattoes represented an improved, genetically enhanced racial type, Thomas explained in *The American Negro,* the direct result of their inheritance of white racial characteristics. In his opinion, "the pure negro people are, by the very nature of their characteristic endowments, precluded from reaching a high degree of efficiency" (409). Because of racial amalgamation during slavery, he said, "slave offspring . . . underwent a physical transformation, and foreign miscegenation changed a sensuous savage animal into a rational human creature, with a possible attainment to manhood and spiritual consciousness" (106).[29]

The freedman, Will wrote confidently, had "an inbred aversion" to his color, and "a ceaseless yearning to supplant it with a lighter hue" (407). He considered "judicious race amalgamation . . . capable of exercising a profound and far-reaching influence upon inferior people. Degenerate people," he added, "are always improved and strengthened by an infusion of virile blood, but the benefits derived from wise race admixture are to be found in transmitted capacity, not color." Mindful of his own racial heritage, Thomas considered "the best examples of negro race admixture . . . those which have an equal inheritance of characteristics from both white and black progenitors, with the initial amalgamation extending back to the third or fourth generation. In such cases we have a degree of intelligence, a poise of judgment, and solidity of character wholly wanting in the extreme of the negro"

(408-9). As elsewhere in his book, Will, probably a third-generation mulatto, obviously was describing himself. But he insisted that "while certain well-defined changes may be wrought in negro physical character by amalgamation . . . an aberrant preference for intensified negro characteristics is not infrequently exhibited" (106-7). He seemed to suggest, then, that even mulattoes could not escape Negro characteristics. The supposed benefits of a racially mixed heritage were undermined by the indelible "mental and physical weakness" inherent in Negroes (107).

Despite his conflicting comments on the rigidity of racial types and the possibilities offered by miscegenation, Thomas identified the behavior and character of Negroes, not their race or color, as the sources of most white racism and discrimination directed against blacks. Painfully cognizant of America's de facto "one-drop rule" that defined anyone with African ancestry as a Negro, he argued that the "lightening" of the black race would accomplish nothing unless accompanied by a major transformation in the basic character of Negroes. For example, clearly referring to his own identification with Negroes, Thomas remarked that "making color the sole criterion of racial distinction" is "a crude and illogical standard." "Obviously," he added, "mental and moral character are not determined by physical accidents, and in every well-ordered community these two qualities are the only recognized endowments of manhood and womanhood" (284). Dark skin, Will continued, was "the chief visible badge of personal degradation" because of the way that Negroes behaved, not because of their biological makeup (296). While he agreed that Negroes who fell short of "manhood and womanhood" deserved their low status, he complained that racial prejudice directed at blacks affected all persons of African descent, including William Hannibal Thomas.

White racists discriminated against all blacks, Will remarked, including people like himself who had overcome their inferior biological heritage and attained "manhood." Significantly, he credited his superiority over Negroes not on his light color but on his sterling character. But no matter how successful Negroes were in ridding themselves of negative race traits, Thomas complained that the contemporary racial system positioned "the competent and incompetent, the trustworthy and untrustworthy negroes . . . apart from their white fellow-men by a distinctive color badge common to all. The caste disabilities . . . with which the deserving members of the race are burdened, become really formidable when we consider what color means to the educated, industrious, competent negro" (69). Thus, despite his insistence on the biologically determined, debased condition of most people of African

descent, Thomas admitted that "the degradation of the race is not characteristic of all persons of negroid ancestry." He worried about the effects of
racial prejudice on the "saving remnant of good men and true women" as
much, or more so, than he did about its impact on the black masses (xxiii).
Thomas's goal, then, in *The American Negro* was to transform the behavior
of Negroes en masse, first by exposing their pathologies and then by suggesting avenues for "radical" racial reform.

In line with contemporary polemical and scholarly writings on race, Thomas
began his discussion of the "Negro problem" with an analysis of African
American slavery. He perceived slavery as a complex institution—one that
simultaneously provided both a beneficial transitionary passage for Africans
to America, and one that imprisoned them. At its paternalistic best, Thomas
said, American slavery offered Africans a life far better than the one they left
in their homeland. Convinced that Africans were biologically and culturally
inferior to Europeans, he asserted that slavery promoted a work ethic among
captured blacks. He considered "their forced industry . . . the earliest uplifting influence which that race encountered in the New World" (7). Thomas
also interpreted the master-slave relationship in an essentially positive light,
arguing that many slaveholders were motivated by Christian duty, not profits, and thus treated their slaves generously. Benevolent masters "left an indelible impress upon many negro men and women, who were ennobled
thereby." In his view, "slavery wrought a salutary transformation" in African
Americans that laid the groundwork for racial regeneration. According to
Thomas, the peculiar institution "made rational men out of savage animals,
and industrious serfs out of wanton idlers. It found the negro rioting in
benighted ignorance, and led him to the threshold of light and knowledge.
It clothed nakedness in civilized habiliments, and taught a jungle idolater of
Christ and immortality" (21). Several forces—forced labor, religious teaching, and contact with whites—provided African Americans with tools necessary for survival in the modern world. Above all, "the fostering care" of
slavery, Thomas argued, protected blacks from their own "savage" instincts
(411). Such arguments positioned Thomas alongside mainstream professional historians of slavery of his day, including Ulrich Bonnell Phillips, who
espoused a strikingly similar proslavery interpretation.[30]

Yet Thomas, unlike Phillips, denounced slavery as an institution that promoted "a monstrous aberration of the sense of human right" (12). It created
an environment—a "licentious carnival"—where "moral integrity" was impossible for masters or slaves (24, 12). In his opinion, slavery, not black las-

civiousness, caused miscegenation. The whites were to blame because they controlled blacks, "debasing their minds and morals, and dominating their persons with execrable legal atrocities" (10). But, Thomas pointed out, the institution corrupted both races.

In the tradition of Hinton Rowan Helper, the Negrophobic North Carolina abolitionist of the 1850s, Thomas argued that slavery proved more harmful to whites than to blacks: "The physical depravity of the enslaved negro exerted a pernicious influence on the white masters; it corrupted their language, warped their moral vision, and swept away the decent and orderly restraints which civilized society imposes on its members. Moral integrity was set aside, the caprice of the individual substituted. Slave-owners became self-indulgent, brutal and lustful, masterful in speech, audacious in action; and throughout the whole saturnalia of chattelism the whites sunk." Yet while critical of slavery's negative effects on both races, Thomas admitted that it elevated the blacks "in moral stamina," providing them Christianity, the law and order of the plantation, and "some knowledge of the duties and obligations of moral living" (12). This again was standard proslavery rhetoric.

Like slavery's white defenders, Thomas also argued that the South's blacks lived happier lives as slaves than as freedpeople. As chattel, he said, they received supervision, guidance, and protection from a "superior" race. Unprepared for freedom, the ex-slaves degenerated morally and mentally. Unlike contemporary blacks, the slaves were a pious, spiritual people. This spirituality, Thomas said, enabled the slaves to endure their bondage and allowed their masters to keep the Africans' barbaric qualities in check. Once their bonds were removed, however, the freedman "had no aspiration to create, no ambition to excel; to him labor was bondage; idleness, freedom" (46). Left unsupervised, the ex-slaves reverted to their inherently irresponsible ways, unleashing "the vulgar, self-asserting, levelling instincts previously latent in negro nature" (423). In Thomas's opinion, the condition of blacks could not be improved until the Negro's "hereditary mental concepts have been uprooted, and replaced by the ideas and realities of modern civilization and culture" (421). Unfortunately, emancipation had failed to accomplish this.

Thomas's assessment of the meaning of emancipation is especially curious. During the Civil War, while serving in Virginia and North Carolina with the U.S. Colored Troops, he had observed the emancipation process firsthand. Following the war he commented on the blacks' joy over their liberation. Yet by 1901 he had concluded that Negroes were virtually passive during their emancipation. The "indifference" of the freedpeople to their liberation, Thomas said, "leads us to conclude that they have neither intelligent knowledge of the magnitude of the boon conferred on the race, nor sensible gratitude" for their emancipators (38). To support his point, Thomas argued erroneously that blacks failed to participate in emancipation celebrations. Any familiarity with the black press of his day, however, would have convinced him otherwise. Throughout the nineteenth and early twentieth centuries black communities north and south commonly commemorated emancipation in various ways. The celebrations helped define the blacks' historical memory and contributed to their group solidarity and pride. According to literary scholar Geneviève Fabre, such celebrations became an important "ritualization of civic life."[31]

Thomas, however, adopted the negative view of emancipation common among postbellum white southerners. In his judgment, the freedpeople were incapable of moving from slavery to freedom. "Such a transition," he said, "fraught with untried responsibilities and unknown duties, carried them beyond their depth." While Will admitted that the ex-slaves had some understanding of their new status, he insisted that blacks could grasp neither its opportunities nor its responsibilities. "To eat, to drink, to sleep, and roam at will, so much was conceivable and eagerly sought," he said, "but that as free men and women they owed duties to each other and society in general, they had no clear conception" (44–45). Thomas regretted that the U.S. government had failed in 1865 to provide a transitionary bridge for the blacks from slavery to freedom akin to serfdom in Europe or apprenticeship in the Caribbean. He considered the results of the slaves' premature emancipation disastrous to the Negroes, the South, and the nation.

In *The American Negro* Thomas described what he considered to be the bitterest fruit of emancipation: the freedpeople. He wrote about them as "others," cataloguing a relentless list of traits, as if classifying an animal species. He delineated what he considered black characteristics with unrelenting force, senseless repetition and, especially for the Victorian age, exceedingly bad taste. Seemingly at every opportunity Will selected words that contained sexual connotations to illustrate the freedmen's deficiencies. His core chapters examined the Negroes under a microscope, focusing minutely on their alleged "Characteristic Traits," "Moral Lapses," and "Criminal Instincts." These chapters provided ammunition aplenty, inflammatory quotes galore, for the most extreme contemporary white racists and hatemongers of every ilk. The severity of his language suggested that he was a man in emotional pain crouched in a metaphorical corner, a lexicon in his only hand, crying out to be heard.

"The negro is a moral pervert," Will exclaimed, "the waste product of American civilization" (220, 371). "The negro represents an intrinsically inferior type of humanity . . . whose predominant characteristics evince an aptitude for a low order of living. While contact with civilization has superimposed on his barbarous nature a superficial conformity to its outward requirements," he said, "such contact has failed to awaken in him a rational sense of personal needs, or to arouse a genuine desire for the realities of truth and right-doing" (139). Summarizing his opinion of Negro life, Thomas wrote: "The social side of negro life has been . . . an open page of execrable weakness, of unblushing shame, of inconceivable mendacity, of indurated folly and ephemeral contrition" (xxi). Unless Negroes charted a new course, he said, submitted to "radical treatment," they were "foredoomed to social destruction" (61).

With a hyperbole that suggested that Thomas wrote while under some physical pain and emotional duress, he identified depravity in virtually every avenue of Negro life. At no place and at no time, Thomas explained, had Negroes "ever created an institution, devised a law, promulgated a science, formulated a philosophy, developed a literature, or instituted conditions of social betterment that had the approval of contemporaries, or the respect of posterity" (354–55). Categorizing the intellectual potential of the race, he argued that "the vacuous-minded negro possesses neither strong mental powers nor intelligent culture" (115). He pointed to a seemingly endless list of negative traits in the freedpeople: "In speech they are silly and vaunting; in their homes, untidy and negligent; in their associations, coarse and vulgar. Their demeanor toward inferiors is pompous and arrogant, while their conduct toward superiors is always servile and craven. Moreover, as they are improvident and idle, their undertakings often begin in folly and shame, and end in sin and crime" (122). And Thomas found still other pejorative qualities in Negroes. He considered them egotistical, shiftless, immoral, impulsive, lazy, cowardly, deceptive, insincere, and totally lacking in judgment and discretion. They were vain, obstinate, self-complacent, unaffectionate, unsympathetic, and overtly sensitive to criticism. His list of negative qualities of Negroes seemed limitless. He insisted that this list was merely "honest race criticism" (142).

Identifying with white supremacists who after Reconstruction created the image of black men as rapists, Thomas went so far as to identify "an imperious sexual impulse" as the foremost characteristic of Negroes (176–77). So degraded were they, he wrote, that it was "almost impossible to find a person of either sex, over fifteen years of age, who has not had actual carnal knowledge" (183). He charged that Negro men readily "lead wives, mothers, sisters, and daughters to the sensuous embraces of white men" (179). Strange women allegedly entered their homes and cohabited with men without protest from their wives. "So great is their moral putridity that it is no uncommon thing for stepfathers to have children by their stepdaughters with the consent of the wife and mother of the girl" (179). Marriage, Thomas wrote, posed no barriers to illicit sex for Negroes. Consciously distancing himself from Negroes, he declared that "so deeply rooted in immorality are *our negro people* that they turn in aversion from any sexual relation which does not invite sensuous embraces . . ." (183, emphasis added).

In *The American Negro,* Thomas, who had abandoned one wife in Pennsylvania and reportedly lived with several women while in South Carolina, considered black women the most degraded representatives of their race. For decades he had seemed to find pleasure in criticizing their supposed low morals. "Fully ninety per cent of the negro women of America," he alleged, were "lascivious by instinct and in bondage to physical pleasure," and that "the social degradation of our freedwomen is without parallel in modern civilization" (195). Specifically, Thomas charged them with being "amenable to impure proposals from their [white] social superiors" (65). In Negro homes they "go about in scanty clothing which invites a familiar caress that is rarely forbidden or resented. . . . Not only does the semi-nude attire of the adult negresses invite lascivious carousal at home, but their young daughters are permitted to parade the streets and visit their associates clad in a scantiness of attire that ought never to be seen outside a bedroom" (177). Reared in this environment, he said, "young negro girls . . . become prematurely old in viciousness" (183). "Women," Thomas noted, "unresistingly betray their wifely honor to satisfy a bestial instinct" (184). Mothers, mired in "ignorance and laziness, filth and squalor," served as "advance agents of intemperance and vice" (199).

Thomas identified the source of the "moral debasement" of black women in their allegedly consensual sexual relationships with white men during the Civil War. During his service with the U.S. Colored Troops he observed many high-ranking white officers, "and some of strong prejudices against the race," who kept black mistresses. "It may have been the outcroppings of gratitude to Federal victors, or reckless abandon to lust, but the inciting cause is immaterial, so long as the shameful fact is true, that, wherever our armies were quartered in the South, the negro women flocked to their camps for infamous riot with the white soldiery." There was no doubt in Thomas's mind that "the present lax morality everywhere observable among negro womenkind is largely due to the licentious freedom which the war engendered among them." In a telling aside, he remarked, "slavery had its blighting evils, but also its wholesome restraints" (14). He conveniently forgot to mention, however, that in 1901 most American mulattoes were the offspring of sexual encounters between black women and their white masters.

Though Thomas held black women in scorn, he nonetheless credited them with assuming enough responsibility to "pay their house rent and feed and clothe their children, while their dissolute husbands roam about in wanton idleness" (188–89). Negro men, however, "crazed by their social freedom," thus ranked even lower than Negro women on his scale of moral turpitude (65). "Soberly speaking," Will wrote in words that were anything but sober, "negro nature is so craven and sensuous in every fibre of its being that a negro manhood with decent respect for chaste womanhood does not exist" (180). Categorizing black men as "bestial," he charged that animal impulse drove them to "abandon themselves without attempt at self-restraint to sexual gratification whenever desire and opportunity arises" (179). He remarked almost casually that black men had a propensity to rape white women and assumed that blacks who were lynched for allegedly raping white women were guilty. "The negro," Will wrote unabashedly, "is of a preeminently sensual race, and one whose male members have an inordinate craving for carnal knowledge of white women" (223). "Lynching will stop," he said, when black men "cease to commit heinous crimes, and when the freed men and women . . . set a higher estimate on morality and chastity" (227).

Thomas placed much of the blame for the alleged degeneracy of black men and women on the race's ministers and educators. Their "specious teachings," he insisted, "wrought havoc" and discouraged the black peasantry from laboring (60). He identified "numberless preachers and teachers so poorly equipped for their chosen vocation that one sees at a glance the physical industries have been deprived of some stalwart laborers" (132). Negro teachers, he asserted, shepherded their students away from useful occupations "to become declaiming pettifoggers, pulpit ranters, quack doctors, and sham teachers" (66). No doubt alluding to Booker T. Washington, Thomas mocked Negro educators who solicited northern philanthropy and then described their schools as indispensable to racial progress. Thomas went so far as to accuse such educators of knowingly accepting as students the mistresses of white men who paid their expenses. Parroting turn-of-the-century whites who denounced "classical" education for blacks as miseducation, he renewed his advocacy of industrial training for blacks. It was imperative to train not their minds but "their hands, the only absolutely available raw material of real value they possess" (61). Since emancipation, Thomas asked, had not Negro education permitted the freedpeople "to riot in a saturnalia of intelligent animalism?" (116).

While he admitted that learning to read and write remained important, Thomas considered other things more essential: the development of "self-respect, self-restraint, prudent forethought, careful industry, honest courage, the grace of patience" and "the nobility of manhood" as well as "the chastity of womanhood" (115–16). These moral qualities, Thomas believed, were the necessary tools for racial development. At the same time, industrial training would provide African Americans with practical skills and presumably teach them "that honest work of whatever kind never degrades a true man or woman, all of whom should learn to labor with patience, accuracy, and fidelity" (264). In Thomas's view, industrial and moral training offered the only long-term solution to the plight of Negro Americans. Their degradation, he believed, required educators to bypass intellectual refinement in favor of physical and moral redemption.

Negro preachers were even more corrupt than teachers, Thomas exclaimed. Borrowing language from "The Characteristics of Negro Christianity," which he published in 1897 in the *Quarterly Review of the United Brethren in Christ,* he accused clerics of transforming churches "into debauching rendezvous, . . . prayer-meetings . . . into séances of sensuous contortions and physical frenzies" (152). Over many years Thomas had attacked the black clergy, accusing them of many sins, so it was not totally surprising that he continued his barrage in *The American Negro,* branding preachers "a significant menace to the civilization of this age" (151). Not only did they reportedly steal sermons from whites, palming them off on Negro congregations as their own, but Thomas purportedly had "personal knowledge of more than a score of negro preachers of high repute who are married to women of known impurity, and of whose immorality they were fully cognizant before marriage" (184–85). Bringing to mind critiques of antebellum camp meetings, Thomas lamented that many young Negroes "can directly trace their downfall to a religious picnic and a clerical seducer" (187).

Thomas in fact believed that black religious life had worsened since emancipation. Under slavery, the desire for freedom helped to maintain a certain level of spiritual purpose and idealism among the slaves. Black liberation destroyed this, replacing it with "a visible degeneration in spiritual appreciation, moral consciousness, candor of belief, and personal integrity" (150).

Postemancipation Negro religion exhibited a "moral obliquity, which condones crimes and approves, or is indifferent to, venality" (164). As with every other aspect of African American life, Thomas asserted that black religion was fundamentally devoid of meaning. To his mind it constituted mere superficial display based solely on physical impulses. The apparent failure of religious belief to transform the race led him to conclude that true "racial regeneration" demanded "a radical change in the religious ideas and actual living of the freedmen" (155).

Though for decades Thomas had concocted reform schemes to lift the race in small steps, in *The American Negro* he attempted to solve America's race problem in one leap. The "radical treatment" he proposed was the complete reformation of the Negro's character, not his color. Convinced that Negroes were locked biologically into a perpetually inferior status, he nevertheless believed that they could be assimilated culturally into the fabric of white American society. Unlike Bishop Henry McNeal Turner of the A.M.E. Church and others, Will rejected the colonization of blacks to Africa as "chimerical expatriation," arguing that not only was black colonization "a physical impossibility" but also insisting that Negroes in all locales always had proven themselves incapable of self-government (335). Negroes were born, he said, not made by their environment. Though at times in *The American Negro* he suggested the ameliorative powers of geography and race mixture, he generally subscribed to the immutability of racial characteristics. Some hope remained for the race, however, if blacks modeled themselves after whites.[32]

As Thomas explained it, "the redemption of the negro is impossible through any process of physical amalgamation; it is possible and assured through a thorough assimilation of the thought and ideals of American [white] civilization" (410). Summarizing the difficult task ahead, he explained: "The negro is immoral; he must be endowed with morality. He is lazy, and therefore needs to be made industrious. He is a coward; he must acquire courage. His conscience is dead, his intellect dense; one must be resurrected, and the other set aflame by the light of heaven" (117). The solution lay in eradicating the Negro's distinctive traits and behaviors.

Though Thomas recognized that this would be an uphill battle, he nonetheless remained confident of success. He recalled Albert Berrien, the ex-slave he met and admired in Rome, Georgia, during Reconstruction. He considered Albert, the natural son of John MacPherson Berrien, attorney general under President Andrew Jackson, the best example of what he thought a Negro could become through "national assimilation." Though born a slave and never educated, Albert was unusually bright, knowledgeable, and judicious. Berrien, Thomas wrote, "was an ideal man, with a genuine luminous soul, who was freed from the bonds of environment and heredity through a complete assimilation of the ideas and habits of a superior influence. Furthermore, though this man was a slave, he was respected and held in the highest esteem by the leading white citizens of the state, as a person of fearless courage and unswerving integrity, and we are confident that his color was never considered in the estimate of his character" (410). Albert Berrien was Thomas's proof that the freedman could be redeemed, his beau ideal of a Negro. Because blacks lacked the will or self-awareness to transform themselves, moral and mental qualities had to be cultivated in them by their white superiors. But how? Thomas believed that to uplift the mass of Negroes to Albert's level required a structured system of racial control. He outlined four "radical" programs but, unlike his previous reform proposals, provided no specific details for their implementation.[33]

First, Thomas advocated restricting the blacks' political rights. Though from Reconstruction through the early 1890s he had insisted that African Americans should vote—and vote Republican—he reversed himself in *The American Negro*. Implicitly repudiating his own service to South Carolina's Republican party, for example, he declared, "southern reconstruction marks the blackest page in American history" (307). He went on to argue that through the years blacks largely had proven themselves incapable of exercising their political rights because, as a racial group, they lacked integrity. The Negro, Thomas explained, "is now, as he was the first day of his enfranchisement, the partisan tool of designing white men" (309). He then alleged that the black voter "is a coward because he is a political parasite. He is corrupt because he is a partisan mendicant. Hence he is the scapegoat of every disorder, the culprit of every crime" (311). Reflecting on Reconstruction, Will considered it a bitter failure, largely because African Americans had been given too much political power. "It was an unpardonable blunder to enfranchise the negro," he explained, because whites manipulated them (309). The best solution, then, in his opinion, was to limit black suffrage and to allow white southerners to "supervise and direct the negro's political education" (332). Thomas concluded that political empowerment was unnecessary—actually an impediment—to black progress and endorsed racial proscription and segregationist laws, arguing that "there are sound reasons for imposing discriminations in a region [the South] where diversity in the social development of its classes is so complex as to forbid unrestricted intercourse" (283).

Second, Thomas proposed the use of severe physical force—what he called "heroic methods in dealing with the outlawries of our civilization"—to regulate Negro behavior (235). Though he believed that whenever possible whites should use "appeals to conscience and reason," to keep blacks in line, he concluded that "it is our duty to back up such commands for right-doing with force. We are, moreover, seriously inclined to the belief that, in a social organism of fixed ethical standards, all in-dwelling, non-conforming inferior types of mankind should be excluded or exterminated" (141). Though he neither explicated the appropriate crimes nor explained his rationale for so severe a punishment, Thomas nevertheless meant that Negro criminals convicted of certain offenses, presumably the rape of white women, should be executed. In his judgment, "our message to Southern civilization is to exterminate by law its lawless white element; at the same time, to exterminate at all hazards and at any cost the savage despoilers of maiden virtue or wifely honor, and do it so thoroughly that the inexorable, remorseless certitude of punishment will make the lives and persons of the women of the South as safe in field, forest, and public highway as in their private homes" (233). "Is this a barbarous suggestion?" he asked. "Assuredly not," Will answered, "so long as we absolve ourselves for summary executions by the plea that the good of society justifies them. It is far better to have individual extermination than national extinction" (141).

Though having already proposed execution as the appropriate penalty for black rapists, Thomas nonetheless revived his 1895 castration plan as punishment for the same crime. (Macmillan's editors apparently missed this contradiction in the text.) He proposed that males, presumably blacks, age fifteen or above, convicted of rape "shall undergo emasculation" and incarceration (234). He emphasized that this proposal incorporated both deterrent and punitive functions. "One is as essential to the well-being of society as the other, and any measure which does not exert a restraining influence upon the vicious classes is of doubtful value." He concluded that his castration proposal was a reform over lynching, replacing "orderly procedure for private passion and revengeful force" (235). No doubt attempting to rationalize the extreme nature of his proposals, Thomas said, "our knowledge of negro nature convinces us that one living example of judicial emasculation would be worth, as a deterrent object-lesson to the race, a thousand summary executions of appalling barbarity" (236).

Thomas argued that "for some offences," presumably lesser ones, "the negro should be whipped." He assumed that blacks would respect the lash when other deterrents would fail. "A judicially administered whipping . . .

would be an efficacious remedy for certain phases of negro crime, and would prove a wholesome deterrent to many who are criminally inclined." He understood that the identification of whipping with slavery would capture the attention of ex-slaves. Such corporal punishment, he reasoned, would render blacks more amenable to law and order and make them think twice before breaking the law. In general, Thomas preferred whipping over imprisonment because "incarceration . . . may be said to involve no punishment for negroes, but rather gives to the idle and vicious desired rest, and in the eyes of their racial friends elevates them to the dignity of martyrs." Whipping, he insisted, was the best mode of racial control for the Negro. "He is an overgrown, irresponsible child, and must be treated as a wilful, untrained child should be; though for sound reasons of public policy all punishment calculated to render a culprit execrable should be inflicted in private" (222).

Third, Will proposed an admittedly impractical but, in his opinion, necessary reeducation program for black children. Suggesting that Negro youth were "viciously environed" by parents incapable of disciplining them, he favored removing children from their parents and placing them in special black orphanages (203). Their teachers, their guardians, would be white. Ideally, he explained, "the process for negro regeneration would be to take its boys and girls under five years of age and train them to maturity in complete severance from all racial contact" (386). Black homes, he concluded, provided environments that exacerbated the worst Negro traits. On a less extreme note, in *The American Negro* Thomas also reiterated his old arguments in favor of land reform and agricultural and industrial training. Finally, like white abolitionists during the emancipation era, Thomas favored sending northern white missionaries to the South as teachers and preachers. They would serve, he said, as role models for two elements of Negro society—its women and its clergy—in desperate need of uplift.

Significantly, all of Thomas's solutions for the elevation of Negroes placed the burden of solving the race "problem" directly on the black man, whose duty was "to conduct himself so worthily as to disarm racial antagonism" (296). Each of his proposals for racial progress centered around the principle of modifying, controlling, and shaping Negro behavior to fit a model of conventional white society. Similar to white racial Radicals of his day, Thomas concluded that the Negro's future depended on white control, supervision, and paternalism. Unless Negroes rid themselves of their inherited and culturally transmitted racial characteristics, he insisted, blacks at best would play a perpetually subordinate role in American society. At worst they would be annihilated by whites who refused to allow their civilization to be contaminated by Negroes. Just "so long as he is by instinctive preference a negro in thought and conduct," Thomas predicted, "he is irrevocably doomed to social and political effacement" (419). In *The American Negro,* he insisted on saving the race by transforming it.

In January 1901, then, as Thomas admired his new book embossed in gold, he had every reason to be satisfied. One of the world's leading English-language presses had just published the work that had consumed his energies for decades while he had been employed as a preacher, teacher, attorney, and journalist. Confident that he had made a major contribution to "negro sociology," he nevertheless predicted "that there may be freedmen who will read this book in a mood of resentment toward the writer and with anger at its disclosures" (xix, xxv). "Should there be any so unwise," he said, "they are kindly advised to re-peruse it in a spirit of calmness, and with a purpose to know the truth. . . . They must demonstrate beyond a reasonable doubt that the negro is a superior being to that which I have made him out to be" (xxv). Thomas, the old soldier and lawyer, was ready for a war of words.

Soon scores of blacks and their white friends met him in battle, condemning Thomas's sweeping, undocumented opinions and generalizations. Like Professor Ripley, they proclaimed *The American Negro* worthless as a contribution to science, censuring it as the most Negrophobic work ever published by a person of color. Considering Thomas a serious threat, fearful that racists would cite *The American Negro* as a definitive text in their white supremacy campaigns, his critics mobilized quickly in early 1901 to counter his arguments point by point. Determined to destroy him, they unearthed the hidden details of his private life and paraded them publicly. By the end of the year an army of furious writers had successfully portrayed the author of *The American Negro* as a hypocrite, a liar, a monster, and more.

Thomas's disturbing book provides a window, albeit a clouded one, to his many inner contradictions and conflicts. It illustrates and contextualizes the alternative reform ideology of a black racial Radical, an ideology diametrically opposed to solutions to the "Negro problem" espoused by such mainstream race leaders as Booker T. Washington and W. E. B. Du Bois. Because he virtually absolved whites and blamed blacks for the "Negro problem," white racial Radicals welcomed Thomas to their ranks. The publishing history of *The American Negro,* especially Macmillan's curious decision to add it to its list after receiving negative readers' evaluations, suggests the centrality and marketability of race and the "Negro problem" at the turn of the century. Throughout 1901 *The American Negro* lay at the heart of the national discourse on race. Though Thomas's African American critics, outnumbered and outgunned by the forces of racial repression, were under attack on several fronts, they would not, could not, tolerate a race traitor in their midst. *The American Negro* served as a rallying cry for angry blacks of all ideological bents who made Thomas their special target. Having cut himself adrift from his race, he left himself exposed. Enemies moved quickly to drive a stake through his troubled soul.

CHAPTER SEVEN

A Man Without a Race

NAWARE OF THE ONSLAUGHT that awaited him, William Hannibal Thomas certainly must have been gratified by the first press notices of *The American Negro*. Early in 1901 one major newspaper after another reviewed his book favorably. Noting Thomas's sense of gloom, his audacity, and his murky prose, nonetheless the *New York Evening Post*, the *St. Louis Globe-Democrat*, the *Chicago Daily Tribune*, the *Boston Evening Transcript*, the *Washington Post*, and other papers judged it a provocative and useful discussion of the race "problem." Reviewers in each newspaper underscored the fact that as a Negro, Thomas could level criticisms at the race that a white man could not. They agreed that his extreme, relentless denunciation of African Americans might in fact do the blacks some good. Featuring his book prominently on its book page, the *New York Times* predicted that *The American Negro* "may possibly do something toward the solution of the race problem . . . as it is written by one who passionately desires that end, and who knows what he is talking about." [1]

The initial reviewers of *The American Negro* complimented Will's sincerity, recognized him as an expert, and interpreted him as a man with a positive mission. "Mr. Thomas," the *Philadelphia Public-Ledger* said, "has acquitted himself of a task only made congenial through a profound conviction." The reviewer added: "No white man interested in the future of the negro, no individual of negro ancestry, can overlook the importance of this book and its wholesome regenerative influence." Devoting an editorial to Thomas's book and dubbing him "A Sensible Negro," the *Richmond Daily Times* wove *The American Negro* into its defense of racial segregation and proscription. The editor declared:

We have never seen a stronger argument from any source for the repeal of the Fifteenth Amendment. It was this stupid blunder that got the negro into trouble and caused the "outrages and miseries of reconstruction," and, as the author of this book says, the negro was not directly responsible. . . . The only way to build up a respectable Republican party in the South is to eliminate, for a time at least, the negro vote. This . . . would be the greatest possible boon to the black man. His right to vote has done him no good, but only harm, and he would have been far better off all these years without it.

The *Savannah News* agreed, interpreting *The American Negro* as "one of the strongest arguments in favor of such disfranchising acts as have been passed by Mississippi, Louisiana and one or two other states, and or repeal of the fifteenth amendment to the constitution."[2]

Not surprisingly, white supremacists relished Thomas and his book. Francis B. Livesey, a fifty-seven-year-old white man from Sykesville, Maryland, declared that Thomas's

great work, "The American Negro," bespeaks him to be the greatest man in the country in the handling of the negro problem, and I, for one, am sorry that the country cannot rise to a proper appreciation of his merits and install him as the savior for the negro in his growing demoralization. . . . The philanthropists of the north who are showering thousands upon Tuskegee should shower leaflet extracts . . . of Col. Thomas' book over the country. One thousand dollars so spent would go further than $10,000 given to Tuskegee.

The popular southern plantation novelist Thomas Nelson Page agreed, describing *The American Negro* as "perhaps the most remarkable study of the Negro which has appeared. . . . No inconsiderable part of its value," Page added, "is owing to the fact that the author, a free colored man, has had both the power to observe closely and the courage to record boldly the results of his observations." Repeating Will's arguments, Page believed that most former slaves had "retrograded" since emancipation and the only hope of the race was "an upper class, founded on . . . pure morals, high character and good manners." Years later Myrta Lockett Avary cited Page and Thomas as twin authorities for the alleged degeneracy of blacks in general and their propensity to rape white women in particular.[3]

Thomas and *The American Negro* also received ringing endorsements from two of the early twentieth century's most venomous "scientific" white racists: Drs. Paul Brandon Barringer (1857–1941) and Robert W. Shufeldt (1850–1934). Both men had medical training and defined African Americans as what historian John S. Haller Jr. describes as "outcasts from evolution."

According to historian Mark Pittenger, such scientists believed that certain races were excluded from evolution, having "suffered evolutionary failures or setbacks which . . . limited their biological and social potentials, dooming them to degeneration and eventual extinction." Blacks considered Barringer and Shufeldt among their most dangerous enemies. As "respectable" men of science, they provided the intellectual foundation for the noxious ideas of an arsenal of white racial Radicals, including Benjamin R. Tillman, James K. Vardaman, and Thomas Dixon Jr.[4]

A North Carolina physician, Barringer chaired the faculty at the University of Virginia and in 1900 published two widely circulated racist pamphlets, *The Sacrifice of a Race* and *The American Negro: His Past and Future*. In the first tract, Barringer concluded that without the guiding hand of slavery, "the negro as a race is reverting to barbarism with the inordinate criminality and degradation of that state." In his second pamphlet he maintained that "the phylogeny of the negro is carrying him back to barbarism." In an unpublished manuscript, "Race Problems in America," Barringer argued that the freedpeople never would overcome what he characterized "the follies of the reconstruction period and its natural results." Barringer explained:

> Go read the work of the one negro who has thus far dared sacrifice himself on the altar of truth, William Hannibal Thomas in his "American Negro." It is a cry of warning that should be sounded from the housetops. It is an appeal for a return to primitive life, the only hope for a primitive people. Dazed, confused, confounded, the negro is but a son of the soil—return him to the soil. Make his education first a moral one and otherwise make it simple enough to keep him on the farm. Here [in the South] there is room for all and he is at least removed from the growing antagonism of industrial competition.

Like Thomas, Barringer identified across-the-board inferiority "anywhere . . . negro blood predominates."[5]

Shufeldt was a widely published U.S. Army surgeon, ethnologist, and field ornithologist. He ranked as one of the strongest proponents of African colonization in the 1890s and after the turn of the century became consumed by the prospect of race mixture. In *The Negro: A Menace to Civilization* (1907) he praised Thomas's "excellent" book, especially his chapter on "Characteristic Traits." Thomas, Shufeldt said, exhibited "the negro race in its true ethnological light. He supports all that I have said . . . in regard to the characteristics of hybrids; he deplores the presence of the negro and his kin in this country." Thomas, according to Shufeldt, was "one-sixteenth part negro" and "a keen and thoughtful observer." But despite his enthusiasm for

The American Negro, Shufeldt was shocked that Thomas proposed the uplift of a race he described as hopelessly backward. Misreading Thomas's vague and contradictory statements regarding racial amalgamation as tacit approval of race mixing, Shufeldt asked: "Has Mr. Thomas ever seen a case of atavism in this country resulting from the very interbreeding he so extravagantly proposes?"[6]

The Reverend Alexander H. Shannon (1869–1968), like Shufeldt, used Thomas's text to preach against the evils of miscegenation. A Methodist minister, chaplain of the Mississippi State Penitentiary, and professor at Millsaps College, Shannon published *Racial Integrity and Other Features of the Negro Problem* (1907) in five editions, the last of which appeared in 1953. Commenting in the 1907 edition on *The American Negro,* specifically its chapters on "Moral Lapses" and "Criminal Instincts," Shannon explained:

> Here will be found sweeping assertions, and details of depravity sufficiently disgusting to excite horror. No where have we found a more realistic portrayal of the sins of the negro, or a darker estimate of his character. While not disposed to commit the injustice of judging a whole race by its worst representatives . . . we know that there is a terribly real basis of fact for such assertions. The saddest feature of the whole situation, the feature which makes the situation all but hopeless, grows out of this almost universal suspension of moral and ethical standards in so far as the negro race is concerned.

For almost half a century, Shannon cited *The American Negro* in his crusade to maintain "race purity."[7]

More moderate white southerners also welcomed Thomas's book. The editor of the *Columbia State,* who admitted not having read *The American Negro,* argued nonetheless that Thomas's dark portrait "is not overdrawn with regard to the negroes as a mass." It allegedly depicted accurately the condition of low-country black South Carolinians among whom Thomas resided in 1890 while in Lincolnville. The *Richmond Dispatch* credited Thomas with possessing the righteousness of Jeremiah. "Thirty years is a long time to wait for a prophet of his own race to arise and tell the negro the unvarnished truth," the editor said, "but he seems to have come at last, and with a tongue as rough as some Old Testament prophets." In the *Louisville Courier-Journal,* critic J. Stoddard Johnston noted the "many points of merit" in Thomas's book but questioned his attacks on the blacks' "inborn instincts." Among southern newspapers with predominantly white readerships, only the *Memphis Commercial Appeal* and the *Atlanta Constitution* found *The American Negro* objectionable. "The true friend of civilization," the reviewer for the *Commercial Appeal* remarked, "is he who strives in uplift, and this can not be accomplished by the malevolent abuse of the submerged by the ultra sacrosanct." Book critic Lucian L. Knight of the *Constitution* feared that Thomas's pessimism might influence northern philanthropists to withdraw financial support from southern schools. Knight suspected "that the mixture of blood" in Thomas's "veins may . . . render his estimates less calmly judicial than would be the case if he were of pure blood."[8]

Ironically, Bill Arp, the race-baiting syndicated columnist and humorist, found Thomas's arguments too draconian. While the Georgian agreed that the Negroes were "getting worse instead of better," he considered Thomas's proposals to employ force and to exterminate the worst element of blacks too extreme. Arp was surprised that Thomas, a northern Negro, "out-Herods Herod in his denunciation of the negro" and that "a reputable publishing house would chaperon it before northern people." Writing tongue-in-cheek, Arp faulted Thomas for failing to

> tell us how to exterminate them, nor where to draw the line between the inferior classes and those who shall be allowed to live and multiply. He exhausts his indignation without defining the mode and manner of the remedy. I suppose we might transport the men and boys over to the Philippines and turn the army loose upon them . . . or we might drive them out west and let them starve . . . or be killed by the Indians. . . . We are doing reasonably well [in the South] . . . for besides the lynchings for the usual crime, which I hope will be kept up diligently, we have retired about 5,000 to private life in the chaingangs of Georgia. . . . That amounts to a partial extermination and is better, for we get their labor during the process.

In a postscript, Arp reminded readers that racial violence occurred not just in the South, but north of the Mason Dixon line too. "We read that extermination has begun at Terre Haute and Indianapolis," he quipped. "I hope Hannibal is happy."[9]

Despite these criticisms, Will savored his apparent success. The *Book Buyer,* announcing publication of *The American Negro,* commented that with the exception of Booker T. Washington, "there is probably no other representative of the colored race better qualified than Mr. Thomas to write with authority on this subject." The magazine's reviewer judged "it impossible to deny the truth of Mr. Thomas' arraignment of his race as a self-contented, lazy, ignorant and superstitious people." Other positive reviews appeared in the *American Monthly Review of Reviews,* the *Journal of Political Economy,* and in two of London's most respected journals—*Spectator* and *Athenaeum*. In mid-March, Will's book served as the topic for discussion at a meeting of the prestigious Johns Hopkins University Historical and Political Science Association in Baltimore.[10]

Though neither sales figures nor Will's royalty statements have survived, *The American Negro* apparently sold well, so well in fact that in March and May 1901 the Macmillan Company reprinted it. Soon after the book's initial release Will received his first royalty check in the amount of one hundred dollars. He was "unspeakably supprised" to get the money, he informed George P. Brett of Macmillan, adding, "you cannot understand how much pleasure it gave me. I thank you with all my heart." Will wrote proudly that in just several days after its release he already had sold nineteen of the twenty-five discounted copies of *The American Negro* that his publisher had sent him, "all of them to scholarly persons, no one has refused me." "Had I been in good health," he continued, "I would have disposed of all of them." His fortunes soon declined, however. After a month Macmillan demanded payment for the books and he could not come up with the money. Eleven of the books, Thomas explained, were "out on credit, and my ill health has so far prevented me from collecting payment for them."[11]

Matters worsened quickly for Thomas on other fronts as well. After the initial flurry of positive reviews of *The American Negro,* an avalanche of negative criticism descended upon him. Influential publications, including the *Springfield Republican,* the *Kansas City Star,* the *Nation,* the *Independent,* and the *Yale Review,* censured him severely. The *Nation,* for example, judged his book "largely a railing accusation, frequently coarse, and generally undiscriminating." Editor William Hayes Ward of the *Independent* predicted that his book would "delight the unreconstructed Southerner." He added: "One would think had he had been soured by failure to recognize his gifts, he is so bitter against his race." William Fremont Blackman of Yale described *The American Negro* as "one-sided, uncritical, bombastic, and tedious with repetition." White Georgian Jabez L. M. Curry, a former Confederate officer and secretary of the John F. Slater Fund, the philanthropy long criticized by Thomas, chided his portrait of southern Negroes as "exaggerated and repulsive."[12]

W. E. Burghardt Du Bois, then a thirty-three-year-old professor of sociology at Atlanta University, blasted *The American Negro* in the *Dial,* the liberal popular magazine where he later critiqued Booker T. Washington's *Up From Slavery* (1901). Du Bois credited Thomas with making "many general observations showing thought and reading, and passing evidence of eccentric originality and no little ability." Having said this, he quickly dismissed his book as of "no great intrinsic importance." It reeked, Du Bois said, of "cynical pessimism, virulent criticisms, vulgar plainness, and repeated and glaring self-contradictions." Ever sensitive to the tone, timbre, and temperament of the race, Du Bois focused on *The American Negro*'s "pitch and passion," describing Thomas's voice as "a wild discordant note." Ironically, Du Bois was disturbed less by Thomas's direful message than by what he diagnosed as his book's "sinister symptom . . . of life which illustrates peculiarly the anomalous position of black men, and the terrific stress under which they struggle." Du Bois argued that years living along the color line had transformed Thomas into a "Negro cynic." He remarked intuitively that his book "means more than it says." [13]

Thomas's siren of despair, according to Du Bois, signaled the metamorphosis of a disillusioned man, one who had lost both his faith and his ideals. Du Bois explained: "He is one of those embodied disappointments of Reconstruction times; one who went South to show the World and the Negro how to do everything in a day, and succeeded only in shattering his ideals, and becoming embittered and dissatisfied with men. Wandering from place to place and from occupation to occupation, he finally settled in Boston, where . . . he published a pamphlet [*Land and Education*] . . . which now, re-written, appears as 'The American Negro.'" To punctuate his point and to embarrass Thomas, Du Bois quoted passages from Thomas's 1890 "pamphlet" and his 1901 book in parallel columns in order to underscore his contradictions. Despite Du Bois's clever attempt to nail Will's coffin shut by quoting the author's own words, the inconsistencies he highlighted were more apparent than real. [14]

In fact Du Bois was intellectually dishonest in his attack on Thomas. He assumed that no one had paid close attention to Thomas's "pamphlet" and that no one would compare it closely with his book. *Land and Education* and *The American Negro* were decidedly different works, and in fairness to Thomas, Du Bois should have underscored and explained this point. They signified very different phases of Thomas's emerging racial ideology. But Du Bois had a political agenda, and he did correctly identify the dramatic shift from Thomas's serious defense of blacks and his attack on whites in 1890 to his wholesale denunciation of his race in 1901. [15]

Du Bois concluded that Thomas, resentful of the new generation of race leaders, lost touch with "the inner strivings of the Negro people" and wrote "with cool ferocity, without pity or restraint" and with "vindictiveness and exaggeration." Unconvinced that Thomas genuinely believed what he wrote in *The American Negro,* Du Bois interpreted it as exposing Thomas's own problems—"a rare exhibition of that contempt for themselves which some Negroes still hold as a heritage of the past." Nonetheless, because the book appeared at a period of heightened anti-black sentiment to which the book would contribute, Du Bois took *The American Negro* seriously. He later described Thomas's arguments as "so palpably false and exaggerated that they do not deserve serious consideration" and denied that Thomas was in any sense an "authority" on the "moral and mental development" of the race. Rather, Du Bois considered him "a thoroughly disreputable man who was cast out by his own race before he was taken up by the whites." Like other critics, Du Bois said that Thomas evaluated "the Negro by his worst and lowest type." "A race has a right to be judged by its best." [16]

It was for just that reason that moderates of both races looked instinctively not to Du Bois but to Booker T. Washington, then America's foremost black spokesman, for guidance in responding to *The American Negro.* In New York City, Columbia University Librarian James Hulme Canfield wrote Washington, describing *The American Negro* as "a terrible book—terrible if false, and far more terrible if true. I instinctively feel that it is a mass of exaggerations, rhetorical and otherwise. But even then its publication must be disastrous in more ways than one." Though Canfield assured Washington that he was "not in a panic at all" over Thomas's book, he simply wanted to know the best manner in which to respond because, he said, "when a blow like this is struck, one must be quickly on guard." [17]

Edgar Gardner Murphy, rector of St. John's Episcopal Parish in Montgomery, Alabama, also expressed alarm over *The American Negro.* A leading southern progressive, Murphy promoted child labor reform and advocated racial harmony, vocally opposing lynching, peonage, and racial proscription. An officer of A Southern Society for the Promotion of the Study of Race Conditions and Problems in the South, he organized its May 1900 Montgomery Race Conference, which ultimately proved ineffectual and reactionary. At first Murphy chose to ignore *The American Negro,* fearful that a public response would only draw attention to it. Though he preached reason, goodwill, and humanitarianism regarding racial matters, Murphy nevertheless was constantly on guard so as not to antagonize white racial Radicals. After the *New York Times* reviewed Thomas's book so prominently and so favorably, however, the clergyman informed his friend Booker T. Washington: "I feel that . . . that my silence is no longer wise." Murphy found the attention to Thomas's book in the *Times* surprising because he assumed that another friend, the Philadelphia businessman and philanthropist Robert C. Ogden, would have used his influence to block "so favorable and conspicuous a review." [18]

On March 2 the *Times* published Murphy's letter, in which he proclaimed *The American Negro* "a calamity." Murphy argued that if Americans accepted the spirit and argument of Thomas's book it "would be little short of a catastrophe." Quoting generously from Thomas's more extreme statements, Murphy declared that his book reeked of "exaggerated pessimism," "morbid denunciations," and "recklessly untrue" generalizations: "Its pages seem aflame with hate." Defending Booker T. Washington and the John F. Slater Fund and its secretary Jabez L. M. Curry from Thomas's not-so-veiled attacks in the book, Murphy questioned the author's familiarity with the conditions of African Americans in the South. The Alabaman hoped that his letter would discredit Thomas, and he took satisfaction "at the thought that the first conspicuous repudiation of the book may come from a Southern white man." After his letter appeared Murphy informed Washington that he hoped that his piece "in some small degree . . . may have removed the impression that the South would be delighted with Thomas's book. I have seen one or two important reviews in which the statement was made that that book represented the view of the Negro which is entertained at the South." [19]

Despite his good intentions, Murphy's quoting *The American Negro* so extensively actually may have served to advertise Thomas's book. Though a racial liberal, Murphy nonetheless was a paternalist who emphasized "racial integrity" and accepted segregation. According to historian Ralph E. Luker, who labels Murphy a "conservative racial separatist," his disdain of individualism, fear of miscegenation, and love of order rendered the Alabaman "his era's most sophisticated intellectual apologist for racial segregation." Historian William A. Link argues that Murphy combined "refined racism and a belief in black progress." For Murphy, "paternalism implied that white responsibility should accompany white supremacy." For example, he favored modifying the Fifteenth Amendment, making "the franchise a local issue in each state." In his letter to the *Times* Murphy admitted being disappointed with the progress of the generation of postwar blacks, lamenting that it had abandoned "the happy simplicity and the quaint piety of the old-time slave." Nevertheless, Murphy was outraged by *The American Negro*'s desperate tone. He urged whites to reject Thomas and welcome optimistic, forward-looking race leaders like Washington, who, Murphy was quick to add, shunned "social equality" in favor of an educational and economic agenda. In Murphy's view, "a dependent race, like a dependent flower or a dependent child, can grow better only in the sunshine." Murphy worried, then, that Thomas's book might cause whites to block the light of limited racial change.[20]

Thomas's world, however, was becoming increasingly cloudy. Soon he was hounded by private investigators and became the target of personal attacks in newspapers and journals. Race leaders as well as ordinary African Americans pummeled him from all sides. "The Colored Citizens" of Memphis held "an indignation meeting" to protest *The American Negro* and then threatened to lynch Thomas if he ever dared to set foot in their city. Blacks would make him pay dearly for selling out to the enemy.[21]

Publication of *The American Negro* hit African Americans like a bombshell, sending them reeling throughout the United States and as far away as Africa. Blacks immediately realized the seriousness of Thomas's allegations. They feared that white supremacists would use *The American Negro* as a racist tract to justify further subjugation of their race. While African Americans mobilized to counter the book's influence, many were not sure just what to make of *The American Negro* and its obscure author.

Writing, for example, in *Howard's American Magazine,* Thomas A. Church marveled how such a book, "breathing all of the venom and spleen of the most confirmed and virulent Negro hater," could be written by a Negro. Sociologist Richard R. Wright Jr. diagnosed *The American Negro* as "thoroughly sensational, and the product of a distorted and immoral imagination." The Reverend Alexander Waters of the A.M.E. Zion Church, president of the National Afro-American Council, summed it up as "a wholesale and unwarranted slander of the negro race." "The unkindest cut of all," according to William H. Councill, president of Alabama State Agricultural and Mechanical College for Negroes, "really the lunge that seems to be from the demon rather than from the man," was Thomas's charge that black school officials used their female students as prostitutes. The vast majority of African American girls, he exclaimed, had "no more criminal carnal knowledge than their traducer will ever have of heaven." And writing from Cape Palmas, Liberia, P. O. Gray wondered "how a Negro . . . can give his talent to help crush his own race."[22]

John H. Wills, a rare book dealer specializing in books by "Negro authors," assumed, like many blacks, that a white person had to have written *The American Negro.* Initially he hypothesized that Thomas plagiarized John H. Van Evrie's vehemently racist tract *Negroes and Negro "Slavery"* (1853). A friend suggested to Wills that Thomas was "merely the assumed author," "a figger to strengthen the position of a white man with his—T's—black color." Wills also noted that in his chapter on "Ethnic Beliefs," Thomas used the phrase "our race" to refer to whites. Another black, John P. Green, who served as U.S. postage stamp agent in President William McKinley's administration, considered Thomas's statements "startling" and admitted that "many of them are true, to a limited degree." Green, however, regretted that Thomas had not exhibited more restraint "when the disposition on the part of certain unfriendly whites to slander and ill treat us is so pronounced." Green believed that at a time when so many whites emphasized the dark conditions of the race, "it would seem the part of charity as well as good judgment" on Thomas's part "to use his learning and talent, in helping to show the bright side."[23]

The Reverend H. T. Johnson, editor of the *Christian Recorder*, also found *The American Negro* alarming, but for different reasons. He considered the book's "great danger . . . not in the fearful arraignment it makes of the race as such, but in the fact that its author is a Negro, and no less a man than our friend, Rev. W. Hannibal Thomas, of New England." Though Johnson admitted that "a great many good things" could be said about Thomas and his book, he concluded that "the evil outweighs the good." Johnson predicted that opponents would try to use the book to harm the race but, he wrote knowingly, it "has shown itself capable of surviving blows from within as well as from without." More unsettling to the editor, however, was that for over three decades Thomas had contributed thoughtful, constructive, though often critical articles to the *Christian Recorder* and the *A.M.E. Church Review*.[24]

Johnson and other blacks had good reason to worry about the impact of *The American Negro*. Editor George L. Knox of the *Indianapolis Freeman* complained that *The American Negro* was so popular that he could not even procure a review copy. He noted that after only a few weeks in print, Macmillan's supply of the book already had been exhausted. "We have heard much talk of the terrible charges this man, Thomas has made against the race," Knox informed influential Cleveland entrepreneur and politico George A. Myers. But, Knox promised Myers, "you can rest assured that the Freeman will take up the cause and do everything in its power to off set such terrible statements."[25]

Other black editors feared that the press might be giving Thomas's book too much publicity. "The fact of the manner," Edward E. Cooper of the *Washington Colored American* said, "is the white papers . . . are in a very effective way making a Benedict Arnold and a Judas Iscariot of this foul demon." This would be just the first of many comparisons black writers would make between Judas Iscariot, the disciple who betrayed Jesus, and William Hannibal Thomas. The Reverend J. W. Smith, editor of the *Star of Zion,* organ of the A.M.E. Zion Church, admonished readers not to buy *The American Negro.* He explained: "We are wondering now whether this Thomas with sprained intellect whose ugly thoughts are maggots bred in his brain is a Christian or an infidel, lawyer and preacher . . . crazy, absent-minded or a fool. . . . Doubtless his satanic majesty may inspire men with meaner malice and slander for the Negro than is shown in this scurrilous book, but it is certain he has never done so. In this book the bottom of meanness has been reached." Smith advised Thomas to carry himself with shame before members of the race and be prepared to "scoot away with break-neck speed." Before Thomas could escape, however, black editors laced into him with an unrelenting fire. He attracted so much attention in fact that one journalist asked, "Will the Hannibal Thomas episode ever close?"[26]

Between February and September 1901, virtually every black newspaper in the country fired broadsides at Thomas and *The American Negro.* Outraged, for example, by his endorsement of disfranchisement and the use of his book by the *Richmond Times,* the *Richmond Planet* asked: "If Mr. Thomas wants his suffrage taken from him, what is he doing in Massachusetts? Why is he not in God forsaken . . . Louisiana and Mississippi and South Carolina where the Negro gets patches on his knees by supplicating God so often for the amelioration of his condition?" Whereas the *Washington Bee* described *The American Negro* as one of the "most filthy and at the same time false books ever published," the *Indianapolis Freeman* judged it "a vile and inexcusable slander upon the Negro people." Writing to the *Freeman* from Chattanooga, J. C. Jones argued that though Thomas might garner "notoriety and money" from his book, posterity would remember him as "Black Judas." The epithet would stick.[27]

No one worked harder to construct Thomas's image as the betrayer of the race than newspaper columnist John Edward Bruce, known as "Bruce Grit," who reportedly assisted Thomas with publishing *The Negro* in Boston in 1886. An ex-slave from Maryland, Bruce was one of the nation's best-known black journalists, contributing weekly columns to numerous newspapers, including the *Washington Colored American.* In 1888 the *New York Age* described Bruce as "the irrepressible free lance and funny man of colored newspaperdom." Impulsive but fiercely committed to racial pride and militant self-help, Bruce lashed out against members of his race who aspired to make themselves "white" in appearance, by their behavior, or by inter-marrying. He opposed integrated schools and espoused an incipient African American cultural nationalism. A gifted writer, by 1901 Bruce had emerged as an outspoken black activist and a chauvinistic social critic known for his barbed prose. Early in February 1901, he declared war on Thomas and gave him no quarter.[28]

Writing in the *Colored American,* Bruce mocked Thomas as a "disgruntled veteran," a failed carpetbagger, and an unsuccessful editor who settled in Massachusetts "to bask in the smiles of his young wife, and write thoughts about things that strike his fancy." Describing *The American Negro* as a "spasmodic and pessimistic outburst," Bruce blasted it as "rank perjury to the race" and emphasized the book's broad negative effects. It would encourage white southerners to continue lynching blacks, alienate moderate whites, and discourage African Americans from pressing forward for civil rights and educational opportunities. Bruce also questioned Thomas's motives for writing a book that defamed, belittled, and depressed his own people. Notoriety and money, Bruce supposed. "This Judas," he said, resembled "his prototype who betrayed our Lord for thirty pieces of silver. . . . Like Cain who murdered his brother Abel," Bruce concluded, "there has been stamped upon the brow of William Hannibal Thomas the word TRAITOR! and unborn generations of the race out of whose loins he came will remember him as Judas."[29]

Over the next three months Bruce investigated Thomas's background and intensified his assault on him. Writing in the *Colored American* he charged that *The American Negro* actually was Thomas's autobiography, a rhetorical argument that Bruce and many other critics later would hammer home. And, Bruce asked, if Negroes were as Thomas alleged, incapable of answering complex questions, how then could he have written a book on so complicated a topic? Bruce wrote that, quite predictably, the Democratic press, especially southern newspapers, had welcomed Thomas "as fulsomely as though he was a six-legged gorilla, something wonderful to contemplate." But, Bruce quipped, white southerners "would hang Thomas, the traitor, as high as he deserves to be hung if he presumed upon their favorable reception of his latest infamy to get into their social class." "Self respecting Negroes," Bruce wrote, "can only treat him with the contempt with which they would treat any biped that fouls its own nest." Referring to Thomas as "the one-armed saddle-colored Judas," Bruce promoted an anti-Thomas tract, *The Critic Revealed,* that he reportedly had written and offered for sale at ten cents per copy.[30]

As soon as he saw the advertisement, Booker T. Washington wired Bruce requesting ten copies of the pamphlet. Acknowledging Washington's order, "Bruce Grit" admitted that he had not yet published the anti-Thomas tract, "and probably will not . . . unless the Negroes show a little more appreciation of the *substantial* kind, of my effort to give the lecherous libertine bail jumper, and pessimistic fraud a black eye." Bruce informed Washington that he was determined "to roast" Thomas "to a turn, and then turn him over and roast him again for his cowardly and dastardly flings at the womanhood of the race." Bruce promised to assail Thomas widely—"in the newspapers [and] in my own way and time." "It occurs to me," Bruce wrote, "that the best thing to do with a viper like thomas is to show the white people who are quoting him that Titus Oates, is a saint compared with him. Testimony against a whole race from a man who consorts with courtesans jumps bail for debt, dishonors his notes; and lives on the earnings of women to whom he is not married, will not be seriously regarded by serious men." Recalling their brief editorial work together in Boston, Bruce said: "I know Thomas, and he knows I know, what I know." In fact, Bruce said, he had published "a few scathing remarks on the reptile" in the *Star of Zion,* the organ of the A.M.E. Zion Church. Consumed with destroying Thomas, Bruce added: "He is the worst onion, that ever came out of the loins, of the black race."[31]

Bruce pulled out all stops in the *Star of Zion,* labeling Thomas "a half caste," "an ethnological betweenity, neither pig nor puppy, but more puppy than pig." Like other mixed breeds, Bruce argued, Thomas was weak and shortsighted. His only way to succeed was to live by his wits as a con man. Thomas reportedly "worked" several scams in Boston, according to Bruce, fleecing the city's finest families "with the skill of a veteran beggar." Though he had no discernible job, Thomas still "wore good clothes, drank good liquor, ate the best food, and lived like a man with an assured income of $1500 or $2000 per annum." Thomas's "glib tongue and persuasive manner and his empty sleeve . . . won the sympathy of the kind-hearted white people [who] . . . put money in his purse." Bruce, who asserted that Thomas had lost his arm in a sawmill accident, obviously had not spent much time with Thomas in Boston or he would have known of his amputation. In any case, he branded Thomas "a white sepulchre" who described himself, not the mass of American blacks, in *The American Negro.*[32]

To prove his point, Bruce published documents in the *Colored American* and an essay in *Howard's American Magazine* that shed more negative light on Thomas's character and thought. Charles W. Chesnutt, the mulatto lawyer and author, Booker T. Washington, and the Reverend C. T. Walker of

New York supplied Bruce with the sordid details of Thomas's problems in Allegheny City and Newberry. Summarizing the information that he and others had amassed, Bruce said that "discriminating people of whatever race will be slow to attach much, if any importance to the learned deliverances . . . found in the autobiography of w. hannibal thomas." Convinced that Thomas was "morally corrupt and has contributed his fair share toward the degradation of the race, which he now criticizes," Bruce continued his unrelenting attack. "I shall keep on hammering him," he informed Whitefield McKinlay, an influential black businessman and prominent Republican politician in the District of Columbia. Regarding Thomas, Bruce quipped: "The only way to kill a viper of his stamp is to *kill* him. He will be kilt, and with printer's ink." [33]

Determined to bury Thomas and destroy whatever credibility he had left, Bruce linked Thomas's questionable "inner life" to contradictions in his writing. Thomas, in his opinion, could not be trusted to judge anything. Just as he was guilty of the "moral delinquencies" that he alleged in Negroes, Thomas's articles and books proved him to be "a shifty, crafty and adroit phrasemonger—a veritable literary cabinetmaker." Comparing, for example, statements in Thomas's "Characteristics of Negro Christianity" (published in *The Negro* in 1886) and *The American Negro,* Bruce showed that Thomas reversed himself regarding the religious, moral, and musical ability of the race. In the fifteen years between these publications, he shifted from a "positive" assessment to one that was "brutally bitter" and "maliciously cowardly in conception and untruthful as to fact." In short, Bruce considered Thomas *"facile princeps* of the new school of literary prevaricators, who have chosen the Negro as their theme." [34]

"Bruce Grit" had a popular following among African American readers, but Booker T. Washington had prestige and influence on both sides of the color line. No sooner had Macmillan published *The American Negro* in January 1901 than Hamilton Wright Mabie, editor of the *Outlook,* asked Washington to contribute a signed review of the book. He agreed. Between November 3, 1900, and February 23, 1901, the *Outlook* had serialized Washington's autobiography *Up From Slavery* to wide acclaim. It appeared in book form in March 1901, two months following the appearance of Thomas's book. "There could not be a greater contrast to the fierce arraignment of the American negro by Mr. W. H. Thomas," the *New York Times* explained, "than is to be found in this simple and unaffected autobiography . . . nor could there be obtained two more diverse impressions of the colored race than those given by their books." Because of its controversial arguments and the timing of its publication, Washington devoted considerable attention to *The American Negro,* especially after Mabie described the book as "the most important book on the subject which has been written."[35]

Once having read Thomas's book "carefully," Washington wrote his private secretary Emmett Jay Scott that *The American Negro* "is by far the worst thing that has been said about the Negro. It is worse by fifty per cent than anything that Dr. [Paul Brandon] Barringer has said." Scott agreed, writing Washington that they had "reason to fear the effect of the Thomas book. It is a terrible indictment—exaggerated and I fear malicious." Scott predicted that "it will be referred to by every man who would malign the race or defend the iniquities that have been visited upon the Negro." Years later one of Washington's operatives in New York warned him that editor T. Thomas Fortune of the *New York Age* planned to smear Washington in an editorial by comparing one of Washington's statements to something Thomas had said in *The American Negro.* The informant wrote Washington knowingly that "it would be more abhorrent to you to have your language compared with that of Hannibal Thomas, than to have it compared with the words of any living man."[36]

Before his review appeared in the *Outlook,* Washington took steps to dig up information on Thomas, assigning Robert Wesley Taylor, Tuskegee Institute's able northern agent, to investigate him. Washington wanted to know all that he could about the man whom Taylor referred to as "that unnamable scoundrel." Taylor soon reported that Thomas had lived in the Boston area, totally dependent on his military pension, since the late 1880s. His neighbors believed that Will merely "assumed" the title of Colonel. He had no law office, Taylor informed Washington, "and so far as is known he is not a lawyer." Until about 1892, Thomas "lived with a woman whom he made believe was his wife and by whom he had a child." Adding more details about Thomas's domestic life, Taylor explained, the woman he lived with "was a poor, ignorant creature who had earned a little money by working out to SERVICE and as soon as he went through with all she had he cast her off—telling her that the marriage ceremony they had was a mock one. While he was living with this woman another came on from Washington to marry him—Miss Barbara Pope . . . but she was saved from his clutches through the intervention of Mrs. A. C. Sparrow. . . . Failing in this effort to get Miss Pope he married the woman with whom he now lives about nine years ago." Taylor added that gossip around Boston credited Thomas with siring "several illegitimate children in South Carolina, all now grown."[37]

By snooping around Boston on Washington's behalf, Taylor filled in many of the gaps in Thomas's biography. "He is a man who has tried to live by his wits," Taylor said. Over the years, he learned, Thomas had worked as a preacher, lecturer, and financial agent "of some Southern School." Since moving to Massachusetts, Thomas reportedly embezzled "a snug sum of money" from Mrs. Mary Stearns of West Medford and, as a salesman for the *Library of the World's Best Literature,* returned neither the money he collected nor the books to the company. Thomas rented a modest home in Everett, subletting a part of it for income. "He has little dealings with colored people," Taylor remarked, "except as he can use them to his own selfish and damnable ends. Not one good word have I heard concerning him, but he is universally decried as a low, mean, contemptible cur."[38]

Taylor informed Washington that although it was rumored in Everett that Thomas was "mentally unsound," he doubted such gossip. Rather, Taylor believed that Thomas "has studiedly and maliciously taken advantage of the present state of the public mind to betray his race into the hands of its enemies." Taylor feared that *The American Negro* would do African Americans "irreparable harm." Spokesmen "of the [Ben] Tillman ilk" would point to Thomas, "a colored man," who wrote as an authority about his race. "Nothing conceivable," Taylor complained to his boss in Alabama, "could come at a more convenient time for our enemies and at such an ill time for us." He added: "The die is cast."[39]

Washington immediately sent copies of Taylor's letter to James Hulme Canfield, the librarian at Columbia, and William Hayes Ward, editor of the *Independent.* Canfield, no doubt, did little to assuage Washington's fears of the potential ill effect of *The American Negro.* The situation was even more serious than Canfield had anticipated. In his view:

There is no abating, I think, the *force* of Thomas's book. What I suspect is that someone else has put it together for him—for it is certainly scholarly and logical and extremely strenuous: beyond almost any other book that I have read for many a day.

But the distrust which at once attaches to its exaggerated statements is quickened and strengthened by a knowledge of the life and habits of the author. I think it will do great harm, but not as much harm when all the facts are known.

At the same time I can well understand that to make any open attack upon him will be to advertise the book and secure its wider circulation. It would be better to let it die—unless a quiet movement could induce the publishers to withdraw their imprint.

Canfield promised to "quote freely" from Taylor's findings at every opportunity, "though of course not disclosing my authority."[40]

Ward also welcomed the information that Taylor had unearthed about Thomas but regretted "at the same time it is not of the kind that can be used" in print. While preparing his own influential review of *The American Negro,* Ward asked Washington if Thomas had been arrested "in connection with the Wilberforce matter" (Thomas's enemies apparently now were aware of this incident) "and also what the schools were that he was agent for." Even without this information, though, Hayes concluded that Thomas was "a common swindler." After the publication of his review of Thomas's book on February 14, Ward informed the Reverend Francis J. Grimké: "No severity can be too great for it." Ward encouraged African American editors to study Thomas's biography carefully and use it against him at every opportunity. Having seen Ward's review, a black chaplain stationed with the U.S. Army in Cuba remarked that "it goes for the author, and rates him as anything but a sane man." Responding philosophically to Thomas's book, the clergyman commented that "it takes all kinds of people to fill the world, and furnish employment for the fool-killer."[41]

Though as late as 1904 Washington worked behind the scenes to suppress *The American Negro,* in March 1901 he criticized it twice publicly, in both instances maintaining the calm and diplomatic language that characterized his writing. Somehow Washington incorporated a rebuttal of Thomas's allegation that ninety percent of African American women were "lascivious by instinct and in bondage to physical pleasure" into his final revisions of *Up From Slavery.* Without identifying Thomas by name or citing the title of his book (thus promoting neither), Washington said: "There never was a baser falsehood uttered concerning a race, or a statement made that was less capable of being proved by actual facts." In his unsigned (again no doubt to draw less attention to Thomas) review in the *Outlook,* Washington chided Thomas for using his African American ancestry to gain an audience, but then only to disassociate himself from the race. Whites, Washington noted, would not respect a man who "seems to withdraw himself from his own race and goes outside of it to emphasize its weak points before an audience of another color."[42]

In contrast to his own steady public optimism, Washington regretted that Thomas exuded pessimism, "an extreme case of the blues." In Thomas's view, "everything is wrong except that which he advocates, but which he himself, it seems, has failed to put into practice anywhere in the South." For example, Washington pointed to industrial and agricultural schools in the

South that already had established programs that Thomas espoused. Some-how, Washington observed, Thomas had missed the widespread progress—material, mental, and moral—that African Americans had achieved since emancipation. Washington explained that Thomas's only constructive argument—that blacks should obtain land and industrial education—had been the agenda of leading educators for more than three decades. More to the point, Washington faulted Thomas's belief in the "old 'forty acres and a mule'" approach to racial progress. Thomas, he said, wanted Negroes to rely on the federal government for assistance. Washington hoped to make them more self-dependent.[43]

Washington charged that Thomas's unsupported, extreme attacks on the morals of African Americans rendered useless whatever "is good and valuable in the book." "A writer, who is unknown and almost unheard of . . . should be careful to fortify himself by giving names, places, and dates." Specifically, Washington charged that Thomas's accusations of immorality among white teachers and black women and children were ludicrous. So too were his allegations that preachers of African descent routinely stole their sermons and practiced voodoo and conjure. *The American Negro,* then, in Washington's judgment, was outrageous, insulting, and rife with unsupported generalizations and obvious contradictions. Unlike his *Up From Slavery,* Thomas's book mapped out no constructive path for blacks to follow. With Thomas clearly in mind, Washington remarked: "It is sad to think of a man without a country. It is sadder to think of a man without a race."[44]

Whereas Washington worked to undo Thomas anonymously, the celebrated mulatto writer Charles W. Chesnutt proved to be Thomas's most formidable public critic. Descended from North Carolina free Negroes, Chesnutt was born in 1858 in Cleveland, Ohio, but returned to Fayetteville, North Carolina, during Reconstruction, residing in the South for fifteen years. As a teacher and school administrator he lived among the freedpeople, experiencing discrimination firsthand and observing the lingering racial etiquette of slavery. Determined to "live down the prejudice" around him by writing, Chesnutt set out to "show to the world that a man may spring from a race of slaves, and yet far excel many of the boasted ruling race." He was motivated to publish "not so much [for] the elevation of the colored people as the elevation of the whites,—for I consider the unjust spirit of caste . . . so insidious as to pervade a whole nation, and so powerful as to subject a whole race and all concerned with it to scorn and social ostracism." Weary of the South's racial mores and reluctant "to think of exposing my children to the social and intellectual proscription to which I have been a victim," in 1883 Chesnutt returned to Cleveland. Four years later he passed the bar and began a lucrative career as a lawyer and legal stenographer. He also published in national magazines, committed to attaining "social recognition and equality" for his race.[45]

In two collections of short stories, *The Conjure Woman* (1899) and *The Wife of His Youth* (1899), and two race-problem novels, *The House Behind the Cedars* (1900) and *The Marrow of Tradition* (1901), Chesnutt used the history of African Americans in slavery and freedom to expose all manner of greed and injustice, pathos and irony, along America's color line. His books explored the complexities of unequal power relationships based on color and caste. Focusing directly on the realities of miscegenation and mulattoes "passing" as whites, Chesnutt's writings sensitized readers to the inner conflicts, ironies, and sufferings wrought by arbitrary, irrational classifications based on skin color. Especially aware of the plight of light-skinned mulattoes, Chesnutt once described himself as "neither fish[,] flesh, nor fowl—neither 'nigger', poor white, nor 'buckrah.' Too 'stuck-up' for the colored folks, and, of course, not recognized by the whites." Years later, in *The Wife of His Youth,* Chesnutt used his character Mr. Ryder, "dean" of the Blue Vein Society, to explain how "we people of mixed blood are ground between the upper and the nether millstone. Our fate lies between absorption by the white race and extinction in the black. The one does n' t want us yet, but may take us in time. The other would welcome us, but it would be for us a backward step."[46]

Though his own very light skin, financial success, and identification with the white elite earned Chesnutt a quick entry to Cleveland's aristocracy of color, he nonetheless described himself as a member of the "radical school" regarding African American rights. People of African descent were entitled to all civil and political rights, he said, and "I do not think that the matter of race or racial development under our constitution and theory of government should be considered by the law at all." Chesnutt viewed "the political and social structure of the South to be destructive of liberty." He also openly avowed racial mixing and opposed all racial distinctions, all racialist language, as unnatural and inaccurate. According to historian Dickson D. Bruce Jr., Chesnutt in fact questioned the entire notion of "race" because, he believed, America already was a racial amalgam. In Chesnutt's opinion, "the ultimate solution to the race problem lay in amalgamation, in the gradual disappearance of the physical tokens of race." Intellectually Chesnutt rejected the notion of "race pride" and all racial barriers.[47]

Significantly, both Chesnutt and Thomas positioned race at the center of their intellectual worlds, but these worlds were in different orbits. Chesnutt was determined to tear down the existing wall between mulattoes, blacks, and whites. Thomas idealized mulattoes and drove a wedge between them, blacks, and whites. Chesnutt (who refused to "pass") looked beyond his mulatto status and yearned for full integration into American society. Convinced that skin color differentiations were "unduly emphasized in the United States," he espoused a broadly based assimilationist ideology, including amalgamation. Thomas (who "passed" occasionally) identified with mulattoes but doubted that racial mixing would cure what he considered indelible, inherited Negroid characteristics. Chesnutt, literary historian Stephen P. Knadler writes, represented the "untragic" mulatto who envisioned full integration and exuded optimism. Though inconsistent in his writings, Chesnutt came close to denying all distinctions based on race. He celebrated "interracial people" and, according to historian Mark Andrew Huddle, predicted optimistically "the inevitability of [the] browning of America." Thomas, like the "tragic" mulatto, marginalized himself and used race as a means to justify his own identity and, ostensibly, to uplift others of African origin. Though Thomas censured Negroes, not mulattoes, his strident racial determinism nonetheless undercut all that Chesnutt stood for. Whereas Thomas was consumed by what he defined as racial differences, Chesnutt "tried desperately to write 'race' out of existence." The two racial thinkers, then, both "race rebels," were on radically different trajectories. By 1901, when Thomas published *The American Negro,* Chesnutt and Thomas were on a collision course.[48]

That year Chesnutt published *The Marrow of Tradition,* a novel based on the notorious November 1898 racial massacre in Wilmington, North Carolina. The book, Chesnutt informed Booker T. Washington, laid out "our side of the Negro question." This was a pivotal moment in the history of race relations, Chesnutt said, when "an obscure jealousy of the negro's progress, an obscure fear of the very equality so contemptuously denied, furnished a rich soil for successful agitation. . . . Constant lynchings emphasized his impotence, and bred everywhere a growing contempt for his rights." The Wilmington riot and Chesnutt's observations of Jim Crow during a tour of the South in 1901 convinced him that members of the race, no matter the shade of their particular skin color, had to unite unequivocally to fight white supremacy and attain racial justice.[49]

Thomas's crude vilification of Negroes and his use of mulattoes as a foil touched a nerve in Chesnutt and he became obsessed with destroying him.

In Chesnutt's opinion *The American Negro* played right into the hands of white racists and pitted members of a struggling race against themselves. From 1901 to 1904 Chesnutt marshaled his legal skills to launch the most thorough, persistent, and devastating investigation of and attack against Thomas. Chesnutt seemingly would not rest until he exposed Thomas's hypocrisy and apostasy and until his book was suppressed. Like a man possessed, Chesnutt first hunted Thomas down, indicted him among his peers, and prosecuted him in a figurative national moot court.

Chesnutt began his one-man crusade to discredit Thomas in February 1901 while on a month-long tour of the South that included visits to Tuskegee Institute and Atlanta University. During his travels Chesnutt systematically examined Thomas's past by visiting places where he had lived, obtaining copies of legal documents from courthouses and soliciting testimony from officials at schools where Thomas had either attended or taught. The more Chesnutt dug into Thomas's past, the more skeletons he uncovered and the more resolved he became to expose and destroy him. Soon Chesnutt amassed the equivalent of a legal brief full enough to try Thomas before a national jury of his peers.[50]

In March 1901, Chesnutt opened his case against Thomas in a penetrating article in the *Boston Evening Transcript* attacking the South's oppressive and pervasive system of Jim Crow. After exposing the "horizontal strata" that separated the races in the South, Chesnutt trained his guns on Thomas. The *Evening Transcript* had given Thomas's book one of its most favorable reviews because, according to editor Joseph Edgar Chamberlin, who wrote the review, "I had never heard of Thomas before, but was bound to assume that the house of Macmillan would not publish a book which was not genuine, or allow a preface to be put forth which contained a false statement of the author's life." Chamberlin considered *The American Negro* "certainly a remarkable, a quite powerful book. If it be false, it should of course be controverted with facts." Chamberlin believed that Thomas's book "goes much further in its condemnation of the negro race than the southern whites go, and it should do good to the negro in bringing the southern whites to the negro's support. If Thomas is a fraud he should be fully exposed, and the house of Macmillan should be riddled for giving him the hearing. If he is what he says he is, he is entitled to the hearing." Chesnutt, angry at the *Evening Transcript*'s seemingly blind endorsement of Thomas's book over Booker T. Washington's *Up From Slavery,* already had uncovered enough information about Thomas to know that the author of *The American Negro* was vulnerable to devastating attack.[51]

Chesnutt cogently inveighed against *The American Negro*, a work he found "in large degree unquotable, and, consisting, as it does, of . . . defamation of a race with which he [Thomas] admits close kinship." Summarizing the book, Chesnutt said that in it Thomas "denies the Negro intellect, character, and capacity for advancement." Chesnutt's recent tour of the South, he said, proved Thomas dead wrong. Throughout the region African Americans were progressing—"in culture, in character, in the accumulation of property, and in the power of organization." Thomas's negative comments about Negro women and children, Chesnutt added, "confute themselves by overstatement." The lawyer placed the burden of proof on Thomas's character, "his truthfulness, his judgment, and his means of observation." Chesnutt was convinced that Thomas was a total fraud.[52]

Even before Chesnutt's piece in the *Evening Transcript* appeared, Jeannette L. Gilder (1849–1916), cofounder and editor of the *Critic*, wired Chesnutt requesting a 1,500-word essay "Scathing Thomas['s] Book." Less than a week later, Chesnutt had a "scathing" review of *The American Negro* in Gilder's hands. "Many many thanks for your promptness," she explained, "and for the article, which is capital. I have trimmed it down a little, as the wicked Thomas might have us up for libel if we printed it just as it stands. I think there is enough left to make him feel ashamed of himself, if he has any feelings left."[53]

In his review in the *Critic*, which literary historian J. Noel Heermance has described as "one of the high points of Chesnutt's early career as racial spokesman," Chesnutt laced into Thomas for defaming his race. Referring to Thomas's "atrocious book," Chesnutt blamed the Macmillan Company for being so ignorant of African American life that the publisher trusted Thomas's opinions totally unsupported by statistics or documentation. Why, he asked, had Macmillan not checked into Thomas's background and his character? "That a reputable publishing house should have issued such a book against any other considerable class of people without such preliminary investigation is incredible."[54]

Chesnutt, however, had looked closely into Thomas's past and, after speaking to many persons who were acquainted with Will, "heard . . . [not] one good word concerning him." Everywhere, Chesnutt explained, people agreed that *The American Negro* "faithfully represents the man." Comparing Thomas to a Jewish antisemite, Chesnutt declared that Thomas had alienated his entire race and would live forever tormented by his betrayal. Chesnutt also drew a parallel between Thomas and the slave who, in his 1888 short story "Po' Sandy," had himself conjured into a pine tree but was sawed into lumber and built into a house that was "ever afterwards haunted by the spirit of the unfortunate victim of an untoward fate." Thomas, too, according to Chesnutt, "transformed himself," in this instance "into white paper and black ink." Thomas, "a mulatto by blood," distanced himself from any Negro racial identification and sadly "bound himself into a book." [55]

Chesnutt denounced every aspect of *The American Negro*. The book resembled a mere catalog of anti-Negro newspaper clippings, he said, littered with imprecise and unclear language. Thomas, quick to identify "race traits" in others, succumbed to "a fondness for big words" which, ironically, Chesnutt remarked, "is supposed to be a trait of his [Thomas's] race." Chesnutt also wondered why in the book Will insisted on referring to contemporary Negroes, long ago emancipated, as "freedmen." Thomas's "thought," Chesnutt joked, "has been swept away by the current of his own eloquence. One must sometimes fish long in this turbid pool to catch a minnow." More serious, though, were Thomas's slanders against African American women and children. No diatribe against the race, Chesnutt explained, surpassed "in untruthfulness and malignity the screed which this alleged reformer has put forth." Some of Thomas's passages were so obscene that Chesnutt believed that the book should be barred from the U.S. mail. "To believe them, one must read the negro out of the human family." He added: "If they are the fruit of this author's observation, one shudders to contemplate the depths of vice which he has fathomed." [56]

For all his anger at Thomas, Chesnutt agreed with his point that African Americans suffered from the social distance that whites imposed between the two races. But, Chesnutt asked, why would whites, or any other race for that matter, wish "to consort with such moral and mental degenerates as Thomas has sought in this book to make of his own people?" Chesnutt concluded his critique by comparing Thomas unfavorably with Judas Iscariot and Benedict Arnold. Whereas these notorious traitors at least had lived virtuous lives before their betrayals, Thomas had made no positive contributions whatsoever. Chesnutt found nothing in Thomas's vaunted career in the South Carolina House of Representatives that certified to his moral character or testified to any valuable accomplishments. Regrettably, Chesnutt mused, "the strongest argument against the negro suggested" in *The American Negro* "is the existence of the book itself." He noted ironically "that a man of color should write such a book is almost enough to make out his case against the negro." [57]

Chesnutt's devastating critique elicited wide response. The *Boston Globe* noted the *Critic* piece favorably, and Professor Kelly Miller of Howard University congratulated Chesnutt for his "flaying of the traitor Thomas." Miller incorporated many of Chesnutt's arguments in his own review of *The American Negro* presented orally in July at the Fifth Hampton Negro Conference. Writing to John E. Bruce, Chesnutt hoped that the outpouring of criticism against Thomas would have a positive effect. In the end, though, Chesnutt added, "our own work is the best answer to his complaints, & the best antidote for his libellous statements."[58]

Having appealed to the court of public opinion to destroy Thomas, Chesnutt next turned his attention to the Macmillan Company. Outraged by Macmillan's complicity in publishing the book, on April 20, 1901, Chesnutt wrote the company, quoting a number of the most extreme statements from *The American Negro*—those accusing Negroes of across-the-board immorality. Chesnutt informed Macmillan that Thomas's book had stirred up a "storm of indignant protest and denial" among blacks and some whites. He explained that because Thomas's allegations were aimed at an entire race, including mulattoes, "unless the book be truthful," it was "nothing less than a crime, from which immunity is secured only by the fact that to libel a whole race is not an offense indictable in any court except that of public opinion." The case pitted Thomas alone on the one side, the Cleveland lawyer said, and virtually the entire race on the other. Unquestionably, Chesnutt judged, Thomas was a gross liar. Chesnutt blasted Macmillan for publishing "so grave an attack upon a class, merely because they are supposed to be poor and ignorant and defenseless." Chesnutt suggested that the company withdraw *The American Negro* from circulation because, he said, "if there was ever a case where decency and fair play demanded it, this seems to me to be one of them."[59]

Chesnutt then presented evidence of Thomas's checkered past to Macmillan in the form of a seven-page document resembling a legal brief, "In Re William Hannibal Thomas, Author of 'The American Negro.'" On his southern trip and from correspondence culled from throughout the nation, Chesnutt had unearthed conclusive evidence that Thomas was "a man notoriously untruthful, without character or standing anywhere, and with a long record in the criminal courts and on the threshold of them." Chesnutt's brief included correspondence documenting Thomas's expulsion from Western Theological Seminary, his misappropriation of Wilberforce University and Clark Theological Seminary funds, and his indictment and conviction for theft in Newberry. Thus, Chesnutt wrote sarcastically, Thomas ended "his career as a preacher of righteousness and instructor of youth, during which he had acquired the alleged knowledge which he so glibly and positively sets forth in his volume." Chesnutt concluded his brief by quoting Butler R. Wilson (1860–1939), one of Boston's most respected African American attorneys. Wilson believed that in writing *The American Negro,* Thomas "published his own biography and misnamed it. It is news to me that he claims to be a lawyer. . . . [He is] financially irresponsible, having posed as editor of [a] magazine in [the] interest of [the] colored race, erstwhile preacher, lecturer, and jack-at-all-trades except one productive of an honest living, he was years ago repudiated in this community. For many years he has been struggling to get his name before the public, and here's hoping that it may be gibbetted." [60]

Responding two days later to Chesnutt's wholesale repudiation of Thomas, George P. Brett first matter-of-factly asked Chesnutt to supply him with page numbers for the extracts he quoted, and then defended Macmillan's decision to publish *The American Negro.* The manuscript, the publisher said, telling only one-half the story, "passed our readers with very considerable praise." Ultimately, though, Brett reminded Chesnutt, authors, not their publishers, were responsible for the statements that appeared in their books. [61]

Thomas, upon receiving Chesnutt's letter via Brett, grew defensive and declared that persons were conspiring against him. "There is on foot an organized effort to discredit" *The American Negro,* Will complained. "Powerful influences are enlisted in the movement. Detectives have been employed to investigate my personal history, and libellous statements have been published." Nevertheless he remained cocky, informing Brett that he had anticipated such a harsh response all along. Thomas assured Macmillan's president that he would "take care of" his critics "in due season." Specifically, he said, the *Critic* already had agreed to publish a rejoinder to Chesnutt's critique and he planned to respond similarly to the critical reviews in the *Outlook* and the *Independent.* Having said this, Thomas then asked Brett for another advance against royalties. Responding to the avalanche of correspondence was proving extremely time-consuming and expensive, he said. "I am harrassed with an enormous correspondence, much of it foolish and abusive. . . . I need money to procure some documents and set myself straight before the public, whom I intend shall have the truth, and the whole truth, regarding myself and what I have written. I am poor but I am not a knave, and I know that no man can bring home to me a dishonorable act." Brett never responded to his request for funds because Thomas already owed Macmillan money. Instead, Brett informed him that he was glad that he would answer his critics, especially Chesnutt. Brett feared that sales might suffer if attacks such as Chesnutt's in the *Critic* went unanswered. Brett also encouraged Thomas to demand that his critics deny their allegations in print, "on threat of suit by the author." [62]

Before Thomas could reply, on April 26 Chesnutt sent Macmillan another letter, supplying page numbers for the quotations he considered to be offensive, adding new criticisms of *The American Negro* and its publisher, and appending a third revised version of "In Re William Hannibal Thomas, Author of 'The American Negro.'" More specific in his criticisms of Thomas than in his previous correspondence, Chesnutt questioned, for example, Thomas's sources for statements imputing syphilis and "moral turpitude" to the entire race. According to Chesnutt, three of Thomas's chapters—"Moral Lapses," "Criminal Instincts," and "Characteristic Traits"—reeked of innuendo, ad hominem attacks, and contradictions. Chesnutt credited Thomas "with a certain ingenuity," the ability to weave together "some incontestable facts with his mass of falsehood." At the very least he was "a corrupt and conscienceless seeker after notoriety." [63]

Chesnutt warned Macmillan that Thomas's sweeping statements had serious implications for contemporary race relations. Already, he reminded Brett, African Americans labored under "a heavy handicap of race prejudice." Thomas's book, carrying the prestigious Macmillan imprint, most certainly would have a "dangerous," "far-reaching and disastrous effect" at a time when race relations were so raw. African Americans stood at a critical juncture in their development, Chesnutt explained, no longer slaves but not yet totally free. He implored Macmillan to recall *The American Negro*. Already the Cleveland Public Library had removed the book from its shelves, fearful that it would exacerbate racial prejudice. Believing that Thomas had duped Macmillan into trusting him as a responsible and informed social critic, Chesnutt asked the publisher to remedy its error. Macmillan, he said, had a "moral" responsibility to remove Thomas's book from its list. Before its publication of *The American Negro*, Thomas "was a man absolutely obscure, who had never done anything toward the world's work which would entitle him to hearing as a spokesman representing a people." Thomas, Chesnutt assumed, "was so obscure . . . that he must have imagined that his past could be concealed, or he never would have risked the inevitable exposure." Chesnutt offered another possible explanation for Thomas's book, however. "He may indeed be so far gone as not to be affected by these disclosures." [64]

Obviously unsure how to respond to Chesnutt's allegations, Brett contacted Professor Franklin H. Giddings, whose enthusiastic reading of Thomas's manuscript had inclined Macmillan to publish *The American Negro* in the first place. Brett sent Giddings Chesnutt's second letter, inquiring whether or not he should reply and, if so, how. *"Unfortunately,"* Brett admitted in an extraordinary statement, *"I have not read . . . [Thomas's] book and am not familiar with it."* Giddings, who continued to evaluate manuscripts for Macmillan at a rapid clip, remained a champion of Thomas's book. Even before Chesnutt's communication with Brett, the Columbia sociologist compared Professor John Roach Straton's "The Race Problem and Its Possible Solution" unfavorably with Thomas's book. "As it stands," Giddings said in his negative reader's report, Straton's manuscript "is inferior on the optimistic side to Booker Washington's work and as a picture of the dark side it lacks the strength and vivid blackness of Thomas' pages."[65]

Giddings advised Brett to respond to Chesnutt directly, suggesting that he admit "that Thomas was a pretty bad lot in his younger days. So," he added, "were very many men who are revered at the present time as the fathers of the Republic." Giddings's point was that an author's private life was irrelevant in editorial decisions. The important questions, he insisted, were whether Thomas's experiences had prepared him to judge Negro life comprehensively and if his statements were accurate. Giddings believed that Macmillan was on solid ground in publishing Thomas's book because "not one of his critics dares to suggest that Thomas doesn't know as much as any man living is likely to know, about the great mass of the negro people, as distinguished from the selected few that Booker Washington and others have been educating; and that few of them show any disposition to offer detailed proof that Thomas has drawn too dark a picture, although they vehemently assert that he has." Giddings predicted that African Americans would continue to assail Thomas, drawing upon the sociological studies of "that well known negro professor, W. E. B. Du Bois." Ironically, Giddings charged, Du Bois "practically admits and deplores, but in veiled English, every thing that Thomas speaks of in English that is unmistakeably plain." He concluded that "The real truth . . . is that the people who are maddest over Thomas' book are precisely those who too well know that the things he says are substantially true."[66]

Armed with Giddings's advice, Brett responded to Chesnutt on May 10, explaining that he considered his letter unfair to both Thomas and Macmillan. Brett, who had admitted to Giddings twelve days before that he had not read Thomas's book, accused Chesnutt of taking extracts out of context that "give a different impression" than "a careful reading of the volume" would provide. Parroting Giddings's recommendation, Brett told Chesnutt that Thomas's private life was of no concern to the press, though it did appear that Thomas "must have passed through a period of his life when much might be said against his character." Further, Brett said, Macmillan's readers, referring to Giddings and William Z. Ripley—"men connected with two of the highest and best educational institutions in this country"—were confident that Thomas both was an authoritative source and that his arguments were substantiated by known facts. Here Brett lied—Ripley had unequivocally opposed publication. Brett then accused Chesnutt of erring by assuming that in *The American Negro* Thomas meant "that all members of the race which it treats are subject to the remarks set forth therein." This point, the publisher added, "if we mistake not the author explicitly so states in the work itself." [67]

While Brett tread water, hopeful that Chesnutt would halt his campaign against Thomas and his publishing company, Chesnutt kept Booker T. Washington informed of his efforts to have Macmillan withdraw *The American Negro* from sale. The Cleveland attorney, "while friendly to Washington," and a supporter of his economic views, "scarcely subscribed to his philosophy" regarding disfranchisement. Nevertheless, the two men shared contempt for Thomas, and Chesnutt sent Washington a copy of "In Re William Hannibal Thomas, Author of 'The American Negro.'" Washington thanked Chesnutt for what he had dug up "describing the character of the execrable William Hannibal Thomas," adding, "I am very glad to learn of your efforts to have this book withdrawn from circulation. I believe that the effort is succeeding because the MacMillans are not pushing it in any of their advertisements as I have taken pains to notice." [68]

While Chesnutt and Brett wrangled over Thomas's *The American Negro*, the book stimulated important debates about race in diverse African American communities throughout the United States. Writing in mid-May, a columnist in the *Boston Evening Transcript* remarked that "the public is still exasperated with that disloyal and inaccurate book, 'The American Negro.'" Black preachers, black teachers, and black women—the three groups that Thomas maligned so egregiously in his book—digested and reflected on his criticisms and then responded in kind. For all its crude racist venom, Thomas's book forced blacks to address basic questions, including racial characteristics, slavery's legacy, industrial versus classical education, the black family, the race's leadership, and many others. Discussions on *The American Negro* at the grassroots level lasted into the summer of 1901, providing important forums for Jim Crow–era blacks to examine themselves and to express their rage at the racial injustice that enveloped them. Ironically, Thomas's book promoted racial solidarity among those he assailed so unjustly. While African Americans might agree on few things, they formed a solid phalanx in condemning Thomas and his rabidly anti-black book.[69]

The Reverend S. Timothy Tice of St. Paul's Church in Cambridge, Massachusetts, led the way in framing the public response to Thomas's *The American Negro.* Educated at the A.M.E.'s Edward Waters College in Jacksonville, Florida, and Wilberforce University, Tice held pastorates in Louisiana, Maryland, and Canada before moving to Massachusetts in 1900. Fiercely proud of his race, for many years Tice preached self-help, communal solidarity, group consciousness, and manual training. Lecturing at Paul Quinn College in 1899, he criticized notions of white superiority as "egotism fallacious and wanton foolishness." Tice saw progress—"material, intellectual, moral and spiritual"—among African Americans wherever he traveled. Only its own divisiveness held the race back. "The greatest enemy to the Negro today is the Negro; the greatest savior of the Negro tomorrow must be the Negro." Two years before he read *The American Negro,* Tice blamed intelligent members of his race for "drawing the color line even among themselves." In 1900 he reminded his brethren that "some of our worst enemies are members of our own race." It was almost as though he prefigured the publication of Thomas's book.[70]

The American Negro outraged Tice. On Monday evening, April 22, 1901, the minister addressed a packed crowd at St. Paul's Church, only three miles from Thomas's home in Everett. The audience gathered to hear Tice and other area ministers smash Thomas's arguments. Speaking "in low measured tones," Tice led off, shocking those in attendance with choice tidbits about Thomas's private life drawn from documents Bruce published in the *Washington Colored American.* Other area African American clergy, Isaac B. Allen, Charles Hall, W. B. Morris, and John Brown, later ascended the pulpit and similarly pilloried *The American Negro.* The audience laughed when Allen joked that he hoped to God that Thomas was there "with two good arms" so that Allen could "give him a lively time." So thorough was Tice's thrashing of Thomas that at the end of the evening the audience donated money to print Tice's address.[71]

In this forty-nine-page pamphlet, Tice acknowledged that he was determined not to abuse Thomas, "with whom I am personally acquainted, and entertain the most friendly relations, socially and otherwise." As proof, he complimented Thomas's analysis of the treatment of the Negroes' social and political rights and colonization. Nonetheless, Tice charged that Thomas, who always had been classified and identified himself as a Negro, was a shameless hypocrite. He was a "demon, black, cold-hearted wretch in human form," the "Judas Iscariot of the Negro race." Thomas's own career was that of "a blank failure as a lawyer, preacher and teacher. He has been a jack-at-all-trades," Tice said, "and a success at none." Thomas had no right, then, to attack the material achievements of the freedpeople. Tice defended African Americans from Thomas's numerous unsupported allegations. His stubborn refusal to recognize their economic contributions proved him "to be a fool and a knave." Negroes, Tice insisted, were no more extravagant, lazy, or shiftless than other races. "When Mr. Thomas rises above his prejudices and biasness, he shows himself as a *Negro* able to state incontrovertible facts, but there is so much of the spirit of chagrin and vindictiveness in him that he cannot write long in this vein." [72]

Tice judged Thomas's chapters on the Negro's basic traits, morals, and alleged criminality most offensive, especially to women. He remained incredulous "How a *Negro* man, born of *Negro* parentage, possessed of *Negro* relatives, married to a *Negro* woman" could defame African American females so thoroughly. Somehow Thomas concocted characteristics in blacks that surpassed even the wildest fantasies of radical white supremacists, and he simply lacked proof for his insulting remarks. "No atheist, infidel or skeptic has ever penned such lines, nor has printer's ink ever before . . . stamped such infamy upon paper." How, Tice asked, could Thomas even purport to be a minister and still attack African American clergymen so unjustly? He responded by charging that Thomas "masqueraded in a garment of seeming righteousness, at the same time being an archangel of fiendish diabolism. He is culpable enough," Tice said, "to take unto himself every charge that he has alleged to the Negro ministry." "Poor, poor, William Hannibal Thomas. Thou are done for!" Tice concluded. By publishing *The American Negro* Thomas had alienated both races. Tice advised him that "since thou are a moral leopard, a traitor like Arnold, a betrayer worse than Judas, it would have been better for thee hadst thou never been born. Thou hast betrayed the innocent,—give up the blood money, and go off and hang thyself: die and be forgotten." [73]

Will, however, neither committed suicide nor accepted Tice's attack passively. In July 1901, he filed a $10,000 damage suit for malicious libel and slander against Tice in Middlesex County Court. According to the *Boston Post*, which described Will inaccurately as "pastor of a colored church in Everett," the case was scheduled to be tried in September. The paper ex-

plained that Will was upset with Tice's attacks on his character, the allegation that he was unfit to write a book on Negroes, and the insinuation that a
white author actually had written *The American Negro*. Will explained that
"the suit is not brought against Tice for money consideration. It is simply to
teach Mr. Tice and others the difference between legitimate criticism and
personal abuse." The *Post* predicted that the trial would "bring out some
amusing incidents." When informed of Thomas's charges, Tice explained
that he was not surprised and remarked: "I hope he will go on with his
suit . . . I am ready for him." Though Tice denied having any malice against
Will, he nevertheless believed that *The American Negro* was so unfair that
it warranted refutation and public debate. After a postponement, the case
never went to trial. Thomas and Tice settled out of court and the case was
dismissed.[74]

No sooner had Tice launched his attack on Thomas in Cambridge than
another black clergyman, the Reverend Charles T. Walker, began a similar
barrage in New York City. The son of a slave deacon and the nephew of two
slave Baptist ministers, Walker was born a slave in Richmond County, Georgia, in 1858. At age fifteen he experienced a religious conversion and joined
the Baptist faith. With financial assistance from Ohio benefactors, Walker
attended Augusta Institute, completing the literary and theological curricula,
and in the 1880s emerged as one of Georgia's most industrious and best-
known preachers. After lecturing in Egypt, Europe, and England in the
1890s, Walker was called to New York City's prominent Mount Olivet Baptist
Church. A gifted evangelist and "an electrifying orator," Walker was, according to an admirer, "without doubt the most eloquent minister in America, if
not in the world." Blacks referred affectionately to both Walker and A.M.E.
Bishop Henry McNeal Turner as the "black Spurgeon." All exaggeration
aside, Walker held a reputation as one of the country's foremost African
American clerics.[75]

In May 1901, Walker used his pulpit at the Mt. Olivet Church as an arena
to reply to Thomas's charges against people of color. Before his large congregation, Walker branded Thomas "The 20th Century Slanderer of The Negro Race." News of Walker's lecture spread quickly throughout the African
American community. To reach an even broader audience, he published the
address as a thirty-one-page pamphlet, distributed it widely, and hit the lecture circuit. Walker led his crusade against Thomas throughout the northeast, speaking in Boston, New Haven, and other cities. "I am trying to organize our people wherever I go to make a fight against Thomas's book in the
libraries," Walker told John Edward Bruce.[76]

Like Tice, Walker depended heavily on the criticisms of others to bolster his indictment of Thomas. He quoted verbatim, for example, Bruce's disclosures about Thomas's sordid past from the *Colored American* and Booker T. Washington's review from *Outlook*. He included a lengthy letter from Mary Church Terrell (1863–1954), president of the National Association of Colored Women, testifying that she never had observed the characteristics that Thomas identified in women of color. Walker also misquoted Bishop Turner who, in an interview, acknowledged knowing Thomas during the Civil War when "some Southern hero shot off one of his arms." In his pamphlet, however, Walker quoted Turner as saying: "And it is a pity he did not shoot his head off."[77]

Walker accused Thomas of frittering his life away, failing repeatedly to help the struggling race that in *The American Negro* "he has so grossly misrepresented and so willfully lied against." Thomas vastly underestimated the material progress of African Americans and grossly insulted their work ethic, morals, and personal habits. Thomas, Walker insisted, conveniently ignored how in the South their race was poorly paid and lacked protection against injustice. He defended black men from Thomas's charges that they preferred white women, explaining, "they have women as good, as pure, and as beautiful as any other race." He judged Thomas's remark—"that . . . decent respect for chaste womanhood does not exist" among Negro men—as sheer slander, "the most sweeping charge ever made against a race of people." Walker asked rhetorically whether Thomas included himself among such men. He could not imagine "that there is not a man living who wants to see a chaste woman—who does not want to see his wife upright, his sisters and his daughters, nor even his mother" live a moral life. On this point Walker charged that Thomas was "an infamous, malicious, unmitigated, pusillanimous liar."[78]

Equally troubling, in Walker's view, was Thomas's labeling of Negroes as "inferior types of mankind [who] should be excluded or exterminated." Drawing on the Old Testament (Esther 3–6), Walker argued: "Like Haaman of old, who desired the extermination of the Jews, William Hannibal Thomas, a disgruntled malcontent, a former 'Carpet-bagger' and office seeker, a man who once claimed that he was called of God to preach the Gospel of the lowly Nazarene—to expound the doctrine of the Golden Rule . . . exceeds heathen philosophers in his recommendation of remedies for existing evils. Let this modern Haaman beware lest he hang on the gallows he is preparing for Mordecai." Ironically, Walker said, members of the race had enough sense to exclude "unworthy" leaders like Thomas from their posts. "He is a statesman without a job." Walker concluded that throughout *The American Negro* Thomas distanced himself from both the Negro and Caucasian races. He was "a man without a race."[79]

Walker blamed Thomas's isolation from his race for sabotaging whatever good might have been accomplished by his writing *The American Negro*. Despite its "false charges, slanderous charges," though, he admitted that Thomas included "important and interesting historical information and other advice that no sensible man will object to." For example, Walker agreed with Thomas's description of railroad trips organized by preachers where "many young girls are brought to grief and shame by them." He also endorsed Thomas's condemnation of Negro social clubs where dancing, drinking, and gambling were rampant. And Walker acknowledged that "many" northerners did periodically visit the South to procure young Negresses for prostitution. "In this Mr. Thomas tells the truth," Walker said. "I have made some investigation concerning this charge and find it to be substantiated."[80]

But the "black Spurgeon" surrendered little else to Thomas. All professions, including the ministry, admitted "unworthy" men, he noted, "for instance, men like Mr. Thomas." Walker wondered whether Thomas was an authority on thievery because of his own criminal record. Did his career as an educator qualify him to criticize the likes of John F. Slater, Charles Avery, and Booker T. Washington? The Republican party per se was not responsible for immorality among the freedpeople, Walker argued. Rather, he blamed opportunistic carpetbaggers, "office seekers, parasites, and hypocrites of the Thomas ilk." Thomas's extreme condemnation of African American achievements in politics, the arts, and religion all betrayed his ignorance and were "in keeping with his slanderous tirade against his own people." In closing Walker reminded blacks that their future lay not in racial mixing or in repatriation schemes, but in developing character, schools, and businesses. Walker warned his people to be cautious of false prophets like Thomas. He was the "modern Haman" in disguise, the "twentieth century Judas Iscariot."[81]

After withstanding withering attack after withering attack, in June 1901 Thomas finally regrouped and stood his ground. Responding to the devastating critiques of Chesnutt and others, in a letter to the *Critic* he insisted that *The American Negro* was an empirical work, "a serious sociological study" based on personal investigations over two decades. He would retract none of his statements. Thomas explained that he had researched the Negro's "mental and social habits" and heretofore had published his findings in periodicals and newspapers read by members of both races. Not until 1901, however, had any furor erupted over his arguments. Thomas suspected that contemporary readers misunderstood his use of the term "Negro." He explained: "That this word is neither an exact nor an inclusive term, and therefore cannot be correctly applied to all persons of color, was presumed to be well understood. It was used, however . . . partly for the sake of brevity, but largely on account of its association with that class of persons under discussion." Attempting to clarify his point, Thomas argued that he never meant to include persons of mixed blood—"of whom the writer of this book is one"—as "Negroes." Rather they were "colored Americans." Such a person, again referring to himself, "neither in blood or bearing, has the influence of a slave." [82]

In his rebuttal, written in a cool and dispassionate voice, Thomas redefined "the pure Negro type of mankind" in terms even more stark, more grotesque, more offensive than he had employed in *The American Negro*. Significantly, as the barrage of his critics intensified, so too had his Negrophobia. In the *Critic* he characterized the Negro, as opposed to a person of mixed blood (Thomas again conspicuously avoided the term "mulatto"), as "not only a physical monstrosity, but of such mental and moral perversion as renders it incapable of self-regeneration, or of any substantial uplift." His description of the "well known" Negroid form revived the most primal nineteenth-century anthropometric caricatures of Africans, gross stereotypes including "broad, flat feet, elongated heels, apelike body, protruding underjaws, wide mouth, thick lips, flat nose, egg-shaped head, stiff, woolly hair, with a brain located in the apex of the cranium, and whose range of mental activities is limited to rudimentary physical wants." Thomas assured his readers that due to generations of amalgamation, the worst of these physical features had been diluted. Nevertheless, Negroes still retained "in a greater or less degree pronounced traces of transmitted mental and moral characteristics." These persons, he explained, were the focus of *The American Negro*. [83]

Thomas reiterated his central theme that behavior and character, not color, determined whether or not a person should be designated a "Negro." He regretted that so many critics had pounced upon his chapter on "Moral Lapses" and generally ignored his findings in the other thirteen chapters. And Will reminded readers that he stated directly that not all "persons of color" were alike. After all, he dedicated *The American Negro* to "men and women of color, of strict integrity and upright living"—these, then, were the adult "men and women of Negroid ancestry who have grown to the full stature of manhood and womanhood." Unwilling to recant, revise, or document his arguments, Thomas remained convinced that most persons of African heritage were Negroes; there were only "perhaps . . . a scant million" who had shed their Negroid traits. He insisted that he held "neither animosity [toward] nor [found] pleasure" in identifying the moral weaknesses of the freedpeople. But he noted with a degree of satisfaction that none of his statements in *The American Negro* "had been refuted" by his critics. In the end, Thomas remained convinced "that Negro inferiority in mind and character is incontrovertible, despite the commendable achievements of individuals of mixed blood." [84]

Not surprisingly, these words did little to quiet Will's detractors. In July 1901 African Americans held a public forum at Hampton, Virginia, on Thomas and *The American Negro* in what amounted to a ritual of denunciation. Black preachers and teachers were determined to try, judge, sentence, execute, and bury Thomas once and for all and then dump dirt on his grave. The setting was the annual Hampton Negro Conference sponsored by Virginia's Hampton Institute. In advance of the July meeting the conference's committee on morals and religion, chaired by the Reverend Francis J. Grimké, polled nearly one thousand leading educators and clergymen of both races, asking them to comment specifically on Thomas's "Moral Lapses" chapter. The committee felt compelled to examine Thomas's serious allegations of widespread immorality among Negroes because, it said, *The American Negro* had received "very wide attention, and, judging from the comments in many of the papers, is accepted by many as true." In its circular letter (see appendix 2) the committee asked: "As you have come in contact with the colored people. . . are these statements true or not? Do they correctly represent the present condition of the race?" Grimké compiled the results in 119 typescript pages of testimony and provided an overview of their contents at the conference.[85]

All but two of the 117 respondents to Grimké's circular letter refuted Thomas's allegations of Negro degeneracy and used their replies as a means to vilify him. One after another explained that *The American Negro* provided insights into Thomas's moral character, not that of the mass of his race. "Can it be," asked the Reverend M. R. Gaines of Austin, Texas, "that he judges all his race from his own case?" The Reverend J. H. M. Pollard of Raleigh, North Carolina, declared: "That some Negroes will lie, is true; Thomas is an example. That some Negroes will steal, is true; Thomas is an example. That some Negroes have no virtue, is true; Thomas is an example. That some Negroes have no honor, is true; Thomas is an example. But the personality of Thomas is not the personality of the race." Archibald H. Grimké wrote from Boston that *The American Negro* was "a monstrous concoction of ability, falsehood, malice, and moral depravity. To vary a little what Henry Ward Beecher said on a certain occasion: Mr. Thomas lies, he knows he lies, and he knows that we know that he lies."[86]

Individuals familiar with Thomas challenged his credentials as a critic of African American morality. Thomas E. Miller (1849–1938), president of the Colored Normal, Industrial, Agricultural and Mechanical College of South Carolina, who served with Thomas in the South Carolina legislature during Reconstruction, concluded that he "reeks in filth . . . has destroyed helpless innocent virtue whenever it has been entrusted to his care . . . has been guilty of nearly every crime in the decalogue; and . . . his book is a monogram of his worthless self. Here in South Carolina he has left a record in immorality as black as midnight." Recalling Thomas's days in Atlanta, the Reverend I. Garland Penn said: "Thomas was a bad Negro in the South, and his relation to women of the race can be proven to be immoral. [In his book he] . . . is talking from his own standpoint. His own depraved nature has led him to believe that others are like him." Writing from Augusta, Lucy C. Laney, principal of Haines Normal and Industrial Institute, remarked that Thomas's "rottenness of character is so well known to many of us here, that we did not for a moment think any thinking person would take the book seriously. I knew the man when I was a girl in school at Atlanta University. Later he was the pastor of an Atlanta church which was glad to be rid of him." In keeping with "his established reputation," she maintained, Thomas "lied."[87]

Theophilus J. Minton, a prominent African American attorney from Philadelphia, also claimed to have known Thomas well enough in South Carolina to doubt his veracity. Thomas's complex personality held the key to understanding *The American Negro,* Minton noted. "Those who are personally acquainted with Mr. Thomas know that credence cannot be given to his ordinary statements of facts . . . his mind constantly tends to the imaginative and the sensational . . . this is so thoroughly a part of his nature that he has long forgotten, if he ever knew, how to speak the truth. . . . I would not believe him on his oath. In character he is Munchausenian. . . . The wonder is that he should have had the effrontery and shamelessness to make such statements in print." Minton said he and other persons of color ultimately had to bear responsibility for Thomas. "The most lamentable act of which I know the Negro race in this country has been guilty," he complained, "is to have produced a William Hannibal Thomas."[88]

Most respondents to the circular letter pointed out that immoral and criminal behavior characterized members of all races and communities. Writing from Shelby, Alabama, the Reverend E. E. Scott observed that "no one doubts or denies" that "demoralizing" conditions existed among African Americans, "but that the race as a whole . . . is morally, sensually, and devilishly corrupt . . . is as far from the truth as wicked, malicious mendacity could put it." President F. G. Woodworth of Tougaloo University considered Thomas's statements "altogether too sweeping and unqualified. . . . He applies to the whole race what is only true of a part of it." Contrary to Thomas, Woodworth identified a definite trend toward moral improvement that was leading "a very considerable portion of the Negro people to a nobler life than Thomas seems to know about." [89]

The respondents to Grimké's questionnaire uniformly charged that Thomas based his judgments not on the highest representatives of the race, but rather on those positioned on the lowest rungs of African American society. They found his book especially offensive because it virtually ignored the achievements of the race's burgeoning middle class. Robert Smalls, U.S. Collector of Customs in Beaufort, South Carolina, who knew Thomas during Reconstruction, wrote that "If any portion of the statements made by him has the color of truth in them, it comes from the fact that he has ever made the lowest class of the race the associates of his bosom, and writes according to his impression of them." Bishop C. R. Harris of the A.M.E. Zion Church agreed, asserting that Thomas had perpetrated "a crime of the deepest dye" by portraying all African Americans as "vicious and immoral." Writing from Harper's Ferry, West Virginia, Dr. N. C. Brackett of Storer College compared Thomas to "other unfriendly critics" who measured African Americans "by the worst specimens of the race." Brackett worried that *The American Negro* would "not only give a false impression of the status" of African Americans but also discourage faith in the idea that every individual "must succeed or fail on his own merits." [90]

In the summary of their report, members of the committee on morals and religion also discussed the possible good that might result from Thomas's damaging statements. They concluded that *The American Negro* "should act as a tonic upon the entire race, in arousing it to a renewed sense of . . . the transcendent importance of character. . . . it ought to put every Negro, man, woman and child in this country on his good behaviour." In the view of the committee, Thomas's charge that the black race was morally depraved had to be proven wrong. Thomas's book "should be a spur, a stimulus to every member of the race, to so live as to give it the lie. After all, the best argument that we can offer in refutation of this book is a pure, upright, consistent life."

In this way, the committee claimed, the controversy about Thomas's book was a salve to the race's open wounds. It united all segments of the black community and demonstrated that "the race is in earnest in its efforts for moral betterment."[91]

While African American women participated in the Hampton Negro Conference and endorsed the Reverend Grimké's findings, many favored a more direct method of getting even with Thomas. As early as April 1901 reports surfaced in the Boston press that Negro club women were mobilizing to ban *The American Negro* from the Boston Public Library. Black women's clubs throughout the country led the way in fostering individual and race pride and setting a high moral standard for their race. The 1901 meeting of the Michigan State Federation of Colored Women's Clubs, for example, asserted that "the capabilities of any race must be judged by the very best that it has produced." Thomas, of course, had focused on what he alleged were the worst qualities of Negro women. This startling charge was not lost on Mary Church Terrell, a leading black female activist who defended African American girls and women from Thomas's scurrilous attacks.[92]

After years of observing and working with women of her race, Terrell, in her vindication of black women, complimented "their intelligence, their diligence and their success." As a teacher in African American schools she had known "hundreds of colored girls, not one of whom, to my knowledge, is leading a life of shame." Among the college-educated black females of her acquaintance, Terrell said, "not one of them is either a giggling idiot or a physical wreck. On the contrary, they are a company of useful, cultured women who would be a blessing and a credit to any race." While Terrell admitted that some girls were "led astray, especially in the South," she attributed such lapses to slavery, which "left its hideous mark for the law of heredity, which affects black and white alike." This condition, however, in no way validated *The American Negro*. According to Terrell, "no one who reads the book can fail to be impressed with the malice and malevolence which are but poorly concealed by the specious logic, and by the bombastic diction employed by the author, to sow his falsehoods broadcast to the world."[93]

Sharing Terrell's outrage, in April a secret committee of Boston-area club women banded together "to defend the honor of colored womanhood" by attacking Thomas and *The American Negro*. Furious over Will's book, Mrs. Gertrude Zenora Lambert of Boston complained to the *Boston Post:*

In my opinion this author has been asleep ever since the declaration of the emancipation. I cannot conceive how it was possible for him to look back thirty-five years and then write . . . such base untruthfulness. His writings are too ridiculous for any clear-minded person to believe. The negro of today has as much understanding and is as brainy as the men of any other race. His great drawback has always been that his face is black. Instead of Mr. Thomas wasting his last days in ridiculing his own race, he should be giving his efforts to a better work.

Another woman, Mrs. M. C. Hall of nearby Chelsea, gave "a stirring speech" attacking *The American Negro* before the town's Women's Protective League. Disgusted because black men had not risen to their defense, Mrs. Hall declared: "Let us women of Chelsea arise and let him [Thomas] see we are women of spirit and will not take such insults and we will see that no such book of defamation is placed in the public library at Boston or elsewhere. Shall we hear the insults of a so-called black man? Never." Mrs. Hall made a special point of comparing Thomas to white supremacist editor John Temple Graves of Georgia.[94]

According to the *Boston Herald,* Mrs. Lambert, Mrs. Hall, and other black women sought to remove *The American Negro* from the shelves of the Boston Public Library and compiled a list of the most offensive passages from the book to present to the library's board of trustees. The women were incensed that Thomas lumped all Negro women together in an immoral mass. One of them asked a reporter: "Does he [Thomas] forget that he had a mother? Would he impugn her memory because she was a negro?" The women objected so strongly to *The American Negro* because they feared that it taught their daughters "that their mothers are immoral women."[95]

Josephine St. Pierre Ruffin (1842–1924), respected president of the Northeastern Federation of Women's Clubs and president of Boston's New Era Club, summarized the attitude of the club women toward *The American Negro.* "The book is a disgrace," she said. "I wouldn't have it come into my house. I wouldn't handle it with a pair of tongs. It is too obscene for anything." Reportedly "undisturbed" by Mrs. Ruffin's comments, Thomas insisted that he understood Negro "traits" and explained: "I do not think there is anything in my book to offend or injure the morals of anyone." He added confidently: "I know the Negro of the North and I know the Negro of the South. I have lived and worked among them here and in every county of every State in the South." Librarian James U. Whitney, who commented without having read *The American Negro,* denied that a petition had been received for the book's exclusion from the Boston Public Library. Though Whitney conceded that some persons might find Thomas's book offensive, he was inclined nonetheless to believe that Thomas was "earnest and had something to say." The librarian judged *The American Negro* a "sociologi-cal" work with "a legitimate place in this library, even though it is unpleasant reading."[96]

In Everett, Massachusetts, Susan A. Armstead, a black Virginian who lived across town from Thomas, was less generous in her assessment of *The American Negro*. The town's Parlin Library added the book to its sociology collection in April 1901, and she was furious. Writing to the editor of the *Everett Republican*, Armstead, a widow, described Thomas as "An Afro-Anglo-Saxon-American author" and blasted him as "a perverted moral." She declared that Thomas undervalued the contributions that Negroes had made to American history while woefully exaggerating the race's shortcomings. Few persons, Mrs. Armstead asserted, would accept Thomas's argument that "the negro race is wholly immoral" and "the white race wholly pure."[97]

Outraged by Thomas's arrogance and the insults he heaped upon her race, she exclaimed: "Such a monster, such an impostor as this would-be white man is not fit to live, and death is too good for him. There is not, and there never was on this earth a race of people more richly abounded in intel-ligence, morality and decency than the negro race." Mrs. Armstead vigor-ously defended black women from Thomas's criticisms, chiding him for judging the mass of African Americans by the behavior of a few. The prob-lem lay with Thomas, she said, not with persons of color. "Because you cannot pluck the flower," Mrs. Armstead informed Thomas, "you pass the sweet scent by. Because you cannot have the stars, you will not see the sky."[98]

Though the campaign to ban *The American Negro* fizzled out in 1901, efforts to suppress the book surfaced again three years later, when Thomas Nelson Page cited Thomas as an authority in two harsh critiques of African Ameri-cans, "The Lynching of Negroes—Its Cause and Its Prevention" and "The Negro: The Southerner's Problem," published in the *North American Re-view* and *McClure's Magazine*, respectively. Blacks were incensed that Page based his writings on Thomas's allegations and ignored sources that assessed their race fairly.[99]

For example, James R. L. Diggs (1867–1923), a professor of Latin and philosophy at Virginia Union University and a radical political activist, pointedly answered Page's defense of lynching in the South. A Maryland native, a Bucknell University graduate, and the ninth African American to receive a Ph.D., Diggs accused Page of discrediting himself by citing Thomas as an authority. "Indeed," Diggs said, "it is by no means compli-mentary to Dr. Page that he should praise this man who would probably have remained unknown but for his general, illogical and scurrilous diatribe against the womanhood of the Negro race." Diggs went so far as to label Thomas a "freak of nature"—unworthy of being mentioned in the same breath as Bishop Henry McNeal Turner or Booker T. Washington, the latter of whom Diggs later criticized publicly.[100]

Editor J. Max Barber of the *Voice of the Negro* also blasted Page for trying to convince white liberals of his fair-mindedness by citing "experts" like Thomas in his articles. Barber insisted, however, that Thomas had no credibility within black or white communities. "A man who will slander the women of his race . . . merits only the execration of decent people everywhere." As late as 1904, Barber said, many still questioned whether Thomas had actually written *The American Negro*. He either had lent his name to the pen of some white racist "or he himself is the most monumental liar of the age." Barber wrote quite candidly that "Negro children ought to be taught to spit upon his name."[101]

Mrs. C. M. Allen, a woman of color from Sherman, Texas, agreed. While she admitted to Page that her race was "very far from the millennium," Mrs. Allen insisted that "there is far more honor in both men and women than observers seem to see." She charged that Page viewed African Americans "from the outside" and erred seriously in relying upon Thomas as an eyewitness. Both races contained their fair share of blackmailers and perjurers, Mrs. Allen said, and Thomas typified the worst of her race. Having lived in South Carolina in her youth, she recalled that Thomas "made an unsavory record" there and was just one of "thousands of professional liars among our race." Nevertheless, Mrs. Allen informed Page, "French or Continental morals . . . are by no means universal among the colored people. . . . We have pure homes . . . and refined, high-souled families living in them." It was impossible for Page to know such facets of African American life, she wrote sarcastically, because "that would be 'social equality'—a thing the best people of both races certainly do not desire." So upset was Mrs. Allen by Thomas and such "slanderers among our people," that she wrote a poem underscoring the importance of respect for African American womanhood.[102]

Having read Page's articles, Robert C. Ogden, the influential Philadelphia department store executive, also worried about the negative effect of Thomas's book on race relations. Ogden, "who served Booker Washington nearly all his life as benefactor and counselor," asked Washington for information on Thomas that might discredit him. Ogden was troubled by the fact that books like *The American Negro* described only one side of conditions among African Americans, providing "exaggerated statements of the worst and . . . very scant knowledge of the best." He promised to pass information on Thomas along to former Civil War general and U.S. Senator Carl Schurz, who reportedly planned to reply publicly to Page's articles. Washington in fact already had informed Schurz that "Thomas has been thoroughly discredited by his publishers and by every one else who knows of his rotten character." Once again Washington ordered Robert Wesley Taylor to prowl around Boston for ammunition to use against Thomas. Washington informed Ogden that the Macmillan Company had "withdrawn the book from the market, having found out the rottenness of his character and the unreliability of his statements." [103]

To supply Ogden with all the weapons against Thomas at his disposal, Washington instructed Chesnutt to send Ogden a copy of "In Re William Hannibal Thomas, Author of 'The American Negro,'" as well as copies of his correspondence with Macmillan. Chesnutt charged Page with basing his articles on the offensive passages that he had identified to Brett in 1901. In these, Chesnutt wrote Ogden, Thomas "deflowered the virginity and defamed the womanhood of an entire race." Chesnutt believed, however, that Macmillan already had withdrawn *The American Negro* from sale as a result of his correspondence with the publisher. "Certainly they tried to get the copies [off the shelves] which they could trace to the city of Cleveland." Chesnutt attacked Page who, like Thomas, failed to offer any specific evidence in his criticisms of African Americans. In conducting his research, Chesnutt said, Page "preferred to keep on his own side of the Chinese Wall of prejudice which separates the races . . . and to take the statements of this man Thomas at second hand." [104]

Armed with the "clues" that Chesnutt had unearthed concerning Thomas's background, in May 1904, Ogden went to work behind the scenes to obtain information about *The American Negro* for Washington. Drawing upon his contacts in the publishing industry, Ogden learned quickly that Chesnutt was wrong about the book's alleged withdrawal. "Inquiry of publishers," Ogden wrote Washington, "indicates that Thomas's book is now selling better than ever before." To this, Washington replied: "The information you give me about the sale of Thomas's book is almost discouraging. I had heard from what I had thought was good authority that the publishers had withdrawn it from the market. It seems almost criminal for a reputable firm to continue to spread such falsehoods through the world." After communicating with Brett, Ogden became cautiously optimistic about the prospects of influencing Macmillan to recall Thomas's book. "Of course, I must be extremely guarded," Ogden informed Washington, "but I will go [as] far as possible in exercising an influence for its suppression." Though Page's articles already were in print, Ogden wrote him nonetheless, offering to send "some important information concerning" Thomas "as an authority upon his subject." Several authors—including Chesnutt's daughter—have alleged that Macmillan stopped selling *The American Negro* in 1904. No documentary evidence, however, exists to support this assertion. Though Macmillan dropped it from its list long ago, the book nonetheless remains available in a reprint edition today.[105]

CHAPTER EIGHT

I Am Alone in the World

LWAYS RECLUSIVE AND SECRETIVE, Will Thomas left few clues of how he coped emotionally with the thorough repudiation of his book and his character by a cadre of furious African Americans and a handful of their white friends. From 1901 to 1935, as throughout his long life, he seemed determined to cover his tracks, leaving only occasional traces of where and how he lived. Evidence of his whereabouts is generally obscure and fragmentary. The problem of constructing Thomas's biography is exacerbated by the presence of numerous other African Americans with the name William H. Thomas with whom he easily could be confused (see appendix 1). To confound matters further, during the last three and one-half decades of his life, as before, Thomas was frequently on the move. In a long-established pattern, when he got into trouble he returned to central Ohio to lose himself in black communities in Delaware or Columbus. Even more confusing, late in life Thomas simultaneously maintained residences in Ohio and Georgia.[1]

Nevertheless, it is certain that he remained in Everett, Massachusetts, until 1910, nine years following the publication of *The American Negro*. During his decade in Everett, the town's population grew from 24,336 to 33,484, including 795 blacks. The landscape of the once bucolic village became dominated by the grimy coke and steel works that towered over the banks of the Mystic and Malden Rivers. While in Everett, Thomas again served as a financial agent for an educational institution, this time representing Union Biblical Seminary, the United Brethren Church's seminary in Dayton, Ohio. Thomas was committed to raising funds for this school, he said, because of its mission to Appalachian whites, reportedly one of his longtime interests.

Thomas also maintained a law office in the house he rented on Tileston Street in Everett. Though he was admitted to the Massachusetts bar in April 1902, it is doubtful that a man in his sixties with serious medical problems and a questionable reputation among people of both races would have had many clients.[2]

Whether or not Thomas practiced law, he nonetheless participated actively in Everett's civic life. He joined the Sons of Veterans, an auxiliary of the Grand Army of the Republic (GAR) founded in 1878 but never fully amalgamated with the parent organization. After the turn of the century, according to historian Stuart Charles McConnell, the GAR "served largely as an organization for the promotion of patriotism and the commemoration of Memorial Day." In some locales former members of the U.S. Colored Troops like Thomas joined the GAR and enjoyed equal status with whites: in 1894, for example, William H. Dupree, a black veteran, commanded a largely white GAR post in Boston. Nonetheless, historian Donald Robert Shaffer concludes that "exclusion was a common fate for African Americans seeking admission into white northern posts." While many African American veterans were relegated to segregated posts, Thomas successfully integrated Everett's James A. Perkins Post. In May 1901, Thomas and Stephen C. Currier, past commander of the post, addressed students at the town's three public schools on the subject of "Memorial Day and What it Teaches." The local newspaper referred to Thomas as "Sergeant W. H. Thomas of the S. of V." The program included a flag ceremony, speeches by Thomas and Currier, and patriotic songs. Thomas, a decorated Civil War veteran and amputee, was a fitting spokesman for the GAR's rhetoric of national salvation. His membership in the Sons of Veterans—a hereditary white organization within an order that generally marginalized blacks—remains yet another inexplicable passage in Thomas's enigmatic biography.[3]

While residing in Everett, Thomas also dabbled in local Republican politics. In 1902 he campaigned successfully for Stephen C. Currier, one of Everett's wealthiest men, for alderman and was appointed to one of the town's commissions. In this capacity Will worked to secure land for a school in one of Everett's school districts. An outspoken Republican in an overwhelmingly Republican town, Thomas also served on Everett's Republican City Committee and, appealing to the temperance ("no license") vote, proved an able ward operative. Despite his service to the party, in December 1905, he failed in his only bid for public office in Massachusetts, a seat on Everett's common council. Always quick to give gratuitous advice, in 1908 Thomas urged president-elect William Howard Taft to read chapter eleven, "Enfranchised Functions," in *The American Negro*. Thomas hoped that Taft would use federal patronage judiciously to strengthen their party in the South. In a characteristic aside, he added: "It may interest you to know that I am a native of Ohio, and knew your father quite well." There is no evidence that Taft read the book.[4]

Despite his flirtation with politics, Will devoted most of his time to writing during the decade following the appearance of *The American Negro*. The devastating criticisms of that book had no effect on his attitudes toward race and contemporary race relations. Writing, for example, in 1904, Thomas reiterated his argument that people of African heritage suffered from unfavorable racial traits and overwhelmingly were backward and inferior to whites. Character, not color, he said, lay at the heart of the race question, and blacks needed to follow white role models. Reflecting on his own unfortunate identification with Negroes, Will remarked: "An inclusive racial prejudice . . . handicaps even the exceptional negroid in search of personal betterment. At the door of opportunity he is often rudely interrogated and turned away on account of his color, though in the end, recognition and appreciation are likely to come to those endowed with tact, capacity, integrity, and true manhood." In addition to these familiar arguments, he again advocated restricting black suffrage and allowing the states to regulate the franchise. Much like Professor William A. Dunning of Columbia University and other historians of his day, Will interpreted Radical Reconstruction as the wrong remedy for the South — an overdose of federal control and a bitter pill for the nation to swallow. In his opinion the Fourteenth and Fifteenth Amendments were mistakes, "since neither freedom nor citizenship was the fruit of zealous negro endeavor, but, like the franchise, a gratuitous conferment of something which has never been rightly appreciated, and, in many respects, grossly abused."[5]

But Thomas devoted most of his time not to racial themes but to a novel and his autobiography. Writing every day, his progress was impeded because he could not afford to hire a stenographer and because the wound from his amputation subjected him to intense and persistent pain. The stump on his right elbow joint had never healed properly. "My physical ills are almost beyond endurance," he wrote in February 1911. Because of numbness in his left hand and rheumatism in his arm, Will learned to use a typewriter slowly and was forced to type with only one finger. Making what for him was an uncharacteristic joke, the humorless Thomas informed a correspondent that he found the typewriter "vastly easier than using a pen." But, referring to three pages laden with typographical errors, he admitted: "I have not quite got the hang of it yet. This, no doubt, you have already discovered."[6]

Despite his difficulties in writing, by 1911 Thomas had drafted five hundred typescript pages of an untitled novel. He was able to do so thanks to the assistance of his wife, Zenette, who wrote at least one chapter of the manuscript. Will decided to dedicate the book to her after she died on July 13, 1906, following a short illness. Though Thomas rarely mentioned literature, he once remarked that he considered Mary Johnston's *The Long Roll* (1911) "a remarkable book, and she a wonderful word painter." With characteristic immodesty, Will described his own manuscript as "something out of the ordinary and entirely unlike anything heretofore found in fiction." When in 1911 the Macmillan Company rejected his novel with "a commendatory letter expressing regret," Thomas quipped: "polite phrases . . . rarely mislead me." Given his past experiences with Macmillan over *The American Negro,* however, Thomas's hope of publishing another book, no matter what its literary merits, with that house was at best a pipe dream. Undaunted, he planned on submitting the novel to Funk & Wagnalls, claiming that Dr. Isaac Kauffman Funk (1839–1912), who established that firm in 1891, was "an old acquaintance." Nonetheless, the book never was published and a copy of the manuscript has not survived. Will, like the characters in his novel, suffered, endured, and then drifted toward oblivion, leaving few traces.[7]

Thomas apparently shared his novel with only one person—South Carolina white conservative Theodore D. Jervey (1859–1947). Though he praised the manuscript's "power of expression," Jervey obviously disliked it and thought that Thomas was out of his element in writing fiction. Jervey, who in 1905 published a novel about race relations during Reconstruction, *The Elder Brother,* considered Thomas's manuscript too slow-paced and packed with too much character development. According to Jervey, Thomas frequently stopped the flow of his narrative to develop ideas peripheral to the story. Jervey encouraged Thomas to write his autobiography. He informed Will that the problems that marred his novel would be strengths in an autobiography.[8]

A Charleston native, Jervey graduated from Virginia Military Institute in 1879 and two years later was admitted to the South Carolina bar. In the 1880s he practiced law and served as an editorial writer for the *Charleston World.* In 1895 Jervey was elected police recorder of the city of Charleston but by 1912 had grown weary of this post. He was determined to publish books that would earn royalties "at least sufficient to enable me to stop putting niggers in jail, six days in the week for a monthly consideration." "My God," he added, "how weary I am of it; but outside of it, my law practice! Ye Gods and little fishes! particularly the latter." Jervey's books, *The Elder Brother, Robert Y. Hayne and His Times* (1909), and *The Slave Trade: Slavery and Color* (1925), never reaped substantial royalties, and as a result, he worked at the police court until 1931. A driving force among South Carolina's Democrats, Jervey attended the party's national conventions in 1892, 1928, and 1944. He was also a leading member of the South Carolina Historical Society, for many years collecting demographic data on black Carolinians. Though an amateur historian and social scientist, Jervey was regarded as an expert on the Old South, a leading "race thinker" and student of the contemporary "Negro problem." In 1919, for example, the prestigious *American Historical Review* asked him to review Ulrich Bonnell Phillips's *American Negro Slavery*. Jervey welcomed Phillips's proslavery interpretation and, not surprisingly, was captivated by Thomas's ringing endorsement of white supremacy.[9]

Like Mississippi cotton planter Alfred Holt Stone, Jervey was a gentleman scholar who participated actively in the historical profession at a time when nonacademic historians still played a serious role in the guild. In December 1909, Jervey presented a paper before the American Historical Association at the session "Reconstruction and Race-Relations Since the Civil War." The panel included Professor Dunning of Columbia University, Judge William Holcombe Thomas of Montgomery, Alabama, and W. E. B. Du Bois. A self-professed "Southern man" and conservative, Jervey informed Harvard University historian Albert Bushnell Hart that he was ambivalent about appearing on the panel with Du Bois. On the one hand, Jervey explained that he frequently had confronted African American lawyers in court and had read Du Bois's *The Souls of Black Folk* (1903) "with great interest." But, Jervey admitted, he was not "devoid of what is called by Dr. [Booker T.] Washington 'color prejudice.'" For example, Jervey explained, "I would not care to be introduced to Professor Du Bois; and while I could listen to him, no doubt, with great benefit, I would not care to debate with him." Jervey was automatically convinced that his arguments would be mainly "historical" and Du Bois's points would be largely "sentimental."[10]

Jervey feared racial unrest as the descendants of the freedpeople acquired education and demanded better jobs, land, education, and social equality. He predicted that whites would resist, resulting in racial conflict. To avoid such a clash, Jervey favored the colonization of African Americans to Haiti.

In his opinion, "Hayti is Afro-American" and could only be redeemed by the Negroes themselves. "The very qualities which make the negro objectionable in the South," he said, "would add to his effective force in Hayti. It is the place for the strenuous Afro-American." Jervey envisioned repatriation as the only viable solution to the race problem. If one million blacks left the South for Haiti and another two and one-half million settled in the North, he said, the condition of those who remained in the South would improve dramatically.[11]

Jervey considered Thomas, second only to Stone, the nation's authority on the "Negro problem." Whereas Stone allegedly benefited from a "wider range," a "stronger mind," and "a fuller culture," Jervey believed that Thomas possessed a "more judicially balanced temperament" and had richer personal experiences to draw upon as evidence. Jervey complimented Will's "powers of observation, which are unusual" and his sense of "judgment which is distinctly admirable." Jervey admired his critical sense, honesty, and candor. Among black writers, only Will was bold enough to criticize northern philanthropists and to subject blacks to "honest race criticism."[12]

Though Jervey and Thomas never met, they nonetheless established a mutually satisfying and unusual friendship. Most unlikely friends, the two men formed a unique intellectual bond—one cemented by shared ultraconservative notions of race. Their correspondence provides important insights into Thomas's thought after he published *The American Negro*. For example, in a 1905 letter to Jervey, Thomas classified himself among "the expansionists," predicting that the United States eventually would control British Columbia, Mexico, and Central America. He favored annexing Haiti, "and everything else in the West Indies that could be got," as additional sites of settlement for America's "surplus negro population." Opposed to earlier colonization projects that sought to repatriate African Americans "under negro guidance," Thomas favored bringing new territories into the Union and administering them under white leadership, thus "on a sound economic and political basis." America's "surplus negro population" needed to be held firmly under white control. Regarding Haiti, he said, "the Haytien people are not now, nor will they ever be capable of self regeneration. Nor do I believe that there is one negro, or ten thousand negroes in the U.S. adequately qualified to lead in their upliftment."[13]

Thomas, who admitted being more pessimistic about race relations than Jervey, warned him that African Americans generally had little interest in and sympathy for black Haitians. "American Negroes," he said, "have no standing in that country, and I include San Domingo as well, the educated natives over there, are infinitely superior to our negroes, upon whom they look with contempt, as well they may." In fact, Thomas continued, Haitians harbored "a more intolerant prejudice against American black people, than the white people of any Southern State have ever shown toward them." The Haitian case, Thomas admitted, illustrated "that racial colors are not always the differentiating line of class distinctions." The salient difference was that in Haiti and other societies "where negroes have sway," he said, "color, in no degree ameliorates the often harsh and brutal relations of master and servant." Thomas's point was that unlike in Haiti, in the United States "a racial spirit" did not exist "among our negro people." [14]

Improbable friends, Thomas and Jervey nonetheless shared essential views regarding sectionalism and racial control. Responding to Jervey's comment that the northern press discriminated against the South, Thomas agreed, remarking that "sectionalism is not dead and prejudice abounds" in the North. "Believe me," Thomas exclaimed, "we are a dreadfully self righteous set up here." The two men also concurred that writers north and south failed to get to the heart of the race problem. According to Thomas and Jervey, agrarian reform and dispersion held the key to the best interests of the South's African American population. After reading one of Jervey's articles, Thomas wrote that white landholders should agree to limit crop production and to employ a permanent group of black families, providing them with schools, teachers, and land to cultivate their own crops. The remaining African Americans—he termed them "the unemployed surplus"—would have to leave the South "through some measure of compulsion." He explained: "If one hundred thousand negroes could be removed from the Carolinas, the racial situation there would be practically relieved of all menacing features." "A systematic dispersion of the surplus negro people throughout the north and west, would be the most convincing object lesson in racial differentiation that the world has ever witnessed." [15]

Having said this, Will nevertheless questioned the practicality of Jervey's proposal to diffuse African Americans throughout North America. For one thing, he doubted that blacks would migrate voluntarily. He also feared that government "herding" would result in the worst features of segregation. "In segregation," Thomas warned, "large bodies of negroes lead double lives, and since submerged influences always controls, such settlements never respond to the teachings of a higher environment." In addition, Will reminded Jervey of the longstanding antipathy in the North toward persons of African descent. For example, in *Robert Y. Hayne and His Times* Jervey cited an 1821 report of the Massachusetts legislature proposing a ban on free Negro migrants. Whereas Jervey interpreted the bill as an example of Yankee hypocrisy, Thomas understood it as a necessary safeguard against the movement of an undesirable element into Massachusetts. "The action itself," Thomas explained, "was wise, and maybe history will repeat itself, if the influx of disreputable Negroes in the state continues." [16]

From 1905 to 1912 Jervey corresponded with Thomas, first encouraging and then repeatedly pressing him to publish his autobiography. Thomas reportedly had been drafting his recollections over the course of many years. Writing to Jervey, Thomas remarked: "I have always had my doubts regarding any intrinsic value . . . an autobiography of mine would possess for the reading public, and apart from certain comments on the men and events of the past, I fail to see how it could be of the slightest interest." Jervey disagreed, admonishing Thomas to publish his recollections because of their value as a historical record, but urging him to cast them in the simple, straightforward literary style of his personal letters, not in the stiff and prolix manner of *The American Negro*. [17]

While the negative response to the book exacerbated Thomas's tendency toward isolation, introspection, and secrecy, exchanging letters with Jervey drew him out of his shell. He considered Jervey "the best type of Southern gentleman" and endorsed his racial views. "Such is my respect for his high character and legal attainments," Thomas said, that in 1889 he urged President Benjamin Harrison to appoint Jervey U.S. Attorney for South Carolina. Jervey, in turn, was intrigued with Thomas, treating him both respectfully and as a curious racial and intellectual "hybrid." Despite Jervey's paternalism, he nonetheless revived Will's flagging spirits, sympathized with his physical and emotional pain, and bolstered his pride and self-esteem. In his letters to Jervey, Thomas dealt with the painful rejection of *The American Negro* and the public airing of his troubled professional and private life by drawing himself close, or as close as he could get to anyone. [18]

Discussing his controversial book with Jervey, Thomas responded obliquely to the avalanche of criticism he received. He brushed aside the harsh reviews with the remark that because reviewers rarely read a book carefully, they consequently misjudged his work. "I welcome honest, intelligent criticism," he told Jervey, "the other sort does not disturb me. I know that every thought and every act of man expresses a true or false conception of an eternal verity; I know that my expressed convictions are demonstrable truths, therefore they will live." Will went on to inform Jervey that *The American Negro* was "the only one written by a colored man in America, that neither owes suggestion nor inspiration to white men." He complained to

Jervey that the Macmillan Company's demand that he cut six of the original twenty chapters resulted in "an incomplete presentation of the subject matter." Thomas considered two of the excised chapters dealing with "racial features"—"Ancestral Environment" and "Physical Variation"—essential to "any adequate apprehension of the negro question." He intended to include them in a second edition of the book, should one ever appear. His critics, Will emphasized in 1910, failed to understand that "the negro is a unique being in whom centiries of sameness has fixed certain habits of mind, incapable of interpretation by their designated standards."[19]

Spurned by his own people, Will thus found solace in establishing a long-distance intellectual relationship with a petit bourgeois white southerner forced to put "niggers in jail, six days in the week" to pay his bills. After the appearance of *The American Negro*, Jervey read Thomas's work in progress and the two men exchanged ideas about all manner of racial themes. In 1905 Jervey gently criticized Thomas's dense and complex writing style. Thomas responded, thanking the South Carolinian for his candor, adding: "I know my limitations and defects better than any one else, and would gladly correct them. But . . . you cannot realize how hard it is for one who is physically disabled and mentally handicapped, to put into terse, vigorous English, the thoughts and emotions that dwell in the soul. The drudgery of writing is appalling, and daily becomes more irksome as age creeps on. I do not have the vigor and vitality that I once had, nor am I so sanguine of results as formerly." Five years later, Thomas confided once more to Jervey: "I know my limitations and realize my defects; my vocabulary is limited hence my ideas are scantily clothed. For much of this, my physical disability is responsible. Finding writing painful and laborious, I have contracted a laconic style, which I fear sometimes, obscures my meaning." "No one but myself," he continued in another letter, "can realize the disadvantages under which I labor, and have for forty years. . . . My situation is not an enviable one, I am alone in the world, there is no one in my vicinity to whom I can turn for sympathy, or help. . . . I am weary of the whole business." A year later Will confided to Jervey: "I am not a vain person . . . and would rather avoid notoriety. In fact had I known the 'American negro,' would have instigated the unjust criticism and malignant abuse that followed its publication, I might have been deterred from writing that book." Jervey provided Thomas with a sympathetic ear. He comforted Will in his loneliness and encouraged him.[20]

Despite his criticisms of Thomas, Jervey considered him a "profound thinker" who possessed the gift of "acute, penetrating observation." Jervey believed that a personal account of Thomas's long life would offer a treasure trove to future historians and would represent his "greatest and best contribution . . . to posterity." More to the point, Jervey overwhelmingly approved of and was intrigued by Thomas's open admission of innate Negro inferiority. The two men—the southern white and the midwestern mulatto—shared a determination to shape and control the future of Negroes. But Jervey never drew Thomas's distinctions between Negroes and mulattoes or between skin color and character. Jervey judged Thomas an unusual authority and a kindred spirit on racial matters, valuing him as a spokesman for white supremacy to be cultivated and nurtured. In 1909 Jervey informed Professor Hart that Thomas, who weathered Reconstruction in South Carolina "unsmirched," ranked as one of America's foremost authorities on the race question. "Why he is not more seriously regarded in the North is a surprise to me."[21]

Convinced of Thomas's importance as a racial thinker, Jervey put him in touch with the white racial conservative William Hemstreet (1834–1920). A native of Oneida County, New York, Hemstreet descended from "an old Free Soil family," served in the Civil War, worked as a journalist, and published widely on the relationship between religion and science. A Republican, he served for thirty-five years as stenographer of the Kings County Court in Brooklyn, New York. Though Hemstreet opposed lynching and professed to have had "agreeable and mutually trusting" relations with African Americans, he found intolerable "unprovoked and unnecessary insolence from a nigger." Like many conservative racial theorists of his day, Hemstreet concluded that the two races could not live together in peace. Writing in the *Arena* in 1903, he argued that "we Americans have the inborn social sentiment of master and slave" and also possess "the natural antipathy of color." As a result, Hemstreet said, "race hatred" in the South resembled "a silent magazine—ready for a touch and havoc." Like other conservative racial theorists, Thomas included, Hemstreet concocted a program to solve the "Negro problem."[22]

He proposed that blacks voluntarily move from areas where they constituted a majority of the population to portions of the unsettled West or, even more ideally, to Cuba. Hemstreet reasoned that once they became a "political minority" among whites, or a political majority among themselves, that "all other questions relating to the races will naturally take care of themselves." Hemstreet described his plan neither as "colonization" nor as "enforced expatriation," but as individual emigration—dispersion and selection as all white peoples do to better their condition." On the mainland, he believed that racial problems only could be resolved by dispersing African Americans throughout the population. A "national Bureau" would buy, equip, and distribute free of charge small farms "to all blacks of the cotton States where their numerical superiority is dreaded." Cuba, however, would be their panacea. In Hemstreet's opinion, there they "would readily assimilate, find themselves a political factor, no color line, a suitable climate, near home . . . help spread the English language, and vote for annexation every time."[23]

Thomas, whose own proposals for agrarian reform in the 1890s had fallen on deaf ears, enthusiastically welcomed Hemstreet's plan. Writing in February 1905, Thomas told Hemstreet: "Your own contribution to our vexatious racial problem is worthy of earnest and thoughtful study by every intelligent and patriotic American citizen. You neither overstate impending dangers, nor suggest Utopian remedies, but what you say goes to the root of the whole question, and with minor modifications, furnishes the only effective solvent of this problem. Land culture and land ownership, under judicious guidance, will do more for negro uplift than all the academic schemes in the Universe." Thomas also informed Hemstreet of his longstanding advocacy of land reform for African Americans, sending him a copy of H.R. 11271, which he had drafted fifteen years earlier. Though Thomas remained committed to "Land for the Landless," he told Hemstreet that "at our ages, and with our resources," it was probable that they would "accomplish little or nothing toward the realization of our ideals." Still, Thomas wrote encouragingly, "we may stand for truth, justice and national honor, and deal righteously with all men."[24]

Examining Thomas's fifteen-year-old land reform proposal carefully, Hemstreet judged it "utterly futile, complicated, costly, paternal," and "fatal." The New Yorker remarked that "only by the government helping the negroes to help themselves can the [race] problem be solved." Specifically, Hemstreet criticized Thomas's plan as a mere "colonization" scheme and asserted that it was both impractical and too expensive for the small number of African Americans involved. Hemstreet suggested that the group nature of Thomas's plan denied the "individuality" of tenants—mixing the interests of the individual with those of the community. Rather than segregating blacks through a paternalistic government plan, Hemstreet proposed that a "self-help" approach be employed, one whereby families of color would live on their own amidst white neighbors, thus failing or succeeding individually. Like Thomas, he implied that blacks required the whites' work ethic as a role model. A segregated African American community would fail, Hemstreet said, because the freedpeople reportedly lacked the capacity to live cooperatively and productively together. Hemstreet further considered Thomas's plan unworkable because "100 families of blacks together . . . would play banjos, dance and quarrel too much." At the same time he feared that white residents in any southern community would resent a government-financed black community dropped in their midst. Finally, Hemstreet offered an alternative proposal that involved "scattering" Negro families through the white community. He argued that the individual "commingling" of the freedpeople among whites in the South would avoid the complexities of a colonization scheme. "If anybody can find a plan better than individual separation of the negroes by government aid," he explained, "I would very much like to see it." Having critiqued Thomas's plan, Hemstreet mailed his copy to Jervey.[25]

Jervey, however, already was very familiar with Thomas and *The American Negro,* describing the book in 1902 as "painstaking," "thorough," "careful," and "truly remarkable." Jervey considered Thomas's foremost contribution to be his delineation of the Negro's characteristic traits—the same chapter of *The American Negro* that so infuriated Will's black critics. Though Thomas realized that amalgamation helped inferior types gain in "transmitted capacity," he understood that racial mixing could only take the race so far. Race improvement depended on what he described as "a thorough assimilation of the thoughts and ideals of American [white] civilization." Jervey also complimented Thomas's land reform proposals and his ability to criticize not only members of his race but northern philanthropists and white southerners as well. "Pessimistic though it be," Jervey explained, "it is questionable whether anything ever has been written of the negro race which gives as much information as" *The American Negro.* He referred to Thomas as a "great negro" and, contrary to his African American critics, declared "that the race could produce one capable of such a masterpiece of mental analysis is of itself the most hopeful sign for the race."[26]

Jervey was so impressed with Thomas that he grouped him, along with Booker T. Washington and W. E. B. Du Bois, as among "those patient, intellectual giants of the race." Despite his genuine respect for Thomas's rivals, Jervey criticized Washington's "cheerful optimism hasty generalization and brisk commercialism," and disagreed with his determination that African Americans remain in the South. In Jervey's opinion Du Bois suffered from an "unutterable longing for social recognition for his race." Thomas, however, exhibited "the most extraordinary view ever entertained by a negro." According to Jervey, Thomas was "the greatest negro thinker this country has ever produced." He defended him from attacks by Washington's "supersensitive admirers" who falsely accused him of opposing industrial training for the freedpeople. Thomas in fact advocated manual training but refused to advance it as a cure-all. Convinced that Thomas's life experiences surpassed those even of Washington in preparing him to advise the race, Jervey credited him with possessing "the absolute truth of a great, if pessimistic mind." Thomas, unlike Washington, believed that people of African descent shared with whites an equal opportunity to develop "from the first era of recorded time." Their racial characteristics, however, doomed them to fall short of whites. Jervey was struck by the fact that though Thomas was in no sense an apologist for the South, his book placed him ideologically close to the darling of white conservatives, Virginia historian Philip Alexander Bruce.[27]

Jervey admitted that though on the surface Will's arguments approximated "the extreme Southern view," on closer inspection Thomas differentiated between the races in ways that transcended such obvious indicators as skin color, hair texture, and educational opportunities. Jervey explained: "To Thomas there is a spiritual difference. There is a negroid spirit and one that is not negroid and the negroid spirit may be absent from a black skinned individual & present in all of its deformity in an almost white." For all of his enthusiasm for Thomas, however, Jervey noted, quite correctly, that Will's "searching analysis" of the freedpeople's alleged deficiencies was far more detailed than his proposed solutions to their problems.[28]

In an unpublished review of *The American Negro,* Jervey lamented that the book had been subjected to "much unfair and misleading criticism." Referring to Thomas as a "hybrid," Jervey interpreted his book as a "hopeful sign for the mixed blood . . . that one of them should have produced a book . . . distinctly judicial in its tone." Thomas, unlike less honest writers, wrote boldly, plainly, and directly of what he considered to be the Negro's vices. "The hybrid is too truthful," Jervey exclaimed. Yes, Jervey admitted, the book was "iconoclastic," but it was no less so than other influential, reform-oriented works. Thomas, according to Jervey, encountered such devastating criticism, especially allegations regarding theft and immoral relations with women, because African American preachers sought to take the focus away from Thomas's accurate observations regarding their "worthlessness."[29]

Jervey went so far as to absolve Thomas from his previous indiscretions. "If a previous sin incapacitates a man from ever preaching and falsehood forever damns him the Negro priest must give up the Epistles of Paul & Peter." Thomas, Jervey said, also refused to pander to mainstream race leaders. Defending Thomas from Washington's anonymous review in the *Outlook,* Jervey ironically praised Thomas for having the courage "not to express belief in the only true and great Negro in the world today"—Booker T. Washington. Had Thomas, Jervey explained, written *The American Negro* for financial gain, as some critics alleged, he simply could have parroted Washington's arguments. Jervey added that Thomas's praise for the North and criticism of the South proved that he was not a mere sycophant of the former Confederate States. Not totally uncritical of Thomas, Jervey took him to task for failing to note the long and positive relationship between African American women and white children placed in their care, for ignoring relations between people of African descent and Jews, and for undervaluing the positive impact of the chain gang as an economic and legal force. All in all, though, Jervey described *The American Negro* as "of incalculable benefit to not only the Negroes but to all those of all races who desire to improve and who are interested in civilization, enlightenment, and progress." "That it should have been misunderstood," Jervey wrote Thomas in 1905, "is not strange, for it is in my judgment . . . a work which must steadily grow in importance." [30]

Two decades later, in *The Slave Trade: Slavery and Color,* Jervey described Thomas as "one of the few Negroes of distinct intellectual force . . . who participated in the struggles of Reconstruction in South Carolina and emerged, uncriticised." Thomas was "the wisest and most neglected Negro in the United States." "What a terrible indictment of the Negro intelligentsia," Jervey added, "is their utter neglect of William Hannibal Thomas, the great Negro who could think of something more than himself and his race, who wished to serve humanity at large." Jervey complimented Thomas's "wonderful clearness of . . . vision" and defended him from Professor Hart, who attacked Thomas's point that African Americans were held back by their "sexual impulse." Though he admitted that Thomas was overly pessimistic, Jervey insisted that his critics were too impatient and failed to dig deeply enough in *The American Negro* to grasp his essential optimism. Jervey argued, for example, that Thomas's emphasis on self-help and industrial education resembled Washington's basic approach to racial uplift. The Charlestonian explained that the differences between the two men were, to some extent, "temperamental." [31]

Jervey's defense of Thomas in *The Slave Trade: Slavery and Color* did not go unnoticed. In 1927 Thomas E. Miller, a mulatto lawyer who served with Thomas in the South Carolina General Assembly, informed Jervey that

> If you would have known the moral turpitude of the miscreant Hanibell Thomas [while in South Carolina], you would not have blotted your book with a single expression about him. To have compared him with Booker Washington is as far fetched as if a scholar should compare Benedict Arnold in any way with the immortal George Washington. No doubt, he is a man of talent and the very fact that one as talented as he is in the Negro race lived the life of a dependent pauper shows that those who knew him abhored him.

Unconvinced by Miller's censure of Thomas, Jervey continued to praise Thomas long after he stopped corresponding with him. Writing African American historian Carter G. Woodson in 1932, Jervey complained that contemporary historians of Reconstruction in South Carolina, including A. A. Taylor, Francis B. Simkins, and Robert H. Woody, had virtually ignored Thomas's "monumental book." Jervey considered it "very strange, that however much all other authors differ concerning other matters," they uniformly ignored Thomas, "one of the few individuals . . . who . . . played a conspicuous part in Reconstruction, without a stain."[32]

In the decade following the publication of *The American Negro*, Thomas became increasingly critical of African American leaders, many of whom had criticized his book so harshly. He believed that men like Booker T. Washington, while promoting "racial identity and racial allegiance," were "despoiling the deluded blacks, and . . . beguiling the foolish whites for the sole purpose of filching money from both classes to minister to their selfish purposes." Thomas hoped to publish, with Jervey's help, "A True History of Tuskegee," in the *Charleston News and Courier*. Convinced that Washington's educational philosophy was flawed and that he was manipulated by whites, Thomas complained that the fundamental problem with black leadership was "the fallacious assumption that a cultivated intellect awakens the soul of man, when . . . it does nothing of the sort." Thomas pointed to "the wide distinction between the verbal and actual ethics of educated negroes," who often employed language to "suggest an inherent . . . veracity, courage, and rectitude," when in fact they were "simply using words." Ironically, numerous reviewers had leveled much the same criticism at Thomas in their critiques of *The American Negro*.[33]

Writing to Jervey early in 1906, Thomas blasted Washington for merely parroting his "white mentor," General Samuel C. Armstrong, who established Virginia's Hampton Institute in 1869. Moreover, he accused Washington of representing white interests at every stage of his career—the launching of Tuskegee Institute in 1881, his incessant "begging" for funds for the school in the North, and his using texts supplied by whites for his many speeches, articles, and books. Specifically, Thomas charged that Max B. Thrasher, who historian Louis R. Harlan acknowledges "wrote or partly wrote nearly all of the articles, books, and sometimes even letters that appeared over Washington's signature," was the principal author of Washington's widely acclaimed *Up From Slavery* (1901). According to Thomas, "not one line of that book did Mr. Washington pen, hence I do not hold him justly chargeable with its many flagrant mendacities." Washington, however, openly acknowledged Thrasher's "painstaking and generous assistance" in writing *Up From Slavery,* and Harlan insists that the book "bears unmistakably the marks of Washington's style and personality." "Washington was to a large degree the author" and Thrasher served primarily as a shorthand stenographer and copy editor.[34]

Thomas missed the mark on Thrasher's role in writing *Up From Slavery* and, as usual, his hyperbole got the better of him. Grossly underestimating Washington's power, influence, and broad political agenda, Thomas asserted that Tuskegee remained "in the remorseless grip of white men" who managed both Hampton and Tuskegee. Thomas assured Jervey that he held no malice toward Washington, whom he considered "not a bad fellow at heart, when left to himself." To the contrary, Thomas said, "I know him well, and thoroughly appreciate his two chief characteristics . . . a fluent tongue and nimble feet." It was, Thomas insisted, Washington's "long training"—his slave background—that rendered him "the verbal phonograph of bigoted and dominating Caucasian thought." Washington, then, according to Thomas, was the tool of white northerners who exploited and controlled the field of "negro education." Fearful that Thomas's criticism of Washington "might be misunderstood," Jervey withheld the piece from the Charleston paper.[35]

Thomas further castigated Washington and others as "Big Negroes" and frauds. "It is not his white, but [his] negro master that the freeman should fear," he added. Such men as Washington, he declared, opposed the elevation of most African Americans because "it would destroy their prominence." Race leaders, Thomas charged, exploited Negroes for reasons of "self aggrandizement" and "personal notoriety," much like whites who commanded regiments of U.S. Colored Troops during the Civil War. Though

Thomas never before had criticized Giles W. Shurtleff and other whites who officered the 5th USCT, in 1910 he confided to Jervey that such men, "most of whom, unable to obtain commissions in their own ranks, were glad to be exalted over black men."[36]

Convinced that powerful men of both races conspired to keep the mass of African Americans oppressed, Thomas became deeply despondent. In March 1910, he confided to Jervey that "in all modesty . . . I know myself to be somewhat of a seer"—that he could predict the future. "I know," he forecasted, "that unless some unlooked for uprising occurs, there will be fifty, aye a hundred years hence, six million negro serfs in the south, as ignorant and shiftless as they are today." Already, Thomas argued, he saw signs of his prophecy. He received correspondence from throughout the South describing "the cruel deceptions practiced by negro leaders on their people." Again and again the freedpeople were "stripped of their scant earnings, by these despicable villains." Thomas also faulted white southern leaders for failing to devise a system to train their former slaves. He alleged that though they "squandered" millions of dollars on "so called education" for the freedpeople, the southern states never established a training system to transform them into an "efficient and trust worthy labor class." Deeply concerned about the future of the freedpeople and despondent because no one had listened to his warnings, Thomas likened himself to John the Baptist as "a voice crying in the wilderness" (Matthew 3:3).[37]

In the summer of 1910 Will left Everett abruptly, placed his books in storage, and returned to Boston to live. He rented two unfurnished rooms on Windsor Street in Roxbury from Mrs. Mary E. Monroe. He lived alone and was listed as a "pensioner" in the Boston city directory. Later, Mrs. Monroe told an investigator looking for him that she knew "nothing about his improper relations with women." While in Boston, Thomas's health, though never good, apparently began to worsen. He suffered from partial paralysis of his hand, which left him "rather helpless," unable to type and incapable of writing more than a dozen lines longhand at any one sitting. Once, in a reflective mood, Will informed Jervey that the weaknesses in his writing resulted both from his physical infirmities and his lack of education. Nonetheless he was determined to revise his novel and to plow ahead with his autobiography, describing himself as "a steady worker" and "a patient waiter." Thomas remarked confidently that the stylistic problems that marred his novel would pose less of a stumbling block in the autobiography because "I have a penchant for making observations." Though he considered work on the autobiography a daunting, "stupendous task," by June 1912, he claimed to have drafted roughly forty chapters. One day that month when Mrs. Monroe was away, Thomas packed up his belongings and skipped town without paying his rent.[38]

From 1912 to 1915 Will's wanderlust continued unabated. Even though he was in his seventies, he established dual residencies in Rome, Georgia, and in Columbus, Ohio. Accompanied by his third wife, Amanda, in July 1912, Thomas returned to Rome, which in 1910 contained 12,099 inhabitants, 31 percent of whom (3,758) were African Americans. Will had lived and worked there in 1871–72 before moving to Atlanta. "Most of the people I knew then," he remarked, "are dead, but their sons and daughters have met me kindly and shown me considerate treatment." He wrote Jervey that after settling in Rome he was determined to complete his autobiography in the winter of 1913. Despite his many assurances to Jervey, however, Thomas neither completed nor published this work. Like his novel, no manuscript of the autobiography has survived.[39]

Although in Rome, as in Everett, Thomas continued to describe himself as an "attorney at law," he never tried a case. Sick and elderly but keen and alert, he wrote Woodrow Wilson in January 1913, informing the president-elect that he had been born on the farm of Wilson's grandmother, Mrs. Harriet L. Woodrow, and offering to send him a copy of *The American Negro*. Thomas, a lifelong Republican, nevertheless wished Wilson "civil and political success during your administration of national affairs." In the presidential election of 1912, other African Americans, including W. E. B. Du Bois, Bishop Alexander Walters, J. Milton Waldron, and William Monroe Trotter, supported Wilson, a southern Democrat, over Theodore Roosevelt and William H. Taft. But whereas other African Americans rejected Wilson once in office, Thomas championed Wilson's presidency.[40]

In July 1913 he praised Wilson's address commemorating the fiftieth anniversary of the Battle of Gettysburg. In Will's opinion, the president's speech, which celebrated sectional harmony, peace, and national greatness but made no mention of race, was "the loftiest utterance spoken by any public official since the days of the immortal Lincoln." Thomas, however, urged Wilson to commit to an even higher level of sectional reconciliation by providing pensions for elderly and infirm former Confederate soldiers. "As a Federal veteran of the civil war," he wrote, "I would approve of any legislative measure that would bring aid and comfort to these brave southern soldiers, who fought a good fight and worthily merit the respect of the American people." In his old age Thomas thus abandoned the Republican party and forgave those whom years ago he had blamed for his empty sleeve.[41]

More than a year later, in November 1914, Thomas once again backed Wilson, this time on a controversial issue regarding discrimination against African Americans. On November 12 Wilson met at the White House with William Monroe Trotter and a delegation of Boston blacks. In 1901 Trotter and George W. Forbes had established the *Boston Guardian,* a newspaper bitterly critical of Booker T. Washington. Over the years Trotter emerged as a leading African American militant, ultimately breaking with Du Bois and the biracial National Association for the Advancement of Colored People (NAACP) and forming his own rival group, the National Equal Rights League, composed only of blacks. During his meeting with the president, Trotter implored Wilson to abolish segregation in government offices in the District of Columbia. Trotter reminded Wilson that he had received African American votes in the last election and that some envisioned him as "perhaps the second Abraham Lincoln." His performance as president, however, disappointed blacks, who, Trotter threatened, might vote against Wilson in the future. In response, the president defended segregation on the ground that it prevented race "friction" and actually helped the race become more independent. Wilson, clearly annoyed at Trotter's boldness, denied that segregation was a "political" question and said that he refused to be blackmailed. Trotter then accused Wilson of bad faith and his subordinates of "race prejudice" and for introducing "a drastic segregation." At this point Wilson, who later regretted having lost his temper, abruptly halted the interview. He found Trotter's argumentative style and passionate tone offensive.[42]

Wilson's abortive interview with Trotter attracted national attention. Whites uniformly faulted Trotter for his "insolence" yet some northern journalists criticized Wilson for sanctioning Jim Crow. African Americans split on the issue. Du Bois praised Trotter's "fearlessness and . . . unselfish devotion to the highest interests of the Negro race." According to Du Bois, Trotter "voiced the feeling of nine-tenths of the thinking Negroes of this country." Writing in the *A.M.E. Church Review,* Forbes agreed, describing Trotter as a "wounded gladiator" unfairly rebuked by Wilson. Robert R. Moton, however, who followed Booker T. Washington as principal of Tuskegee Institute in 1915, found Trotter's conduct embarrassing to the race. His behavior, Moton said, was not representative of the vast majority of African Americans. He sent Wilson his apology for Trotter's actions "and the regrets of ninety nine percent of the thoughtful Negroes of this land."[43]

Though Will would not have wanted to have been included in such company, he nevertheless agreed with Moton's assessment of Trotter and his delegation. Writing to Wilson's secretary, Joseph P. Tumulty, a day following the incident, Thomas congratulated the president on his treatment of Trotter. He blasted Trotter as "a person of some education," but one who possessed "an unappeasable craving for notoriety, and I fear is sadly wanting in common sense." Like other "colored democrats" in the North, these men were "mercenary creatures, without civic or social integrity, and intent solely on self aggrandizement." They joined the Democratic Party in 1912 only for financial gain and were willing "to sell their votes to the highest bidder." Thomas judged their statements to Wilson "ill bred and delusive" and advised the president against subjecting himself to meeting black leaders again. According to Thomas, "there is no such thing as personal leadership among the colored people of the north, despite all that the self constituted colored vandals may say to the contrary."[44]

Thomas left Rome, Georgia, early in 1915 to settle permanently in Columbus, Ohio. Columbus had a long history in the nineteenth century of relatively "fluid" race relations. Following the Civil War African Americans routinely attended integrated schools, gained access to public and private custodial institutions, and entered theaters, restaurants, and hotels equally with whites. Yet, according to historian David A. Gerber, racial lines frequently were drawn, and "affluent, prominent blacks" were "favored where facilities were generally closed to Negroes." In the 1880s conditions gradually worsened as African Americans from the South migrated to Columbus and encountered de facto segregation in public transportation, asylums, and poor houses. The African American, according to historian Richard Clyde Minor, "was no longer a thing of glamour—a principle for which one might risk his life and even die. He was a mouth to feed, a workman to exploit. He was even a potential voter. He was not an abstraction but a human being." By 1913, historian Frank U. Quillin explained, Columbus whites exhibited an extreme hostility toward people of color. He observed that "all classes of whites are banded together against the negroes." Excluded almost totally from decent neighborhoods, hotels, restaurants, soda fountains, and saloons, blacks also were kept out of skilled jobs and unions. Most toiled in menial positions—as janitors, waiters, barbers, and domestic servants. Nonetheless, "better-class negroes" sought good relations with whites and wanted to uplift their race.[45]

Most of Columbus's black population lived two blocks north of the city's main business district, between East Long Street and Mt. Vernon Avenue. This African American enclave was settled by Virginians in the 1880s who

worked in the nearby Pennsylvania Railroad shops and as servants for affluent whites to the south on East Broad Street. In 1921 Roderick Duncan
McKenzie described the East Long Street neighborhood as "a city of blacks
within the larger community." In addition to their own social and political organizations, residents supported "colored" hotels, stores, churches,
schools, moving picture theaters, and pool rooms. The "better-class negroes" that Quillin identified—physicians, dentists, clergymen, druggists,
and undertakers—established themselves there as well. In the 1920s members of Columbus's black bourgeoisie ran more than one hundred businesses
along East Long Street and bought property as far east as Woodland Avenue.
The racial tensions that Quillin described flared up regularly over public
transportation, control of property, and access to Franklin Park. Whereas
whites pointed to African American migrants from the South as the source
of Columbus's "Negro problem," local people of color praised them for their
determination to lead decent lives and to own their own homes and
businesses.[46]

Though living part of the year in Rome, Georgia, in 1912 Will established
residency in downtown Columbus in a small house on East Elm Street in a
racially mixed neighborhood. The Columbus city directory listed him as a
"colored" janitor. After leaving Rome for good in early 1915, Thomas lived
in the house on East Elm Street until August 27, 1915, when he entered St.
Francis' Hospital to be treated for a gastric carcinoma. Thirty-seven days
later, when his condition failed to improve, Thomas was discharged.[47]

Meanwhile, Jervey, having not heard from Thomas since he moved to
Georgia in 1912, became obsessed with finding him. Suspecting that he had
returned either to Ohio or Massachusetts, Jervey employed Clement L.
Martzolff, professor of history and director of extension work at Ohio University in Athens, and Calvin W. Lewis, a private investigator in Brookline,
Massachusetts, to track down the peripatetic Thomas. Police in Columbus
and Dayton could not find him. Nor could Lewis, who combed the streets
of Boston and Everett searching for him. In April 1917, Lewis contacted
Butler R. Wilson, one of Boston's leading African American lawyers and a
founding member of the NAACP, concerning Thomas's whereabouts. Wilson,
who had supplied information on Thomas to Charles W. Chesnutt in 1901,
reported erroneously that Thomas had died three or four years earlier. Others, too, informed Lewis that Thomas had died somewhere in the South. "I
find," Lewis wrote Jervey, "that the colored people [of Boston] are down on
Thomas's book; furthermore, they state that he was a libertine and a low-
down specimen of humanity generally—in fact, they represent him to have

been almost, if not quite, a moral degenerate." Lewis recounted the story that when he departed Boston, Thomas left behind an unpaid bill for his lodging. Another informant told Lewis that Thomas was "not dead but very much 'alive,'" reportedly having resided in Columbus with his brother Walter until the fall of 1916, when he relocated to Cleveland. But Will neither roomed with his brother nor lived in Cleveland: since March 1914, Walter also had unsuccessfully been searching for him. As usual, Thomas had eluded his pursuers.[48]

Journalist George W. Forbes, Trotter's former partner at the *Boston Guardian* and a librarian in Boston, held the key to the erroneous report of Thomas's death. A gifted polemicist, Forbes contributed a quarterly column to the A.M.E. *Church Review* where, in April 1914, he happily but erroneously published a tongue-in-cheek obituary of Thomas based on vague reports from "some Southern or Western paper" of Will's demise in Texas. Forbes, who admitted that he was "not seriously agitated by" the news of Thomas's death, laced into him with caustic satire: "Colonel Thomas was not a man you could become enthusiastic over at first sight, and he failed to improve . . . with time and proximity. Though living in Boston long before and after writing his notorious book . . . he was little known . . . and towards the last went almost wholly unnoticed. Running on a small percentage of friendship . . . he reached in the end the point where none felt so poor as to do him honor." Commenting on *The American Negro*, Forbes recalled that the book "dropped like a bomb in the camp of the more intelligent colored people."

> Every one felt humiliated by it. Its contents were so vile and lurid that even the colonel's young wife (herself long dead) wept as she typewrote it. Ben Tillman bought up a hundred copies . . . for distribution among his constituency. Efforts were made then, as with Dixon's "Leopard Spots" since, to keep the public libraries from circulating the book. Yet today we wonder what it was all about. Nobody reads that silly book now. It contained so much that was nauseating that people soon tired of it, or felt that they were reading the experiences of one man only. . . . There never was a better illustration of a book proving the antidote for its own poison.[49]

James Young, an African American from Malden, Massachusetts, "whose niece," probably Zenette Thomas, Will "married as one of his wives," corroborated the story of Thomas's death. Young informed Forbes that Will's body was discovered in a river in North Carolina. Authorities reportedly were unsure whether Thomas's death resulted from "a case of foul play or of accidental drowning." When informed that Will was indeed alive, Forbes "laughed" about his bogus obituary and remarked that it "had given him a chance to take a shot at" Thomas. Indeed, the death announcement had been based on wishful thinking, not fact.[50]

Following his release from St. Francis' Hospital, Will worked in Columbus as a janitor, at different times renting rooms on East Broad, North Young, and East Long Streets. Living in the heart of Columbus's African American community, Thomas was surrounded by stores, barber shops, hotels, and restaurants owned by people of color. In 1920 he dropped out of sight again, probably moving to Dayton to enter the Central Branch, National Home for Disabled Volunteer Soldiers. Established in 1867, the Central Branch was the largest and most prestigious of the various National Homes scattered across the country. It served as both a temporary way station for veterans to recover their strength as well as a facility for long-term, permanent medical care. The Central Branch reminded A.M.E. Bishop Daniel A. Payne of the Hotel des Invalides in Paris. Both served superannuated soldiers. Will most likely was an inmate at the Central Branch. If so, he lived in a highly regimented, military-oriented, and racially segregated environment.[51]

No exact record exists of Will's whereabouts in the early to middle 1920s. Incredibly, in March 1922, approaching his seventy-ninth birthday, Thomas appeared in Washington, D.C., at the U.S. Supreme Court, where he took the oath of office and signed the roll of attorneys and was thereby admitted to the Supreme Court bar. This hypothetically permitted him to argue cases there but he never did so. Thomas listed as his address the Citizens Trust Savings Bank, Columbus, Ohio. Four years later, giving his address as the Bank of Westerville, Ohio, he petitioned for an increase in his military pension from $75 to $90 a month. In making this request, Thomas explained the various medical problems that plagued him. "I am in my 84th year, I have but one arm and by reason of my disabled hand, I need daily assistance in dressing, undressing, eating and drinking. My right foot, and leg below the knee, is a source of much pain when walking, nor can I use a crutch, owing to the loss of my right arm. For more than a score of years, I have had no normal movement of my bowels. I am therefore compelled to have recourse to medical and mechanical means for every intestinal evacuation." Dr. Ben R. Kirkendall of Columbus, Thomas's physician for ten years, documented that Will suffered from a left inguinal hernia that required him to wear a truss, "obstinate constipation," and transitory numbness and partial loss of feeling in his left arm and right leg. These conditions, Dr. Kirkendall said, rendered Thomas's "general health . . . below par, so much so, that he is kept from any active physical duties." Thomas exhibited "marked nervous tremor in hand when held with the fingers separated." Kirkendall concluded that Will had been "more or less helpless since the loss of his arm."[52]

Despite these maladies, in his eighties and nineties Thomas somehow worked as a janitor. He did so, according to Columbus businessman Eldon W. Ward, with the support of Columbus African Americans who viewed him as an elderly man in need of help. Dependent on his military pension, Will relied on whatever he earned from his custodial work to pay for his room, board, and medical bills. In addition, Thomas marketed packages of Civil War–era souvenir prints, engravings, and photographs. In 1909 he copyrighted a print of Thomas Hovenden's "The Last Moments of John Brown." Two decades later he prepared for sale a collection of prints, including illustrations of Abraham Lincoln, Ulysses S. Grant, and Appomattox Court House. Though he may have been enfeebled, Thomas remained remarkably lucid into his nineties. Writing in 1934, Willard W. Bartlett, Otterbein College's historian, remarked that Thomas's "mind is exceedingly keen and his memory for events which can be checked, both in national history and in the history of Otterbein College, is so accurate that the writer has placed a high degree of confidence in his statements." Bartlett interviewed Thomas, then almost ninety and living on Nineteenth Street in Columbus, in January and April 1933 when researching his institutional history of Otterbein. Bartlett added that "in recent years" Thomas "has been very friendly toward Otterbein College."[53]

In spite of his painful experiences at what a half-century earlier had been called Otterbein University, Thomas retained fond memories of his days in Westerville. Some time following the publication of *The American Negro,* he recalled his "cherished associations . . . with an institution of learning, founded in freedom and perpetuated by integrity, whose teachings gave inspiration and guidance to a struggling youth." While still living in Boston, Thomas remembered his youth in central Ohio positively and decided "to be associated with a church which he knew in his boyhood, and when the end shall come, desiring to repose in Otterbein Cemetery." In 1908 he formally joined the United Brethren in Christ congregation on the corner of West Main and Grove Streets in Westerville across from the Otterbein campus. Through the years he had frequently traveled back and forth to Ohio from Pennsylvania, Georgia, South Carolina, and Massachusetts, so it was not out of character for him to join a church in Westerville over seven hundred miles from his Boston home.[54]

William Hannibal Thomas
at Otterbein College on the occasion
of the College's Diamond Jubilee
75th Anniversary, May 15, 1922.
Courtesy Otterbein College Archives.

On June 14, 1916, Otterbein honored Thomas, along with all of the school's Civil War veterans, with an inscription on a granite and bronze memorial on the grounds of Towers Hall. Thomas was Otterbein's only student who had served in an African American unit. Almost six years later, on May 15, 1922, he returned to Otterbein to attend a ceremony in which Vice President Calvin Coolidge presented an address celebrating the college's Diamond Jubilee 75th Anniversary and placed a wreath on the Civil War monument that bore Thomas's name. During this event Thomas had his picture taken in front of Towers Hall. Like many Civil War veterans who lived into the 1920s and beyond, Will wore a Civil War commemorative medal at the ceremony. In this photograph he fastened the heart-shaped badge of the Twenty-Fourth Army Corps to his coat. As always, he pinned up the right sleeve of his suit jacket just below his amputation. Almost eighty years old, he continued to display his war wound with pride. In this photograph Thomas looked significantly more gaunt than he had two decades earlier in the publicity brochure for *The American Negro*. His remaining white hair was long and unkempt. Will's most dominant feature remained the dark, deeply set sockets around his eyes. His return visits to Otterbein no doubt helped ease his painful memories of the racial disturbance his presence ignited at the school in 1859, and they offered a sense of closure to one of the major emotional traumas of his life.[55]

In his last years Thomas lived quite comfortably at one of Columbus's leading African American residences, the Litchford Hotel. In 1991, Columbus businessman Eldon W. Ward explained that the hotel's benevolent owners and patrons looked after Thomas, enabling him to live rent-free. Located in a fashionable neighborhood on the corner of Elm and North Fourth Streets, not far from Will's previous boarding houses, this three-story brick structure opened in 1906 and contained twenty-six rooms, a bar, and dance hall. Middle-class blacks took their families there to dine and to listen to such touring jazz legends as Cab Calloway, Duke Ellington, and Count Basie. According to the *Colored American Magazine*, the Litchford Hotel ranked as "one of the best furnished, most substantially built, and best conducted hotels in the country designed for the accommodation of the colored traveling public." James W. Bryant, whose father ran his oil and gas business out of offices in the Litchford Hotel, also lived there in the early 1930s. He remembered Thomas as "slender in body size with light complexion and white hair." Thomas lived in and took his meals at the hotel. Quiet and introspective, he kept to himself, performed odd jobs, and did occasional custodial work. Living at the Litchford Hotel provided Thomas with fellowship and a sense of family that had often been missing throughout his long life. In an interesting twist of fate, Negroes succored and protected him as one of their own in his old age. Were they aware of Thomas's controversial life, especially his authorship of *The American Negro*?[56]

By November 1935, Thomas's physical condition—complicated by myocarditis and senility—had deteriorated seriously and he needed constant care. During his last days Mrs. Frances Jones, housekeeper at the Litchford Hotel, nursed him, loaned him money, and paid his bills. On November 15, 1935, Thomas died at age ninety-two from myocarditis and general debility. According to Amanda Murray of Washington, D.C., his niece and only known relative, Will requested that he be buried at the Otterbein Cemetery in Westerville. There he was laid to rest on November 19. The Reverend J. S. Innerst, pastor of the United Brethren Church, delivered Thomas's last rites. Documents filed after Thomas's death shed little light on the life of this shadowy man. Had he been alive, however, Thomas would have cringed at one detail included on his death certificate. It described him as a "Negro."[57]

A Tragic Mulatto and a Tragic Negro

A FTER HIS DEATH IN 1935 William Hannibal Thomas remained forgotten and ignored. His remains lay in an unmarked grave in Otterbein Cemetery for forty-two years until 1977, when Brian Green, an Otterbein College student, applied to the Veterans Administration to erect a marble headstone for the deceased Civil War soldier. Green became intrigued by Thomas as a historical subject while conducting research for Professor Harold B. Hancock, author of the only modern biographical account of Thomas published before 1996. Despite Green's best efforts, the Veterans Administration erred, engraving on the cemetery marker Thomas's year of birth as 1893, not 1843, his military rank as first lieutenant, not sergeant, and his Civil War unit as the 5th Ohio Infantry, not the 5th U.S. Colored Troops. Hard to pin down during his long and troubled life, Thomas's identity remained uncertain even in death.[1]

Any account of Thomas's life must by necessity be incomplete, just as he would have willed it. Comparing his fate to that of "Hannibal, the great Carthaginian general" at the hands of the Romans, Thomas considered the historian his enemy and seemingly went out of his way to destroy or conceal evidence that might explain not only his motivations but the simplest details of his life. Thomas's biographer's most difficult task has been reconstructing his genealogy and childhood from mere scraps of information. His later years, however, were only slightly less difficult to untangle and interpret. Frequently in trouble and on the run, Thomas lived a mysterious and sketchy life, often in the interstices between white and black societies. Through much of his life Will had neither friends nor family, and he purposely left only snippets of autobiographical information, often erroneous and exaggerated fragments of questionable value. After almost fifteen years of research on this obscure and secretive man, no "smoking gun" has surfaced to explain his erratic behavior, his contradictory racial ideology, and his complex life.[2]

Thomas nonetheless was a man of intelligence, erudition, ability, and resourcefulness—a man who ultimately used his gifts against his people and himself. His contradictions alone render him a challenging and interesting subject for an intellectual biography. And no matter how disturbing one finds *The American Negro*, both the man and his book deserve thorough and judicial analysis. For thirty years he worked to lead and inspire black people, imploring them to establish roots, maintain stability, and prove their worth. Yet all the while Thomas was rootless, unstable, and untrustworthy. In *The American Negro* he set forth a radically negative and utterly pessimistic assessment of African American life that contradicted much of what he had argued over three decades. The book underscored Thomas's hyperbolic, self-destructive personality and his seemingly limitless hypocrisy. As his many critics explained, he preached character but practiced sin. Thomas's evolution from a constructive, mainstream black social critic to what historian Joel Williamson has termed a Radical racist raises the essential question: Why did Thomas write *The American Negro*?[3]

Given the scant evidence, the jagged contours of his enigmatic life, his extreme statements, and the daunting complexity inherent in attempting to explain human behavior, answers to this question must necessarily remain speculative and certainly not definitive. But there are answers to be sure. They cluster around two points: Thomas's self-concept and intention in writing *The American Negro*, and the unconscious forces rooted in his life history.

As Thomas's numerous articles suggest, for decades he considered himself a serious social critic, an observer armed with the necessary experience among and insight into those people who, in 1901, he still termed the "freedmen." In a long tradition of African American authors, Thomas spoke of "the Negro" in the singular and assumed that he could assess the race as a whole. Even by contemporary standards, however, he was no systematic student of the "Negro problem" in general or of black southerners in particular. In his early writings and in *The American Negro*, Thomas described and criticized black behavior—but failed to explain it—in what was mostly illogical and prolonged rant. Thomas never analyzed such basic socioeconomic elements of African American life as sharecropping, the black church, black education, and black public health. His writings are largely void of blacks as parents, partners, farmers, businessmen, and industrial workers—as people with strengths and weaknesses—men and women who sometimes failed but who also eked out victories small and large against the overwhelming power of whites in Jim Crow America.[4]

Instead Thomas described the "freedmen" as a hopelessly inferior monolithic class that remained unchanged, locked in what he termed "mental density" and "moral turpitude" since emancipation. Certainly aware of black people's history and the range of conditions under which they lived, he told only one side of the story, repeatedly underscoring the blacks' weaknesses and providing vague or impractical solutions to what he termed, quite literally, the "Negro problem." To argue his points Thomas employed no systematic sociological method, no scientific or demographic data, such as W. E. B. Du Bois used in researching, among others, such contemporary works as *The Philadelphia Negro* (1899), *The College-bred Negro* (1900), *The Negro Common School* (1901), *The Negro Artisan* (1902), and *The Negro Church* (1903). Lacking any training in social science analysis, Thomas nevertheless convinced the Macmillan Company that *The American Negro* was a worthy contribution to "negro sociology." When attacked publicly by Charles W. Chesnutt in the *Critic*, Thomas continued to insist that his book was "a serious sociological study; the matured fruit of personal observation and painstaking analysis of the mental and social habits of the Negro and negroid types of people."[5]

Macmillan's decision to publish *The American Negro* was perhaps not surprising. In 1901 there were few other competing sociology texts on race. Sociologist James B. McKee notes that in the 1890s, when sociology became established as a discipline, sociologists conspicuously avoided racial questions and the "Negro problem." "Though they were deeply committed to the study of social issues, and their basic stance was one of social reform, for them, as for the many social reformists both inside and outside the university, race was not a reformable issue. They wrote no books on the race problem and only a scattering of articles; a few brief comments on race appeared in some books, such as those by Franklin H. Giddings, E. A. Ross, and Lester F. Ward." Giddings, one of the nation's most influential sociologists, played the decisive role in Macmillan's decision to publish *The American Negro*. The Columbia University professor enthusiastically shared Thomas's 1901 notions of racial superiority and inferiority. Both Giddings and Thomas based their understandings of race on Darwinian evolutionary theory and on the Lamarckian theory of the inheritance of acquired characteristics, and both stressed character over color. The mixing of the two theories was common among Social Darwinists, especially in America, until the 1920s. Given the racial climate of the day, Giddings and Macmillan were convinced that a book critical of blacks by a black author would fill a scholarly void and sell well. They were right at least on the second point.[6]

After years of working in relative obscurity, Thomas no doubt welcomed the recognition that publishing a book, especially one carrying the prestigious Macmillan imprint, would bring. In 1901 he was immensely proud of *The American Negro* and never comprehended the fury with which his black critics denounced him. A decade after the book's publication, however, Thomas wrote disingenuously to Theodore D. Jervey: "I am not a vain person . . . and would rather avoid notoriety. In fact had I known that the 'American negro,' would have instigated the unjust criticism and malignant abuse that followed its publication, I might have been deterred from writing that book." These were the self-deluded words of an emotionally and physically wounded man. In 1901, however, Thomas believed what he wrote. He sought recognition for his ideas, and, like any other author, he wanted his book to succeed. Thomas considered *The American Negro* his foremost accomplishment. It brought him both a meteoric rise and a deep and sudden fall.[7]

Macmillan Company records provide only a few clues as to the book's actual success. Thomas received no advance payment against future royalties, and several weeks before publication, he informed George P. Brett, Macmillan's president, "I have no idea that I shall realize any unusual sum out of this book." Such rhetoric aside, in the last extant correspondence between Thomas and Macmillan, in July 1901, the publisher informed him that he owed them $36.40. There is more to the story, however, because the book in fact sold extremely well.[8]

After about two weeks on the market, *The American Negro*, which retailed for two dollars, sold at least five hundred copies. This is documented by the fact that Macmillan paid Will one hundred dollars in royalties (his author's royalty rate was ten percent) on January 22, 1901. Convinced of its sales potential, Macmillan quickly reprinted the book in March and then again in May. How much did Will ultimately earn from the book? What did he do with the money? Because sales figures and royalty statements have not survived, there is no way to know how much Thomas profited from his controversial book. The evidence, in fact, suggests that he was always in financial difficulty. It was thanks only to the generosity of African Americans in Columbus, Ohio, that Thomas was able to live out his last years in relative comfort.[9]

It would be unfair to Thomas, however, to conclude that he wrote *The American Negro* solely with the intention of making money. Since 1865 he had worked as a preacher, teacher, lawyer, trial justice, state legislator, and journalist in an effort to uplift the race. Like other black reformers, Thomas employed the "jeremiadic tradition," emphasizing the freedpeople's failings, suggesting roads to redemption, and employing the "harsh judgmental tones and strident condemnation" that, according to historian David Howard-Pitney, constitute "essential elements of the jeremiad." Like Frederick Douglass, Booker T. Washington, and Du Bois, Thomas directed jeremiads at African Americans because of their alleged failure to organize, to take advantage of opportunities, to advance as a race, and to initiate self-reform. Unlike Douglass and Du Bois, Washington and Thomas aimed their jeremiad reform rhetoric only at persons of African descent. After 1894, however, Thomas broke with Washington and the black "jeremiadic tradition" when he became utterly pessimistic about the future of American blacks. Castigating them in gross and intemperate language, Thomas abandoned "the jeremiah's optimistic formula." His program of racial redemption was far more extreme than any of his peers.[10]

Though Thomas's arguments in *The American Negro* were outlandish even by the standards of his day, it is essential to frame them within contemporary debates among African Americans about race. Thomas was one of many blacks at the turn of the century who wrestled with questions of racial identity and racial makeup. They often did so in self-contradictory and unclear terms. Nor was Thomas the only person of African descent to take critical, sometimes unpopular stands on a broad range of questions concerning race traits, racial identification, and skin color differentiation. Racial spokesmen had a long tradition of self-reflection, self-criticism, and debate on these topics. In "Race and the Wider Identity," psychoanalyst Erik H. Erikson identified a distinct pattern of *"negative* identity elements" among African American writers, including Du Bois, James Baldwin, and Ralph Ellison. Just as black musicians used the blues to transcend painful conditions that enveloped the race, so too did black writers employ "the negative and the confused" as a constructive force for racial protest, uplift, and growth.[11]

In 1884, for example, Frederick Douglass sparked a national dispute over racial intermarriage when he married Helen Pitts, his white former secretary. Responding to criticism from blacks as well as whites, Douglass declared that "there is no division of races. God Almighty made but one race." Five years later, Butler R. Wilson, the Boston lawyer and civil rights activist who in 1901 supplied Charles W. Chesnutt with negative information on Will Thomas, expressed alarm over divisions among black Bostonians over color. "If color prejudice exists to-day among any colored people in Boston," he argued, "it can be traced to the work of men who failing in ability, in patriotism and a broad grasp of affairs appeal to this diseased state of the uneducated, non-reading portion of the people, who are easily swayed by the oily, lying tongues of demagogues." Had Wilson written these words a decade later, he no doubt would have aimed this attack squarely at Thomas.[12]

In 1904, three years after Thomas published *The American Negro,* Nannie H. Burroughs (1879–1961), leader of the Woman's Convention of the National Baptist Convention, identified a widespread pattern of self-hate among blacks. Titling an article in the *Voice of the Negro* "Not Color But Character," Burroughs complained that "many Negroes have colorphobia as badly as the white folk have Negrophobia." Quite possibly responding to Thomas's book, she insisted that "it has never been shown" that mulattoes were superior to blacks, "nor never will, as long as we present in the majority such superior types of manhood and womanhood found in thoroughbred Negro men and women throughout the world." And in 1912 novelist James Weldon Johnson, a thoughtful and insightful analyst of life along the color line, described a "desperate class" of blacks who "conform to the requirements of civilization much as a trained lion with low muttered growls goes through his stunts under the crack of the trainer's whip." Traveling through the backwoods South, Johnson's protagonist in *The Autobiography of an Ex-Coloured Man* is disheartened by "these dull, simple people—the great majority of them hard working, in their relations with the whites submissive, faithful, and often affectionate, negatively content with their lot." Johnson compared these folk "with those of the race who had been quickened by the forces of thought."[13]

Long before he published *The American Negro,* Thomas had established himself as a consistently candid, sometimes harsh, and often irascible critic of blacks, especially black preachers and teachers. While he apparently had few friends, black or white, according to the A.M.E.'s *Christian Recorder,* Thomas nonetheless had earned the respect of members of the race. As diabolical as he appeared to blacks in 1901, and as offensive as we might find his racial views today, it is essential that we, unlike his black contemporaries, not transform Will Thomas into the devil incarnate. *The American Negro* was reprehensible in the age of Jim Crow and remains so today. We nonetheless must analyze its author within the context of his day, not ours, and judge him fairly, as we would anyone of any time or any place regardless of race.

Several historians have underscored the importance of assessing African Americans in a fair and balanced manner. In her discussion of Martin R. Delany, a conservative associate of Thomas's in Reconstruction-era South Carolina, Nell Irvin Painter emphasized the value in analyzing those who took minority positions. Some have considered Delany, like Thomas, "a traitor to his race or a man who had been whitewashed." But Delany, Painter explains, like Thomas, "believed sincerely that he held the interests of black people paramount. He had not been bribed or misled, and he was not alone among his black peers." In a similar vein, Clarence E. Walker has stressed the importance of deromanticizing our analyses of African Americans. "In dealing with black people," he insists, "historians must get beyond the romantic notion that oppression produced a class of people who were inevitably kind and generous to their peers" or were of a heroic mold. "The falseness of this notion," Walker adds, "can be seen most clearly in the racial self-hatred and oppositions based on color that have historically divided black America." Most recently, Colin A. Palmer has argued that by emphasizing black resistance against white oppression and, implicitly, transforming all black historical subjects into heroes, we trivialize the contributions and complexities of African American life. "A maturing historiography of black America," Palmer writes, should "eschew hagiography if only because it diminishes the humanity of the people being studied and make caricatures of their struggles, vulnerabilities, successes, and failures." These sober reminders of Painter, Walker, and Palmer are useful in contextualizing Thomas's complex and often inconsistent racial ideology.[14]

Though Thomas was a black race critic among many, contemporary reviewers noted that he was no ordinary race critic. "Why a negro should write such a book," editor William Hayes Ward of the *Independent* said, "is a problem in psychology." Reflecting on *The American Negro,* an unidentified reviewer in the *Political Science Quarterly* remarked: "Mr. Thomas's book has been much discussed, and by a large proportion of those who have entertained a rosy faith in the negro's prospects it has been severely condemned. It should be regarded, we think, as an interesting psychological fact. If the dark view it offers of negro intelligence and morals is even approximately true, that truth should be known. If it is all a lie, the liar is one of the most interesting personalities that have ever taken to authorship." If Thomas lied, he did so unconsciously, because there is every reason to believe that he wrote *The American Negro* from the heart. His book was no scam. It articulated a racial ideology premised on Negro inferiority and outlined steps for what he termed the race's "feasible regeneration." Though he had exhibited questionable ethics and outright dishonest behavior before, *The American Negro* was his sincere attempt to solve the "Negro problem." Thomas's "interesting" personality, however, holds the key to explaining why he resorted to such an extreme denunciation of his race in his attempt to redeem it. His adult behavior, like *The American Negro,* was characterized by "antisocial personality disorder"—unlawful acts, "deceitfulness," "impulsivity," "aggressiveness," "consistent irresponsibility," and "lack of remorse." [15]

But if the bare bones of Thomas's life and thought have proven difficult to piece together, how then can one analyze the concealed, fragile, and intricate skeleton of his personality? It is impossible, of course, to put him on the couch or to analyze his dreams. Nonetheless, elements of Thomas's personality, at least the bits that the spotty available evidence allow us to interpret, beg for analysis. His personality offers important clues into his thought and behavior—specifically why he led a self-destructive life, why he wrote *The American Negro,* and why he disassociated himself from his race.

Insufficient information on Thomas's family and childhood prevents us from identifying what Erik Erikson referred to as "the major crisis of adolescence," one's "*identity* crisis." We know little about Will's identity formation, his perception of self. His parents moved frequently in the Old Northwest, he wrote lovingly of his mother, and he referred only once to his father. What was Will's relationship with Henry Whiting and his family? Did some black person close to Thomas, possibly a relative, treat him harshly during his youth? And if so, did that person become "the Negro" in his unconscious? Will's persistent and consistently bizarre remarks on the alleged immorality of African Americans in general, and about black women and their sexuality in particular, suggest that he may have experienced as a child some abusive or traumatic sexual experience connected with a Negro. Thomas's remark, for example, that "the negro is of a preeminently sensual race, and one whose male members have an inordinate craving for carnal knowledge of white women" cries out for interpretation. It could be Will Thomas describing Will Thomas. It could be Thomas reliving an early childhood experience. But to speculate regarding Thomas's psyche without a significant "life history" would amount to what one of Erikson's critics termed "psychological reductionism . . . empirically questionable from the viewpoint of historical research." [16]

Without a diagnostic model to explain Thomas's motivations, his behavior is in the end largely inexplicable. At best we can describe Thomas's actions and interpret his words. Yet evidence from Thomas's scant biography and *The American Negro* itself attest that he was a troubled man with a deep-seeded animus against blacks—and against those parts of himself that he identified as "Negro"—that surfaced full-blown in 1901 in *The American Negro*. In that book he revealed such wild fantasies as black women aggressively seducing the unwary, black men routinely serving as pimps, and black stepfathers incestuously abusing their stepdaughters with their wives' permission. As solutions to the "Negro problem," Thomas proposed such extreme measures as castrating or executing black rapists, whipping those who commit lesser crimes, and reeducating African American youth by segregating them in Negro orphanages. No matter how degraded Thomas may have judged individual blacks in his acquaintance, such distorted images of blacks mirrored elements from his own life experience, *not* that of the race. There was considerable truth, then, to his black critics' allegation that *The American Negro* was Thomas's autobiography, not a "sociological" study of African Americans at the turn of the century.

Without resorting to undue speculation, one may conclude that Thomas experienced three major traumas during his young adulthood that influenced his thought and behavior: the racial disturbance caused by his enrollment and forced sudden departure from Otterbein University in 1859 (age sixteen), the refusal on racial grounds of his offer to join the U.S. Army in 1861 (age eighteen), and his Civil War amputation in 1865 (age twenty-two). Each was a violent shock, a wound that had consequences that affected Thomas deeply, so much so that he commented on them as major signposts in his life. These life events left deep emotional scars.

The Otterbein experience "humiliated and angered" him, a conflict that Thomas did not resolve until the 1920s, when he was in his late seventies. His rejection by the army, Thomas said, was "one of not a few instances where color has militated against me." While he went on to a distinguished career in the segregated U.S. Colored Troops, a service that strengthened his identification with blacks, it also heightened Thomas's ambivalence about his own racial identification. His Civil War amputation had the most devastating effect of all, altering Will's life in countless ways. "My physical ills are almost beyond endurance," he wrote in February 1911. To be sure, pain became a way of life for Thomas following his battlefield surgery in February 1865. He suffered for years with a neuroma on his right stump, a condition that results after severed nerves heal and their ends grow into a convoluted ball, sending "pain messages to the brain which are not actually related to any damaging event in the stump." Thomas's amputation also caused degenerative paralysis in his left hand and wrist. At times his hand was virtually useless to him and he had access to but one finger.[17]

Years before, as early as 1894 and probably earlier, the severe emotional and physical pain resulting from white racism and his Civil War amputation pushed Thomas over the edge. To be sure, racism affects each individual differently, and scholars generally discount it as a source of self-hatred responses in blacks. Few minorities do indeed come to hate themselves or become self-destructive as a result of racial oppression. In Thomas's case, however, the combination of white racism and physical pain transformed him into a bitter, pessimistic man who lashed out at others and projected an arrogant exterior to the world—what his critics considered "a sick mind."[18]

Will's cycle of self-destruction began many years before the appearance of The American Negro, soon after his amputation—in fact as early as the 1868 episode at Western Theological Seminary and another the following year at Wilberforce University. Through the years Thomas repeatedly exhibited rage, mistrust of the motives of others, and a damaged identity and self-esteem. His failure to recover from his traumas or, more important, the impact they had on his behavior, culminated in the 1901 publication of his book. This, Thomas's final self-destructive act, resulted from his acting out of anger at being identified with blacks and his intense physical pain.[19]

Unquestionably Thomas exhibited posttraumatic symptoms common to amputees—hostility, superficial self-confidence, rationalization, compulsivity, extreme pessimism, delusion, and the setting of excessively high goals—characteristics especially observable in those unable to tolerate a prosthesis. Military doctors repeatedly encouraged Thomas to wear an artificial limb, but he refused, arguing that his stump was too painful to accommodate one. According to Dr. Lawrence W. Friedmann, "the adjustment to a prosthesis depends upon the patient's personal adjustment to amputation; upon the basic personality of the amputee and his . . . integration of the prosthesis into his . . . personality structure. A prosthesis may be considered as assisting in personality reintegration in a number of ways." While a prosthesis might have helped him physically and emotionally, Thomas's case once more goes against the grain of the scholarly literature.[20]

Over the course of many years Thomas accepted, not rejected, his amputation. Pinning up and displaying, not hiding, his empty sleeve, he transformed it into a badge of honor, not a mark of inferiority. Though he used his amputation rhetorically—to gain sympathy for himself and the Republican party—Thomas never complained about having served in the U.S. Colored Troops. He always considered his military service one of his greatest accomplishments, having willingly sacrificed his arm for the cause of freeing the slaves and keeping the Union intact. But the amputation left him with a physical trauma, a frightfully painful wound that never healed, and a psychical trauma that confronted him with "a totally new reality" and forced him to develop "a corresponding new definition of self." One manifestation of this was Will's postwar pattern of self-destructive behavior.[21]

This can possibly be explained by "repetition compulsion," a process whereby a person unconsciously positions himself in distressing circumstances and then repeats the experience. Thomas repeatedly ran afoul of authorities, including the law, reestablished himself in a different setting, and then repeated the process. Because in only one instance, his expulsion from the South Carolina legislature in 1877, did Thomas ever address his past conflicts, his behaviors cannot be analyzed at the level of concrete psychopathology, and we cannot observe how he dealt with them. He left no record, for example, of his problems in Allegheny City, Wilberforce, Monongahela City, or Atlanta. In his reminiscence of his days in South Carolina, Thomas conveniently omitted his indictment for stealing a bale of cotton in Newberry and blamed a turncoat "negro Republican" and white and black Democrats for his ouster. He probably had no recognition of his pattern of behavior and understood each situation as the result of unique circumstances of the moment. He expressed no remorse, no empathy, no guilt for the impact of his malevolence.[22]

Another symptom of Thomas's altered "self" was his projection of his unethical and dishonest personal and professional behavior onto others. This is most evident in *The American Negro,* in which Thomas displaced his rage from white to black perpetrators. Identifying negative racial traits in "others" provided a defense against characteristics that he was afraid to recognize in himself. The catalog of negatives he heaped upon African Americans in chapters on "Characteristic Traits," "Moral Lapses," and "Criminal Instincts" allowed Thomas to accomplish two things.

First, it freed him from acknowledging and accepting his past behaviors. Employing the mechanism of projection, Thomas obsessed on the "many despicable traits" of Negroes—the very characteristics that he observed in himself and repressed. Blaming "others"—Negro women, preachers, and teachers—for the failures of the race and, unconsciously, for his own personal and professional defeats enabled Thomas to purge his own guilt. The problem, however, as psychiatrist Joel Kovel observed in his study of white racism, is that "threatening and contradictory" ideas "will not disappear, since the basic conflicts which give rise to danger are continued within, and they are unyielding."[23]

Second, projecting undesirable traits onto Negroes enabled Thomas to establish his own identity separate and apart from others of the race. He envisioned a highly select subgroup among Negroes, an elite who shared mulatto "character" traits—*his* "character" traits. A prophet who would lead blacks out of the wilderness, Thomas was conspicuously silent about who, with the exception of former Georgia slave Albert Berrien, would qualify as members of the elect. As Thomas explained, "degradation of the race is not characteristic of all persons of negroid ancestry . . . the common, indiscriminate inclusion of all persons of color in the same category is an unjust classification, which acts with great severity against a saving remnant of good men and true women." Having linked Negro identity ("race") to character, not color, Thomas marked out special racial terrain reserved for mulattoes—but not necessarily for all mulattoes, only those whom he described as exhibiting non-Negro, and to his mind, positive, characteristics.[24]

Though Thomas always identified with mulattoes, not until 1901 did he clearly favor a separate mulatto leadership class. As he explained in *The American Negro*,

> the pure negro people are, by the very nature of their characteristic endowments, precluded from reaching a high degree of efficiency. Whatever the freedmen has achieved in the way of intelligence and character is due to alien qualities incorporated into his being through race amalgamation. His change in color is, however, merely an incident of miscegenation; the fundamental outcome is the displacement of characteristic instincts, and the introduction of new traits, a thing that is not always accomplished through physical admixture.

Typically vague on just what he meant by racial "amalgamation," Thomas added: "The redemption of the negro is impossible through any process of physical amalgamation; it is possible and assured through a thorough assimilation of the thought and ideals of American civilization." Thomas seemed to imply intellectual and cultural amalgamation by some sort of osmosis.[25]

According to Thomas, then, it was not race after all that was the Negro's problem, but rather what he vaguely termed "character." It was not enough to look like a mulatto, he said, one had to act like one. Writing in 1926, sociologist Jerome Dowd observed that Thomas's "attitude toward the Negro problem is like that of the religious evangelist toward the unconverted. He believes that regeneration is entirely a matter of will power of the individual. He, therefore, minimizes all efforts at regeneration through laws or other external means." Rigid color or race differentiation and identification, Thomas maintained, was wrong because it discriminated "against a saving remnant of good men and true women"—most specifically William Hannibal Thomas.[26]

Though Thomas described himself as a mulatto, and others classified him as a mulatto, he nevertheless was ambivalent about this status, careful to argue that light skin alone was not necessarily an indicator of "character." Will often said that he preferred to be considered a "colored American." Based on his rather general and popularized understanding of Darwinian and Lamarckian theories, he classified mulattoes "hybrids" with all the strengths and weaknesses of mixed breeds in animal and natural life. Whites of Thomas's day generally viewed America's mixed-race populations with suspicion. Writing in 1910, E. H. Randle argued that mulattoes

> have less physical endurance, and less procreative ability than either the negroes or the whites. This is a slow elimination of the less fit to maintain the struggle for life. The mulatto is quicker and brighter [than the black man] and often has all the aspirations of a white man, and he is dissatisfied with his place in nature. Being made up of unlike and discordant elements of character he has a nature warring with itself, restless and discontented. It is so with all mixed races and breeds of men and beasts.

In 1917, Edward B. Reuter, then a graduate student at the University of Chicago and later one of the nation's authorities on racial mixing, remarked that "in the American mulatto the evolution of a superior race may be seen in process." Because he had his own doubts about precisely where mulattoes stood on the evolutionary ladder, Thomas rarely mentioned them. While identifying with mulattoes as a vague leadership group, he nevertheless shared the same suspicions of mulattoes that white racial Radicals held. It is surprising that Radicals such as Thomas Nelson Page and Dr. Paul Brandon Barringer did not react negatively to Thomas's cryptic references to "amalgamation" and "assimilation." Dr. Robert W. Shufeldt certainly did not fail to see the implications for "atavism" in Thomas's alleged endorsement of "interbreeding." Having disassociated himself from Negroes by writing *The American Negro* and unwilling to position himself squarely in the mulatto camp, Thomas, according to Booker T. Washington, was "a man without a race."[27]

Washington's remark was a political attack, designed to discredit Thomas and, given the contemporary importance of race, especially to Washington, was pure rhetoric. Like Washington, Thomas's critics never responded to him as an intellectual but always responded to him on his terms, with an onslaught of ad hominem attacks. African Americans obviously took Thomas and his book seriously. They considered him a deviant, a dangerous outsider, and mobilized to suppress his deviance. Curiously, the demographic data on blacks at Du Bois's fingertips, documenting dramatic progress of the race against difficult odds, easily could have destroyed the credibility of *The American Negro* in one fell swoop. But black intellectuals feared that Thomas and his blasphemous book had already received too much publicity, and more attention to it might lead to even more ammunition for white supremacists. Blacks wanted Thomas's book off the shelves. They simply wanted him to disappear.[28]

"At the beginning of the twentieth century," historian Elazar Barkan reminds us, "the term 'race' had a far wider meaning than at present, being used to refer to any geographical, religious, class-based or color-based grouping." In 1890, for example, the Bureau of the Census instructed census enumerators to "be particularly careful to distinguish between blacks, mulattoes, quadroons, and octoroons. The word 'black' should be used to describe those persons who have three-fourths or more black blood; 'mulatto,' those persons who have from three-eighths to five-eighths black blood; 'quadroon,' those persons who have one-fourth black blood; and 'octoroon,' those persons who have one-eighth or any trace of black blood." Though racial boundaries in what literary scholar Werner Sollors has aptly described "the calculus of color" were commonly blurred, turn-of-the-century Americans focused closely on skin color classifications. Will Thomas, obsessed with skin color, fashioned a racial ideology around an elite mulatto classification— not an economic class but one vaguely defined by "character." Thomas's most serious betrayal of his race was not his insulting list of alleged race "traits" but rather his strategy of raising the status of mulattoes by lowering that of blacks.[29]

But Thomas misread the times. No matter what arbitrary decisions census enumerators and others had made regarding fractions of "black blood" in people, the United States, unlike other former slave societies in the Western Hemisphere, was essentially biracial, not multiracial. Even as blacks and whites debated the merits of *The American Negro,* Americans had begun to obliterate skin color differentiations among persons of African descent. The

1920 U.S. Census was the last federal census to enumerate mulattoes as a separate class of people. The tangled web Thomas spun ultimately trapped him. His plea for greater recognition of mulattoes, really just the recognition of one mulatto—William Hannibal Thomas—appeared at the very moment when African Americans of every shade were under severe attack. White American society defined Thomas not as he would have preferred, as a mulatto, but rather as a Negro. Thomas *was* the American Negro he vilified so thoroughly in *The American Negro*.[30]

Suffering from the bite of white racism, at an early age Thomas inculcated the white man's definition of skin color as his own. This was the basic source of his contradictions, inner tensions, and inner torments. Probably before, but definitely after the 1859 disturbance at Otterbein, Thomas agonized over society defining him as a Negro, not as a mulatto, and this established his conflicted sense of racial identity. After 1865 his racial ambivalence was exacerbated, and certainly by 1894 transformed into hatred, by Will's emotional and physical suffering. He was an emotional time bomb with a long fuse, one that ignited in the 1890s and exploded in a rage of racial hate: *The American Negro*. His self-imposed marginality—feeling at ease neither as a black nor as a mulatto—kept Thomas always uncomfortable with being identified with either group, especially with race leaders (he termed them "Big Negroes") like Washington and Du Bois who tended to be light-skinned. Whereas most mixed-race people confront what historian Leo Spitzer has called the "predicament of marginality" because of external "barriers" to privilege and power, Thomas largely constructed his own.[31]

Thomas's biography, and his greatest success and greatest failure, *The American Negro*, underscore the power, in his case a destructive force, that dominant societal definitions of "race" and "civilization" can hold over people. Though he never glorified whites and never even hinted at being "white," Thomas nonetheless thoroughly internalized and incorporated what Elaine K. Ginsburg has described as "the dominant culture's racial definitions and characterizations." His African origins, his identification with blacks both by others and by himself, gnawed at Thomas deeply, rendering him dysfunctional, unable to see what he was doing and leaving him with a twisted and tortured mind. His rootlessness, his multiple identities and careers, and ultimately the publication of *The American Negro* signified a man at war with himself. Thomas's claims to superiority over Negroes masked his feelings of inferiority and his loathing for those parts of himself that he identified with blacks.[32]

Ironically, throughout his long life, Thomas successfully overcame white racism, repeatedly reaching positions of respect and responsibility only to sabotage himself because of his racial ambivalence, his dishonesty, and his deep emotional and severe physical pain. For all of Thomas's preoccupation with race, his problems resulted less from his racial classification as a mulatto or as a Negro than from his failure to accept responsibility for his actions. He repeatedly blamed his manifest failures in life on his identification with blacks. This in turn led him to attack blacks, creating an insurmountable distance between him and them. Thomas manipulated the concept of "race," using it as an excuse, a convenient scapegoat in the highly polarized era of Jim Crow to suit his psychological needs. Without diminishing the power and significance of race in that violent and turbulent age, it was his character, not his color, that led to Will Thomas's demise, precisely what he found faulty in members of his race. He was both a tragic mulatto and a tragic Negro. William Hannibal Thomas was "Black Judas" and *The American Negro* was the story of his life.

The Multiple William H. Thomases

IN 1975, when analyzing several of William Hannibal Thomas's religious articles in the *A.M.E. Church Review,* historian David Wood Wills remarked that "biographical information about Thomas seems . . . surprisingly hard to locate." Having found one short biographical sketch, Wills concluded that in the years 1887 to 1888 Thomas "apparently was an A.M.E. pastor serving somewhere in the New York Conference." Despite his careful research, Wills confused Thomas with another A.M.E. minister, the Reverend William Henry Thomas (1847–1903), who also had published in the *A.M.E. Church Review.* Wills's error is perfectly understandable and underscores just one of several problems that confront anyone examining William Hannibal Thomas's life and thought.[1]

During his long and complex life, people frequently confused William Hannibal Thomas with other black men, especially because he commonly referred to himself and signed his publications with variants of his name—as William H. Thomas, Will Thomas, Will H. Thomas, Will Hannibal Thomas, W. Hannibal Thomas, Wm. Hannibal Thomas, William Hannibal Thomas, W.H. Thomas, and also "Hannibal," "Hannible," and "Hanible." While trying to track Thomas down in Boston in 1917, Charleston lawyer Theodore D. Jervey learned that one of Will's relatives had erroneously concluded that he had died because of a newspaper story "that a man of Thomas's name" had been stabbed in the back in Virginia. The misidentification of Thomas obviously posed difficulties for his contemporaries as well as his biographer.[2]

The multiple William H. Thomases have exacerbated the problems of piecing together Thomas's lengthy life from mere scraps of information. At one point in my research, I had identified twenty-six men with the name W. H. Thomas or William H. Thomas who, either because of their work or when or where they lived, could possibly have been confused with William Hannibal Thomas. Over the course of my work I eliminated many other Thomases either because they were white or because internal evidence suggested that they could not have been William Hannibal Thomas. Thomas has often been confused with as many as nineteen black contemporaries with the name William H. Thomas, including one man who served in Will's Civil War regiment and also resided in Delaware, Ohio. To confound matters even further, nine of the black Thomases, like Will, also were ministers in either the A.M.E. Church or the Methodist Episcopal Church. Will Thomas held affiliations in both denominations.[3]

This appendix includes sketches of African American men who at one time or another have been confused with William Hannibal Thomas. As much as possible, these men are identified by name, a place, date, or some other information that explains their possible misidentification with William Hannibal Thomas, and a brief biographical sketch based on all available information. Like William Hannibal Thomas, most of these Thomases left a sparse documentary trail and have fallen through the cracks of African American history.

1. W. H. Thomas (New York, 1889; North Carolina, 1890)

A highly respected A.M.E. pastor in Albany, New York, and in Wilmington, North Carolina, W. H. Thomas attracted national attention while serving in Wilmington. In an 1891 article in the *Christian Recorder,* Thomas attacked Booker T. Washington and Bishop Daniel A. Payne's criticisms concerning the qualifications of A.M.E. ministers. In the same year Thomas wrote former president Rutherford B. Hayes informing him of his interest in the work of the John F. Slater Fund and describing himself "as a Minister of the Gospel, laboring in the interest of the Negro."[4]

2. William H. Thomas (Florida, 1893)

The Reverend William H. Thomas served an A.M.E. church in the Enterprise District, Florida, in 1893. The district met in Palatka, Florida.[5]

3. William H. Thomas (Texas, 1878)

In 1870 William H. Thomas joined "on trial" the West Texas Conference of the Methodist Episcopal Church, a conference composed entirely of African Americans. According to conference minutes, Thomas served churches in Lavernia and Helena, Texas, before his name disappeared from the conference roll in 1875. This man may actually have been named Washington Thomas.[6]

4. William Thomas (Georgia, 1876)

On February 8, 1876, the Reverend William Thomas of Marietta, Georgia, wrote President Ulysses S. Grant addressing what he considered to be the great suffering of African Americans. Thomas proclaimed that the "time of liberty and prosperity is dead with us as a colored people," and he requested that African Americans receive equal protection under the law. "We have tried it long enough to know," Thomas wrote, "that we can't live here under the present administration of the law any longer without a change and that a big one. We now stand as the fox in the dens of the mountains." Apologetic for his spelling and writing, Thomas asked that Grant heed him and answer his letter.[7]

5. William H. Thomas (Georgia, 1879)

Born in Fairfax County, Virginia, in 1836, the Reverend William H. Thomas served both the Savannah and Washington Conferences of the Methodist Episcopal Church. In 1879 he was admitted "on trial" to the Savannah Conference while he served the Savannah City Mission. Admitted to "full connection" in 1881, Thomas became a traveling deacon of the first class in the Brunswick Circuit. He transferred to the Washington Conference in 1883 to serve a church in Giles, Virginia. Elected and ordained an elder in 1885, Thomas moved to Thaxton Switch, Virginia, where he died on October 13, 1885.[8]

6. William M. Thomas (South Carolina, 1868–77)

Despite their different middle initials, many contemporaries confused William M. Thomas with William Hannibal Thomas. Both men were affiliated with the Republican Party and with the A.M.E. Church in South Carolina during Reconstruction. The Reverend William M. Thomas, a presiding elder of the Columbia Conference, was born in South Carolina. He represented Colleton County in the state's 1868 constitutional convention and in the South Carolina House of Representatives, 1868–76. Like William Hannibal Thomas, he also was appointed an officer in the South Carolina militia and was an active leader among African Methodists. In 1876 he served as one of South Carolina's alternate delegates to the Republican National Convention.[9]

7. William H. Thomas (54th Massachusetts Volunteer Infantry)

On March 19, 1863, twenty-two-year-old William H. Thomas, a porter from Baltimore, joined the first African American regiment raised in Massachusetts: the 54th Massachusetts Volunteer Infantry. Thomas served with the regiment until he was mustered out on August 20, 1865. This unit, perhaps the most famous African American regiment to serve in the war, fought at Fort Wagner, Charleston, the Florida coast, and Savannah.[10]

8. William Thomas (Flushing, Ohio)

On June 7, 1863, William Thomas, an eighteen-year-old farmer and resident of Flushing, Ohio, enlisted in the 55th Massachusetts Volunteer Infantry, the sister unit of the 54th Massachusetts Volunteer Infantry. Ohio sent more recruits to this African American regiment than any other state. Thomas served until July 7, 1865.[11]

9. William H. Thomas (New Jersey, 1895)

In 1895 William H. Thomas, a Philadelphia native, passed the civil service examination and was placed at the head of a list of eligible appointees. Later that year he was appointed a watchman in the U.S. Customs Service. In 1897 Thomas was fired from his position for "insubordination" after he had complained that he was forced to perform work not in keeping with his job description. Thomas, an African American, made numerous complaints, arguing that he was fired by the McKinley Administration both because of racial discrimination and because he was a Democrat. Writing to President Woodrow Wilson's private secretary, Joseph P. Tumulty, in 1915, Thomas described himself as "one of those Negroes who cultivate the thought that we live in an era where all that is most desired, is in the custody of the white or superior race. And that the better element of that race with whom you are identified, are always willing to accord, to those of my race, such recognition as they may merit." Even an appeal based on Thomas's Democratic party affiliation failed to sway the Wilson Administration. Thomas was not reinstated.[12]

10. William H. Thomas (Liberia, 1883-85)

Though the Methodist Episcopal Church first expressed interest in establishing missions in Africa as early as 1833, not until the 1880s did the church emphasize its African program. The Reverend William H. Thomas was one of the first Methodist missionaries who sought to "redeem" Africa. In 1883 the church posted Thomas to the Basha District in Liberia, a conference composed entirely of Africans. Thomas continued in the Liberia Conference and was ordained a deacon in 1885. After this, however, Thomas failed to appear in the minutes of the conference and was discontinued due to poor health.[13]

11. W. H. Thomas (Haiti, 1861)

In February 1861, W. H. Thomas boarded the brig *Mary A. Jones* in Boston bound for Haiti. The ship carried forty emigrants and nine cabin passengers, including Thomas. In a letter to the *New York Weekly Anglo-African,* Thomas wrote that he found the passage pleasant. He claimed to be going to the Caribbean to work for the government of Haiti.[14]

12. William H. Thomas (Boston, 1895)

Listed in the city directories of Boston as a printer, this William H. Thomas wrote a venomous anti-Catholic pamphlet in 1895, *The Roman Catholic in American Politics.* In the pamphlet Thomas called himself a journalist and mentioned his travels to Rome and the City of Panama. In acrimonious language, Thomas blamed Catholics for undermining politics by corrupting public men, debauching the public service, promoting class warfare, and introducing religion into the affairs of state and government. Thomas denounced Irish Catholics as a criminal element that perpetrated the 1863 New York City draft riots as well as other crimes in the United

States. He asserted that the Catholic Church promoted hostility by discouraging the use of public schools in favor of parochial schools. Convinced that Catholics voted in blocs at the behest of their priests, Thomas warned that the only way to check the growing power of papal authority in America was to cross party lines and vote for Protestants. Thomas's polemic suggests the intense anti-Catholic sentiment among many African American Protestants.[15]

13. William H. Thomas (Delaware, 1877-95)

The Reverend William H. Thomas, born in Hollidaysburg, Pennsylvania, in 1855, answered the call to enter the ministry of the Methodist Episcopal Church. Admitted to the Delaware Conference (composed entirely of African Americans) in 1877, Thomas served several churches in Maryland, New Jersey, and Delaware. By 1880 he reached the rank of deacon second class. Church minutes revealed that Thomas ran afoul of the church authorities when "grave rumors" concerning his conduct forced the conference to investigate his actions. The 1895 minutes simply stated that Thomas was permitted to withdraw from the conference under the charges against him. No specifics of the case ever surfaced.[16]

14. W. H. Thomas (Liberia, 1909)

The Baptist Church, like the Methodist Episcopal Church, conducted missionary work in Liberia. In 1897 the Lott Carey Baptist Foreign Mission Convention, named for the first African American missionary to Liberia, opened a mission in Liberia. The convention, composed largely of southern Baptists, grew slowly and gradually funded more projects in Liberia. In 1909 the convention sent two North Carolinians—the Reverend W. H. Thomas and his wife, Cora A. Pair Thomas, both graduates of Shaw University in Raleigh, to Brewerville, Liberia. He served as a missionary teacher and she taught in an industrial school. Thomas's station presided over the establishment of the first religious newspaper published by Liberian Baptists, the *Watchman*. The Thomases spent eleven years in Liberia, convinced that African Americans had a special calling to evangelize Africa. Thomas criticized European colonialism in Africa for ruthlessly exploiting the indigenous population, making "rigorous and exacting demands upon the defenseless creatures." He blasted the low morality of many European white missionaries. In his opinion, "they in many respects out-heathen the heathen." Thomas believed that African Americans held a special kinship with Africans that enhanced their effectiveness as missionaries. He labored in Africa for three decades and died in 1942.[17]

15. William H. Thomas (Ohio, 1831-95)

Ironically, the 5th U.S. Colored Troops contained two mulattoes from Ohio named William H. Thomas. Whereas William Hannibal Thomas enrolled in the regiment in September 1863 and was mustered into Company I in October, William H. Thomas, a thirty-two-year-old farmer, already had joined the unit's Company C in

Chillicothe, Ross County, Ohio, on June 22, 1863. Born in Hardin County, Virginia, William H. Thomas was promoted to corporal in July 1864 and by September 1865, had risen to the rank of sergeant. Lieutenant Joseph J. Scroggs and Sergeant Milton M. Holland served along with Thomas in Company C. He was wounded at Fort Gilmer in September 1864 and suffered severe frost bite in January 1865 while performing pioneer duty during the second Fort Fisher campaign. Thomas mustered out of the service with his company on September 20, 1865. After the war he returned to Delaware, Ohio, unable to perform manual labor because of chronic rheumatism and deafness that resulted from his military service. Thomas lived with his wife and daughter before entering the Ohio Soldiers' and Sailors' Home in Erie County, Ohio, in July 1893. He died September 30, 1895.[18]

16. William H. Thomas (Pittsburgh, Brooklyn, Boston, Philadelphia, 1847-1903)

The Reverend William H. Thomas, a distinguished A.M.E. clergyman, no doubt bore the brunt of the burden of being most frequently confused with William Hannibal Thomas. Indeed, on the surface the two men shared many similar experiences, so much so that contemporaries sometimes went to great lengths to differentiate between them, to ensure that no confusion existed as to which "Thomas" they referred. In 1880, for example, two decades before William Hannibal Thomas published *The American Negro,* a correspondent from the A.M.E.'s New England Conference remarked that at a meeting in New Haven, Connecticut, "the Missionary Sermon . . . was preached by Rev. W. H. Thomas (*not 'Hannibal'*)." Apparently readers of the *Christian Recorder* were familiar with the two men. Both in fact had published in the A.M.E. *Church Review* and appeared frequently in the *Christian Recorder.* Though more moderate and less outspoken than William Hannibal Thomas, William Henry Thomas also advocated reforms within the A.M.E. Church.[19]

William Henry Thomas was born on June 27, 1847, in New York City, descended from John Thomas and Eliza Gray Thomas, a former Maryland slave. Thomas's mother allegedly made her way to freedom in Philadelphia via the underground railroad and became one of the first women to join the city's Mother Bethel A.M.E. Church. Her son graduated from Lincoln University in 1869, attended Princeton Theological Seminary, and then ministered a congregation in Utica, New York (1870-73). While in Pittsburgh (1873-78), as pastor of Grace Memorial Presbyterian Church, Thomas attended Western Theological Seminary. The seminary's *General Biographical Catalogue* (1927) erroneously listed him as enrolling in the seminary from 1865 to 1868, the years when William Hannibal Thomas attended the school. Someone in the registrar's office no doubt confused the two men.[20]

William Henry Thomas next served churches in Providence (1878-79) and Newport (1879-83), Rhode Island; Brooklyn (1883-87) and Buffalo (1887-93), New York; Providence, Rhode Island (1893-98); and Boston, Massachusetts (1898-1902). In 1888 he unsuccessfully petitioned President Grover Cleveland for the post of U.S. Minister to Liberia. In 1901, when William Hannibal Thomas published *The American Negro,* Edward B. Jourdain, an attorney from New Bedford, Massachusetts, noted that the faculty at Western Theological Seminary somehow had "confounded Wm. Henry Thomas, a man and minister, with this libertine and criminal [William Hannibal Thomas]."[21]

At the time of his death (February 15, 1903) William Henry Thomas served as pastor of Philadelphia's Mother Bethel A.M.E. Church, the church to which his mother had belonged and the most prestigious congregation within the denomination. At each of his many posts Thomas received praise for his dedicated church work. African Methodist clergy singled him out many times for his devoted labors to their New England Conference. William Henry Thomas earned a reputation as a popular and respected minister in the African American community—just as William Hannibal Thomas became known as its "Black Judas." In a eulogy for his friend William Henry Thomas, Washington attorney and historian Archibald H. Grimké indirectly compared the two Thomases. Grimké described the minister as "no hypocrite, no humbug, no fraud. He spoke as he believed and he practiced what he professed. He fought in the open, not under cover. He struck hard but he struck fair." In 1903 no African American would have said the same of William Hannibal Thomas.[22]

17. William H. Thomas Jr. (1871–?)

The son of the Reverend William Henry Thomas described above, William H. Thomas Jr. also became a leading A.M.E. minister. Born October 22, 1871, in Utica, New York, Thomas earned his undergraduate and theological degrees at Lincoln University (1894 and 1897, respectively). He also took postgraduate work at Boston University (1897–99). During his ministerial career Thomas served churches at Chelsea (1897–1900) and New Bedford (1900–1903), Massachusetts; Newport, Rhode Island (1903–6); Boston, Massachusetts (1906–10); and Kansas City, Missouri (1910–14). While in Kansas City, he participated in the Methodist Ministers' Alliance. In 1914, as part of this committee, Thomas and two other ministers wrote President Woodrow Wilson expressing their concerns over segregation and discrimination against African Americans employed by the national government. The Methodist Ministers' Alliance resolved to fight racial discrimination, to further Christian principles, and to work for the uplift of all mankind. The organization informed Wilson that "segregation is out of harmony with the best ideals of a Christian civilization, that it imposes an unnecessary humiliation upon those affected, as well as indirectly upon all men of color; besides being unAmerican and undemocratic, and totally at variance with the real spirit, purpose, and destiny of our institutions."[23]

After serving a church in Denver, Colorado, the Reverend Thomas was reassigned as pastor of the Metropolitan A.M.E. Church, in Washington, D.C. In 1930 he delivered the commencement address at Washington's Frelinghuysen University. Established in 1906, in its early years Frelinghuysen "operated as a galaxy of satellite 'home schools' with educational centers at several locations" for African Americans throughout the District of Columbia. By 1930, when Dr. Anna Julia Cooper became president, Frelinghuysen offered a broad range of classes, from elementary through the college level.[24]

18. William H. Thomas (Dayton, 1843–?)

This mulatto veteran of the 43rd U.S. Colored Infantry was an inmate at the Central Branch, National Home for Disabled Volunteer Soldiers, in Dayton, Ohio, in 1919. Born in Maryland, he was literate, married, and entered the home in 1918. This William H. Thomas and William Hannibal Thomas *may* have been inmates at the facility at the same time.[25]

19. William H. Thomas (Columbus, 1921–32)

Like William Hannibal Thomas, during the 1920s and 1930s this William H. Thomas also worked as a janitor in Columbus. He and his wife Lida resided in the heart of Columbus's African American community.[26]

Circular Letter From the Committee
on Morals and Religion for 1901,
Hampton Negro Conference

Dear Sir:—

William Hannibal Thomas, in a book entitled, "The American Negro," makes the following statements:

"Soberly speaking, Negro nature is so craven and sensuous in every fiber of its being that a Negro manhood with decent respect for chaste womanhood does not exist."

"It is almost impossible to find a person of either sex, over fifteen years of age, who has not had actual carnal knowledge. But not only do the young Negro girls who grow up in idleness become prematurely old in viciousness, but even those better reared are amazingly yielding to licentious overtures, especially if a proposed meeting-place is sufficiently secluded to render detection improbable."

"Innate modesty is not a characteristic of the American Negro women. On the contrary, there is observable among them a willing susceptibility to the blandishments of licentious men, together with a widespread distribution of physical favors among their male friends."

"Marriage is no barrier to illicit sexual indulgence, and both men and women maintain such relations in utter disregard of all their plighted troth. In fact, so deeply rooted in immorality are our Negro people, that they turn in aversion from any sexual relation which does not invite sensuous embraces, and seize with feverish avidity upon every opportunity that promises personal gratification."

"Most Negro women marry young; when they do not their spinsterhood is due either to physical disease, or sexual morbidity, or a desire for unrestrained sexual freedom." . . . . "Nor is female ante-nuptial knowledge a bar to marriage among Negroes, especially in the alliance of a fair woman to a black man, while illegitimate motherhood is rather a recommendation in the eyes of a prospective husband."

"Marital immoralities are not confined to the poor, the ignorant, and degraded among the freed people, but are equally common among those who presume to be educated and refined."

"There is no school of prominence in Negro training which has not had among its pupils young freedwomen sustaining immoral relations with white men, whose school expenses have been, in many instances, defrayed by such persons with the knowledge and consent of the school authorities."

"In view of all the known facts at our command, we shall be justified in assuming that not only are ninety per cent of the Negro women of America lascivious by instinct and in bondage to physical pleasure, but that the social degradation of our freedwomen is without a parallel in modern civilization."

"So visibly universal is the strife for personal adornment that Negro mothers cannot be held blameless for the immoralities of their daughters, and there is at least ground for believing that sexual impurity is deliberately inculcated in them, since, in many instances, their maternal guardians appear to be never so pleased as when the physical charms of their daughters have procured for them dress and jewels beyond the ability of their parents to provide. Nor do girls themselves appear to be abashed by any publicity of their immoralities."

"The Negro is of a preeminently sensual race, and one whose male members have an inordinate craving for carnal knowledge of white women."

As you have come in contact with the colored people, and as far as your knowledge goes, are these statements true or not? Do they correctly represent the present condition of the race? Please state in full what your convictions are on the matter— and how long you have been laboring among the colored people. Let us hear from you at your earliest convenience. By so doing you will greatly oblige the Committee on Morals and Religion of the Hampton Conference.

Francis J. Grimké, Chairman,
1526 L. Street, N. W.
Washington, D.C.[1]

Notes

Abbreviations

American Missionary Association Archives
  American Missionary Association Archives, Amistad Research Center, Tulane University

Applications and Recommendations, RG 59
  Applications and Recommendations for Public Office, Administrations of Hayes, Garfield, and Arthur, 1877–1885, Record Group 59, National Archives and Records Administration

Bartlett Interview Notes
  Notes of Willard W. Bartlett Interview of William Hannibal Thomas, Columbus, Ohio, Otterbein College Archives, Westerville, Ohio

Directory of Pittsburgh & Allegheny
  Directory of Pittsburgh & Allegheny Cities, The Adjacent Boroughs, and Parts of the Adjacent Townships (Pittsburgh: George H. Thurston, various years)

Directory of Pittsburgh and Allegheny Cities
  Directory of Pittsburgh and Allegheny Cities and Parts of Adjoining Townships (Pittsburgh: George H. Thurston, various years)

Hampton Report
  "Report of the Committee on Morals and Religion for 1901 on W. H. Thomas's Book, *The American Negro,* Hampton Negro Conference, July, 1901," unpublished typescript, Carter G. Woodson Papers, Manuscript Division, Library of Congress

NIMS
  The Negro in the Military Service of the United States, 1639–1886, National Archives Microfilm M-858

Official Records

U.S. War Department, *The War of the Rebellion: A Compilation of the Official Records of the Union and Confederate Armies,* 127 vols. and index (Washington, DC: Government Printing Office, 1880–1901)

Records of the Adjutant General's Office, RG 94

Records of the Adjutant General's Office, Colored Troops Division, Record Group 94, National Archives and Records Administration

Records of the BRFAL, RG 105

Records of the Superintendent of Education for the State of Georgia, Bureau of Refugees, Freedmen, and Abandoned Lands, 1865–1870, Record Group 105, National Archives and Records Administration

SCHS

South Carolina Historical Society

SCDAH

South Carolina Department of Archives and History

Sessions Journal, Newberry County

Sessions Journal, Newberry County, Clerk of Court, Minutes of the Court of General Sessions, 1873–1883, SCDAH

Thomas Pension File, RG 15

William H. Thomas Pension File, Record Group 15, National Archives and Records Administration

WTS Faculty Minutes

Western Theological Seminary Faculty Minutes, April 17, 1868, Pittsburgh Theological Seminary Library

Introduction. An African American Enigma

1. Booker T. Washington, *Up From Slavery: An Autobiography* (Garden City: Doubleday, 1901), 318; Gunnar Myrdal, *An American Dilemma: The Negro Problem in American Democracy,* 2 vols. (New York: Harper, 1944), 1:63; Jessie Carney Smith and Carrell Peterson Horton, eds., *Historical Statistics of Black America: Agriculture to Labor & Employment* (New York: Gale Research, 1995), 494; Leon F. Litwack, *Trouble in Mind: Black Southerners in the Age of Jim Crow* (New York: Knopf, 1998), xvi.

2. Myrdal, *An American Dilemma,* 2:1187 n.13.

3. Thomas, *The American Negro: What He Was, What He Is, and What He May Become* (New York: Macmillan, 1901), v.

4. See, for example, Arthur W. Calhoun, *A Social History of the American Family from Colonial Times to the Present,* 3 vols. (Cleveland: Arthur H. Clark, 1917–19), 3:30–31, 44–45; Benjamin Brawley, *A Social History of the American Negro* (New York: Macmillan, 1921), 325; E. Franklin Frazier, *The Negro Family in Chicago* (Chicago: University of Chicago Press, 1932), 6–7; Bertram Johannes Otto Schrieke,

Alien Americans: A Study of Race Relations (New York: Viking, 1936), 202; John G. Van Deusen, *The Black Man in White America* (Washington, DC: Associated Publishers, 1938), 21, 128; Everett V. Stonequist, "Race Mixture and the Mulatto," in *Race Relations and the Race Problem,* ed. Edgar T. Thompson (Durham: Duke University Press, 1939), 265n; Robert Austin Warner, *New Haven Negroes: A Social History* (New Haven: Yale University Press, 1940), 164; Otto Klineberg, ed., *Characteristics of the American Negro* (New York: Harper, 1944), 15; Arnold M. Rose, *The Negro's Morale: Group Identification and Protest* (Minneapolis: University of Minnesota Press, 1949), 29–30, 86; John Dollard, *Caste and Class in a Southern Town* (New York: Doubleday Anchor, 1957), 398n–399n; Abram Kardiner and Lionel Ovesey, *The Mark of Oppression: Explorations in the Personality of the American Negro* (Cleveland: World Publishing Co., 1962), 362; James Graham Cook, *The Segregationists* (New York: Appleton-Century-Crofts, 1962), 356; I. A. Newby, *Jim Crow's Defense: Anti-Negro Thought in America, 1900–1930* (Baton Rouge: Louisiana State University Press, 1965), 26; Harold B. Hancock, "Otterbein's First Black Student: William Hannibal Thomas," *Otterbein Miscellany* 8 (May 1972): 7–12; Florette Henri, *Black Migration: Movement North, 1900–1920* (New York: Anchor, 1975), 188; J. Noel Heermance, *Charles W. Chesnutt: America's First Great Black Novelist* (Hamden, CT: Archon, 1974), 93–94; Dwight W. Hoover, *The Red and the Black* (Chicago: Rand McNally, 1976), 523; David Gordon Nielson, *Black Ethos: Northern Urban Negro Life and Thought, 1890–1930* (Westport: Greenwood Press, 1977), 159–60; Thomas, "Race Problems," 62.

5. Bertram Wilbur Doyle, "Racial Traits of the Negro as Negroes Assign Them to Themselves" (M.A. diss., University of Chicago, 1924), 3, 10, 11; Thomas, *The American Negro,* 123–24; Bertram Wilbur Doyle, *The Etiquette of Race Relations: A Study in Social Control* (1937; New York: Schocken Books, 1971), 175. On Doyle, see Stow Persons, *Ethnic Studies at Chicago, 1905–45* (Chicago: University of Chicago Press, 1987), 72, 151 n.26, and James B. McKee, *Sociology and the Race Problem: The Failure of a Perspective* (Urbana: University of Illinois Press, 1993), 150–51.

6. August Meier, "Negro Racial Thought in the Age of Booker T. Washington, Circa 1880–1915" (Ph.D. diss., Columbia University, 1957), 972; idem, *Negro Thought in America, 1880–1915* (1963; Ann Arbor: University of Michigan Press, 1966).

7. Lawrence J. Friedman, *The White Savage: Racial Fantasies in the Postbellum South* (Englewood Cliffs: Prentice-Hall, 1970), 147; James M. McPherson, *The Abolitionist Legacy: From Reconstruction to the NAACP* (Princeton: Princeton University Press, 1975), 341; Ralph E. Luker, *The Social Gospel in Black and White: American Racial Reform, 1885–1912* (Chapel Hill: University of North Carolina Press, 1991), 294.

8. The reformer Mary White Ovington referred to Thomas as "a renegade Negro." See "Reminiscences," *Baltimore Afro-American,* October 1, 1932, [24].

9. See "The Democratic Return to Power—Its Effect?" *A.M.E. Church Review* 1 (January 1885): 213–50.

10. "The American Negro," London *Spectator* 86 (March 23, 1901): 427.

Chapter One. Student, Servant, Soldier

1. Thomas, *The American Negro: What He Was, What He Is, and What He Will Become* (New York: Macmillan, 1901), xi.

2. Thomas Pension File, RG 15; Thomas, *The American Negro*, xi–xii.

3. Rebecca Thomas Interment Record, Oak Grove Cemetery, Delaware County Historical Society, Delaware, OH; James H. Rodabaugh, "The Negro in Ohio," *Journal of Negro History* 31 (January 1946): 9–10; *History of Delaware County and Ohio* (Chicago: O. L. Baskin & Co., 1880), 647; Schedule of the Whole Number of Persons, 1830 Federal Census of Ohio, Muskingum County, Wayne Township, p. 293, Ohio Historical Society; Robert E. Chaddock, *Ohio Before 1850: A Study of the Early Influence of Pennsylvania and Southern Populations in Ohio* (New York: Columbia University Press, 1908), 16, 15, 18.

4. Thomas, *The American Negro*, xii; Schedule 1—Free Inhabitants in Jackson Township in the County of Pickaway, State of Ohio, 1850, p. 242, Seventh Census of the United States, Ohio Historical Society; Schedule 1—Free Inhabitants in Jackson Township in the County of Pickaway, State of Ohio, 1860, p. 294, Eighth Census of the United States, Ohio Historical Society; Bartlett Interview Notes, April 18, 1933; Thomas to Woodrow Wilson, January 8, 1913, Woodrow Wilson Papers, Manuscript Division, Library of Congress. On Mrs. Woodrow, see William Bayard Hale, *Woodrow Wilson: The Story of His Life* (Garden City: Doubleday, 1912), 16–19.

5. Winkle, *The Politics of Community: Migration and Politics in Antebellum Ohio* (Cambridge: Cambridge University Press, 1988), 11, 78. Scant information also remains on the Whitings. Henry Whiting was not listed in the 1840 census for Pickaway County. He most likely came to Ohio about the same time as Thomas's parents. See Freda M. Corcoran, comp., *Muhlenberg Township, Pickaway County, 1870 Census, Cemeteries, Maps* [Circleville, OH: n.p., 1989], 17.

6. *Compendium of the Enumeration of the Inhabitants and Statistics of the United States, as Obtained at the Department of State, From the Returns of the Sixth Census* (Washington, DC: Thomas Allen, 1841), 77, 78; Mary Norris, "Places That Didn't Make the Guidebook," *New York Times*, January 3, 1993, section 5, 23; *The Seventh Census of the United States: 1850* (Washington, DC: Robert Armstrong, Public Printer, 1853), 843, 818; *Population of the United States in 1860; Compiled From the Original Returns of the Eighth Census* (Washington, DC: Government Printing Office, 1864), 390, 378, 380, 397.

7. *History of Franklin and Pickaway Counties, Ohio, With Illustrations and Biographical Sketches* (Cleveland: Williams Brothers, 1880), 33, 51, 56–57, 173; Francis P. Weisenburger, *The Passing of the Frontier: 1825–1850, History of the State of*

Ohio, Volume III (1941; Columbus: Ohio Historical Society, 1969), 18; Ronald E. Shaw, *Canals for a Nation: The Canal Era in the United States, 1790–1860* (Lexington: University Press of Kentucky, 1990), 128–29, 158–59; *Annual Report of the Commissioner of Statistics to the General Assembly of Ohio for the Year 1860* (Columbus: Richard Nevins, State Printer, 1861), 568; Chaddock, *Ohio Before 1850,* 24; Robert Leslie Jones, *History of Agriculture in Ohio to 1880* (Kent: Kent State University Press, 1983), 50–51, 53, 60, 113, 125, 163.

8. James Buchanan, comp., *The Blacks of Pickaway County, Ohio, in the Nineteenth Century* (Bowie, MD: Heritage Books, 1988), iii; Carter G. Woodson, *Free Negro Heads of Families in the United States in 1830* (Washington, DC: Association for the Study of Negro Life and History, 1925), 128–29; Schedule 1—Free Inhabitants of Jackson Township, 1860, p. 294; Lee Soltow, "Inequality Amidst Abundance: Land Ownership in Early Nineteenth Century Ohio," *Ohio History* 88 (spring 1979): 147n; idem, *Men and Wealth in the United States, 1850–1870* (New Haven: Yale University Press, 1975), 54.

9. *Williams' Circleville and Lancaster Directory, City Guide, and Business Mirror, Volume 1—1859–'60* (Circleville: L. N. Olds, 1859), 13; Alexander W. Wayman, *Cyclopaedia of African Methodism* (Baltimore: Methodist Episcopal Book Depository, 1882), 36; A[mzi] D[oolittle] Barber, *Report on the Condition of the Colored People of Ohio* (Massillon, OH: n.p., 1840), 5, 6–7; "The North and the South," *Circleville Herald,* June 16, 1854, 2:2; "Capture of a 'Fugitive' in Pickaway Co.," ibid., February 28, 1851, 2:1; "Murder of a Fugitive Slave," ibid., June 9, 1854, 2:2; "Another Infernal Outrage," ibid., October 21, 1859, 1:6. For Ohio's black laws, see Stephen Middleton, *The Black Laws in the Old Northwest: A Documentary History* (Westport: Greenwood Press, 1993), 9–141.

10. O. Brainard Hanby, *The Remarkable Life Of a Song Writer* [Benjamin R. Hanby] (n.p., [1936]), 5, Otterbein College Archives; Wilbur H. Siebert, *The Underground Railroad From Slavery to Freedom* (1898; New York: Russell & Russell, 1967), 134–35, 428; "Africa: Hamlet Recalls the Glory Days," *Westerville News,* November 26, 1986, 1, 30; Alan Miller, "Slaves' Route to Freedom Depended on Help Here," *Columbus Dispatch,* February 11, 1987, 1E, 2E (clippings deposited in Local History Resource Center, Westerville Public Library, Westerville, OH).

11. Thomas, "Memories of Otterbein Half a Century Ago," *United Brethren Review* 16 (July/August 1905): 201; John A. Hardon, *The Protestant Churches of America,* rev. ed. (Garden City: Image Books, 1969), 297–300; Frank S. Mead, *Handbook of Denominations in the United States* (New York: Abingdon-Cokesbury Press, 1951), 84; Elmer T. Clark, *The Small Sects in America,* rev. ed. (New York: Abingdon-Cokesbury Press, 1937), 68; Jack M. Tuell, *The Organization of the United Methodist Church* (Nashville: Abingdon Press, 1970), 16–17. In 1946 the UBC merged with The Evangelical Church to form The Evangelical United Brethren Church. In 1968 this denomination joined with the Methodist church to form the United Methodist Church.

12. Emma Lou Thornbrough, *Indiana in the Civil War Era, 1850–1880* (Indianapolis: Indiana Historical Bureau & Indiana Historical Society, 1965), 15; Eugene H. Berwanger, *The Frontier Against Slavery: Western Anti-Negro Prejudice and the Slavery Extension Controversy* (1967; Urbana: University of Illinois Press, 1971), 20, 45, 56; Thomas, "Memories of Otterbein Half a Century Ago," 201; Charles Kettleborough, *Constitution Making in Indiana: A Source Book of Constitutional Documents With Historical Introduction and Critical Notes*, 4 vols. (1916; Indianapolis: Indiana Historical Bureau, 1971), 1:360–63; Emma Lou Thornbrough, *The Negro in Indiana: A Study of a Minority* (Indianapolis: Indiana Historical Bureau, 1957), 69–70. Thomas's references to his family's early relocations were extremely vague. In 1905 he wrote that after moving to Indiana "in his seventh year [1850]," his parents "soon" returned to Ohio. Based on internal evidence I conclude that they returned to Ohio in 1851. See "Memories of Otterbein Half a Century Ago," 201.

13. Thomas, *The American Negro,* xiv; idem, "Memories of Otterbein Half a Century Ago," 201. Again, Thomas's vague accounts of his early life make it impossible to pinpoint the precise dates of his family's travels. He remarked that after their initial return to Ohio in the early 1850s, they departed to Michigan only "[a] few years later." But then he explained that he first attended school, presumably in Ohio, in his "thirteenth year [1856]." Thomas obviously was confused regarding the racial composition of his first district school. In 1905 he complained that schools such as the first one he attended were "not always open to colored children." See ibid.

14. Ronald P. Formisano, "The Edge of Caste: Colored Suffrage In Michigan, 1827–1861," *Michigan History* 56 (spring 1972): 19, 21, 30. For Michigan's black laws, see Middleton, *The Black Laws in the Old Northwest,* 349–71.

15. *The Seventh Census of the United States: 1850,* 892, 886; John C. Dancy, "The Negro People in Michigan," *Michigan History Magazine* 24 (spring 1940): 228; *Population of the United States in 1860,* 236, 242; Charles N. Lindquist, *Lenawee Reflections* (Adrian: Lenawee County Historical Society, 1992), 48–50; William Lloyd Garrison to Helen E. Garrison, October 10, 1853, in *The Letters of William Lloyd Garrison,* 6 vols., ed. Louis Ruchames (Cambridge: Harvard University Press, 1971–81), 4:262; "Wells Brown Reading," *Adrian Expositor,* March 14, 1857, 2:4.

16. *Brown's City Directory of Adrian, Michigan* (Adrian: Adrian Times and Expositor Steam Printing Office, 1870), 38–39; *Pathways to Knowledge: The Foundation and Growth of Adrian Public Schools, 1828–1988* (Adrian: Adrian Public Schools, 1989), 29; "The City of Adrian—Its Present Resources and Future Growth: Number VII, Our Public Buildings," *Adrian Expositor,* May 2, 1857, 2:3; "Meeting of the Adrian Sabbath School Union," ibid., July 18, 1857, 2:5; Thomas, "Memories of Otterbein Half a Century Ago," 201; idem, *The American Negro,* xxi. The UBC Church was not listed in Adrian's 1859–60 or 1870 city directories. See

Williams' Adrian & Hudson Directory, City Guide, and Business Mirror (Adrian: C. S. Williams, 1859), n.p.; *Brown's City Directory of Adrian, Michigan,* 47–48. The latter source listed two local black institutions—the Second Baptist (Colored) Church and the St. John's Masonic Lodge, No. 7 (Colored). See pp. 47, 49.

17. Thomas, "Memories of Otterbein Half a Century Ago," 201–2; Harold B. Hancock, "Otterbein University During the Civil War," 8, Local History Resource Center, Westerville Public Library; idem, *Westerville Heritage, 1806–1986* (Westerville: Otterbein College Print Shop, 1986), 9–10; Peter H. Odegard, *Pressure Politics: The Story of the Anti-Saloon League* (New York: Columbia University Press, 1928), 73; K. Austin Kerr, *Organized for Prohibition: A New History of the Anti-Saloon League* (New Haven: Yale University Press, 1985), 126; Harold B. Hancock, *The History of Westerville, Ohio* (Westerville: Otterbein Press, 1974), 40, 50.

18. Thomas, "Memories of Otterbein Half a Century Ago," 202–3.

19. Ibid., 202; *The Seventh Census of the United States: 1850,* 827; *Population of the United States in 1860,* 380; *Ninth Census—Volume I. The Statistics of the Population of the United States* (Washington, DC: Government Printing Office, 1872), 230; Hanby, *The Remarkable Life of a Song Writer,* 3–5; Hancock, *Westerville Heritage,* 10–11; idem, *The History of Westerville, Ohio,* 50; Willard W. Bartlett, *Education for Humanity: The Story of Otterbein College* (Westerville: Otterbein College, 1934), 38; Miller, "Slaves' Route to Freedom Depended on Help Here," 2E; Siebert, *The Underground Railroad,* 421; Gara, *The Liberty Line: The Legend of the Underground Railroad* (1961; Lexington: University of Kentucky Press, 1967), 6.

20. Thomas, *The American Negro,* xii–xiii.

21. Thomas, "Memories of Otterbein Half a Century Ago," 202; Hanby, *The Remarkable Life Of a Song Writer,* 7, 17–18; Bartlett Interview Notes, January 26, 1933.

22. Thomas, *The American Negro,* xiv; idem, "Memories of Otterbein Half a Century Ago," 202. Aside from Thomas's writings, no documentary record exists of blacks attending Westerville schools before 1859. See Harold B. Hancock, "The Westerville Public Schools: 130 Years of Service, 1855–1985" (unpublished manuscript, December 1, 1985), 3–5, 11–13, Local History Resource Center, Westerville Public Library.

23. Hancock, *The History of Westerville, Ohio,* 50; Thomas, "Memories of Otterbein Half a Century Ago," 203; idem, *The American Negro,* xiv; "Hannible," "Letter From Hannible," January 29, 1866, *Christian Recorder,* February 10, 1866, 1:5–7.

24. James O. Horton, "Black Education at Oberlin College: A Controversial Commitment," *Journal of Negro Education* 54 (fall 1985): 484n; Thomas, "Memories of Otterbein Half a Century Ago," 203–4; Hancock, "Otterbein University During the Civil War," 8.

25. Thomas, "Memories of Otterbein Half a Century Ago," 201, 206, 203, 202.

26. Hancock, "Otterbein University During the Civil War," 8.

27. Donald G. Tewksbury, *The Founding of American Colleges and Universities Before the Civil War* (1932; Hamden, CT: Archon, 1965), 25, 72, 76–78; Frederick Rudolph, *The American College and University: A History* (New York: Vintage, 1962), 54–55, 57; Henry Garst, *Otterbein University, 1847–1907* (Dayton: United Brethren Publishing House, 1907); Bartlett, *Education for Humanity;* Harold B. Hancock, *The History of Otterbein College, 1930–1972* (Kansas City: American World Book Press, 1971).

28. Bartlett, *Education for Humanity,* 38; Hancock, *The History of Otterbein College, 1930–1972,* 2; *Annual Catalogue of the Officers and Students of Otterbein University, for the Year Ending June 27th, 1860* (Dayton: United Brethren Printing Establishment, 1860), 15.

29. Hancock, *The History of Westerville, Ohio,* 41; Robert Samuel Fletcher, *A History of Oberlin College: From Its Foundation Through the Civil War,* 2 vols. (Oberlin: Oberlin College, 1943), 2:918, 536; Horton, "Black Education at Oberlin College," 480–82; Ellen N. Lawson and Larlene Merrill, "The Antebellum 'Talented Thousandth': Black Education at Oberlin College," *Journal of Negro Education* 52 (spring 1983): 142, 151–52.

30. Garst, *Otterbein University,* 129–30, 136–38, 130, 136.

31. Board of Trustee Minutes, June 20, 1854, p. 57, Minutes of the Otterbein University Board of Trustees, 1846–1866, Otterbein College Archives; "Younker," "To Whom It May Concern," *Religious Telescope,* February 23, 1859, 99:1.

32. Weaver, "'To Whom It May Concern,'" ibid., March 9, 1859, 106:7; Bartlett, *Education for Humanity,* 38–39.

33. Otterbein University Faculty Minutes, November 11, 18, 1859; Otterbein University Board of Trustees Executive Committee Minutes, November 14, 1859, Otterbein College Archives; Hancock, "Otterbein's First Black Student: William Hannibal Thomas," *Otterbein Miscellany* 8 (May 1972): 7.

34. Thompson, testimonial for William Hannibal Thomas, August 30, 1877, Applications and Recommendations, RG 59; [Thompson], *A Brief History of "The Otterbein University of Ohio," Located at Westerville, Franklin Co., Ohio, Prepared for the Centennial Exhibition, at Philadelphia, Pa., 1876* (1876; Westerville: Otterbein College Press, 1974), 9–10. In 1880 the National Prohibition Reform Party nominated Thompson for vice president. See Mrs. M. M'Clellan Brown, *Biographical Sketch of Rev. H. A. Thompson, D.D.* (New York: Prohibition Reform Party, [1880]).

35. *Annual Catalogue of the Officers and Students of Otterbein University,* 12; Thomas, "Memories of Otterbein Half a Century Ago," 204.

36. Thomas, "Memories of Otterbein Half a Century Ago," 204; Bartlett Interview Notes, January 26, 1933. For conflicting accounts of Thomas's admission and experiences at Otterbein, see Bartlett, *Education for Humanity,* 39; "OC Integrated—1847," Otterbein College *Tan and Cardinal,* September 27, 1968, 4:1–2;

Hancock, *History of Otterbein College,* 2; idem, "Otterbein's First Black Student: William Hannibal Thomas," 7–8.

37. Thomas, "Memories of Otterbein Half a Century Ago," 204–5.

38. Garst, *Otterbein University,* 136. Many years later Thomas recalled that his discussion with Hanby occurred three weeks after his admittance to Otterbein, not the day following the chapel incident. See Bartlett Interview Notes, April 18, 1933.

39. Thomas, "Memories of Otterbein Half a Century Ago," 205, 206.

40. Ibid., 205, 206, 205; Thomas to Theodore D. Jervey, February 5, 1910, Theodore D. Jervey Papers, SCHS.

41. Thomas, "Memories of Otterbein Half a Century Ago," 205; Bartlett Interview Notes, January 26, 1933. Thomas's name never appeared on the membership roll of the Philomathean Society. See Journal, Philomathean Society, Otterbein University, 1859–1911, Otterbein College Archives.

42. Bartlett, *Education for Humanity,* 39; Thomas, "Memories of Otterbein Half a Century Ago," 201–2; idem, *The American Negro,* xiv–xv; Hanby testimonial for Thomas, n.d., Applications and Recommendations, RG 59; Harold B. Hancock, "William H. Fouse, 1868–1944," *Interesting Personalities in Westerville History* [1986]; Bob Dreitzler, "Black Educator Broke Racial Barriers," *Columbus Dispatch,* February 22, 1989 (clippings deposited in Local History Resource Center, Westerville Public Library). Bartlett recorded Prescott S. Thomas's rejection at Otterbein in his Interview Notes (undated). During his interview with Thomas on January 26, 1933, Bartlett recorded that following Thomas's departure from Otterbein, "no other colored student [attended the college] for 20 years." Otterbein's financial records erroneously list Thomas attending the university from November 16, 1859 to April 16, 1860. See Otterbein University Treasurer, Scholarships, Tuition, Incidentals Journal, 1859–1864, Otterbein College Archives.

43. Thomas, "Memories of Otterbein Half a Century Ago," 206.

44. Ibid.

45. Thomas, "Retrospection," *Christian Recorder,* April 28, 1866, 1:4–5; Thomas to Erastus Milo Cravath, August [?], 1871, American Missionary Association Archives; idem, *The American Negro,* xi, xiv.

46. Thomas, "Memories of Otterbein Half a Century Ago," 205–6; Schedule 1—Free Inhabitants in Jackson Township in the County of Pickaway, Ohio, July 17, 1860, p. 294; Schedule 1—Inhabitants in Delaware, in the County of Delaware, State of Ohio, Enumerated 1870, p. 328, Ohio Historical Society; *History of Delaware County and Ohio,* 647; *Population of the United States in 1860,* 372, 367, 396; Sylvia Brooks, "Delaware Roots," *Columbus Dispatch,* October 10, 1982, B2:1–6. "B. F." Thomas was born in 1847 and began his apprenticeship in Delaware, Ohio, in 1864 before entering the U.S. Colored Troops. He also referred to himself as "Frank." Walter S. Thomas was born in 1857. Another brother, John W. Thomas, apparently never lived with his family. See Lowell Dwight Black, "The Negro Volunteer Militia Units of the Ohio National Guard, 1870–1954: The Struggle for Military Recogni-

tion and Equality in the State of Ohio" (Ph.D. diss., The Ohio State University, 1976), 371.

47. Charles H. Wesley, *Ohio Negroes in the Civil War* (Columbus: The Ohio State University Press, 1962), 15–16, 26; Thomas, *The American Negro*, xv.

48. Thomas, *The American Negro*, xv; R. R. Wright, ed., *The Encyclopedia of the African Methodist Episcopal Church*, 2d ed. (Philadelphia: Book Concern of the AME Church, 1947), 533; Edward D. [*sic*] Davis to the editor, April 6, 1863, *Christian Recorder*, April 18, 1863, 2:4; B. W. Arnett and S. T. Mitchell, *The Wilberforce Alumnal, A Comprehensive Review of the Origin, Development and Present Status of Wilberforce University* (Xenia: The Gazette, 1885), 4–6; Frederick A. McGinnis, *A History and an Interpretation of Wilberforce University* (Wilberforce, OH: n.p., 1941), 25–28.

49. Bertram Wyatt-Brown, "Abolitionism and Antislavery in Hudson and Cleveland: Contrasts in Reform Styles," in *Cleveland: A Tradition of Reform*, ed. David D. Van Tassel and John J. Grabowski (Kent: Kent State University Press, 1986), 102; George A. Singleton, *The Romance of African Methodism: A Study of the African Methodist Episcopal Church* (New York: Exposition Press, 1952), 92; James J. Burns, *Educational History of Ohio* (Columbus: Historical Publishing Co., 1905), 350; William Cheek and Aimee Lee Cheek, *John Mercer Langston and the Fight for Black Freedom, 1829–65* (Urbana: University of Illinois Press, 1989), 94, 109, 126n.

50. Cheek and Cheek, *John Mercer Langston*, 126n–127n; Brown testimonial for William Hannibal Thomas, November 12, 1877, Applications and Testimonials, RG 59; Davis to the editor, *Christian Recorder*, April 18, 1863, 2:4; Daniel A. Payne, *History of the African Methodist Episcopal Church* (Nashville: Publishing House of the A.M.E. Sunday-School Union, 1891), 283, 284, 296, 308, 323, 325, 399; Singleton, *The Romance of African Methodism*, 92.

51. Daniel A. Payne, *Recollections of Seventy Years* (1888; New York: Arno, 1969), 225; Grace Naomi Perry, "The Educational Work of the African Methodist Episcopal Church Prior to 1900" (M.A. thesis, Howard University, 1948), 27, 29n, 38, 43, 83; Charles Denmore Killian, "Bishop Daniel A. Payne: Black Spokesman for Reform" (Ph.D. diss., Indiana University, 1971), 112–13. Because of mismanagement, the A.M.E. Church never received the funds from the sale of Union Seminary.

52. Thomas, "Memories of Otterbein Half a Century Ago," 205–6; idem, "Retrospection," 1:5–6; "Hannibal," "Letter From the Fifth Regiment, U.S.C.T.," October 27, 1865, *Christian Recorder*, November 4, 1865, 1:5–7.

53. Thomas, *The American Negro*, xv; Chauncey N. Olds to J. D. Cox, July 2, 1869, Applications and Recommendations, RG 59; U.S. War Department, *Revised Regulations for the Army of the United States, 1861* (Philadelphia: George W. Childs, 1862), 112, 351; U.S. War Department, *Index of General Orders Adjutant General's Office, 1862* (Washington, DC: Government Printing Office, 1863), 16; William Cullen Bryant II, ed., "A Yankee Soldier Looks at the Negro," *Civil War History* 7 (June 1961): 138; Wiley, *The Life of Johnny Reb: The Common Soldier of the Confed-*

eracy (1943; Indianapolis: Bobbs-Merrill Charter Books, 1962), 327–28; Willard B. Gatewood, ed., *Slave and Freeman: The Autobiography of George L. Knox* (Lexington: University Press of Kentucky, 1979), 9; Gary R. Kremer, *James Milton Turner and the Promise of America: The Public Life of a Post–Civil War Black Leader* (Columbia: University of Missouri Press, 1991), 16; Stewart Sikakis, *Who Was Who in the Civil War* (New York: Facts on File, 1988), 314.

54. F. H. Mason, *The Forty-Second Ohio Infantry: A History of the Organization and Services of that Regiment in the War of the Rebellion* (Cleveland: Cobb, Andrews & Co., 1876), 259; Whitelaw Reid, *Ohio in the War: Her Statesmen, Her Generals, and Soldiers,* 2 vols. (Cincinnati: Moore, Wilstach & Baldwin, 1868), 2: 266–68; Garfield to J. Harrison Rhodes, December 17, 1861, in *The Wild Life of the Army: Civil War Letters of James A. Garfield,* ed. Frederick D. Williams (East Lansing: Michigan State College Press, 1964), 49; Charles G. Williams, ed., "Down the Rivers: Civil War Diary of Thomas Benton White," *Register of the Kentucky Historical Society* 67 (April 1969): 134–74; Garfield, "My Campaign in Kentucky," *North American Review* 143 (December 1886): 525–35; Joseph D. Carr, "Garfield and Marshall in the Big Sandy Valley, 1861–1862," *Filson Club History Quarterly* 64 (April 1990): 247–63; *The Military History of Ohio. Its Border Annals, Its Part in the Indian Wars, in the War of 1812, in the Mexican War, and in the War of the Rebellion* (New York: H. H. Hardesty, 1886), 152; *Official Records,* series 1, vol. 7, pp. 25–39, 46–47, 501, 503, 602–3, 663–65; ibid., vol. 10, part 1, pp. 33, 72–74; ibid., vol. 10, part 2, pp. 9, 17–18.

55. Ira Berlin, ed., *Freedom: A Documentary History of Emancipation, 1861–1867, Series I, Volume III* (Cambridge: Cambridge University Press, 1990), 21; Olds to Cox, July 2, 1869, Applications and Recommendations, RG 59; Mason, *The Forty-Second Ohio Infantry,* 192, 198, 262; Earl S. Miers, *The Web of Victory: Grant at Vicksburg* (New York: Knopf, 1955), 155–57; *Official Records,* series 1, vol. 24, part 1, pp. 585, 591.

56. Thomas, *The American Negro,* xv; Reid, *Ohio in the War,* 2:527–30; *Official Records,* series 1, vol. 16, part 1, pp. 909, 918–23, 928–30; ibid., vol. 16, part 2, p. 436; "The Battle of Richmond," in *Madison County: 200 Years in Retrospect,* ed. William E. Ellis, H. E. Everman, and Richard D. Sears (Richmond, KY: Madison County Historical Society, 1985), 181–208; *Official Records,* series 1, vol. 20, part 2, p. 290.

57. *Official Records,* series 1, vol. 24, part 1, pp. 751–58, 761–64, 766, 769–71; ibid., vol. 24, part 2, pp. 285–88, 620–22; Edwin C. Bearss, "The Armed Conflict, 1861–1865," in *A History of Mississippi,* 2 vols., ed. Richard Aubrey McLemore (Jackson: University & College Press of Mississippi, 1973), 1:468–79; Reid, *Ohio in the War,* 2:529; Stephen A. Hurlbut to the President, March 30, 1878, Applications and Recommendations, RG 59; Thomas, *The American Negro,* xv; Thomas to Howard, April 24, 1889, Oliver Otis Howard Papers, Bowdoin College.

58. Frank Levstik, "Robert A. Pinn: Courageous Black Soldier," *Negro History*

Bulletin 37 (November 1974): 305; Paul Comstock, "Two Black Yankees Among Local Medal of Honor Winners," *Delaware Gazette,* June 6, 1990, 8:1–3; Joseph B. Mitchell, "Negro Troops at Chaffin's Farm," *The Badge of Gallantry: Recollections of Civil War Congressional Medal of Honor Winners* (New York: Macmillan, 1968), 132–43; Hondon B. Hargrove, *Black Union Soldiers in the Civil War* (Jefferson, NC: McFarland & Co., 1988), 216–17.

59. William F. Fox, *Regimental Losses in the American Civil War, 1861–1865* (Albany: Albany Publishing Co., 1898), 48, 53, 521–24. On the 5th USCT, see Frank R. Levstik, "The Fifth Regiment, United States Colored Troops, 1863–1865," *Northwest Ohio Quarterly* 42 (fall 1970): 86–98; Versalle Freddrick Washington, "Eagles on Their Buttons: The Fifth Regiment of Infantry, United States Colored Troops in the American Civil War" (Ph.D. diss., The Ohio State University, 1995); and Noah Andre Trudeau, *Like Men of War: Black Troops in the Civil War, 1862–1865* (Boston: Little, Brown, 1998).

60. Cheek and Cheek, *John Mercer Langston,* 406; Thomas, "A Reminiscence of the War," September 27, 1865, William A. Bourne Papers, Manuscript Division, Library of Congress; idem, "Retrospection," 1:5–6; "Hannibal," "Letter From the Fifth Regiment, U.S.C.T.," 1:5–7. On matters of unequal pay and other forms of discrimination by the army against black troops, see Berlin, ed., *Freedom: A Documentary History of Emancipation, 1861–1867, Series II* (Cambridge: Cambridge University Press, 1982), chaps. 7 and 9.

61. Patton testimonial, October 1, 1877, Applications and Recommendations, RG 59; Company I Descriptive Book and Descriptive Books, Companies F to K, 5th U.S. Colored Troops; 5th U.S. Colored Infantry, Regimental Returns, Company I Muster Roll, November and December, 1863, May and June, 1864, Records of the Adjutant General's Office, RG 94; Craig J. Blaine, "Forgotten Men: A Collective Biography of Black and White Ohioans in the Ranks of the Union Army" (M.A. thesis, Kent State University, 1973)," 99–100; Joseph T. Glatthaar, *Forged in Battle: The Civil War Alliance of Black Soliders and White Officers* (New York: Free Press, 1990), 72; Berlin, ed., *Freedom: A Documentary History of Emancipation, Series II,* 20–21, 303–4, 29, 440–41; Thomas to Theodore D. Jervey, March 10, 1910, Jervey Papers.

62. Berlin, ed., *Freedom: A Documentary History of Emancipation, Series II,* 303n, 310; Company I, 5th U.S. Colored Troops Regimental Returns, November, 1863; Company I, 5th U.S. Colored Troops Muster Roll, November and December, 1863; Special Orders No. 10, December 25, 1863, Regimental Orders and Letters, 5th U.S. Colored Troops; Company I, 5th U.S. Colored Troops Muster Roll, May and June, 1864, Records of the Adjutant General's Office, RG 94.

63. Edward Longacre, "Brave Radical Wild: The Contentious Career of Brigadier Edward A. Wild," *Civil War Times Illustrated* 19 (June 1980): 9–19; Richard Reid, "General Edward A. Wild and Civil War Discrimination," *Historical Journal of Massachusetts* 13 (January 1985): 14–29; idem, "Raising the African Brigade: Early Black Recruitment in Civil War North Carolina," *North Carolina Historical*

Review 70 (July 1993): 266–97; "Hannibal," "Letter From the Fifth Regiment, U.S.C.T.," 1:5–7.

64. Washington, "Eagles on Their Buttons," 111; Trudeau, *Like Men of War,* 220–27; "Hannibal," "Letter From the Fifth Regiment, U.S.C.T.," 1:5–6; Levstik, "The Fifth Regiment, United States Colored Troops, 1863–1865," 93; Thomas to Theodore D. Jervey, July 30, 1911, Jervey Papers; Joseph J. Scroggs Diary [typescript], July 30 [1864], p. 7, *Civil War Times Illustrated Collection,* U.S. Military History Institute, Carlisle Barracks, PA; Ulysses L. Marvin, "General Shurtleff," *Oberlin Alumni Magazine* 7 (June 1911): 318.

65. Trudeau, *Like Men of War,* 286.

66. Report of Alonzo G. Draper, October 6, 1864, in *Official Records,* series 1, vol. 42, part 1, pp. 819–20; Scroggs Diary, September 29, 1864, p. 18; Dudley T. Cornish, *The Sable Arm: Negro Troops in the Union Army, 1861–1865* (1956; New York: Norton, 1966), 279–80; Draper to John A. Andrew, December 15, 1864, NIMS, reel 3, frame 568.

67. "Hannibal," "Letter From the Fifth Regiment, U.S.C.T.," 1:5–7; Richard J. Sommers, *Richmond Redeemed: The Siege at Petersburg* (Garden City: Doubleday, 1981), 86–87, 485; Shurtleff to Edward H. Merrell, October 22, 1864, Edward H. Merrell Papers, State Historical Society of Wisconsin; Scroggs Diary, September 29, 1864, p. 20.

68. Jack D. Foner, *Blacks and the Military in American History: A New Perspective* (New York: Praeger, 1974), 40; Butler to E. M. Stanton, October 3, 1864, in *Private and Official Correspondence of General Benjamin F. Butler, During the Period of the Civil War,* 5 vols. (Norwood, MA: Plimton Press, 1917), 5:215; Charles Johnston, "Attack on Fort Gilmer, September 29th, 1864," *Southern Historical Society Papers* 1 (June 1876): 438; Marvin testimonial, June 30, 1869; Shurtleff testimonial, October 30, 1865, Applications and Recommendations, RG 59; Berlin, ed., *Freedom: A Documentary History of Emancipation, Series II,* 29.

69. Butler to Whom it May Concern, July 22, 1869, and to Dear Sir, June 7, 1877, Applications and Recommendations, RG 59; Thomas to O. O. Howard, September 16, 1891, Howard Papers; John Mercer Langston, *From the Virginia Plantation to the Nation's Capitol or the First and Only Negro Representative in Congress from the Old Dominion* (Hartford: American Publishing Co., 1894), 217; Benjamin F. Butler, *Butler's Book* (Boston: A. M. Thayer and Co., 1892), 742–43; John E. Stanchak, "Butler Medal," in *Historical Times Illustrated Encyclopedia of the Civil War,* ed. Patricia L. Faust (New York: Harper, 1986), 99.

70. Thomas, "The Incidents of a Day's March," September 27, 1865, Bourne Papers. On the 5th USCT at Fair Oaks, see Trudeau, *Like Men of War,* 304–9; Thomas, *The American Negro,* xxi. On members of the 5th USCT voting in this election, see R. J. M. Blackett, ed., *Thomas Morris Chester: Black Civil War Correspondent, His Dispatches from the Front* (Baton Rouge: Louisiana State University Press, 1989), 188–89.

71. 5th U.S. Colored Infantry Field and Staff Muster Roll, Records of the Adjutant General's Office, RG 94; Scroggs Diary, December 10, 1864, p. 30; Edwin S. Redkey, ed., "'Rocked in the Cradle of Consternation': A Black Chaplain in the Union Army Reports on the Struggle to Take Fort Fisher, North Carolina, in the Winter of 1864–65," *American Heritage* 31 (October/November 1980): 74–79; Rowena Reed, *Combined Operations in the Civil War* (Annapolis: Naval Institute Press, 1978), 350; Chris Eugene Fonvielle Jr., "To Forge a Thunderbolt: The Wilmington Campaign, February, 1865" (M.A. thesis, East Carolina University, 1987), 30–41; idem, *The Wilmington Campaign: Last Rays of Departing Hope* (Campbell, CA: Savas Publishing, 1997), chap. 4.

72. Report of Rear Admiral David D. Porter, December 31, 1864, in *Official Records of the Union and Confederate Navies in the War of the Rebellion,* 30 vols. plus index (Washington, DC: Government Printing Office, 1894–1922), series 1, vol. 11, pp. 266–67; Fonvielle, "To Forge a Thunderbolt," 41–46, 47; idem, *The Wilmington Campaign,* chap. 5; 5th U.S. Colored Infantry Company I Muster Roll; 5th U.S. Colored Infantry Field and Staff Muster Roll, Records of the Adjutant General's Office, RG 94; Scroggs Diary, December 25, 1864, pp. 32–33, 36–37; Black, "The Negro Volunteer Militia Units of the Ohio National Guard," 161, 164; Shurtleff to wife, December 30, 1864, Giles W. Shurtleff Papers, Oberlin College Archives.

73. Scroggs Diary, January 5, 13, 15, 1865, pp. 37, 39; Extract from the Return of the U.S. Forces at Fort Fisher, North Carolina, Commanded by Major General Alfred H. Terry, for the Month of January 1865, NIMS, reel 4, frame 534; Report of Brigadier General Charles J. Paine, January 20, 1865, in *Official Records,* series 1, vol. 46, part 1, pp. 404, 423–24; Shurtleff to Mary, January 20, 1865, Shurtleff Papers; Fonvielle, "To Forge a Thunderbolt," 50–54, 298; idem, *The Wilmington Campaign,* chap. 7.

74. Thomas, *The American Negro,* xvi; Fonvielle, "To Forge a Thunderbolt," 120–21; idem, *The Wilmington Campaign,* chap. 10; Speed to Will Speed, February 12, 1865, Thomas Speed Letterbook, The Filson Club, Louisville.

75. Fonvielle, "To Forge a Thunderbolt," 175, 185–88; Scroggs Diary, February 20, 1865, p. 42; Report of Brigadier General Charles J. Paine, April 24, 1865, in *Official Records,* series 1, vol. 47, part 1, pp. 924–26; Marvin testimonial, June 30, 1869, Applications and Recommendations, RG 59. For a useful narrative and map of the Battle of Forks Road, February 20, 1865, see Fonvielle, *The Wilmington Campaign,* 396–98.

76. Case number 354 in George A. Otis and others, compilers, *The Medical and Surgical History of the War of the Rebellion (1861–65),* 3 parts, 2 vols. each (Washington, DC: Government Printing Office, 1870–88), part 2, vol. 2, p. 745; William H. Thomas Certificate of Disability for Discharge, July 25, 1865, Thomas Pension File, RG 15; George W. Adams, *Doctors in Blue: The Medical History of the Union Army in the Civil War* (New York: Henry Schuman, 1952), 114–15, 118, 124, 133–34; James O. Breeden, *Joseph Jones, M.D.: Scientist of the Old South* (Lexington: University

Press of Kentucky, 1975), 226; *The Medical and Surgical History of the War of the Rebellion (1861–65)*, part 2, vol. 2, p. 877; Peter Josyph, ed., *The Wounded River: The Civil War Letters of John Vance Lauderdale, M.D.* (East Lansing: Michigan State University Press, 1993), 28. On Thomas's amputation, also see his carded medical records, 5th U.S. Colored Troops, "Thom—," Records of the Adjutant General's Office, RG 94. Some confusion exists as to the day Thomas was injured. In *The American Negro*, xvi, he wrote erroneously that it occurred "On the evening of the 21st of February, 1865." Ohio's official records reported erroneously that Thomas was wounded on February 22. See William H. Thomas Muster Roll Jacket, July 14, 1891, Ohio Adjutant General, Civil War Muster Rolls, U.S. Colored Troops, reel 2057, Ohio Historical Society. Federal record keepers made the same error. See 5th U.S. Colored Infantry Company Muster-Out Roll, September 20, 1865, Records of the Adjutant General's Office, RG 94. A 1932 memorandum in the Adjutant General's Office correctly recorded that Thomas received his wound on February 20. See Rosafy-ORD/med/wilmarth to Mrs. Parquette, August 30, 1932.

77. *The London and Provincial Medical Directory, 1855* (London: Reynell and Weight, 1855), 300; *List of the Fellows, Members, and Licentiates in Midwifery of the Royal College of Surgeons of England* [London: n.p., 1859], 91; John A. Shepherd, "The Surgeons in the Crimea, 1854–1856," *Journal of the Royal College of Surgeons of Edinburgh* 17 (September 1972): 4, 6, 14, 16; Dr. H. C. Merryweather Medical Autobiography, August 24, 1863; Henry C. Merryweather Individual Muster-In Roll, September 29, 1863, 5th U.S. Colored Infantry, Records of the Adjutant General's Office, RG 94; Commissioned Officers of the 5th USCT to Gov. David Tod, November 13, 1863, Personal Papers, Medical Officers and Physicians, Records of Adjutant General's Office, RG 94; J. W. Mitchell To Whom It May Concern, November 7, 1864, Records of the Adjutant General's Office, RG 94. For Dr. Merryweather's amputations, see Otis and others, compilers, *The Medical and Surgical History of the War of the Rebellion*, part 2, vol. 2, pp. 572, 679, 718, 745; part 3, vol. 2, pp. 233, 236, 256, 469, 473, 474, 480, 488, 510, 886.

78. Glatthaar, *Forged in Battle*, 194–95; Blaine, "Forgotten Men," 84, 86; Glatthaar, *Forged in Battle*, 193.

79. Thomas, *The American Negro*, xvi; Otis and others, compilers, *The Medical and Surgical History of the War of the Rebellion*, part 1, vol. 2, p. 74; Rosafy-ORD/med/wilmarth to Mrs. Parquette, August 30, 1932; 5th U.S. Colored Infantry Company I Muster Rolls, January–August 1865; Hospital Muster Roll, May and June 1865, Records of the Adjutant General's Office, RG 94; Certificate of Disability for Discharge, July 25, 1865, Thomas Pension File, RG 15; Dr. Read [Smyth?] To Whom it May Concern, July 30, 1865, Applications and Recommendations, RG 59; Company I Regimental Returns; Company I Muster-Out Roll, September 20, 1865; Discharge Certificate, September 20, 1865, Records of the Adjutant General's Office, RG 94. Because of a bureaucratic error, Thomas was mustered out of the service—for a second time—on September 20, 1865 at Carolina City, North Carolina.

Thomas's carded medical records, RG 94, state that he was discharged from service on July 28, 1865. On April 8, 1878, a War Department official noted on Thomas's second (September 20, 1865) discharge certificate: "Canceled. This soldier was discharged on Surgeon's Certificate of Disability, July 25, 1865." On G. H. McKim's Mansion, see Entry 544, Field Records of Hospitals, McKim's Mansion, Records of the Adjutant General's Office, RG 94; Otis and others, compilers, *The Medical and Surgical History of the War of the Rebellion,* part 1, vol. 2, p. 329; part 3, vol. 1, pp. 910–11.

80. Laurann Figg and Jane Farrell-Beck, "Amputation in the Civil War: Physical and Social Dimensions," *Journal of the History of Medicine and Allied Sciences* 48 (October 1993): 470–71; "Hannibal," "Letter From the Fifth Regiment, U.S.C.T.," 1: 5–7; Thomas, "Retrospection," *Christian Recorder,* April 28, 1866, 1:5–6.

81. Thomas, "Letter From the Fifth Regiment, U.S.C.T.," 1:5–7. Thomas neither organized a veterans group of the 5th USCT nor joined the Grand Army of the Republic, a predominantly white organization that reluctantly accepted some blacks but generally relegated them to segregated posts.

82. Ibid.

Chapter Two. Questions of Character

1. "Hannibal," "Letter From Delaware, Ohio," *Christian Recorder,* August 19, 1865, 1:4–5; Glatthaar, *Forged in Battle: The Civil War Alliance of Black Soldiers and White Officers* (New York: Free Press, 1990), 242; William H. Thomas Application for an Artificial Limb, October 14, 1870; Surgeon General's Office Certificate, January 3, 1871; Declaration for the Increase of an Invalid Pension, February 18, 1909, Thomas Pension File, RG 15. In October 1865 Thomas applied for his pension under the general law pension system initiated by Congress in 1862. He first appeared on the pensioner's roll in January 1866 and continued to draw a disability pension for the next sixty-nine years. Because his disability was described as "total," in 1866 he was awarded $8 a month. His monthly amount was increased regularly: to $15 in 1867, to $18 in 1872, to $24 in 1874, to $30 in 1883, to $36 in 1886, to $46 in 1904, to $65 in 1920, to $75 in 1926, to $90 in 1927, to $100 in 1930. See William H. Thomas Claim for an Invalid Pension, n.d.; Claims for Increased Invalid Pension, August 3, 1872, July 24, 1874, April 7, 1904, May 11, 1926, February 4, 1931, Thomas Pension File, RG 15.

2. Thomas, "Memories of Otterbein Half a Century Ago," *United Brethren Review* 16 (July–August 1905): 206.

3. *Delaware Gazette,* October 6, 1865, 3:1; "Observer," "Arrival and Reception of the 55th Delaware (Ohio) [*sic*] Regt.," *Christian Recorder,* October 21, 1865, 2: 4–5; A. C. Luca, "Soldiers, Welcome Home," *New York Weekly Anglo-African,* December 23, 1865, 1:6–7. Communities with large black populations commonly greeted the USCT veterans with parades and other celebrations. See Richard Severo

and Lewis Milford, *The Wages of War: When America's Soldiers Came Home—From Valley Forge to Vietnam* (New York: Simon and Schuster, 1989), 128.

4. Thomas to Whipple, August 7, 1865, American Missionary Association Archives. As early as September 1861, the American Missionary Association had established a school among the freedmen in Hampton, Virginia. On Whipple and the American Missionary Association, see Joe M. Richardson, *Christian Reconstruction: The American Missionary Association and Southern Blacks, 1861–1890* (Athens: University of Georgia Press, 1986).

5. Charles F. Cooney, "'I Was . . . Eager to Become a Soldier,'" *Manuscripts* 26 (fall 1974): 280.

6. Thomas, "A Reminiscence of the War" and "The Incidents of a Day's March," September 27, 1865, William A. Bourne Papers, Manuscript Division, Library of Congress. One version of Thomas's text appears in his own handwriting, obviously penned with his left hand. Giles W. Shurtleff, colonel of the 5th USCT, transcribed a more legible copy.

7. Glatthaar, *Forged in Battle*, 237; Berlin, ed., *Freedom: A Documentary History of Emancipation, 1861–1867: Series II, The Black Military Experience* (Cambridge: Cambridge University Press, 1982), 32; Laurann Figg and Jane Farrell-Beck, "Amputation in the Civil War: Physical and Social Dimensions," *Journal of the History of Medicine and Allied Science* 48 (October 1993): 465; Thomas to William Hemstreet, February 23, 1905, Theodore D. Jervey Papers, SCHS.

8. R. R. Wright, ed., *The Encyclopedia of the African Methodist Episcopal Church*, 2d ed. (Philadelphia: Book Concern of the AME Church, 1947), 352; Gilbert Anthony Williams, "The *A.M.E. Christian Recorder*: A Forum for the Social Ideas of Black Americans, 1854–1902" (Ph.D. diss., University of Illinois at Urbana-Champaign, 1979); "To Our Correspondents," *Christian Recorder*, February 23, 1867, 2:5; "By the Editor," *Christian Recorder*, August 24, 1872, 4:1. In addition to "Hannibal," Thomas signed his articles as "Hannible," "Hanible," and variants of his first and middle name. In 1869 he joked that his temporary absence from the *Christian Recorder* had not resulted from his leading military campaigns like his namesake, Hannibal, "much as I should like to follow in the footsteps of my illustrious *predecessor*." "Hannibal," "A Letter From Hannibal," *Christian Recorder*, April 17, 1869, 1:3–4.

9. "Hannibal," "Letter From Delaware, Ohio," 1:4–5; "Town and County," *Delaware Gazette*, September 10, 1869, 3:1; ibid., June 16, 1871, 3:2; "List of Letters," ibid., September 27, 1877, 1:5; ibid., January 10, 1884, 6:4; [William Hannibal Thomas], "A Letter from Hannibal," *Christian Recorder*, July 31, 1873, 5:3.

10. Figg and Farrell-Beck, "Amputation in the Civil War: Physical and Social Dimensions," 468, 473; Figg, "Clothing Adaptations of Civil War Amputees" (M.S. thesis, Iowa State University, 1990), 19, 20; Severo and Milford, *The Wages of War*, 129–31, 137–42; "Population of Delaware," *Delaware Gazette*, September 24, 1869,

3:2; *Ninth Census—Volume I: The Statistics of the Population of the United States* (Washington, DC: Government Printing Office, 1872), 56; *Statistics of the Population of the United States at the Tenth Census* (Washington, DC: Government Printing Office, 1883), 404, 423; *Negro Population, 1790–1915* (Washington, DC: Government Printing Office, 1918), 218. Because he resided in Pittsburgh at the time, Thomas was not listed in the 1870 manuscript census for Delaware County. It identified his mother and siblings as mulattoes. Hattie, age thirty-three, was listed as a native of Canada and her father of "foreign birth." Because the 1880 manuscript census listed her father as a native of Virginia, it is unclear, therefore, whether she was Will's sister or half-sister. Benjamin, age twenty-three, and Walter, age fourteen, were Ohio natives. Thomas's brother, Prescott, died during the war and their father died some time before 1880. The 1880 manuscript census listed Mrs. Thomas as a widow. See Schedule 1—Inhabitants in Delaware, in the County of Delaware, State of Ohio, Enumerated 1870, p. 328, Ohio Historical Society; Tenth Census of the United States, 1880, Delaware, Ohio, Schedule 1—Inhabitants, p. 17, Ohio Historical Society; Paul E. Nitchman, *Blacks in Ohio, 1880,* 6 vols. (Decorah, IA: Anundsen Publishing Co., 1985–86), 3:100.

11. "Hannibal," "Letter From Delaware, Ohio," 1:4–5.

12. "Hannibal," "A Letter From Delaware, Ohio," *Christian Recorder,* September 23, 1865, 1:3–4. On Quinn, see George A. Singleton, *The Romance of African Methodism: A Study of the African Methodist Episcopal Church* (New York: Exposition Press, 1952), 27–28, 34–35, 71.

13. "Church Directory," *Delaware Gazette,* November 27, 1868, 3:1; ibid., December 17, 1869, 3:1; *History of Delaware County and Ohio* (Chicago: O. L. Baskin and Co., 1880), 407, 621, 411; "The A.M.E. Sabbath School," *Delaware Gazette,* August 23, 1877, 4:3; "Colored People on Temperance," ibid., August 3, 1874, 3:7; "Local Intelligence," ibid., July 24, 1868, 3:1; ibid., February 19, 1869, 3:1; "Town and Country," ibid., July 16, 1869, 3:1; "Jubilation," ibid., April 15, 1870, 3:2; "Town and Country," ibid., September 23, 1870, 3:1; "Emancipation Celebration," ibid., August 29, 1873, 3:3; Benjamin Frank ("B. F.") Thomas Interment Record No. 3812, Oak Grove Cemetery, Delaware County Historical Society, Delaware, OH; "Local Intelligence," *Delaware Gazette,* February 5, 1869, 3:1–2; "Lecture by Fred. Douglass," ibid., March 11, 1870, 3:2.

14. "Hannibal," "Letter From Delaware, Ohio," 1:4–5; idem, "Progress of the Colored People in Delaware, Ohio," *Christian Recorder,* September 29, 1866, 2:3.

15. "Mrs. R. Thomas," *Delaware Gazette,* May 29, 1879, 4:2; "Mrs. Rebecca Thomas," ibid., November 23, 1882, 3:3; Walter S. Thomas to the President, January 30, 1878, Applications and Recommendations, RG 59; William Hannibal Thomas, *Land and Education: A Critical and Practical Discussion of the Mental and Physical Needs of the Freedmen* (Boston: Wallace Spooner, 1890), [ii]. On the "Exodusters," see Nell Irvin Painter, *Exodusters: Black Migration to Kansas After Reconstruction* (1976; New York: Norton, 1979).

16. "Hannibal," "Letter From Hannibal," *Christian Recorder,* September 22, 1866, 1:3–4; *Minutes of the Forty-Ninth Session of the Ohio Annual Conference of the African Methodist Church* (Springfield, OH: Republic Printing Co., 1879), 46; *Minutes of the Fiftieth Session of the Ohio Annual Conference of the African Methodist Church* (Columbus: J. F. Earhart and Co., 1880), 53; *Minutes of the Second Session of the North Ohio Annual Conference of the African Methodist Episcopal Church* (Lima, OH: Allen County Democrat Press, 1883), 11; "Delaware Doings," *Cleveland Gazette,* April 3, 1886, 1:4.

17. David A. Gerber, *Black Ohio and the Color Line, 1860–1915* (Urbana: University of Illinois Press, 1976), 36; V. Jacque Voegeli, *Free But Not Equal: The Midwest and the Negro During the Civil War* (1967; Chicago: University of Chicago Press, 1970), 182, 173.

18. Philip S. Foner and George E. Walker, eds., *Proceedings of the Black National Conventions, 1865–1900,* 2 vols. (Philadelphia: Temple University Press, 1986), 1:49; Gerber, *Black Ohio and the Color Line,* 35–40; C. Peter Ripley, ed., *The Black Abolitionist Papers,* 5 vols. (Chapel Hill: University of North Carolina Press, 1985–92), 5:374, 376; Donald Charles Swift, "The Ohio Republicans, 1866–1880" (Ph.D. diss., University of Delaware, 1967), 74–75; Robert D. Sawrey, *Dubious Victory: The Reconstruction Debate in Ohio* (Lexington: University Press of Kentucky, 1992), 114–17, 134–35; Felice A. Bonadio, *North of Reconstruction: Ohio Politics, 1865–1870* (New York: New York University Press, 1970), 79–106; idem, "Ohio: A 'Perfect Contempt of All Unity,'" in *Radical Republicans in the North: State Politics During Reconstruction,* ed. James C. Mohr (Baltimore: Johns Hopkins University Press, 1976), 90, 92; William Gillette, *The Right to Vote: Politics and the Passage of the Fifteenth Amendment* (1965; Baltimore: Johns Hopkins University Press, 1969), 26, 32, 140–44; Gerber, *Black Ohio and the Color Line,* 194, 237–43.

19. "Hannibal," "Letter From the Fifth Regiment, U.S.C.T.," *Christian Recorder,* November 4, 1865, 1:5–7; Thomas, "Retrospection," ibid., April 28, 1866, 1:5–6.

20. "Hannibal," "Letter From Delaware, Ohio," 1:4–5; "Local Intelligence," *Delaware Gazette,* May 31, 1867, 3:1.

21. "Meeting of Colored Citizens," *Delaware Gazette,* March 4, 1870, 2:4.

22. "Colored Citizens for Grant," ibid., July 5, 1872, 2:5.

23. "A Meeting of Colored Citizens," ibid., July 31, 1871, 3:3; "Personal Mention," ibid., August 7, 1879, 4:2; Tenth Census of the United States, 1880, Schedule 1, p. 17; *History of Delaware County and Ohio,* 647; W. S. Thomas and others, "An Address to the Colored Voters of Ohio," *Delaware Gazette,* October 4, 1883, Supplement, 2:4–5; "Ohio Republicans," *Cleveland Gazette,* June 13, 1885, 2:4; "Personal," *Christian Recorder,* March 11, 1886, 2:4; "New Papers," *New York Freeman,* January 15, 1887, 2:3; "Local News," *Delaware Democratic Herald,* November 15, 1887, 3:3; Thomas to Benjamin Harrison, January 13, 1892, Benjamin Harrison Papers, Manuscript Division, Library of Congress; Thomas to Grover Cleveland, April 12, 1893, Grover Cleveland Papers, Manuscript Division, Library

of Congress; *Cleveland Gazette,* November 1, 1884, 2:3; Lowell Dwight Black, "The Negro Volunteer Militia Units of the Ohio National Guard, 1870–1954: The Struggle for Military Recognition and Equality in the State of Ohio" (Ph.D. diss., The Ohio State University, 1976), 366; J. C. D. Maldsne [?] to the President, May 28, 1877, J. B. Foraker to the President, April 26, 1889, Thomas to Grover Cleveland, September 8, 1893, Applications and Recommendations, RG 59; Republican State Executive Committee, *Ohio Republican Speakers* (n.p.: Republican State Executive Committee, 1901), 12.

24. Joseph F. Rishel, *Founding Families of Pittsburgh: The Evolution of a Regional Elite, 1760–1910* (Pittsburgh: University of Pittsburgh Press, 1990), 123; "Editorial Correspondence. Pittsburgh, March 20, 1870. The Cities," *Christian Recorder,* April 2, 1870, 1:1–2; Francis G. Couvares, *The Remaking of Pittsburgh: Class and Culture in an Industrializing City, 1877–1919* (Albany: State University of New York Press, 1984), 9–10, 32–33, 82, 106; *Population of the United States in 1860; Compiled From the Original Returns of the Eighth Census* (Washington, DC: Government Printing Office, 1864), 413, 414; *Ninth Census—Volume I,* 243, 244; *Ninth Census of the United States: Statistics of Population, Tables I to VIII Inclusive* (Washington, DC: Government Printing Office, 1872), 380. Pittsburgh annexed Allegheny City in 1907.

25. Glasco, "Double Burden: The Black Experience in Pittsburgh," in *City at the Point: Essays on the Social History of Pittsburgh,* ed. Samuel P. Hays (Pittsburgh: University of Pittsburgh Press, 1989), 73–74; Ann Greenwood Wilmoth, "Pittsburgh and the Blacks: A Short History, 1780–1875" (Ph.D. diss., The Pennsylvania State University, 1975), 12; *Population of the United States in 1860,* 413, 414; *Ninth Census—Volume I,* 243, 244; "Pittsburgh, PA.," *Christian Recorder,* February 16, 1867, 2:2; "The Negro In Pittsburgh, 1939–41" (unpublished manuscript, n.d.), Record Group 41, Records of the WPA Pennsylvania Historical Survey, Ethnic Survey, 1938–41, Pennsylvania Historical and Museum Commission, roll no. 2, chap. 5 [Final Manuscript], 65; Couvares, *The Remaking of Pittsburgh,* 91.

26. Paul J. Lammermeier, "Family and Occupational Structures in the Upper Ohio Valley: 1850–1880, A Comparative Study of Six Large and Small Urban Black Communities" (unpublished paper, Brockport Conference on Social and Political History, September, 1972), 9, 10, 15, 18, copy in Portsmouth, Ohio, Public Library; Michael Fitzgibbon Holt, *Forging a Majority: The Formation of the Republican Party in Pittsburgh, 1848–1860* (New Haven: Yale University Press, 1969), 263; H. H. G., "The Free Land Once More," *New York Weekly Anglo-African,* September 16, 1865, 4:3; Jacqueline Welch Wolfe, "The Changing Pattern of Residence of the Negro in Pittsburgh, Pennsylvania, With Emphasis on the Period, 1930–1960" (M.A. thesis, University of Pittsburgh, 1964), 10, 17, 18, 20, 23. Garnet toured Pittsburgh after visiting the South to report on the conditions of the freedpeople during the first months of Reconstruction. See Earl Ofari, *"Let Your Motto Be Resis-*

tance": The Life and Thought of Henry Highland Garnet (Boston: Beacon Press, 1972), 117–19.

27. John Bodnar, Roger Simon, and Michael P. Weber, *Lives of Their Own: Blacks, Italians, and Poles in Pittsburgh, 1900–1960* (Urbana: University of Illinois Press, 1982), 74–75, 78–79; Peter Gottlieb, *Making Their Own Way: Southern Blacks' Migration to Pittsburgh, 1916–30* (Urbana: University of Illinois Press, 1987), 66–67; "The Negro in Pittsburgh, 1939–41," chap. 7 [Prefinal Manuscript], 3–7; Samuel Watts, "Letter From Allegheny City, Pa.," *Christian Recorder*, February 20, 1864, 2:3; idem, "Demonstration in Brown Chapel Charge," ibid., December 10, 1864, 1:2–3; "Africana," "Letter From Pittsburgh," ibid., February 4, 1865, 1:4–5; Watts to the editor, ibid., April 15, 1865, 3:1; Alexander W. Wayman, *Cyclopedia of African Methodism* (Baltimore: Methodist Episcopal Book Depository, 1882), 14, 129; "Hannible," "Letter From Hannible," *Christian Recorder*, February 10, 1866, 1:5–7; "Avery College, Allegheny City, Penna." [advertisement], ibid., May 14, 1864, 3:7; R. J. M. Blackett, ed., *Thomas Morris Chester: Black Civil War Correspondent* (Baton Rouge: Louisiana State University Press, 1989), 8. During Reconstruction the Avery Fund also established Avery Normal Institute in Charleston, South Carolina. See Edmund L. Drago, *Initiative, Paternalism, and Race Relations: Charleston's Avery Normal Institute* (Athens: University of Georgia Press, 1990), 50–51.

28. Frank D. McCloy, "The Mount of Sacred Science," in William Wilson McKinney, ed., *The Presbyterian Valley* (Pittsburgh: Davis & Warde, Inc., 1958), 365–66, 371, 372; C. Peter Ripley, ed., *The Black Abolitionist Papers*, 3:439; 5:130; "Editorial Correspondence," *Christian Recorder*, April 9, 1870, 2:2–3; ibid., May 21, 1870, 2:2–3; Daniel A. Payne, *Recollections of Seventy Years* (1888; New York: Arno, 1969), 205. In 1959 Western Seminary, affiliated with the Presbyterian Church U.S.A., and Pittsburgh-Xenia Seminary, affiliated with the United Presbyterian Church in North America, merged to become Pittsburgh Theological Seminary, Presbyterian Church (U.S.A.).

29. Thomas, *The American Negro: What He Was, What He Is, and What He May Become* (New York: Macmillan, 1901), xvi; *Triennial Catalogue of the Western Theological Seminary of the Presbyterian Church at Allegheny, Penn'a, 1863–1866* (Pittsburgh: W. S. Haven, 1866), 32–33; *Annual Catalogue of the Western Theological Seminary at Allegheny City, Pa., 1866–1867* (Pittsburgh: W. S. Haven, 1867), 8; *Annual Catalogue of the Western Theological Seminary of the Presbyterian Church at Allegheny City, Pa., 1867–1868* (Pittsburgh: W. S. Haven, 1868), 7, 12, 13.

30. "The Late Prof. A. A. Hodge," *The Christian* no. 916 (August 19, 1887): 722; Benjamin B. Warfield, "William Miller Paxton," *Princeton Theological Review* 3 (April 1905): 225–29; Thomas to Woodrow Wilson, January 8, 1913, Woodrow Wilson Papers, Manuscript Division, Library of Congress; J. H. Turpin, "Western

Theological Seminary, Allegheny City," *Christian Recorder,* September 23, 1865, 3: 2; "Hannibal," "Letter From Hannibal," ibid., October 7, 1865, 1:2. Turpin (1836–1882), who later was licensed both by the Ohio Presbytery and the A.M.E. Church, had a controversial career, abandoning the A.M.E. Church for the Baptist faith in 1870 before returning to the A.M.E. Church as secretary of its Book Concern Committee. He later served congregations in South Carolina and the West Indies. See "Meeting of the Book Concern Committee," *Christian Recorder,* November 26, 1870, 1:5–6; "Obituary," ibid., September 21, 1882, 3:3.

31. "Hannibal," "Letter From Hannibal," *Christian Recorder,* October 7, 1865, 1:2; Turpin, "Letter From Allegheny," ibid., May 5, 1866, 1:7; "Hannibal," "Pittsburg [*sic*] Correspondence," ibid., June 2, 1866, 1:4. On the "love feast," see Wright, ed., *The Encyclopedia of the African Methodist Episcopal Church,* 412.

32. "Hannible," "Letter From Allegheny City," *Christian Recorder,* November 25, 1865, 1:6–7. On Vashon, see Catherine M. Hanchett, "George Boyer Vashon, 1824–1878: Black Educator, Poet, Fighter for Equal Rights," *Western Pennsylvania Historical Magazine* 68 (July and October 1985): 205–19, 333–49. Garnet replaced Vashon as president of Avery College in 1868.

33. "Hanible," "Letter From Hanible," *Christian Recorder,* October 21, 1865, 2:4; "Hannibal," "Letter From the Fifth Regiment, U.S.C.T.," ibid., November 4, 1865, 1:5–6.

34. "Hanible," "Letter From Hanible," 2:4; "Hannibal," "Letter From the Fifth Regiment, U.S.C.T.," 1:5–6. Johnson's speech appears in the *New York Times,* October 11, 1865, 1:3–4 and Paul H. Bergeron, ed., *The Papers of Andrew Johnson,* 14 vols. to date (Knoxville: University of Tennessee Press, 1967–), 9:219–23. For an analysis, see David Warren Bowen, *Andrew Johnson and the Negro* (Knoxville: University of Tennessee Press, 1989), 146–48.

35. "Hanible," "Letter From Hanible," December 28, 1865, *Christian Recorder,* January 6, 1866, 1:3–6; William H. Thomas, "Retrospection," ibid., April 28, 1866, 1:5–6. On Thomas's identification with the Republican Party, see his "Letter From Pittsburgh," ibid., October 24, 1868, 1:3–4.

36. "Hannibal," "Letter From Hannibal," July 25, 1866, ibid., August 4, 1866, 2:6–7; idem, "Traces of the Old Leaven," ibid., October 1, 1870, 1:5–6. The last article appeared originally in the *Christian Radical.*

37. "Hannibal," "Letter From Allegheny," July 25, 1867, *Christian Recorder,* August 3, 1867, 1:2–3.

38. "Hannible," "Letter From Hannible," December 6, 1866, ibid., December 15, 1866, 2:5–6; idem, "Letter From Hannible," January 29, 1866, ibid., February 10, 1866, 1:5–7; idem, "Politeness," ibid., January 30, 1869, 1:2–3.

39. "Hannibal," "Letter From Hannibal," November 9, 1867, ibid., November 16, 1867, 2:5; Delany, "The Negro in Holy Writ. The Similitude of Divine Attributes," in Benjamin Tucker Tanner, *An Apology for African Methodism* (Baltimore: n.p., 1867), 383–86. Tanner, a Pittsburgh native, was educated at Avery Col-

lege and, like Thomas, at Western Theological Seminary. He had a long and distinguished career in the A.M.E. Church, editing the *Christian Recorder* from 1868 to 1884 and founding, then editing, the *A.M.E. Church Review* from 1884 to 1888. He was elected bishop in 1888. See Wright, ed., *The Encyclopedia of the African Methodist Episcopal Church*, 602. Delany, the son of a slave, studied medicine briefly at Harvard, edited antislavery newspapers, and was a leader in Pittsburgh's black community until 1856. In *The Condition, Elevation, Emigration and Destiny of the Colored People of the United States* (1852), he espoused black nationalism. See Victor Ullman, *Martin R. Delany: The Beginnings of Black Nationalism* (Boston: Beacon Press, 1971); and Dorothy Sterling, *The Making of an Afro-American: Martin Robison Delany, 1812–1885* (Garden City: Doubleday, 1971).

40. "Hannibal," "Pittsburg [*sic*] Correspondence," *Christian Recorder*, July 28, 1866, 1:1–2.

41. "Hannibal," "Letter From Hannibal," January 8, 1867, ibid., January 19, 1867, 1:1–2; "Hannibal," "To the Clergy of the A.M.E. Church," ibid., October 12, 1867, 2:2–3.

42. "Hannibal," "The Future of the A.M.E. Church, No. 1, The Episcopacy," ibid., January 18, 1868, 1:1–3; idem, "The Future of the A.M.E. Church, No. 2, The Ministry and Theology," ibid., February 8, 1868, 1:3–4.

43. WTS Faculty Minutes, p. 28; Schedule 1—Inhabitants in 2nd Ward, Allegheny City, in the County of Allegheny, State of Pennsylvania, 1870, p. 72, Ninth Census of the United States, Historical Society of Western Pennsylvania; *Directory of Pittsburgh & Allegheny, 1869–70* (1869), 432; *Directory of Pittsburgh & Allegheny, 1870–71* (1870), 460; *Directory of Pittsburgh & Allegheny, 1871–72* (1871), 496; *Directory of Pittsburgh and Allegheny Cities, 1873–74* (1873), 537; *Directory of Pittsburgh and Allegheny Cities, 1874–1875* (1874), 601; *Directory of Pittsburgh and Allegheny for 1876–7, Embracing a General Directory of the Residences of Citizens* (Pittsburgh: Thurston & Foster, 1876), 605; *Directory of Pittsburgh and Allegheny Cities, 1880–81. Embracing a General Directory of the Residences of Citizens* (Pittsburgh: W. W. Lewis, 1880), 657; Louis R. Harlan, ed., *The Booker T. Washington Papers*, 14 vols. (Urbana: University of Illinois Press, 1972–89), 4:328n. The author has not succeeded in obtaining biographical information on Martha Thomas.

44. Eugene H. Roseboom, *The Civil War Era: 1850–1873, A History of the State of Ohio, Volume IV* (1944; Columbus: Ohio Historical Society, 1968), 195; "Wilberforce University and the Baltimore District," *Christian Recorder*, December 2, 1865, 3:1.

45. David Smith, *Biography of Rev. David Smith of the A.M.E. Church, Being a Complete History, Embracing Over Sixty Years' Labor in the Advancement of the Redeemer's Kingdom on Earth. Including "The History of the Origin and Development of Wilberforce University"* (Xenia, OH: Xenia Gazette Office, 1881), 111; Daniel A. Payne, "Wilberforce University," in *Proceedings at the Quarter-Century Anniversary of the Society for the Promotion of Collegiate and Theological Education at the*

West, Held at Marietta, Ohio, Nov. 7–10, 1868 (New York: Trow & Smith Book Manufacturing Co., 1868), 173; Wright, ed., *The Encyclopedia of the African Methodist Episcopal Church,* 533.

46. Report of the Committee on Wilberforce, *Minutes of the Thirty-fifth Session of the Ohio Annual Conference of the African M. E. Church* (Pittsburgh: n.p., 1865), 26; "Episcopal Address," *Christian Recorder,* February 20, 1869, 1:1–5; Daniel A. Payne, "To the Trustees of Wilberforce University," ibid., February 19, 1870, 3:1. Shorter Hall was not rebuilt until 1878.

47. Wayman, *Cyclopedia of African Methodism,* 180, 8, 85; Foner and Walker, eds., *Proceedings of the Black National and State Conventions, 1865–1900* (Philadelphia: Temple University Press, 1986), 70; Smith, *Biography of Rev. David Smith,* 117–20; Daniel A. Payne, *History of the African Methodist Episcopal Church* (Nashville: Publishing House of the A.M.E. Sunday-School Union, 1891), 428, 431–32, 446n; "Episcopal Address," *Christian Recorder,* February 20, 1869, 1:1–5.

48. Entries for January 28, March 17, June 26, 29, 1868, Minutes Book, Wilberforce University Board of Trustees, 1865–1878, pp. 68, 70, 80–81, 98, Wilberforce University Archives; "Editorial Items," *Christian Recorder,* July 18, 1868, 2:3.

49. WTS Faculty Minutes, p. 28.

50. Ibid., pp. 28–29; Western Theological Seminary Matriculation Record Book, 1828–1947, Pittsburgh Theological Seminary Library; Thomas, *The American Negro,* xvi; Wilson testimonial, June 12, 1869, Applications and Recommendations, RG 59; T. H. Robinson to Chesnutt, n.d., in Chesnutt, "In Re William Hannibal Thomas, Author of 'The American Negro'" (unpublished manuscript, [1901]), 1, Charles W. Chesnutt Papers, Fisk University; T. H. Robinson to John Edward Bruce, April 21 [*sic*], Edward B. Jourdain to Bruce, April 5, 1901, in John Edward Bruce, "The Critic Revealed," *Washington Colored American,* April 13, 1901, 1:4, 9:1–3.

51. Daniel Schindler Alumni Record and Biographical Data Card, Hamma Divinity School Archives, Wittenberg University; *Portrait and Biographical Album of Greene and Clark Counties, Ohio* (Chicago: Chapman Brothers, 1890), 304–5; *The Semi-Centennial Souvenir of Wittenberg College* (Springfield, OH: The Class of Ninety-Six, 1895), unpaginated; "Christian Radical," *Christian Radical,* October 15, 1868, 1:5, 8; "The Degraded Preacher," ibid., June 24, 1871, 4:2–3; "*The Christian Radical,*" ibid., August 12, 1869, 4:4–5; "Our Own," *Wittenberger* 2 (January 1875): 29. Following the collapse of the *Christian Radical,* Schindler served as professor of rational psychology, Latin, and theology at Adrian College, Michigan, edited *Living Christianity,* and held pastorates in Pennsylvania, Ohio, and Virginia. See *Calendar of Adrian College for 1875–76* (n.p., n.d.), 37; *Adrian College Recorder* 1 (March 1876): 42–43; ibid., (April 1876): 55.

52. Thomas, *The American Negro,* xvi; *Christian Radical,* July 29, 1869, 4:4; ibid., September 30, 1869, 4:3–6; "Don't Understand," ibid., April 20, 1871, 4:2–3; "Christian Union," ibid., November 24, 1870, 6:1–2; Schindler to Ulysses S.

Grant, March 5, 1877, Applications and Recommendations, RG 59; "The Ex-Master and Ex-Slave," *Christian Radical*, November 19, 1868, 4:1–3; "Georgia Over Again," ibid., August 12, 1869, 7:1; "The Disorder of the South," ibid., March 23, 1871, 4:2–4; ibid., April 21, 1870, 4:5–6; "The Ku Klux Klan in Tennessee: Whipping Negro Preachers," ibid., September 30, 1869, 1:6.

53. W. Hannibalt [*sic*] Thomas, "A Plea for the Bible," *Christian Radical*, March 17, 1870, 5:3–4; W. Hannibal Thomas, "Traces of the Old Leaven," ibid., September 1, 1870, 1:4–5. Thomas also published the latter article in the *Christian Recorder*, October 1, 1870, 1:5–6.

54. Thomas, "Meeting of the Western College Society," *Christian Recorder*, December 5, 12, 1868, 1:1–2, 1:1–3.

55. *Minutes of the First Pittsburgh Annual Conference of the African M.E. Church, Held at Pittsburgh, Penn'a, April 3d to 9th, 1869* (Pittsburgh: W. S. Haven & Co., 1869), 9; "To the Honorable the [*sic*] Senate and House of Representatives of the United States, in Congress Assembled," [printed petition with signatures, March 14, 1870], Records of the U.S. Senate, 41st Congress, Record Group 46, National Archives and Records Administration; Smith, *Biography of Rev. David Smith*, 126.

56. Entries for June 29, 1869, Minutes Book, Wilberforce University Board of Trustees, 1865–1878, pp. 98–102, 103–5; Jones to Chesnutt, April 4, 1901, in Chesnutt, "In Re William Hannibal Thomas," 6.

57. *Minutes of the Pittsburgh Annual Conference of the African M.E. Church, Held in Wylie St. A.M.E. Ch[urch], Pittsburgh, April 9th to 18th 1870* (Pittsburgh: W. S. Haven & Co., 1870), 5, 21, 6, 9, 22, 8. Although the Reverend West was eventually exonerated from the complaints raised against him, he was nonetheless replaced by Thomas. See ibid., 8, 12, 15. The *Missionary Record* (1868–79) was published by the Reverend Richard Harvey Cain, a leading A.M.E. minister and South Carolina Republican politician. His newspaper fused theological news with pro-Republican political opinion. See Clarence E. Walker, *A Rock in a Weary Land: The African Methodist Episcopal Church During the Civil War and Reconstruction* (Baton Rouge: Louisiana State University Press, 1982), 121.

58. *Minutes of the Pittsburgh Annual Conference of the African M.E. Church, Held at Brownsville, Penn'a., April 15th to 20th, 1871* (Pittsburgh: W. S. Haven & Co., 1871), 4, 20, 18, 24, 8.

59. Ibid., 16.

60. Ibid., 20, 10.

61. Ibid., 10, 15; "Hannibal," "A Letter From Hannibal," *Christian Recorder*, April 17, 1869, 1:3–4. The Reverend Hunter served as pastor of the Wylie Street Church. During the Civil War he had served as chaplain of the 4th USCT. The Reverend Jones, of the Wheeling District, served as pastor of the Washington Circuit.

62. "Hannibal," "The Future of the A.M.E. Church, No. 2," 1:3–4.

Chapter Three. Missed Opportunities and Unresolved Allegations

1. Thomas, *The American Negro: What He Was, What He Is, and What He May Become* (New York: Macmillan, 1901), xvi; W. H. T. [William Hannibal Thomas], "Letter From Chicago," *Christian Radical,* June 10, 1871, 2:4–5; Thomas to Howard, July 31, 1871, Oliver Otis Howard Papers, Bowdoin College; John A. Carpenter, *Sword and Olive Branch: Oliver Otis Howard* (Pittsburgh: University of Pittsburgh Press, 1964), 157.

2. Thomas to Cravath, August 1, [?], 1871, American Missionary Association Archives; Joe M. Richardson, *Christian Reconstruction: The American Missionary Association and Southern Blacks, 1861–1890* (Athens: University of Georgia Press, 1986), 98–99.

3. Thomas to Cravath, November 6, December 18, 1871, American Missionary Association Archives; Thomas to Theodore D. Jervey, December 23, 1910, Theodore D. Jervey Papers, SCHS; Thomas, *The American Negro,* 410. The elder Berrien was a rice planter from Savannah and it is unknown when his son migrated to Rome. See Anthony Gene Carey, *Parties, Slavery, and the Union in Antebellum Georgia* (Athens: University of Georgia Press, 1997), 23.

4. Will H. Thomas, "Sauntering," *Christian Recorder,* September 25, 1873, 1:5–6.

5. Harvey H. Jackson III, *Rivers of History: Life on the Coosa, Tallapoosa, Cahaba, and Alabama* (Tuscaloosa: University of Alabama Press, 1995), 108; H. J. Adams, "Rome District, North Georgia Conference," *Southern Christian Advocate* 33 (April 8, 1870): 54; "Romulus," "Rome: As She Was—As She Is—As She May Be," *Rome Weekly Courier,* April 14, 1871, 2:6–7; O. S., "Circular to Northern Men," ibid., May 19, 1871, 2:1; Roger Aycock, *All Roads to Rome* (Rome: Rome Area Heritage Foundation, 1981), 76; Robert Preston Brooks, "The Agrarian Revolution in Georgia, 1865–1912," *Bulletin of the University of Wisconsin, History Series,* 3 (1914), 468, 472, 519; Steven Hahn, *The Roots of Southern Populism: Yeoman Farmers and the Transformation of the Georgia Upcountry, 1850–1890* (New York: Oxford University Press, 1983), 45; Michael P. Johnson, *Toward a Patriarchal Republic: The Secession of Georgia* (Baton Rouge: Louisiana State University Press, 1977), 60–61, 73n.

6. Jackson, *Rivers of History,* 131; Aycock, *All Roads to Rome,* 76, 79, 95–109; Walter L. Fleming, *Civil War and Reconstruction in Alabama* (1905; Gloucester, MA: Peter Smith, 1949), 156; Robert C. Black III, *The Railroads of the Confederacy* (Chapel Hill: University of North Carolina Press, 1952), 158–59; *Official Records,* series 1, vol. 38, part 4, p. 260; Albert Castel, *Decision in the West: The Atlanta Campaign of 1864* (Lawrence: University Press of Kansas, 1992), 198; Wade Bannister Gassman, "A History of Rome and Floyd County, Georgia in the Civil War" (M.A. thesis, Emory University, 1966), 6–8, 75–76, 117–19, 121, 124–25; Clark G. Reynolds, "Confederate Romans and Bedford Forrest: The Civil War Roots of the Towers-Norton Family," *Georgia Historical Quarterly* 77 (spring 1993): 30, 34–35.

On the process of statewide agricultural adjustment, see Paul A. Cimbala, *Under the Guardianship of the Nation: The Freedmen's Bureau and the Reconstruction of Georgia, 1865–1870* (Athens: University of Georgia Press, 1997), 130–38.

7. Aycock, *All Roads to Rome*, 135.

8. Hahn, *The Roots of Southern Populism*, 177, 218; Reuben S. Norton Diary [typescript], May 13, July 25, 1865, pp. 101, 104, John H. Towers Papers, Manuscript Division, Library of Congress; Gassman, "A History of Rome and Floyd County, Georgia in the Civil War," 127; Alan Conway, *The Reconstruction of Georgia* (Minneapolis: University of Minnesota Press, 1966), 127; John Horry Dent Farm Journals and Account Books (microfilm), vol. 9, December 30, 1871, p. 73; vol. 10, February 8, 1872, p. iii, Troy State University.

9. *Ninth Census—Volume I: The Statistics of the Population of the United States* (Washington, DC: Government Printing Office, 1872), 102; Joseph P. Reidy, *From Slavery to Agrarian Capitalism in the Cotton Plantation South: Central Georgia, 1800–1880* (Chapel Hill: University of North Carolina Press, 1992), 285n; Allen W. Trelease, *White Terror: The Ku Klux Klan Conspiracy and Southern Reconstruction* (New York: Harper, 1971), 67, 75, 117, 226; "The Disorder of the South," *Christian Radical*, March 23, 1871, 4:2–4.

10. *Proceedings of the Freedmen's Convention of Georgia Assembled at Augusta, January 10th, 1866* (Augusta, GA: The Loyal Georgian, 1866), 29; Elizabeth Studley Nathans, *Losing the Peace: Georgia Republicans and Reconstruction, 1865–1871* (Baton Rouge: Louisiana State University Press, 1968), 29–30; Ruth Currie-McDaniel, *Carpetbagger of Conscience: A Biography of John Emory Bryant* (Athens: University of Georgia Press, 1987), 57–66; Numan V. Bartley, *The Creation of Modern Georgia*, 2d ed. (Athens: University of Georgia Press, 1990), 49; Russell Duncan, *Entrepreneur for Equality: Governor Rufus Bullock, Commerce, and Race in Post–Civil War Georgia* (Athens: University of Georgia Press, 1994), 54.

11. George C. Rable, *But There Was No Peace: The Role of Violence in the Politics of Reconstruction* (Athens: University of Georgia Press, 1984), 73–74, 110–11; Lee W. Formwalt, "The Camilla Massacre of 1868: Racial Violence as Political Propaganda," *Georgia Historical Quarterly* 71 (fall 1987): 399–426; Conway, *The Reconstruction of Georgia*, 174; Bartley, *The Creation of Modern Georgia*, 64; *Proceedings of a Meeting of the State Central Committee of the Union Republican Party of Georgia, Held at Atlanta, Wednesday, November 24, 1869* (Atlanta: New Era Job Office, 1869), 11.

12. Duncan, *Entrepreneur for Equality*, chaps. 6 and 7.

13. Alfred M. Pierce, *A History of Methodism in Georgia, February 5, 1736–June 24, 1955* (n.p.: North Georgia Conference Historical Society, 1956), 165–69; A. V. Huff Jr., "Methodist Church, The," in *Encyclopedia of Religion in the South*, ed. Samuel S. Hill (Macon: Mercer University Press, 1984), 469. On the work of the Freedmen's Aid Society, see R. S. Rust, *Educational Work in the South by the Freedmen's Aid Society of the Methodist Episcopal Church* (Cincinnati: Western Meth-

odist Book Concern, 1882), 1–16, and Ralph E. Morrow, *Northern Methodism and Reconstruction* (East Lansing: Michigan State University Press, 1956), 155–61.

14. Clarence E. Walker, *A Rock in a Weary Land: The African Methodist Episcopal Church During the Civil War and Reconstruction* (Baton Rouge: Louisiana State University Press, 1982), 72–81; Hildebrand, *The Times Were Strange and Stirring: Methodist Preachers and the Crisis of Emancipation* (Durham: Duke University Press, 1995), xviii, 72, 86. On the diverse missionary activity among the freedpeople, see William E. Montgomery, *Under Their Own Vine and Fig: The African-American Church in the South, 1865–1900* (Baton Rouge: Louisiana State University Press, 1993), 38–96.

15. Willam B. Gravely, "James Lynch and the Black Christian Mission During Reconstruction," in *Black Apostles at Home and Abroad: Afro-Americans and the Christian Mission From the Revolution to Reconstruction,* ed. David W. Wills and Richard Newman (Boston: G. K. Hall, 1982), 161–88; Morrow, *Northern Methodism and Reconstruction,* 137, 139, 169; "The M. E. Church in the South," *Atlanta Methodist Advocate,* June 2, 1869, 86:1–2; J. P. Powell, "An Appeal From Georgia," *Zion's Herald* 46 (July 1, 1869): 305; "Missionary Anniversary, M.E. Church (North)," *Southern Christian Advocate* 32 (December 10, 1869): 198; John H. Caldwell, *Reminiscences of the Reconstruction of Church and State in Georgia* (Wilmington, DE: J. Miller, 1895), 8; Albea Godbold, "Table of Methodist Annual Conferences (U.S.A.)," *Methodist History* 8 (October 1969): 36.

16. *Minutes of the Annual Conferences of the Methodist Episcopal Church for the Year 1872* (New York: Nelson & Phillips, 1872), 91, 92, 126; Harold Lawrence, ed., *Methodist Preachers in Georgia, 1783–1900* (Tignall, GA: Boyd Publishing Co., 1984), 549; Jones, *Soldiers of Light and Love: Northern Teachers and Georgia Blacks, 1865–1873* (Chapel Hill: University of North Carolina Press, 1980), 37; *The Methodist Almanac for the Year of Our Lord 1868* (Cincinnati: Poe & Hitchcock, 1868), 39.

17. Thomas, "Christian Union," *Christian Recorder,* February 10, 1872, 1:3–4; Hildebrand, *The Times Were Strange and Stirring,* 93; Jones, *Soldiers of Light and Love,* 16, 209.

18. Lucius C. Matlack, "The Methodist Episcopal Church in the Southern States," *Methodist Quarterly Review* 54 (January 1872): 112, 124; Rust, "Methodist Freedmen's Aid Society," *Zion's Herald* 45 (December 17, 1868): 610.

19. Paul A. Cimbala, "Making Good Yankees: The Freedmen's Bureau and Education in Reconstruction Georgia, 1865–1870," *Atlanta Historical Journal* 29 (fall 1985): 8; Morrow, *Northern Methodism and Reconstruction,* 162–63, 170; Carpenter, *Sword and Olive Branch,* 155.

20. "Tabular Statement of Schools in Ga[.], Supt. of Education, Atlanta, Ga.," 4, 12, Miscellaneous Lists and Memoranda, 1865–70, Records of the BRFAL, RG 105; *Report of the Freedmen's Aid Society of the Methodist Episcopal Church* (Cincinnati: Methodist Book Concern, 1868), 15; William B. Higginbotham, "Sibley School, Rome, Ga.," *Atlanta Methodist Advocate,* July 7, 1869, 107:1; Ronald E.

Butchart, *Northern Schools, Southern Blacks, and Reconstruction: Freedmen's Education, 1862–1875* (Westport: Greenwood Press, 1980), 42; Daniel Wesley Stowell, "The Failure of Religious Reconstruction: The Methodist Episcopal Church in Georgia, 1865–1871" (M.A. thesis, University of Georgia, 1988), 75, 82; J. W. Lee, "Georgia Conference—Our Educational Work," *Atlanta Methodist Advocate,* January 6, 1869, 1:3; "Rome, Ga., A. W. Caldwell," ibid., April 21, 1869, 63:1; "At Rome Also," ibid., May 26, 1869, 82:3; "Rome, Ga. Conf., A. W. Caldwell," ibid., July 14, 28, 1869, 111:1, 119:2; Dent Farm Journals and Account Books, vol. 7, June 3, 1867, p. 143; Wesley Prettyman, "Rome District, Georgia Conference," *Atlanta Methodist Advocate,* October 13, 1869, 162:5; Teacher's Monthly School Report for the Month of May, 1870, Rome, Floyd County, Georgia, Records of the Superintendent of Education for the State of Georgia, Records of the BRFAL, RG 105.

21. *Fifth Annual Report of the Freedmen's Aid Society of the Methodist Episcopal Church* (Cincinnati: Western Methodist Book Concern Print, 1872), 13; "Fourth Annual Report of [the] Freedmen's Aid Society," in *Atlanta Methodist Advocate,* December 28, 1870, 206:3–5; "Anniversary of the Freedmen's Aid Society," ibid., March 6, 1872, 37:2–4; Morrow, *Northern Methodism and Reconstruction,* 165; Carpenter, *Sword and Olive Branch,* 161–62; "The School at Rome," *Atlanta Methodist Advocate,* November 8, 1871, 178:5.

22. "The School at Rome," 178:5; Matlack, "The Methodist Episcopal Church in the Southern States," 122; Charles Andrux Talbert, "The Methodist Episcopal Church and the Negro During Reconstruction (1865–1885)" (M.A. thesis, Garrett Biblical Institute, 1932), 56; Caldwell, *Reminiscences of the Reconstruction of Church and State in Georgia,* 8; Daniel W. Stowell, "'The Negroes Cannot Navigate Alone': Religious Scalawags and the Biracial Methodist Episcopal Church in Georgia, 1866–1876," in *Georgia in Black & White: Explorations in the Race Relations of a Southern State, 1865–1950,* ed. John C. Inscoe (Athens: University of Georgia Press, 1994), 76–77; *Seventh Annual Report of the Freedmen's Aid Society of the Methodist Episcopal Church* (Cincinnati: Western Methodist Book Concern, 1874), 14. Formerly a member of the M.E. Church, South, John H. Caldwell helped to establish the M.E. Church in 1866. On Caldwell and other "religious scalawags," see Daniel W. Stowell, *Rebuilding Zion: The Religious Reconstruction of the South, 1863–1877* (New York: Oxford University Press, 1998), 58, 60–61, 131–36, 152–53. On the organization of the M.E. Church in Georgia, see Edmund Jordan Hammond, *The Methodist Episcopal Church in Georgia* (n.p., 1935), 105–18.

23. W. H. T. [William Hannibal Thomas], "Theological Institute," *Atlanta Methodist Advocate,* January 31, 1872, 18:5–6; "Barrows, Lorenzo D.," in Matthew Simpson, *Cyclopedia of Methodism* (Philadelphia: Louis H. Everts, 1881), 91.

24. W. H. T., "Theological Institute," 18:5–6.

25. Thomas to Garfield, May 18, 1872, James A. Garfield Papers, Manuscript Division, Library of Congress; *Proceedings of the National Union Republican Convention Held at Philadelphia* (Washington, DC: Gibson Brothers, 1872), 5; Olive

Hall Shadgett, *The Republican Party in Georgia: From Reconstruction Through 1900* (Athens: University of Georgia Press, 1964), 166–67.

26. "Decoration Day at Marietta," *Atlanta Methodist Advocate,* June 5, 1872, 90: 5. On Langston and the 5th USCT, see William Cheek and Aimee Lee Cheek, *John Mercer Langston and the Fight for Black Freedom, 1829–65* (Urbana: University of Illinois Press, 1989), 396–408.

27. "Decoration Day at Marietta."

28. Akerman to Wilson, June 28, 1872, Applications and Recommendations, RG 59; Will H. Thomas, "General John F. Hartranft," *Christian Recorder,* August 24, 1872, 5:1–2; "Hannibal," "Note from 'Hannibal,'" ibid., October 12, 1872, 2:3; Will H. Thomas to Rev. W. H. Hunter, October 16, 1872, in ibid., October 26, 1872, 4:4; idem, "Saunterings IV," ibid., November 30, 1872, 1:1–2. In October 1872, Hartranft defeated Charles R. Buckalew and served as governor of Pennsylvania from 1873 to 1879. On Akerman, see William S. McFeely, "Amos T. Akerman: The Lawyer and Racial Justice," in *Region, Race, and Reconstruction: Essays in Honor of C. Vann Woodward,* ed. J. Morgan Kousser and James M. McPherson (New York: Oxford University Press, 1982), 395–416.

29. Will H. Thomas, "Saunterings," *Christian Recorder,* November 2, 1872, 1:1–3.

30. Will H. Thomas, "Saunterings II," ibid., November 9, 1872, 1:1–2. On Blyden's antipathy toward mulattoes, see Hollis R. Lynch, *Edward Wilmot Blyden: Pan-Negro Patriot, 1832–1912* (1967; New York: Oxford University Press, 1970), 105–6.

31. Will H. Thomas, "Saunterings VI," *Christian Recorder,* February 6, 1873, 1:1–2.

32. Will H. Thomas, "Saunterings VII," *Christian Recorder,* February 20, 1873, 1:1–2; idem, "Saunterings V," ibid., January 30, 1873, 1:4–5.

33. James D. Anderson, *The Education of Blacks in the South, 1860–1935* (Chapel Hill: University of North Carolina Press, 1988), 28; *Fifth Annual Report of the Freedmen's Aid Society of the Methodist Episcopal Church,* 21.

34. *Sixth Annual Report of the Freedmen's Aid Society of the Methodist Episcopal Church* (Cincinnati: Western Methodist Book Concern Print, 1873), 28, 33; Wesley Prettyman, "North Georgia District," *Atlanta Methodist Advocate,* May 21, 1873, 83: 1; *Seventh Annual Report of the Freedmen's Aid Society of the Methodist Episcopal Church,* 19; S. W. Williams, ed., *The Methodist Almanac for the Year of Our Lord 1875* (Cincinnati: Hitchcock & Walden, 1875), 27; Rust, *Educational Work in the South by the Freedmen's Aid Society,* 4; "Floyd County Georgia in 1880, With a List of the Principal Businesses," *Northwest Georgia Historical and Genealogical Society Quarterly* 16 (winter 1984), [15]; Dorothy Orr, *A History of Education in Georgia* (Chapel Hill: University of North Carolina Press, 1950), 301–2; Henry Morrison Johnson, "The Methodist Episcopal Church and the Education of Southern

Negroes, 1862–1900" (Ph.D. diss., Yale University, 1939), 406. For glimpses into black religious life in Rome, Georgia, following Reconstruction, see J. T. Jenifer, "The New South and the Negro," *Christian Recorder*, November 18, 1886, 1:4–5; W. Decker Johnson, "The Rome District of Georgia," ibid., July 23, 1896, 5:5.

35. Howard N. Rabinowitz, "Continuity and Change: Southern Urban Development, 1860–1900," in *The City in Southern History: The Growth of Urban Civilization in the South*, ed. Blaine A. Brownell and David R. Goldfield (Port Washington, NY: Kennikat Press, 1977), 97, 99; John Tyler Dennett, *The South As It Is: 1865–1866*, ed. Henry M. Christman (New York: Viking, 1965), 268; John Dittmer, *Black Georgia in the Progressive Era, 1900–1920* (Urbana: University of Illinois Press, 1977), 12; *Ninth Census—Volume I*, 102; *Statistics of the Population of the United States at the Tenth Census (June 1, 1880)* (Washington, DC: Government Printing Office, 1883), 417; James Michael Russell, *Atlanta, 1847–1890: City Building in the Old South and the New* (Baton Rouge: Louisiana State University Press, 1988), 267; Jerry Thornbery, "The Atlanta Freedmen, 1865–69," *Prologue* 6 (winter 1974): 236–44, 251.

36. Rabinowitz, "Continuity and Change," 100–101; Grigsby Hart Wotton Jr., "New City of the South: Atlanta, 1843–1873" (Ph.D. diss., The Johns Hopkins University, 1973), 316; Philip Noel Racine, "Atlanta's Schools: A History of the Public School System, 1869–1955" (Ph.D. diss., Emory University, 1969), 14; David R. Goldfield, *Cotton Fields and Skyscrapers: Southern City and Region, 1607–1980* (Baton Rouge: Louisiana State University Press, 1982), 109; Russell, *Atlanta, 1847–1890*, 176–81.

37. Thornbery, "The Atlanta Freedmen, 1865–69," 245–50; idem, "The Development of Black Atlanta, 1865–1885" (Ph.D. diss., University of Maryland, 1977), 80–84, 87n, 148, 150; "Clark University," *Atlanta Methodist Advocate*, July 5, 1871, 106:6; J. W. Lee, "Georgia Conference—Our Educational Work," ibid., January 6, 1869, 1:3; "Clark University," ibid., August 18, 1869, 130:2; D. W. Hammond, "Clark University," ibid., September 1, 1869, 139:1. The M.E. Church established Clark Chapel in 1867. By the early 1870s its congregation numbered over 300. See Wotton, "New City of the South," 334. Summer Hill School continued into the 1880s as a public school for blacks as a separate entity from Clark University.

38. R. S. Rust, "Freedmen's Aid Society: Normal Schools," *Atlanta Methodist Advocate*, December 22, 1869, 201:3–4; *Third Annual Report of the Freedmen's Aid Society of the Methodist Episcopal Church* (Cincinnati: Western Methodist Book Concern Print, 1869), 8–9; R. S. Rust, "Atlanta Training School," *Atlanta Methodist Advocate*, August 11, 1869, 126:6; *Fourth Annual Report of the Freedmen's Aid Society of the Methodist Episcopal Church* (Cincinnati: Western Methodist Book Concern Print, 1871), 9; *Fifth Annual Report of the Freedmen's Aid Society*, 18; Charles Edgeworth Jones, *Education in Georgia* [Bureau of Education Circular of

Information No. 4, 1888] (Washington, DC: Government Printing Office, 1889), 149; Alphonso A. McPheeters, "The Origin and Development of Clark University and Gammon Theological Seminary" (Ed.D. diss., University of Cincinnati, 1944), 61.

39. Morrow, *Northern Methodism and Reconstruction*, 166, 171; "Clark University," *Atlanta Methodist Advocate*, January 18, 1871, 10:1; Lee, "Education and Our Schools in Atlanta," ibid., July 9, 1873, 109:5–6; James P. Brawley, *Two Centuries of Methodist Concern: Bondage, Freedom and Education of Black People* (New York: Vantage, 1974), 6; McPheeters, "The Origin and Development of Clark University and Gammon Theological Seminary," 66; *Eighth Annual Report of the Freedmen's Aid Society of the Methodist Episcopal Church* (Cincinnati: Western Methodist Book Concern Print, 1875), 31; *Tenth Annual Report of the Freedmen's Aid Society of the Methodist Episcopal Church* (Cincinnati: Western Methodist Book Concern, 1878), 23; Robert C. Morris, *Reading, 'Riting, and Reconstruction: The Education of the Freedmen in the South, 1861–1870* (1976; Chicago: University of Chicago Press, 1981), 172.

40. J. H. Knowles, "Clark Theological Seminary," *Atlanta Methodist Advocate*, January 31, 1872, 18:3–4; "Opening of Clark Theological Seminary, Atlanta, Ga.," ibid., February 14, 1872, 26:6; *Fifth Annual Report of the Freedmen's Aid Society*, 18–21; Rupert Talmage Mallory, "The Freedmen's Aid Society of the Methodist Episcopal Church" (B.D. thesis, Duke University, 1939), 65; Jones, *Education in Georgia*, 149; James P. Brawley, *The Clark College Legacy: An Interpretive History of Relevant Education, 1869–1975* (Atlanta: Clark College, 1977), 15; McPheeters, "The Origin and Development of Clark University and Gammon Theological Seminary," 53, 48–49. The Loyd Street Church held separate religious services for whites and blacks. In 1875 the African American congregations of Clark Chapel and Loyd Street Church merged and white Methodists established their own church on Marietta Street. See Arthur Reed Taylor, "From the Ashes: Atlanta During Reconstruction, 1865–1876" (Ph.D. diss., Emory University, 1973), 181, 188.

41. "Clark Theological Seminary" [advertisement], *Atlanta Methodist Advocate*, August 20, 1873, 135:6; "Anniversary of the Freedmen's Aid Society," 37:2–4; *Sixth Annual Report of the Freedmen's Aid Society*, 27–28.

42. *Fifth Annual Report of the Freedmen's Aid Society*, 21; *Minutes of the Annual Conferences of the Methodist Episcopal Church for the Year 1872*, 127, 298; "Personals," *Atlanta Methodist Advocate*, December 11, 1872, 199:1; "The Opening," ibid., February 28, 1872, 34:1; "Anniversary of the Freedmen's Aid Society," 37:2–4; *Sixth Annual Report of the Freedmen's Aid Society*, 27–28; Hammond, *The Methodist Episcopal Church in Georgia*, 121, 132; Brawley, *Two Centuries of Methodist Concern*, 229; Willard Range, *The Rise and Progress of Negro Colleges in Georgia, 1865–1944* (Athens: University of Georgia Press, 1951), 226. Barrows returned to the North in 1873. Lee served as president of Clark Theological Seminary until fall 1874, when Lansing replaced him. Haven, an outspoken racial egalitarian and social reformer, was appointed bishop in 1872 and assigned to Atlanta. See McPheeters, "The Ori-

gin and Development of Clark University and Gammon Theological Seminary," 56; *Eighth Annual Report of the Freedmen's Aid Society,* 27; Brawley, *The Clark College Legacy,* 16.

43. J. W. Lee, "Georgia Conference," *Atlanta Methodist Advocate,* November 6, 1872, 178:4–5; William B. Gravely, *Gilbert Haven: Methodist Abolitionist* (Nashville: Abingdon Press, 1973), 200–203; Will H. Thomas, "Christianity—What It Is," *Atlanta Methodist Advocate,* May 1, 1872, 69:2–3.

44. Will H. Thomas, "Christianity—What It Is," *Christian Recorder,* August 10 [*sic*] [17], 1872, 7:1–2; "By the Editor," ibid., August 24, 1872, 4:1; ibid., December 7, 1872, 4:6; ibid., January 2, 1873, 4:4. Tanner referred to the difference between a Dahlgren cannon—a large naval gun—and a Springfield rifle musket—the principal infantry weapon employed by both U.S. and Confederate armies during the Civil War.

45. "Georgia Conference Education Reports—Clark Theological Seminary," *Atlanta Methodist Advocate,* November 12, 1873, 181:4; *Sixth Annual Report of the Freedmen's Aid Society,* 27–29.

46. Will H. Thomas, "Saunterings VI."

47. W. H. T. [William Hannibal Thomas], "Editorial Correspondence," *Christian Recorder,* August 17, 1872, 4:3–4; Will H. Thomas, "Clark Theological Seminary," *Atlanta Methodist Advocate,* April 16, 1873, 61:2–3.

48. W. H. Thomas to the editor, *Christian Recorder,* August 10, 1872, 8:1; idem, "Clark Theological Seminary," 61:2–3.

49. Thomas, "Clark Theological Seminary," 61:2–3; idem, "Saunterings," *Christian Recorder,* October 23, 1873, 1:3–5; *Eighth Annual Report of the Freedmen's Aid Society,* 28; Carl R. Osthaus, *Freedmen, Philanthropy, and Fraud: A History of the Freedman's Savings Bank* (Urbana: University of Illinois Press, 1976), 178–79; Alfred M. Pierce, *A History of Methodism in Georgia,* 169. Grigsby Hart Wotton Jr. argues that though Clark University practiced complete integration, Atlanta's white M.E. clergy segregated their congregations. He also asserts that blacks who attended Clark "became members of a Negro elite increasingly separate from the Negro masses." See "New City of the South," 307–9.

50. Ware to Cravath, August [?], 1872; Thomas to Cravath, February 1, September 29, 1873, American Missionary Association Archives. In 1865 the Avery trust granted the American Missionary Association an endowment of $100,000 with the requirement that the income be expended only on African missions. The Association opened Atlanta University in 1869. Before 1872 it offered only preparatory classes and, in that year, initiated college work. See "Atlanta University," *American Missionary* 17 (August 1873): 173–74; ibid., 18 (September 1874): 197–98; Richardson, *Christian Reconstruction,* 105, 134.

51. "Our Swivel," *Christian Recorder,* July 31, 1873, 4:4; [William Hannibal Thomas], "A Letter from Hannibal," ibid., July 31, 1873, 5:3; Will H. Thomas, "Saunterings," ibid., August 28, 1873, 5:1–2; idem, "Saunterings," ibid., Septem-

ber 11, 1873, 1:2–3; ibid., September 25, 1873, 1:5–6; ibid., October 16, 1873, 8:1–2; idem, "Saunterings," ibid., October 23, 1873, 1:3–5; Thomas to Cravath, September 29, 1873, American Missionary Association Archives.

52. *Minutes of the Seventh Session of the Georgia Annual Conference of the Methodist Episcopal Church Held at Atlanta, Ga., Beginning October 15, 1873* (Atlanta: James P. Harrison, 1873), 10; "Georgia Conference, Seventh Session," *Atlanta Methodist Advocate,* October 29, 1873, 174:4–5; *Minutes of the Annual Conferences of the Methodist Episcopal Church for the Year 1873* (New York: Nelson & Phillips, 1873), 141–42; "Arrest of a Negro Preacher on Two Criminal Warrants—The Justice's Courts," *Atlanta Constitution,* October 26, 1873, 8:2; Grand Jury Minute Book J, Fulton County Superior Court, Fall Term, 1873, January 1873–December 1873, p. 577, Fulton County Court House, Atlanta, Georgia.

53. Thomas to Cravath, October 29, 1873, American Missionary Association Archives.

54. Thomas to Cravath, November 2, 1873, American Missionary Association Archives; Grand Jury Minute Book J, Fulton County Superior Court, p. 633; Chesnutt to The Macmillan Company, April 26, 1901, and enclosed in "In Re William Hannibal Thomas, Author of 'The American Negro'" (unpublished manuscript, [1901]), 1–3, Macmillan Company Papers, New York Public Library; Chesnutt to Robert C. Ogden, May 27, 1904, Charles W. Chesnutt Papers, Fisk University Library. Fulton County Superior Court criminal dockets did not survive for 1873, making it impossible to determine the exact disposition of Thomas's case.

55. Ware to Cravath, December 1, 1873, American Missionary Association Archives.

56. Rust to Cravath, December 2, 1873, American Missionary Association Archives.

57. George Lansing Taylor, "Southern Correspondence—Our Work in the South," *Cincinnati Western Christian Advocate* 41 (April 22, 1874), 121:2–4; Thomas, "Christianity—What It Is," *Atlanta Methodist Advocate,* 69:2–3.

Chapter Four. Lawyer and Legislator in South Carolina

1. Thomas to Erastus Milo Cravath, November 2, December 2, 1873, American Missionary Association Archives; Daniel Augustus Straker, *The New South Investigated* (Detroit: Ferguson Printing Co., 1888), 58.

2. Thomas to Cravath, November 2, December 2, 1873, American Missionary Association Archives.

3. Thomas H. Pope, *The History of Newberry County, South Carolina, Volume One: 1749–1860* (Columbia: University of South Carolina Press, 1973), 92, vii–viii, 73, 105, 112; Ulrich Bonnell Phillips, *A History of Transportation in the Eastern Cotton Belt to 1860* (New York: Columbia University Press, 1908), 343–47; Rachel N. Klein, *Unification of a Slave State: The Rise of the Planter Class in the South Carolina Backcountry, 1760–1808* (Chapel Hill: University of North Carolina Press,

1990), 251; Lacy K. Ford Jr., *Origins of Southern Radicalism: The South Carolina Upcountry, 1800–1860* (New York: Oxford University Press, 1988), 46.

4. Pope, *The History of Newberry County, South Carolina, Volume One,* vii, 114, 115, 285.

5. Thomas H. Pope, *The History of Newberry County, South Carolina, Volume Two: 1860–1990* (Columbia: University of South Carolina Press, 1992), 9, 10, 19, 29, 32, 44, 19, 31; Immigration Society of Newberry, September 6, 1869 [broadside], Thaddeus S. Boinsett Collection, Duke University; *Ninth Census—Volume I. The Statistics of the Population of the United States, Embracing the Tables of Race, Nationality, Sex, Selected Ages, and Occupations* (Washington, DC: Government Printing Office, 1872), 60, 260. In 1875 Newberry County contained 16,185 blacks and 7,141 whites. *Recent Election in South Carolina. Testimony Taken by the Select Committee on the Recent Election in South Carolina,* 44th Congress, 2nd Session. House of Representatives Miscellaneous Document 31 (Washington, DC: Government Printing Office, 1877), part 1, p. 135; part 2, p. 62.

6. *Recent Election in South Carolina,* part 2, p. 56; part 1, p. 133; Christian H. Suber quoted in Julie Saville, *The Work of Reconstruction* (Cambridge: Cambridge University Press, 1994), 176; Pope, *The History of Newberry County, South Carolina, Volume Two,* 27, 38, 46, 52, 57, 62.

7. A. W. Wayman, "Bishop Payne," *A.M.E. Church Review* 10 (January 1894): 410; Saville, *The Work of Reconstruction,* 165.

8. A. Weston, "How African Methodism Was Introduced In The Up County," in *Proceedings of the Quarto-Centennial Conference of the African M.E. Church of South Carolina, at Charleston, S.C., May 15, 16 and 17, 1889,* ed. Benjamin W. Arnett (n.p., 1890), 70–71; *A.M.E. Church Review* 10 (January 1894): 410; Stephen Ward Angell, *Bishop Henry McNeal Turner and African-American Religion in the South* (Knoxville: University of Tennessee Press, 1992), 7; Pope, *The History of Newberry County, South Carolina, Volume Two,* 291; *Minutes of the Tenth Session of the South Carolina Annual Conference of the African Methodist Episcopal Church Held at Newberry, S.C.* (Columbia: Republican Printing Co., 1874), 12, 69, 80.

9. George P. Rawick, ed., *The American Slave: A Composite Autobiography, Volume 2: South Carolina Narratives, Parts 1 and 2* (Westport: Greenwood Publishing Co., 1972), 17; Lewis J. Bellardo, "A Social and Economic History of Fairfield County, South Carolina, 1865–1871" (Ph.D. diss., University of Kentucky, 1979), 270–71; Robert S. Seigler, *A Guide to Confederate Monuments in South Carolina . . . Passing the Silent Cup* (Columbia: South Carolina Department of Archives and History, 1997), 422–25.

10. Lou Falkner Williams, *The Great South Carolina Ku Klux Klan Trials, 1871–1872* (Athens: University of Georgia Press, 1996), 17; Martin Abbott, "County Officers in South Carolina in 1868," *South Carolina Historical Magazine* 60 (January 1959): 35; Peggy Lamson, *The Glorious Failure: Black Congressman Robert Brown Elliott and the Reconstruction in South Carolina* (New York: Norton, 1974),

82, 131; Saville, *The Work of Reconstruction*, 193–94; Pope, *The History of Newberry County, South Carolina, Volume Two*, 24–25, 33, 47, 49, 50, 51, 54.

11. Thomas H. Pope to John David Smith, June 15, 1990, in possession of the author; Pope, *The History of Newberry County, South Carolina, Volume Two*, 28, 225, 451n, 179, 76, 453n, "Notice," *Newberry Herald*, September 25, 1867, 3:6; Deed Book NN, October 10, 1869, pp. 463–64, Clerk's Office, Newberry County, Newberry, South Carolina; Pope to Smith, September 23, 1990, in possession of the author; John Schreiner Reynolds, *Reconstruction in South Carolina, 1865–1877* (Columbia: The State Co., 1905), 237. On Hoge, see *Biographical Directory of the United States Congress, 1774–1989* (Washington, DC: Government Printing Office, 1989), 1199–1200. When, in 1890, Newberry established a graded school system, the town set up male and female academies for whites and relegated the Hoge Institute for blacks. Pope to Smith, June 15, 1990.

12. "Hoge School," *Newberry Herald*, June 9, 1875, 3:2; Deed Book SS, pp. 759–60, Clerk's Office, Newberry County, SCDAH; William Hayes Ward to John Edward Bruce, March 19, 1901, John Edward Bruce Papers, Schomburg Center for Research in Black Culture, New York Public Library; Chesnutt, "In Re William Hannibal Thomas, Author of 'The American Negro'" (unpublished manuscript [1901]), 4–5, Charles W. Chesnutt Papers, Fisk University; E. W. Screven to E. A. Webster, March 1, 1901, in John Edward Bruce, "The Critic Revealed," *Washington Colored American*, April 13, 1901, 1:4, 9:1–3. There is no recorded conveyance from Thomas regarding his land purchase. According to Pope, Thomas probably mortgaged the property and a foreclosure resulted. The property may have been sold for nonpayment of taxes when Thomas fled Newberry in 1877. Pope to Smith, June 12, 1990, in possession of the author.

13. *Minutes of the Twelfth Session of the South Carolina Annual Conference of the African Methodist Episcopal Church, held at Charleston, South Carolina* (Charleston: Walker, Evans and Cogswell, 1876), 12; "South Carolina Electoral College," *Christian Recorder*, July 1, 1875, 6:6; Angell, "Henry McNeal Turner and Black Religion in the South, 1865–1900" (Ph.D. diss., Vanderbilt University, 1988), 318–19, 343; "General Conference," *Missionary Record*, April 1, 1876, 2:3–5.

14. J. R. Oldfield, "A High and Honorable Calling: Black Lawyers in South Carolina, 1868–1915," *Journal of American Studies* 23 (December 1989): 396; "Special and Local," *Newberry Herald*, February 4, 1874, 3:1; Pope to Smith, June 8, September 3, 1990, in possession of the author; Pope, *The History of Newberry County, South Carolina, Volume Two*, 225; Thomas, *The American Negro: What He Was, What He Is, and What He May Become* (New York: Macmillan, 1901), xvi–xvii; idem, "Making a President: An Episode of 1876," *United Brethren Review* 11 (March/April 1906): 85; List of Attorneys, November Term, 1876, Supreme Court of South Carolina, Roll of Attorneys, 1865–1950, no page, SCDAH. Despite Thomas's claims, except in "extraordinary cases," South Carolina law required applicants for the bar to have read law in the office of a practicing attorney for two years or to have

graduated from a law school. See *The Constitution of South Carolina Adopted April 16, 1868, and the Acts and Joint Resolutions of the General Assembly Passed at the Special Session of 1868* (Columbia: John W. Denny, 1868), 96.

15. "Report of the Adjutant and Inspector General of the State of South Carolina, November 1870," in *Reports and Resolutions of the General Assembly of the State of South Carolina at the Regular Session, 1870-'71* (Columbia: Republican Printing Co., 1871), 542; Office of Adjutant and Inspector General, List of Commissions Issued, 1874, pp. 52–53, Office of Adjutant and Inspector General, List of Commissions Issued, 1875, pp. 32–33, Office of Adjutant and Inspector General, List of Commissions Issued, 1876, pp. 80–81, SCDAH; Joel Williamson, *After Slavery: The Negro In South Carolina During Reconstruction, 1861-1877* (Chapel Hill: University of North Carolina Press, 1965), 261, 262, 263; Pope, *The History of Newberry County, South Carolina, Volume Two*, 48; Thomas, *The American Negro*, xvii; William Hannibal Thomas's business cards, Theodore D. Jervey Papers, SCHS, and enclosed with Thomas to Joseph P. Tumulty, July 5, 1913, Woodrow Wilson Papers, Manuscript Division, Library of Congress. After leaving office, Governor Moses admitted that less than twenty-five percent of the persons on the South Carolina National Guard muster rolls at any one time rendered any military service. See Otis Singletary, *Negro Militia and Reconstruction* (Austin: University of Texas Press, 1957), 149.

16. Thomas to Howard, March 5, 1874, Oliver Otis Howard Papers, Bowdoin College.

17. Notary Public appointment, May 7, 1874, Governors Moses and Chamberlain Abstracts of Letters Received, 1872–1877, p. 181, SCDAH; *Newberry Herald*, May 13, 1874, 3:5; Trial Justice Appointment, May 22, 1874, Governors Moses and Chamberlain Abstracts of Letters Received, 1872–1877, p. 185, SCDAH; Pope, *The History of Newberry County, South Carolina, Volume One*, 60 and idem, *The History of Newberry County, South Carolina, Volume Two*, 42, 48; *Constitution of the Commonwealth of South Carolina Ratified April 16, 1868* (Columbia: Charles A. Calvo Jr., State Printer, 1885), 29–30; Holt, *Black Over White: Negro Political Leadership in South Carolina During Reconstruction* (Urbana: University of Illinois Press, 1977), 98. Early in 1875 a debate erupted over the appointment of trial justices. Governor Daniel H. Chamberlain insisted that in accord with the 1868 state constitution they be elected. See Chamberlain to R. H. Gleaves, January 26, 1875, General Assembly Papers, Legislative System, 1866-77 (Messages), SCDAH; *Journal of the House of Representatives of the State of South Carolina, 1874-75* (Columbia: Republican Printing Co., 1875), 230–32, and Chamberlain to the editor, *Greenville Republican*, February 4, 1875, in *Columbia Daily Union-Herald*, February 14, 1875, 1:4.

18. "The Independent Movement in Newberry," *Newberry Herald*, October 7, 1874, 2:2. See Carol K. Rothrock Bleser, *The Promised Land: The History of the South Carolina Land Commission, 1869-1890* (Columbia: University of South Carolina Press, 1969), 54–63, 100–101.

19. "Public Speaking," *Newberry Herald,* September 30, 1874, 3:3; Francis Butler Simkins and Robert Hilliard Woody, *South Carolina During Reconstruction* (Chapel Hill: University of North Carolina Press, 1932), 466–68; Holt, *Black Over White,* 17, 59, 61, 144, 176–78; Joel Williamson, *New People: Miscegenation and Mulattoes in the United States* (New York: Free Press, 1980), 86–87.

20. John Dwight Warner Jr., "Crossed Sabres: A History of the Fifth Massachusetts Volunteer Cavalry, an African-American Regiment in the Civil War" (Ph.D. diss., Boston College, 1997), iii, iv, 441–46; Richard Nelson Current, *Those Terrible Carpetbaggers: A Reinterpretation* (New York: Oxford University Press, 1988), 91–98, 214–28, 328; "Moses-Chamberlain," *Charleston News and Courier,* August 28, 1874, 2:3.

21. "Newberry," "The Way It Was Done in Newberry," *Columbia Daily Union-Herald,* October 2, 1874, 1:2.

22. "United for Reform! The Independent Republican Convention," *Charleston News and Courier,* October 3, 1874, 1:1–3; "The Independent Republican Convention," *Columbia Daily Union-Herald,* October 4, 1874, 4:3; Simkins and Woody, *South Carolina During Reconstruction,* 471–72; "An Unholy Alliance," *Columbia Daily Union-Herald,* October 4, 1874, 4:4. In the 1874 campaign, the Democrats nominated a candidate neither for governor nor for lieutenant governor.

23. For versions of Thomas's speech, see "Daybreak, at Last! The Independent Republicans Nominate Green for Governor," *Charleston News and Courier,* October 5, 1874, 1:1–5; "United for Reform! The Independent Republican Convention," ibid., October 3, 1874, 1:3; "The Independent Republican Convention," *Newberry Herald,* October 7, 1874, 2:2; "Reform," ibid., October 14, 1874, 2:3–4. Chamberlain's *Columbia Daily Union-Herald* mocked Thomas's speech. See Ira, "Our Charleston Letter," October 6, 1874, 1:3–4.

24. "Daybreak, at Last! The Independent Republicans Nominate Green for Governor," 1:1–5; "The Independent Republican Convention," *Charleston News and Courier,* October 5, 1874, 2:1–2; "The Colored Republicans and the Carpet-bag Thieves," ibid., October 21, 1874, 2:2–3. On Conservatives and the fusion ticket, see William C. Hine, "Frustration, Factionalism and Failure: Black Political Leadership and the Republican Party in Reconstruction Charleston, 1865–1877" (Ph.D. diss., Kent State University, 1979), 374–79.

25. Removed as Trial Justice, October 6, 1874, Governors Moses and Chamberlain Abstracts of Letters Received, 1872–1877, p. 219, SCDAH; "City Notes," *Columbia Daily Union-Herald,* October 7, 1874, 4:1; *Newberry Herald,* October 14, 1874, 2:3; Pope, *The History of Newberry County, South Carolina, Volume Two,* 60; "Campaign Notes," *Charleston News and Courier,* October 8, 1874, 1:3.

26. Thomas, "To the People of Newberry County," October 6, 1874, in *Newberry Herald,* October 7, 1874, 2:3–4.

27. Ibid.

28. Ibid.

29. Pink, "Glorious News from Georgetown and Newberry," *Charleston News and Courier*, October 13, 1874, 1:1; "Monday's Speaking," *Newberry Herald*, October 14, 1874, 2:2; Pink, "A Glorious Prospect Inspiring Effect of the Certainty of a Fair Election," *Charleston News and Courier*, October 26, 1874, 1:1; "Newberry and the Cause," *Columbia Daily Herald-Union*, October 13, 1874, 1:4; "The Canvass," in ibid., October 24, 1874, 2:1–4; "A Regular," "The Laurens Republicans at Work," in ibid., October 28, 1874, 1:3–4; Pink, "The Doom of the Thieves," *Charleston News and Courier*, October 28, 1874, 1:1.

30. "Atrocious Murder," *Columbia Daily Union-Herald*, October 21, 1874, 1:5; "The Newberry Trouble," in ibid., October 23, 1874, 1:1; Pope, *The History of Newberry County, South Carolina, Volume Two*, 61–62; F. J. Moses Jr., "Governor's Proclamation," *Columbia Daily Union-Herald*, October 24, 1874, 1:5–6; "Changes in the Board of Commissioners," *Newberry Herald*, October 28, 1874, 3:3; Appointed Trial Justice, October 29, 1874, Governors Moses and Chamberlin Abstracts of Letters Received, 1872–1877, p. 222, SCDAH; "Special and Local," *Newberry Herald*, Novem-ber 18, 1874, 3:1.

31. "The Election," *Newberry Herald*, November 8, 1876, 2:2; "Official Vote in the State," *Charleston News and Courier*, November 20, 1874, 1:3; Simkins and Woody, *South Carolina During Reconstruction*, 473n (election returns); "Fraudulent Voting," *Charleston News and Courier*, November 12, 1874, 2:2; chart, *Newberry Herald*, November 18, 1874, 3:3–4; Holt, *Black Over White*, 175, 178; William Gillette, *Retreat from Reconstruction, 1869–1879* (Baton Rouge: Louisiana State University Press, 1979), 245–58. Holt refers erroneously to Thomas as "an Independent Republican candidate from Charleston in the 1874 election." See *Black Over White*, 78.

32. Eric Foner, *Reconstruction: America's Unfinished Revolution, 1863–1877* (New York: Harper, 1988), 543–44, 547; Holt, *Black Over White*, 178–80, 183, 190–92; *Inaugural Address of Gov. D.H. Chamberlain Delivered before the General Assembly of South Carolina, December 1, 1874* (Columbia: Republican Printing Co., State Printers, 1874), 15–16; Trial Justices Revoked, December 3, 1874, Governors Moses and Chamberlin Abstracts of Letters Received, 1872–1877, p. 231, SCDAH.

33. Thomas to Chamberlain with enclosed petition, December 10, 1874, Governor Chamberlain Letters Received, SCDAH; "Appointments," *Columbia Daily Union-Herald*, February 6, 1875, 4:1; Thomas to Chamberlain, March 4, 1876, Governors Papers, Daniel H. Chamberlain, SCDAH.

34. Thomas to Theodore D. Jervey, May 22, 1905, Jervey Papers; Chamberlain to the President, May 9, 1877, Applications and Recommendations for Public Service, RG 59.

35. "State News," *Columbia Daily Union-Herald*, April 22, 1875, 1:2; Thomas, "To the Editor of the Newberry *Herald*" (with enclosure from *Charleston News and Courier*, n.d.) in *Newberry Herald*, January 6, 1875, 2:1–2.

36. Foner, *Reconstruction: America's Unfinished Revolution*, 546; Thomas, "To

the Editor of the Newberry *Herald*," 2:1-2. Compare Delany's plan with one proposed in 1868 by the Reverend Cain and the program of the South Carolina Land Commission established in 1869. See Bleser, *The Promised Land*, 19-21, 25-46.

37. "Mr. Wm. H. Thomas," *Delaware Gazette*, September 16, 1875, 4:5; Thomas, *The American Negro*, xvii.

38. Sessions Journal, Newberry County, January 18, 1876; "Presentment of the Grand Jury," *Newberry Herald*, January 26, 1876, 3:4; Walter R. Jones to Thomas, March 9, 1876, D. H. Chamberlain Letter Book, SCDAH; Sessions Journal, Newberry County, May 11, 1876; *Newberry Herald*, May 17, 1876, 2:7.

39. Lipscomb to Chamberlain, July 7, 1876, W. R. Smith to Chamberlain, August 9, 1876, Thomas to Chamberlain, August 8, 1876, Daniel H. Chamberlain Papers, SCDAH; Pope, *The History of Newberry County, South Carolina, Volume Two*, 66, 431-32.

40. Sessions Journal, Newberry County, entries for January 12, March 25, April 2, 1875; January 11, 12, 13, 21, May 3, 4, 8, 9, 16, 1876.

41. Richard Zuczek, "The Last Campaign of the Civil War: South Carolina and the Revolution of 1876," *Civil War History* 42 (winter 1996): 18-31; and idem, *State of Rebellion: Reconstruction in South Carolina* (Columbia: University of South Carolina Press, 1996), 159, 209; Pope, *The History of Newberry County, South Carolina, Volume Two*, 68-69; Cain, "The Political Outlook in the State," *Charleston Missionary Record*, April 1, 1876, 3:2-3.

42. Eric Foner, *Nothing But Freedom: Emancipation and Its Legacy* (Baton Rouge: Louisiana State University Press, 1983), 92-102; Edward A. Miller Jr., *Gullah Statesman: Robert Smalls from Slavery to Congress, 1839-1915* (Columbia: University of South Carolina Press, 1995), 104-6.

43. Orville Vernon Burton, *In My Father's House Are Many Mansions: Family and Community in Edgefield, South Carolina* (Chapel Hill: University of North Carolina Press, 1985), 29-31, 289-90.

44. Williamson, *After Slavery*, 268.

45. *An Address to the People of the United States, Adopted at a Conference of Colored Citizens, held at Columbia, s.c., July 20 and 21st, 1876* (Columbia: Republican Printing Co., State Printers, 1876), 3, 10; "An Address to the People of the United States, Adopted at a Conference of Colored Citizens, Held at Columbia, s.c., July 20 and 21, 1876," *Columbia Union-Herald*, July 29, 1876, 2:1-5; Lamson, *The Glorious Failure*, 237-38.

46. Thomas to Chamberlain, August 8, 1876, Chamberlain Papers, SCDAH; Chamberlain quoted in Walter Allen, *Governor Chamberlain's Administration in South Carolina: A Chapter of Reconstruction in the Southern States* (New York: Putnam, 1888), 377, 378, 486; Pope, *The History of Newberry County, South Carolina, Volume Two*, 69; *Recent Election in South Carolina*, part 1, p. 307; Keith Ian Polakoff, *The Politics of Inertia: The Election of 1876 and the End of Reconstruction* (Baton Rouge: Louisiana State University Press, 1973), 191-93. The Republicans nominated Chamberlain on September 13. On the Democrats' tactic of forcefully "divid-

ing time" with Republican speakers, see Hampton M. Jarrell, *Wade Hampton and the Negro: The Road not Taken* (Columbia: University of South Carolina Press, 1949), 67.

47. Simkins and Woody, *South Carolina During Reconstruction,* 489; Williamson, *After Slavery,* 405–6; Pope, *The History of Newberry County, South Carolina, Volume Two,* 69; Current, *Those Terrible Carpetbaggers,* 354. On the Ellenton riot, see Mark M. Smith, "'All is not Quiet in our Hellish County': Facts, Fiction, Politics, and Race—The Ellenton Riot of 1876," *South Carolina Historical Magazine* 95 (April 1994): 142–55. On the Cainhoy riot, see Melinda Meek Hennessey, "Racial Violence During Reconstruction: The 1876 Riots in Charleston and Cainhoy," ibid., 86 (April 1985): 100–112. George C. Rable analyzes the context of political violence in South Carolina in *But There Was No Peace: The Role of Violence in the Politics of Reconstruction* (Athens: University of Georgia Press, 1984), 164–69.

48. "The Republican County Convention," *Newberry Herald,* October 11, 1876, 3:2; Celsus, "Radical Nominations in Newberry," *Columbia Register,* October 8, 1876, 2:4–5; "Special and Local," *Newberry Herald,* November 8, 1876, 3:2–3.

49. Thomas, "Making a President," 87; "Special and Local," *Newberry Herald,* November 8, 1876, 3:2–3.

50. A South Carolinian [Belton O'Neall Townsend], "The Political Condition of South Carolina," *Atlantic Monthly* 39 (February 1877): 187; *Recent Election in South Carolina,* Appendix, pp. 49, 24; Pope, *The History of Newberry County, South Carolina, Volume Two,* 69. For a firsthand account of violence against black voters and black candidates, see William H. Heard, *From Slavery to the Bishopric in the A.M.E. Church* (1908; New York: Arno, 1969), 40–44.

51. "The Election," *Newberry Herald,* November 8, 1876, 2:2; Holt, *Black Over White,* 174; Simkins and Woody, *South Carolina During Reconstruction,* 515; Polakoff, *The Politics of Inertia,* 219; Foner, *Reconstruction: America's Unfinished Revolution,* 575. For a summary of the forms of intimidation directed at blacks, see U.S. Congress, *Congressional Record: Containing the Proceedings and Debates of the Forty-Fourth Congress, Second Session, Volume V* (Washington, DC: Government Printing Office, 1877), Appendix, p. 230.

52. Simkins and Woody, *South Carolina During Reconstruction,* 516–22; *Recent Election in South Carolina,* Appendix, pp. 76, 108, 119; John S. Reynolds, *Reconstruction in South Carolina, 1865–1877* (Columbia: The State Co., 1905), 393 (chart), 396; "Our County Officers," *Newberry Herald,* November 29, 1876, 2:3. Republicans, after voiding returns from certain counties, claimed 86,216 votes for Chamberlain and 83,071 for Hampton. Democrats claimed 92,261 votes for Hampton and 91,127 votes for Chamberlain. In Newberry, Keitt led candidates for the House with 2,789 votes while Thomas and Bridges received, respectively, 2,765 and 2,760 votes. According to an 1875 state census, South Carolina contained 925,145 persons, including 110,744 colored voters and 74,199 whites. The report also stated that on September 30, 1876, there were only 589 U.S. troops in the state. See *Recent Election in South Carolina,* part 2, p. 23.

53. "South Carolina Legislature," *Columbia Union-Herald,* November 28, 1876, 1:2-3; Thomas, "Making a President," 89. For the opposing sides, see *Report of the Special Committee of the House of Representatives of South Carolina, Relative to the Organization of that Body, and the Constitutional Validity Thereof. Adopted December 21, 1876* (Columbia: Republican Printing Co., 1876) and *A Reply to the Special Committee of the Mackey "House of Representatives" of South Carolina. Shewing That the Organization of That Body was Without Constitutional Validity, and That Its Acts are Consequently Void* (Charleston: News and Courier Job Presses, 1877). On the role of the federal troops, see Brooks D. Simpson, "Ulysses S. Grant and the Electoral Crisis of 1876-77," *Hayes Historical Journal* 11 (winter 1992): 6-7.

54. Alfred B. Williams, *Hampton and His Red Shirts: South Carolina's Deliverance in 1876* (Charleston: Walker, Evans and Cogswell, 1935), 404; Simkins and Woody, *South Carolina During Reconstruction,* 526-27.

55. Thomas, "Making a President," 89, 90, 91, 92-93. Thomas referred to the disputed presidential election of 1876 in which Democratic candidate Samuel J. Tilden received a popular vote margin of 250,000 over Hayes but without the contested electoral votes of South Carolina, Louisiana, Oregon, and Florida fell one vote short of the necessary majority.

56. "The Legislature," *Newberry Herald,* December 6, 1876, 2:5; Thompson, *Ousting the Carpetbagger from South Carolina* (Columbia: R. L. Bryan, 1926), 143-44, 146; Josephus Woodruff Diary, November 29, December 3, 10, 1876, SCDAH.

57. "Organization of the 'Rump,'" *Columbia Register,* November 29, 1876, 2:2-3; *Journal of the House of Representatives of the State of South Carolina for the Regular Session of 1876-77* (Columbia: Republican Printing Co., State Printers, 1876), 4, 14, 16, 17, 19, 34-37, 42, 57, 62, 65; "Which Was The Rump?" *Columbia Union-Herald,* December 1, 1876, 1:2-3; "The Way Opened," *Columbia Register,* December 1, 1876, 3:2; "In A Dead Lock!" ibid., December 2, 1876, 3:2; "The Third Day's Session," ibid., December 3, 1876, 3:2; "Legislative Proceedings," *Columbia Union-Herald,* December 5, 1876, 1:2-3; "Legislative Proceedings," ibid., December 7, 1876, 1:3; "The Gay Rump," *Columbia Register,* December 7, 1876, 3:2; "Cast-Iron Cheek," ibid., December 8, 1876, 3:2; "Legislative Proceedings," *Columbia Union-Herald,* December 8, 1876, 1:2; "Legislative Proceedings," ibid., December 9, 1876, 1:2; "The Legislature," *Newberry Herald,* December 13, 1876, 2:2.

58. "The Unlawful Rump," *Columbia Register,* December 9, 1876, 3:2; "Carpet-Baggery," ibid., December 14, 1876, 3:3.

59. "C.," "Thomas, of the Rump," *Columbia Register,* December 12, 1876, 2:6; *Newberry Herald,* December 13, 1876, 3:1; editorial, ibid., December 6, 1876, 2:6; Pope to Hampton, December 23, 1876, Hampton Correspondence File, SCDAH.

60. Simkins and Woody, *South Carolina During Reconstruction,* 517, 529-34.

61. Current, *Those Terrible Carpetbaggers*, 360; Thomas to Chamberlain, March 26, 1877, Chamberlain Papers, SCDAH, copy in William Hannibal Thomas Collection, Otterbein College Library.

62. Thomas to Hayes, April 2, 1877, Applications and Recommendations, RG 59.

63. Ibid.

64. Ibid.

65. Ibid.

66. Ibid.

67. Babbitt to Thomas, April 9, 1877, Chamberlain Letter Book, SCDAH; Simkins and Woody, *South Carolina During Reconstruction*, 540–41. For the complex circumstances that led Hayes to withdraw the U.S. troops, see Vincent P. DeSantis, "Rutherford B. Hayes and the Removal of the Troops and the End of Reconstruction," in *Region, Race, and Reconstruction: Essays in Honor of C. Vann Woodward*, ed. J. Morgan Kousser and James M. McPherson (New York: Oxford University Press, 1982), 417–50.

68. Holt, *Black Over White*, 209; William J. Cooper Jr., *The Conservative Regime: South Carolina, 1877–1890* (Baltimore: Johns Hopkins University Press, 1968), 25; "Doings of the Legislature," *Charleston News and Courier*, May 2, 1877, 1:1–3; Thomas, "Making a President," 94; "EXIT THOMAS!" *Newberry Herald*, May 2, 1877, 2:6; *Journal of the House of Representatives of the State of South Carolina, Being the Special Session, Commencing April 24, 1877* (Columbia: Presbyterian Publishing House, 1877), 36–37, 40–41; Walter B. Edgar, ed., *Biographical Directory of the South Carolina House of Representatives, Volume I, Session Lists, 1692–1973* (Columbia: University of South Carolina Press, 1974), 426–27; Thomas, "Making a President," 93–95.

69. "The Leaders of the Rascality to Suffer," *Columbia Register*, May 2, 1877, 3:2; "Doings of the Legislature," *Charleston News and Courier*, May 2, 1877, 1:1–3. Thomas of course was from Ohio, not Massachusetts, and had no direct connection to Sumner. In a highly racist poem, Robert McKay noted Thomas's conspicuous leadership in the Mackey House of Representatives. See "South Carolina Redeemed, 1865–1887," unpublished manuscripts, Robert McKay Papers, South Caroliniana Library, University of South Carolina.

70. Bruce, "The Critic Revealed," 9:2; "Notes From Newberry: A County That Has Hardly a Single Official Who Knows Whether His Title to His Office is Sound," *Charleston News and Courier*, May 16, 1877, 1:5; "Special and Local," *Newberry Herald*, May 16, 1877, 3:2; "Special and Local," ibid., May 23, 1877, 3:2; "Special and Local," ibid., May 30, 1877, 3:4.

71. *The State v Will H. Thomas*, Sessions Journal, Newberry County, September 6, 10, 1877, February 4, 5, 8, June 3, 7, December 5, 1878, February 3, June 2, November 10, 1879, November 11, 1880, and February 8, 1881, pp. 312, 322, 336, 340, 352, 353, 356, 361, 375, 380, 399, 424, 461, 518, 526; "Court," *Newberry Her-*

ald, February 13, 1878, 3:3; "Special and Local," ibid., June 12, 1878, 3:2. On postredemption prosecutions of other Republicans, see Williamson, *After Slavery,* 414–16.

72. Holt, *Black Over White,* 144, 150–51, 162; idem, "Negro State Legislators in South Carolina During Reconstruction," in *Southern Black Leaders of the Reconstruction Era,* ed. Howard N. Rabinowitz (Urbana: University of Illinois Press, 1982), 236, 240; Thomas, *The American Negro,* xvii. Holt omits Thomas from his "Summary of Biographical Data for Negro Legislators, 1868–76," *Black Over White,* Table 5, as does Eric Foner in *Freedom's Lawmakers: A Directory of Black Officeholders During Reconstruction* (New York: Oxford University Press, 1993).

73. Miller in Hampton Report, 39–40; Thomas, "Making a President," 94.

74. Theodore D. Jervey, *The Slave Trade: Slavery and Color* (Columbia: The State Co., 1925), 271.

Chapter Five. U.S. Consul and Racial Reformer

1. Untitled article in *Columbia Register,* March 29, 1877, 2:1.

2. William S. McFeely, *Frederick Douglass* (New York: Norton, 1991), 334–45; Dickson D. Bruce, *Archibald H. Grimké: Portrait of a Black Independent* (Baton Rouge: Louisiana State University Press, 1993), 67–77; Allison Blakely, "Black U.S. Consuls and Diplomats and Black Leadership, 1880–1920," *Umoja: A Scholarly Journal of Black Studies* n.s., 1 (spring 1977): 1–16.

3. Charles Stuart Kennedy, *The American Consul: A History of the United States Consular Service, 1776–1914* (Westport: Greenwood Press, 1990), vii–viii, 144–45, 187, 189.

4. Ibid., 140, 129, 149, 188, 146. On the system of compensation by fees, see William Barnes and John Heath Morgan, *The Foreign Service of the United States: Origins, Development, and Functions* (Washington, DC: Department of State, 1961), 77, 129, 149.

5. The testimonials are deposited in Applications and Recommendations, RG 59.

6. Beatty to Secretary of State, July 5, 1867; Redpath testimonial, n.d.; Hayes testimonial, July 2, 1869; Hayes to Whom it May Concern, November 3, 1871; Butler to Whom it May Concern, July 22, 1869; Butler to Dear Sir, June 7, 1877, ibid.

7. W. Hannibal Thomas to Grant, n.d.; Will. Hannibal Thomas to Grant, n.d.; Thomas to Grant, July 8, 1869; Thomas to Grant, October 29, 1869, ibid.

8. Schindler to Grant, March 5, 1877; Lawrence to Hayes, March 28, 1877; Thomas to Hayes, April 10, 1877; Chamberlain to the President, May 9, June 29, 1877, ibid.

9. "The A.M.E. Sabbath School," *Delaware Gazette,* August 23, 1877, 4:3; Thomas to O. O. Howard, [September 5], 1877, Oliver Otis Howard Papers, Bowdoin College; Howard testimonial, March 1, 1878, Garfield to R. B. Hayes, November 18, 1877, Applications and Recommendations, RG 59.

10. Mackey testimonial, February 13, 1878; Blythe to R. B. Hayes, February 7,

1878; Jillson to the President, December 19, 1877, Applications and Recommendations, RG 59.

11. Thomas to the President, October 11; Thomas to Dear Sir, November 20, 1877, Applications and Recommendations, RG 59.

12. Thomas to Dear Sir, November 20, 1877, ibid.

13. Ibid.

14. Department of State Consular Cards, St. Paul de Loanda, Portuguese S.W. Africa, General Records of the Department of State, Record Group 59, National Archives and Records Administration; *Register of the Department of State Corrected to December, 1878* (Washington, DC: Government Printing Office, 1878), 12, 29; Blakely, "Black U.S. Consuls and Diplomats," 11.

15. James Duffy, *Portuguese Africa* (Cambridge: Harvard University Press, 1959), 49–50, 73, 78, 80–81, 96; Joachim J. Monteiro (1875) quoted in Gerald J. Bender, *Angola Under the Portuguese: The Myth and the Reality* (Berkeley: University of California Press, 1978), 77; D. C. Platt, *The Cinderella Service: British Consuls Since 1825* (Hamden, CT: Archon, 1971), 28. The Portuguese spelled the name of the district São Paulo de Luanda, and the city Luanda. Today Luanda serves as the capital of both Angola and Luanda province.

16. Bender, *Angola Under the Portuguese*, 46, 52, 68; Jackson to F. W. Seward, February 10, March 1, April 29, 1878; Robert Scott Newton to [?], [?, 1878], Despatches From United States Consuls in St. Paul de Loanda, 1854–1893, vol. 3, January 2, 1870–August 14, 1882, Records of the State Department, Record Group 59, National Archives and Records Administration.

17. Bender, *Angola Under the Portuguese*, 66, 67.

18. *Register of the Department of State Corrected to December, 1878*, 12; Peter Duignan and L. H. Gann, *The United States and Africa: A History* (Cambridge: Cambridge University Press, 1984), 114–16; R. J. Hammond, *Portugal and Africa, 1815–1910: A Study in Uneconomic Imperialism* (Stanford: Stanford University Press, 1966), 73–74; *Register of the Department of State for the Year 1869-'70* (Washington, DC: Government Printing Office, 1869), 10, 34; *Register of the Department of State, Containing a List of Persons Employed in the Department and in the Diplomatic, Consular, and Territorial Service of the United States* (Washington, DC: Government Printing Office, 1870), 13, 25; ibid. (1871), 13, 30; ibid. (1873), 31; *Register of the Department of State Corrected to December, 1877* (Washington, DC: Government Printing Office, 1877), 12, 29; ibid. (1878); ibid. (1879), 12, 30; ibid. (1880); ibid. (1882), 13, 33.

19. "Special and Local," *Newberry Herald*, July 3, 1878, 3:1; Thomas to Seward, July 5, August 8, 1878; Thomas to Hale, October 21, 1878, Despatches From United States Consuls in St. Paul de Loanda.

20. McConnicle to Hayes, November 16, 1878, Despatches From United States Consuls in St. Paul de Loanda; J. J. C., Consular Bureau Report in the Case of Wm. H. Thomas, Consul, St. Paul de Loando. *Subject:* "Charges Against W. H.

Thomas, U.S. Consul, St. Paul de Loanda," November 25, 1878, Applications and Recommendations, RG 59. As late as 1897 Martha continued to seek support from Thomas's military pension. See file jacket, July 1, 1897, Thomas Pension File, RG 15.

21. Newton to Sir, February 21, 1879, Despatches From United States Consuls in St. Paul de Loanda. On Newton, see *Register of the Department of State for the Year 1869–'70*, 34, and *Register of the Department of State Corrected to December, 1877*, 12.

22. Thomas to Seward, March 21, 1879, Despatches From United States Consuls in St. Paul de Loanda; Hayes to the Senate of the United States, February 4, 1879, Nomination File 572, Records of the U.S. Senate, Record Group 46, National Archives and Records Administration; *Journal of the Executive Proceedings of the Senate of the United States of America, From March 5, 1877, to March 3, 1879, Inclusive* 21 (Washington, DC: U.S. Government Printing Office, 1901), 507, 565.

23. Thomas to Seward, March 21, 1879, Despatches From United States Consuls in St. Paul de Loanda.

24. "Personal Mention," *Delaware Gazette*, May 8, 1879, 4:6; "Religious Notes," ibid., August 28, 1879, 4:4; Frank M. Marriott to Dear Sir, May 26, 1879 and ticket receipt dated April 17, 1879; M. Moore to W. C. Beckwith, April 30, 1879; Moore to Sir, May 20, 1879; Marriott to Gentlemen, May 28, 1879; Ward Brothers to Seward, June 9, July 28, 1879, Despatches From United States Consuls in St. Paul de Loanda; Seward to Ward Brothers, October 29, 1879, Domestic Letters of the Department of State, Record Group 59, National Archives and Records Administration.

25. Newton to Sir, January 12, 1880, Despatches from St. Paul de Loanda; Newton to United States Minister Resident, Monrovia, August 2, 1880, Despatch Books, U.S. Consulate, Loanda, Record Group 84, National Archives and Records Administration; Hale to Sir, March 12, 1880, Despatches from United States Consuls in St. Paul de Loanda. To determine Thomas's whereabouts during the period of Thomas's alleged consular service, the author researched documents at the Arquivo Nacional da Torre do Tombo and the Arquivo Historico Ultramarino, Lisbon, Portugal. No passenger lists remain for ships between Lisbon and São Paulo de Luanda.

26. *Directory of Pittsburgh and Allegheny Cities, 1880–81* (1881), 657; Kennedy to John David Smith, July 12, 1991, in possession of the author; Verge to J. C. Bancroft Davis, March 10, 1882, Despatches From United States Consuls in St. Paul de Loanda; Department of State Consular Cards, St. Paul de Loanda.

27. Newton to Sir, November 20, 1878; Newton to Department of State, November 23, 1881, Despatches From United States Consuls in St. Paul de Loanda.

28. Thomas to Howard, April 24, 1889; Howard to Thomas, April 26, 1889; Thomas to Howard, September 16, 1891, Howard Papers; Thomas to Richard Olney, February 12, 1897, Applications and Recommendations for Public Office, Administration of Grover Cleveland, 1893–1897, RG 59.

29. "Hannibal," "Miscellaneous Echoes From the South," *Christian Recorder,*

April 12, 1877, 1:6–7; December 27, 1877, 4:2–3; May 30, 1878, 2:7. In his second article Thomas responded to the attack by "An Exile" against Atlanta University. See "The Schools in Atlanta," ibid., October 11, 1877, 2:6.

30. Thomas, *The American Negro: What He Was, What He Is, and What He May Become* (New York: Macmillan, 1901), xviii. Harold Hancock suggests that in these years Thomas "probably taught and preached in Massachusetts and the South." See "Otterbein's First Black Student: William Hannibal Thomas," *Otterbein Miscellany* 8 (May 1972): 9.

31. William H. Thomas, Claim for Increased Invalid Pension, May 17, 1883, Thomas Pension File, RG 15; "Personal," *Christian Recorder,* December 11, 1884, 2:2.

32. Thomas, "The Democratic Return to Power—Its Effect?" *A.M.E. Church Review* 1 (January 1885): 225–27; idem, "The Hero of Appomattox," *Christian Recorder,* July 30, 1885, 2:3; idem, "The Burial of General Grant," ibid., August 20, 1885, 2:6–7; idem, "Independence in Politics," *Cleveland Gazette,* January 30, 1886, 2:2.

33. Thomas, "The Humanity of Religion," *Christian Recorder,* January 22, 1885, 1:3–4; idem, "Denominational Finance," ibid., February 4, 1886, 1:1–2; idem, "Preachers as Politicians," ibid., February 25, 1886, 1:2–3; idem, "What Answer?" ibid., January 20, 1887, 1:2–4; idem, "Common Sense Religion," ibid., September 30, 1886, 1:1–2; idem, "The Humanity of Religion," ibid., January 22, 1885, 1:3–4; idem, "Colored Men as Jurors," ibid., March 5, 1885, 1:2–3. Responding to "The Humanity of Religion," the Reverend B. F. Lee, editor of the *Christian Recorder,* remarked that Thomas presented "a rather severe criticism [of the race]; one that is exceedingly painful and serious, if correct." Responding to "Denominational Finance," Lee remarked that "Colonel W. Hannibal Thomas makes some good suggestions relative to our finance" but questioned the practicality of Thomas's proposals. See *Christian Recorder,* January 22, 1885, 2:1–2; February 4, 1886, 2:2.

34. Thomas, "Seminaries or Universities?" *Christian Recorder,* February 17, 1887, 1:1–3; idem, "Some Methods of Education," ibid., December 24, 1885, 1:1–3; idem, "Co-Operative Land Purchase," ibid., November 18, 1886, 1:5–6; idem, "Shall Negroes Become Land-Owners?" *A.M.E. Church Review* 4 (July 1887): 484. In 1882 John F. Slater, a Rhode Island textile manufacturer, endowed $1 million for black education. Thomas criticized the Slater Fund for omitting blacks from its board of trustees and its general agent, Atticus G. Haygood, for not being "in sympathy, in a broad and liberal sense, with negro learning." The fund largely supported industrial education. See John E. Fisher, *The John F. Slater Fund: A Nineteenth Century Affirmative Action for Negro Education* (Lanham, MD: University Press of America, 1986); and Roy E. Finkenbine, "'Our Little Circle': Benevolent Reformers, The Slater Fund, and The Argument For Black Industrial Education, 1882–1908," *Hayes Historical Journal* 6 (fall 1986): 6–22.

35. "Local Chit-Chat," *Delaware Democratic Herald,* January 17, 1888, 5:3; "Massachusetts Nominees. A New Magazine Devoted to Race Issues," *New York*

Freeman, October 9, 1886, 1:1–2; Thomas, "Introduction," *The Negro* 1 (July 1886): 4.

36. William Hayes Ward to Booker T. Washington, March 21, 1901, in *The Booker T. Washington Papers,* 14 vols., ed. Louis R. Harlan (Urbana: University of Illinois Press, 1972–89), 6:56; John Edward Bruce, "The Critic Revealed; or, The Deadly Parallel," *Howard's American Magazine* 6 (April 1901): 366; Penelope L. Bullock, *The Afro-American Periodical Press, 1838–1909* (Baton Rouge: Louisiana State University Press, 1981), 77; Douglass to Thomas, July 16, 1886, Frederick Douglass Papers, Manuscript Division, Library of Congress. Thomas printed the letter as "A Misnomer," *The Negro* 1 (August 1886): 33–34.

37. Douglass to Thomas, July 16, 1886; "Our Colored Exchanges," *Indianapolis World,* n.d., quoted in *Christian Recorder,* August 19, 1886, 3:1; "Personal," ibid., October 21, 1886, 2:5.

38. Lee, "Afmerica," *The Negro* 1 (July 1886), 5–9; Pope, "Truth Versus Hypocrisy," ibid., (August 1886): 37–40; Ward, "Aunt Harriet," ibid., 43–47. Lee's poem appeared originally in the A.M.E. *Church Review* 2 (July 1885): 55–59.

39. W. L. M., "The Poor Whites of the South," *The Negro* 1 (July 1886): 25–30; Thomas, "Strikes," ibid., (August 1886): 34–36; Thomas, "Black Laws," ibid., 42.

40. Thomas, "Notes," ibid., (July 1886): 30; idem, "Characteristics of Negro Christianity," ibid., 19; idem, "Race Problems," ibid., (August 1886): 50, 52, 59; "Boston's Labor Movement. The True Lesson of Judge Ruffin's Funeral," *New York Freeman,* December 11, 1886, 1:1–2.

41. See Thomas, "A National Forecast," *Christian Recorder,* August 22, 1889, 1: 1–3; idem, "Unsolved Negro Problems," *Our Day* 5 (February 1890): 89–103; idem, "Negro Problems," A.M.E. *Church Review* 6 (April 1890): 388–402; idem, "Negro Problems: Political Domination," A.M.E. *Church Review* 7 (October 1890): 166–82.

42. Thomas, "Some Observations on Southern Industrial Development," A.M.E. *Church Review* 4 (January 1888): 259–68; [idem], "Industries of the South," *New York Age,* February 4, 1888, 2:4–5; idem, "Toil and Trust," A.M.E. *Church Review* 4 (April 1888): 369, 371; Thomas, "Till Another King Arose, Which Knew Not Joseph," A.M.E. *Church Review* 5 (April 1889): 341, 342–43.

43. Thomas, "Till Another King Arose, Which Knew Not Joseph," 337.

44. Wills, "Aspects of Social Thought in the African Methodist Episcopal Church, 1884–1910" (Ph.D. diss., Harvard University, 1975), 212; "The A.M.E. Church Review," *Cleveland Gazette,* August 20, 1887, 3:2; *Christian Recorder,* July 7, 1887, 2:3; "New Publications," *New York Freeman,* July 23, 1887, 1:3; "A.M.E. Church Review," *New York Age,* January 21, 1888, 1:6; "Magazine Literature," ibid., May 4, 1889, 2:4; "Magazine Literature," ibid., May 10, 1890, 2:3; "Literary Notes," *Christian Recorder,* October 16, 1890, 5:2; *Boston Herald,* n.d., in ibid., November 13, 1890, 3:2; ibid., April 9, 1891, 4:2.

45. Thomas to Hayes, September 16, 1891, Rutherford B. Hayes Correspon-

dence, Rutherford B. Hayes Presidential Center, Fremont, Ohio; Leslie H. Fishel Jr., "The 'Negro Question' at Mohonk: Microcosm, Mirage, and Message," *New York History* 74 (July 1993): 282–88, 306; James M. McPherson, *The Abolitionist Legacy: From Reconstruction to the* NAACP (Princeton: Princeton University Press, 1975), 137n. Thomas never received an invitation to speak at Mohonk. Black bibliographer Monroe N. Work, for example, omitted *Land and Education* from his comprehensive *A Bibliography of the Negro in America and Africa* (1928).

46. Thomas, *Land and Education: A Critical and Practical Discussion of the Mental and Physical Needs of the Freedmen* (Boston: Wallace Spooner, 1890), 70, 67.

47. Ibid., 68, 71, 5, 8, 6, 67, 68.

48. Ibid., 16, 11, 12.

49. Ibid., 26, 16, 29, 30, 32, 48, 49, 50, 67, 9, 11.

50. Ibid., 8, 6–7.

51. Ibid., 10, 11, 12.

52. Ibid., 10, 64, 66, 36.

53. Du Bois, "The Storm and Stress in the Black World," *Dial* 30 (April 16, 1901): 263; Thomas, "Land and Education," A.M.E. *Church Review* 7 (January 1891): 322–33; "Book Notices," *Our Day* 5 (June 1890): 500–502; Moore, "*Land and Education:* A Worthy Contribution to Our Race Literature by Col. Wm. Hannibal Thomas," *New York Age,* February 14, 1891, 2:4–5.

54. *Christian Recorder,* n.d., in *New York Age,* April 26, 1890, 2:6; Thomas to Dear Sir [printed letter and printed bill], "A Bill to establish industrial training schools and to provide land for Negroes to be held under lease with privilege of subsequent purchase" [July 7, 1890], H.R. 11271, Original House Bills, 51st Congress, Record Group 233, National Archives and Records Administration; Thomas to Hayes, June 9, 1890, Hayes Correspondence.

55. Thomas, "A Bill to establish industrial training schools."

56. Ibid.

57. U.S. Congress, *Congressional Record,* 51st Congress, 1st Session, vol. 21, part 7, July 7, 1890 (Washington, DC: Government Printing Office, 1890), 7014.

58. Thomas to Hayes, June 9, 1890, Hayes Correspondence; Thomas, *Land and Education: A Practical Method of Industrial Training for the Freedmen* (n.p., [1891]), [1]; Thomas to Hayes, April 24, 1891, Hayes Correspondence. Thomas's FLEF proposal also appears in *Teach the Freedmen: The Correspondence of Rutherford B. Hayes and the Slater Fund for Negro Education, 1881–1887,* 2 vols., ed. Louis D. Rubin Jr. (Baton Rouge: Louisiana State University Press, 1959), 2:196–97.

59. Thomas, *Land and Education: A Practical Method of Industrial Training for the Freedmen,* [2].

60. Ibid., [3].

61. Ibid., [3–4].

62. Thomas to Hayes, September 16, 1891, Hayes Correspondence. In 1901 Thomas faulted the Slater Fund, charging that it "failed to produce those results which the friends of negro education had a right to expect from its use." See *The American Negro*, 267.

63. "Editorial Notes," *Our Day* 5 (February 1890): 183; "Personals," *Christian Recorder*, April 17, 1890, 4:4; William D. Johnson, "Our Education," ibid., May 14, 1891, 1:3–4; idem, "Charleston and Other Points," ibid., June 1, 1893, 6:4. On Lincolnville, see Joel Williamson, *After Slavery: The Negro in South Carolina During Reconstruction, 1861-1877* (Chapel Hill: University of North Carolina Press, 1965), 207; Peggy Lamson, "Cain, Richard Harvey," in *Dictionary of American Negro Biography*, ed. Rayford W. Logan and Michael R. Winston (New York: Norton, 1982), 85; and Bernard E. Powers Jr., *Black Charlestonians: A Social History, 1822-1885* (Fayetteville: University of Arkansas Press, 1994), 208, 224.

64. "Fresh Ohio News—Delaware," *Cleveland Gazette*, August 16, 1890, 2:5; Schedule 1—Population, Middlesex County, Everett, Massachusetts, 1900, p. 10; Twelfth Census of the United States, Parlin Memorial Library, Everett, Massachusetts; Zenette Thomas, "Massachusetts," *Christian Recorder*, November 12, 1891, 6:1; idem, "Rambles in the South," ibid., February 16, 1893, 3:3–4; idem, "How to Make Home Happy," ibid., April 13, 1893, 3:1. Many of Zenette's points appear in *The College of Life, or Practical Self-Educator: A Manual of Self-Improvement for the Colored Race* (1895; Miami: Mnemosyne Publishing, 1969), 153–62.

65. "Personals," *Christian Recorder*, February 5, 1891, 4:5; Thomas, "Virginia: Portsmouth," ibid., January 1, 1891, 5:3; "Personals," ibid., January 12, 1893, 4:4; Thomas, "Religious Characteristics of the Negro," A.M.E. *Church Review* 9 (April 1893): 402; "Personals," *Christian Recorder*, October 25, 1894, 2:2; "General Conference Delegates," ibid., October 24, 1895, 6:2; Abram Grant, "The Historic and Literary Congress for the First Episcopal District of the A.M.E. Church," ibid., August 13, 1896, 5:5–6; Thomas, "Some Pertinent Suggestions," ibid., January 16, 1896, 1:1–2; idem, "Christianity, True and False," ibid., October 15, 1896, 1:4–6; "Concentration of Departments," ibid., January 2, 1896, 2:2.

66. Thomas, "Southern Barbarisms, White and Black," *Quarterly Review of the United Brethren in Christ* 5 (July 1894): 259–60; John Addison Porter to Thomas, July 22, 1897, William McKinley Papers, Manuscript Division, Library of Congress; Thomas to Washington, September 13, 1897, in Harlan, ed., *The Booker T. Washington Papers*, 4:328.

67. *The Boston Directory* no. 92 (Boston: Sampson & Murdock, 1896), 1490; William H. Thomas file jacket, 1897, Thomas Pension File, RG 15; *The Boston Directory* no. 93 (Boston: Sampson & Murdock, 1897), 1518; *Report on Population of the United States at the Eleventh Census: 1890, Part 1* (Washington, DC: Government Printing Office, 1895), 461; Dudley P. Bailey and Walter L. Colby, *Everett Souvenir* (Everett, MA: Everett Souvenir Co., 1893), 4, 8; "Everett," *Boston Courant*, January 6, 1900, 3:2; *Malden and Everett Directory, 1897* (Boston: W. A. Greenough,

1897), 747; Schedule 1—Population, Middlesex County, Everett, Massachusetts, 1900, p. 10; Joan Williams to John David Smith, February 21, 1991, in possession of the author.

68. Thomas, "Southern Barbarisms, White and Black," 248–49, 250, 252, 253, 258.

69. Thomas, "Characteristics of Negro Christianity," *Quarterly Review of the United Brethren in Christ* 8 (July 1897): 217, 218–19, 220, 228, 227, 229.

70. Thomas to Tourgée, [1895], Albion W. Tourgée Papers (microfilm), Chautauqua County Historical Society, Westfield, NY.

71. *An Act: Entitled an Act to prevent and punish Criminal Assaults on Female Chastity, and other Felonious Acts* [printed draft bill], Tourgée Papers. A copy also appears in the Theodore D. Jervey Papers, schs.

72. Ibid.

73. Thomas to Dear Sir, [1895] [printed cover letter], Tourgée Papers.

74. Ibid.

75. Ibid.

76. Ibid.; Leon F. Litwack, *Trouble in Mind: Black Southerners in the Age of Jim Crow* (New York: Knopf, 1998), 278, 285; Joel Williamson, *The Crucible of Race: Black-White Relations in the American South Since Emancipation* (New York: Oxford University Press, 1984), 214; Thomas, *The American Negro,* 234.

77. John Herbert Roper, *C. Vann Woodward, Southerner* (Athens: University of Georgia Press, 1987), 100.

78. Surgeon's Certificate, August 17, 1887; Thomas to Commissioner of Pensions, January 30, 1904; Surgeon's Certificate, March 14, 1904, Application for Increase in Invalid Pension, April 10, 1909, Thomas Pension File, RG 15; S. Weir Mitchell, *Injuries of Nerves and Their Consequences* (1872; New York: Dover, 1965), 342–68; Royce C. Lewis Jr., "Amputations and Amputees," in *Medical and Psychological Aspects of Disability,* ed. A. Beatrix Cobb (1973; Springfield, IL: Charles C. Thomas, 1977), 150, 157, 161, 163; Laurann Figg and Jane Farrell-Beck, "Amputation in the Civil War: Physical and Social Dimensions," *Journal of the History of Medicine and Allied Sciences* 48 (October 1993): 460–64; Thomas to James R. Garfield, December 20, 1908; Declaration for the Increase of an Invalid Pension, February 18, 1909, Thomas Pension File, RG 15.

Chapter Six. Author of *The American Negro*

1. Rayford W. Logan, *The Negro in American Life and Thought: The Nadir, 1877–1901* (London: Dial, 1954); Leon F. Litwack, *Trouble in Mind: Black Southerners in the Age of Jim Crow* (New York: Knopf, 1998), 284.

2. Thomas, *The American Negro: What He Was, What He Is, and What He May Become* (New York: Macmillan, 1901), 43–44. See Joshua 3:7–17.

3. Joel Williamson, *New People: Miscegenation and Mulattoes in the United States* (New York: Free Press, 1980), 108.

4. Thomas, *The American Negro*, x.

5. Joel Williamson, *The Crucible of Race: Black-White Relations in the American South Since Emancipation* (New York: Oxford University Press, 1984), 6.

6. Willard B. Gatewood, *Aristocrats of Color: The Black Elite, 1880–1920* (Bloomington: Indiana University Press, 1990), 10, 95; Victoria Marie Grieve, "Any Perceptible Trace: Representations of the 'Mulatto' in the United States Census, 1850–1920" (M.A. thesis, University of Georgia, 1996), 15, 84; Williamson, *New People*, 114; Grace Elizabeth Hale, *Making Whiteness: The Culture of Segregation in the South, 1890–1940* (New York: Pantheon, 1998), 23.

7. Thomas, *The American Negro*, 196; Thomas to Theodore D. Jervey, March 23, 1905, December 23, 1910, Theodore D. Jervey Papers, SCHS.

8. Thomas to Gentlemen, September 22, 1899; Macmillan Company to Thomas, September 23, 1899; Thomas to Macmillan Company, September 25, 1899, Macmillan Company Papers, New York Public Library. Fulkerson's work appears in John David Smith, ed., *Anti-Black Thought, 1863–1925: "The Negro Problem,"* 11 vols. (New York: Garland Publishing, 1993), 10:119–237. For an analysis of this tract, see p. xxviii.

9. John L. Gillin, "Franklin Henry Giddings," in *American Masters of Social Science*, ed. Howard W. Odum (New York: Henry Holt, 1927), 191–228; Franklin H. Giddings, "Use of the Term 'Race' in Anthropology and Sociology," *American Anthropologist* n.s., 4 (April–June 1902): 362–63; George W. Stocking Jr., "American Social Scientists and Race Theory: 1890–1915" (Ph.D. diss., University of Pennsylvania, 1960), 190–91; Franklin H. Giddings, *The Principles of Sociology* (New York: Macmillan, 1896), 18.

10. Vernon J. Williams Jr., *From a Caste to a Minority: Changing Attitudes of American Sociologists Toward Afro-Americans, 1896–1945* (Westport: Greenwood Press, 1989), 15; Giddings, *Principles of Sociology*, 324, 828; Carl N. Degler, *In Search of Human Nature: The Decline and Revival of Darwinism in American Social Thought* (New York: Oxford University Press, 1991), 17–18; Franklin H. Giddings, "Race Improvement Thru Civilization," *Independent* 61 (February 14, 1906): 384; idem, "Race War Coming, Dr. Giddings Says," *New York Times,* September 26, 1912, 5:4–5.

11. Giddings to Macmillan Company, October 2, September 9, 1899, Macmillan Company Papers. Calhoun's work was published in 1902 and appears in Smith, ed., *Anti-Black Thought, 1863–1925,* 11:231–401. For an analysis of this book, see p. xxix.

12. Giddings to Macmillan Company, October 10, 1899, Macmillan Company Papers.

13. Brett to Thomas, October 10, 1899; Thomas to Brett, October 12, 13, 14, 1899, ibid.; Contract Between Colonel William Hannibal Thomas and The Macmillan Company, October 14, 1899, Macmillan Publishing Company Archives, New York, New York; Brett to Ripley, October 13, 1899, Macmillan Company Papers.

14. Stocking, "American Social Scientists and Race Theory," 143–44, 220n, 227–28, 258–64, 274, 372; idem, *Race, Culture, and Evolution: Essays in the History of Anthropology with a New Preface* (Chicago: University of Chicago Press, 1982), 64–65; William Z. Ripley, *The Races of Europe: A Sociological Study* (New York: Appleton, 1899), 570; John Higham, *Strangers in the Land: Patterns of American Nativism, 1860–1925* (1955; New York: Atheneum, 1970), 154–55; Ripley to Du Bois, May 14, 1907, W. E. B. Du Bois Papers, University of Massachusetts, Amherst.

15. Ripley to Brett, October 19, 1899; Brett to Ripley, October 21, 1899, Macmillan Company Papers.

16. Compilation of readers reports on "The American Negro" [typescript], n.d., memorandum attached to copies of Thomas-Macmillan correspondence, n.d., ibid.

17. Thomas to Brett, January 17, 1900; Brett to Thomas, January 23, 1900; Thomas to Brett, January 25, 1900, ibid.

18. Brett to Thomas, January 27, 1900; Thomas to Brett, January 30, 1900, ibid. Ironically, modern scholars consider these three writers among the most racist of turn-of-the-century white polemicists. On Page and Bruce, see John David Smith, *An Old Creed for the New South: Proslavery Ideology and Historiography, 1865–1918* (Westport: Greenwood Press, 1985), 174, 200, 206, 211, 286 (Page), 173–77, 181 (Bruce). On Graves, see Smith, "'No negro is upon the program': Blacks and the Montgomery Race Conference of 1900," in *A Mythic Land Apart: Reassessing Southerners and Their History,* ed. Smith and Thomas H. Appleton Jr. (Westport: Greenwood Press, 1997), 135–37, 143, 148n.

19. Brett to Thomas, February 2, 1900, Macmillan Company Papers.

20. Thomas to Brett, February 5, June 19, August 22, 1900; Macmillan Company to Thomas, July 11, 1900, ibid.

21. Macmillan Company to Thomas, August 28, 1900; Thomas to Brett, August 29, 1900; Brett to Thomas, August 31, 1900, ibid.

22. Thomas to Brett, September 1, 1900, and enclosed table of contents, ibid.

23. Thomas to Brett, October 24, 1900; Macmillan Company to Thomas, October 25, 1900; Thomas to Macmillan Company, October 27, 1900; Thomas to Miss Stephens, November 21, 1900; Thomas to Brett, December 26, 1900; Brett to Thomas, December 12, 1900, ibid.

24. Thomas to Brett, December 14, 1900; Brett to Thomas, December 20, 1900, ibid.

25. "Books and Authors," *New York Daily Tribune,* January 5, 1901, 10:3.

26. *Boston Evening Transcript,* January 26, 1901, 18:1; Thomas to Brett, February 22, 1901, Macmillan Company Papers; illustrated flier for *The American Negro* in William Howard Taft Papers, Manuscript Division, Library of Congress; flier for *The American Negro* and William Hannibal Thomas's business cards in Jervey Papers and enclosed with Thomas to Joseph P. Tumulty, July 5, 1913, Woodrow Wilson Papers, Manuscript Division, Library of Congress.

27. Thomas, *The American Negro,* xxiv, xxv, [v]; Commons, "Racial Composi-

tion of the American People," *Chautauquan* 38 (November 1903): 234. Hereinafter all page references to *The American Negro* in this chapter will be parenthetical.

28. Williamson, *New People,* 108.

29. Thomas, "Southern Barbarisms, White and Black," *Quarterly Review of the United Brethren in Christ* 5 (July 1894): 247.

30. See Smith, *An Old Creed for the New South,* 201, and chap. 8.

31. Geneviève Fabre, "African-American Commemorative Celebrations in the Nineteenth Century," in *History & Memory in African-American Culture,* ed. Fabre and Robert O'Meally (New York: Oxford University Press, 1994), 87. For the broader, comparative meaning of emancipation rituals, see B. W. Higman, "Remembering Slavery: The Rise, Decline and Revival of Emancipation Day in the English-speaking Caribbean," *Slavery and Abolition* 19 (April 1998): 90–105.

32. See Stephen Ward Angell, *Bishop Henry McNeal Turner and African-American Religion in the South* (Knoxville: University of Tennessee Press, 1992), chap. 11.

33. Thomas to Jervey, December 23, 1910, Jervey Papers.

Chapter Seven. A Man Without a Race

1. "Books and Reading," *New York Evening Post,* January 11, 1901, 6:5; "In Literary By-Ways," *St. Louis Globe-Democrat,* January 19, 1901, 13:1; "Among the New Books," *Chicago Daily Tribune,* January 21, 1901, 7:3–4; Joseph Edgar Chamberlain, "Books of the Day," *Boston Evening Transcript,* January 23, 1901, 12:1–2; "New Books," *Washington Post,* January 23, 1901, 7:2–3; "W. H. Thomas on the American Negro," *Springfield Republican,* February 17, 1901, 8:4–5; "The Negro Arraigned," *New York Times Saturday Review of Books and Art,* February 23, 1901, 113–14.

2. "New Publications," *Philadelphia Public-Ledger,* January 31, 1901, 7:2–3; "A Sensible Negro," *Richmond Daily Times,* January 30, 1901, 4:1–2; "A Negro on the Negro," *Savannah News,* February 18, 1901, Hampton University Peabody Collection, Hampton University.

3. Ledger of Marriages, 1893–1894, Carroll County Court House, Westminster, MD; "Thomos [*sic*] vs. Booker Washington," *Everett Republican,* May 17, 1902, 8:5; Page, *The Negro: The Southerner's Problem* (New York: Charles Scribner's Sons, 1904), 82; Page to Charles R. Chiles, C. Fade Martin, May 9, 1904, Thomas Nelson Page Papers, University of Virginia; Myrta Lockett Avary, *Dixie After the War: An Exposition of Social Conditions Existing in the South, During the Twelve Years Succeeding the Fall of Richmond* (1906; New York: Negro Universities Press, 1969), 385n. In an unpublished paper, Thomas Bland Keys cited Thomas as a source for what he termed the "widespread impregnation of many thousands of southern Negro females by white Union soldiers." See "Yankee Miscegenation in the Confederate States" (unpublished paper, n.d., South Carolina Joint Legislative Membership Research Committee files, Columbia).

4. John S. Haller Jr., *Outcasts from Evolution: Scientific Attitudes of Racial Infe-*

riority, 1859–1900 (Urbana: University of Illinois Press, 1971), vi–ix; Mark Pittenger, *American Socialists and Evolutionary Thought, 1870–1920* (Madison: University of Wisconsin Press, 1993), 174; Kelly Miller, *Radicals and Conservatives and Other Essays on the Negro in America* (1908; New York: Schocken Books, 1968), 125; Joel Williamson, *The Crucible of Race: Black-White Relations in the American South Since Emancipation* (New York: Oxford University Press, 1984), 177, 275; Benjamin Brawley, *A Social History of the American Negro* (1921; New York: Macmillan, 1970), 325.

5. John David Smith, ed., *Anti-Black Thought, 1863–1925: "The Negro Problem,"* 11 vols. (New York: Garland Publishing, 1993), 4:238, 7:457; Barringer, "Race Problems in America" (unpublished manuscript, n.d.), Paul Brandon Barringer Papers, University of Virginia. On Barringer, see John David Smith, "An Old Creed for the New South: Southern Historians and the Revival of the Proslavery Argument, 1890–1920," *Southern Studies: An Interdisciplinary Journal of the South* 18 (spring 1979): 80–81 and idem, "'No negro is upon the program': Blacks and the Montgomery Race Conference of 1900," in *A Mythic Land Apart: Reassessing Southerners and Their History,* ed. John David Smith and Thomas H. Appleton Jr. (Westport: Greenwood Press, 1997), 130–32, 135–36, 138, 141–45.

6. Edgar Erskine Hume, *Ornithologists of the United States Army Medical Corps: Thirty-Six Biographies* (Baltimore: The Johns Hopkins Press, 1942), 390–412; Donald K. Pickens, *Eugenics and the Progressives* (Nashville: Vanderbilt University Press, 1968), 172; Robert W. Shufeldt, *The Negro: A Menace to American Civilization* (Boston: Gorham Press, 1907), 49, 93, 94–95, 131; "Race Fusion," *New York Times,* December 23, 1907, 8:4. Shufeldt restated his argument, including his praise and criticism of Thomas, in *America's Greatest Problem: The Negro* (Philadelphia: F. A. Davis, 1915), 64, 113, 114–15, 123–24, 146–49, 153–58.

7. "Dr. A. H. Shannon Rites Set; Was Minister, Author," *Nashville Banner,* May 14, 1968, clipping in Millsaps College Archives; "Shannon, Professor A. H.," n.d., Historical Research Project, Works Projects Administration Subject File, Mississippi Department of Archives and History; A. H. Shannon, *Racial Integrity and Other Features of the Negro Problem* (Nashville: Publishing House of the M.E. Church, South, 1907), 16–17, 42–45, 64–65, 68–69; idem, *The Racial Integrity of the American Negro* (Nashville: Lamar & Barton, 1925), 34–35; idem, *The Racial Integrity of the American Negro* (Washington, DC: Public Affairs Press, 1953), 56, 174. Also see Shannon, *The Negro in Washington: A Study in Race Amalgamation* (New York: Walter Neale, 1930), 75–76, 105, 214–15.

8. "A Negro on the Negro Race," *Columbia State,* February 20, 1901; "New Books," *Richmond Dispatch,* March 3, 1901, clippings in Hampton University Peabody Collection; "The American Negro," *Louisville Courier-Journal,* February 16, 1901, 5:3–4; "A Negro's Book," *Memphis Commercial Appeal,* February 15, 1901, 4:1–2; Knight, "Is There No Hope for the Negro?" *Atlanta Constitution* (Sunday Supplement), March 10, 1901, p. 6.

9. [Charles Henry Smith], "Bill Arp's Letter," *Atlanta Constitution,* March 11,

1901, Hampton University Peabody Collection. On Arp as a white supremacist, see Thomas D. Clark, *The Southern Country Editor* (Indianapolis: Bobbs-Merrill, 1948), 58, 311, 317, and David B. Parker, *Alias Bill Arp: Charles Henry Smith and the South's "Goodly Heritage"* (Athens: University of Georgia Press, 1991), chap. 7.

10. *Book Buyer* 22 (February 1901): 10; F.F.S., "More About The American Negro," ibid., (March 1901): 93, 143–44; "Sociology and Politics," *American Review of Reviews* 23 (March 1901): 374–75; C. C. Closson in *Journal of Political Economy* 10 (March 1902): 316–18; "The American Negro," *Spectator* 86–87 (March 23, 1901): 427–28; *Athenaeum* no. 3834 (April 20, 1901): 492–93; Marvin E. Gettleman, ed., *The Johns Hopkins University Seminary of History and Politics: The Records of an American Educational Institution, 1877-1912,* 5 vols. (New York: Garland Publishing, 1988–90), 4:592.

11. George P. Brett to Thomas, January 22, 1901; Thomas to Brett, January 24, February 22, 1901, Macmillan Company Papers, New York Public Library.

12. "W. H. Thomas on the American Negro," *Springfield Republican,* February 17, 1901, 8:4–5; "Two Studies of the Negro," *Kansas City Star,* March 24, 1901, in Southern Education Board Papers, Southern Historical Collection, University of North Carolina at Chapel Hill; *Nation* 72 (March 7, 1901): 202–3; [William Hayes Ward], "The American Negro," *Independent* 53 (February 14, 1901): 393–94; William Fremont Blackman in *Yale Review* 10 (May 1901): 112–13; Jabez L. M. Curry, "Report of the Chairman of the Educational Committee," *Proceedings of the John F. Slater Fund for the Education of Freedmen, 1901* (Baltimore: n.p., 1901), 10.

13. W. E. B. Du Bois, "Storm and Stress in the Black World," *Dial* 30 (April 16, 1901): 262–63. Du Bois's review of Washington's book became the famous chap. 3 of *The Souls of Black Folk* (1903), "Of Mr. Booker T. Washington and Others."

14. Du Bois, "Storm and Stress in the Black World," 263.

15. Ibid.

16. Ibid.; David Levering Lewis, *W. E. B. Du Bois: Biography of a Race* (New York: Henry Holt, 1993), 276; Du Bois in Hampton Report; Du Bois to A. G. Thurman, February 25, 1908, W. E. B. Du Bois Papers, University of Massachusetts, Amherst; Du Bois, ed., *The Negro American Family* (1909; Cambridge: M. I. T. Press, 1970), 64–65.

17. Kelly Miller to Washington, January 27, 1901; Canfield to Washington, January 25, 1901, in *The Booker T. Washington Papers,* 14 vols., ed. Louis R. Harlan (Urbana: University of Illinois Press, 1972–89), 6:17–18, 21–22. For a partisan editorial comparing Thomas unfavorably with Washington, see "The American Negro," *Southern Workman* 30 (March 1901): 139–40.

18. Hugh C. Bailey, *Edgar Gardner Murphy: Gentle Progressive* (Miami: University of Miami Press, 1968), 30, 34, 36; Smith, "'No negro is upon the program,'" 125–50; Murphy to Washington, February 25, 1901, Booker T. Washington Papers, Manuscript Division, Library of Congress.

19. Murphy, "W. H. Thomas on Negroes. An Exaggerated Arraignment Likely

to Do Harm" (unpublished manuscript, February 24, 1901), Edgar Gardner Murphy Papers, Southern Historical Collection, University of North Carolina at Chapel Hill; Murphy to Washington, March 20, 1901, in Harlan, ed., *The Booker T. Washington Papers,* 6:53–54. Murphy's letter appeared as "Mr. Thomas on Negroes. An Exaggerated Arraignment Likely to Do Harm," *New York Times,* March 2, 1901, 141:1–2.

20. Dewey W. Grantham, *Southern Progressivism: The Reconciliation of Progress and Tradition* (Knoxville: University of Tennessee Press, 1983), 232–34; Ralph E. Luker, *The Social Gospel in Black and White: American Racial Reform, 1885–1912* (Chapel Hill: University of North Carolina Press, 1991), 283, 286–87; William A. Link, *The Paradox of Southern Progressivism, 1880–1930* (Chapel Hill: University of North Carolina Press, 1992), 69, 77; Murphy to Washington, March 28, 1900, in Harlan, ed., *The Booker T. Washington Papers,* 5:475; Murphy, "W. H. Thomas on Negroes," Murphy Papers. On the potential negative impact of Murphy's letter, see Harlan, ed., *The Booker T. Washington Papers,* 6:46n.

21. John N. Abby, "Hit 'im Again," *Star of Zion* 25 (February 21, 1901): 5; editorial in ibid., (February 28, 1901): 4.

22. Church, "A Question of the Hour," *Howard's American Magazine* 6 (April 1901): 383; Wright in *American Journal of Sociology* 6 (May 1901): 852; Waters, "Negro Progress," *Independent* 53 (March 14, 1901): 651; Councill, "The American Negro: An Answer," *Publications of the Southern History Association* 6 (January 1902): 40–44; Gray, "'Much Learning Doth Make Him Mad,'" *Voice of the People* 1 (September 1, 1901), 4:1–2.

23. Wills to John E. Bruce, April 11, 1901, John Edward Bruce Papers, Schomburg Center for Research in Black Culture, New York Public Library; Green to George A. Myers, February 20, 1901, George A. Myers Papers, Ohio Historical Society.

24. "The American Negro," *Christian Recorder,* January 31, 1901, 2:3; editorial, ibid., February 21, 1901, 2:3; "Good From Evil," ibid., March 21, 1901, 2:2; "The Publications Department," *A.M.E. Church Review* 18 (July 1901): 76–77.

25. Knox to Myers, February 7, 1901, Myers Papers. On Knox, see Willard B. Gatewood Jr., *Slave and Freeman: The Autobiography of George L. Knox* (Lexington: University Press of Kentucky, 1979).

26. Cooper to Myers, February 18, 1901, Myers Papers; "A Dirty Book—Don't Buy It," *Star of Zion* 25 (February 14, 1901): 4; *Indianapolis Freeman,* May 11, 1901, 4:3. For other early examples of the Judas metaphor applied to Thomas, see Lewis H. Douglass, "Judas and His Book," *New York Age,* February 21, 1901; "Iscariot," ibid., March 21, 1901; J. Francis Robinson to the editor, February 24 [1901], ibid., n.d., clippings in Hampton University Peabody Collection.

27. "Two Kinds of Negroes," *Richmond Planet,* February 2, 1901, 4:2–3; *Washington Colored American,* February 2, 1901, 8:3; *Wichita Searchlight,* February 23, 1901, 2:1; "William Hannibal Thomas," *Bulletin of Atlanta University* no. 116 (Feb-

ruary 1901): 4; "William Hannibal Thomas," *Washington Bee,* February 9, 1901, 4: 1; "The Black Sheep," *Cleveland Gazette,* March 9, 1902, 2:1; "Politics in Ohio," *Washington Colored American,* March 2, 1901, 14:2; "Little Nuggets," *Kansas City American Citizen,* March 1, 1901, 1:7; *Indianapolis Freeman,* April 27, 1901, 2:3; *Washington Colored American,* April 6, 1901, 8:3; "Bishop Walters Defends His Race with Facts and Figures," *Kansas City American Citizen,* April 5, 1901, 1:6–7; "Progress of the Negro," *Milwaukee Wisconsin Weekly Advocate Devoted to the Interests of the Negro Race,* April 11, 1901, 1:1; Charles Alexander, "Our Journalists and Literary Folks," *Indianapolis Freeman,* May 11, 1901, 2:3–4; "Chips," *Chicago Broad Ax,* May 25, 1901, 1:4; "Hannibal is Hustling," *Washington Colored American,* July 27, 1901, 8:1; Jones, "A Black Judas," *Indianapolis Freeman,* July 13, 1901, 4:3–4.

28. "Men and Matters," *New York Age,* March 17, 1888, 2:6; William Glenn Cornell, "The Life and Thought of John Edward Bruce" (M.A. thesis, University of North Carolina, 1970), 11, 17, 23, 32–37, 42, 47, 49. On Bruce, see Bettye Collier-Thomas and James Turner, "Race, Class and Color: The African American Discourse on Identity," *Journal of American Ethnic History* 14 (fall 1994): 16–18. On Judas as Antichrist, see Sidney Tarachow, "Judas, the Beloved Executioner," *Psychoanalytic Quarterly* 29 (October 1960): 547.

29. John Edward Bruce, "He Defames The Race," *Washington Colored American,* February 2, 1901, 2:1–3. An emended version of Bruce's column appeared in *Star of Zion,* February 14, 1901, 1:1–2.

30. John Edward Bruce, "The Passing Throng," *Washington Colored American,* February 23, 1901, 2:2–3; idem, "Bruce on Business," ibid., March 16, 1901, 9:1.

31. Washington to Bruce, March 20, 1901, Bruce Papers; Bruce to Washington, March 20, 1901, Washington Papers. Bruce never issued *The Critic Revealed,* publishing instead two articles with that title. Titus Oates (1649–1705) was the English imposter who instigated the Popish Plot scare.

32. John Edward Bruce, "An Ethnological Betweenity. The Most Venomous and Spiteful Liar of the Negro Race. Sparks and Such," *Star of Zion,* March 14, 1901, 4: 3–5. William Hayes Ward, editor of the *Independent,* criticized Bruce's piece in the *Star of Zion* as "a blatherskitey," "hastily" prepared article filled with inaccuracies about Thomas's past. Though outraged by Thomas's book, Ward had little patience with Bruce's purple prose. See Ward to Booker T. Washington, March 21, 1901, in Harlan, ed., *The Papers of Booker T. Washington,* 6:56; Ward to Bruce, March 19, 1901, Bruce Papers.

33. John Edward Bruce, "The Critic Revealed," *Washington Colored American,* April 13, 1901, 1:4, 9:1–3; Bruce to McKinlay, April 17, 1901, Whitefield McKinlay Papers, Manuscript Division, Library of Congress.

34. Bruce, "The Critic Revealed," 365–70.

35. Mabie to Washington, January 8, 1901, in Harlan, ed., *The Booker T. Washington Papers,* 6:3–4; "'Up From Slavery,'" *New York Times Saturday Review of Books and Art,* March 9, 1901, 145:3.

36. Washington to Scott, January 24, 1901; Scott to Washington, January 28, [1901]; Charles William Anderson to Washington, May 27, June 2, 1904, in Harlan, ed., *The Booker T. Washington Papers*, 6:14, 22; 7:515, 518.

37. Taylor to Washington, January 29, 1901, in Harlan, ed., *The Booker T. Washington Papers*, 6:24.

38. Ibid., 25.

39. Ibid.

40. Canfield to Washington, February 8, 1902, in Harlan, ed., *The Booker T. Washington Papers*, 6:28–29.

41. Ward to Washington, February 8, 1901, in Harlan, ed., *The Booker T. Washington Papers*, 6:29; [Ward], "The American Negro," 393–94; Ward to Grimké, February 21, 1901, in Carter G. Woodson, ed., *The Works of Francis J. Grimké*, 4 vols. (Washington, DC: Associated Publishers, 1942), 4:69; William J. Anderson to George A. Myers, March 14, 1901, Myers Papers.

42. Thomas, *The American Negro*, 195; Booker T. Washington, *Up From Slavery: An Autobiography* (New York: Doubleday, 1901), 249; [Booker T. Washington], "The American Negro," *Outlook* 67 (March 30, 1901): 736. An autograph draft of Washington's review appears in Washington's papers at the Library of Congress, therefore suggesting that Washington, not his ghostwriter Max Bennett Thrasher, wrote the piece. See Harlan, ed., *The Booker T. Washington Papers*, 6:75n.

43. [Washington], "The American Negro," 736, 734.

44. Ibid., 734–36.

45. Charles W. Chesnutt, *The Journals of Charles W. Chesnutt*, ed. Richard Brodhead (Durham: Duke University Press, 1993), 93, 139, 172, 140.

46. Ibid., 157–58; Chesnutt, *The Wife of His Youth and Other Stories of the Color Line* (1899; Ann Arbor: University of Michigan Press, 1968), 7.

47. Chesnutt to Robert C. Ogden, May 27, 1904, and enclosed in "In Re William Hannibal Thomas, Author of 'The American Negro'" and copies of Macmillan Company correspondence (unpublished manuscript [1901]), 13, Charles W. Chesnutt Papers, Fisk University; Michael Flusche, "On the Color Line: Charles Waddell Chesnutt," *North Carolina Historical Review* 53 (January 1976): 19; Dickson D. Bruce Jr., *Black American Writing From the Nadir: The Evolution of a Literary Tradition, 1877–1915* (Baton Rouge: Louisiana State University Press, 1989), 173–74.

48. Chesnutt, "What is a Negro?" n.d., Chesnutt Papers; Stephen P. Knadler, "Untragic Mulatto: Charles Chesnutt and the Discourse of Whiteness," *American Literary History* 8 (fall 1996): 443–44; 18; Mark Andrew Huddle, "Intersections Along the Color Line: The Search for an Interracial America in the Writings of Charles W. Chesnutt," unpublished paper in possession of the author, 2, 5–6, 17, 18, 19. For suggestive discussions on the "tragic mulatto" paradigm, see: Judith R. Berzon, *Neither White Nor Black: The Mulatto Character in American Fiction* (New York: New York University Press, 1978), 100; Hazel V. Carby, *Reconstructing Womanhood: The Emergence of the Afro-American Woman Novelist* (New York: Oxford

University Press, 1987), 89; Susan Gillman, "The Mulatto, Tragic or Triumphant? The Nineteenth-Century American Race Melodrama," in *The Culture of Sentiment: Race, Gender, and Sentimentality in Nineteenth-Century America,* ed. Shirley Samuels (New York: Oxford University Press, 1992), 221; and Werner Sollors, *Neither Black Nor White Yet Both: Thematic Explorations of Interracial Literature* (New York: Oxford University Press, 1997), 220–45.

49. William Gleason, "Voices at the Nadir: Charles Chesnutt and David Bryant Fulton," *A. L. R.: American Literary Realism* 24 (spring 1992): 23, 25, 30; Chesnutt to Washington, October 8, 1901, in Harlan, ed., *The Booker T. Washington Papers,* 6:235–36; Charles W. Chesnutt, *The Marrow of Tradition* (1901; Ann Arbor: University of Michigan Press, 1969), 238.

50. Chesnutt, "The White and the Black," *Boston Transcript,* March 20, 1901, 13:5–6.

51. Chesnutt, "The White and the Black," 13:5–6; Chamberlin to Chesnutt, February 1, 1901, Chesnutt Papers; Frances Richardson Keller, *An American Crusade: The Life of Charles Waddell Chesnutt* (Provo, UT: Brigham Young University Press, 1978), 210–11. In an earlier letter to Chesnutt, Chamberlin remarked that "Race problems have always been pretty near to my heart, for various reasons." Chamberlin to Chesnutt, January 21, 1900, Chesnutt Papers.

52. Chesnutt, "The White and the Black," 13:5–6. On Chesnutt's southern trip, see Chesnutt to Booker T. Washington, in Harlan, ed., *The Booker T. Washington Papers,* 6:51.

53. Gilder to Chesnutt, March 15, 1901, Chesnutt Papers.

54. J. Noel Heermance, *Charles W. Chesnutt: America's First Great Black Novelist* (Hamden, CT: Archon, 1974), 94–95; Chesnutt, "A Defamer of His Race," *Critic* 38 (April 1901): 350.

55. Chesnutt, "A Defamer of His Race," 350. For "Po' Sandy," see Chesnutt, *The Conjure Woman* (1899; Ann Arbor: University of Michigan Press, 1969), 36–63.

56. Chesnutt, "A Defamer of His Race," 351.

57. Ibid.

58. "New Literature," *Boston Globe,* April 4, 1901, 2:4; Miller to Chesnutt, April 5, 1901, Chesnutt Papers; N. B. Young, "Fifth Annual Session of the Hampton Negro Conference," *Indianapolis Freeman,* August 3, 1901, 4:5; Miller, "Review of W. Hannibal Thomas' Book 'The American Negro,'" *Hampton Negro Conference* 5 (July 1901): 64–74; Chesnutt to Bruce, May 6, 1901, Bruce Papers.

59. Chesnutt to Macmillan Company, April 20, 1901, and enclosed in "In Re William Hannibal Thomas, Author of 'The American Negro'" (unpublished manuscript, [1901]), Macmillan Company Papers, New York Public Library. Different versions of Chesnutt's brief against Thomas appear in the Macmillan Company Papers and in the Chesnutt Papers, Fisk University.

60. Chesnutt to Macmillan, April 20, 1901, and enclosed in "In Re William Han-

nibal Thomas, Author of 'The American Negro,'" 1–7. Chesnutt erroneously dated Thomas's affiliation with Wilberforce University in the mid-1870s, not in 1869. In a slightly different version of his brief, Chesnutt misquoted Thomas's description of himself as a "teacher of righteousness and prophet of wisdom." Compare copy in Chesnutt Papers, 5, and Thomas, *The American Negro*, 247.

61. Brett to Chesnutt, April 22, 1901, Macmillan Company Papers.

62. Thomas to Brett, April 24, 1901; Brett to Thomas, April 25, 1901; Macmillan Company to Thomas, July 23, 1901, ibid.

63. Chesnutt to Macmillan Company, April 26, 1901, and enclosed in "In Re William Hannibal Thomas, Author of 'The American Negro,'" ibid.

64. Chesnutt to Macmillan Company, April 26, 1901, ibid.

65. Brett to Giddings, April 29, [1901] (emphasis added); Giddings to Macmillan Company, April 8, 1901, ibid. In February 1901, Straton sent his manuscript to Washington to read, hopeful that he ultimately would accept "some proposition looking to racial separation." Straton to Washington, February 18, 1901, in Harlan, ed., *The Booker T. Washington Papers*, 6:42. Straton, who taught at Mercer University, never published his book. For his paternalistic racial views, see "Will Education Solve the Race Problem?" *North American Review* 170 (June 1900): 785–801.

66. Giddings to Brett, May 7, 1901, Macmillan Company Papers. On Giddings's ideological and methodological differences with Du Bois, see Lewis, *W. E. B. Du Bois*, 202.

67. Brett to Chesnutt, May 10, 1901, Chesnutt Papers.

68. Willard B. Gatewood, *Aristocrats of Color: The Black Elite, 1880–1920* (Bloomington: Indiana University Press, 1990), 305; Chesnutt to Washington, April 27, 1901, in Harlan, ed., *The Booker T. Washington Papers*, 6:98; Chesnutt to Washington, May 10, 1901, Washington Papers; Washington to Chesnutt, May 3, 1901, Chesnutt Papers.

69. Elia W. Peattie, "A Real Study of a Race," *Boston Evening Transcript,* May 15, 1901, 2:4. Glenda Elizabeth Gilmore notes that Thomas's book encouraged white educators in North Carolina to reflect on the condition and morality of their black female pupils. See *Gender & Jim Crow: Women and the Politics of White Supremacy in North Carolina, 1896–1920* (Chapel Hill: University of North Carolina Press, 1996), 140–41.

70. S. Timothy Tice, "Incidents of Our Trip," *Christian Recorder,* September 24, 1891, 5:5–6, 6:1; "Personals," ibid., November 5, 1896, 2:4; Charles Spencer Smith, *A History of the African Methodist Episcopal Church* (Philadelphia: A.M.E. Book Concern, 1922), 217; Tice, "'Shall the Negro Share the Glory That Awaits Africa?' Reply to Dr. J. M. Henderson," *Christian Recorder,* January 12, 1893, 1:3–5; idem, "Negro Education in Maryland—State Industrial and Normal School Bill," *Baltimore Negro Appeal,* February 16, 1900, 2:1; "Revolution of Negroes," *Voice of the People* 1 (November 1, 1902): 1:2; Tice, "The Benefits of Social Settlements and Industrial Church Work in the Cities," in *The United Negro: His Problems and His*

Progress, ed. I. Garland Penn and J. W. E. Bowen (Atlanta: D. E. Luther Publishing Co., 1902), 217; "Afro-American Council," *Minneapolis Afro-American Advance,* June 17, 1899, 1:2; Tice, *The Negroes' Star of Hope, in the Midnight Skies* (Waco, TX: n.p., 1899), 10–13; idem, "Race Notes," *Baltimore Negro Appeal,* February 16, 1900, 2:3–4.

71. "Rev. Thomas Scored," *Washington Colored American,* April 27, 1901, 10: 1–2. Tice presented a similar paper on Thomas at the A.M.E. Church's New England Annual Conference in Providence, Rhode Island, June 4, 1901. See "The Annual N.E. Conference," ibid., June 22, 1901, 3:1–4.

72. S. Timothy Tice, *The American Negro, What He Was, What He Is and What He May Become; a Critical and Practical Rejoinder to William Hannibal Thomas* (Cambridgeport, MA: n.p., 1901), 30, 7, 41, 42, 45, 6–7, 24, 12 (emphasis added).

73. Ibid., 35–36, 24 (emphasis added), 29, 24, 33, 49.

74. "Clergymen in $10,000 Libel Suit. Author W. H. Thomas of 'The American Negro' Brings Action. Rev. S. T. Tice Defendant," *Boston Post,* July [6], 1901, [8: 3], clipping in Chesnutt Papers; "Rev. Mr. Tice Not Surprised," *Boston Post,* July 7, 1901, 4:7; "Pastor Sues Pastor," *Everett Republican,* July 13, 1901, 1:3; *Thomas v Tice,* July, 1901, Docket #8410, Middlesex Superior Court for Civil Business, Supreme Judicial Court Archives, Boston, Massachusetts. The *Everett Republican* also referred to Thomas erroneously as "pastor of a colored church in Everett."

75. Silas Xavier Floyd, *A Sketch of Rev. C. T. Walker, D. D.* (Augusta, GA: Sentinel Publishing Co., 1892), 2–8; idem, *Life of Charles T. Walker, D. D.* (1902; New York: Negro Universities Press, 1969); Samuel William Bacote, ed., *Who's Who Among the Colored Baptists of the United States* (1913; New York: Arno, 1980), 46; Stephen Ward Angell, *Bishop Henry McNeal Turner and African-American Religion in the South* (Knoxville: University of Tennessee Press, 1992), 281n; William E. Montgomery, *Under Their Own Vine and Fig Tree: The African-American Church in the South, 1865–1900* (Baton Rouge: Louisiana State University Press, 1993), 289. Charles H. Spurgeon (1834–92) was one of England's leading eighteenth-century Baptist evangelists.

76. Charles T. Walker, *Reply to William Hannibal Thomas (Author of the American Negro): The 20th Century Slanderer of The Negro Race* (n.p., [1901]); "Negro Defends His Race," *New York Sun,* April 19, 1901; "A Good Showing," *Bridgeport Standard,* May 9, 1901, clippings in Southern Education Board Papers; Floyd, *Life of Charles T. Walker, D.D.,* 143; Walker to Bruce, May 13, 1901, Bruce Papers.

77. Walker, *Reply to William Hannibal Thomas,* 20–21; Turner, interview in *Atlanta Age,* March 30, 1901, quoted in Bruce, "The Critic Revealed," 367; Walker, *Reply to William Hannibal Thomas,* 17.

78. Walker, *Reply to William Hannibal Thomas,* 1, 4–5, 13, 3–4, 18.

79. Ibid., 15, 17, 18. Haman, prince at the court of Ahasuerus, was hanged upon the exposure of his plot to destroy the Jews. This event is remembered in the Jewish festival of Purim.

80. Ibid., 21, 2, 21.

81. Ibid., 23, 22, 23, 31, 25. For another example of a black minister who preached a sermon condemning Thomas, see the Reverend Jenkin Lloyd Jones in Hampton Report, 112–13. Also see Jones's "'The Souls of Black Folk,'" *Unity* 51 (May 7, 1903): 148.

82. Thomas, "Mr. William Hannibal Thomas Defends his Book," *Critic* 38 (June 1901): 548, 550.

83. Ibid., 548. The best analyses of these stereotypes remain John S. Haller Jr., *Outcasts from Evolution: Scientific Attitudes of Racial Inferiority, 1859–1900* (Urbana: University of Illinois Press, 1971); and Stephen Jay Gould, *The Mismeasure of Man* (New York: Norton, 1981).

84. Thomas, "Mr. William Hannibal Thomas Defends his Book," 549–50.

85. Hampton Report, 1, 3; Francis J. Grimké to Dear Sir, n.d. [circular letter from Committee on Morals and Religion for 1901, Hampton Negro Conference], Francis J. Grimké Papers, Moorland Spingarn Research Center, Howard University; "The Hampton Negro Conference," *Southern Workman* 30 (August 1901): 428. W. E. B. Du Bois published some of the responses to Grimké's letter in *The Negro Church* (Atlanta: Atlanta University Press, 1903), 176–85.

86. Hampton Report, 78, 34, 91. On Grimké in this period, see Dickson D. Bruce Jr., *Archibald Grimké: Portrait of a Black Independent* (Baton Rouge: Louisiana State University Press, 1993).

87. Hampton Report, 40, 58, 55–56.

88. Ibid., 108. Karl Friedrich Hieronymus Münchhausen (1720–97) was a German soldier, adventurer, and teller of tales.

89. Ibid., 67, 74.

90. Ibid., 45, 88, 25. On Smalls in this period, see Edward A. Miller Jr., *Gullah Statesman: Robert Smalls from Slavery to Congress, 1839–1915* (Columbia: University of South Carolina Press, 1995).

91. Hampton Report, 117, 118.

92. "'The American Negro,'" *Boston Transcript*, April 3, 1901, 10:4; Mary Taylor Blauvelt, "The Race Problem as Discussed by Negro Women," *American Journal of Sociology* 6 (March 1901): 662–72; "Colored Womens' Clubs," *Boston Transcript*, April 9, 1901, 8:5.

93. Terrell, "Negro Women," *Independent* 53 (March 14, 1901): 633; idem, "Refutation of Charges Against Colored Women," *Howard's American Magazine* 6 (April 1901): 350–51.

94. "Mrs. Lambert on Thomas," *Boston Post*, April 6, 1901, 6:6; "Colored Woman Angry," *Boston Traveler*, April 22, 1901, Hampton University Peabody Collection.

95. "Arrayed Against a Book: Colored Women Fiercely Assail 'The American Negro,'" *Boston Herald*, April 6, 1901, 12:1.

96. "Mrs. Ruffin Honored Again," *Boston Post*, August 3, 1901, 2:3; John Dan-

iels, *In Freedom's Birthplace: A Study of the Boston Negroes* (1914; New York: Negro Universities Press, 1968), 209–10; Floris Loretta Barnett Cash, "Womanhood and Protest: The Club Movement Among Black Women, 1892–1922" (Ph.D. diss., State University of New York at Stony Brook, 1986), 46–47, 58, 208, 292–93; Mark R. Schneider, *Boston Confronts Jim Crow, 1890–1920* (Boston: Northeastern University Press, 1997), 94–103; "Talk of Thomas' Book," *Boston Globe,* April 5, 1901, 11:5; "Not Excluded From the Library," *Boston Evening Transcript,* April 5, 1901, 9:5–6.

97. Schedule 1—Population, Middlesex County, Everett, Massachusetts, 1900, p. L50A, Twelfth Census of the United States, Parlin Memorial Library, Everett, Massachusetts; "New Books at the Parlin Library," *Everett Republican,* April 13, 1901, 2:3; Armstead to the Editor, April 23, 1901, in ibid., April 27, 1901, 8:6.

98. Armstead to the Editor, April 23, 1901, *Everett Republican,* April 27, 1901, 8:6. On Thomas both as an unfair critic of African American women and as one of many men of both races who blamed black females for the alleged weaknesses of the race, see Addie Hunton, "Negro Womanhood Defended," *Voice of the Negro* 1 (July 1904): 280–82, and Deborah Gray White, *Too Heavy a Load: Black Women in Defense of Themselves, 1894–1994* (New York: Norton, 1999), 61, 62–63, 64, 69.

99. Page, "The Lynching of Negroes—Its Cause and Its Prevention," *North American Review* 178 (January 1904): 33–48; "The Negro: The Southerner's Problem," *McClure's Magazine* 23 (May 1904): 96–102.

100. *Diamond Jubilee of the General Association of Colored Baptists in Kentucky* (Louisville: American Baptist, 1943), 36–37; Randall K. Burkett, *Black Redemption: Churchmen Speak for the Garvey Movement* (Philadelphia: Temple University Press, 1978), 99–100; James R. L. Diggs, "Is It Ignorance or Slander? The Answer to Thomas Nelson Page," *Voice of the Negro* 1 (June 1904): 228–29. See also Diggs's "The Necessity for High Moral Character in the Teachers," in *The United Negro: His Problems and His Progress,* 410–12.

101. Editorial, "The Pessimism of Page," *Voice of the Negro* 1 (June 1904): 216. For similar criticism, see "Thomas Nelson Page on the Negro," *Southern Workman* 33 (June 1904): 325, and "Mr. Page and Negro Morality," *Southwestern Christian Advocate* 38 (July 7, 1904): 1, 8.

102. Allen to Page, May 2, 1904, Page Papers.

103. Ogden to Washington, May 21, 1904, Washington Papers; Ogden to Kelly Miller, October 24, 1904, Robert C. Ogden Papers, Manuscript Division, Library of Congress; Louis R. Harlan, *Booker T. Washington: The Making of a Black Leader, 1856–1901* (New York: Oxford University Press, 1972), 62; Washington to Schurz, May 18, 1904, Carl Schurz Papers, Manuscript Division, Library of Congress; Taylor to Washington, May 10, 1904, Washington Papers; Washington to Ogden, May 24, 1904, Chesnutt Papers. In his May 10 letter to Washington, Taylor said that he would approach Professor William Z. Ripley, then teaching at Harvard Univer-

sity. Washington must have learned that Ripley had recommended that Macmillan not publish *The American Negro*.

104. Ogden to Washington, May 21, 1904, Washington Papers; Washington to Ogden, May 24, 1904; Chesnutt to Ogden, May 27, 1904, and enclosed in "In Re William Hannibal Thomas, Author of 'The American Negro,'" 8, 12, and copies of Macmillan Company correspondence, Chesnutt Papers; Chesnutt to Washington, May 28, 1904, Washington Papers.

105. Ogden to Washington, May 27, 1904; Washington to Ogden, May 31, 1904; Ogden to Washington, June 2, 1904, Washington Papers; Ogden to Page, July 1, 1904, Thomas Nelson Page Papers, Duke University; Helen M. Chesnutt, *Charles Waddell Chesnutt: Pioneer of the Color Line* (Chapel Hill: University of North Carolina Press, 1952), 162–63; Sylvia Lyons Render, *Charles W. Chesnutt* (Boston: G. K. Hall, 1980), 117; Ernestine Williams Pickens, *Charles W. Chesnutt and the Progressive Movement* (New York: Pace University Press, 1994), 26, 28.

Chapter Eight. I Am Alone in the World

1. Through the years Thomas had maintained ties in Columbus, supporting the St. Paul A.M.E. Church. See *Minutes of the Fifty-Ninth Session of the Ohio Annual Conference of the African Methodist Episcopal Church* (Xenia: Aldine Printing House, 1889), 77.

2. *The Everett Directory, 1904, 1906, 1908* (Salem, MA: Henry M. Meek, 1904, 1906, 1908), 106, 111, 471, 256; *Thirteenth Census of the United States Taken in the Year 1910: Volume I, Population* (Washington, DC: Government Printing Office, 1913), 256; Elmer E. Spear, "Historical Sketch of Everett," in *Welcome Home Souvenir Book in Honor of Everett's Soldiers and Sailors* (Everett: City of Everett, 1919), 188; Thomas to Dear Sir, [circular letter, n.d.]; H. A. Thompson To Whom It May Concern, October, 1905; Thomas to Theodore D. Jervey, December 14, 1905, Theodore D. Jervey Papers, SCHS; display advertisement for Thomas's law office, *The Everett Directory, 1904,* 470; "Round the City," *Everett Republican,* May 3, 1902, 3:4.

3. Stuart Charles McConnell, *Glorious Contentment: The Grand Army of the Republic, 1865–1900* (Chapel Hill: University of North Carolina Press, 1992), 202–5, xiii, 183; Donald Robert Shaffer, "Marching On: African-American Civil War Veterans in Postbellum America, 1865–1951" (Ph.D. diss., University of Maryland, 1996), 252; "For Alderman," *Everett Republican,* February 8, 1902, 1:5–6; "Noble Lesson," ibid., June 1, 1901, 1:4.

4. Thomas, "A Word for Mr. Currier," *Everett Republican,* February 8, 1902, 1:5–6; "Stephen C. Currier, Candidate for the Republican Nomination for Alderman," ibid., November 15, 1902, 8:1; "Republicans Victorious," ibid., December 13, 1902, 1:4–5; "Late in Commencing . . . the Mayor Appoints New Commission," ibid., February 28, 1903, 1:6; "Annual Budget Passed," ibid., March 14, 1903, 8:4; "The Papers Filed," ibid., September 19, 1903, 8:5; "Ward Five is Ready,"

ibid., October 10, 1903, 1:3; "Big Republican Rallies," ibid., December 5, 1903, 1: 4–5; "Tribute of Citizens," ibid., January 9, 1904, 1:3; "Papers Were Filed," ibid., September 16, 1905, 1:3; Thomas to Jervey, December 14, 1905, Jervey Papers; "Round the City," *Everett Republican,* November 18, 1905, 5:4; "The Citizens' Candidate," ibid., December 16, 1905, 8:5; Thomas to Taft, November 11, 1908, William Howard Taft Papers, Manuscript Division, Library of Congress. Taft's father, Alphonso Taft (1810–91), was a veteran Cincinnati, Ohio, jurist, U.S. Secretary of War (1876), and U.S. Attorney General (1876–77).

5. Thomas, "The Heart of the Negro Problem," *United Brethren Review* 15 (January–February 1904): 8–9, 10; idem, "Suffrage Question," *Everett Republican,* December 31, 1904, 2:2–3; idem, "Secession and Reconstruction—A Retrospect," *United Brethren Review* 16 (January–February 1905): 28, 30.

6. Thomas to Jervey, June 6, [1910], February 27, [1911], November 20, 1909, January 20, 1911, Jervey Papers. In *The Slave Trade: Slavery and Color* (Columbia: The State Co., 1925), 343, Jervey noted that Thomas was "utterly lacking" in a sense of humor.

7. Thomas to Jervey, August 6, 13 [1910], January 20, 26, February 27, 1911, Jervey Papers; "Obituary," *Everett Republican,* July 21, 1906, 5:4; Thomas to Jervey, July 30, 1911, February 5, 1910, June 26, 1911, Jervey Papers.

8. Thomas to Jervey, February 5, 1910, Jervey to Thomas, July 21, 1910, Thomas to Jervey, August 6, [1910], Jervey Papers.

9. George Armstrong Wauchope, *The Writers of South Carolina* (Columbia: The State Co., 1910), 62; Jervey to Yates Snowden, December 1, 1912, Yates Snowden Papers, South Caroliniana Library, University of South Carolina; "Rites for Jervey, Former Recorder, Scheduled Today," *Charleston News & Courier,* January 25, 1947, 2:4; "T. J. Jervey, Charleston Recorder For Life, Dies," *Columbia State,* January 26, 1947, 2A:8; "Necrology," *South Carolina Historical and Genealogical Magazine* 49 (January 1948): 66–67; *American Historical Review* 25 (October 1919): 117–18.

10. "The New York Meeting of the American Historical Association," *American Historical Review* 15 (April 1910): 488–89; "Twenty-Fifth Annual Meeting of the American Historical Association," *Annual Report of the American Historical Association for the Year 1909* (Washington, DC: Government Printing Office, 1911), 36–37; Jervey to Hart, November 11, 1909, Jervey Papers. Much to his surprise, Jervey found Du Bois's landmark revisionist paper, "Reconstruction and Its Benefits," to be quite objective. See Jervey to Thomas, January 2, 1910, Jervey Papers; Jervey, *The Slave Trade,* 274–75. Du Bois's paper appeared in the *American Historical Review* 15 (July 1910): 781–99.

11. Theodore D. Jervey, *Migration of the Negroes: A Study of the U. S. Census Tables* (n.p., 1895), 1; idem, *The Negro Problem: A Study* (n.p., 1902), 7, 8; idem, "The Migration of the Negroes" (unpublished manuscript, n.d.), 11, 12, Jervey Papers. In *Migration of the Negroes* (1895) Jervey identified "a movement . . . among

the negroes and hybrids from and out of the South," with the highest percentage of increase (53 percent) in the "Pacific slope": New Mexico, Arizona, California, Washington, and Oregon. From these figures he concluded that "the negro problem is in a fair way to a solution." See pp. 1–4. Seven years later, in *The Negro Problem: A Study*, Jervey noted that Thomas generally opposed his advocacy of the "diffusion" of African Americans through North and Central America. See pp. 4, 7.

12. Jervey, *The Slave Trade*, 212; Thomas, *The American Negro: What He Was, What He Is, and What He May Become* (New York: Macmillan, 1901), 268, 142.

13. Thomas to Jervey, March 23, August 9, 1905, January 4, 1906, Jervey Papers.

14. Thomas to Jervey, May 22, 1905, ibid.

15. Thomas to Jervey, November 20, 1909, March 23, 1905, ibid.

16. Thomas to Jervey, January 4, 1906, February 5, 1910, ibid.; Jervey, *Robery Y. Hayne and His Times* (New York: Macmillan, 1909), 114–15; Thomas to Jervey, November 20, 1909, Jervey Papers.

17. Thomas to Jervey, February 5, 1910; Jervey to Thomas, March 14, August 9, 1910, Jervey Papers.

18. Thomas to William Hemstreet, February 23, 1905; Thomas to Jervey, March 23, 1905, ibid.

19. Thomas to Jervey, March 23, 1905, June 6, [1910], ibid.

20. Jervey to Thomas, June 22, 1905; Thomas to Jervey, August 9, 1905, March 10, June 6, [1910]; Jervey to Thomas, July 21, 1910; Thomas to Jervey, June 26, 1911, ibid.

21. Jervey to Thomas, May 28, March 14, December 8, 1910; Jervey to Hart, May 18, 1909, ibid.

22. "Colonel William Hemstreet," *New York Times*, October 16, 1920, 13:4; "Col. W. Hemstreet Dies in 87th Year," miscellaneous newspaper clippings, vol. 121, p. 84, Brooklyn Historical Society, New York; Hemstreet, "The Problem of the Blacks," *Arena* 29 (January 1903): 495–97.

23. Hemstreet, "The Problem of the Blacks," 498. For a contemporary rival proposal, see John David Smith, "Out of Sight, Out of Mind: Robert Stein's 'Deafricanization' Scheme to 'Hopeland,'" *Phylon* 46 (spring 1985): 1–15.

24. Thomas to Hemstreet, February 23, 1905, Jervey Papers. In 1909 Thomas continued to espouse government-sponsored land distribution—"20 millions of small land owners, scattered throughout the country." See Thomas to Jervey, November 20, 1909, ibid.

25. Hemstreet to Jervey, February 26, [1905], and enclosed notes on H. R. 11271, ibid.

26. Jervey, *The Negro Problem: A Study*, 2–3; Thomas, *The American Negro*, 408, 410; Jervey, *The Negro Problem: A Study*, 2–3.

27. Jervey, *The Negro Problem: A Study*, 7, 2, 3; idem, "Essay on the Negro Problem as Viewed by Booker T. Washington, W. E. B. Du Bois, and W. H. Thomas," unpublished manuscript, c. 1902, pp. 7–8, 5, 7, Jervey Papers.

28. Jervey, "Essay on the Negro Problem," 6, 7, Jervey Papers.

29. Unpublished book review of William Hannibal Thomas, *The American Negro*, c. 1901, pp. 4, 5, 4, 9, 8, 14, ibid.

30. Ibid., 14, 6, 9–10, 14–15, 17; Jervey to Thomas, March 14, 1905, ibid.

31. Jervey, *The Slave Trade*, 209, 275, 277, 301; Albert Bushnell Hart, *The Southern South* (1910; New York: Negro Universities Press, 1969), 134; Thomas, *The American Negro*, 165, xi, 264; Jervey, *The Slave Trade*, 211.

32. Miller to Jervey, December 28, 1927, Jervey Papers; Jervey to Woodson, November 18, 1932, Carter G. Woodson Papers, Manuscript Division, Library of Congress.

33. Thomas to Jervey, May 22, 1905, December 14, 1905, January 4, 1906, Jervey Papers.

34. Thomas to Jervey, January 4, 1906, ibid.; Louis R. Harlan, *Booker T. Washington: The Making of a Black Leader, 1856–1901* (New York: Oxford University Press, 1972), 246; Washington, *Up From Slavery: An Autobiography* (New York: Doubleday, 1901), viii; Harlan, "Introduction" in Washington, *Up From Slavery* (1901; New York: Penguin, 1986), xxii, xxvi, liii.

35. Thomas to Jervey, January 4, 1906, Jervey to Thomas, January 13, 1906, Jervey Papers.

36. Thomas to Jervey, March 10, 1910, ibid.

37. Ibid.

38. Thomas to Jervey, December 23, 1910, ibid.; *The Everett Directory, 1910–1911* (Salem, MA: Henry M. Meek, 1910), 404; *The Boston Directory* no. 108 (Boston: Sampson & Murdock, 1912), 1783; Calvin W. Lewis to Jervey, June 11, 1917; Thomas to Jervey, July 16, August 6, August 13, [1910]; Thomas to Jervey, December 23, 1910, June 26, 1911, June 20, 1912; Lewis to Jervey, June 11, 1917, Jervey Papers.

39. *Thirteenth Census of the United States Taken in the Year 1910. Volume II, Population* (Washington, DC: Government Printing Office, 1913), 401; Thomas to Jervey, December 6, 1912, Jervey Papers; *Rome, Georgia, City Directory, 1913, Vol. V* (Asheville, NC: Piedmont Directory Co., 1913), 256.

40. Thomas to Wilson, January 8, 1913, Woodrow Wilson Papers, Manuscript Division, Library of Congress; August Meier, *Negro Thought in America, 1880–1915* (1963; Ann Arbor: University of Michigan Press, 1971), 187–88.

41. Thomas to Joseph P. Tumulty, July 5, 1913, Wilson Papers; Wilson, "An Address at the Gettysburg Battlefield," [July 4, 1913], in *The Papers of Woodrow Wilson*, 69 vols., ed. Arthur S. Link (Princeton: Princeton University Press, 1966–94), 28:23–26.

42. "An Address to the President by William Monroe Trotter," [November 12, 1914]; "Remarks by Wilson and a Dialogue," November 12, 1914; "A News Report: President Resents Negro's Criticism," [November 12, 1914], in Link, ed., *The Papers of Woodrow Wilson*, 31:298–309; Stephen R. Fox, *The Guardian of Boston: William Monroe Trotter* (1970; New York: Atheneum, 1971), 140, 179–82; "Negro Com-

plaints Displease President," unidentified clipping, November 12, 1914, Wilson Papers.

43. Fox, *The Guardian of Boston*, 182–85; "Mr. Trotter and Mr. Wilson," *Crisis* 9 (January 1915): 119–27; W. E. B. Du Bois, "William Monroe Trotter," ibid., 9 (December 1914): 82; Forbes, "President Wilson, Trotter and the American People," A.M.E. *Church Review* 31 (January 1915): 309–18; Moton to Wilson, November 14, 1914, Wilson Papers.

44. Thomas to Tumulty, November 13, 1914, Wilson Papers.

45. Gerber, *Black Ohio and the Color Line, 1860–1915* (Urbana: University of Illinois Press, 1976), 53; James H. Rodabaugh, "The Negro in Ohio," *Journal of Negro History* 31 (January 1946): 19; Mary Louise Mark, *Negroes in Columbus* (Columbus: The Ohio State University Press, 1928), 10, 27; Richard Clyde Minor, "The Negro in Columbus, Ohio" (Ph.D. diss., The Ohio State University, 1936), 6; Frank U. Quillin, *The Color Line in Ohio: A History of Race Prejudice in a Typical Northern State* (Ann Arbor: George Wahr, 1913), 146, 145, 148–49, 150–51, 153.

46. Mark, *Negroes in Columbus*, 16–18; Roderick Duncan McKenzie, "The Neighborhood: A Study of Local Life in the City of Columbus, Ohio," *American Journal of Sociology* 27 (September 1921): 148 (map), 154–55; W. A. McWilliams, *Columbus Business & Professional Negro Directory* (Columbus: W. A. McWilliams, 1930), 14; Nimrod B. Allen, "East Long Street," *Crisis* 25 (November 1922): 12–16.

47. *Columbus City Directory, 1911–1912, Volume 36* (Columbus: R. L. Polk, 1911), 1399; *Columbus City Directory, 1912–1913, Volume 37* (Columbus: R. L. Polk, 1912), 1312; *Columbus City Directory, 1913, Volume 38* (Columbus: R. L. Polk, 1913), 1439; *R. L. Polk & Company's Columbus City Directory, 1914, Volume 39* (Columbus: R. L. Polk, 1914), 1536; *R. L. Polk & Company's Columbus City Directory, 1915, Volume 40* (Columbus: R. L. Polk, 1915), 1231; F. W. Copeland to U.S. Pension Bureau, May 29, 1916, Thomas Pension File, RG 15; Sisters of the Poor, of St. Francis' Hospital, to C. L. Martzolf[f], July 24, 1916, Jervey Papers. Based on city directories Thomas apparently resided at the locations cited in this paragraph. There is no way to know for sure, however, because at least one other William H. Thomas, also an African American and a janitor, lived in Columbus during these years. See appendix 1.

48. Julia L. Cable to Jervey, August 28, 1916, and enclosures; Lewis to Jervey, April 26, 30, June 11, 1917, and enclosures, Jervey Papers; W. L. Curry to G. M. Saltzgaber, March 27, 1914; Saltzgaber to Curry, April 10, 1914, Thomas Pension File, RG 15. On Wilson, see Dickson D. Bruce, *Archibald Grimké: Portrait of a Black Independent* (Baton Rouge: Louisiana State University Press, 1993), 43, 176. Walter S. Thomas lived amongst mostly white neighbors on East Spring Street, Columbus. See Fourteenth Census of the United States: 1920—Population, Columbus, Ward 12, 6A.

49. Lewis to Jervey, June 11, 1917, Jervey Papers; Forbes, "Within the Sphere of Letters," A.M.E. *Church Review* 30 (April 1914): 355–56. Forbes dissolved his part-

nership with Trotter in November 1903, following the July 30 "Boston Riot." See Fox, *The Guardian of Boston*, 29–30, 64, 66.

50. Lewis to Jervey, June 11, 1917, Jervey Papers.

51. G. M. Saltzgaber to F. W. Copeland, June 28, 1916, Thomas Pension File, RG 15; *R. L. Polk & Company's Columbus Directory, 1916, Volume 41* (Columbus: R. L. Polk, 1916), 1339; *R. L. Polk & Company's Columbus Directory, 1917, Volume 42* (Columbus: R. L. Polk, 1917), 1331; *R. L. Polk & Company's Columbus Directory, 1918, Volume 43* (Columbus: R. L. Polk, 1918), 1268; *R. L. Polk & Company's Columbus Directory, 1919, Volume 44* (Columbus: R. L. Polk, 1919), 1074; John David Smith telephone interview with Sam Roshon, Columbus Metropolitan Library, January 4, 1991, notes in possession of the author; George L. Cutton, *The National Military Home, Dayton, Ohio: Eighty Three Years of Service to Veterans* (Dayton: Vernon Roberts Post 359 of the American Legion, 1951); Judith Gladys Cetina, "A History of Veterans' Homes in The United States, 1811–1930" (Ph.D. diss., Case Western Reserve University, 1977), 97, 108, 174, 417, 457; Daniel A. Payne, *Recollections of Seventy Years* (1888; New York: Arno, 1969), 199–200; Patrick J. Kelly, "Creating a National Home: The Postwar Care of Disabled Union Soldiers and the Beginning of the Modern State in America" (Ph.D. diss., New York University, 1992), 140, 184; idem, *Creating a National Home: Building the Veterans' Welfare State, 1860–1900* (Cambridge: Harvard University Press, 1997), 98–99. While Thomas does not appear in any of the records of the Central Branch, an Ohio-born mulatto of his approximate age, "William Thomas," was listed in the 1920 census as an inmate there. See Fourteenth Census of the United States: 1920—Population, Ohio, Montgomery County, Jefferson Township, 31A. Coincidentally, another mulatto Civil War veteran, William H. Thomas, 43rd U.S. Colored Infantry, resided at the Central Branch at the same time. See appendix 1. The Central Branch had a long history of teaching men with amputated right arms to write with their left hands. See Cetina, "A History of Veterans' Homes in The United States, 1811–1930," 283.

52. Attorney Rolls, 1924, U.S. Supreme Court Records, 1790–1961, Record Group 267, National Archives and Records Administration; Thomas to Commissioner of Pensions, November 23, 1926; Kirkendall to Commissioner of Pensions, November 22, 1926; Certificate of Medical Examination, February 9, 1927, Thomas Pension File, RG 15.

53. Ward to John David Smith, February 13, 1991, in possession of the author; "John Brown Kissing a Negro Child on his Way to Execution" (1909) and "Memorial Souvenirs of Grant and Lincoln" (1929), Otterbein College Archives; Willard W. Bartlett Note Cards and Research Notes, Otterbein College Archives; Willard W. Bartlett, *Education for Humanity: The Story of Otterbein College* (Westerville, OH: Otterbein College, 1934), 39n.

54. Thomas, inscription in presentation copy of *The American Negro*, Otterbein College Archives; Henry Garst, *Otterbein University, 1847–1907* (Dayton: United

Brethren Publishing House, 1907), 297; Membership Book, 1908, United Brethren Church, Westerville, Ohio. The membership roll is deposited with the records of the Church of the Master, United Methodist Church, Westerville. This congregation became affiliated with the United Methodist Church in 1968. Garst believed that Thomas was "a prominent colored attorney of Boston, who spent some of his youthful days in Westerville, and for a time was a student in Otterbein University." He recalled that Thomas "requested to have his name enrolled as a member of the United Brethren Church here, desiring to be associated with a church which he knew in his boyhood."

55. *Soldiers' Memorial, Otterbein University, Westerville, Ohio, Cut of Proposed Marker* (n.p., [c. 1914–15]); *Invitation and Program of the Unveiling of the Soldiers Memorial, Otterbein University, Westerville, Ohio* (n.p., 1916), Otterbein College Archives; Otterbein College *Tan and Cardinal*, May 22, 1922, 1:4, 2:2–3; Melinda Gilpin to John David Smith, December 15, 1993, in possession of the author; Stanley S. Phillips, *Civil War Corps Badges and Other Related Awards, Badges, Medals of the Period* (Lanham, MD: S. S. Phillips, 1982), v, 97. Veterans of the Tenth and Eighteenth Corps were entitled to wear the badge of the Twenty-Fourth Corps. Thomas served in both corps.

56. *Polk's Columbus (Ohio) City Directory, 1929, Volume 53* (Columbus: R. L. Polk, 1929), 1563; *Polk's Columbus (Ohio) City Directory, 1931, Volume 55* (Columbus: R. L. Polk, 1931), 1267; *Polk's Columbus (Ohio) City Directory, 1934, Volume 58* (Columbus: R. L. Polk, 1934), 1054; "Litchford Hotel, Columbus, O.," *Colored American Magazine* 14 (November 1908): 585–88; Eldon Ward oral history interview, February 12, 1991, Columbus, Ohio, cassette tape in possession of the author; Ward to Smith, February 13, 1991, in possession of the author. Ward communicated Bryant's testimony about Thomas to the author.

57. Certificate of Death No. 66082, State of Ohio, Franklin County, November 15, 1935; Graves Registration Card (photostat), Veterans Service Commission, Columbus, OH; Lot and Burial Record, Otterbein Cemetery, November 19, 1935; Amanda Murray, Affidavit, November 21, 1935; Kenneth R. Fichner, Application for Reimbursement, December 14, 1935; Mrs. Francis Jones to E. L. Bailey, January 14, 1936; Murray to Bailey, February 9, 1936; Public Voucher for Burial, Funeral, and Transportation of Body of Deceased Veteran, February 7, 1936; William H. Thomas Death Certificate, December 17, 1935, Thomas Pension File, RG 15. For obituaries, see "Early Otterbein Grad Dies at 92," *Columbus Dispatch*, November 17, 1935, 2B: 1; "Rites Tuesday," *Columbus Ohio State Journal*, November 18, 1935, 2:3; "William Hannibal Thomas," *Columbus Citizen*, November 18, 1935, 13:7; "William H. Thomas Dies at Age of 92," *Westerville Public Opinion*, November 21, 1935, 1:2; Harold Hancock, "Otterbein's First Black Student: William Hannibal Thomas," *Otterbein Miscellany* 8 (May 1972): 11. Myocarditis is the inflammation of the muscular substance of the heart.

Epilogue. A Tragic Mulatto and a Tragic Negro

1. "Otterbein's First Black to be Commemorated," *Columbus Dispatch,* June 5, 1977, B-5:1-2; "Black Student Remembered" ibid., October 30, 1977, B-5:1-2; Ray Adams, "Guest Column," *Westerville Public Opinion,* November 8, 1991, 4-5; Brian Green, "William Hannibal Thomas, Esq." (unpublished paper, March 1978), Otterbein College Archives; Hancock, "Otterbein's First Black Student: William Hannibal Thomas," *Otterbein Miscellany* 8 (May 1972): 7-12; John David Smith, "Thomas, William Hannibal," in *Encyclopedia of African-American History,* 5 vols., ed. Jack Salzman, David Lionel Smith, and Cornel West (New York: Macmillan, 1996), 5:2650-51. Also see John David Smith, "Thomas, William Hannibal," in *American National Biography,* 24 vols., ed. John A. Garraty and Mark C. Carnes (New York: Oxford University Press, 1999), 21:530-31.

2. Thomas, "Race Problems," *The Negro* 1 (August 1886): 62.

3. Williamson, *The Crucible of Race: Black-White Relations in the American South Since Emancipation* (New York: Oxford University Press, 1984), 6-7.

4. Nell Irvin Painter, "A Different Sense of Time," *Nation* 262 (May 6, 1996): 38.

5. Thomas, *The American Negro: What He Was, What He Is, and What He May Become* (New York: Macmillan, 1901), xxii, xix, 114, 191; W. E. B. Du Bois, *On Sociology and the Black Community,* ed. Dan S. Green and Edwin D. Driver (Chicago: University of Chicago Press, 1978); Thomas, "Mr. William Hannibal Thomas Defends his Book," *Critic* 38 (June 1901): 548.

6. James B. McKee, *Sociology and the Race Problem: The Failure of a Perspective* (Urbana: University of Illinois Press, 1993), 24, 28, 61; George M. Fredrickson, *The Black Image in the White Mind: The Debate on Afro-American Character and Destiny, 1817-1914* (New York: Harper, 1971), 312-15. On the diversity and synthesis of evolutionary thought, see Ernst Mayr, *The Growth of Biological Thought: Diversity, Evolution, and Inheritance* (Cambridge: Harvard University Press, 1982), especially chap. 12, and Peter Bowler, *Evolution: The History of an Idea* (1983; Berkeley: University of California Press, 1989), chap. 10.

7. Thomas to Jervey, June 26, 1911, Theodore D. Jervey Papers, SCHS.

8. Macmillan Company to Thomas, October 25, 1900; Thomas to Brett, December 26, 1900; Brett to Thomas, January 22, 1901; Thomas to Brett, January 24, February 22, 1901; Macmillan Company to Thomas, July 23, 1901, Macmillan Company Papers, New York Public Library.

9. Contract Between Colonel William Hannibal Thomas and The Macmillan Company, October 14, 1899, Macmillan Publishing Company Archives, New York, New York.

10. Wilson Jeremiah Moses, *Black Messiahs and Uncle Toms: Social and Literary Manipulations of a Religious Myth* (University Park: Pennsylvania State University Press, 1982), 4, 31; Sacvan Bercovitch, *The American Jeremiad* (Madison: Univer-

sity of Wisconsin Press, 1978), 23–24; David Howard-Pitney, *The Afro-American Jeremiad: Appeals for Justice in America* (Philadelphia: Temple University Press, 1990), 22, 54, 67, 69, 93–104.

11. Erik H. Erikson, "Race and the Wider Identity," in *Identity: Youth and Crisis* (1968; Boston: Faber and Faber, 1983), 296, 300.

12. "God Almighty Made But One Race: An Interview Given in Washington, DC on 25 January 1884," in *The Frederick Douglass Papers, Series One: Speeches, Debates, and Interviews,* 5 vols. to date, ed. John W. Blassingame and John R. Mc-Kivigan (New Haven: Yale University Press, 1979–), 5:145–47; Wilson, "Prejudice Among the Race," *New York Age,* August 10, 1889, 1:4–5.

13. Nannie H. Burroughs, "Not Color But Character," *Voice of the Negro* 1 (July 1904): 277; James Weldon Johnson, *The Autobiography of An Ex-Coloured Man* (1912; New York: Hill and Wang, 1960), 76–77, 169–70.

14. Nell Irvin Painter, "Comment," in *The State of Afro-American History: Past, Present, and Future,* ed. Darlene Clark Hine (Baton Rouge: Louisiana State University Press, 1986), 87–88; Clarence E. Walker, *Deromanticizing Black History: Critical Essays and Reappraisals* (Knoxville: University of Tennessee Press, 1991), xvi; Colin A. Palmer, "Slave Resistance," *Reviews in American History* 26 (June 1998): 372.

15. [William Hayes Ward], "The American Negro," *Independent* 53 (February 14, 1901): 394; "Book Notes," *Political Science Quarterly* 17 (September 1902): 547. On the diagnostic features of "antisocial personality disorder," see American Psychiatric Association, *Diagnostic and Statistical Manual of Mental Disorders,* 4th ed. (Washington, DC: American Psychiatric Assn., 1994), 645–50.

16. Erik Erikson, *Young Man Luther: A Study in Psychoanalysis and History* (1958; New York: Norton, 1962), 14; Thomas, *The American Negro,* 223; George A. Lindbeck, "Erikson's *Young Man Luther:* A Historical and Theological Reappraisal," in *Encounter with Erikson: Historical Interpretation and Religious Biography,* ed. Donald Capps, Walter H. Capps, and M. Gerald Bradford (Missoula, MT: Scholars Press for The American Academy of Religion, 1977), 25. For an analysis mostly of the pros, and a few of the cons, of employing psychoanalytic insights in the writing of history, see Peter Gay, *Freud for Historians* (New York: Oxford University Press, 1985), especially chap. 1.

17. Thomas, "Memories of Otterbein Half a Century Ago," *United Brethren Review* 16 (July/August 1905): 204; idem, *The American Negro,* xv; Thomas to Jervey, February 27, [1911], Jervey Papers; Roberto H. Barja and Richard A. Sherman, *What to Expect When You Lose a Limb* (Washington, DC: U.S. Government Printing Office, 1986), 18.

18. John D. McCarthy and William L. Yancey, "Uncle Tom and Mr. Charlie: Metaphysical Pathos in the Study of Racism and Personal Disorganization," *American Journal of Sociology* 76 (January 1971): 648–72; Alexander Thomas and Samuel

Sillen, *Racism & Psychiatry* (1972; Secaucus, NJ: Citadel Press, 1979), 45–56; Joseph A. Baldwin, "Theory and Research Concerning the Notion of Black Self-hatred: A Review and Interpretation," *Journal of Black Psychology* 5 (February 1979): 51–77; James M. McPherson, *The Abolitionist Legacy: From Reconstruction to the NAACP* (Princeton: Princeton University Press, 1975), 341.

19. On the process of recovery, see Judith Herman, *Trauma and Recovery: The Aftermath of Violence—From Domestic Abuse to Political Terror* (New York: Basic, 1992).

20. American Psychiatric Association, *Diagnostic and Statistical Manual of Mental Disorders* (Washington, DC: American Psychiatric Assn., 1987), 247; Sidney Fishman, "Amputee Needs, Frustrations, and Behavior," *Rehabilitation Literature* 20 (November 1959): 326–27; idem, "Amputation," in *Psychological Practices with the Physically Disabled,* ed. James F. Garrett and Edna S. Levine (New York: Columbia University Press, 1962), 21–22; Lawrence W. Friedmann, *The Psychological Rehabilitation of the Amputee* (Springfield, IL: Charles C. Thomas, 1978), 20.

21. Mary Jo Deegan, "Living and Acting in an Altered Body: A Phenomenological Description of Amputation," *Journal of Sociology and Social Welfare* 5 (May 1978): 343; Laurann Figg and Jane Farrell-Beck, "Amputation in the Civil War: Physical and Social Dimensions," *Journal of the History of Medicine and Allied Sciences* 48 (October 1993): 468; Sybil J. Kohl, "Emotional Coping with Amputation," in *Rehabilitation Psychology,* ed. David W. Krueger (Rockville, MD: Aspen Systems, 1984), 276.

22. Edward Bibring, "The Conception of the Repetition Compulsion," *Psychoanalytic Quarterly* 12 (October 1943): 486–519; Thomas, "Making a President: An Episode of 1876," *United Brethren Review* 11 (March/April 1906): 93–94.

23. Thomas, *The American Negro,* xx; Joel Kovel, *White Racism: A Psychohistory* (1970; New York: Vintage, 1971), 263.

24. Thomas, *The American Negro,* xxiii. My interpretation of Thomas's "projection" both borrows from and departs from Nancy Leys Stepan and Sander L. Gilman, "Appropriating the Idioms of Science: The Rejection of Scientific Racism," in *The Bounds of Race: Perspectives on Hegemony and Resistance,* ed. Dominick La Capra (Ithaca: Cornell University Press, 1991), 90–91. For my use of "projection" see J. Laplanche and J.-B. Pontalis, *The Language of Psycho-Analysis* (New York: Norton, 1973), 351.

25. Thomas, *The American Negro,* 409, 410. Compare Thomas's use of "American civilization" as a racial or cultural paradigm with that of Franz Boas, who used Europe as his racial and cultural benchmark. See Carl N. Degler, *Culture Versus Biology in the Thought of Franz Boas and Alfred L. Kroeber,* German Historical Institute Annual Lecture Series No. 2 (New York: Berg Publishers, 1989), 9.

26. Jerome Dowd, *The Negro In American Life* (1926; New York: Negro Universities Press, 1968), 332–33; Thomas, *The American Negro,* xxiii.

27. E. H. Randle, *Characteristics of the Southern Negro* (New York: Neale Pub-

lishing Co., 1910), 117; Edward B. Reuter, "The Superiority of the Mulatto," *American Journal of Sociology* 23 (July 1917): 106; [Booker T. Washington], "The American Negro," *Outlook* 67 (March 30, 1901): 736. On the broad range of attitudes on mulattoes in this period, see John G. Mencke, *Mulattoes and Race Mixture: American Attitudes and Images, 1865–1918* (Ann Arbor: University of Michigan Research Press, 1979), 123, 125; Leonard Richard Lempel, "The Mulatto in United States Race Relations: Changing Status and Attitudes, 1800–1940" (Ph.D. diss., Syracuse University, 1979), 278–79; and Bettye Collier-Thomas and James Turner, "Race, Class and Color: The African American Discourse on Identity," *Journal of American Ethnic History* 14 (fall 1994): 17.

28. My use of "deviant" and "deviance" derives from Kai T. Erikson, *Wayward Puritans: A Study in the Sociology of Deviance* (New York: John Wiley and Sons, 1966), chap. 1.

29. Elazar Barkan, *The Retreat of Scientific Racism: Changing Concepts of Race in Britain and the United States Between the World Wars* (Cambridge: Cambridge University Press, 1992), 2; Carroll D. Wright, *The History and Growth of the United States Census Prepared for the Senate Committee on the Census* (Washington, DC: Government Printing Office, 1900), 187; Werner Sollors, *Neither Black Nor White Yet Both: Thematic Explorations of Interracial Literature* (New York: Oxford University Press, 1997), chap. 4.

30. Victoria Marie Grieve, "Any Perceptible Trace: Representations of the 'Mulatto' in the United States Census, 1850–1920" (M.A. thesis, University of Georgia, 1996), 15, 84. On the changing significance of the terms "black" and "mulatto" in the federal census, see Department of Commerce, Bureau of the Census, *Negro Population, 1790–1915* (Washington, DC: Government Printing Office, 1918), chap. 11.

31. Paul R. Spickard, *Mixed Blood: Intermarriage and Ethnic Identity in Twentieth-Century America* (Madison: University of Wisconsin Press, 1989), 329; Leo Spitzer, *Lives in Between: Assimilation and Marginality in Austria, Brazil, West Africa, 1780–1945* (Cambridge: Cambridge University Press, 1989), 4.

32. Elaine K. Ginsburg, "Introduction: The Politics of Passing," in *Passing and the Fictions of Identity,* ed. Ginsburg (Durham: Duke University Press, 1996), 9.

Appendix 1. The Multiple William H. Thomases

1. David Wood Wills, "Aspects of Social Thought in the African Methodist Episcopal Church, 1884–1910" (Ph.D. diss., Harvard University, 1975), 212n.

2. Calvin W. Lewis to Theodore D. Jervey, June 11, 1917, Theodore D. Jervey Papers, SCHS.

3. Several of these men are sorted out in Randall K. Burkett, Nancy Hall Burkett, and Henry Louis Gates Jr., eds., *Black Biography, 1790–1950,* 3 vols. (Alexandria: Chadwyck-Healey, 1991), 2:499–500.

4. "An Albany Pastor," *New York Age,* November 23, 1889, 1:5; A. W. Wayman, "Notes by the Way," *Christian Recorder,* December 4, 1890, 2:1; Thomas, "Reso-

lutions," ibid., March 5, 1891, 2:1–2; and "Personals," ibid., January 29, 1891, 4:2; Thomas to Hayes, October 19, 1891, Rutherford B. Hayes Correspondence, Rutherford B. Hayes Presidential Center, Fremont, Ohio. Hayes was a member of the board of trustees of the Slater Fund.

5. William H. Berry, "District Conference," *Christian Recorder,* June 22, 1893, 2:6.

6. Information supplied by Mary-Louise Mussell, Drew University and the General Commission on Archives and History, The United Methodist Church.

7. William Thomas to Mr. President, February 8, 1876, Letters to the President, Department of Justice, Record Group 60, National Archives and Records Administration.

8. *Minutes of the Twenty-Third Session of the Washington Annual Conference of the Methodist Episcopal Church* (Baltimore: Steam Press of Oliver W. Clay & Co., 1886), 38–39; *Minutes of the Annual Conference of the Methodist Episcopal Church Fall Conference of 1879* (New York: Phillips & Hunt, 1879), 93; *Minutes of the Annual Conferences of the Methodist Episcopal Church Spring Conference of 1883* (New York: Phillips & Hunt, 1883), 27, 29; *Minutes of the Annual Conferences of the Methodist Episcopal Church Spring Conference of 1884* (New York: Phillips & Hunt, 1884), 23; *Minutes of the Annual Conference of the Methodist Episcopal Church Spring Conference of 1885* (New York: Phillips & Hunt, 1885), 22; *Minutes of the Annual Conferences of the Methodist Episcopal Church Spring Conference of 1886* (New York: Phillips & Hunt, 1886), 25; Harold Lawrence, ed., *Methodist Preachers in Georgia, 1783–1900* (Tignall, GA: Boyd Publishing Co., 1984), 549.

9. "Appointments of [the] South Carolina Conference," *Christian Recorder,* March 6, 1873, 2:1; *Proceedings of the Republican National Convention, Held at Cincinnati, Ohio, 1876* (Concord, NH: Republican Press Assn., 1876), 29; P. W. Jefferson, "Word From South Carolina," *Christian Recorder,* March 15, 1877, 1:4–5; Alexander W. Wayman, *Cyclopedia of African Methodism* (Baltimore: Methodist Episcopal Book Depository, 1882), 161; Lawrence Chesterfield Bryant, *South Carolina Negro Legislators: A Glorious Success* (Orangeburg, SC: L. C. Bryant, 1974), 101; Thomas Holt, *Black Over White: Negro Political Leadership in South Carolina During Reconstruction* (Urbana: University of Illinois Press, 1977), 72, 189n, [240], 252; Clarence E. Walker, *A Rock in a Weary Land: The African Methodist Episcopal Church During the Civil War and Reconstruction* (Baton Rouge: Louisiana State University Press, 1982), 121; Eric Foner, *Freedom's Lawmakers: A Directory of Black Officeholders During Reconstruction* (New York: Oxford University Press, 1993), 211.

10. Massachusetts Adjutant-General's Office, *Massachusetts Soldiers, Sailors, and Marines in the Civil War,* 8 vols. (Norwood, MA: Norwood Press, 1932), 4: 656–57, 679; Peter Burchard, *One Gallant Rush: Robert Gould Shaw and His Brave Black Regiment* (New York: St. Martin's, 1965); Russell Duncan, ed., *Blue-Eyed Child of Fortune: The Civil War Letters of Colonel Robert Gould Shaw* (Athens: University of Georgia Press, 1992).

11. Thomas Truxtun Moebs, *Black Soldiers–Black Sailors–Black Ink: Research Guide on African-Americans in U.S. Military History, 1526–1900* (Chesapeake Bay: Moebs Publishing Co., 1994), 505; Norwood P. Hallowell, *The Negro as a Soldier in the War of the Rebellion* (Boston: Little, Brown, 1897), 8.

12. Thomas to Joseph P. Tumulty, January 4, 1915; Patrick R. Griffin to Tumulty, June 15, 1915, Woodrow Wilson Papers, Manuscript Division, Library of Congress; *Official Register of U.S. Government Military/Civilian Employees* (Washington, DC: Government Printing Office, 1897), 209.

13. *Minutes of the Annual Conferences of the Methodist Episcopal Church Spring Conferences of 1885* (New York: Phillips & Hunt, 1885), 17; *Minutes of the Liberia Annual Conference Held in the Methodist Episcopal Church, Monrovia, January 1885* (Monrovia: T. W. Howard, 1885), 7, 10, 25, 28; *Minutes of the Liberian Annual Conference Held in the Methodist Episcopal Church, Lower Buchanan Bassa County, January 1883* (Monrovia: T. W. Howard, 1883), 9, 19; John H. Reed, *Racial Adjustments in the Methodist Episcopal Church* (New York: Neale Publishing Co., 1914), 138–40, 174.

14. "For Hayti," *New York Weekly Anglo-African*, March 9, 1861, 2:3; "Foreign Correspondence," ibid., April 6, 1861, 3:3–4.

15. *The Boston Directory* (Boston: Sampson & Murdock Co., 1895), 1417; William H. Thomas, *The Roman Catholic in American Politics. By an American Journalist* (Boston: Albion Printing Co., 1895), 1–32.

16. Robert R. Doherty, *Representative Methodists. Biographical Sketches and Portraits of the Members of the Twentieth Delegated General Conference of the Methodist Episcopal Church, Held in the City of New York, May, 1888* (New York: Phillips & Hunt, 1888), 132; *Minutes of the Thirty-first Session of the Delaware Annual Conference, of the Methodist Episcopal Church, Held at Ezion M.E. Church, Wilmington, Del., April 11, 1894* (Philadelphia: M. E. Book Room, 1894), 4, 7, 11, 18; *Minutes of the Annual Conferences of the Methodist Episcopal Church Spring Conference of 1895* (New York: Hunt & Eaton, 1895), 68.

17. Edward A. Freeman, *The Epoch of Negro Baptists and The Foreign Mission Board, National Baptist Convention, U.S.A., Inc.* (Kansas City, KS: Central Seminary Press, 1953), 112; Sandy D. Martin, *Black Baptists and African Missions: The Origins of a Movement, 1880–1915* (Macon, GA: Mercer University Press, 1989), 174–75, 177–80; Leroy Fitts, *Lott Carey: First Black Missionary to Africa* (Valley Forge, PA: Judson Press, 1978), 106–8; William H. Thomas, *Glimpses of West Africa* (Raleigh: The Capital Printing Co., 1921), 25, 110, 115; "Pioneer Missionary Dies in Liberia," *Norfolk Journal and Guide*, December 9, 1942, clipping in Moorland-Spingarn Research Center, Howard University.

18. 5th U.S. Colored Infantry Muster-In Roll, June 22, 1863, and Muster-Out Roll, September 20, 1865; Company Descriptive Book, Company C, 5th U.S. Colored Infantry, Adjutant General's Office, Record Group 94, National Archives and Records Administration; Tenth Census of the U.S., 1880, Delaware, Ohio, Sched-

ule 1—Inhabitants, p. 4, Ohio Historical Society; William H. Thomas Pension File, Record Group 15, National Archives and Records Administration; Application and Discharge of William H. Thomas, Register No. 2075, Ohio Veterans Home Archives, Sandusky, Ohio; "Graves Registration Card," Oak Grove Soldiers Cemetery, Delaware County, Ohio.

19. "Editorial Correspondence—New England Conference," *Christian Recorder,* June 24, 1880, 2:3, emphasis added; William Henry Thomas, "The Ministry We Need," A.M.E. *Church Review* 1 (July 1884): 61–65; "Needs of Our Editorial and Publishing Interests," *Christian Recorder,* March 26, 1896, 3:1–3.

20. "Mortuary," *Christian Recorder,* April 17, 1902, 6:2; Horace Mann Bond, *Education for Freedom: A History of Lincoln University, Pennsylvania* (Lincoln University, PA: Lincoln University, 1976), 364; "Sketches of Delegates," *Christian Recorder,* April 16, 1896, 1:1; *General Biographical Catalogue. The Western Theological Seminary of the Presbyterian Church, Pittsburgh, Pennsylvania, 1827–1927* (Pittsburgh: Western Theological Seminary, 1927), 143.

21. "Testimonials to Rev. W. H. Thomas," *New York Freeman,* May 29, 1886, 2:4; W. H. Thomas, "African Methodism in Boston, Mass.," *Christian Recorder,* April 11, 1901, 7:1–2; Wm. H. Thomas to Cleveland, March 12, 1888, Applications and Recommendations for Public Office, Administrations of Cleveland and Harrison, 1885–1893, Record Group 59, National Archives and Records Administration; *The Boston Directory, Numbers 95–99* (Boston: Sampson & Murdock, 1899–1903), 1550, 1601, 1627, 1651, 1770; R. R. Wright, ed., *The Encyclopedia of the African Methodist Episcopal Church,* 2d ed. (Philadelphia: Book Concern of the AME Church, 1947), 342, 343; Jourdain to John E. Bruce, April 5, 1901, in C. T. Walker, *Reply to William Hannibal Thomas . . . The 20th Century Slanderer of the Negro Race* (n.p., n.d.), 28.

22. "The Late Dr. W. H. Thomas," A.M.E. *Church Review* 19 (April 1903): 757–58; Archibald H. Grimké, "Rev. Wm. H. Thomas, D. D.," unpublished eulogy, n.d., pp. 7–8, Archibald H. Grimké Papers, Moorland-Spingarn Research Center, Howard University.

23. Richard R. Wright Jr., *Centennial Encyclopaedia of the African Methodist Episcopal Church* (Philadelphia: n.p., [1916]), 225; R. R. Wright Jr., ed., *Who's Who in the General Conference, 1924* (Philadelphia: n.p., 1924), 86–87; Horace Talbert, *The Sons of Allen* (Xenia, OH: The Aldine Press, 1906), 93; *The Boston Directory, Number 109* (Boston: Sampson & Murdock, 1913), 1821; W. H. Peck, W. H. Thomas, and W. E. Griffin to Woodrow Wilson and enclosure, November 24, 1914, Wilson Papers.

24. Louise Daniel Hutchinson, *Anna J. Cooper: A Voice From the South* (Washington, DC: Smithsonian Institution, 1981), 160, 164.

25. *Record of Changes in Membership of the National Home for Disabled Volunteer Soldiers, 1919* (Washington, DC: Government Printing Office, 1920), 365; Fourteenth Census of the United States: 1920—Population, Ohio, Montgomery County, Jefferson Township, 11B.

26. This William H. Thomas lived on Clifton Avenue and Johnson Street. The two Thomases are differentiated in *Polk's Columbus (Ohio) City Directory, 1929, Volume 53* (Columbus: R. L. Polk, 1929), 1563.

Appendix 2. Circular Letter From the Committee on Morals and Religion for 1901, Hampton Negro Conference

1. Francis J. Grimké to Dear Sir, n.d. [circular letter from Committee on Morals and Religion for 1901, Hampton Negro Conference], Francis J. Grimké Papers, Moorland-Spingarn Research Center, Howard University.

Index

Adrian, Mich., 7–8

Adrian Expositor, 8

"African Church," 42, 43, 44–45, 46–47

African Methodist Episcopal Church, xxiv, 5, 42, 49–50, 51, 57, 61, 62, 63, 65, 67, 72, 74–75, 83, 90, 138, 139, 140, 154, 155, 160, 162, 279–80; Book Concern, 55–56, 64; and educational reform, 42, 141; and political activism, 96. *See also* "African Church"; African Methodist Episcopal Zion Church; Allen's A.M.E. Chapel; *A.M.E. Church Review;* Bethel A.M.E. Church (Ohio); Bethel A.M.E. Church (S.C.); Brown's A.M.E. Chapel; *Christian Recorder;* church reform; Emanuel A.M.E. Church; Monongahela Circuit A.M.E. Church; Newberry A.M.E. Church; New England A.M.E. Conference; North Ohio Annual A.M.E. Conference; Ohio Annual A.M.E. Conference; Pittsburgh Annual A.M.E. Conference; Sabbath schools; St. Paul A.M.E. Church (Mass.); St. Paul A.M.E. Church (Ohio); South Carolina A.M.E. Conference; Union Seminary; Wilberforce University; Wylie Street A.M.E. Church

African Methodist Episcopal Zion Church, 49, 72, 204. See also *Star of Zion*

agrarian reform, 109, 141, 143, 156, 188, 208–9, 241; and African American migration, 241, 245–46; and the federal government, 145, 150–53, 245, 355 (n. 24). See also *Land and Education* (Thomas)

Akerman, Amos T., 79

Allegheny City, Pa., 39, 43, 46, 47, 59, 66, 89, 124, 137, 139, 205; African Americans in, 48–49, 52; African Methodist Episcopal Church community in, 58

Allegheny Institute and Mission Church. *See* Avery College

Allen, Isaac B., 220

Allen, Mrs. C. M., 232

Allen's A.M.E. Chapel, 49, 58

amalgamation, 176–78, 185, 194, 210, 225, 273–74. *See also* assimilation

A.M.E. *See* African Methodist Episcopal Church

A.M.E. Church Review, xxiv, 138, 139, 145–46, 149, 201, 253, 256, 279, 284

The American Commonwealth (Bryce), 173

American Historical Review, 239

American Missionary Association, 39–40, 67–68, 83–84, 89, 92, 93–94, 305 (n. 4), 321 (n. 50). *See also* Atlanta University; freedmen education

miscegenation (*continued*)
amalgamation; castration; execution;
integration: sexual; lynching;
mulattoes; rape
Mohonk Conference, 146, 336–37 (n. 45)
Monongahela Circuit A.M.E. Church, 63–
65, 173
Monroe, Mary E., 251–52
Montgomery, Charles W., 95
Moore, Mamie, 136
Moore, W. H. A., 150
morality, African American, 156–59, 180–
85, 192–94, 209, 226–28, 248, 269,
287–88; and criminal character, 165,
180, 188, 192, 194, 221; and economic
position, 153, 221. *See also* women,
African American: morality of
Morrill, H. R., 97
Morris, J. W., 65
Morris, Robert C., 85
Morris, W. B., 220
Morrow, J. W., 73, 76
Moses, Franklin J., Jr., 99, 108; accused
of corruption, 101, 102, 103, 325 (n. 15);
and William Hannibal Thomas, 100,
105, 107
Moses, Franklin J., Sr., 119
Moses, Montgomery, 99, 110
Moton, Robert R., 253–54
Mt. Olivet Baptist Church, 222
Mt. Vernon Place Methodist Church, 81
mulattoes: identification with, xxv, 1–2,
149, 160, 163, 273–74; and politics,
101–2, 113, 125; problems of, 19, 162,
164, 168; perceived superiority of, xx–
xxi, 1, 39, 101–2, 164, 166, 176–77, 211,
273, 275–76. *See also* "hybrids"; racial
identification; skin color differentiation
Murphy, Edgar Gardner, 198–200
Murphy picnic, 43, 130
Murray, Amanda, 261
Myers, George A., 201
Myrdal, Gunnar, xix–xx

NAACP, 253, 255
namedropping, William Hannibal
Thomas and, 89, 108, 121, 123, 128–29,
237, 238, 252

Nance, Lee A., 97
Nation, 196
National Afro-American Council, 200
National Association for the
Advancement of Colored People
(NAACP), 253, 255
National Equal Rights League, 45–46,
253. *See also* Equal Rights League
(Delaware, Ohio)
National Guard Service of South
Carolina, 99–100, 112, 281
National Home for Disabled Volunteer
Soldiers (Central Branch), 257, 286,
358 (n. 51)
nationalism, African American, 203
The National Temperance Advocate, 77
The Negro, xxv, 141–44, 202
The Negro: A Menace to Civilization
(Shufeldt), 193
*The Negro: As He Was, As He Is, As He
Will Be* (Fulkerson), 165
"The Negro: The Southerner's Problem"
(Page), 231
The Negro Church (Du Bois, ed.), 351
(n. 85)
Negroes and Negro "Slavery" (Van Evrie),
200
Negro Militia, 99–100, 112, 281
"Negro Problem," 167, 178, 240, 263;
African American responsibility for,
xx, xxvi, 146, 156, 161, 163, 255;
solving the, 168, 269–70, 273–74, 354–
55 (n. 11); white responsibility for, 141–
45, 149, 156, 158–59, 189
Negro Thought in America, 1880–1915
(Meier), xxii
neo-slavery, 52, 60, 64, 104, 121, 143–44,
217, 244
New Bern, N.C., 36
Newberry, S.C.: African American
community in, 95, 113, 125; African
Methodist Episcopal Church
community in, 96, 98–99; and
Confederate defeat, 94–95; and
Democrats, 95–96, 97, 107–8, 111,
113–15, 120; and election of 1874, 105–
7; and Hoge Institute, 97–98, 324
(n. 11); Republicans in, 95–96, 97, 99–

Thomas, William Hannibal (*continued*)
(n. 6), 359 (n. 57); biographical trail
of, xxiii, 25, 65, 98, 125, 173, 235,
262–63, 270, 279–80; called "Black
Judas," xxvi, 201–3, 214, 224, 277, 285;
character of, xxv, 27, 30–31, 36, 58–
59, 91–92, 98, 102, 116, 119, 129–30,
137–38; childhood and youth, 2–3, 5,
6, 7–11, 294 (n. 13); confused with men
with similar names, 279–81, 284–85,
357 (n. 47), 358 (n. 50), 367 (n. 26);
criminal warrants for, 90–91, 140, 173,
215; death, 255–57, 261–62, 279;
denounced as a Benedict Arnold, 201,
214, 221, 249; education, 7–8, 10–12,
14–18, 38–39, 49–52, 53–56, 58–59,
109–10; as educator, 20–22, 39, 42,
67–68, 72, 74, 76–77, 82, 86–88, 97–
98, 335 (n. 30); emotional traumas, 39,
59, 160, 180–81, 243, 260, 270–72,
276–77; family, 1–3, 6, 7–12, 19–
20, 39, 41, 44, 68, 134–35, 136, 138,
269, 297 (n. 46), 305–6 (n. 10); and
finances, 44–45, 56–57, 62, 64–65,
90–91, 110, 119, 124, 136, 172, 207, 216,
247, 252, 257, 261, 265; geographic
mobility of, 41, 66, 67–68, 81, 89, 93,
135–38, 154, 235, 252, 255–58, 294
(n. 12); and historians, xix, xxi–xxii,
xxiii–xxiv, 262; as janitor, 257–258,
357 (n. 47); as journalist, xxv, 46, 59–
61, 68, 141–42, 160, 216; as lawyer, 39,
99, 109–11, 169, 216, 236, 252, 257,
324–25 (n. 14); as manual laborer, 5, 11,
19, 38; military service, xxiv–xxv, 22–
40, 41–42, 46–47, 100, 129, 131, 260,
271–72, 302–3 (n. 76), 303–4 (n. 79),
359 (n. 55); as minister, xxv, 39, 46,
59, 62–65, 77–78, 93–94, 216, 335
(n. 30), 350 (n. 74); personal attacks
on, xx, 200–32, 255–56, 275, 348–
49 (n. 60); politics and political
appointments, 45, 86, 99–132, 236, 325
(n. 17), 329 (n. 52); and relations with
women, 18, 44, 98, 119, 138, 206, 251–
52, 261; and self destruction, xxiv–
xxvi, 23, 59, 160, 263, 269, 271–72,
276–77

Thomas, William Henry, 155, 279, 284–
85
Thomas, William Holcombe, 239
Thomas, William M., 95, 96, 112, 281
Thomas, Zenette, 154, 155–56, 165,
238, 256
Thompson, Henry A., 15, 296 (n. 34)
Thompson, Henry T., 118
Thompson, William B., 75
Thornbrough, Emma Lou, 7
Thrasher, Max Bennett, 250, 347
(n. 42)
Tice, S. Timothy, 220–22, 350 (n. 71)
Tilden, Samuel J., 330 (n. 55)
Tillman, Benjamin R., 164, 193, 207,
256
Tod, David, 46
Tomlinson, Reuben, 101, 107
Torrence, Felix, 96
Tourgée, Albion W., 157–58, 159
Trescott, William H., 107
Trotter, William Monroe, 252–54,
357–58 (n. 49)
Trudeau, Noah Andre, 29
"A True History of Tuskegee"
(Thomas), 249–50
Tumulty, Joseph P., 254, 282
Turner, Henry McNeal, xxiv, 140, 185,
222–23, 232
Turner, James Milton, 23
Turpin, Jeremiah H., 51, 309–10
(n. 30)
Tuskegee Institute, 21, 141, 155, 192,
249, 250, 253
Tyler, Tex., 155

UBC. *See* United Brethren in Christ
Church
Underground Railroad, 5–6, 9–10,
284
Union Biblical Seminary, 235
Union League, 71
Union Republicans, 101–7
Union Seminary, 20–22, 42, 56–57, 63.
See also Wilberforce University
United Brethren in Christ Church, 6, 8–
9, 12–13, 14–15, 235, 258, 261, 293
(n. 11), 358–59 (n. 54). See also